C0-AVY-430

A COMMENTARY ON GALATIANS

PILGRIM CLASSIC COMMENTARIES

VOLUMES IN THE SERIES

The Geneva Bible
A Commentary on Galatians
William Perkins

A COMMENTARY ON GALATIANS

William Perkins

INTRODUCTORY ESSAYS BY
BREVARD S. CHILDS
GERALD T. SHEPPARD
JOHN H. AUGUSTINE

EDITED BY
GERALD T. SHEPPARD

THE PILGRIM PRESS
NEW YORK

William Perkins' *Commentary on Galatians* is reproduced by permission of General Theological Seminary, New York, from a copy in their collection at St. Mark's Library.

This Pilgrim Press volume has been reproduced from a seventeenth-century text and reflects the condition of that original volume.

Library of Congress Cataloging-in-Publication Data

Perkins, William, 1558–1602.
[Commentarie or exposition upon the five first chapters of the Epistle to the Galatians]
A commentary on Galatians / William Perkins : edited by Gerald T. Sheppard : introductory essays by Brevard S. Childs, Gerald T. Sheppard, John H. Augustine.
p. cm. — (Pilgrim classic commentaries)
Commentary on the final chapter of Galatians added by the original editor of the manuscript, Ralph Cudworth.
Facsim. of: A commentarie or exposition upon the five first chapters of the Epistle to the Galatians. London : Printed by Iohn Legatt, 1617.
Includes bibliographical references.
ISBN 0–8298–0790–X. — ISBN 0–8298–0786–1 (pbk.)
1. Bible. N.T. Galatians—Commentaries. I. Sheppard, Gerald T., 1946– . II. Childs, Brevard S. III. Augustine, John H. IV. Cudworth, Ralph, d. 1624. V. Title. VI. Series.
BS2685.P37 1989
227'.407—dc20 89-35504

The Pilgrim Press, 475 Riverside Drive, New York, N.Y. 10115

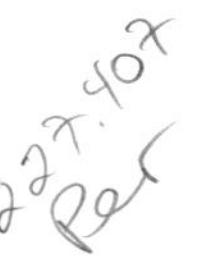

Contents

INTRODUCTORY ESSAYS TO THE PILGRIM PRESS EDITION

William Perkins' Exposition Among Seventeenth-Century Commentaries 1600–1645

GERALD T. SHEPPARD

William Perkins' *Commentary on Galatians* is presented here as the second volume in the Pilgrim Classic Commentaries series, which was inaugurated with the publication of the Geneva New Testament (1602) in the Spring of 1989. This facsimile of the 1617 edition of Perkins' work includes modest grammatical changes and some standardization of spellings from the initial publication of the commentary in 1604. The *Commentary on Galatians* is the last book written in Perkins' own hand, though it was edited cautiously by Ralph Cudworth and further expanded by him with commentary on the last chapter. When Cudworth, the father of the famed Cambridge neo-Platonist of the same name, was appointed in 1603 to lecture on this Epistle at Cambridge, he was invited by Perkins' executors to complete the commentary. As an adoring editor, Cudworth confesses plainly his anxiety of influence in a manner that elicits our trust but also alerts us to differences between himself and Perkins. In a lengthy dedicatory epistle, Cudworth reviews the state of biblical commentary and delineates the fundamental Protestant principles of exegesis. The result for the critical reader is some remarkably candid commentary on commentary, as well as an opportunity to read the only comprehensive treatment of a Pauline Epistle by Perkins. Written by Perkins for lectures and, therefore,

Gerald T. Sheppard is associate professor of Old Testament Studies at Emmanuel College of Victoria University of the University of Toronto.

more accurate than the edited transcriptions of lectures so typical of publications in this period, this work retains the true quality of oral discourse common to Perkins' public "expositions" of scripture. Perkins, a master of the "plain style" of preaching, became famous for his sermons, "not so plain but that the piously learned did admire them, nor so learned but that the plain did understand them."[1]

Modern scholars have called William Perkins "the first theologian of the reformed Church of England to achieve an international reputation" and "the principal architect of Elizabethan puritanism." He remained the "dominant influence in Puritan thought" for forty years after his death.[2] Perry Miller avers that "the seventeenth century, Catholic as well as Protestant, ranked him with Calvin."[3] Perkins' various intellectual strengths as a man of letters, rhetorician, expositor, and theologian are amply demonstrated in his exposition on Galatians. He gained a reputation as one who read "so speedily that one would think he read nothing, so accurately, one would think he read all."[4] He was thoroughly conversant with the humanistic traditions, often reflecting both the revived interest in syllogistic logic and, even more, the newer alternative rhetorical proposals such as that of his Cambridge colleague Peter Ramus. Though often characterized as a "Calvinist" and nearly "presbyterian" in some of his views, he showed great affection for established Anglican and Lutheran writers, as well as for the Latin and Greek traditions of the Catholic Church.[5] As a post-Reformation scholar, prized by "puritans" whose label he disdained, Perkins' works were renowned both in England and New England. Samuel Morison remarks that "your typical Plymouth Colony library comprised a large and a small Bible, Ainsworth's translation of the Psalms, and the works of William Perkins, a favorite theologian."[6] Perry Miller assures us, "Anyone who reads the writings of early New England learns that Perkins was indeed a towering figure in their eyes."[7]

William Perkins (1558–1602) was born in England and raised "on the borderline of the gentry," entering Christ's College, Cambridge, as a pensioner in 1577. His tutor, Laurence Chaderton, gained notoriety in the Elizabethan period as "the pope of Cambridge puritanism." Though Perkins remained a conforming, at most "moderate," Puritan, his association with Chaderton incited suspicions among his antagonists later. Upon completing a B.A. degree (1581) and an M.A. (1584), Perkins served as both lecturer (preacher) at St. Andrew's Church parish, Cambridge, from 1584 until his death, and a Fellow of Christ's College from 1584 to 1595.[8] Those influenced directly by his teaching and preaching include William Ames and John Cotton.[9] Since Perkins wrote no commentary on Romans or any other Pauline Epistle, his role as a "restorer of the Gospel" is perhaps best exhibited in this work on Galatians which alone illustrates the full force of his biblical interpretation in defense of a Protestant view of justification by faith.

The scholarly significance of publishing Perkins' *Commentary on Galatians* alongside the Geneva New Testament with its annotations and other selected commentaries from the seventeenth century is far ranging. The Pilgrim Classic Commentaries series provides an unparalleled resource for studies in English Protestant and Puritan social and political history, the Reformation in England and its legacy in New England, history of biblical interpretation, and assessments of Westminster Assembly and Confession. It also provides specific sources for the study of the renaissance heritage of Protestant poetics. A reprint series of this scope has not been undertaken since the well-known Nicholas series in the mid-nineteenth century.

In Sydney E. Ahlstrom's *A Religious History of the American People,* the late Yale historian argued persuasively that the inheritance from seventeenth-century England in America had not been adequately recognized. Ahlstrom calls for greater attention to ways in which "the Reformation was being carried out of Great Britain," precisely because from this heritage "come the colonial impulses—imperial, commercial, and evangelistic—which would form the chief foundations—political, economic, and religious—of the American tradition." A stridently Protestant America, with little regard for the massive Catholic presence in its midst, grew out of this "Protestant synthesis," giving rise to the Great Puritan Epoch that Ahlstrom thinks came to a close only in the 1960s. English Protestant religious themes of election and predestination of a chosen people composing a "New Israel" took on a powerful political thrust in the milieu of the colonies, further fueled by the Great Awakening and the American Revolution in the century that followed. What emerged was a uniquely American form of Evangelical Protestantism as spontaneously political as it was religious. Because of this profound connection between England and New England, with a history of persistent influence from the English Protestant Reformation, this series concentrates specifically on commentaries that passed from England to New England, playing a definitive role in the perception of religion and society both in the history of the United States and in some parts of eastern Canada.

Unlike biblical commentaries in the twentieth century, their antecedents in seventeenth-century England and New England pervasively influenced every level of intellectual, artistic, social, and political life. Books such as Jeremiah, Hosea, and Jonah challenge the assumption of God's continuous covenantal relationship with Israel: English Protestant commentaries on these same books sought to show under what circumstances England (or New England) might be a nation chosen like Israel or similarly rejected by God. Every aspect of social and political life invited a critique from a divine point of view—the role of the king in church affairs, the propriety of owning slaves, the use of East Indians as sources of cheap labor, the pros and cons of tobacco, and so forth. In this "Golden Age of Preaching," the commentaries fully reflected the vibrancy of the lecture hall and pulpit. Those who did not read commentaries heard them quoted, praised, or condemned. "Search the scriptures" (John 5:39) was the rallying cry of the English Protestant Reformation. Because the Bible represented, at least rhetorically, the fulcrum on which the fate of the world rested, biblical commentaries covered a vast range of contemporary issues and often wedded the highest aesthetic gifts to pragmatic concerns of daily life and politics.

When considering commentaries during this period, the editors are aware that the milieu is still largely that of a Latin church. Older Latin commentaries, including many contemporary Roman Catholic volumes, continued to be treasured by many Protestants alongside the new English contributions. Moreover, the task of selecting which works to include in this collection was complicated by an awareness of the popularity of some continental Reformation commentaries (for example, those on Isaiah, Jeremiah, and the

Gospels), which explains the tendency of English expositors to neglect certain major biblical books. In many cases a choice was made in favor of the more original contributions rather than the compilations because they better reflect an indigenous appropriation of continental Reformation themes, cast in uniquely English forms.

Because these commentaries antedate the full impact of the Enlightenment and its modern critical approach to history, they remain among the few extant English works that sustain the biblical text as a literary and coherent whole. At the same time, the seventeenth century was not, by and large, an age of sermons or of interpretations of Scripture for any but controversial and polemical purposes. Rather than resolve inner-biblical tensions or contradictions by a speculative appeal to different and autonomous authors/editors, the commentators more often found in these instances an opportunity to understand the equally perplexing tensions and contradictions of their own daily and national life. By means of this vision of a canonical text, English Protestant commentators sought to discover within the past tense of Christian Scripture a realistic and pragmatically compelling present tense, ripe with implications for their own time. Accordingly, these works warrant a distinct place in the history of English commentary and prove particularly provocative to scholars concerned with a post-modern literary interpretation of the Bible or how it was read as canonized "Scripture" within Christian faith.

Theological students will find in these commentaries a primary source for understanding the implications of the famous Westminster Assembly. Many of these same volumes were collected at Union Theological Seminary in New York City by Old Testament scholar Charles Briggs, at the end of the nineteenth century. Briggs drew on them for his defense in his historic heresy trial as a minister in the Presbyterian Church. Relying on these commentaries and a copy of the *Westminster Annotations,* Briggs argued that the Westminster Confession did not deny the value of modern historical-critical investigations of biblical texts. The close association in the commentaries between exposition of biblical claims and the value placed on the illumination of historical inquiry confirmed for Briggs that the Westminster Divines were at most "pre-critical" rather than "anti-clerical" or fundamentalistic in their approach. In the current foment over Bible and history, these volumes mark a pivotal moment in Christian interpretation.

The influence of these commentaries on English literature remains seriously underestimated. For example, when John Milton defends a controversial point in the *Tetrachordon,* he can confidently assert that "I say we conclude no more than what *the common expositors* themselves give us, both in that which I have recited, and much more hereafter." Most English Protestant commentaries did not bury the biblical text under the debris of arcane historical details or linguistic minutiae. Artistic and literary features were central elements within their style. As part of their commenting on Scripture, the expositors often rendered the scriptural text in the form of a poetic paraphrase, transforming the alien traces of Hebrew poetry into the familiar register of rhyme and meter of the great English poets. In this way the aesthetic circle was complete. As the Bible influenced the poets and great prose artists, so the Bible was itself paraphrased to meet the approval of a fastidious cultural idea of literary beauty. Without the aid of the Bible and the guide of these commentaries, English literature in this period is easily distorted.

For literary scholars these commentaries have drawn increasing attention to the long-neglected influence of Reformed theology on English and American literature and culture. Students of the seventeenth century are often hampered by a lack of primary source materials. This Pilgrim Classic Commentary series provides precisely the materials necessary to study biblical typology, English Protestant defenses of poetry, the art of biblical translation and paraphrase, the "plain style," the complex manner in which the Bible affords a literary model for Protestant poetry and prose, as well as the intertextual nature of the commentaries themselves. Literary scholars conversant with the great literature and poetry in the seventeenth century will be particularly interested in this series for it provides essential background material that will bring precision to studies of how Reformed theology directly influenced the poetry and prose of the period.

Grateful acknowledgment is made to David Green, director of St. Mark's Library, General Theological Seminary, for his assistance and for permission to reprint this edition of Perkins' work, and to Eva Kushner, president of Victoria University, and to the Northrop Frye Centre, for a generous research grant.

NOTES

1. Thomas Fuller, *The Holy State and the Profane State* (London, 1642; new ed., 1841), with notes by James Nichol, 81.

2. Ian Breward, "The Significance of William Perkins," *Journal of Religious History* 4 (1966): 113; John Eusden, *Puritans, Lawyers, and Politics* (New Haven: Yale University Press, 1958), 11; Christopher Hill, *Society and Puritanism in Pre-Revolutionary England* (1964; reprint, London: Panther Books, 1969), 216.

3. Perry Miller, *The Marrow of Puritan Divinity,* Publications of the Colonial Society of Massachusetts 23 (1936), 255.

4. Fuller, *The Holy State,* 82. See also Samuel Clarke, *A Marrow of Ecclesiastical Historie* (London, 1654).

5. See Donald McKim, *Ramism in William Perkins' Theology* (New York: Peter Lang, 1987), 11–12.

6. Samuel Eliot Morison, *The Intellectual Life of Colonial New England,* 2d ed. (New York: New York University Press, 1956), 134.

7. Perry Miller, *Errand into the Wilderness* (1956; reprint, New York: Harper & Row, 1964), 57.

8. On the social status of young Perkins, see Breward, "The Significance of William Perkins," 116. For an excellent summary of the life and work of William Perkins, see McKim, *Ramism,* 5–13.

9. H. C. Porter, *Reformation and Reaction in Tudor Cambridge* (Cambridge University Press, 1958; reprint, New York: Archon Books, 1972), 269.

Reflections on the Reissue of William Perkins' *Commentary on Galatians*

BREVARD S. CHILDS

The reissuing of William Perkins' famous commentary on Galatians is a happy occasion. It has long been out of print and virtually inaccessible to all but a few scholars. Perhaps most important in the publication is the strong affirmation that there is something of lasting value in these Puritan commentaries.

One can, of course, mount a fully legitimate argument for reissuing such a commentary by stressing its historical significance. Although the English Puritans expended much of their energy in writing commentaries on the Bible, modern scholarly interest in the Puritans has tended to neglect this genre and focus rather on those areas that seem to stand in some direct continuity with modern political, social, or economic institutions. Yet from a strictly historical perspective the commentaries contain a wealth of fresh material that is basic to understanding the Puritan mentality. Indeed, one of the best ways to see the effect of the American experience on Puritanism is to compare later editions of commentaries published in the New World with the original English editions.

It seems to me, however, that the strongest reasons for republishing commentaries such as Perkins' are theological. Particularly at this time in the late twentieth century, when confidence in scientific biblical scholarship has begun to erode and a wide-

Brevard S. Childs is Professor of Old Testament Interpretation at the Divinity School, Yale University.

spread uncertainty reigns regarding the interpretation and use of the Bible, these commentaries serve as a rich resource for fresh reflection on the problem of biblical interpretation in general.

One should quickly add that this venture can obviously be misunderstood. There can be no simple repristination of the past, nor can Perkins' exegesis be read without critical reflection. Indeed, the challenge to the modern reader is to gain the skill and competence needed to distinguish between the valuable and the worthless in the very particularity of a seventeenth-century context. Because most modern Christians judge the controversy between Geneva and Rome in a different light than did Perkins, there is need for critical understanding, both of his concrete historical situation and the limitations of his polemic. Yet because doctrinal precision was for Perkins a matter of life and death, his stance is not to be easily dismissed as merely theological narrowness, which the adherents of the Enlightenment once imagined.

Several specific features in Perkins' commentary are marks of its particular excellence. First, there is a sober attempt to deal with the text in its literal sense. Admittedly, this is not carried out with great philological learning; nevertheless, the author shows a genuine sense for the literature and careful attention to the details of the text. For example, Perkins is concerned to discuss in the context of chapter 2 the number of actual visits made by Paul to Jerusalem. In addition, he seeks to follow carefully the argument of the entire epistle, which he continually outlines with great clarity.

Second, one of the greatest strengths of his exposition is that he seeks to penetrate specific texts to the larger theological issues at stake. Much like Calvin, he moves consciously from the verbal sense of the text to explore the theological substance of the issue at stake. Invariably, he relates Paul's controversy with the Galatians to the larger theological issues of Christian liberty, justification by faith, and Christian peace and concord. Perkins moves with great ease through the whole of the Old Testament as well as the New in such a way that his commentary serves as a kind of biblical theology. Admittedly, in his Galatians commentary Perkins makes rather infrequent use of the church fathers, which stands in contrast, say, to Calvin or Bucer.

Third, the commentary has an immanently practical goal which informs his exposition and remains the hallmark of great Puritan writing. Perkins has in mind a Christian audience whom he is consciously instructing in the ways of God and in the vocation of righteous response. Often he reserves his practical application to a subsection entitled "use," but frequently he moves to application in other parts of the exposition without a sharp distinction. There is a deftness and remarkable confidence in the way in which Perkins passes from the description of Paul's world to a concrete application to his congregation. His parenesis is not to be confused with flat moralism, but reflects an earnest struggle with the imperatives of the Christian faith on a very practical level.

Finally, a word of congratulations is due to The Pilgrim Press for this bold venture which makes it possible for a strong Christian voice out of the past to speak again to the future.

Authority and Interpretation in Perkins' *Commentary on Galatians*

JOHN H. AUGUSTINE

William Perkins devoted a large portion of his works to the interpretation of Scripture.[1] These biblical commentaries often originated as sermons he preached at Great St. Andrew's Church in Cambridge.[2] In writing commentaries, Perkins followed the tradition of Melanchthon, Bucer, Calvin, and other Reformers who attempted to direct the new freedom of interpretation gained through the break with the Roman Catholic church. Although the Reformers embraced the new familiarity with Scripture attained through the publication of the Bible in English, it was apparent that such a broad distribution of Bibles created its own problems: there were as many interpretations of Scripture possible as there were readers.

For Reformed Protestants this situation raised an issue of authority. They felt compelled to attack the policy of the Roman Catholic church that forbade personal interpretation and discouraged translation, yet they also had to try to stem the tide of extreme interpretations fostered in part by their own insistence on the importance of a particular individual's reading of Scripture. Consequently, English divines were forced to become authoritative scriptural expositors themselves, and thus risked assuming the very authority they sought to avoid. An examination of Perkins' treatment of issues of scriptural interpretation and authority in his *Commentary on Galatians* within the context of a broader discussion

John H. Augustine is an associate fellow at Pierson College of Yale University.

of Reformed ideas of biblical interpretation in Renaissance England will demonstrate Perkins' attempt to ascribe authority to the Word of God rather than to himself as an interpreter. An orientation to the *Commentary* itself and its rhetorical strategies will precede a discussion of Perkins' references to apostolic authority, the authority of Scripture, the authority of the literal sense, and the authority of Christ and the Holy Spirit in his interpretation of Galatians.

AUTHORITATIVE RHETORICAL STRATEGIES

Ralph Cudworth (d. 1624), a fellow of Emmanuel College and friend of Perkins, prepared the *Commentary on Galatians* (1604, 1617) for publication shortly after Perkins' death in 1602. In addition to being a fellow of Emmanuel College, Cudworth was a minister at St. Andrew's Church in Cambridge, where Perkins often preached. In 1603 Cudworth was appointed as lecturer in Cambridge on the *Epistles to the Galatians*. He later became a royal chaplain to James I. His son, Ralph Cudworth (1617–88), was the noted Cambridge Neoplatonist. Perkins' *Commentary on Galatians,* as Cudworth claims, is unmatched by any previous commentary on Galatians, and he compares it to Luther's *Commentary on Galatians* (1535), predicting that Perkins' work "will find the like favour and acceptance" (A4v).[3]

Cudworth's "Dedicatory Epistle" to Perkins' *Commentary* attempts to justify the use of scriptural commentaries while preserving the authority of Scripture itself. Rather than "contemne the simplicitie of the Scriptures" as did certain novices in the universities, he characterized the Scriptures as possessing "great majestie joyned with simplicity, and as great difficultie mixed with plainnes and facilitie" (A3r). Just as catechisms are necessary for gathering the "plaine and easie places," so commentaries are necessary for understanding "such places as are more abstruse and difficult" (A3v). Moreover, Cudworth argues that scriptural commentaries are authorized by the precedent and practice of Scripture itself, for "Our Saviour Christ (the great Doctor of the Church) hath by his owne practise given us a president hereof in expounding the lawe. Matth. 5. in expounding all hard parables to his disciples a part: for the text saith, that he *unfolded* or *expounded them unto them.* Mark 4:33" (A3v). "But," Cudworth warns, "how Commentaries ought to be written, it is not so easie to define, there beeing such difference as well in regard of the manner of writing, as of the measure" (A3v). He blames "fantasticall Anabaptists" on the one hand and "prejudicate Papists" on the other for misunderstanding the purpose and role of scriptural commentaries. In addition to misconstruing the "foure severall senses of the Scripture," Roman Catholic commentators, for instance, "take occasion to enter into infinite frivolous questions, *which breede strife rather than godly edifying which is by faith*" (A3v). Further, he claims that such excursions obscure the dialectic between the reader and the Holy Spirit that is essential to the understanding of Scripture: "Which tedious discourses, and impertinent excursions from the text, serve for no other ende but to cast a mist before the eyes of the reader, and drawe (as it were) the veile of Moses over his face, so that he cannot see the meaning of the holy Ghost" (A4r).

The "Epistle to the Reader," also by Cudworth, describes the occasion of the writing of Perkins' *Commentary* and praises Perkins as an exemplary Christian and expositor of Scripture. The *Commentary on Galatians* consists of adaptations from three years of Sunday sermons, which, in Cudworth's view, deserve special attention because they were "penned the last of all his workes, beeing come to ripenes of judgement: and that upon mature deliberation after his Sermons (as his manner was)." In addition, they were "written with his own hand" (A5r), unlike Perkins' other works which, with the exception of some of the shorter treatises, were transcribed by others. Consequently, Cudworth claims that they exceed his other works and "that they surpasse in this kinde all the moderne writers that have gone before them: so that he which will vouchsafe to read them shall not greatly neede nor desire any other Interpreter upon this Scripture" (A5r). Like Chaucer's cleric who "first he wroughte, and afterward he taughte," Cudworth commends Perkins' consistent application of his teachings to his own life. Yet he considers it unnecessary to point this out since Perkins is already well known and sufficiently commended by others for "soundnes of doctrine, and integritie of life: which (whilst he was living) did parallel each other, his doctrine beeing a patterne of his life, and his life a counterpaine of his doctrine" (A5v). Frequently invoking tropes of humility, Cudworth also notes that since Perkins was unable to complete the exposition of Galatians before his death, Cudworth was called upon to finish the task. Cudworth testifies that he was "neither chosen out of purpose to make ostentation of witt, reading, or invention: but left as a necessary task to be performed by some for the perfecting of the worke and the good of the Church: (if this poore mite may conferre any thing to the Treasurie of the Lords temple") (A5v).

After praising Perkins for his personal integrity and astute interpretation of Scripture, Cudworth prescribes what he considers to be the proper method of scriptural interpretation. The "manner" of biblical commentary is clear to Cudworth and other Reformed Protestants: the literal sense must be the basis of doctrinal interpretation. As for what he calls the "measure" of biblical commentary, Calvin's maxim of *perspicua brevitas* holds true: they should be clear, concise, and relevant. In a crucial passage, Cudworth describes the proper "manner" of scriptural commentary:

> But as for the manner: the literall sense (which our author here followeth) is the onely sense intended by the Spirit of God: the Allegoricall, Tropologicall, Anagogicall, beeing but severall uses and applications thereof: For the Scripture (consisting in the sense not in the letters) is profitable to teach, and improove, as *Paul* saith: whereas from the Allegorical sense no necessary argument can be taken (as their owne doctors consent) either to confirme or confute any point of doctrine: and therefore much lesse from the Tropologicall, or Anagogicall. (A4r)

Immediately following, he describes the "measure" appropriate for interpreting Scripture:

> And as for the measure, in regard of brevitie or prolixity, the golden meane hath alway beene judged by the learned to be the best, which is not onely to give the bare meaning paraphrastically, but to make collection of doctrine and application of uses; yet briefly, rather pointing at the cheife, then dwelling long upon any point. (A4r)

Furthermore, Cudworth follows Perkins and places special emphasis upon the need for the application of doctrine for "confutation, correction, instruction, and consultation" (A4v).

Perkins' sermons—now transcribed as commentary—reflect the technique and cadence of oral address while Cudworth's *Supplement* conveys the style and texture of commentary, intended to be read. Filled with polysyndeton, correlation, emphatic conjunction, and the mnemonic force of repetition, Perkins' speech-based prose progresses as a series of loosely coordinated sentencelike structures rather than as a series of clearly defined sentences. This creates a sense of disjointedness not present in Cudworth's *Supplement*. However, this very same loose coordination of phrases and sentences produces a sense of immediacy. As did the author of the Pauline Epistles, Perkins uses frequent references to apostolic authority to enforce the importance of his case. In addition, he follows the Pauline Epistles by combining a logical with an emotional appeal in an attempt to persuade his readers to respond to scriptural injunctions. For instance, after defining and dissecting the meaning of faith and related ideas (113–14), Perkins discusses the meaning of a phrase from Gal. 2:20, "I am crucified with Christ." In vivid detail, he calls for the reader to "apply thy selfe to Christ crucified, hand to hand, foot to foot, heart to heart; and thou shalt feele in thy selfe a death of sinne, and the heat of spiritual life to warme and inflame thy dead heart" (124–25).

In discussing the work of William Tyndale, *The Obedience of a Christian Man* (1528) in particular, Janel Mueller makes a similar point about the use of apostolic authority in her analysis of Tyndale's method of persuasion: "The theological paradigm duly becomes a compositional paradigm, as the Scripturalism of Tyndale's own style manifests itself in the assimilation of native resources of expression to the sentence forms and rhetorical devices that characterize the Pauline Epistles where apostolic authority takes the guise of an irresistible call for a feeling response."[4] Mueller takes the analysis a step further by claiming that Tyndale was directly influenced not only by Paul's appeals to his authority but by the sentence forms and rhetorical devices of the Pauline Epistles themselves. Accordingly, Mueller uses the term "Scripturalism" to denote "a writer's absorption with the text of the Bible and with rendering its meaning in English—an absorption so intense as to mark the writer's own style with the impress of Biblical modes of expression."[5] Like Barbara K. Lewalski's treatment of the Bible as a literary model for poets in *Protestant Poetics and the Seventeenth-Century Religious Lyric,* Mueller emphasizes "a writer's molding of his thought and language forms after a recognizable mode or model from the Old or New Testament."[6] Though Perkins' *Commentary on Galatians* is filled with everything from full quotations of scriptural texts, to brief allusions to scriptural phrases, it rarely reflects the type of stylistic influence described by Mueller. Perkins' use of Scripture is much more detached and deliberate, often taking the form of a long catalog of scriptural citations or a paraphrase of a scriptural text. He differentiates clearly between scriptural text and commentary. In addition, his extremely ordered textbook style, with its seemingly endless lists and divisions, mitigates against allowing a particular scriptural style to develop.

Perkins crafts a number of evocative images designed to enforce various doctrinal positions. These images often take the form of similes. For example, in a discussion of Gal. 3:1 he likens the Galatians to "a peece of waxe without all forme: fit to take the forme and print of any religion" (138). Earlier, he uses the extended simile of a hand to assist in his comparison of faith, hope, and love:

> Faith is like an hand, that opens it selfe to receive a gift, and so is neither love, nor hope. Love is also an hand, but yet an hand that gives out, communicates, and distributes. For as faith receives Christ into our hearts: so love opens the heart, and pouers out praise and thanks to God, and all manner of goodnesse to men. Hope is no hand, but an eye that wishly looketh, and waiteth for the good things, which faith beleeveth. Therefore it is the onely propertie of faith to claspe and lay hold of Christ, and his benefits. (113–14)

In a discussion of the importance of a reliance on grace rather than the law for salvation, he calls Gal. 5:3–4 a "thunderbolt against all Popery" (331). This combination of vivid imagery and frequent similes helps to lighten the enormous load of definitions, classifications, and catalogs as well as the characteristic interrogative exchanges that abound in Perkins' *Commentary.* Donald McKim demonstrates that Perkins' work followed a Ramist pattern or method that was characterized by highly schematized charts and divisions. Though McKim perhaps overstates his conclusion by the assertion that "Perkins' biblical commentaries show that he approached the Scriptural books with the tools of the Ramist philosophy firmly in hand" (70), it is evident that Perkins used a very deliberate strategy of working by careful division and classification in his explication of Paul's Epistle to the Galatians.

A number of organizational strategies are apparent in Perkins' long and detailed *Commentary*. With the text of the Epistle to the Galatians from the Geneva Bible prominently in view, Perkins examines the Epistle through a detailed verse-by-verse analysis.[7] However, he is careful even in statements describing his method to point out that he is merely following the example of his authority, the apostle Paul:

> In Paul's example, we see what it is to search the Scriptures, not onely to consider the scope of whole bookes, and the parts thereof; but to ponder and weigh, every sentence, and every part of every sentence, and every circumstance of time, place, person. This is the right forme of the studie of divinitie to be used of the sonnes of the Prophets. (187)

Perkins' concern stems in part from his desire to link his method of exposition to the precedent established by the apostle Paul and thus lend credence to his commentary without detracting at all from the authority of the Scripture itself.

In a discussion of the "plain style" of preaching (Gal. 3:1), Perkins suggests that three things are most important for effective preaching:

> The first is, true and proper interpretation of the Scripture, and that by it selfe: for Scripture, is both the glosse, and the text. The second is, savorie and wholesome doctrine, gathered out of the Scriptures truly expounded. The third, is, the Application of the said doctrine, either to the information of the judgement, or to the reformation of the life. (140–41)

Perkins uses these three categories—meaning, doctrine, and application—to organize his discussion of each verse or group of verses.[8]

However, Perkins in the *Commentary* and Cudworth in the *Supplement* approach their discussion of the meaning, doctrine, and application of the text in different ways.

Perkins divides the Epistle into three parts: preface, instruction, and conclusion. The preface (1:1–5) introduces the reader to Paul and the situation in Galatia. The instruction section is divided into two parts: doctrine (1:6—5:12) and manner (5:13—6:11). The "summe" of the "doctrine" section provides "a reproofe of the Galatians for revolting from the Gospel" (15). According to Perkins, the "manner" section begins that portion of the Epistle dealing not with issues "touching the faith of the Galatians" but with issues "touching good life" (351). The "ground," or guiding principle for maintaining this "good life" is contained in the words, *"Brethren yee have been called to libertie"* (351). Two rules follow from this guiding principle: "One in these [words], *use not your libertie as an occasion to the flesh:* the other in these, *Doe service one to another by love* (351). The conclusion (6:12–18), as Cudworth writes in his *Supplement,* repeats the main points of consideration in the Epistle:

> First, that neither circumcision is necessary to justification, nor the ceremoniall law to salvation. Secondly, that the false Apostles urging the observation of the lawe as a thing necessary to salvation, sought not herein Gods glorie, or the edification of their hearers, but their owne ease, and freedome from the crosse, and persucution. Thirdly, that Christ crucified is the onely thing that justifies a sinner without the workes of the Lawe. Fourthly, that the true religion standeth not in outward things, but in the renovation of the inward man. (538)

In the first half of Perkins' exposition of Galatians 1—5, each exposition of a verse or group of verses contains a summary discussion of the particular verse or verses, often within the context of the rest of the Epistle, followed by a paraphrase of the passage. For instance, in a discussion of Gal. 2:19 Perkins first explains the meaning of the passage and then paraphrases the passage:

> In these words, *Paul* sets downe a second reason, to prove Christ to be no minister of sinne, in abolishing the justice of the law. And the reason is framed thus: We Jewes, justified by

> Christ, are dead to the law, not to live as we list, but live to the honour of God. Therefore Christ in taking away the justice of the law, is not the minister of sinne. (118)

In another instance, he discusses Gal. 3:26–28 in the context of the chapter and then paraphrases the passage:

> If we Jewes were still under the law as under a schoolemaster, then we should be still after the manner of servants: but we are not after the manner of servants: because we are children: for even ye Galatians, and that all of you are children of God, not by Circumcision, or by the keeping of the law, but by faith in Christ. Againe, that they are children of God, he prooves it thus: Ye are baptized into Christ, and in baptisme ye have put on Christ, in that ye are joyned with him, and have fellowshippe with him, who is the naturall Sonne of God: therefore ye are sonnes of God. (205–6)

The initial introduction and paraphrase are followed by a long section that examines the doctrines raised by a particular passage. At this point, Perkins usually begins the often lengthy process of uncovering numerous layers of ideas that will then be examined in numerical order. For example, he follows his paraphrase of Gal. 3:26–28 with the following order of discussion:

> In these words, I consider two things. The first is, the benefit or gift bestowed on the Galatians, which is sonne-ship, Adoption, or the condition of Gods children. The second is, the description of this benefit by foure arguments. The first is, by the circumstance of the persons, *ye all are children of God*. The second is, the inward meanes, namely, *faith in Christ Jesus*. The third is, the outward meanes, or the pledge of adoption, *ye are all baptised into Christ*. The last is, the foundation of adoption, and that is *to put on Christ,* or, *to be one with him*. (206)

These categories are further divided and subdivided in his process of exposition. Since Perkins considers that the authoritative interpretation of Scripture is provided by other passages of Scripture ("both the glosse and the text"), his discussions often involve incidental references to related doctrines in other passages or to long digressions on doctrines that are only alluded to in the Epistle itself. These divisions and digressions often take the form of answers to questions or objections raised in the text by unnamed advocates of another view. Perkins' often heated responses to these hypothetical questions reflect not only his own disputatious stance but the increasingly dogmatic nature of theological discussion in the period. Other questions serve as a guide to Perkins' examination of the implications of the text at hand. For instance, in his discussion of Gal. 4:1–7, Perkins' introduction to a series of questions and answers contains his explanation for this Socratic method: "The first, the sending of the Sonne, is in these words, *In the fulnesse of time, God sent forth his Sonne*. That we may attaine to the sense of this great Mysterie, sixe questions are to be propounded" (245). Yet another instance of this interrogative method exhibits the pervasiveness of Perkins' attempt to attribute the authority of interpretation to the Scripture rather than to himself: "For a more ful declaration of this authoritie, I propound these three questions" (241). In a highly ordered fashion, Perkins explains the meaning, doctrine, and application of a scriptural passage. He supports his interpretation by the paraphrase and dissection of a particular text as well as by placing his interpretation within the context of other scriptural texts.

In his exposition of chapters 4 and 5, Perkins introduces another method of organization. While this approach still relies on the three broad categories of meaning, doctrine, and application, he occasionally begins by defining the important words in a verse before expanding his perspective to examine what he calls the "sense" of the doctrines under discussion, the "scope" of the passage in relation to the rest of Scripture, and, finally, the "use" or application of the text to the reader's life.[9] In these chapters Perkins relies upon what he considers to be analogous texts to authorize his definitions of words used in particular verses. Likewise, Cudworth uses other scriptural passages to support his case for the definition of words used in the text.

Cudworth's less polemical, more analytical exposition of chapter 6 covers similar ground, though he pays much greater attention to the etymology of words and their original definitions in Greek.

For example, he discusses the use of the word "burdens" in Gal. 6:2: "The Apostle calleth slippes, infirmities, and sinnes, by the name of *burdens,* taking his metaphor from travellers, who use to ease one another, by carrying one anothers burden, either wholly, or in part: that so they may more cheerefully, and speedily goe on in their journey" (432). At one point Cudworth outlines his approach, explaining what he calls the "rule" or doctrine at hand. His comments refer to Gal. 6:6, but they serve as a guide for the rest of his exposition of chapter 6: "In handling of the rule, I will first shewe the meaning of the words; secondly, the reasons of the rule: thirdly, the objections against it: lastly, the doctrine, and uses, that are to be gathered from it" (467). Unlike Perkins, Cudworth maintains a high, formal style, and relies on quieter, more extended images that invite a reader to enter into a consideration of the idea or doctrine under discussion. Rather than comparing our sinful state to being imprisoned, as Perkins does (195–96), Cudworth paints a picture of a peacock and calls his readers to consider their own sinful state: "In so doing we shall with the Peacocke, now and then cast our eyes downeward, to our feete, the fowlest and ugliest things we have: and not alway stand in admiration of our gay feathers, and glorious traine" (453). His extended comparison of a minister to a ship captain exemplifies Cudworth's gentler approach as opposed to Perkins' polemics, as well as the evocative character of Cudworth's imagery:

> The master of the ship (a man would thinke) were idle, and did nothing: he stands not to the tackling, he stirreth not the pumpe; he driveth not the oares, he foundeth not the deepe, he rideth not the ropes; but onely sitteth still at the sterne, and looketh to the pole-starre, and guideth the compasse; yet his labour passeth all the rest: were it not for him, the shippe would runne her selfe under the water, or strike upon the rockes, or be split upon the sands, or fall foule with another (as marriners speake). Even so for all the world fareth it with the Ministers of the word: they seeme to sit still, to be at ease, to doe nothing; and yet their labour is double and treble to other mens bodily labour, except they be unfaithfull, and doe the worke of the Lord negligently. (472)

In addition, Cudworth includes broader allusions to classical culture (450), though he openly agrees with Perkins that human learning should be used sparingly in sermons (478). The basis of authority remains, for Cudworth as well as for Perkins, in Scripture itself. In a discussion of Gal. 6:2, Cudworth attacks the "frivolous distinction[s] forged by the Schoolemen" because they lack "the warrant of Scripture or consent of Antiquitie" (443).

For both Perkins and Cudworth the third and most important category of scriptural exposition—after meaning and doctrine—is the application of Scripture to the life of the believer. This emphasis on the practical application of the meaning and doctrine of the verse under discussion receives consistent attention throughout both the Commentary and the Supplement. The "use" or application follows directly from the doctrinal explanation:

> Thus we see how God sent forth his Sonne: the use followes. This act of God in sending, declares his infinite love: for this sending was for their sakes that were the enemies of God. And it further signifies unto us the most free love of God. For nothing in us mooved him to send, but his owne goodnesse. This love of God must moove us to love God againe, and to be thankfull. (247)

In fact, Perkins goes so far as to make understanding Scripture contingent to some degree upon the practice of an individual's beliefs or "baptisme":

> Commentaries are needfull to the studie of the Scriptures: and the best Commentarie to a mans owne selfe is his owne baptisme. For if a man have learned to know ought and to practise his owne baptisme, he shall the better be able to understand the whole: and without this helpe, the Scriptures themselves shall be as a riddle unto us. (231–32)[10]

The practical application of Christian doctrine to a believer's life is so important to Perkins that he alludes to James 1:22, "But be ye doers of the word, and not hearers only, deceiving your own selves" (AV), in a number of key places as part of his authoritative context for interpretation (1:6–7, p. 19; 2:20, p. 124; 5:19–21, p. 383). In the closing lines of Cudworth's "Dedicatory Epistle" to his *Supplement,* he too emphasizes a connection between the understanding of Scripture and its application: "The comfortable meaning of the Scriptures is better understood, then by all the speculations of the most curious Skeptikes: as the sweetnes of hony is better knowne in a moment by him tha[t] tasteth it, then by those that spend many houres in the contemplation and discourse of it" (Dd3r). To strengthen the case for the importance of the practical application of scriptural teaching to a believer's life, Perkins supports his reading of Galatians with references to the authority of the apostle Paul.

APOSTOLIC AUTHORITY

In Perkins' opening "Argument" to his *Commentary,* he describes the "occasion" of Paul's Epistle to the Galatians and defines what he calls the "scope" of the letter.[11] The situation that motivated Paul to write his Epistle arose when "certain false Apostles" challenged the authority of his calling as an apostle which, in turn, raised questions about the veracity of his teachings. These "false Apostles" intended to seduce "the Churches of Galatia persuading them that justification and salvation was partly by Christ and partly by the Lawe" (1). Perkins presents Paul's response to this challenge to his authority and the "scope" of the Epistle in the form of a broad outline of the Epistle:

> The Scope of the Epistle is in three things. First the Apostle defends his calling in the first and second Chapters. Secondly, he defends the truth of his doctrine, teaching justification by Christ alone. And upon this occasion he handles the greatest question in the world, Namely, what is that Justice whereby a sinner stands righteous before God, in the 3. and 4. and in the beginning of the fift. Thirdly, he prescribes rules of good life in the fift and sixt chapters. (1)

Perkins ascribes apostolic authority—"one called to be a planter & founder of the Church of the new Testament among the nations" (1)—to Paul and places particular emphasis on the title "Apostle" throughout his *Commentary.* He anchors his discussion of Paul's argument for justification by faith in Paul's defense of his authority as an apostle. Moreover, he identifies the special nature of revelation in apostolic teaching, "the immediate word of God" (4), with the special nature of revelation in Scripture in order to support an authoritative role for both the apostle and the whole context of Scripture itself in the process of interpreting Scripture.

Cudworth pays less attention to issues of authority, though he maintains a characteristically Protestant emphasis on the authoritative role of the "scope," or the broader shape, context, and purpose of Scripture itself and the "simplicity that is in Christ" (478) in interpreting Scripture (6:8). He contrasts the Reformed method of what he calls the "clearing of this text" (468) with those whose four levels of biblical interpretation merely obscure the true teachings of Christ in Scripture. He claims in graphic images that

> the maine scope of the ministery, is, to preach the word purely, and to applie it powerfully to the consciences of men: and it condemnes all deceitfull handling of the word, and all huckster-like dealing, in mingling wine and water together, wheat and chaffe, gold and drosse, in perverting it with aguish and fottish conceits, in wrestling it with allegories, tropologies, and anagogies, & in wringing the text till they make it bleede, and so (as an ancient writer saith) presse the two dugges of the Scriptures, the old and new Testament, that in stead of milke they drinke nothing but blood. (478)

In the process of establishing the relevancy of Paul's divine calling as an apostle to scriptural interpretation, Perkins considers the unique status of an apostle as one called directly or "immediately" by God. He frequently cites the direct calling of the apostle Paul by God in an attempt to lend authority to the message of the Epistle. For example, Perkins emphasizes Paul's appeal to his apostleship by referring to the apostle's direct calling from God in a syllogism that provides a "summe" of the body of the *Commentary*, or what Perkins calls the "doctrine" section of the Epistle:

> *If I be immediately called of God to teach, and my doctrine be true, ye ought not to have revolted from my doctrine.*
>
> *But I was called immediately of God to teach, and my doctrine is true. Therefore ye should not have revolted from my doctrine. (15)*

Later, in a restatement of "the principall argument of the Epistle" (155) at the beginning of his discussion of Gal. 3:1, Perkins again bases his appeal on the divine calling of the apostle: "That we may see how this chapter depends on the former, we must repeat the principall argument of the Epistle: If I was called of God, and my doctrine be true, then ye should not have revolted to an other Gospel: but I was called of God, and my doctrine is true: therefore ye should not have revolted to an other Gospel" (136).

Unlike ordinary ministers, who are called of God by the ministry of others, an apostle is one called not by people "but by Christ immediatly" (4). Perkins then explains what it means to be called by "the immediate word of God" (4). The apostles are directly taught by the Holy Spirit and thus their teachings, the "word of God," are infallible: "For in that they were called immediately, they were also taught by immediate inspiration, and also aided by the infallible assistance of Gods spirit" (4).

An important qualification for proper biblical interpretation accompanies Perkins' confidence in expositing Scripture. He claims that the Spirit directed the apostles and prophets in writing the Scripture, and he notes that the Scripture must be enlivened by the faith of the reader in order to become the Word of God: "The essentiall note of the Church is faith: faith stands in relation to the word of God: and the word of God is no word unto us unlesse we know it to be so: and we know it to be so, because it was written by the Apostles, who in preaching and writing could not erre" (4). With this distinction in mind, Perkins points out the difference between the inspired Word of God and the mere word of humans. He writes,

> The doctrine of the Apostles is the immediate word of God, because it was given by inspiration both for matter and wordes: whereas the doctrine of the Church in sermons, and the decrees of Councels is both the word of God and the word of man. The word of God, as it agrees with the writings of the Apostles and Prophets: the word of man, as it is defective, and as it is propounded in tearmes devised by man. (4)

The obedience required in response to the "immediate word of God" helps to explain Perkins' concern for the application or "use" of the apostle's teaching. Hence, for Perkins as well as for Cudworth, the authority of the apostolic writer establishes warrants for the authority and proper interpretation of Scripture.

THE AUTHORITY OF SCRIPTURE

The doctrine of the apostle's "immediate word of God" and the interpreter's admixture of the Word of God and the word of man explains Perkins' desire to subordinate his exposition to Scripture itself. Repeatedly he stresses the authority of the biblical Word enlivened by the Holy Spirit. Paul the apostle, in preaching and writing, represented the direct authority of God, for "God puts his owne authoritie into the word which he [Paul] uttered: and he was assisted by the extraordinary, immediate, and infallible assistance of Gods spirit" (23). Consequently, the written word of God, when enlivened by the Spirit, authorizes itself, and God's written word stands

> in excellency & authority, above al men and angels. And hence it followes, that the Church and Councels cannot authorize the word of God, in the mind and conscience of any man. For the inferiour and dependent authority, addes nothing to that which is the principall, and superior authoritie. Therefore the opinion of the Papist is false, that we cannot knowe the scripture to be the word of God, but by the testimony of the church: as though the letter of a Prince could not be knownen to be so, without the testimony of the subjects. The principall authority is sufficient in it selfe, to authorize it selfe, without externall testimony. (24).

In an important discussion of Gal. 4:13–16, Perkins reiterates his earlier claims for the authority of Scripture and explains why the form as well as the content reflect the "immediate word of God":

> Here Paul notably expresses the Authority and Honour of an Apostle, which is to be heard even as Christ himselfe: because in preaching he is the mouth, and in writing the hand of God. This authority is to be maintained: and the consideration of it is of great use. The Papists say, we know the scripture to be the

> word of God, by the testimonie of the Church: but indeede the principall meanes whereby we are assured touching the truth of Scripture, is, that the books of scripture were penned by men, whose writings, and sayings, we are to receive, even as from Christ himselfe, because they had either Propheticall or Apostolicall authoritie, and were immediately taught and inspired in writing: and all this may be discerned, by the matter, forme, and circumstances of the foresaid books. (286)

Perkins' "ordinarie ministers" who are "called of God by the ministerie of men" (4) lack the authority of an apostle called directly by God. In the same way, Perkins the commentator shifts the authority away from himself as preacher and biblical expositor of Scripture to the Scripture itself.

Perkins' emphasis on the "immediate word of God" stands in direct opposition to the Roman Catholic church's emphasis on the roles of priest and pope, and explains his constant polemic against the Catholic church. He claims that the Catholic church attempts to steal the authority from the Word of God:

> Lastly, seeing it is the propertie of an Apostle to be called immediatly by Jesus Christ, hence it follows, that the authority, office, and function of apostles ceased with them, and did not passe by succession to any other. Therefore it is a falsehood that the Pope of Rome succeedes *Peter* in Apostolicall authoritie, and in the infallible assistance of the spirit, when he is in his Consistory. (5)

To further establish the Scripture's authority, Perkins, writing as a biblical expositor, frequently refers to familiar Protestant principles of biblical interpretation. One claim echoes throughout his commentary: "Scripture is both the glosse and the text. And the principall meanes of the interpretation of scripture, is scripture it selfe" (311). To an objection that the sense of the written word must be authorized by the church, Perkins repeats the familiar maxim that "Scripture it selfe is both *the glosse,* and *the text*" (311), and explains at greater length that his interpretive principles are based on a firm conviction of the primacy of the literal sense:

> Scripture is the best interpreter of it selfe. And the sense which is agreeable to the words of the text, to the scope of the place, to other circumstances, and to the analogie of faith: in the plainer places of Scripture, is the proper and infallible sense of Scripture. Thus fetching the sense of Scripture from it selfe, we shall keepe our selves within the limits of Scripture, and in the matter of our salvation have certentie of faith, which we shall never have, if we listen to reason, tradition, and the authority of men. (383)

Perkins' references to the importance of the broad context of Scripture indicate both the importance of the literal sense to his interpretation as well as the ability of Scripture to interpret itself.

THE AUTHORITY OF THE LITERAL SENSE OF SCRIPTURE

Methods of scriptural interpretation in Renaissance England remained quite diverse and reflected equally diverse theological perspectives. The various points of view led to serious disagreement regarding the proper aims of literary interpretation. Roman Catholics continued to prize allegorical interpretation of the Scripture, while most Protestants disagreed with this position. A number of important theological debates demonstrate the positioning of traditions. In *A Disputation on Holy Scripture Against the Papists* (1588), William Whitaker, a Calvinist and scriptural expositor, defends the English Protestant doctrine of the authority of Scripture against the attacks of the Jesuit Robert Bellarmine and Thomas Stapleton, an English Catholic.[12] William Fulke, a Puritan theologian famous for his part in the Vestiarian Controversy at Cambridge, fought with three Catholics, D. Heskins, D. Sanders, and M. Rastell, over issues of scriptural interpretation (1579).[13] In addition, there was some dissension in the Protestant church over multiple levels of biblical interpretation.

The Protestant biblical expositors shared a new interest in the literal interpretation of Scripture. While not all Protestants practiced the same method of scriptural interpretation, the differences were, nonetheless, minimal since they shared the same general approach. Distinction existed, however: William Tyndale, William

Whitaker, and Perkins emphasize varying aspects of the Protestant position on biblical interpretation.

Tyndale examines allegorical methods of biblical interpretation in *The Obedience of a Christian Man* (1528), chiefly asserting that "the scripture hath but one sense, which is the literal sense."[14] He protects the literal sense from a purely naturalistic reduction of it by affirming that the "literal sense is spiritual."[15] In addition, he assails the Catholic "sophistes with their anagogical and chopological sense," who claim "that the scripture serve[s] but to feign allegories," (307), for they have made the literal sense "become nothing at all"; they "not only say the literal sense profiteth not, but also that it is hurtful."[16] Allegories by themselves in Tyndale's view are insignificant unless supported by other biblical passages in their proper literal context.

By allowing only those allegorical interpretations "where the text offereth thee an allegory," Tyndale maintained a position similar to Martin Luther's.[17] Despite Luther's commitment to the literal sense, he was willing to permit some allegorization of the literal sense as an aid to preaching. He suggests,

> Allegories doe not strongly prove and persuade in Divinitie, but as certaine pictures they beutifie and sette out the matter. . . . For as painting is an ornament to set forth and garnish an house already builded; so is an allegorie the light of a matter which is already otherwise proved and confirmed.[18]

A clear description of the literal sense was given by William Whitaker, who articulated exegetical positions closely reflecting Luther's and Tyndale's on this issue. He discusses in his *Disputation* how "allegories, tropologies and anagoges are . . . various collections from one sense, or various applications and accommodations of that one meaning." He claims that there is "but one true, proper and genuine sense of scripture, the literal."[19] In addition, Whitaker explains his avoidance of the allegorizing of the Catholics, who "say that all the sense mentioned above are to be found in every passage of scripture."[20]

Calvinists like Perkins were more guarded about the use of allegorical interpretation. Calvin stepped beyond Luther's hermeneutics and was extremely careful about any use of allegory in scriptural interpretation. A discussion of Gal. 4:22–24 in his *Commentary on Galatians,* translated into English in 1581 by R. Vaux, provides an important text for Calvin's principles of scriptural interpretation.

> Hee [Saint Paul] writeth these things to have an Allegorical meaning. Origen and many other more with him snatche occasion hereby to wrest the Scripture this way and that way from the naturall sence, for thus they gathered, that the literall sence was to lowe and to base: that therefore under the barke of the letter, there laye hidden greater misteries, which otherwise could not be got out but by devising allegories. . . . The scripture, say they, is plentifull, and therefore bringeth forth manifold sences or meaning, I confesse that the scripture is a very bountifull fountayne of al wisedome and such as cannot be drawn drie: but I denie that the bountie thereof consisteth in divers and contrary sences, such as every man may devise of his own braine.[21]

The principles of interpretation according to the literal sense were applied throughout Calvin's commentaries.

Perkins stresses the importance of the literal sense in scriptural interpretation. "The Church of Rome maketh 4 senses of the Scriptures," he says, "but this her device of the fourfold meaning of Scripture must be exploded and rejected. There is only one sense, and the same is the literall."[22] Like Calvin, Perkins explains his position on the literal sense in his discussion of Gal. 4:24–25:

> Here that Papists make a double sense of Scripture, one *literall,* the other *spirituall*. . . . *Spirituall* senses they make three. One *allegoricall,* when things in the old Testament are applied to signifie things in the new Testament. The second, is *Tropologicall;* when scripture signifies something touching maners. The third, is *Anagogicall,* when things are in scripture applied to signifie the estate of everlasting life. Thus Jerusalem properly is a citie: by allegorie, the Church of the new Testament: in a tropologicall sense, a state well ordered: in an anagogicall sense, the estate of eternall life. These senses they use to applie to most places of the Scripture, specially to the historie. But I

> say to the contrary, that there is but one full and intire sense of every place of Scripture, and that is also the literall sense, sometimes expressed in proper, and sometimes in borrowed or figurative speaches. To make many senses of scripture is to overturne al sense, and to make nothing certen. As for the three spirituall sense (so called) they are not sense, but applications or uses of scripture. (304–5)

Perkins follows Calvin in rejecting an allegorical interpretation of Gal. 4:24–25 as a primary sense of the text. He likens such an interpretation to "the madnesse of men that hence gather Transsubstantiation, or the reall conversion of bread into the body of Christ. They might as well gather hence the conversion of Agar into mount Sinai" (306). Yet the insistent Perkins does recognize that "the Scripture is not only penned in the proper tearmes, but also in sundry divine figures and allegories" (305). Citing specific examples of scriptural figures and allegories, he suggests that Scripture is only to be understood figuratively when "the proper signification of the words be against common reason, or against the analogie of faith, or against good manners" (305). Luther calls this passage from Galatians "a wonderful allegory"[23] which indicates the human bondage created by the law. Still, he views the allegory as merely ornamental, comparing it to certain pictures that "beautify and set out the matter."[24]

Reformed Protestants placed great value on the literal meaning of Scripture. Their perception of the literal sense of Scripture differs from the medieval exegetes', who thought that the literal sense was the most simplistic level of interpretation.[25] They also claimed that certain allegorical interpretations were used to support doctrinal positions that ran counter to the Reformation. The Protestant would tend to see in Scripture literal and historical truth where the Roman Catholic would also sense allegorical resonance that could be used to support a particular doctrinal position.

For the Reformers, the literal meaning was simply the plain sense in contrast to allegorical meanings that often altered the literal sense of the word: "That is the true sense of the scripture, which is natural and simple: and that let us embrace, and hold with tooth and nayle."[26] Figurative meanings, if they were required by the text, were considered part of the literal sense. "The Scripture," writes Tyndale, "useth proverbs, similitudes, riddles, or allegories . . . but that which the proverb, similitude, riddle, or allegory signifieth, is ever the literal sense."[27] The Reformers, however, did not abandon a christological interpretation of Scripture. The Word of God was Christ as revealed in Scripture through the action of the Holy Spirit.

THE AUTHORITY OF CHRIST AND THE HOLY SPIRIT

For Perkins, Scripture's ultimate authority comes from its ability to convey the teachings of Christ. He claims that "in the New Testament, there is but one rule and order for all men, and that is the rule of Christ" (296). The "rule of Christ" determines our interpretation of Scripture because Christ is "the true object of our faith" (142). Thus "the bookes of Scripture are not bookes of policy (as Atheists suppose) to keepe men in awe, but they are the very word of God" (35). However, when Perkins speaks of Scripture he is referring not merely to the text alone but to what the literary historian John R. Knott calls the "dynamic interaction of Spirit and Word."[28]

Perkins' references to the Word of God recall similar references by other Reformed Protestants and indicate the important role played by the Holy Spirit in Protestant hermeneutics. These discussions help to explain the basis for Perkins' understanding of the Scripture's authority. Following Calvin and the early Reformers, William Whitaker argues, in his *Disputation on Holy Scripture,* that Scripture became the authoritative Word of God only through the work of the Holy Spirit:

> The sum of our opinion is, that the scripture is *autopistos,* that is, hath all its authority and credit from itself; is to be acknowledged, is to be received, not only because the church hath so determined and commanded, but because it comes from God: and that we certainly know that it comes from God, not by the church, but by the Holy Ghost.[29]

Whitaker claims that the Spirit confirms the authority of the "living" Word of God.

A number of Reformed Protestants, including Perkins, use a metaphor of vision to explain the role of the Spirit in scriptural interpretation. In another passage from the *Disputation,* Whitaker discusses the importance of "the eyes of faith" to the interpretation of Scripture. Whitaker claims, following Calvin, that Scripture generates its own light for those who look with the "eyes of faith."[30] Whitaker's use of vision imagery refers to a particular view of the text available only by faith and the work of the Spirit. The Elizabethan poet Sir Philip Sidney uses a similar metaphor in his *Apology for Poetry* (1595) to indicate a relation between an individual's spiritual life and the enjoyment of the aesthetic dimensions of the psalmist's poetry. He writes that "unspeakable and everlasting beauty" can be "seen by the eyes of the mind, only cleared by faith." This vision, too, depends on the work of Christ, for in order to see properly, the sinful "eyes of the mind" require forgiveness gained by faith in Christ.[31] To be thus justified by faith, according to Protestants, involved the illumination of the Spirit. Using metaphors similar to those used by Whitaker and Sidney, Calvin explains these connections in a section of the *Institutes of the Christian Religion* entitled, "The Word becomes efficacious for our faith through the Holy Spirit":

> And this bare and external proof of the Word of God should have been amply sufficient to engender faith, did not our blindness and perversity prevent it. But our mind has such an inclination to vanity that it can never cleave fast to the truth of God; and it has such a dullness that it is always blind to the light of God's truth. Accordingly, without the illumination of the Holy Spirit, the Word can do nothing.[32]

Perkins develops the metaphor of the eye of faith to a greater extent than either Whitaker, Calvin, or Sidney. In fact, he uses the metaphor to explain Gal. 3:1. Both posing and responding to questions about how believers are to understand the meaning of Christ's crucifixion for their own lives, Perkins stresses the importance of an active, heartfelt faith and the important role of the minister or expositor in establishing the gospel of Christ in the hearts of believers:

> And how must we behold him? by the eye of faith, which makes us both see him, and feele him, (as it were) crucified in us. Here note, that implicit faith, (which is to beleeve as the Church beleeves,) is a blind faith: for by it we cannot contemplate and behold Christ. And the common fault is here to be noted, whereby men neglect and passe by this contemplation of Christ. There is among us the evill eye that devoureth all it seeth: there is the adulterous eye: but where is the eye of faith to behold Christ? where is the force of this eye to be seene, which maketh the thing which it beholdeth to be ours, and us like unto it? Wee love to tricke and paint our bodies, and some to set fine complexions on their faces (and therefore complexions at this day are made a kind of merchandise) but away with such vanities. If ye love to be painted, I will tell you what ye shall doe. The office of the Ministers is to describe, and paint out Christ unto us: let them paint Christ crucified in the heart, and set up his image there, and then shalt thou have a favourable complexion in the eye both of God, and man. (142)

As the Spirit enlivens the text, it becomes the "living" Word of God. For instance, Calvin writes in the *Institutes* that "the Scriptures obtain full authority among believers only when men regard them as having sprung from heaven, as if there the living word of God were heard."[33] Elsewhere, Calvin explains his view that the Word and Spirit belong inseparably together: "For by a kind of mutual bond the Lord has joined together the certainty of his Word and of his Spirit so that the perfect religion of the Word may abide in our minds when the Spirit, who causes us to contemplate God's face, shines; and that we in turn may embrace the Spirit with no fear of being deceived when we recognize him in his own image, namely, in the Word."[34] Knott traces the use of this idea of what he calls "the kinetic quality of the Word" in the writings of other Reformed Protestants and he discusses the extensive authority thus attributed to this "living" Word in Renaissance England. Knott claims that "all English Protestants would agree that in some sense the Bible expressed the 'living' Word of God. . . . A sense of the divine presence in Scripture led many of them to pay minute attention to the details of the text and to allow its authority to extend to virtually every aspect of their lives."[35]

Cudworth describes the place of scriptural commentary in relation to the authoritative and "living" Word of God. He explains in his "Dedicatory Epistle" preceding the *Supplement* to Perkins' *Commentary on Galatians* that both an outward guide, or commentary, and an inward guide are required for the reading and interpretation of Scripture because "to goe alone is not so safe" (Dd3r). In language that recalls Calvin's frequent references in the *Institutes* to "the internal testimony of the Spirit," Cudworth identifies the "inward guide" as the Holy Spirit and claims that it is indispensable for the understanding of Scripture. He writes that

> *The inward guide, is the spirit of Revelation, which dwelleth onely in a humble, docible, & obedient heart, which whosoever bringeth, hath a promise that he shall know the truth, John 7.17 and understand the secrets of God. Psal. 25.14. and without which the Scriptures are but as a riddle or a clasped booke.* (Dd3r)

To provide "outward" or intellectual guidance for interpreting Scripture, Cudworth recommends a commentary, *"especially,"* he writes, *"such a one as a sanctified spirit hath much breathed upon: seeing it is the best learning the Theorick of him which is skilfull in the Practicke"* (Dd3r).

CONCLUSION

The purpose of this essay has been to show how certain concerns about authority and interpretation dominate Perkins' *Commentary on Galatians.* These concerns have been examined within the context of a general introduction to the respective styles and rhetorical strategies of Perkins and Cudworth. By emphasizing in Galatians Paul's appeals to his apostolic authority, as well as Protestant principles of scriptural interpretation that emphasize the vital role the living Word of God plays in the process of interpreting Scripture, Perkins sought to ascribe authority to the Word of God rather than to himself as an interpreter. In other words, Perkins was careful not to cite his own learning and interpretations as authoritative in themselves; he avoided any forms of self-promotion related to the use of his knowledge in order to avoid detracting from the Holy Spirit's work in the Word of God.[36]

NOTES

1. William Perkins was a prolific and articulate spokesperson for Reformed Protestants in Renaissance England. R. T. Kendall notes that "by the end of the sixteenth century Perkins had replaced the combined names of Calvin and Beza as one of the most popular authors of religious works in England," witnessing the publication of "seventy-six editions (including repeated issues) during his lifetime, seventy-one of which came after 1590" (*Calvin and English Calvinism to 1649,* Oxford Theological Monographs [Oxford: Oxford University Press, 1982], 52–53). Moreover, Peter Lake claims that "like so much else in the Puritan tradition it was in many ways summed up in the works of William Perkins" (*Moderate Puritans and the Elizabethan Church* [Cambridge: Cambridge University Press, 1982], 297).

Nevertheless, the works of the Anglican Perkins have been largely overlooked in this century. In the 1940s Louis Wright commented, "The writings of the Reverend William Perkins . . . have not been republished since the seventeenth century; no modern anthology includes anything from his pen; few teachers of history, literature, or theology mention his name in their classes. Yet this man's works were once so popular that they appeared in English, Latin, Dutch, Spanish, Welsh, and Irish, and they influenced the lives of thousands of Englishmen on both sides of the Atlantic" ("William Perkins: Elizabethan Apostle of 'Practical Divinitie,'" *Huntington Library Quarterly* 3 [1940]: 171). Wright would have been familiar with studies involving Perkins by William Haller, *The Rise of Puritanism* (1938; New York: Columbia University Press, 1957); Perry Miller, *The New England Mind: The Seventeenth Century* (1939; Boston: Beacon Press, 1961); and W. Fraser Mitchell, *English Pulpit Oratory from Andrewes to Tillotson* (1932; New York: Russell & Russell, 1962). The situation, however, is gradually changing. Several recent books, including Donald McKim, *Ramism in William Perkins' Theology,* American University Studies 7, Theology and Religion 15 (New York: Peter Lang, 1987), a number of articles in various theological and literary journals, and two new editions of portions of Perkins' works indicate a renewed awareness of the importance of Perkins to seventeenth-century culture in England and America. The books include Harry C. Porter, *Reformation and Reaction in Tudor Cambridge* (Cambridge: Cambridge University Press, 1958); Charles George and Katherine George, *The Protestant Mind and the English Reformation* (Princeton: Princeton University Press, 1961); Norman Pettit, *The Heart Prepared: Grace and Conversion in Puritan Spiritual Life* (New Haven: Yale University Press, 1966); John A. Coolidge, *The Pauline Renaissance in England* (Oxford: Clarendon Press, 1970); Kendall, *Calvin and English Calvinism to 1649;* Nicholas Tyacke, *Anti-Calvinists: The Rise of English Arminianism c. 1589–1640,* Oxford Historical Monographs (Oxford: Clarendon Press, 1987). McKim lists a number of recent articles on Perkins (pp. 245–46). The two editions are *The Work of William Perkins,* ed. Ian Breward, Courtenay Library of Reformation Classics 3 (Appleford, Eng.: Sutton Courtenay Press, 1970); and *William Perkins, 1558–1602, English Puritanist: His Pioneer Works on Casuistry,* ed. Thomas Merrill (Nieuwkoop, Neth.: B. De-Graaf, 1966).

2. Although it is not unusual for Perkins to be called "the greatest of the sixteenth-century Puritan theologians," or "the prince of the puritan theologians," he considered himself to be in the mainstream of the established Church of England (Horton Davies, *Worship and Theology in England: From Cranmer to Hooker* [Princeton: Princeton University Press, 1970], 424; Patrick Collinson, *The Elizabethan Puritan Movement* [Berkeley and Los Angeles: University of California Press, 1967], 403). Like John Jewell, who appealed to the church fathers against Rome, Perkins attacks the papists on the one side and the separatists on the other (*The Workes of that Famous and Worthy Minister of Christ in the University of Cambridge, M. William Perkins,* 3 vols. [London, 1626–31]). Thomas Fuller, the historiographer of the moderate Protestant tradition, took Perkins as his model for the faithful pastor (*The Holy State* [Cambridge, 1642]). Most current studies of Perkins consider him to represent a moderate rather than radical form of Protestantism. In fact, the religious historian Peter Lake argues that Perkins is a product of "precisely the moderate puritan tradition with which this study is concerned"; his study is entitled *Moderate Puritans and the Elizabethan Church* (10). See also Porter, *Reformation and Reaction,* 238, 260, 267–68; Kendall, 51–76; and Tyacke, *Anti-Calvinists,* 5, 29–33.

3. William Perkins, *A Commentarie or Exposition, upon the five first Chapters of the Epistle to the Galatians: penned by the godly, learned, and judiciall Divine, Mr. W. Perkins. Now published for the benefit of the Church, and continued with a Supplement upon the sixth Chapter, by Ralph Cudworth, Bachelour of Divinitie* (Cambridge, 1617). Subsequent references to this work are cited parenthetically in the text. I have silently regularized i/j and u/v.

4. Janel Mueller, *The Native Tongue and the Word: Developments in English Prose Style 1380–1580* (Chicago: University of Chicago Press, 1984), 192.

5. Ibid., 40.

6. Ibid., 245. Barbara K. Lewalski discusses Protestant sermon theory in *Protestant Poetics and the Seventeenth-Century Religious Lyric* (Princeton: Princeton University Press, 1979). She suggests that these theories "shed considerable light on the poetics of the religious lyric in the seventeenth century" (p. 214). Although she notes that Scripture is the primary resource for the preacher's sermon (p. 226), her concern is not with how Scripture functioned in sermons but with how Scripture functioned as a stylistic model for preachers and, by extension, for poets of the seventeenth-century religious lyric. She writes, "English Protestants of all parties appealed even more directly and centrally than had Augustine to Biblical texture and style as the model for, or at least as a determinant of, the preacher's appropriate art. This appeal does not lead to artlessness or to the abnegation of art in the presentation of sacred subject matter, but rather to the development of an art whose precepts may be derived, and whose stylistic features may be imitated, from the scriptures" (219). For further discussion of the role of Protestant sermons in Elizabethan England, see Mitchell, *English Pulpit Oratory;* Porter, *Reformation and Reaction;* Horton Davies, *Worship and Theology in England: From Cranmer to Hooker* (Princeton: Princeton University Press, 1970), 133–87; and idem, *Like Angel from a Cloud: The English Metaphysical Preachers: 1588–1645* (San Marino: Huntington Library, 1986), 227–54, 294–348.

7. This attention to the treatment of individual verses is reflected in the fact that both the 1604 and 1617 editions of the *Commentary* conclude with three indexes: "Common Places Handled in this Commentarie" (Pp6r–v), "A Table of all those places of Scripture which are briefly expounded in this Commentarie" (Pp7r–v), and "An exact Table of all particulars contained in this Commentarie" (Pp8r–Rr4r).

8. Perkins defines the "plain style" of preaching at great length in his exposition of Gal. 3:1: "Here first, we are to observe, the properties of the Ministerie of the word. The first, that it must be plaine, perspicuous, and evident, as if the doctrine were pictured, and painted out before the eyes of men. Therefore the Church of Rome deales wickedly, in keeping the Scriptures in an unknowne tongue. For this is to cover that from the people, which is to bee painted before the eye of their minds. Againe, that kind of preaching is to be blamed, in which there is

used, a mixed kind of varity of languages, before the unlearned. For this is a singe to unbeleevers. I Cor. 14.22. And in this kind of preaching we doe not paint Christ, but we paint out our owne selves. It is a byword among us: *It was a very plaine sermon*. And I say againe, *the plainer, the better*" (140).

9. See Perkins' discussion, e.g., of Gal. 5:9 (343–45), 5:10 (345–47), and 5:11–12 (347–51).

10. In his discussion of Gal. 3:26–28, Perkins provides an extended discussion of baptism (211–38).

11. For a discussion of the use of the term "scope," see Gerald T. Sheppard's article in this volume.

12. William Whitaker, *A Disputation on Holy Scripture Against the Papists,* trans. William Fitzgerald, Parker Society Publications 46 (Cambridge, 1849), 403–10, 467–73. This was published in Latin in 1588 and reprinted in 1610. It is a series of lectures on John 5:39, "Search the Scriptures." Whitaker gave the lectures at Cambridge while he was Regius Professor of Divinity and Master of St. John's College. In his address to the reader, Whitaker explains the method used in editing the lectures: "The style is that which was used in delivering them orally, scholastic and concise, suitable not for expansion (which was little suited to our design), but for argument. They are published as they were taken down by some of my constant and attentive auditors, and have afterwards been reviewed by myself." Barbara K. Lewalski calls Whitaker's works "central to English hermeneutics" in *Donne's "Anniversaries" and the Poetry of Praise* (Princeton: Princeton University Press, 1973), 156. See also Charles K. Cannon, "William Whitaker's *Disputatio de Sacra Scriptura:* A Sixteenth-Century Theory of Allegory," *Huntington Library Quarterly* 25 (1962): 129–38; and Victor Harris, "Allegory to Analogy in the Interpretation of Scriptures," *Philological Quarterly* 45 (1966): 1–23.

13. Fulke's *Heskins Parleament repealed* is contained in *D. Heskins, D. Sanders, and M. Rastel accounted . . . three pillers . . . of the Popish Synagogue* (1579).

14. William Tyndale, *Doctrinal Treatises and Introductions to Different Portions of the Holy Scriptures,* ed. Rev. Henry Walter, Parker Society Publications 43 (Cambridge: Cambridge University Press, 1848), 304.

15. Ibid., 309.

16. Ibid., 307, 308.

17. Ibid., 307, 305.

18. Martin Luther, *A Commentary on St. Paul's Epistle to the Galatians,* 1535, trans. 1575, ed. Philip S. Watson (London: James Clarke, 1953), 206v.

19. Whitaker, *Disputation on Holy Scripture,* 404.

20. Ibid., 405.

21. John Calvin, *Commentaries on The Epistles of Paul to the Galatians and Ephesians,* trans. William Pringle (Edinburgh: Calvin Translation Society, 1854), 104.

22. *The Workes of that Famous and Worthy Minister of Christ in the University of Cambridge, M. William Perkins,* 3 vols. (London, 1626–31), 2.737.

23. Luther, *Galatians,* 419.

24. Ibid., 417.

25. For a more extended comparison of the Reformers' method of exegesis with that of medieval exegetes', see C. S. Lewis, "The Literary Impact of the Authorised Version," in *Selected Literary Essays by C. S. Lewis,* ed. Walter Hooper (1950; Cambridge: Cambridge University Press, 1969), 127–30.

26. Calvin, *Galatians,* 104.

27. Tyndale, *Doctrinal Treatises,* 304.

28. John R. Knott, *The Sword of the Spirit: Puritan Responses to the Bible* (Chicago: University of Chicago Press, 1980), 35. Knott discusses the complex relation between the Word of God and the Holy Spirit and the way it was handled by the early Reformers (pp. 13–41). Heinrech Heppe traces the unraveling of the distinction in Reformed theology between the "living" Word of God and the text of Scripture: "The later dogmaticians on the contrary, separating the idea of inspiration from that of revelation unanimously teach that the 'Word of God' rests, not upon God's personal acts of revelation, but upon the manner of their recording, upon inspiration. On this view the 'Word of God' is 'the word brought to record by inspiration,' whereby the concepts 'Word of God' and 'Holy Scripture' were identified." Heppe claims that this change was taking place at about the time it is thought that Perkins delivered his sermons on *Galatians.* He writes that "as early as the end of the sixteenth century the conception of inspiration had changed; it was now completely severed from the idea of revelation. Scripture was therefore now regarded as inspired, purely because it was dictated to the Biblical authors by God" (*Reformed Dogmatics: Set Out and Illustrated from the Sources,* trans. G. T. Thomson, ed. Ernst Bizer [1950; Grand Rapids: Baker Book House, 1978], 15, 17).

29. Whitaker, *Disputation on Holy Scripture,* 279–80.

30. Ibid., 290.

31. Philip Sidney, *An Apology for Poetry,* ed. Geoffrey Sheppard (London: Nelson, 1965), 99.

32. John Calvin, *Institutes of the Christian Religion,* trans. Ford Lewis Battles, ed. John T. McNeil (Philadelphia: Westminster Press, 1960), 3.2.33. Citations are to book, chapter, and section.

33. Ibid., 1.7.2.

34. Ibid., 1.9.3.

35. Knott, *Sword of the Spirit,* 39–40.

36. Numerous significant areas of Perkins' work remain to be discussed. In addition to the essential work of examining the influence of this *Commentary* by Perkins on the literature and theology of both England and America, the *Commentary* itself contains treatments of central Christian doctrines; for instance, Protestant doctrines of Holy Eucharist (1:2, pp. 6–7), divine election (3:11–12, pp. 168–72; 4:8–9, p. 271), assurance of salvation (4:1–7, pp. 258–65; 4:8–9, pp. 271–73), law and gospel (3:18, p. 187), original sin (3:21–22, pp. 196–97), and baptism (3:26–28, pp. 211–38) are all treated at length. Other issues such as church polity (1:2, pp. 6–7), the possible corruption of certain editions of Scripture (3:1, pp. 138–39), a minister's role in church and society, and the use of humane learning in sermons (6:6, p. 478) are also discussed by Perkins and Cudworth in the *Commentary* and *Supplement.*

Between Reformation and Modern Commentary: The Perception of the Scope of Biblical Books

GERALD T. SHEPPARD

At several crucial places in his commentary William Perkins employs a technical hermeneutical term, what he calls the "scope" of a biblical text. As a participant in the post-Reformation effort to attain new self-consciousness and precision in literary interpretation, Perkins is not casual in his use of scope, but seeks to preserve in his own time a feature he considers essential to the vision of the Scripture as reestablished by the Reformation. He contends that the "Church of Rome" controls biblical interpretation by "meanes" of "Tradition, Councels, Fathers," and that Rome assumes Protestants have "nothing but the private interpretation of *Luther, Melanchthon, Calvin, etc.*" In response, Perkins declares that Scripture is "both the glosse [annotative commentary] and the text." According to Perkins, Scripture is itself the means of interpretation, "when places of Scripture are expounded by the anologie of faith, by the words, scope, and circumstances of the place."[1] This formula conveys Perkins' definition of the "literal sense" of Scripture. He distinguished the scope of Scripture both from a summary of the Bible's doctrinal content, as expressed in the analogy of faith, and from the words and grammar of the text, what we might call today

Gerald T. Sheppard is associate professor of Old Testament Studies at Emmanuel College of Victoria University of the University of Toronto.

its "surface structure." In addition, Perkins differentiated the "scope" of a text from the "circumstances of the place," that is, from the "occasion" of the text when it is read as a period piece incited by the incidental events of an ancient time. However, by the end of the nineteenth century Perkins' understanding of "scope" became rare. The term "scope," when it was retained, became a mere synonym for "aim" or "purpose" and played almost no role at all in the late modern hermeneutical terminology that predominated in the twentieth century. Nevertheless, since the 1970s, features of the biblical text that Perkins and his contemporaries sought to identify as a text's scope have gained renewed attention, though often expressed in other, uniquely late modern terms.

In this essay I will examine commentaries on Galatians by Luther and Calvin in order to establish a precedent for Perkins' vision of the biblical text; then, I will describe Perkins' use of the term "scope" in relation to the "literal sense" of Scripture. Finally, I will show how in the modern period interpreters lost and then began to rediscover what Perkins had called the scope of a text, referring to it as the "canonical context" or the "shape" of biblical books. Rather than offering a minor corrective note in the history of interpretation, this essay claims to recover an important link between Reformation and modern ideas about literary coherence in the Bible, a link that has broad implications for our understanding of the history of religion, literary interpretation, biblical hermeneutics, and theology.

A RECOVERY OF THE LITERAL SENSE

Christians have traditionally affirmed that Scripture plays a normative role in the reception, articulation, and defense of doctrine. The Reformers sought freedom from the accumulation of normative postbiblical traditions and the authority of the Pope by reaffirming the superior authority of the literal sense. They objected to the use of "spiritual senses" as sufficient proof for the authority of church traditions, creedal confessions, or binding papal declarations. Ralph Cudworth, in his preface to Perkins' commentary, assesses these circumstances historically and hermeneutically, asserting that the "literall sense (which our author here followeth) is the only sense intended by the Spirit of God." The other senses—allegorical, tropological, and anagogical—are, at their best, "but several uses and applications" of the literal. In Cudworth's view, this position is more than merely a Protestant novelty, for "as their own [Roman Catholic] doctors confess" allegory provides "no necessarie argument . . . either to confirm or confute any point of doctrine: and therefore much lesse from the Tropologicall, or Anagogical."[2] Because Roman Catholic and some Protestant commentaries moved so quickly from close observations on the literal sense of the biblical text to extensive discourses on spiritual senses and marginally related dogmatic questions, Cudworth complains that except for a "few Glosses" there has not been "one poore Comment on the Bible for divers hundred years."[3] This negative judgment is remarkable since nearly half a century had passed since the continental Reformation. Clearly, by comparison, English Reformation commentary arrived late, but perhaps it benefited by its isolation from some of the worst of Protestant scholasticism in other parts of Europe.[4] Due to these international circumstances, English Protestant commentaries provide unique insight into the history of post-Reformation biblical interpretation. Here we have potentially fresh exposition along the lines of the Reformation, with some maturity and without the worst of the philosophical abstraction and controversy that preoccupied Protestants elsewhere.

The Reformers' appeal to the literal sense had its precedent in church history and proved effective as a way to question the authority of certain doctrines and the binding power of the Roman church. However, it introduced new problems. For example, if this position allowed Protestants to dismiss the papal claim of apostolic succession, it also reopened older questions about how plainly the Bible supported an orthodox conception of the Trinity (not a biblical term) or the dual nature of Christ. Underlying these debates were fundamental hermeneutical issues regarding how expositors should properly construe the literal sense, so that they preserved a normative vision of the Scripture shared with the early church. Advances in the sciences, history, and rhetoric, they thought, should lead to a heightened acuity of that same text rather than to a distortion or loss of it. In this regard, the modern approach consists of only a sharpening of these nascent questions. Mid-nineteenth century advocates of modern historical criticism shared these assumptions when they defended their approaches on grounds that the Protestant tradition accepted only the literal sense as normative, and identified this literal sense strictly with the historical author's original intent.[5] The debate over the nature of the literal sense of Scripture has persisted through these periods as a key issue, and one related to a discernment of biblical authority.[6]

As resources for an examination of what constitutes the literal sense of Scripture, commentaries have two advantages over theological treatises: first, their organization requires text-oriented descriptions, and, second, they must exhibit explicitly the relationship between an effective vision of the biblical text and its interpretation. In this way, an expositor's theory of interpretation is accompanied by a record of how the act of interpretation corresponds practically to the literary and historical elements within a particular vision of the text as "scripture." Viewing William Perkins as a prime representative of English Protestants in this period, we can consider how well his conception of scope reflects or goes beyond an older hermeneutical formulation of the literal sense and is aided or encumbered by advances in philological, literary, and historical knowledge. My aim is to show what was at stake in the attempt Perkins made to define the literal sense of the scriptural text in a manner he thought consonant with the older church tradition and, at the same time, in a manner supportive of an advance in the Christian understanding of true doctrine, especially the doctrine of justification by faith.

LUTHER'S AND CALVIN'S DESCRIPTIONS OF THE ARGUMENT OF GALATIANS

A comparison of the overall structure of Martin Luther's and John Calvin's commentaries on Galatians with Perkins' reveals some striking similarities. All three commentaries follow a similar format. Perkins begins, as did Luther (see the 1515 and 1539 editions) and Calvin (1548) more than a half-century before, with a short statement regarding "The Argument" of the book, followed by a lengthy commentary upon individual verses or clusters of verses.[7] The term "argument" is appropriate for two reasons: first, there is assumed to be a pattern or unified *logos* within the biblical text indicating how it makes a claim upon the reader; second, and concurrently, the reader, as a faithful interpreter of the Bible, is engaged in a contemporary defense of true Christian doctrine.

Luther's introductions to his two commentaries on Galatians confirm the absence of a formal dichotomy within the literal sense between what a text historically meant in the past and what it means for the present. In the lengthy Dedication and very brief statement of the "subject" of his 1515 commentary, Luther names and satirizes his opponents; in the commentary of 1535, his "argument" becomes virtually synonymous with a "summary" of doctrine.[8] He offers no consistently detached description of the Book of Galatians but seizes upon what he regards to be its chief concern, the doctrine of justification by faith. Luther freely draws upon passages from other Pauline letters to distinguish "Christian righteousness" from righteousness by obedience to the law, including obedience to the revealed law of God. Luther's implicit assumption is that the Pauline epistles as a whole offer the most immediate resource for the elucidation of a doctrine that finds its clearest expression in Romans and Galatians. Moreover, he reflects a view articulated as early as Irenaeus, which allows at most a pedagogical value to the law while distinguishing sharply the dispensations of the Old Testament from those of the New Testament: "When He (Christ) came, Moses and the Law stopped."[9]

Luther knows, of course, that in the context of the "New Testament" the Pauline epistles belong after the Gospels. He observes that it is "the devil's habit" to "set against us," who have understood justification by faith, "those passages in the Gospel in which Christ Himself requires works from us and with plain words threatens damnation to those who do not perform them."[10] Luther's solution to this problem is to recall the explicit teaching in the epistles of "two kinds of righteousness" and to apply this teaching as an aid to interpret properly what the Gospels claim. The law taught by Christ can pertain to our obedience only if it is kept strictly within "its limits" of "dominion only over the flesh" and never recommended to us as a means of our salvation or as a tormentor of our conscience. Within the context of Scripture the Pauline epistles function as commentary on the Gospels and show that "Christ is not a lawgiver." In sum, Galatians is interpreted by Luther as belonging to a subcollection within a larger Scripture. As such it provides a primary witness to a doctrine—justification by faith—further elaborated in the context of other Pauline epistles. It also supplies dogmatic commentary even on the Gospel narratives which, if read in isolation from the Pauline epistles, might allow a contrary assessment in matters pertaining to how the Gospel relates to the law. Luther's "argument" adjudicates in this way a claim about Scripture by construing the place of the Book of Galatians within a comprehensive vision and corresponding shape of Christian Scripture as a whole.

Calvin is far more ready to describe the literary dimensions of the biblical text and to define how the text's form and function support the argument it sustains in the context of Scripture. After he has "ascertained what was the design of the writing," Calvin provides a sketch of "the order in which it [the design of the argument] is treated." First, we will examine how he perceives "the design," and, then, how he recognizes "order" within it.

Calvin begins his presentation of the "argument" of the book on a decidedly historical question: he discusses the size and location of Galatia and then speculates about the ethnographic origins of the Galatians themselves. Calvin conceives such details as pertinent only as an aid to his interpretation of the text. He comments, after his historical digression, that "more than enough has now been said as to the origin of the nation, so far as relates to the present passage."[11] By qualifying his use of historical information in terms of how well it "relates to the present passage," Calvin seeks to sustain the biblical text itself as that upon which he comments rather than simply viewing the text as one among many resources that refer us outside of Scripture to a world of ancient geography and historical events.

Calvin's subsequent comments about the "design" of Galatians should be observed closely in order to detect his implicit assumptions about the relation of the scriptural context to his exposition:

> At the time of the Apostle Paul they were under the dominion of the Romans. He had purely and faithfully instructed them in the Gospel; but false apostles had entered, during his absence, and had corrupted the true seed by false and erroneous doc-

> trine. They taught that the observation of ceremonies was still necessary. This might appear to be a trivial matter; but Paul very properly contends as for a fundamental article of the Christian faith. It is no small evil to quench the light of the Gospel, to lay a snare for consciences, and to remove the distinction between the Old and New Testaments. He perceived that these errors were also connected with a wicked and dangerous opinion as to the manner in which justification is obtained. This is the reason why he fights with so much earnestness and vehemence; and, having learned from him the important and serious nature of the controversy, it is our duty to read with greater attention.[12]

Calvin's opening two sentences illustrate again the limited though important role of historical knowledge for his exposition. After mentioning in the first sentence a purely historical circumstance of Roman domination in "the time of Apostle Paul," Calvin shifts in the second sentence to a historical-theological affirmation that Paul's teaching of the Gospel has fallen prey to false "doctrine" among the Galatians. After Calvin describes this error of the Galatians, he characterizes Paul's response as a defense of "an article of Christian faith," as though the apostle were participating in debates of a later period. Next, Calvin moves entirely out of the narrow circumstances of the historical controversy with the Galatians by observing that the opponents of Paul sought to "remove the distinction between the Old and the New Testaments," a distinction technically alien to their time. The historical Paul gives no indication that he thinks his letter is a book of "scripture," much less a part of a "New Testament," a term first used a century later. Finally, from this assessment of the design Calvin draws insight into the "nature of the controversy" that ought to inform how we read other details of the book "with greater attention."

We see clearly that Calvin uses historical information here, as he does typically in his other commentaries, to illuminate elements in the text of Galatians, but he finds "The Argument" of the book by appeal to its form and function as a part of a larger Christian Scripture.[13] Therefore, the effective text that Calvin interprets is not restricted to its original historical import as an ancient letter.

Rather, the design of the present passage of Galatians corresponds to Calvin's vision of the text of Galatians as a scriptural book within the context of a New Testament that functions as an authoritative guide to "an article of Christian faith."

Calvin additionally describes an "order" to this "design" of the book. He concludes that in chapters 1 and 2 Paul asserts his authority as an apostle and "touches on the main point," "man's justification," which is "directly argued" in the third chapter. Calvin, then, focuses on the chief feature of the argument in the first two chapters as a response to the question, Why (does) he labor so hard in establishing his own claim to respect? Calvin shows precisely how the content of each of these chapters relates to the others.[14] He relates the third chapter (on justification by faith) to the fourth chapter (on the subject of the proper use of ceremonies, concluding with "a beautiful allegory") and to the fifth (concerning holding fast to their liberty, not allowing ceremonial disputes to distract them from "matters of real importance"). The composition of the Book of Galatians has, for Calvin, a design that, by the order of its content, circumscribes a particular argument in relation to the whole of Scripture and Christian doctrine.

Calvin can demarcate clearly the various subsections that belong to the larger design and constitute a single, dogmatic argument. The subsections (here, Galatians 1—2, 3, 4, 5) are depicted as little units of tradition with their own appropriate beginnings and endings. For example, Calvin comments on chapter 3 as a subsection: "He [Paul] pursues this topic till the end of the third chapter." Concerning the fourth chapter, Calvin opens with the observation, "In the commencement . . . he inquires into . . ." and finishes his treatment of this unit by noting, "Towards the close of the chapter his argument is enlivened by a beautiful allegory."[15] A significant difference from Luther's treatment is that Calvin does not appeal to other Pauline epistles to understand nuances of internal literary descriptions. His approach can be further distinguished from Luther's by observing his closer attention to the immediate context of the biblical Book of Galatians and his effort to describe the specific literary devices and historical motivations corresponding to the "design" of the text, indicative of its argument. Like Perkins, both Luther and Calvin maintain that the literary territory of Scripture should be properly described prior to the explication of its significance for Christian doctrine.

THE NATURE OF COMMENTARY IN PERKINS' TIME

Cudworth's preface acknowledges the difficulty in the task and nature of "commentary." He distinguishes "easie and plaine places" in Scripture from "difficult places." The first allow the pastor to compose catechisms, while the second "require interpretation, and the commentaries of the learned." The commentary is to offer "some rule" to help the reader "trie the spirits, consonant to the Analogy of faith, and doctrine of the Orthodoxe Fathers of the Church." In the New Testament, this analogy of faith or true doctrine expressed by Scripture is said to have a certain "form" (Rom. 2:20; Rom. 6:17) or "pattern" (2 Tim. 1:13). Therefore, an implicit issue for any commentary must be how the form or pattern of the literal sense of a biblical text corresponds to the form or pattern integral to the analogy of faith. Likewise, Cudworth recognizes three concerns for commentary. First, he admits that "how" commentaries should be written remains "not so easie to define," in terms of both style and length. Commentaries that engage too many dogmatic "questions" risk "the setting aside" of Scripture in deference to "vain speculations."[16] Second, he notes that the opposite extreme might be to concentrate only on exposition of the literal sense, failing to explore any of its practical "uses" and "application." But since not every reader of commentaries is a "prophet," the expositor must "cut" up the meat of the word into small pieces so that the readers, "as babes," can be nourished by it.[17] Third, Cudworth emphasizes that the commentator must "divide the word aright," and here we have a hint of what concerns us most. In brief, how an expositor envisions the pattern of a biblical text in relation to a larger conception of the truth of that text represents a fundamental matter within the history of interpretation. This issue becomes extremely significant to English Protestants in the late sixteenth and seventeenth centuries.

Regarding the earlier commentaries by Luther on Galatians,

Cudworth notes that changing circumstances have caused them to lose some of their "strength," compounding the inevitable dilution that results when a work is translated into English. By the dawn of the seventeenth century, the contemporary English counterparts to these earlier "restorers of the Gospell" had won their own major battles and now sought to refine, sustain, and, above all, defend the Protestant faith. It seems fair to say that by Perkins' time the reexamination of the Bible by English Protestants became more polemical than that of their predecessors. However, English commentary had to express itself in a very different climate, with a more self-consciously hermeneutical defense of now well-established Protestant interpretations. The expositor sought to refine the hermeneutical vocabulary of the preceding period in order to respond relevantly to the modifications in the Roman Catholic Counter-Reformation after the Council of Trent (1545) and against other Protestants of the radical Reformation who often asserted quite independent views. In the heat of these later controversies, by Perkins' time commentators often employed Aristotelian logic and rhetoric to explain nuances of the argument of a biblical book in ways that would appear novel in comparison with Luther and, especially, Calvin. For this reason, Protestants in Perkins' day have often been described by historians as "scholastic Protestants," though the labels "Post-Reformation Protestants" or, in New England, colonial "Puritans" have become typical in more recent studies, especially in reference to scholars such as Cudworth and Perkins.

PERKINS' VIEW OF THE OCCASION AND SCOPE OF A TEXT

In the same manner as Luther and Calvin, Perkins begins his commentary on Galatians with a statement of the argument; he demonstrates, however, an explicit methodological precision missing in his predecessors. "Two things," he asserts, lead him to discover the argument: "the occasion of the Epistle and the scope."[18]

The Occasion

For Perkins "the occasion in Galatians is the attack by Paul's opponents on his calling and, therefore, on his status as an apostle and the truth of "his doctrine." Paul's antagonists put forward their own doctrine "that justification and salvation was partly by Christ, and partly by the Law." This presentation of the occasion so thoroughly expresses it as a confrontation between incompatible "doctrines" that it resembles Luther's expression of "the argument" of the book as a transhistorical, primarily theological debate. Conversely, Calvin had considered particular historical features more rigorously by making observations about the secular history of the Galatians and by defining the issue in terms of whether the gentile churches should observe the same "ceremonies" as those familiar in the Jerusalem church. According to Calvin, such observances would not have presented a major problem were it not for a "wicked and dangerous" doctrinal assumption that they were necessary for salvation.[19]

The issue of Paul's calling provides Perkins with an opportunity to distinguish between ordinary ministers who are called "by the ministry of [Christian] men" and apostles who are called "not by men, but by Christ immediately." Paul, therefore, possesses "immediate inspiration," with the aid of "God's Spirit," so that "in preaching and writing [he] could not erre." When Paul states that he writes some things not "from the Lord," Perkins argues that the apostle means that those particular teachings came through the apostle's own interpretation of Scripture aided by the Holy Spirit rather than by direct command of God. Both what Paul calls a direct word from God and what he says is not "from the Lord" become equally inspired Scripture; for Perkins, "the immediate and meere word of God" must be interpreted as though all of it were written "by the finger of God."[20]

Perkins here distinguishes "immediate inspiration," a temporal gift belonging only to "apostles," from other types of inspiration he hopes for ordinary ministers whose preaching he calls elsewhere "the art of prophesying." Perkins' strong affirmations about the inspiration of Scripture often seem to circumvent questions of human "accommodation" in the biblical witness, though he points to a key problem seized upon later by historical critics. Authors of biblical tradition may, as in the case of Paul, seem to deny divine inspiration and authority for some of their words, or, more commonly, they may not claim any special revelation or divine authority at all. Perkins' solution, citing 1 Cor. 7:40 for support, entails precarious historical speculation. By expressing his response in the form of a paraphrase from Paul himself—"but I by collection and interpretation of scripture, and that by the assistance of God's Spirit"—Perkins implies that Paul intended his entire letter to be special revelation on a par with the Old Testament Scripture, a position increasingly made dubious by historical criticism. For our purpose, it is significant that in Perkins' statements about the occasion of the Book of Galatians, he is mostly concerned with historical proofs of Paul's authority and with the special inspiration of the letter as a whole, while the description of the book's warrants as a resource for understanding doctrine belongs more to a treatment of its scope.

The Scope

Perkins describes the "scope" of a biblical text as an indicator of how the content can be read in support of an authoritative argument. This technical use of the term "scope" became commonplace among English expositors from the middle of the sixteenth until the end of the nineteenth centuries, and is highly significant because it indicates the debt this period owes to the Greek church fathers rather than to the influence of classical Greek rhetoric.[21] The term *skopos* corresponds to the verb "to oversee," "to survey," or "to aim at (a target or goal)." As a noun it conveys the sense of one who watches, is a lookout, guard, watcher, or marksman, so that the word "bishop" *(episkopos)* signifies an official who watches over or, in its Latinate synonym, "supervises" the church. Denoting what a lookout can see, "scope" commonly could designate a large tract of land. By means of the "scope," one discerns the center of a target at which one aims a weapon, or, in hermeneutical terms, one can determine the aim, intent, or central purpose of a text. All of these uses of the term were common in Perkins' time.

In the early Christian Greek fathers' interpretation of Scripture *skopos* occurs frequently.[22] Athanasius used *skopos* regularly in his refutation of the Arians in the fourth century. In this older usage, the *skopos* of Scripture, close to the *upothesis* used by Irenaeus, corresponds to the credal core found clearly within the larger context of Scripture and, from this vantage point, delimits the purpose of any part of Scripture on the basis of the whole. In this way, the description of a text's scope vacillates between a vision of the larger context and appeals to the core content of Christian Scripture, so that the latter resembles a restatement of some element in the rule or analogy of faith. As an example, Athanasius contends that the Arians find biblical support for their Christology from a narrow reading of biblical texts in the Old Testament and in the Gospels because they have missed "the scope" of all these texts, which is the dual nature of Christ, as shown clearly elsewhere in the New Testament.[23]

When in the argument Perkins describes the scope of the entire Book of Galatians, he states that it consists "in three things." These "things" belong to three subsections of the literary context, corresponding generally to Galatians 1—2, 3—4, and 5—6. That these "things" conform to literary units within the larger compositional "argument" becomes apparent by how Perkins ascribes the relation of the content of each to its author, Paul. In the first section, Paul "defends" his calling; in the second, the truth of the doctrine of justification by faith. In the last section, Paul "prescribes rules of the good life."[24] This depiction of the scope addresses both the form and function of the book within the larger implicit context of Christian Scripture. Its focus is on what the biblical author, Paul, seems to assert intentionally about the subject matter of Scripture. In the commentary itself, Perkins further elaborates the scope of each part by inner-biblical evidence from the other Pauline epistles as well as from other non-Pauline biblical books in the Old and New Testaments. Hence, his description of "the scope" is concerned with how the parts of the whole book interrelate and correspond to the purpose of the book within Scripture generally.

The special character of the scope of the book becomes evident when we note how Perkins describes the epistle itself in terms of its genre as an ancient Greek letter.[25] Perkins finds three parts, not related directly to the three things of its scope. These conventional features—preface (1:1–5), instruction, and conclusion (6:11–18)—can be further subdivided. The preface, for instance, comprises both an inscription and a salutation. Even as Perkins refers throughout his commentary to the occasion as a means of illuminating the scope of Galatians, so, too, he often employs information about the surface structure of Galatians as a letter in order to delineate more precisely the scope. A subtle though significant difference exists, therefore, between the structure of Galatians as an isolated period piece, that is, as an antique letter, and its form and function as one of several Pauline letters which now also serve as books within a collection of books comprising the Bible (from *ta biblia,* lit. "the books"). The epistolary form of Galatians is clearly not identical with its scope. Nonetheless, both the occasion of the letter and its structure as a letter prove to be essential elements for Perkins, because, like the words and grammar of the text, they constitute the actual circumstances and literary vehicle within which the scope of the normative literal sense finds expression.

The crucial role played by scope is demonstrated further in Perkins' treatment of Paul's allegorical interpretation in Gal. 4:21–30.[26] In v. 21, Paul asks, "Do you not hear the law?" According to Perkins, the apostle is implying that there is a proper way to interpret the law that can be distinguished from how his opponents who are "under the law" hear it. Perkins explains, "Ye reade and heare in deed, but ye understand not the scope and drift of that which you read." Citing Romans 10, 2 Cor. 3:14, and the rich young ruler's question to Jesus, Perkins argues that the Galatians, the Jews, and the Papists all err by "mistaking and misconceiving the true scope of the law." Instead of considering that "Christ was the scope of the law," those who misunderstand the law have "a veille before their eyes in the reading of the law." This usage by Perkins is similar to what we found earlier in Luther and Calvin. The explicit teaching of the Pauline epistles on the subject of the relation of the law and gospel to justification by faith becomes the scope for a proper reading of both the Gospels and the Old Testament. Otherwise, Perkins fears even the Gospels might be wrongly interpreted as "an instrument to make us keepers of the law."[27]

In his understanding of the nature of the literal sense of Scripture, Perkins is careful to distinguish scope from both the analogy of faith and "the words . . . and circumstances of the place." Galatians 4:21–30 provokes Perkins to confront the issue of whether a biblical text has two senses, one "proper and literall," and another "spiritual or mysticall." His answer is that the literal sense, what he also calls "the full sense of the Holy Ghost," is "not only the bare history, but also that which is thereby signified." Proper and figural expositions of the literal sense "are not two senses, but two parts of one ful and intire sense." Yet Perkins has no desire to misuse "Rhetorricke" in a way that will "turne all of the Bible into Allegory," so he proposes criteria to help the expositor determine when a text in its literal sense must be read either properly or figuratively. A figural interpretation is recommended if "the signification of the words be against cōmon reason, or against the analogie of faith, or against good manners."[28] It is noteworthy that he does not list "scope" here, because scope belongs to a more preliminary step in the activity of interpretation. Conversely, as we observed at the beginning of this essay, when Perkins describes the full hermeneutical arsenal that helps one discern and expound the literal sense itself he includes scope in a significantly different list: "by the analogie of faith, by the words, scope, and circumstances of the place."[29] In both cases the "analogie of faith" alone is a common denominator.

While a grasp of the scope of a biblical text alone may not guarantee an orthodox theology, it could perhaps ensure that first, the perception of the text would be that of a scripture and, therefore, would have continuity with the same text as envisioned by earlier church tradition; second, an allowance could be made for some discontinuity with the past vision of the biblical text which could be considered constructive—indicative of more rather than less acuity in the perception of the literal sense—insofar as the Renaissance expositor made proper use of knowledge superior to earlier generations of interpreters in areas, for example, of rhetoric, history, the sciences, text criticism, or philology; and third, the text could be envisioned as a discrete arena of rhetorical elements whose semantic import may accordingly be, as Cudworth says, "both obscure and perspicuous." In other words, the significance of the scope is that it maps out the territory of the text so that the reader finds Scripture in some places to be an open book and at other places a "clasped or sealed booke" (cf. Isa. 29:11).[30] Recognition of the scope guarantees a perspective from which each of these options becomes discernible and provides an occasion for theologically profound rather than trivial interpretation of Scripture.

In sum, by describing the scope Perkins seeks to indicate the contours of the literal sense of the book. This perception of the literal sense holds together the words of the book with their subject matter of biblical revelation which finds its complete expression in terms of the analogy of faith. The analogy of faith is a logical summary of this revelation symmetrically related to the literal sense of Scripture. For Perkins, it is only after recognizing the proper scope that the Bible can be read biblically and function as a sure guide to correct doctrine.

THE SCOPE OF THE LITERAL SENSE, OLD AND NEW

Throughout the history of biblical interpretation there has been little consistency in the hermeneutical language that is concerned with how to describe the larger context of the biblical text as literature and as a vehicle of revelation. In Protestant interpretation from the sixteenth century on, the use of the biblical text to reject the authority of various church traditions naturally required precise descriptions of scriptural texts in order to support the Protestant defense of the analogy of faith. Advances in the humanistic study of philology, literature, and rhetoric raised other questions and possibilities for both Protestant and Roman Catholic interpreters. Perkins' great indebtedness to the rhetorical theories of Peter Ramus regarding how exposition of a text could be most convincing confirms the respect Protestants maintained, as had Calvin, for humanistic insights.[31]

The need for some refinement in technical terminology concerning the literary design and purpose of biblical texts became evident in the period immediately after the Reformers and as part of the response to the Counter-Reformation. The strenuous Lutheran response of Martin Chemnitz, including his effort to differentiate Scripture from various authoritative "traditions," points in this same direction.[32] In the first half of the sixteenth century the term "scope" became attractive in its older Greek sense because of the rejuvenation of studies in Neoplatonic rhetoric, especially at Cambridge University. This possibility from the side of philosophical studies surely complemented the frequent occurrence of the term in works of the Greek church fathers avidly read by the English Protestants.

The continental Lutheran theologian Matthias Flacius Illyrius (1520–1575) was a pioneer in such Protestant hermeneutical refinements. As a student of Luther he became one of the forerunners of modern hermeneutical theory, despite his vitriolic reputation earned in heated conflicts with Melanchthon. In his massive *Clavis Scripturae Sacrae* (1st ed., Basel, 1567), Flacius includes his previously circulated eight rules for "How one should read the Holy Scripture." His first rule states:

> When you start to read a book, try so far as possible, from the beginning, to keep in mind first of all, the scope ("scopum"), purpose ("finem"), or intention of the whole book/work which is, as it were, its head ("kaput") or face ("facies"). Often this can be done in a few words, and not seldom it is indicated in the superscription. This is either one, if the whole book constitutes a single body, or it is several, if it comprises several parts which are not coherent at all.[33]

Flacius proceeds to relate the scope to the argument, just as does Perkins. Moreover, he describes the scope of the text as analogous to the anatomy of a body, with the relation of chest and limbs to the head and face, as well as to a land in which one knows the compass directions and location of specific rivers, mountains, and territories.

One of the first known occurrences in English literature of scope in this sense is attributed to Hugh Latimer around the middle of the sixteenth century. In a sermon published in 1584 he states, "Every parable hath certum statum, a certayne scope, . . . it is enough for us when we have the meaning of the principall scope, and more needeth not."[34] In a similar manner, scope became a technical hermeneutical term common among preachers throughout the seventeenth century. We know that Perkins read the works of Latimer and the above-mentioned hermeneutical treatise of Flacius, because he cites them in his own writing.[35] At a minimum, the use of scope by Perkins and by other English Protestants is not an idiosyncrasy inspired by the Greek fathers but reflects a wide-ranging, text-oriented proposal common to a perception of the textuality of Scripture during the post-Reformation period in Europe, England, and New England.

Protestant introductions to biblical hermeneutics in the nineteenth century still gave an important place to recognizing the scope of a biblical text. Thomas Horne, in his impressive four-volume

Introduction to the Study of Scripture (1818), devotes an entire section to "scope" which he defines accordingly:

> The scope, it has been well observed, is the soul or spirit of a book; and that being once ascertained, every argument and every word appears in its right place and is perfectly intelligible: but, if the scope be not duly considered, everything becomes obscure, however clear and obvious its meaning may really be.[36]

Horne suggests that the interpreter consult the beginnings and endings of books, subdivisions, titles (e.g., of some psalms), repetitions, and summaries within a book. Only then can a particular passage within the book be correctly understood. Horne asserts the same for the Bible as a whole: "Thus the scope and end of the whole Bible, collectively is contained in its manifold utility, which St. Paul expressly states in 2 Tim. iii. 16, 17, and also in Rom. xv. 4."[37] Only toward the end of the nineteenth century does this usage of scope disappear, surviving merely as a vestigial referent to the intended goal or aim of an author.

THE LOSS OF SCOPE IN MODERN COMMENTARY

Perkins assumed that the biblical presentation of Paul as an author could be considered evidence in support of a cumulative argument found in the witness of the Pauline epistles of Christian Scripture. Although Perkins often explicitly states that the author of Scripture is God or the Holy Spirit, he is equally certain that the historical Paul actually wrote the letters attributed to him, and he interprets nuances by recalling an idiosyncracy of Paul or by using what Paul said plainly in other letters to clarify points in the exposition of any particular letter. Accompanying Perkins' assertion that there is only one literal sense is his repeated assumption that the expression of the Word of God coincides (without error) with the intent of the apostle as found in these letters.

Protestants in the modern period often justified the primacy of historical criticism by recalling the traditional formulation, found also in Perkins, that the literal sense of Scripture coincides with the human author's intent.[38] Likewise, the same defense of historical criticism as the primary method for recovering the normative sense of a biblical text is found in a Roman Catholic encyclical of Vatican II, Divino Afflante Spiritu (1943). Since both Protestants and Roman Catholics, as Cudworth acknowledges in his own time, agree that the literal sense is the principal, normative sense of Scripture, modern historical critics could appear both to accept the traditional formulation and to offer objective and neutral common ground preliminary to dogmatic disputation. Building on the older pre-critical assumption that the author's intent implied a historical author, the newer methods sought to deconstruct the biblical text in order to reconstruct the original sources or oral units of tradition underlying the Bible and, in turn, more accurately reflect their genuine authors, in contrast to additions by later editors or glossators. These methods found descriptions of the scope of a book crude and historically untrustworthy as guides to the intent of such recovered historical authors. Against these liberal assessments of authors stood the modern fundamentalists who endeavored to defend the historicity of the biblical authors as they are presented in Scripture. As a part of the historical debate within modernity, fundamentalists presupposed the same rigorous identification of the historical author's intent with the literal sense and usually found the older appeal to scope similarly awkward and historically unreliable.

Consequently, for modern commentators, both conservative and liberal, a common historicism led to a shared neglect of what Perkins and interpreters for nearly two centuries described as the scope of a biblical text. The older conception of scope finds its modern counterpart only in commentary subsections labeled the "aim" (Perkins also would end some sections with the aim, but reserved scope for another preliminary analysis). Though examples may be cited from the work of many modern commentators and theologians, a technical vocabulary to express this dimension of the text has gained no new consensus. In the exegetical portions of Karl Barth's *Church Dogmatics,* for example, we find an implicit attention, similar to Perkins', to the scope of biblical books.[39] However, even G.C. Berkouwer, who tries to retain an important role for scope, is apologetic and underestimates its textually descriptive potential:

> The comprehension of the goal is not a simple matter. But fear of this idea of *scopus* is fruitless, for Scripture disintegrates into

> many words without the goal, and its God-breathed character is thereby neglected.[40]

At most, Berkouwer can cite as instances of the scope of Scripture the classic summarizing statements about the gospel in John 20:31, Rom. 4:23–24, 1 Cor. 10:11, and 2 Tim. 3:16. The concept of a pattern or design within texts that would be indicative of their scope as a part of Scripture has been almost entirely lost.

Corresponding to the abandonment of the older view of scope, the modern period similarly replaced what had once been called "exposition," derived from Latin, with something called "exegesis," taken from Greek roots. Prior to the nineteenth century the English word "exegesis" indicated only an explanatory note and did not embrace the full activity of interpretation expected of an expositor. By the end of the twentieth century, exegesis came to signify a more scientific approach aimed at determining, as Milton S. Terry (1890) states, "the exact ideas intended by the author" which was the same as the "meaning" of the words. This information allows one to ascertain "the scope and plan of each writer, and brings forth the grammatico-historical sense of what each book contains." "Exposition," though often "used synonymously" with exegesis, ought to build on the work "of critics and exegetes" in order to set "in fuller form, and by ample illustration, the ideas, doctrines, and moral lessons of Scripture."[41] Here, scope has come to mean what the exegete can find only after recovering "the exact ideas" of the historical author. It now belongs to a hermeneutical activity called exegesis prior to exposition, and reflects a goal, aim, or purpose discernible within the historical intentionality rather than denoting the discovery of a text-oriented set of internal warrants within Scripture itself. In the place of an intertext established by the scope, such grammatico-historical exegesis often reduces the significance of the biblical text to a recovery of historical persons interacting with one another and with some common historical traditions.

Modern historical criticism has proven that not all of the Pauline letters can be regarded as originally written by the historical Paul, and even so-called genuine letters, for instance 1–2 Corinthians, are probably edited from two or more earlier Pauline letters by a later deutero-Pauline school. In the place of the biblical presentation of an author, historical criticism has discovered an intricate tapestry of authors and editors so that the Paul as presented in Scripture can be compared and contrasted with the Paul of a modern historical reconstruction. In this way, advances in historical interpretation have correctly undermined Perkins' presupposition that the historical Paul is the author of each of the biblical letters that carries his name. Perkins' theories about Paul's historical view of his own inspiration now seem quaint and indefensible. In the place of Perkins' appeal to the scope of a biblical book, modern exegetes have tended to let a reconstruction of ancient rhetorical or form-critical features provide the normative structure that discloses the meaning of the scriptural text.[42] What has not been as carefully considered in the modern period is the import and hermeneutical status of the biblical presentation of Paul in the formation of Scripture itself.

SCOPE AND THE FUTURE OF MODERN COMMENTARY

The genius of the appeal to the scope of a text by Perkins and his contemporaries lay in its descriptive, relatively objective character and in its persuasive appeal to a design in biblical books that indicates something about their authoritative form and function as parts of a scripture. I believe that the use of scope has been neglected in modern hermeneutical theory for two reasons: first, the inaccurate assumption that a historical reconstruction of a biblical author's intent is the same as the literal sense of Scripture, and second, an inadequate historical-critical appreciation for the semantic transformation that takes place when prescriptural traditions conjoin to form parts of a scripture in Judaism and Christianity.

Only in the modern period did a sharp distinction arise between original historical authors or redactors and biblical authors as persons presented in association with biblical texts. Only the biblical authors perform an integral syntactical function in the context of Scripture in order to demarcate which texts circumscribe key topical divisions within Scripture (e.g., Moses and the five-book Torah, Solomon and the wisdom books) as well as how traditions have been assigned a specific scriptural intertext (e.g., David of the Samuel narratives and the Psalms, and Paul in relation to a collection of the Pauline epistles).[43] On the same modern critical grounds that must question a direct historical connection between the presentation of a figure and that same figure in history, a new recognition has arisen regarding the importance of the biblical presentation in that it plays an integral role in determining the organization and context of Scripture. In this way, clues are found regarding how prescriptural traditions came to be read and heard as Scripture, so that the loss of these clues, as warrants to the scriptural function of ancient prescriptural traditions, would mean the loss of Scripture itself.

It appears that the modern pursuit of a historically reconstructed author and his or her intent inevitably atomizes the biblical books by shifting focus away from what was traditionally considered the literal sense of Scripture, that which Perkins and his predecessors sought to sustain, in order to pursue some other historical senses pertinent to selected, prebiblical traditions and their historical authors. Such a modern historical reconstruction of the intents of historical figures behind the biblical figures may naively and often unconsciously substitute for Scripture some other prescriptural text or collection of ancient traditions. From these modern reconstructions one might attempt to construe a history of religious ideas or, anachronistically, theologies, in the place of the logic, design, or scope of the canonical context of Scripture. Even in the case of Galatians, which modern historians attribute as a whole to Paul, the biblical context of the apostle Paul as author constitutes for Scripture an essential sign that warrants a search for how the scope of Galatians relates to the scope of the entire collection of Pauline letters. Using the Bible as a resource for the recovery of the religious ideas of the historical Paul, as valuable as that may be, is not identical with reading the Bible biblically as a norm of Christian revelation.

Furthermore, modern critical studies of major world religions have shown that, with the possible exception of Mani and the fourth-century Manichean scriptures, almost no one sets out to write a scripture. In his letters, the apostle Paul never claims to be writing parts of a scripture. The expressions "New Testament" and "Old Testament" as terms for the Bible do not arise before the middle of the second century A.D. From a rigorously historical perspective, prescriptural traditions become scriptural often against, in spite of, or beyond the historical author's original intents.[44] Consequently, the prophetic claims of a historical author must be subtly distinguished from the attribution of inspiration to a scriptural text that now includes both originally prophetic and non-prophetic traditions. The nature of Scripture presupposes a textual unity or an intertextuality not anticipated by the original authors of traditions caught up within it. In Perkins' account of the occasion of the Book of Galatians, he advances dubious historical theories about Paul's intent to regard self-consciously his sayings "not from the Lord" as just as "inspired" and authoritative as those he assigns to prophetic audition. Perkins considers all that Paul writes to be as "from the finger of God" in a manner that presumes the cooperation of historical events without any interference or semantic difference. These dogmatic historical statements were all vulnerable to a more sophisticated conception of history found later in the modern period.

Robert Robinson describes carefully a remarkable shift that occurred when modern interpreters compounded Perkins' naive historical assumptions by declaring that the historical author's intent should itself become the main criterion for the "literal sense," rather than, as found more typically in the traditional formulation, the other way around.[45] Likewise, Whitaker in his monumental *Disputation on Holy Scripture* suggests "we ought to consider the scope, end, matter, circumstances (that is, as Augustine says, the persons, place, and time), the antecedent and consequents of each passage."[46] Flacius, cited above, illustrates well this older order of interpretation in his list: "primary scope, purpose, or intention." Even for Thomas Aquinas, Robertson argues, the literal sense and, subsequently, what was construed as the author's intent could be found by a grammatical-contextual assessment rather than only by historical reconstruction at the expense of the literary context of Scripture. I would add to Robinson's claim a clarification that in the premodern period expositors such as Perkins assumed that the author, in the traditional definition of the literal sense, signified the biblical author, or the author as presented as a *persona* in the context of Scripture. The modern recognition that the biblical presentation of an author and the historical author of parts of a biblical book are not identical has introduced a modern problem that Perkins could not have anticipated. For this reason, Perkins can never be cited in support of modern fundamentalist assumptions about the biblical text and history; but neither can his statements about author's intent justify a dismissal of the scope of a biblical text as merely a naive, premodern way of referring to a historical-critical reconstruction of the original author.

In his monumental study of eighteenth- and nineteenth-century biblical hermeneutics, Hans Frei sought to describe a feature integral to interpretation of Scripture in the period of the Reformation that had been lost in most of modern biblical commentary and theological studies. He described this lost feature as "narrative realism," a characteristic of the "history-like narratives" found in Scripture. Depending on Eric Auerbach's assessment of "serious modern realism" in both the Victorian novel and the style of biblical narratives, Frei argues for a rediscovery of the realistic dimension typical of biblical narrative which by its own cumulative depiction makes a tyrannical claim about the nature of reality. The reader is thereby rendered a figure within this universal history of Scripture.[47]

In Frei's analysis the primary mode of understanding congruent to Scripture depends not so much on Scripture's capacity to refer outside of the text to ancient history as much as on its capacity to render reality, to make a claim about how things were, are, and shall be that lies beyond the limits and pretense of a modern history. Frei's groundbreaking study points in a promising direction but could have found even greater support in the use of scope that embodies the element of biblical realism while allowing for the multigenre nature of Scripture. By not considering Flacius or most of the late sixteenth and seventeenth centuries, Frei has perhaps allowed the later, modern preoccupation with history to induce him to focus too excessively on a biblical-literary counterpart to history, namely, realistic narrative. The term "narrative" does not play an explicit hermeneutical role in any of these periods, while "scope" does reflect an effort to describe the realistic feature as well as the literary character of the literal sense.[48]

The conception of a text's scope as put forth by Perkins closely resembles a number of recent efforts by biblical scholars to describe the shape or the composition of biblical books in their canonical context or canon-conscious redactions within the formation of Scripture.[49] All of these efforts employ specialized descriptions dependent on historical-critical advances foreign to Perkins' day, though in support of what he and his colleagues aptly recognized about the nature of Scripture and its literal sense. The challenge of any period of textual interpretation includes the need to show that there is a common text that both past and present interpreters have sought to illuminate. This matter entails a question of whether there is any genuine continuity over time in the effective vision of a text among its temporal interpreters and how they estimate any progress or advantage that might be achieved through, for example, philological gains or, in the case of the modern period, new historical knowledge. The modern period brought dramatic changes to an interpreter's understanding of the biblical prehistory that earlier generations could not have foreseen.

The perception of differences in the biblical text during the modern period must necessarily differ from that of earlier generations and therefore the perception of both continuity and discontinuity within the literal sense of Scripture must also change. In order to sustain the same vision of a text, the modern period must claim to find, as did the Reformers, a new precision in how it envisions the text in comparison with the vision of the same text in earlier times. In these terms, Perkins' use of scope as a text-oriented description corresponds well to recent modern attempts to describe the canonical context and to measure the semantic transformation that takes place when prescriptural traditions become part of a scripture. Perkins understood better than some modern historians that the capacity of a scripture to render reality for religious believers depends, in part, on its own peculiar intertext and scope. In the late modern period we have learned that historicity does not alone determine the capacity of a text to render reality and that even a modern concept of history itself entails its own wedding of myth and reality in service to a valuable, sapiential conception of human existence different from the claims about the revelation of ultimate reality so integral to the aspirations of religion and theology.

NOTES

1. Perkins, *Galatians,* 311.

2. Ibid., A4.

3. Ibid., A2.

4. For a pejorative assessment of the biblicism, scholasticism, and debates over abstract doctrine especially among Lutheran, post-Reformation Protestants, see Frederick Farrar, "Post-Reformation Epoch," in a reprint of his Bampton Lectures of 1885 entitled *History of Interpretation* (Grand Rapids: Baker Book House, 1961), 357–95. Farrar's assessment reflects his support for modern historical criticism at a time when conservative scholars often tried to argue against it by appeal to statements in support of the inerrancy of the Bible or its dictation from God that could be found in the works of early post-Reformation Protestants. However, for a more careful interpretation of how such language about the Bible should not support a naive biblicism, see Robert Preus on the term "dicto," in his *The Theology of Post-Reformation Lutheranism* (St. Louis: Concordia Publishing House, 1970), 290; and Henning Graf Reventlow, "The Age of the Puritans," in his *The Authority of the Bible and the Rise of the Modern World,* trans. John Bowden (London: SCM Press, ET 1984), 91–184.

5. E.g., W. Robertson Smith, *The Old Testament in the Jewish Church: Twelve Lectures on Biblical Criticism* (Edinburgh: A. & C. Black, 1881). After Vatican II, the same argument became commonplace among the newer Roman Catholic historical critics; see esp. Raymond Brown, *The Sensus Plenior of Sacred Scripture* (Baltimore: St. Mary's University, 1955); and his "Hermeneutics," in *The Jerome Biblical Commentary* II, ed. R. Brown, J. Fitzmyer, et al. (Englewood Cliffs, New Jersey: Prentice-Hall, 1968), 606–23.

6. Cf. Brevard S. Childs, "The Sensus Literalis of Scripture: An Ancient and Modern Problem," in *Beiträge zur Alttestamentlichen Theologie: Festscrift für Walter Zimmerli,* ed. H. Donner, R. Hanhart, and R. Smend (Göttingen: Vandenhoeck & Ruprecht, 1976), 80–95.

7. John Calvin, *Commentaries on the Epistles of Paul to the Galatians and Ephesians,* trans. William Pringle (Grand Rapids: Wm. B. Eerdmans, 1948), 13–20.

8. Martin Luther, *Lectures on Galatians 1519,* trans. Jaroslav Pelikan, in *Luther's Works* (St. Louis: Concordia Publishing House, 1963), 27:153–62; and his *Lectures on Galatians 1535,* trans. Jaroslav Pelikan, *Luther's Works,* 26:13. In Luther's 1519 edition, he prefers "The Subject of St. Paul's Epistle to the Galatians," though in the 1535 edition he

describes this same section as "The Argument of St. Paul's Epistle to the Galatians."

9. Luther, *Galatians* (1535), 7.

10. Ibid., 10f.

11. Calvin, *Galatians,* 14.

12. Ibid., 14–15.

13. Jack B. Rogers and Donald McKim, *The Authority and Interpretation of the Bible: An Historical Approach* (New York: Harper & Row, 1979), 89–116 and the selected bibliography on pp. 145–46. An impressive recent study is that of Thomas F. Torrance, *The Hermeneutics of John Calvin* (Edinburgh: Scottish Academic Press, 1988). On Calvin's limited use of the term "scope," see 51–138.

14. Calvin, *Galatians,* 15–18.

15. Ibid., 19.

16. Perkins, *Galatians,* A2–3.

17. Ibid., A4.

18. Perkins, *Galatians,* 1.

19. Calvin, *Galatians,* 14–15.

20. Perkins, *Galatians,* 4–5. For a discussion of the issue of authority in relation to the inspiration of Scripture, see John H. Augustine's article in this volume.

21. "Scopos" and its verbal counterparts do occur in Neoplatonic philosophy, often more applicable to particulars while "theoria" pertained to universals. Cf. Henry George Liddell and Robert Scott, *A Greek-English Lexicon,* rev. H. S. Jones (Oxford: Clarendon Press, 1968), 1613–14. However, it does not appear to be a key term in Greek rhetoric as shown by its absence in major studies of the same. Cf. James J. Murphy, *Rhetoric in the Middle Ages* (Berkeley and Los Angeles: University of California Press, 1974); and Wilbur S. Howell, *Logic and Rhetoric in England, 1500–1700* (New York: Russell & Russell, 1961); and studies of the rhetoric of Ramus and its influence on Perkins (see n. 18). On the specific character of rhetoric in the period of Perkins, see Barbara Lewalski, "The Poetic Texture of Scripture," in her *Protestant Poetics and the Seventeenth-Century Religious Lyric* (Princeton: Princeton University Press, 1979), 72–110. Regarding the origin of "scopus" from the Patristic tradition and the use of it by John Major, a teacher of both Calvin and Erasmus, see Torrance, *Hermeneutics,* 51; and esp. Marjorie O'Rourke Boyle, *Erasmus and Language and Method* (Toronto: University of Toronto Press, 1977), 72.

22. On the use of "skopos" among the Greek fathers, see especially

the entry and illustrations in *A Patristic Greek Lexicon,* ed. G.W.H. Lampe (Oxford: Clarendon Press, 1961), 1241.

23. Cf. Georges Florovsky, "St. Athanasius and the 'Scope of Faith,'" in his *Bible, Church, Tradition: An Eastern Orthodox View* (Belmont, Mass.: Nordland, 1972), 80–83; and H.E.W. Turner, *The Pattern of Truth* (London, 1954), 193–94.

24. Perkins, *Galatians,* 1.

25. Ibid.

26. Ibid., 298–319.

27. Ibid., 300–301.

28. Ibid., 305.

29. Ibid., 311.

30. Ibid., A3.

31. Cf. Perry Miller, *The New England Mind: The Seventeenth Century* (1939; Boston: Beacon Press, 1954); Walter J. Ong, *Ramus, Method, and the Decay of Dialogue* (1958; New York: Octagon Books, 1974); and Donald K. McKim, *Ramism in William Perkins' Theology* (New York: Peter Lang, 1987).

32. Martin Chemnitz, sections on "Concerning Traditions; From the First Decree of the Fourth Session of the Council of Trent," in his *Examination of the Council of Trent, Part 1,* trans. Fred Kramer (St. Louis: Concordia Publishing House, 1971), 217–307.

33. My translation from the reprint of parts of the 1719 print of the Clavis: Matthias Flacius Illyricus, *De Ratione Cognoscendi Sacras Literas: Über den Erkenntnisgrund der Heiligen Schrift,* ed. Lutz Geldsetzer (Dusseldorf: Stern-Verlag Janssen & Co., 1968), 91.

34. See the entry "scope," in *The Compact Edition of the Oxford English Dictionary* (Oxford: Oxford University, 1971), 2:2671–72.

35. Cf. McKim, 11. Perkins identifies a quotation as from "Illyricus in his booke of the way to understand Scriptures. Tract I." See *The Workes of that famous and worthy Minister of Christ in the Universitie of Cambridge, Mr. William Perkins* (Cambridge, 1618), 2:669.

36. Thomas Hartwell Horne, *An Introduction to the Critical Study and Knowledge of the Holy Scriptures,* 2d ed. (New York: Hurst & Co., 1834), 1:337. As do the earlier English Protestant interpreters, he treats this subject in a section entitled "#3 Of the Scope," pp. 339–40, under a chapter concerned with the scriptural context and the *usus loquendi* of a text and not in his lengthy section on special interpretation related to matters of figural speech, tropes, poetics generally, and other rhetorical features (pp. 355–82).

37. Ibid., 337.

38. Smith, *Old Testament in the Jewish Church,* 12–27.

39. Regarding the relation of historical reference in Barth's biblical commentary to the depictive realism of the biblical text, see George Hunsinger, "Beyond Literalism and Expressivism: Karl Barth's Hermeneutical Realism," *Modern Theology* 3/3 (1987): 209–23.

40. G. C. Berkouwer, *Studies in Dogmatic: Holy Scripture* (Grand Rapids: Wm. B. Eerdmans, 1975), 124–25, 184.

41. Milton S. Terry, *Biblical Hermeneutics: A Treatise on the Interpretation of the Old and New Testaments,* rev. ed. (New York: Eaton & Mains, 1890), 19.

42. See Brevard S. Childs, "Galatians," in his *The New Testament as Canon* (Philadelphia: Fortress Press, 1984), 297–310; and esp. his criticism, pp. 300–304, of the Hermeneia Series commentary on *Galatians* by Hans Dieter Betz (Philadelphia: Fortress Press, 1979).

43. Regarding the integral relationship between the presentation of Paul and the existence of a biblical collection of Pauline epistles, see Childs, *New Testament as Canon,* discussion of the authorship of 2 Thessalonians, pp. 361–72, and his treatment of the pastoral epistles in general, pp. 373–95. See also Raymond Brown's distinction between the "literal sense" and the "canonical sense" of Scripture in his *The Critical Meaning of the Bible* (New York: Paulist Press, 1981), 30–35.

44. Cf. Wilfred C. Smith, "The Study of Religion and the Study of the Bible," *Journal of the American Academy of Religion* 39/2 (1971): 131–40; and my article "Canon," in *The Encyclopedia of Religion,* ed. Mircea Eliade (New York: Macmillan Co., 1987), 3:62–69.

45. Robert Robinson, *Roman Catholic Exegesis Since Divino Afflante Spiritu: Hermeneutical Implications,* SBL Dissertation Series, 3 (Atlanta: Scholars Press, 1988), 23–24.

46. William Whitaker, *A Disputation on Holy Scripture, 1558,* trans. William Fitzgerald (Cambridge: Cambridge University Press, 1849), 470.

47. Hans W. Frei, *The Eclipse of Biblical Narrative: A Study in Eighteenth and Nineteenth Century Hermeneutics* (New Haven: Yale University Press, 1974), esp. 13–16.

48. For a criticism of this use of narrative and "narrative theology," see Eberhard Jüngel, *God as the Mystery of the World,* trans. Darrell L. Guder (Grand Rapids: Wm. B. Eerdmans, 1983), 309–14.

49. For bibliography, Henning G. Reventlow, *Problems in Biblical Theology in the Twentieth Century,* trans. John Bowden (Philadelphia: Fortress Press, 1986), 132–44; and see esp. Brevard S. Childs, *The New*

Testament as Canon; and idem, *The Old Testament as Scripture* (Philadelphia: Fortress Press, 1979); Rolf Rendtorff, *The Old Testament: An Introduction* (Philadelphia: Fortress Press, 1984); James Sanders, *Torah and Canon* (Philadelphia: Fortress Press, 1972); and on "canon conscious redaction" see my article "Canonization: Hearing the Voice of the Same God in Historically Dissimilar Traditions," *Interpretation* 34/1 (1982): 21–33; and idem, *Wisdom as a Hermeneutical Construct: A Study in the Sapientializing of Old Testament Traditions,* Beihefte zur *Zeitschrift für die alttestamentliche Wissenschaft* (Berlin: Walter de Gruyter, 1980).

A COMMENTARIE, *OR,* EXPOSITION VPON the fiue first Chapters of the Epi- *stle to the Galatians: penned by the* godly, learned, and iudicious Diuine, Mr. William Perkins.

NOW PVBLISHED FOR THE BEnefit of the Church, and continued with a Sup- *plement vpon the sixt Chapter, by* Ralfe Cudworth Bachelour of Diuinitie.

Printed at London by *Iohn Legatt*, Printer *to the Vniuersitie of* Cambridge.
1617.

MELIORA SPERO
A. Gifford, D.D.
of the Museum.

TO THE RIGHT HONORABLE, RIGHT VERTVOVS, AND MOST TRVLY RELIGIOVS LORD,

ROBERT, Lord RICH, Baron of Leeze,&c. Grace and peace.

HE holy Scriptures (Right Honourable) giuen by diuine inspiration, and penned by the holy men of God, Prophets, Apostles, and Apostolike writers, not by priuate motion, but as they were guided by the holy Ghost; are not onely commended by God, and left vnto the Church as a pretious *depositum* carefully to be kept in their integritie (for which cause the Church is called *the ground and pillar of truth. 1. Tim, 3. 15.*) not to be defended onely by the sword of the Magistrate, against Heretikes, Schismatikes, and men of scandalous life, in which respect he is called (and that truly,) *Custos vtriusque tabulæ*: but also to be the pillar and foundation whereon to rest our faith; the touch-stone of truth; the shoppe of remedies for all spirituall maladies; an anker in the blasts of Temptation, and waues of affliction; a two edged sword to foyle and put to flight our spirituall enemies; the onely Oracle to which we must haue recourse, and whereat we are to enquire the will of God: In a word, the bread and water of life, whereon our soules are to feede vnto eternall life. Therefore we are commanded to search the Scriptures as for siluer, and to seeke in them as for treasures, to reade in them continually, to meditate of them day and night, to vse them as bracelets vpon our armes, and frontlets betweene our eyes; to teach them to our posteritie, and to talke of them when we are in our houses, and when we walke by the way, when we lie downe, and when we are vp. And great reason there is of this commandement, seeing that (as an ancient writer saith) *Quicquid in eis docetur veritas est: quicquid præcipitur bonitas est: quicquid promittitur fœlicitas est*: that is, *Whatsoeuer is taught in them, is truth it selfe: whatsoeuer is commanded, is goodnesse it selfe: whatsoeuer*

2. Tim. 3. 16.
2. Pet. 1. 20.
1. Tim. 6. 20.
Eph. 6. 17.
Esa. 8. 20.
Ioh. 5. 39.
Psal. 1. 2.
Deut. 6. 8.
Hugo de S. Vict. de Script. & Scriptor. sacris. lib. 1. cap.

is promised, is happines it selfe. They being of such perfection, that nothing may bee added vnto them, nor any thing taken from them: of such infallible certainty, that heauen and earth shall sooner passe away, then one title fall to the ground: so pleasant and delightfull, that they exceed the hony and the hony combe: and so profitable, that no treasures may be compared vnto them; seeing they are able to make vs wiser then our enemies, then the aged, then our teachers: to make vs wise vnto saluation; to giue vs an inheritāce among them that are sanctified: nay, able to saue our soules. Which being so; I cannot sufficiently wonder, that any calling themselues Christians, should make lesse account of the booke of God, then the Romanes in old time did of their twelue Tables, and other Heathens of their Rituall books: or then the Iewes at this day doe of their Talmud, the Turks of their Alcoran, the Æthiopians of their Abetelis: especially that those which professe themselues Diuines, should so distaste the holy scripture, that leauing it, the cleare fountaine of the water of life, they should betake themselues to the troubled streames of mens deuises, and digge vnto themselues pits which will hold no water. Wherein the Schoolemen (I meane the Sententiaries, the Summists, and Quodlibetaries) are chiefly (if not only) to be censured, who setting aside the scriptures, haue vanished away in vaine speculations in their Questions vpon *Lombard* the Master of the Sentences, & vpon *Thomas* their new Master. So that had it not bene for some few *Glosses* (which notwithstanding like the glosse of Orleans doe often corrupt the text) *Nicolaus de Lyra*, *Hugo de S. Charo*, and *Peter Comestor* (whom I should haue named first, being so good a text man, that (as his name importeth) hee did eate vp the text, as the poore mans horse drank vp the Moone) we should not haue had among such a multitude of writers, one poore Comment vpon the Bible for diuers hundred yeares. And no maruaile, seeing it is an ordinary thing for yong nouices in Popish Vniuersities (and I would it were but there only) not to lay the foundation of their studie in Diuinitie vpon the rocke, but vpon the waters: that is, not vpon the Scripture, but vpon *Aquinas*, or some such Summist: & to reade the Scriptures no further then they giue them light for the vnderstanding of their Schoole-Doctours. Witnes one of their own writers, who testifieth of himselfe, that he had studied Schoole-diuinity and the Canon Law for the space of 16. yeres, and yet neuer so much as saluted either the Scriptures or the Fathers. Which course they take, either because they presume to vnderstand, aboue that which is written, contrary to the commandement of the Apostle, *Rom.* 12.3. or for that they iudge the Scrip-

Margin notes: Deut. 4.2. Matth. 5.18. Psal. 19.10. Psal. 119 98. &c. 2 Tim. 3 15. Act. 20.32. Iam. 1.21. Iere. 2.13. Ferdinand. Vellosil. Episc. Luc. in praef. in aduer. Schol. Theol. Nec Script. nec Doctores vel à limine salutasse.

tures

tures too simple and shallow for them to wade in, as not affording them sufficient matter for their wits to worke vpon. Not conside-ring that whilst they contemne the simplicity of the Scriptures, & looke beyond the Moone, in the meane time with *Thales* they fall into the ditch: and that whilest they striue with the wings of their wit to soare aboue the cloudes of other mens conceyts, they sinke into a Sea of absurdities and errors. Nor yet remembring that the Scripture hath great maiesty ioyned with simplicity, and as great difficulty mixed with plainenesse and facility: and therefore not vnfitly resembled by S. *Gregorie*, to the maine Ocean in which the lambe may wade and the Elephant may swimme. For the spirit of God hath in wonderfull wisdome so tempered the Scriptures, that they are both obscure and perspicuous: in some places like *a clasped* or *sealed booke*, *Isay.* 29.11. in other places like *a booke that is opened*, *Apoc.* 5.5. being both *easie* and *difficult*. *Easie*, in that *the entrance into the word, giueth light and vnderstanding to the simple*, *Psal.* 119. 130. *Difficult*, in that *some things are hard to bee vnderstood*, 2. *Peter.* 3. 16. and *hard to bee interpreted*, *Hebrewes* 5.11. *Easie*, to inuite vs to reade and learne them: *Difficult*, to exercise vs lest we should con-temne them. From the easie and plaine places are gathered princi-ples of religion, both articles of faith and rules of good life, which wee call *Catechismes*. The difficult places require interpretation, and the *Commentaries* of the learned. Both which are necessa-rie in the Church of God. *Catechismes* haue a necessarie vse, both in regard of the simple, who are to bee fedde with milke, beeing but babes in Christ: and of the learned who are strong men in Christ, that they may haue some rule, whereby to trie the spirits, consonant to the Analogie of faith, and doctrine of the Orthodoxe Fathers of the Church: which *Paul* calleth *The forme of knowledge. Rom.* 2.20. and *The forme of doctrine. Rom.* 6.17. and *a paterne of wholesome words.* 2. *Tim* 1.13. which formes of doctrine were in vse in the primitiue Church in the Apostles dayes, as it is manifest, *Heb.* 6.1. where the Apostle sets downe the principall points of the Catechisme, calling them *the doctrine of the beginning of Christ.* And after the Apostles, we finde that they were vsed by the learned Fathers, both of the Greeke and Latine Church. *Clement Alex.* had his Pedagogue. *Cyril* of *Ierusalem* his Catechisme and Mystagog. books. *Origen* (that famous Catechist) his * bookes of principles. *Theodoret* his Epitome θείων δογμάτων. *La-ctantius* his Institutions. *Augustine* his Enchiridion. *Hugo de S. Victore* his books of the Sacraments, or mysteries of christian religion. And it were greatly to bee wished, that as in other reformed Churches

Laert. de vit. Philos. lib. 1 in Thal.

Epist. ad Leander.

μόρφωσιν γνώσεως.

τύπον διδαχῆς.

ὑποτύπωσιν ὑγιαινόντων λόγων.

* περὶ ἀρχῶν.

 beyond

beyond the Sea, they haue a set Catechisme which all men follow; and in the Church of Rome one approoued by the Councell of Trent: so there were an vniforme Catechisme inioyned by publicke authority to be vsed in all Families, Schooles, and Churches in this land, that we might all with one mind and one mouth, iudge and speake the same thing.

Now as *Catechismes* gathered out of plaine and easie places are necessary for the simple: so *Commentaries* are as necessary for the vnderstanding of such places as are more abstruse and difficult. Our Sauiour Christ (the great Doctor of the Church) hath by his owne practise giuen vs a president hereof in expounding the law, *Math.5.* in expounding all hard parables to his disciples apart: for the text

[ἐπέλυε. διερμήνευε. διήνοιγε.]

saith, that he *vnfolded* or *expounded them vnto them. Mark.*4.33. That *he interpreted vnto them in all the scriptures the things which were written of him. Luk.*24.27. That *he opened vnto them the scriptures.* v.32. And they haue bin alwaies so accounted in the Church of God. For the Iewes (as we know) had their *Perushim*, the Greeke church their *Scholia*, the Latine Church their *Glosses*, with other Paraphrases, & Expositions. Neither was it euer called in question by any, saue by

[Sleidan.lib.6.]

the fantasticall Anabaptists, who rest onely vpon immediate reuelations: And some preiudicate Papists, who hold the consent of all

[Coster.Ench. controuers.c.1]

Catholikes to be the true Scripture, both *the glosse*, and *the text*; the written word, but inky Diuinity, and a dead letter. And certaine arrogant spirits who with *Nestorius* skorne to reade any Interpreters.

[Socrat.lib.7. cap.32.]

But how Commentaries ought to be written, it is not so easie to define, there beeing such difference as well in regard of the manner of writing, as of the measure. For besides that the Popish writers make foure seuerall senses of the Scripture, commending *Ierome* to excell in the Litterall, *Origen* in the Allegoricall, *Ambrose* in the Anagogicall, *Chrysostome* in the Tropologicall; they haue aboue fifty seuerall wayes of expounding the Scripture, as their owne writers

[Sixt.Senens. in præfat.in Bib.]

doe record. In the measure, we finde some too tedious, as the two *Alphonsi*, *Tostatus*, and *Salmeron*, who vpon euery small occasion digresse from the text, or rather take occasion to enter into infinite

[1.Tim.1.4.]

triuolous questions, *which breede strife rather then godly edifying which is by faith*. For there is not so short a Chapter in the Bible, vpō which

[Sixt.Sen. Bibl. lib.4.]

the former mooueth not aboue eight score questions: whereupon his volumes grow to that bignesse, that one contracting his Com-

[Petrus Ximenes Episc. Cauriens.]

mentary vpon S. *Mat.* and drawing it into an Epitome, yet could not so abridge it, but that it contained aboue a thousand pages *in folio* in the largest volume, & smallest character. The other is so short with his 12. volumes vpon the Euangelists, that he might well haue

contra-

contracted leaues into lines, and lines into letters. Which tedious discourses, and impertinent excursions from the text, serue for no other end but to cast a mist before the eyes of the reader, and draw (as it were) the veile of *Moses* ouer his face, so that he cannot see the meaning of the holy Ghost. Others on the contrarie are too short, and compendious, offending as much in breuitie, as the former in prolixitie: by name, *Emmanuel Sa* the Iesuit, whose Commentaries vpon the Bible are shorter then the text it selfe, like to those of Apollinaris, of whom *Ierom* writeth, that a man which readeth them, would thinke he read *Contents of chapters, rather then Commentaries.* But as for the manner: the literall sense (which our author here followeth) is the onely sense intended by the Spirit of God: the Allegoricall, Tropologicall, Anagogicall, beeing but seuerall vses and applications thereof: For the Scripture (consisting in the sense not in the letters) is profitable to teach, and improoue, as *Paul* saith: whereas from the Allegoricall sense no necessarie argument can be taken (as their own doctors confesse) either to confirme or confute any point of doctrine: and therefore much lesse from the Tropologicall, or Anagogicall. And as for the measure, in regard of breuitie or prolixity, the golden meane hath alway beene iudged by the learned to be the best, which is not onely to giue the bare meaning paraphrastically, but to make collection of doctrine & application of vses; yet briefly, rather pointing at the chiefe, then dwelling long vpon any point. Some are of opinion that a Commentor is onely to giue the literal sence of the place, without making further vse of application, or instruction: To which I could easily subscribe, if all the Lords people could prophesie, or if all were able to handle the word of God, the sword of the spirit: For as to an expert Musitian who is acquainted with the concords or rules of discant, it is as good a direction to haue onely the ground as if he had euery point pricked out vnto him, being inured to the diuision vpon euery point, as it falleth out in the ground: So to him that is acquainted with the word of God, a short & concise handling of the Scripture, may be as good a direction as if euery point were discoursed at large. But because all readers are not strong men in Christ, some being but babes, who must haue euery thing minced, and cut smal vnto them before they can receiue it. Neither all teachers expert, and prompt Scribes, like to *Ezra*, nor mightie in the Scripture as *Apollos*, such as are able to diuide the word aright, and applie it fitly as they ought: (Some being *deceitfull workemen* peruerting it to their owne destruction, in pressing the two dugges of the Scripture, the Old and New Testament, that in steed of milke, they suck nothing but

2. Cor. 3.

Non tam Commentarios quàm indicia capitulorum. Hieron. prooem. in 1. Comment. in Esai.

2. Tim. 3. 16.

Symbolica Theologia non est argumentatiua. Thom.

2. Cor. 11. 13.

Volusian. ad Nicol. 1.

2.Pet.3.16. but bloud: Others, *vnskilfull*, casting wild Coloquintida into the pot of the childrē of the prophets, being too hasty to learne, & too ignorant to know of themselues, what they should haue gathered.) Therefore to help the ignorance of the one, and hinder the malice of the other (and so to profit the most) beside the meaning, he hath briefly drawne out such doctrines as naturally arise from the text, shewing withall, how they ought to be applied for confutation, correction, instruction, consolation. Which he hath done with such dexterity (artificially matching together two things, heretofore insociable, *Breuity*, and *Perspicuity*) that the like (I take it) hath not bin performed heretofore by any Expositer vpon this Epistle: which we may well call the key of the new Testament, in that it handleth the weightiest points of doctrine, whether we consider the necessary knowledge thereof, or the controuersies of these times. Therfore *Luther* after he had once publikely expounded it, toke it in hand againe, and interpreted it the second time, beginning (as himselfe
Ecclef.18.6. saith) where he ended, according to the saying of *Syracides*, *When a man hath done what he can, he must beginne againe*. Which *Commentary*, seeing it hath found such good intertainement amongst vs, beeing but a forrainer, and hauing lost much of his strength, and taken winde by changing from language to language, as wine from one vessell to another: I doubt not but this, beeing a free denizen, will find the like fauour and acceptance, the rather, if it will please your Honour to vouchsafe it your countenance: To whose protection and patronage I here commed it, as S *Luke* did his Histories to the most noble *Theophilus*: desiring hereby to testifie my humble duty vnto your Honour, and my thankfulnes to God for the riches of his grace bestowed vpon you in the mystery of the Gospell, for your zeale of Gods glory, your loue of the truth, and of all those that vnfainedly embrace the truth.

And thus fearing to hinder the course of your more serious cogitations & actions, I humbly take my leaue: Desiring the Lord,
1.Sam.2.30. who hath promised to honour those that honour him, that as hee hath made you Honourable in your noble progenitors, so he would make you thrise Honourable in your future successors, and long cōtinue you a notable instrument vnder his Highnes, of the peace and welfare of your country, as hitherto he hath done, acomplishing all your desires for present prosperity and future felicity. From *Emmanuel* colledge in Cambridge: August. 10. 1604.

Your Honours most humbly deuoted

Rafe Cudworth.

To

TO THE COVRTEOUS Reader.

I Heere offer to thy view (gentle Reader) a Comment, and a Supplement: the Comment begun by an excellent workman, and drawne in excellent proportion, in all points suting to the analogie of faith, and the doctrine of the Orthodoxe Fathers of the Church, being the substance of his three yeares Lectures vpon the Lords day. If his former workes either of positiue Diuinitie in sundry of his Treatises, or Controuersall Diuinitie in his Reformed Catholique, or Case-Diuinitie in his Cases of Conscience, haue ministred any comfort vnto thee, or giuen thee content: I doubt not but these Commentaries will abundantly satisfie thy expectation. For (to omit the varietie of matter) as also the breuitie and admirable perspicuitie, in regard of the manner, being the chiefe commendation of Oecumenius, or any Interpreter) in them as in a mirrour thou mayest more clearely see his knowledge in the mysterie of Christ; and his Ephes.3.4.
dexteritie in exemplifying that by practise which hee had formerly taught by * precept, then in any of his writings besides: as hauing a double eminency * In his Prophetica.
aboue the rest. First, in that they were penned the last of all his works, being come to ripenesse of iudgement: and that vpon mature deliberation after his Sermons, (as his manner was.) Secondly, it that they were written with his owne hand, whereas all his other writings (except some short Treatises) were taken by some diligent auditors, and perused by himselfe. Herein re- Gal.6.11.
sembling the Epistle it selfe, which was written with Pauls owne hand: all the rest (except that short one to Philemon) by his scribes. And as they doe Philem. v.18.
exceed his other writings, so I might say (perhaps more truly then discreetly) that they surpasse in this kind all the moderne writers that haue gone before thẽ: so that he which wil vouchsafe to reade them, shal not greatly need nor desire any other interpreter vpon this Scripture: the which I speake not as esteeming of Antiquitie no better worth then to be put vnder a bushell, that Noueltie might be set vpon the candlesticke: but for that I see not, but that John Baptist the last of all the prophets, was as goodly a burning & shining Iohn 5.35.
candle, as any of the rest: & that he pointed forth Christ more distinctly then Iohn 1.36.
the rest. But I hope I shall not need to vse many wordes in commendation

either

either of the worke, or of the Authour, being so well knowen and sufficiently commended by others, for soundnes of doctrine, and integrity of life: which (whilest he was liuing) did parallell each other, his doctrine being a patterne of his life, and his life a counterpaine of his doctrine. And now being dead, his sauory writings which he hath left behinde him, breathing foorth (as it were) the sweet smell of a sanctified spirit (like a field which the Lord hath blessed) hath got him a name neuer to be forgotten: which giueth him after his death a second life.

I am further to aduertise thee (good Reader) that there were some places in the originall copy, to which the Authour would (no doubt) haue giuen some reuiew and correction, if God had drawne out the line of his life but a little longer: which I haue filed and polished according to my poore skill, though very sparingly, in such places onely as were obscure, or had any phrase of doubtfull construction, or otherwise seemed to be mistaken: pointing and interlining the rest to fit it for the Presse. It may be my vnskilfull handling of them hath depriued them of their due lustre, yet sure I am it hath giuen them no tincture.

Touching the Supplement: it was my purpose at the first to haue made a supply of that which was wanting, out of the Authors owne writings, as it hath bene done in Aquinas *Summes & others: but afterwards perceiuing that his workes already extant, would not affoard mee sufficient matter to furnish out that Argument, I was inforced to take another course, and to make a supply with courser stuffe of mine owne, as I could. Which if it shall seeme not to sute the former in all points, I shall desire thee to consider that it is not so easie a matter for* Asclepiodorus *accustomed to draw with a cole or chalke only, to finish a picture begun by* Apelles *with so curious a pensill: and that it is an argument wherein (I confesse) I haue not beene so much conuersant as perhaps in some other: neither chosen out of purpose to make ostentation of wit, reading, or inuention: but left as a necessary taske to bee performed by some for the perfecting of the work, & the good of the Church: (if this poore mite may confer any thing to the treasury of the Lords Temple.) And thus hoping that these respects may entreat for a friendly acceptance at thy hands, and that thou wilt affoord me thy good word for my good will, and a fauourable construction for my paines: I commend it to the blessing of the Almighty, and thee to his gracious protection, vnfainedly wishing to thee as to my selfe, the mercy of God in Christ Iesus.* August. 10.

Thine in the Lord Iesus,

R. C.

THE EPISTLE OF S. PAVL TO THE GALATIANS.

THE ARGVMENT.

TWo things are generally to bee considered, the occasion of this Epistle, and the scope. The occasion that mooued Paul to write this Epistle was, because certaine false Apostles slaundered him both in respect of his calling, as also in respect of his doctrine; teaching that hee was no Apostle, and that his doctrine was false. And by this meanes they seduced the Churches of Galatia, perswading them that iustification and saluation was partly by Christ, and partly by the Law. The scope of the Epistle is in three things. First the Apostle defends his calling in the first and second Chapters. Secondly, he defends the truth of his doctrine, teaching iustification by Christ alone. And vpon this occasion he handles the greatest question in the world, Namely, what is that iustice whereby a sinner stands righteous before God, in the 3. and 4. and in the beginning of the fift. Thirdly, he prescribes rules of good life in the fift and sixt Chapters.

1 *Paul an Apostle (not of men, nor by man, but by Iesus Christ, and God the Father, who raised him from the dead.)*

THE Epistle hath three parts, a *Preface*, an *Instruction*, and the *Conclusion*. The Preface is in the fiue first verses: and it hath two parts, an *Inscription*, and a *Salutation*.

The *inscription* sets downe the persons that write the Epistle, and the persons to whom it is sent. The persons that write are two; *Paul* and the *Brethren*.

Paul is mentioned in the first verse. In which, in comely and decent maner he commends himselfe to the Galatians by his office and function [*an Apostle*] that is, one called to be a planter & founder of the Church of the new Testament among the nations. And because the title of an Apostle in generall signification may agree to all teachers, therefore he goes further, and sets downe the cause of his Apostleship. And first he remoues the false causes in these words [*not of men*] that is, not called by men as by authors of my calling, or not called by the authoritie of men. And in this *Paul* op-

poseth

poseth himselfe to the false Apostles, who were called not by God, but by men. Againe he saith[*not by man*] that is, not called of God in and by the ministery of any meere man. And in this *Paul* opposeth himselfe to all ordinary ministers of the Gospel whatsoeuer, who are called of God by man. This done, he propounds the true cause and author of his Apostleship, of whom he was called immediatly. Against this it may bee obiected, that *Paul* was ordained to be an Apostle by the imposition of hands of the Church of Antioch. I answer, that this imposition was rather a confirmation then a calling. Secondly, they of Antioch had not imposed handes on *Paul*, but that they were commanded by the spirit of God. Further *Paul* addes that he was called by Christ[*and God the father*] for three causes. The first, was to signifie the consent of will in the Father & Christ. The second was to teach vs how wee are to conceiue of God, namely that he is the Father, and Iesus Christ, and the holy Ghost: for the Godhead may not be conceiued out of the Trinitie of persons. The third is, because the Father is the fountaine of all good things that come to vs by Christ. Lastly, he sets down the effect or action of the Father[*who raised him from the dead*] & that for two causes. One was to prooue Christ to be the natural Sonne of God, for he professed himselfe to be so: & that was one cause why he was crucified and put to death. Now when he was dead, if hee had not bin the Son of God indeed, he had neuer risen againe but perished in death. And in that the Father raised him againe to life, he gaue testimony that he was his owne naturall Son. And there- Rom.1.5. fore *Paul* saith that *Christ was declared to be the Sonne of God by the resurrection from the dead*: and hee applies the wordes of the Psalme, Act.13.33. (*thou art my sonne this day haue I begotten thee*) to the time of Christs resurrection. Againe, *Paul* mentions the resurrection of Christ, to note the time of his owne calling: for though the rest of the Apostles were called when Christ was in the estate of humiliation, yet *Paul* was called afterwards, when Christ was entred into his kingdome, and sate at the right hand of his Father.

The vse. First, wheras *Paul* in the very forefront of his Epistle, begins with his owne calling, I gather, that euery minister of the Gospel ought to haue a good and lawful calling. A man cannot preach Rom.10.14. *vnles he be sent.* Christ took not vnto him the office of a Mediator til he was called and sent of the Father. Therefore the opinion of the Anabaptists is foolish and fantasticall, who thinke that euery man may preach that wil without any special calling. They alledge that 1.Cor.16.15 *the house of Stephanas ordained themselues to the ministery of the Saints.* ἔταξαν. Answere, the meaning of the place is not that they called themselues,

ſelues, but that they ſet themſelues apart to the miniſterie of the Saints, in the purpoſe and reſolution of their owne hearts. Againe they alledge, that all Chriſtians in the new Teſtament *are Kings and Prieſtes*, and the office of the Prieſt is to teach. I anſwere, all are Prieſts in that they are to offer themſelues in ſacrifice to God: and to teach priuatly within their places and callings, as the maſter his ſeruants, the father his children, &c. and to make a confeſſion of their faith, when they are called ſo to doe. Thirdly, they alleadge, that the power of the keies is giuen to the Church. I anſwer, it is indeed; yet ſo as the vſe and adminiſtration thereof belongs to the Miniſters alone, in the diſpenſation of the word. Apoc. 5. 10.

Secondly, whereas *Paul* ſaith (*Not of men, but of Chriſt*) I gather that euery lawfull calling is of God, and not of men as authours thereof: and that the right to call belongs to God. The Father thruſts forth labourers into his vineyard: the Sonne giues Paſtors and teachers: the holy Ghoſt makes ouerſeers. It may be alledged that the Church hath authoritie to call and ordaine Miniſters. I anſwere, that the Churches authoritie is no more but a miniſterie or ſeruice, whereby it doeth teſtifie, declare, and approoue whom God hath called. Matth. 9. 38. Ephe. 4. 11. Act. 20. 28.

Thirdly, whereas *Paul* thus proclaimes his calling, (*Paul an Apoſtle of Ieſus Chriſt*) I gather that the callings of the Miniſters of the Goſpel muſt be manifeſt to their owne conſciences, & the conſciences of their hearers, and that for diuers weighty cauſes. Firſt, they are emballadors, inſtruments, and the mouth of God: and for this cauſe they are to ſpeak in the name of God, & this they cannot do, vnleſſe they know themſelues to be called. Secondly, that the calling of the miniſtery may tend to edification, there is required the aſſiſtance of Gods ſpirit in the teacher, the protection of him & his miniſtery, the effectuall operation of the ſpirit in the hearts of the hearers. And hee that wants the aſſurance of his calling, cannot pray to God in faith for theſe things: neither can hee apply the promiſes of God to himſelfe. Thirdly, the knowledge of our callings breeds conſcience of our dueties, diligence, and the feare of God. Laſtly, knowledge of our callings in the conſciences of the hearers, breeds a reuerence in their hearts, and obedience to the miniſterie of the word. Vpon this, ſome may demaund, how they may knowe that they are called of God to the miniſterie of the word. Anſwere: they may know it, if they finde three things in themſelues: the firſt is the teſtimony of their conſciences, that they entred not for praiſe, honour, lucre, but in the feare of God, with a deſire to glorifie him, and to edifie the Church.

The

The ſecond is a facultie to do that to which they haue a deſire and will. In this facultie are two things, knowledge of God and his wayes, and aptneſſe to deliuer that which they know. The third is the Ordination of the Church, which approoues and giues teſtimony of their wil and abilitie. He that hath theſe things, is certainly called of God. Now put the caſe, a man wants the firſt of theſe three, becauſe he entred with euill conſcience, being caried with ambitious and couetous deſires: then I anſwer, that his calling ſtill in reſpect of the Church, is good and lawfull, and when he repents of his bad conſcience, it is alſo accepted of God.

The fourth point to be obſerued is, that Paul makes three kinds of callings in the Church. One is when men are called by men, and not by God: and thus are all falſe teachers called. The ſecond is, when men are called of God by the miniſtery of men: thus are all ordinary Miniſters of the word called. The third is, when men are called not by men, but by Chriſt immediatly. And *Paul* heere ſignifieth, that he himſelfe and the reſt of the Apoſtles were called according to this third way. And in this reſpect hee puts a difference betweene the Apoſtles, and all the Miniſters of the new Teſtament. For in that they were called immediatly, they were alſo taught by immediate inſpiration, and alſo aided by the infallible aſſiſtance of Gods ſpirit. And of all this they had promiſes, *Matt.* 10. 19, 20. *Luke* 10, 16. Hence we may gather the certaintie of our Religion. The eſſentiall note of the Church is faith: faith ſtands in relation to the word of God: and the word of God is no word vnto vs, vnleſſe we know it to be ſo: and we know it to be ſo, becauſe it was written by the Apoſtles, who in preaching and writing could not erre. Secondly, hence I gather, that the doctrine of the Apoſtles is the immediate word of God, becauſe it was giuen by inſpiration both for matter and wordes: whereas the doctrine of the Church in Sermons, and the decrees of Councels is both the word of God and the word of man: The word of God, as it agrees with the writings of the Apoſtles and Prophets: the word of man, as it is defectiue, and as it is propounded in tearmes deuiſed by man. It may be obiected, that *Paul* ſpake ſome things of himſelfe, and not from the Lord, 1. *Cor.* 7. 12. *Not the Lord, but I.* Anſwere: the meaning is, Not the Lord by any expreſſe commaundement, but I by collection and interpretation of Scripture, and that by the aſſiſtance of Gods ſpirit, v. 40. Seeing then the writings of the Apoſtles are the immediate and meere word of God, they muſt be obeied as if they had bene written without man by the finger of God.

Laſtly,

Laſtly, ſeeing it is the propertie of an Apoſtle to be called immediatly by Ieſus Chriſt, hence it followes, that the authoritie, office, and function of Apoſtles ceaſed with them, and did not paſſe by ſucceſſion to any other. Therefore it is a falſhood that the Pope of Rome ſucceeds *Peter* in Apoſtolicall authoritie, and in the infallible aſſiſtance of the ſpirit, when he is in his Conſiſtory.

And where *Paul* ſaith he was called by Ieſus Chriſt, and not by man, that is, meere man, he giues a pregnant teſtimony that Chriſt is both God and man.

And whereas *Paul* was called by Chriſt raiſed from the dead, hence I gather the dignitie of the Apoſtle *Paul* aboue all other Apoſtles, in that he was called after the reſurrection of Chriſt, when he was entred into his kingdome.

The Text.

2. *And all the brethren that are with mee, to the Churches of Galatia.*

The Expoſition.

By brethren wee are to vnderſtand ſuch as ſeparated themſelues from the Pagans, and receiued the faith of Chriſt, 1. *Cor.*5.11. And heere more ſpecially ſuch as taught and profeſſed the faith, that is, both Paſtors and people, whether of Antioch (as ſome thinke) or of Rome, as others.

And *Paul* writes his Epiſtle as well in their names as in his owne, and with their conſent, for two cauſes. One was, that hee might not bee thought to deliuer any priuate doctrine deuiſed of his owne head. And this care he had alwayes: and therfore taught nothing but that *which was in the writings of Moſes and the Prophets, Actes* 26.22. And this was the care of Chriſt: who ſaith, *My doctrine is not mine, but his that ſent me, Ioh.*7.16. And at this day, this muſt be the care of the Miniſters of the Goſpel, to deliuer nothing of their owne. Firſt therefore their doctrines muſt be founded in the writings of the Prophets and Apoſtles: and ſecondly, that they may be ſure of this, they muſt haue the conſent of the true Church, ſpecially of ſuch as haue beene the reſtorers of the Goſpell in this laſt age. This rule *Paul* giues to *Timothie, to continue in the things which he had learned* of *Paul* and the reſt of the Apoſtles, 2. *Tim.*3.14. Hence it appeares to be a fault in ſundry priuate perſons, when they reade the Scriptures, to gather priuate opinions, to broach them to the world. This practiſe hath beene the foundation of hereſies and ſchiſmes in the Church.

Secondly, *Paul* writes with conſent, that hee might the better mooue and perswade the Galatians to receiue his doctrine which he is now to deliuer.

Hence it appeares, that the Consent of Pastors and people is of great excellency. For the better conceiuing of it, and the meaning of the text, I will handle three points. The first is, what is the force of consent? wherein stands it? and where it is now to bee found? For the first: Consent is of force to prepare the heart, and to mooue it to beleeue: as *Augustine* saith, *I had not beleeued the Gospell, except the authoritie of the Church had mooued me.* And this is all it can doe. For it is the word, that is the obiect and the cause of our faith: the word it selfe workes in vs that faith whereby it is beleeued. And *Paul* in this place vseth consent, not to worke a faith in the Galatians, but onely to stirre vp a liking of his doctrine. Two errors of the Church of Rome must here bee auoided. One, that Consent is a certaine marke of the Church. It is false: for Consent may bee among the wicked, in the kingdome of Antichrist, *Reuel.* 13.16. In the kingdome of darkenesse, all is in peace. Againe, dissention may bee among the godly; as betweene *Paul* and *Barnabas. Paul* and *Peter*: in the church of Corinth there were schismes 1.*Cor.*11. Consent therefore simply, vnlesse it bee ioyned with true faith and true doctrine, is not of force to declare vnto vs the true Church. The second errour is that the catholike consent of beleeuers in points of religion is the true and liuely scripture, and that the written word is but a dead letter to it, and to bee iudged by it for his sense and meaning. But all is contrary. For the written word is the first, and perfect patterne of the minde and will of God: and the inward consent of the hearts of men, is but a rude and imperfect extract, and draught of it.

The second point is wherein stands this consent? It must haue his foundation in Christ, and thence flow to the members, as the oyle from *Aarons* head, to his garments, *Psal.*133. and it stands in three things, consent in one faith and doctrine: consent in affection, whereby men be of one heart, *Act.*2.47. consent in speach, 1.*Cor.* 1. 10.

The third point is where it is now to bee found? The Papists say that they haue true and perfect consent among themselues, and that Fathers and Councells bee on their side: and that we haue no consent among our selues. I answer first, that they haue not the consent which they pretend, for the proper points of Popery were not knowne to the Apostles nor to the Apostolicall Churches, but were taken vp in the ages following by little and little. Secondly, such doctrines as the Papists make articles of faith, are but opinions and coniectures in the fathers & Councels. Thirdly, the things which the Papiſtes hold, are the ſame peraduenture in name, but they are not the ſame indeed with that which the fathers hold, neither are they holden in the ſame maner: as for example, the purgatory which the fathers hold, is a thing far different from the purgatory of the Papiſts, and ſo all the reſt. Of conſent they may brag, but they cannot ſhew it. As for our ſelues, wee all conſent in the foundation of religion. There is difference about the deſcent of Chriſt into hell. The thing we all hold, namely a deſcent: the difference is in the manner, whether it be vertually or locally. There is difference about the paines of Chriſt in his agony and paſſion: yet all acknowledge the infinite merite and efficacie of the death of Chriſt. There is difference about the gouernment of the viſible Church on earth. For the ſubſtance of gouernement all agree, but for the maner of execution and adminiſtration, they doe not. That Chriſt is preſent in the Euchariſt, & that his body and blood is there to bee eaten and drunken, all our churches agree: and the difference is onely touching the manner of his preſence; namely, whether it be ſpirituall or locall. And this is the mercy of God, that in all our differences the foundation of religion is not raſed. Let vs pray for the continuance, and increaſe of this conſent.

Thus much of the perſons that write: now follow the churches to which the Epiſtle is ſent [*to the Churches of Galatia.*] At this time the Galatians had made a reuolt, and were fallen from iuſtification by the obedience of Chriſt: ſo as *Paul was afraid of them, Chap.*4. and yet he called them Churches ſtill, vſing great meekeneſſe and moderation. His example muſt wee follow in giuing iudgement of churches of our time. And that we may the better doe this, and the better relieue our conſciences, marke three rules. The firſt is, that we muſt rightly conſider of the faults of the Churches. Some are faults in manners, ſome in doctrine. If the faults of the church bee in manners, and theſe faults appeare both in the liues of miniſters & people, ſo long as true religion is taught, it is a church, and ſo to be eſteemed: and the miniſters muſt be heard, *Mat.*23.1 Yet may we ſeparate from the priuate company of bad men in the church, 1.*Cor.*5.11 and, if it be in our libertie and choiſe, ioyne to Churches better ordered. If the errour be in doctrine, we muſt firſt conſider whether the whole church erre, or ſome few therin. If the error be in ſome, and not in all, it remains a Church ſtill, as Corinth did, where ſome denied the reſurrection; becauſe a Church is named of the better part. Secondly, wee muſt conſider whether the church erre in the foundation or no: If the error or errors be beſide the

the foundation of religion, *Paul* hath giuen the sentence that they which build vpon the foundation hay and stubble of erronious opinion may be saued, 1. *Cor.* 3 15. Thirdly, inquiry must bee made whether the Church erre of humane frailtie, or of obstinacy. If it erre of frailty, though the error be in the foundation, yet it is still a Church, as appears by the example of the Galatians. Yet if a church shal erre in the foundation openly, and obstinatly, it separates from Christ, and ceaseth to be a Church, and wee may separate from it and may giue iudgement that it is no Church. When the Iewes resisted the preaching of *Paul*, and had nothing to say but to raile, *Paul* then separated the church of Ephesus, and Rome from them, *Act.* 19.8. & 28.28. It may here be demaunded, why *Paul* writes to the Galatians as brethren, and cals them Churches, seeing they haue erred in the foundation, and are as he saith, vers. 6. *remooued to another Gospell.* I answer, he could doe no otherwise. If a priuate man shall erre, he must first bee admonished, and then the Church must be told of it. If he heare not the Church, then iudgement may bee giuen that he is as a Publican, & not before: much more then, if the Church shall erre, there must first be an examination of the errour, and then sufficient conuiction: and after conuiction, followes the censure vpon the Church, and iudgement then may be giuen, and not before. And *Paul* had now only begun in this Epistle to admonish the Church of Galatia. Great therfore is the rashnes, and want of moderation in many, that haue bene of vs, that condemne our Church for no church, without sufficient conuiction going before. If they say that we haue bene admonished by bookes published: I say againe, there be grosser faults in some of those bookes, then any of the faults that they reprooue in the Church of England: and therefore the bookes are not fit to conuince, specially a Church.

And though *Paul* call the Galatians Churches of God, yet may we not hence gather, that the church of Rome is a church of God. The name it may haue; but it doeth in truth openly, and obstinatly oppugne the manifest principles of Christian religion.

If any demaund what these Chuches of Galatia are? I answere, that they were a people of Asia the lesse: and though they were famous Churches in the dayes of the Apostle, yet now the Countrey is vnder the dominion of the Turke. This shewes, what God might haue done to vs in England long agoe for the contempt of the Gospell. This againe shewes, what desolation will befall vs vnlesse we repent, and bring foorth better fruites of the Gospell.

3 *Grace bee with you and peace from God the Father, and from our Lord Ieſus Chriſt.*

4 *Who gaue* ——————

Here is laid downe the ſecond part of the Preface, which is the *Salutation* propounded in the forme of a prayer, *Grace and peace, &c.* Grace here mentioned is not any gift in man, but grace is Gods, and in God. And it ſignifies his gracious fauour and good will, whereby he is well pleaſed with his elect, in, and for Chriſt. Thus *Paul* diſtinguiſheth the grace of God from *the gift that is by grace, Rom.* 5.v.15. and ſets grace before the gift as the cauſe of it. Heere comes the error of the Papiſts to be confuted, which teacheth that the grace which makes vs gratefull to God, is the infuſed gift of holineſſe and charity: wheras indeed we are not firſt ſanctified, and then pleaſe God: but firſt we pleaſe God by grace in Chriſt, and then vpon this we are ſanctified, and indued with charitie.

Peace is a gift not in God, but in vs: and it hath three parts. The firſt is peace of conſcience, which is a quietneſſe and tranquility of minde, ariſing of a ſenſe and apprehenſion of reconciliation with God, *Rom.* 5.v.1. The ſecond is peace with the creatures: and it hath fiue branches. The firſt is, peace with Angels, for man is redeemed by Chriſt, and by meanes of this redemption, ſinfull man is reconciled to good Angels, *Coloſſ.* 1.20. The ſecond is, peace with the godly, who are all made of *one heart and minde, Iſai.* 11.9. The third is, peace with our ſelues: and that is a conformitie of the will, affections, and inclinations of mans nature to the renewed minde. The fourth is, peace in reſpect of our enemies. For the decree of God is, *Touch not mine anointed, and doe my Prophets no harme.* Againe, Pſal. 105.15. *All things turne to the good of them that loue God.* The fift is, peace Rom.8.28. with the beaſts of the field. God makes a couenant with them for his people, *Oſe.* 2.18. The creatures deſire and wait for the deliuerance of Gods children, *Rom.* 8. They that truſt in God, ſhall walke vpon the Lion and the Baſiliske, *Pſal.* 91.

The third part of peace, is proſperitie and good ſucceſſe: whatſoeuer the righteous man doeth, it proſpers. And all things proſpered in the houſe of *Potipher*, when *Ioſeph* was his ſteward, becauſe he feared God, *Gene.* 39.1,2.

To proceed, *Paul* ſets downe the cauſes of grace and peace, and they are two, God the Father, and Ieſus Chriſt. And heere it muſt bee remembred, that the Father and Chriſt, as they are one God, they are but one cauſe: and yet in regard of the maner of working, they are two diſtinct cauſes. For the Father giues grace from none but himſelfe, by the Son; and Chriſt procures grace and peace, and he giues it vnto men from the Father. Furthermore Chriſt is deſcribed by his property, *Our Lord*, and by his effects in the next verſe.

The vſe. Wheras *Paul* begins his praier with grace, we learne that Grace in God is the firſt cauſe and beginning of all good things in vs. *Election is of grace, Rom.* 11.v.5. *Vocation to God is of grace*, 2. *Tim*. 1.9 *Faith is of grace, Phil.* 1.29. *Iuſtification is freely by grace, Rom.* 3.24 *Loue is by grace*, 1 *Iohn* 4.9. *Euery good inclination is of grace, Phil.* 2.13. *Euery good worke is of grace, Ezech*. 36.27. *Ephe*. 2.10, *Life euerlaſting is of grace, Rom* 6.23. To auoide any euill is the leaſt good, and euery good is of God. It may be ſaid, that will in man is the cauſe and beginning of ſome good things. Anſwer: In the creating or imprinting of the firſt grace in the heart, wil is no cauſe at all, but a ſubiect to receiue the grace giuen. After the firſt grace is giuen, will is an agent in the receiuing of the ſecond grace, and in the doing of any good worke. Yet this muſt be remembred, that when the will is an agent, it is no more but an inſtrument of grace, and grace in God is properly the firſt, middle, and laſt cauſe of grace in vs, & of euery good acte. Hence it followes, that there bee not any meritorious works that ſerue to prepare men to their iuſtification: and that the cooperation of mans wil with grace in the act of conuerſion, wherby we are conuerted of God, is but a fiction of the braine of man. Laſtly, this doctrine is the foundation of humilitie: for it teacheth vs to aſcribe all to grace and nothing to our ſelues.

Secondly we learne, that the chiefe good things to bee ſought for, are the fauour of God in Chriſt, and the peace of a good conſcience. Conſider the example of *Dauid, Pſal.* 4.v.7. & *Pſal.* 73.v. 24, 25. and of *Paul*, who accounted all things dung for grace and peace in Chriſt. And the peace of good conſcience is as a guard to keepe our hearts and mindes in Chriſt. *Phil.* 4.7. The fault of moſt men is, They ſpend their dayes and their ſtrength in ſeeking riches, honors, pleaſures: and they think not on grace & peace. After the maner of beaſts, they vſe the bleſſings of God, but they look not at the cauſe; namely, the grace of God. Our dutie. Aboue all things to ſeeke for grace & peace. The reaſon: true happines, which all men deſire, conſiſts in peace, and is founded in grace: they are ſaid to be happie & bleſſed that mourne, & ſuffer perſecution for iuſtice ſake, *Matt*. 5. becauſe in the midſt of their ſorrows & miſeries, they haue the fauour of God, & the peace of good conſcience.

Thirdly, in that grace and peace are ioyned, we learne, that peace without grace is no peace. *There is no peace to the wicked, ſaith my God, Iſai.* 57. laſt. They which make a couenant with hell & death,

are

are ſooneſt deſtroyed, *Iſai.*28.18. *Laughter* (ſaith *Salomon*) *is madnes:* namely, when it is ſeuered from grace and peace. *When men ſay, peace peace, then comes deſtruction*, 1.*Theſſ.*5. The proſperitie of the men of this world, ends in perdition, reade *Pſal.*73.

Paul ſaith not ſimply that grace and peace comes from God, but from God the Father, and from Ieſus Chriſt: that hee may teach vs rightly to acknowledge and worſhip God. For God is to be acknowledged and worſhipped in the Father, in Chriſt, and in the holy Spirit. It was the fault of the Pagans, and it is the fault of ſundrie Chriſtians to worſhip an abſolute God, without the Father, and without Chriſt. This fault muſt be amended, for it turnes God to an Idol.

Againe when *Paul* ſaith, that grace proceeds firſt from the Father, and ſecondly from Ieſus Chriſt: he ſets down the order which God obſerueth in the communication of grace and peace. The Father is the fountaine of grace, & giues it from none but from himſelfe. Chriſt againe is (as it were) a conduit or pipe, to conuay grace from the Father to vs. *Of his fulneſſe we receiue grace for grace, Iohn* 1. *In him we are complete, Col.*2. Election, Iuſtification, Saluation, & all is done in, and by Chriſt, 2.*Tim.*1.9. The vſe. I. Let them that trauel vnder the burden of a bad conſcience, and a bad life, come to Chriſt by turning from their ſinnes, & by beleeuing in him, and they ſhall obtaine grace, and find reſt to their ſoules. II. In our miſeries our hearts may not be troubled ouermuch, but we muſt alwaies moderate our ſorrowes. For if we beleeue in Chriſt, we ſhall alwaies haue grace & peace. Reade *Iob.*14.27. III. We muſt moderate our cares for this life. For if we truſting in Chriſt, haue grace and peace, wee ſhall want nothing, reade *Pſal.*4.v.6,7.

Ieſus Chriſt that giues grace and peace, is called, *our Lord* for two cauſes. One is to teach vs to acknowledge Chriſt aright, and that is as well to acknowledge him to be our Lord, as well as our Sauiour. He is a Prieſt to procure life, a prophet to teach the way of life, a Lord to command them to walke in the way of life. The fault of our times: All men profeſſe Chriſt: yet many allow of no Chriſt, but of their owne deuiſing: namely, a Chriſt that muſt bee a Sauiour to deliuer them from hell, but not a Lord to command them; that they cannot brooke. The ſecond cauſe why Chriſt is called *our Lord*, is to ſignifie the perſons to whom grace and peace belong, and they are ſuch as acknowledge Chriſt for their Lord, and yeeld ſubiection to him in heart & life. They find reſt to their ſoules, that take vp the yoke of Chriſt in new obedience, and the patient bearing of the Croſſe, Matth.11.v.29.

4. *Who gaue himſelfe for our ſinnes, that he might deliuer vs out of this preſent euill world, according to the will of God our Father.*

5. *To whom be glorie for euer and euer, Amen.*

In theſe wordes the ſecond argument is propounded, whereby Chriſt is deſcribed, namely the effect of Chriſt, which is, *that hee gaue himſelfe.* And hee is ſaid to giue himſelfe for two cauſes. Firſt, becauſe he preſented himſelfe as a price and ſacrifice for ſinne to God the Father, *Matth.* 20.28. *Epheſ.* 5.2. 1.*Tim.* 2.6. The ſecond, becauſe he did publikely propound and ſet foorth himſelfe to the world, as a ſacrifice and price of redemption. *Rom.* 3.25. *Iohn* 3.14. and *Actes* 4. 12.

In this giuing there are fiue things to be conſidered. The firſt, the giuer, Chriſt: the ſecond, the thing giuen, and that is Chriſt himſelfe. The third is, the end of his giuing, for ſin, that is, that hee might make ſatiſfaction for our ſinnes. The fourth is, another end of his giuing, that hee might deliuer vs out of this preſent euill world. Here the preſent world ſignifies the corrupt eſtate of men, that liue according to the luſts of their owne hearts, 1. *Iohn* 2.16. And men are here ſaid to be deliuered and taken out of the world, when they are ſeuered from the condition of ſinfull men by ſanctification and newnes of life, and by diuine protection, whereby they are preſerued from euill after they are ſanctified, *Tit.* 2.14. and *Iohn* 17.15. And this deliuerance is not in this life in reſpect of *place*, but in reſpect of *qualitie*. The fift thing, is the cauſe that mooued Chriſt to giue himſelfe, and that is the will of God.

In the fifth verſe there is ſet downe a corollary or concluſion, which containes the praiſe of God.

The vſe followes. Whereas Chriſt is the giuer of himſelfe, hence it followes that his death and ſacrifice was voluntarie. And this he ſhewed in two things. When he was to bee attached, hee fled not, but went to a garden in the mount, as his cuſtome was, which was knowne to *Iudas*, *Iohn* 18.2. And in the very ſeparation of body and ſoule, hee cried with a loude and ſtrong voice, which argued that he was Lord of death, and died becauſe his will was to die. This muſt be remembred. For otherwiſe his death had not bene a ſatisfaction for ſinne.

In that Chriſt gaue himſelfe to be a ſacrifice, wee learne many things. Firſt, that the worke of redemption exceedes the worke of creation. For in the creation, Chriſt gaue the creatures to man; in the redemption he gaue himſelfe, and that as a ſacrifice. Second-

ly,

ly, in that he gaue himſelfe, it appeares that he gaue neither Angel, nor meere man, nor any thing out of himſelfe; and that all merits of life, and ſatisfactions for ſinne, are to be reduced to the perſon of Chriſt: and conſequently that there be no humane ſatiſfactions for ſin, nor meritorious works done by vs: becauſe they pertaine not to the perſon of Chriſt, but to our perſons: and they were neuer offered of Chriſt vnto God as merits and ſatiſfactions, becauſe he gaue nothing but himſelfe, and the things which appertained vnto his owne perſon. Thirdly, in that Chriſt giues himſelfe, wee muſt take, and receiue him with lingring hearts. Nay he is to ſuffer violence of vs, and the violent are to take him to themſelues. Laſtly, in that he giues himſelfe to vs, we againe muſt giue our bodies and ſoules vnto him in way of thankefulneſſe, and dedicate all that wee haue or can doe to the good of men. The creatures at our tables preſent vs with their bodies: and ſo muſt we preſent our bodies and ſoules to God.

The firſt end of this giuing is, that Chriſt might be a ſacrifice & ranſome for ſin. The knowedge of this point is of great vſe. Firſt, it works loue in vs on this maner. We muſt in mind & meditation come to the croſſe of Chriſt. Vpon the croſſe wee are to behold Chriſt crucified, and in his death and paſſion, his ſacrifice, in his ſacrifice for the ſins of his enemies, his endleſſe loue: and the conſideration of this loue will mooue vs to loue him againe, and the Father in him. Secondly, the conſideration of his endleſſe paines for our ſinnes in the ſacrifice of himſelfe, muſt breed in vs a godly ſorrow for them; for if he ſorrow for them, much more we. Thirdly, this knowledge is the true beginning of amendement of life. For if Chriſt gaue himſelfe to redeeme vs from iniquitie, wee muſt take vp a purpoſe of not ſinning, and neuer wittingly ſinne more. Laſtly, this knowledge is the foundation of comfort in them that truely turne to Chriſt. For the price is paid for their ſinnes: and they which are eaſed of their ſinnes are bleſſed, *Pſal.* 32.1. And in temptation, they may boldly oppoſe the ſatisfaction of Chriſt againſt hell, death, the law, and the iudgement of God; and if at any time they ſinne, they muſt recouer themſelues and remember that they *haue an Aduocate with the Father, Ieſus Chriſt the iuſt*, 1. *Iohn* 2.1.

And whereas *Paul* ſaith, *that Chriſt gaue himſelfe for our ſinnes*, he teacheth that euery man muſt apply this gift and ſacrifice of Chriſt to himſelfe. This applying is done by faith: and the right maner of application is this. Wee muſt turne to Chriſt, and in turning by faith apply: and when wee apply Chriſt by faith, wee muſt withall turne. Faith goeth before conuerſion in order of nature, yet in the order of teaching, and practiſe, they are both together. They which vſe to apply Chriſt and his benefites vnto themſelues, and yet will not turne themſelues to Chriſt, miſapply, and preſume: becauſe the right apprehenſion of Chriſt, is in the exerciſes of inuocation, and repentance.

The ſecond end, for which Chriſt gaue himſelfe, is that he might take vs out of this euill world. And hence wee are taught three things. Firſt, that we muſt be grieued and diſpleaſed at the wickednes of the world as *Lot* was, 2. *Pet.* 2.7. Secondly, that we muſt not faſhion our ſelues to the wicked liues of the men of this world: but wee muſt in all things *prooue what is the good will of God*, and doe it. Thirdly, ſeeing we are taken out of this world, wee muſt not dwell in it, but our dwelling muſt be in heauen. *Reuel.* 13.6. the beaſt out of the ſea perſecutes them that dwell in heauen, that is, ſuch as dwel on earth, and for affection haue their conuerſation in heauen. And ſeeing this muſt be ſo, wee muſt not loue the world, but loue the comming of Chriſt, and euery day prepare our ſelues againſt the day of death, that we may enter into our owne home.

Rom. 12.2.

And whereas *Paul* cals this world *an euill world*, hee doeth it to ſignifie that there is nothing in men but ſinne, till they be regenerate, yea that ciuill vertues, and ciuill life, that are excellent in the eyes of men, are no better then ſinnes before God. It is the errour of the Papiſts, that men may thinke and do ſome thing that is morally good without grace.

The cauſe that moued Chriſt to giue himſelfe, is the will of God. Hence it appeares that God giues Chriſt to no man for his foreſeen faith, or works. For there is no higher cauſe of the will of God. The foreknowledge of things that may come to paſſe, goes before will; but the foreknowledge of things that ſhal come to paſſe, and therfore the foreknowledge of faith and workes, followes the will of God. Becauſe things that ſhall come to paſſe, are firſt decreed, and then foreſeene.

The will here mentioned, is ſaid to be the wil of God, that is, the firſt perſon the Father: for when Chriſt is oppoſed to God, then God ſignifies the Father. And hee is moſt commonly called God, becauſe he is God without communication of the godhead from any: whereas the Sonne and holy Ghoſt are God, by communication of godhead from the Father.

And this God is called *our Father* by *Paul*. And hereby he ſignifies that the ſcope of the Goſpel is; firſt, to propound God vnto vs not only as a creator, but as a Father: ſecondly, to inioyne vs to acknowledge him to be our Father in Chriſt: and conſequently to

carry

carry our selues as dutiful children to him in all subiection and obedience. They which doe not this, know not the intent of the Gospel: and if they know it, in deed they deny it.

The conclusion annexed to the salutation (*To whom bee glorie for euer*) teacheth vs so oft as we remember the worke of our redemption by Christ, so oft must we giue praise and thanks to God: yea all our liues must be nothing else but a testimony of thankfulnesse for our redemption. And all our praise and thankes to God, must proceed from the serious affection of the heart, signified by the word, *Amen*: that is, so be it.

6. I maruell that you are so soone remooued away to another Gospell, from him that hath called you in the grace of Christ.

7 Which is not another Gospell: but that some trouble you, and intende to ouerthrow the Gospell of Christ.

Here beginnes the second part of the Epistle, in which he giues instruction to the Galatians. And it hath two parts: one concernes doctrine, the other manners. The first part touching doctrine, beginnes in the sixt verse, and continues to the thirteenth verse of the 5. chapter. The summe of it is a reproofe of the Galatians for reuolting from the Gospell: and it is disposed in this syllogisme.

If I be immediatly called of God to teach, and my doctrine be true, yee ought not to haue reuolted from my doctrine.

But I was called immediatly of God to teach, and my doctrine is true.

Therefore ye should not haue reuolted from my doctrine.

The proposition is not expressed: because it was needelesse. The *minor* is handled, through the whole Epistle. The Conclusion is in the 6. and 7. verses, the meaning whereof I will briefely deliuer. *So soone*] that is, presently after my departure. *remooued*] carried away by the perswasions of false teachers, *to another Gospell.*] to another doctrine of saluation, which in the speech and opinion of the false teachers, is another manner of Gospell, more sufficient and more excellent, then that which *Paul* hath deliuered. *From him*] that is, from me beeing an Apostle, who haue called you by preaching the Gospell of Christ, *In the grace*] that is, haue called you freely, without any desert of yours, to bee partakers of the fauour of God in Christ. *Which is not another*] which pretended Gospell of the false Apostles, is not indeed another gospell from that of *Paul*, because there is but one; but it is an inuention of the braine of man. *But there bee some*] that is, but I plainely perceiue the cause of your reuolt, that some trouble you, and seeke to ouerthrow the Gospell of Christ.

In

In theſe words,two points are to be conſidered. The firſt is, the manner which *Paul* vſeth in reproouing the Galatians.He tenders their good,and ſaluation,and ſeekes by all meanes their recouery. And therefore in his reproofe he doth two things. Firſt, he reprooues them with meekeneſſe,and tenderneſſe of heart, following his owne rule,*Gal.6.1.*for he might iuſtly haue ſaid, ye may be aſhamed,that ye are remooued to another Goſpell,but he ſaith only,I maruell,that is,I was well perſwaded of you,and I hoped for better things,but I am deceiued,and I wonder at it.Secondly, hee frames his reproofe with great warineſſe,and circumſpection : for he ſaith not,ye of your ſelues doe remooue to another Goſpell,but ye are remooued : and thus he blames them but in part, and laies the principal blame on others.Againe,he ſaith not ye were remooued,but in the time preſent,*ye are remooued*, that is,ye are in the act of Reuolting,and haue not as yet altogether reuolted.And hereby he puts them in mind,that although they be in a fault,yet there is nothing done,which may not eaſily be vndone. According to his example,we are in all Reproofes,to ſhew loue, and to keepe loue: to ſhew loue to the party reprooued,and to frame our reproofe, ſo as we may keepe his loue.

The ſecond point is the fault reprooued,and that is, the Reuolt of the Galatians:which was a departure from the calling, whereby they were called to the grace of Chriſt. If it be demanded, what kind of Reuolt this was?I anſwer,there be two kinds of reuolt,*particular* and *generall*. *Particular*, when men profeſſe the name of Chriſt, and yet depart from the faith, in ſome principall points thereof.Of this kinde was the Apoſtacy of the tenne tribes, and ſuch is the Apoſtacy of the Romane Church. A *generall* reuolt is, when men wholly forſake the faith and name of Chriſt. Thus doe the Iewes,and Turkes at this day.Againe,a reuolt is ſometime of weakeneſſe,and humane frailty,and ſometime of obſtinacie. Now the reuolt of the Galatians was onely particular in the point of iuſtification,and of weakeneſſe,,and not of obſtinacie : and this *Paul* ſignifies when he ſaith,they were carried by others.Of this Reuolt, foure things are to be conſidered. The time,*ſo ſoone* : from whom, or what ? *from the doctrine of Paul*, and conſequently the grace of Chriſt. To what ? *to another Goſpell*. By meanes of whom ? *but ſome trouble you, &c.*

Touching the time,it was ſhort, They were ſoone caried away. This ſhewes the lightneſſe and inconſtancy of mans nature,ſpecially in matter of religion. While *Moſes* taried in the mount, *Aaron* and the people ſet vp a golden calfe,and departed from God. *Oſea*

ſaith,

ſaith, The righteouſneſſe of the Iſraelites, was like the morning dewe, which the riſing of the Sunne conſumeth, cha. 6.4. *Iohn* was a burning light, and the Iewes reioyced in this light: that is well; but marke what is added: *for an houre or moment. Iohn* 5.35. They which cried *Oſanna to the Sonne of Dauid*, ſhortly after cried, *Crucifie him, crucifie him.* The croſſe and perſecution, will make men call the Goſpel in queſtion, if not forſake it, *Luke* 8.13. The multitude of people among vs are like waxe, and are fit to take the ſtampe, and impreſſion of any religion: and it is the law of the land that makes the moſt imbrace the Goſpell, and not conſcience. That wee may conſtantly perſeuere in the profeſſion of the true faith, both in life and death, firſt wee muſt receiue the Goſpel ſimply for it ſelfe, becauſe it is the Goſpel of Chriſt, and not for any by-reſpect. Secondly, we muſt be mortified, and renued in the ſpirit of our minds, and ſuffer no by-corners in our hearts, where ſecret vnbeleefe, ſecret hypocriſie, and ſpirituall pride may lurke, and lie hid from the eyes of men, *Heb.* 3.12. Thirdly, wee muſt not onely be hearers of the word, but alſo doers of it in the principall duties to be practiſed, of faith, conuerſion, and new obedience.

To come to the ſecond point: when *Paul* ſaith, the Galatians were remooued from him that called them, that is, himſelfe; hee ſhewes Chriſtian modeſtie: becauſe ſpeaking things praiſe-worthy of himſelfe, he ſpeakes in the third perſon: *from him that hath called, &c.* The like he doeth, 2. *Cor.* 12. *I know a man taken vp into the third heauen*: that is himſelfe. And *Iohn* ſaith, *the diſciple that leaned on the breaſt of Chriſt, whom Chriſt loued*, asked whom he meant, *Ioh.* 13.23. After this practiſe, we are to giue praiſe to God, and to his inſtruments, but neither to praiſe nor diſpraiſe our ſelues. This is Chriſtian ciuility to be ioyned with our faith.

Secondly, when he ſaith, *who hath called you in the grace of Chriſt*, we learne, that the ſcope of the Goſpell is to bring men to the grace of Chriſt. To this very end God hath vouchſafed vs in England the Goſpel more then fourtie yeares. And therefore our words, and deedes, and liues, ſhould bee ſeaſoned with grace, and ſauour of it: and ſhew forth the grace of God. Secondly, we owe vnto God great thankfulnes, and wee can neuer be ſufficiently thankefull for this benefit, that God calles vs to his grace. But it is otherwiſe, the ſunne is a goodly creature; yet becauſe wee ſee it daily, it is not regarded; and ſo it is with the grace of God.

Thirdly, the Galatians are remooued not onely from the doctrine of *Paul*, but alſo from the grace of God. And the reaſon is, becauſe they ioyned the workes of the law with Chriſt & his grace

in

in the cauſe of their iuſtification,and ſaluation.Here it muſt be obſerued,that they which make an vnion of grace,and workes,in the cauſe of iuſtification,are ſeparated from the grace of God. Grace admits no partner,or fellow.Grace muſt be freely giuen euery way, or it is no way grace. Hence it followes, that the preſent Church of Rome is departed from the grace of God, becauſe it makes a concurrence of grace,and workes,in the iuſtification of a ſinner before God: and we may not make any reconciliation with that Church in religion: becauſe it is become an enemy of the grace of God.

The third point is,to what thing the Galatians reuolt? *to another Goſpel*,that is,to a better goſpel,then that which *Paul* taught,compounded of Chriſt and the workes of the law. And this forged goſpell the falſe Apoſtles taught, and the Galatians quickely receiued. Here we ſee the curious niceneſſe and daintineſſe of mans nature,that cannot be content with the good things of God,vnles they be framed to our minds:and if they pleaſe vs for a while,they doe not pleaſe vs long, but we muſt haue new things. Our firſt parents not content with their firſt eſtate, muſt needes be as God.
Leu.10.1. *Nadab* and *Abihu* offer ſacrifice to God, but the fire muſt bee of
2.Reg.16.11. their owne appointment. King *Achas* will offer ſacrifice to God,but
Reu.2.24. the altar muſt be like the altar at Damaſcus. Falſe teachers beſide the doctrine of the Apoſtles,had profound learning of their owne. The Iewes beſide the written law of *Moſes*,muſt haue their *Cabala*, containing,as they ſuppoſed,more myſticall & excellent doctrine. The Papiſts beſide the written word, ſet vp vnwritten Tradition which they make equall with the Scripture. We that profeſſe the Goſpel,are not altogether free from this fault. We like,that Chriſt ſhould be preached: but Sermons are not in common reputation learned,neither doe they greatly pleaſe the moſt, vnleſſe they bee garniſhed with skill of arts,tongues,and variety of reading: this curiouſneſſe and diſcontentment the Lord condemnes, when he
Deut.22.9. forbids *plowing with the oxe,and the aſſe,and the wearing of garments of linſi-wolſie*. And it is the worſt kind of diſcontentment, that is in
2.Tim.4.5. things pertaining to ſaluation. It is called by *Paul*, *the itching of the eare*,and it is incident to them that follow their owne luſts. The remedy of this ſinne,is to learne the firſt leſſon that is to be learned of them that are to be good ſchollers in the ſchoole of Chriſt: and that is to feele our pouerty, and in what extreame neede we ſtand of the death and paſſion of Chriſt:and withall to hunger and thirſt after Chriſt,as the bread and water of life. Reade *Iſa.*44.3. *Ioh*,7.37 *Pſal.*25.11.the example of *Dauid*,*Pſal.*143.6. When the heart and con-

conſcience hath experimentally learned this leſſon, and not the braine, and tongue alone : then ſhall men beginne to ſauour the things of God, and diſcerne of things that differ, and put a difference betweene grace, and workes, mans word, and Gods word, and for the working of our ſaluation,eſteeme of mans workes,and mans word,as offals that are caſt to dogges.

Paul addes,*which is not another Goſpel*,that is,though it be another goſpel in the reputation of falſe teachers,yet indeede it is not another, but is a ſubuerſion of the Goſpell of Chriſt. Hence I gather, that there is but one Goſpell,one in number and no more.For there is but one way of ſaluation by Chriſt, whereby all the Elect are ſaued, from the beginning of the world to the end. *Act*.15.11. 1.*Cor*.10.3. It may be demanded,how they of the old Teſtament, could be partakers of the body, and blood of Chriſt, which then was not.*Anſwer*.The body,and blood of Chriſt,though then it was not ſubſiſting in the world,yet was it then preſent to all beleeuers, two waies : firſt, by diuine acceptation : becauſe God did accept the incarnation and paſſion of Chriſt to come, as if it had beene accompliſhed.Secondly,it was preſent to them by meanes of their faith,which is a ſubſiſtance of things that are not ſeene ;and conſequently it makes them preſent to the beleeuing heart.

Againe,hence it appeares,to be a falſhood, that euery man may be ſaued in his owne religion,ſo be it, he hold there is a God, and that he is a rewarder of them that come vnto him. For there is but one Goſpel : and if the former opinion were true,then ſo many opinions,ſo many goſpels.*Paul* ſaith,that the world by her wiſdome could not know God in his wiſedome, and for this cauſe he ordained the preaching of the word to ſaue men,1.*Cor*.1 21. And though he that comes to God muſt beleeue that he is, and that he is a rewarder of them that come to him : yet not euery one that beleeues generally that there is a God,and that he is a rewarder of them that come to him,comes to God : for this the diuells beleeue.

The fourth point,is concerning the Authors of this Reuolt:and *Paul* chargeth them with two crimes. The firſt is,that they trouble the Galatians,not onely becauſe they make diuiſions, but becauſe they trouble their conſciences ſetled in the goſpell of Chriſt. It may be alleadged,that there be ſundry good things which trouble the conſcience,as the preaching of the law, the cenſure of excommunication, the authority of the Magiſtrate in compelling Recuſants to the congregation.I anſwer,theſe things indeede trouble the conſciences of men,but they are euill conſciences:& the end of this trouble is that they may be reformed,& made good. But the crime wherewith the falſe Apoſtles are charged,is,that they trouble the conſciences of the godly, or the good conſciences of men. Here then is ſet downe a note,whereby falſe, and erroneous doctrines, may be diſcerned: namely, that they ſerue onely to trouble, and diſquiet the good conſcience. And by this we ſee the Romane religion to bee corrupt and vnſound: for a great part of it tends this way. Iuſtification by workes is a yoke that none could euer beare, *Act.*15. The vow of ſingle life is as a ſnare, or as the nooſe in the halter to ſtrangle the ſoule. 1.*Cor.*7. 34. So is the doctrine which teacheth that men after their conuerſion, muſt ſtill remaine in ſuſpence of their ſaluation: and that pardon of ſinne is neceſſarily annexed to confeſſion in the eare,and to ſatiſfaction for the temporall puniſhment of ſinne in this life,or in purgatory.

On the contrary, the Goſpell of Chriſt (as here it appeares) troubles not the good conſcience, but it brings peace and perfect ioy. *Ioh.*15.11.*Rom.*15 4.And the reaſon is plaine: for it miniſters a perfect remedy for euery ſinne, and comfort ſufficient for euery diſtreſſe. And this is a note whereby the Goſpell is diſcerned from all other doctrines whatſoeuer.

The ſecond crime wherewith the falſe Apoſtles are charged, is that they ouerthrow the Goſpel of Chriſt:the reaſon of this charge muſt be conſidered. They did not teach a doctrine flat contrary to the Goſpell of Chriſt: but they maintained it in word, and put an addition to it of their owne out of the law, namely iuſtification, and ſaluation, by the workes thereof. And by reaſon of this addition; *Paul* giues the ſentence,that they peruert,and turne vpſide downe the Goſpell of Chriſt. Vpon this ground it appeares that the Popiſh religion is a flat ſubuerſion of the Goſpell of Chriſt, becauſe it ioynes iuſtification by workes, with free iuſtification by Chriſt. The excuſe, that the workes that iuſtifie, are workes of grace, and not of nature, will not ſerue the turne. For if Chriſt by his grace make workes to iuſtifie, then is he not onely a Sauiour, but alſo an inſtrument to make vs Sauiours of our ſelues: he being the firſt,and principall Sauiour,and we ſubordinate Sauiours,vnto him. But if Chriſt haue a partner in the worke of iuſtification, and ſaluation,he is no perfect Chriſt.

8. *But though we,or an Angell from heauen, preach vnto you otherwiſe, then that which we haue preached vnto you, let him be accurſed.*

9. As we said before, so say I now againe, if any man preach vnto you otherwise then ye haue receiued, let him be accursed.

An obiection might bee made against the former conclusion, thus: But the most excellent among the Apostles, *Iames, Peter, Iohn* (by your leaue) teach another Gospel then that which *Paul* had preached. To this obiection hee makes answere in this verse negatiuely, that whosoeuer teacheth another Gospel, is accursed, whatsoeuer he be. In this answere three things are to be considered: a sinne, the punishment thereof, and a supposition seruing to amplifie the sinne.

The sinne is to preach in the cause of our iustification, any other thing *besides that*, or *diuers to that* which *Paul* taught the Galatians, though it bee not contrary. Thus much the very wordes παρ' ὅ. import: and the same wordes are againe vsed in the next verse. And *Paul* bids *Timothie, Auoid them that teach otherwise*, that is, any diuers doctrine as necessarie to saluation, besides that which hee taught, 1.*Tim*.6.3. And the reason of this sinne is: because God hath giuen this commaundement, Wee may not depart from his word, to the right hand, or to the left; neither may we adde thereto, or take therefrom, *Iosu*.1.v.7,8. *Deut*.4.& 12. Before I gather any doctrine hence, this ground is to be laid down, that *Paul* preached *all the counsell of God*, *Act*.20.27. And that which he preached, being necessarie to saluation, he wrote, or some other of the Apostles *Iohn* 20.31. This being graunted (which is a certaine trueth) two maine conclusions follow. One, that the Scriptures alone by themselues, without any other word, are *abundantly sufficient to saluation*, whether we regard doctrines of faith, or maners. For he that deliuers any doctrine out of them, and beside them, as necessary to be beleeued, is accursed.

The second conclusion, is, that vnwritten Traditions, if they be tendered to vs, as a part of Gods word, and as necessary to saluation, they are *abominations*, because they are doctrines beside the Gospell that *Paul* preached. And the Romane religion goes to the ground: because it is founded on Tradition, out of, and beside the written word. Learned Papistes, to helpe themselues, make a double answere. One is, that they are accursed which preach otherwise then *Paul* preached, and not they which preach otherwise then he writ. But it is false which they say, for that which he preached, he writ. *Augustine* hauing relation to the text in hand, saith, *that hee is accursed which preacheth any thing* * *beside that which we haue receiued in the Legall and Euangelicall Scriptures.* Againe he saith, *that he*

* Præter quã. contra Petilian.l.3.c.6. De bono viduitatis.c.1.

* Non aliud quid amplius?

*he must * not teach any more, or any other thing; then that which is in the Apostle, whose words he must expound.*

The second answere is, that to preach otherwise, is to preach contrary. Because (as they say) precepts and doctrines may bee deliuered if they be diuerse, and not contrary. As the Gospell of *Iohn*, and the *Apocalyps*, were written after this Epistle to the Galatians, which are diuers to it, though not contrary: the like they say of the canons of councells: and that *Paul*, *Rom.* 16. 18 put [παρ' ὃ] *beside*, for *contrarie*. I answer thus: The preposition (παρὰ) translated beside or otherwise, signifieth thus much properly: and wee are not to depart from the proper signification of the words, vnlesse we be forced by the text. And the place in the Romans in his proper and full sense, must be turned thus: *Obserue the authors of offences, besides the doctrine which ye haue learned.* And *Pauls* mind is, that they should bee obserued, that teach any other diuers, or distinct doctrine, though it bee not directly contrary. The Gospell of *Iohn* and the *Apocalyps*, written afterward, propound not any diuers doctrine pertaining to the saluation of the soule, but one and the same in substance, with that which *Paul* wrote. The Canons of Councels, are traditions touching order and comelinesse, and they prescribe not any thing, as necessary to iustification, and saluation. Againe, the Embassadour that speakes any thing beside his commission, is as wel in fault, as he that speakes the contrary: though not so much.

The second point is, the punishment [*Let him be accursed*] Here are three things to be considered. The first, what is it to be accursed? *Ans.* God hath giuen to the Church, the power of binding, and it hath foure degrees, *Admonition*, *Suspension* from the Sacraments, *Excommunication*, *Anathema*. And this last is a censure or iudgement of the Church, whereby it pronounceth a man seuered from Christ, and adiudged to eternal perdition, *Rom.* 9. 5. 1 *Cor.* 16. 22. And hee is here said to be accursed, that stands subiect to this censure. The second part is, who are to be accursed? *Ans.* Hainous offenders, and desperate persons, of whose amendmentt here is no hope. And therefore this iudgement is seldome pronounced vpon any. We finde but one example in the new Testament: *Paul* accursed *Alexander* the Copper-smith, 2. *Tim.* 4. 14. And the Church afterward accursed *Iulian* the Emperour. Other examples we finde not any.

The third point, how the Church should accurse any man, and in what order? *Answer.* In this action, there be foure iudgements. The first is Gods, which is giuen in heauen, whereby he doth accurse obstinate and notorious offenders. The second iudgement, per-

pertaines to the Church vpon earth, which pronounceth them accurſed, whom God accurſeth. It may bee ſaid, how comes the Church to know the iudgement of God, whereby hee accurſeth? *Anſwer.* The word ſets downe the condition of them, that are accurſed; and experience, and obſeruation findes out the perſons, to whom theſe conditions are incident. The third iudgement is giuen in heauen, whereby God ratifies and approoues the iudgement of the Church, according to that, *Whatſoeuer yee binde in earth, ſhall bee bound in heauen.* The laſt iudgement pertaines to euery priuate perſon, who holds him in execration, whom God hath accurſed, and the Church hath pronounced ſo to be. If hee heare not the Church, the Church pronounceth him to bee as a Publican and heathen: *and then* (ſaith Chriſt) *let him bee as a Publican to thee.* Thus muſt the text be vnderſtood.

Hence we are taught, to be carefull in preſeruing the puritie of the Goſpel: becauſe the corrupters therof, are to be accurſed as the damned ſpirits. Hence againe it appeareth, that the Church in accurſing, doth but exerciſe a Miniſtery, which is, to publiſh and teſtifie, who are accurſed of God. Laſtly, hence we learne, that priuate perſons muſt ſeldome vſe curſing: becauſe God muſt firſt accurſe, and the Church publiſh the ſentence of God; before we may with good conſcience vtter the ſame. They therefore which in a rage accurſe themſelues and others, deale wickedly. We are called ordinarily to bleſſing, and not to curſing.

The third point is, the ſuppoſition of things impoſſible, on this manner. Put the caſe, that I *Paul*, or any other of the Apoſtles, ſhould teach otherwiſe then I haue taught you: neither I nor they muſt bee beleeued, but be accurſed. Againe, put the caſe, that an Angel from heauen ſhould come and preach, otherwiſe then *Paul* preached to the Galatians, who muſt bee beleeued? *Paul*, or the Angel? the anſwer is, not the Angel, but *Paul*: and the Angel muſt be accurſed. And the reaſon is, becauſe *Paul* in preaching and writing, did repreſent the authoritie of God, and God puts his owne authoritie into the word which he vttered: and he was aſſiſted by the extraordinary, immediate, and infallible aſſiſtance of Gods ſpirit. From this ſuppoſition, ſundry things may bee learned. The firſt, that the word preached and written by *Paul*, is as certaine, as if it had been written by God himſelfe, immediatly. It may bee obiected, that *Paul* ſaith, 1. *Cor.* 7. 12. *To the remnant, I ſpeake, not the Lord.* I anſwer, *Paul* ſaith, *I, not the Lord*, not becauſe he was deceiued in his aduiſe, for hee ſpake by the Spirit of God, c. 7. v. 40. but becauſe hee gaue counſell in a caſe of mariage, whereof the Lord had made no expreſſe law. The meaning then is this, I ſpeake by collection from the law of God, and not the Lord, by any particular and expreſſe Law.

Secondly it appeares hence, that the articles of faith, or the doctrine of the Goſpel, is in excellency & authority aboue al men and Angels. And hence it followes, that the Church and Councels cannot authorize the word of God, in the mind and conſcience of any man. For the inferiour and dependent authoritie addes nothing to that which is the principall, and ſuperiour authority. Therefore the opinion of the Papiſts is falſe, that we cannot know the ſcripture to be the word of God, but by the teſtimony of the church: as though the letter of a Prince could not be knowen to bee ſo, without the teſtimony of the ſubiects. The principall authority is ſufficient in it ſelfe, to authorize it ſelfe, without externall teſtimony.

Thirdly, ſince the dayes of the Apoſtles, ſundrie doctrines haue beene receiued and beleeued, touching interceſſion of Saints, prayer to the dead, and for the dead, Purgatorie, and ſuch like: and theſe doctrines haue bene confirmed by ſundrie reuelations. And heere we learne, what to iudge both of the doctrines, and of the reuelations; namely, that they are accurſed: becauſe the doctrines are beſide the written word, and the reuelations tend to ratifie and confirme them.

Laſtly, hence we learne, what to thinke of the writings of Papiſts, and Schoolemen, whereof ſome are called, *Seraphicall, Cherubicall*, or *Angelicall Doctours*. They broach and maintaine ſundrie things, beſide that which the Apoſtles preached, and wrote; as iuſtification by works, and a mixture of the law and the Goſpel: they giue too little to grace, and too much to mans will. In this regard, *Paul* hath giuen the ſentence, that they are accurſed. For this cauſe ſtudents of diuinitie, are warily to reade them with prayer, that they be not led into temptation, and they are to vſe them onely in the laſt place. And they are greatly to bee blamed, that preferre them almoſt aboue all writers: they ſhew that they haue little loue of the Goſpel in their hearts.

9 *As we ſaid before, ſo ſay I now againe: if any man preach vnto you otherwiſe then ye haue receiued, let him be accurſed.*

In theſe wordes *Paul* repeates againe that which he ſaid before: and the repetition is not in vaine, but for three weightie cauſes; the firſt is, to ſignifie that he had ſpoken not raſhly, but aduiſedly, what ſoeuer he had ſaid before: the ſecond is, that the point deliuered, is an infallible truth of God: the third is, to put the Galatians & vs in

minde,

minde,that we are to obserue and remember that which hee hath said,as the foundation of our religion,namely,that the doctrine of the Apostles,is the only infallible trueth of God, against which we may not listen to Fathers,Councels,or to the very Angels of God. If this had bin remembred and obserued,the Gospel had continued in his puritie after the daies of the Apostles.

In this verse one thing is to be obserued. Before, *Paul* said,they are accursed which teach otherwise then hee had taught: here he saith, they are accursed which teach otherwise then the Galatians had receiued. Whereby it appeares,that as *Paul* preached the Gospel of Christ,so the Galatians receiued it. And they receiued it,first in that they had care to know it: secondly, in that they gaue the assent of faith vnto it,as to a trueth: against which the very Angels could take no exception. And for this also are the Thessalonians commended,that the Gospel was to them *in power & much assurance.* The great fault of our times is, that where as the Gospel is preached,it is not accordingly receiued. Many haue no care to know it: and they which know it,giue not vnto it the assent of faith,but only hold it in opinion. And this is the cause that there is so small fruit of the Gospel. This sinne will at length haue his punishment. The places that are not seasoned by the waters of the Sanctuarie, are turned to salt-pits, *Ezech.*47.v.11.

10 *For now whether preach I men or God? or seeke I to please men? for if I should yet please men, I were not the seruant of Christ.*

The interogations in this place, *doe I preach?* and, *doe I please?* are in stead of earnest negations: *I doe not preach, I doe not please.* And when he saith, *do I now preach men,or God?* his meaning is this: Heretofore I haue preached the Traditions of men, but now being an Apostle,I preach not the doctrine of men,but of God. And when he saith, *doe I seeke to please men?* his meaning is this; I doe not make this the scope of my ministerie, to frame and temper my doctrine so,as it may be sutable and pleasing to the affections of men. For otherwise *wee are to please men in that which is good, and for their good,* 1.*Cor.*10.33. *Rom* 15.2.

This verse containes a double reason of his former speach, and of the repetition thereof. The first is this. Though heretofore I taught the Traditions of men; yet now I teach the word not of men,but of God: and therefore I accurse them that teach otherwise. The second is framed thus. If I should yet please men,I were not the seruant of God: but I am the seruant of God: therefore I ſeeke not to pleaſe men,but,if need ſhall be,I will denounce curſes againſt them.

Here firſt we ſee the proper nature of the Miniſtery,which is not the word or doctrine of man,but of God. By this the Miniſters of the Goſpel are taught to handle their doctrine with modeſtie, and humilitie,without oſtentation,with reuerence, and with a conſideration of the maieſtie of God whoſe the doctrine is which they vtter,that God may be glorified,1.*Pet*.4.11.

Secondly, the hearers in hearing are to know that they haue to deale with God: and that they are to receiue the doctrine taught *not as the word of man,but as the very word of God,* as the Theſſalonians did,1.*Theſſ*.2.13. The want of this conſideration,is the cauſe that ſome contemne the miniſtery of the word, as others are not touched and mooued in hearing.

Againe, heere is ſet downe the right manner of diſpenſing the word, which muſt not bee for the pleaſing of men,but of God. Hence it appeares,that Miniſters of the Goſpel muſt not be menpleaſers,nor apply and faſhion their doctrine to the affections,humors,and diſpoſitions of men,but keep a good conſcience,and do their office. The Lord tels *Ieremie*, hee muſt not turne *to the people, but the people muſt turne to him,Iere*.15.19. Thus God ſhall bee with them,and they ſhall bring forth much fruite.

And the people muſt know it to bee a good thing for them,not to be pleaſed alwaies by their Miniſters. The miniſtery of the word muſt be as a ſacrificing knife,to kill & mortifie the old *Adam* in vs, that we may liue vnto God. A ſicke man muſt not alwaies haue his mind,but he muſt often be croſſed,and reſtrained of his deſire:and ſo muſt we that are ſicke in our ſoules in reſpect of our ſinnes. It is a fault therefore of men that deſire to be pleaſed, and to haue matters ſmoothed ouer of their Teachers. This is *Dauids* balme,which he wiſheth may neuer be wanting to his head,*Pſal*.141.5.

The end of this verſe ſets downe a memorable ſentence,That if we ſeek to pleaſe men,we cannot be the ſeruants of God. Hence I gather,that our nature is full of rebellion, & enmitie againſt God; becauſe they which pleaſe men,cannot pleaſe God. Againe,here is ſet downe what is the hurt that comes by pride,and ambition. It keepes men that they cannot be the ſeruants of Chriſt; *Yee beleeue not*(ſaith Chriſt)*becauſe ye ſeeke glory one of another, Ioh*.5.44. Ambition ſo fils the mind with vanitie,& the heart with worldly deſires, that it cannot thinke, or deſire to pleaſe God. Wherefore hee that would be a faithfull Miniſter of the Goſpel,muſt deny the pride of his heart, and bee emptied of ambition,and ſet himſelfe wholly to

ſeeke

ſeeke the glory of God in his calling. And generally, he that would be a faithfull ſeruant of Chriſt, muſt ſet God before him as a Iudge, and conſider that he hath to deale with God: and he muſt turne his mind and ſenſes from the world, and all things therein, to God: and ſeeke aboue all things to approoue his thoughts, deſires, affe-ctions, and all his doings vnto him.

Laſtly, the profeſſion of the ſeruant of God, is here to be obſer-ued in the example of *Paul*, who ſaith, *Doe I now preach men?* and, *doe I yet pleaſe men?* as if he had ſaid, I haue done thus and thus, I haue preached the traditions of men heretofore, and I haue pleaſed men in perſecuting the Church of God: but I doe not ſo ſtill, nei-ther wil I. And he that can ſay the like with good conſcience, I haue ſinned thus and thus heretofore, but now I doe not, neither will I ſinne as I haue done, is indeed the ſeruant of God.

11 *Now I certifie you, brethren, that the Goſpell which was preached by me, was not after man.*

The meaning is this: that it may the better appeare that I haue iuſtly accurſed them which teach any other Goſpel, and iuſtly re-prooued you for receiuing it: I giue you to vnderſtand, *that the Go-ſpel which I preached was not after man,* that is, not deuiſed by man, or preached of mee by mans authoritie, but it was from God, and preached by the authoritie of God. And this ſenſe appeares by v. 10. and 12.

In theſe words is laid down the reaſon of the concluſion, or the aſſumption of the principall argument, which was on this maner: If I bee called to teach, and that immediatly of God, and my do-ctrine be true, then ye ought not to haue reuolted from the Goſpel which I preached: but I was called to teach immediatly of God, and my doctrine is true. The firſt part of the aſſumption is here ſet downe, and handled to the end of the ſecond chapter: and the con-cluſion (as we haue heard) was ſet downe in the premiſes.

Hence two maine points of doctrine that are of great conſe-quent, may be gathered. The firſt is this: it is a thing moſt neceſſa-ry, that men ſhould be aſſured & certified that the doctrine of the Goſpel, and the Scripture, is not of man, but of God. This is the firſt thing which *Paul* ſtands vpon in this Epiſtle. It may be deman-ded, how this aſſurance may be obtained. I anſwer, thus. For the ſetling of our conſciences, that Scripture is the word of God, there be two teſtimonies. One is the euidence of Gods Spirit, imprinted and expreſſed in the Scriptures: and this is an excellencie of the word of God aboue all wordes and writings of men, and Angels, and containes 13. points. The firſt, is the purity of the law of *Moſes*, wheras the lawes of men haue their imperfections. The ſecond is, that the Scripture ſetteth down the true cauſe of all miſery, namely ſinne, and the perfect remedie, namely, the death of Chriſt. The third is, the antiquitie of Scripture, in that it ſets downe an hiſtorie from the beginning of the world. The fourth is, prophecies of things in ſundrie bookes of Scripture, which none could poſſibly foretell but God. The fift is, the confirmation of the doctrine of the Prophets and Apoſtles by miracles, that is, workes done aboue, and contrarie to the ſtrength of nature, which none can doe but God. The ſixt is, the conſent of all the Scriptures with themſelues, whereas the writings of men are often at iarre with themſelues. The ſeuenth is, the confeſſion of enemies; as namely of heretikes, who in oppugning of Scriptures, alledge Scriptures, and thereby confeſſe the trueth thereof. The eight is, an vnſpeakable deteſtation, that Sathan and all wicked men beare to the doctrine of Scripture. The ninth is, the protection and preſeruation of it, from the beginning to this houre, by a ſpeciall prouidence of God. The tenth is, the conſtant profeſſion of Martyrs, that haue ſhed their blood for the Goſpell of Chriſt. The eleuenth is, that fearefull puniſhments and iudgements haue befallen them, that haue oppugned the word of God. The twelfth is, holines of them that profeſſe the Goſpel. The laſt is, the effect and operation of the word: for it is an inſtrument of God, in the right vſe whereof, wee receiue the teſtimony of the ſpirit of our adoption, and are conuerted vnto God. And yet neuertheleſſe, the word which conuerteth, is contrary to the wicked nature of man.

The ſecond teſtimony is from the Prophets and Apoſtles, who were Embaſſadors of God, extraordinarily to repreſent his authoritie vnto his Church, and the pen-men of the holy Ghoſt, to ſet downe the true and proper word of God. And the Apoſtles aboue the reſt, were eye-witneſſes, and eare-witneſſes of the ſayings and doings of Chriſt: and in that they were guided by the infallible aſſiſtance of the Spirit, both in preaching and writing: their teſtimonie touching the things which they wrote, muſt needes bee Authenticall. If it be ſaid, that counterfeit writings may be publiſhed to the world vnder the name of the Apoſtles. I anſwere, if they were in the daies of the Apoſtles, they by their authoritie cut them off: and therefore *Paul* ſaith, *If any teach otherwiſe, let him bee accurſed.* And they prouided, that no counterfeits ſhould be foiſted vnder their names, after their departure. And heereupon *Iohn*, the laſt of the Apoſtles, concludes the New Teſtament with this

clauſe,

clauſe, *If any man ſhall adde vnto theſe things, God ſhall adde vnto him the plagues that are written in this booke, Reuel.*22.18. If any demaund, of what value is the teſtimonie of the Church. I anſwer, conſider the Church diſtinct from the Apoſtles, and then the teſtimonie thereof is farre inferiour to the Apoſtolicall teſtification, concerning the word of God. For the Church is to be ruled by the teſtimonie of the Apoſtles, in the written word: and the ſentence of the Church is not alwaies, and altogether certain, nor ioyned with that euidence of the ſpirit, wherewith euery teſtimonie Apoſtolical is accompanied.

Furthermore, that we may be capable of theſe two teſtimonies, and take the benefit therof, we our ſelues for our parts, muſt yeeld ſubiection and obedience to the word of God. In this our obedience, ſhall wee be aſſured, that it is indeed of God, as our Sauiour Chriſt ſaith, *Iohn* 7.v.17

This doctrine touching the certaintie of the word, is of great vſe. For when the minde and conſcience, by meanes of the double teſtimony before mentioned, plainly apprehends it, there is a foundation laid of the feare of God, and of iuſtifying faith: and before we be aſſured that the Scripture is the word of God, it is not poſſible that wee ſhould conceiue, and hold a faith in the promiſes of God. And the want of this certaintie in many, is an open gap to hereſie, Apoſtacie, Atheiſme, and all iniquitie. Secondly, by this it appeares, that the Church of Rome erreth groſſely, in teaching that we cannot know the Scripture to be the word of God, without the teſtimony of the Church, in theſe latter times, and that without it, wee could haue no certaintie of religion; whereas the teſtimony of the ſpirit, or the euidence thereof in Scripture, with the teſtimonie of the Apoſtles, will doe the deed ſufficiently, though the Church ſhould be ſilent.

The ſecond maine point is, That it is neceſſary, that men ſhould be aſſured in their conſciences, that the calling and authoritie of their teachers, is of God. It may bee demaunded, how we in theſe daies ſhould be aſſured thereof. I anſwere thus: a diuers conſideration muſt be had, of the firſt Miniſters of the Goſpel, & of their ſucceſſors. Touching the firſt Miniſters & planters of the Goſpel, within theſe 80. yeares, wee muſt conſider, that a calling is of two ſorts: Ordinarie, and Extraordinarie. Ordinarie is, when God calls by the voices, and conſent of men, following the lawes of his word. Extraordinarie is, when God calles otherwiſe. And this he doeth three waies; firſt, by immediate voice. Thus God called *Abraham*, and *Moſes*, and thus were the Apoſtles called. The ſecond is, by the meſſage of a creature. Thus *Aaron* and the tribe of *Leui* was called by *Moſes*: *Elizæus*, by *Elias*: *Philip* was called by the Angel to baptize the Eunuch, *Actes* 8.26. The third is, by inſtinct. Thus *Philip* a Deacon preached in Samaria, *Act*.8.14. Thus the men of Cyprus and Cyrene preached among the Gentiles, and the hand of God was with them, though otherwiſe they were but priuat perſons, *Act*.11.19 20. Of this kind was the calling of the firſt preachers of the Goſpel. It may bee obiected, that they did not confirme their callings and doctrine by miracles, which they ſhould haue done, if their callings had bene extraordinary. I anſwer: they preached no new doctrine, but the old & ancient doctrine of the Prophets and Apoſtles, which they had heeretofore confirmed by miracles. Now old doctrine needs no new miracles, but new doctrine ſuch as are the Popes decrees and decretals. Againe, it may bee alledged, that men may falſly pretẽd extraordinary calling. I anſwer, if 3. rules be obſerued, they cannot. The firſt is, that extraordinary neuer takes place, but when there is no roome for ordinary. The ſecond, that they which plead a calling extraordinarily, muſt bee tried by the word, both for doctrine & life: for this is an infallible way to diſcouer falſe teachers, *Mat*.7.22. *Deu*.13.1,5. *Iohns* authority is ſaid to be frõ heauen, becauſe his baptiſme, that is, his doctrine was ſo, *Luk*.20.2. The third is, that extraordinary teachers in theſe laſt daies, after they haue brought men to receiue the Goſpel, are to be ordained as other ordinary miniſters after the lawes of Gods word. For they are not extraordinary in reſpect of their doctrine, which is the doctrine of the word, nor in reſpect of their office or function, in which regard they are paſtours and teachers, & not Apoſtles or Euangeliſts: but their callings are extraordinary, in reſpect of the common abuſe of the office of teaching, & in reſpect of the cõmon corruption of doctrine. Theſe 3. rules as caueats obſerued, we may eaſily perceiue who are called extraordinarily, who not: & they are all fully verified in the firſt preachers of the Goſpel.

Thirdly, it is obiected, that they which are lawfully called, are ordained by them, whoſe anceſtors haue bene ſucceſſiuely ordained by the Apoſtles. I anſwer: Succeſſion is threefold. The firſt is, of perſons and doctrine iointly together: and this was in the Primitiue Church. The ſecond is, of perſons alone, and this may be among infidels and heretikes. The third is, of doctrine alone. And thus our Miniſters ſucceed the Apoſtles. And this is ſufficient. For this rule muſt be remembred, that the power of the Keies, that is, of order and iuriſdiction, is tied by God, and annexed in the New Teſtament to doctrine. If in Turkie, or America, or els where, the

Goſpell ſhould be receiued of men,by the counſell and perſwaſion of priuate perſons, they ſhall not neede to ſend into Europe for conſecrated Miniſters,but they haue power to chooſe their owne Miniſters from within themſelues: becauſe where God giues the word,he giues the power alſo.

Touching the Succeſſours of the firſt Preachers, their calling was altogether ordinary,and they were ordained of their predeceſſours. It is obiected,that their callings are corrupt. I anſwer thus. All actions Eccleſiaſticall,that tende to binding or looſing,appertaine properly to the perſon of Chriſt, and men are but Miniſters, and inſtruments thereof. And therefore to call men to the miniſtery and diſpenſation of the Goſpell,belongs to Chriſt, who alone giueth the power,the will,the deede. And the Church can doe no more but teſtifie,publiſh,and declare whom God calleth, by Examination of parties for life and doctrine,by Election, and by ordination. This is for ſubſtance all that the Church can doe: and all this is allowed, and preſcribed by the lawes of this Church, and land. And therefore our callings for their ſubſtance are diuine, whatſoeuer defects there be otherwiſe.

This aſſurance that our callings are of God, is of great vſe. It cauſeth the Miniſter to make a conſcience of his duty: it is his comfort in trouble,*Iſa.*49.2. 2.*Cor.*2.15. And to the hearers it is a meanes of great reuerence,and obedience.

12 *For neither receiued I it of man, neither was I taught it, but by the reuelation of Ieſus Chriſt.*

The meaning is this. *Paul* here ſaith,he *receiued not the Goſpell of man*: becauſe he receiued not the office to teach and preach the Goſpel from any meere man. For here he ſpeakes of himſelfe as he was an Apoſtle: and then an Apoſtle properly is ſaid to receiue the Goſpell,when he receiues not onely to know and beleeue it, but alſo to preach it. And he addes further, that he was not taught it, that is,that he learned the Goſpel not by the teaching of any man, as formerly he learned the law at the feete of *Gamaliel*. The laſt words[*but by the reuelation of Ieſus Chriſt*]carry this ſenſe; but I learned it and receiued it of Chriſt who taught me by reuelation. Further,Reuelation is twofold,one ordinary,the other extraordinary. Ordinary is,when Chriſt teacheth men by the word preached,and by his ſpirit. In this ſenſe the holy Ghoſt is *called the ſpirit of reuelation,Eph.*1.17. Extraordinary is,with the word preached, and that foure waies. Firſt,by voice. Thus God taught *Adam* and the Patriarkes. The ſecond, by dreames, when things reuealed were represented to the mind in sleepe. The third is vision, when things reuealed are represented to the outward senses of men being awake. The fourth is instinct, when God teacheth by inward motion and inspiration. Thus did God vsually teach the Prophets, 2.*Pet.*1.21. Now the reuelation which *Paul* had, was not ordinary, but extraordinary, and that partly by vision, partly by voice, and partly by instinct, *Act.*9. & 22. It may heere be demanded, where Christ was, whether on earth, or in heauen, because *Paul* heard his voice, and saw him visibly. I answer, he was not on earth, but in heauen: and that *Paul* both saw him, and heard him, it was by miracle; whereas *Stephen* in like maner saw Christ, hee saw him not on earth, but standing at the right hand of God in heauen: for otherwise the opening of the heauens had bene a needlesse thing.

These words then are a confirmation of the former verse, on this maner. The authoritie whereby I teach, and the doctrine which I teach, I first receiued and learned it, not of man, but immediatly of Christ: therefore the Gospel which I preach is not humane, but diuine, and preached not by humane, but by diuine authoritie.

In the scope and sense of the words, many points of doctrine are contained. The first, that Christ is the great Prophet and Doctour of the Church, *Matt.*17.6. *Heare him*, and 23.8. *One is your Doctor, namely, Christ.* And he is called *the great Shepheard of the sheepe*, *Heb.* 13. 20. His office is in three things. The first is, to manifest and reueale the will of the Father touching the redemption of mankind, *Ioh.*1.18. & 8.26. This hee hath done from the beginning of the world (the Father neuer speaking and appearing immediatly but in the Baptisme and Transfiguration of Christ:) and this he doeth to *Paul* in this place. The second is, to institute the ministerie of the word, and to call and send Ministers. *As my Father sent mee, so send I you*, *Iohn* 20.21. He it is that giues *some to bee Pastours, some to bee Teachers*, *Ephes.*4.11. And thus appoints *Paul* to be an Apostle. The third is, to teach the heart within, by illuminating the mind, and by working a faith of the doctrine which is taught. He openeth the vnderstanding of his Disciples, that they may vnderstand the Scriptures, *Luke* 24.45. Thus heere he inlightneth and teacheth *Paul*.

Furthermore, it must be obserued, that this office of teaching, is inseparably annexed to the person of Christ, and is by him accordingly executed euen after his ascension, as appeares in the conuersion of *Paul*. And therefore *Isai* saith, *they shall be all taught of God*, *Isa.*54.13. As for the Ministers of the Gospel, they in teaching are no more but instruments of Christ, to vtter and pronounce the word to the eare: this is all they can doe. Therefore *Paul* ſaith, *hee that plants or waters is not any thing, but God that giueth the increaſe.* The teacher then properly in the miniſtery of the new Teſtament to the very end of the world, is Chriſt himſelfe. This muſt teach vs reuerence in hearing Gods word, and care with diligence in keeping of it. *Hebr.*2.1,2,3,&c. Secondly this teacheth vs, that they which imbrace not the Goſpell among vs, are contemners of Chriſt, and ſhall endure eternall condemeation. *Ioh.*3.18.& *Heb.*12.25. Thirdly, if we want vnderſtanding, we muſt pray to Chriſt for it; and becauſe we haue ſo excellent a teacher, we muſt pray vnto him that he would giue vnto vs hearing eares, that is, hearts tractable, and obedient to his word, that we may be fit diſciples for ſo worthy a maſter.

The ſecond is, that there be two waies whereby Chriſt teacheth thoſe that are to be teachers. One is immediate reuelation; the other is ordinary inſtruction in ſchooles by the meanes and miniſtery of man. The like ſaith *Amos, I was neither Prophet, nor ſonne of a Prophet, but the Lord ſent me to prophecie to Iſrael. Amos.*7.4.

The third point is, that they which are to be teachers muſt firſt be taught; and they muſt teach that which they haue firſt learned themſelues, 2.*Tim.*3.14. *Abide in the things which thou haſt learned.* Chriſt taught that which he heard of the Father; the Apoſtles that which they heard of Chriſt: ordinary miniſters that which they haue learned of the Apoſtles. This is the right Tradition: and if it be obſerued without addition or detraction, the Goſpell ſhall remaine in his integrity. Here our Aunceſtours are greatly to bee blamed, who haue not contented themſelues with that which they haue learned of the Apoſtles, but haue deliuered things of their owne which they were neuer taught. Hence ſprang vnwritten traditions, and the corruption of religion. Againe, ſuch are here to be blamed, that take vpon them to be teachers of the Goſpel, and were neuer taught by reuelation, or by any ordinary way. Thirdly, priuate perſons are much more to be blamed, that broach and deliuer ſuch doctrines, and opinions, as they themſelues neuer learned by any miniſtery. For teachers themſelues muſt firſt learne, and then teach.

The fourth point is, that they which are to be teachers are firſt to be taught, and that by men, where reuelation is wanting. This kind of teaching is the foundation of the ſchoole of the Prophets, and it hath beene from the beginning. The Patriarkes till *Moſes* were Prophets in their families, and they taught not onely their families in generall, but alſo their firſt borne, that they might

ſucceede

ſucceed as Prophets after them. There were 48. cities of the Leuites diſperſed through all the tribes, where not onely the people were taught, but alſo ſchooles erected that they might be taught, which were to be Prieſts and Leuites, *Num.* 37. One city among the reſt is called *Cireath ſephar, Ioſu.* 15. 15. that is, *the citie of bookes*, or as we ſay, *the Vniuerſitie. Samuel* a yong man was ſent to the Tabernacle in Shilo, to be taught, and trained vp of *Eli* the Prieſt. *Samuel* when he was iudge of Iſrael erected Colledges of Prophets, and ruled them himſelfe, 1 *Sam.* 10. In the decaied eſtate of the ten tribes, *Elias* and *Elizeus* ſet vp ſchooles of the Prophets in Bethel, Carmel, &c. and the yong ſtudents were called *the ſonnes of the Prophets*, 2. *King.* 2. 3. Chriſt himſelfe beſide the ſermons made to the people, trained vp and taught himſelfe his twelue Apoſtles, and his ſeuenty Diſciples. *Paul* commands *Timothie* to *teach that which he had learned, to ſuch as ſhall be fit to teach others*, 2. *Tim.* 2, 2. Furthermore, this teaching is of great vſe. For it ſerues to maintaine the true interpretation of ſcripture, the purity of doctrine: and it is a meanes to continue the miniſtery to the end of the world. The meaneſt arte or trade that is, is not learned without great teaching: then much more teaching is required in diuinity, which is the arte of all arts. The true interpretation of ſcripture, and the right cutting of the word is a matter of great difficulty, and a matter (whatſoeuer men thinke) of the greateſt learning in the world. Therefore it is neceſſary, that teachers ſhould firſt be taught, and learne aright the Goſpel of Chriſt. Eleauen hundred yeares after Chriſt, men began to lay aſide *Moſes*, and the Prophets, and the writings of the new Teſtament, and to expound the writings of men, as the Sentences of *Peter Lumbard.* Hence ignorance, ſuperſtition, & idolatry come headlong into the world. Seeing then the teaching of them that are to be teachers, is of ſuch antiquity, and vſe, all men are to be exhorted to put to their helping hands, that this thing may goe forward. Princes are to maintaine it, by their bountifulneſſe, and authority, as they haue done, and doe ſtill: and that which they doe, they muſt doe it more. Parents muſt dedicate the fitteſt of their children to the ſeruice of God, in the miniſtery, and not to vſe it in the laſt place for a ſhift, as they doe. For commonly, the eldeſt muſt be the heire, the next the lawyer, the yongeſt the diuine. Students muſt loue and affect this calling aboue all other, 1. *Cor.* 14. 1. Laſtly, all men muſt make prayer, that God would proſper and bleſſe all Schooles of learning, where this kind of teaching is in vſe.

Here againe it appeares, that Chriſt is God, and more then a meere man, becauſe he is oppoſed to man: and that *Paul* receiued

authority

authoritie, and the keies of the kingdome of heauen, immediatly of Christ, as well as *Peter.*

13 *For ye haue heard of my conuersation, in times past, how that I persecuted the Church of God extremely, and wasted it.*

14 *And profited in the Iewish religion, aboue many of my companions, of mine owne nation, and was much more zealous of the Traditions of my fathers.*

In the former verse, the Apostle set downe, that hee learned the Gospell, not of man, but of Iesus Christ, immediatly. This in the next place he goes about to prooue at large. His reason is framed thus. If I learned the Gospel of any man, I learned it either before, or after my conuersion: but I learned it neither before, nor after my conuersion of any man. The first part of his reason is here confirmed thus: before my calling and conuersion, I professed Iudaisme, and I liued accordingly, persecuting the Church, and suppressing the Gospell of Christ, and profiting in my religion aboue many others: therefore I was not then fit to heare and learne the Gospell of Christ of any man. This argument he further confirmes by the testimony of the Galatians thus: That this was my conuersation in Iudaisme, ye are witnesses: for ye haue heretofore heard as much.

In the example of *Paul*, two points are generally to be considered. The first, that the distinction of man and man, ariseth not of the will, or naturall disposition of man, but of the grace and mercy of God. For *Paul* an Elect vessell for nature and disposition, before his conuersion, is as wicked as any other. And he saith, *Rom* 9. 11. that the difference betweene man and man before God, is *not in him that willeth, nor in him that runneth, but in God that sheweth mercie.* Therefore it is a Pelagian errour, to thinke that men, doing that which they can, doe by nature occasion God to giue them supernaturall grace. The second point is, that *Paul* here makes an open, and ingenuous confession of his wicked life past. And hence I gather that this Apostle, and consequently the rest, writ the scriptures of the new Testament by the instinct of Gods spirit, and not by humane policie, which (no doubt) would haue mooued them to haue couered and concealed their owne faults, and not to haue blazed their owne shame to the world. And therefore the bookes of Scripture, are not bookes of policy (as Atheists suppose) to keepe men in awe, but they are the very word of God. Againe, the end of this plaine confession is, that *Paul* might thereby confirme,

and

and iuſtifie his owne calling, to the office of an Apoſtle. This ſerues to giue a checke to ſuch perſons as vſe to ſitte and rehearſe their wicked liues paſt in boaſting and reioycing manner.

In *Pauls* example there be two things to be conſidered, his profeſſion before his calling, and his conuerſation. His profeſſion was Iudaiſme: and this hindred him from imbracing the goſpel. It may here be demanded, what Iudaiſme, or the Iewiſh religion is? *Anſw.* In the daies of Chriſt, and the Apoſtles, there were three ſpeciall ſects among the Iewes, Eſſeis, Saduceis, and Phariſes. And the Phariſes were the principall, and their doctrine was commonly imbraced of the Iewes. And therefore by Iudaiſme (as I take it) Phariſeiſme is here meant. Now the principall doctrines of the Phariſes were theſe, I. They held that there was one God, and that this God was the Father, without any diſtinction of perſons: for when Chriſt mentioned the diſtinction of the Father, and the Son, they would not acknowledge it, *Iohn* 8.19. II. They acknowledged in the Meſſias but one nature: for when it was asked them how Chriſt being the ſonne of *Dauid*, ſhould neuertheleſſe be his Lord; they could not anſwer. *Math.*22. III. They held that the kingdome of the Meſſias, was an earthly kingdome: and with this opinion, the Diſciples of Chriſt were tainted. IV. They held, that the keeping of the morall law, ſtood in externall obedience, as appeares by the ſpeeches of Chriſt, reforming their errours, *Math.*5.6.7. chap. V. They maintained a naturall freedome of the will, in the obſeruing of the law. *Luk.*18. *Lord I thanke thee* (ſaith the Phariſie) *I doe thus and thus*. VI. They held a iuſtification by the workes of the law, without the obedience of the Meſſias. *Rom.*9,3. VII. Beſide the written word and law of *Moſes*, they had many vnwritten traditions, which they obſerued preciſely: and the obſeruation of them was accounted the worſhip of God, *Math.*15.3.9. Other points they held, but theſe are the principall. It may further be demanded, how the Iewes could hold ſuch hereticall, and damnable opinions, and yet be the people of God? *Anſwer.* They had for their parts forſaken God: but God had not forſaken them, becauſe the Temple was yet ſtanding, and the ſacrifices with the outward worſhip, yet remained among them. In this regard, they were ſtill a reputed people of God. Againe, they are called a people of God, not of the bigger, but of the better part: and the better part was a ſmall remnant of them, that truely feared God, and beleeued in the Meſſias. Of which ſort, were *Ioſeph*, *Marie*, *Zacharie*, *Elizabeth*, *Simeon*, *Anna*, *Ioſeph* of Arimathia, *Nicodemus*. Againe, it may be demanded, how the Iewes beeing ſuch a people of God ſhould fall away to ſo damnable a religion. *Anſwer.* They neither loued, nor obeyed the doctrine of *Moſes*, and the Prophets: and therefore God in iudgement left them to the blindeneſſe of their owne mindes, and hardneſſe of their owne hearts. *Iſai.* 6. The like may be our caſe. If we loue and obey not the Goſpell, more then we haue done, our religion may end in ignorance, ſuperſtition, and prophaneneſſe, as theirs hath done.

The ſecond thing in *Pauls* example, is his conuerſation, whereby he liued and conuerſed according to his religion. The like ſhould be in vs. For the profeſſion of the faith, and godly conuerſation are to goe together, *Phil.* 1.27. Faith in the heart is a light, and workes are the ſhining of this light, *Matth.* 5. 16. Chriſt hath redeemed them that beleeue *from their vaine conuerſation*, 1. *Pet.* 1.18. Here many of vs doe amiſſe, disioyning faith, and good life. And this fault is the greater, becauſe it is an occaſion to our aduerſaries to miſlike, and reiect our religion.

Pauls conuerſation hath two parts, his perſecution of the church, and his profiting in his religion.

Perſecution properly is the afflicting of the people of God for their faith and religion. In this we are not to follow *Paul*, but to doe the contrarie, that is, by all meanes to ſeeke the good of the church. After Gods glory immediatly, we are to ſeek the comming and aduancement of the kingdome of God. Now this kingdome is a certaine eſtate and condition of men, whereby they ſtand ſubiect to the word & ſpirit of God. And this ſubiection to God and Chriſt, is the propertie of them that bee members of the Church of God. All, both rich and poore conferred ſome thing (according to their abilitie) to the building of the Temple, which figured the Church of God. The fault of our times is, that we build our ſelues, and our worldly eſtates, and little reſpect the common good of the Church.

In the perſecution of the Church by *Paul*, two points are to bee conſidered, the manner and meaſure, or accompliſhment. The manner is, that hee perſecuted the Church *extreamely*, or *aboue meaſure*. That which *Paul* did in his religion, wee muſt doe in ours. The good things that we are to doe, we muſt doe them *with all our might*, *Eccleſ.* 9. 10. Our duetie is to keepe our hearts in the feare of God, and we muſt doe it *with all diligence*, *Prou.* 4. 24. It is our duetie to ſeeke Gods kingdome, and we muſt *take it with violence*. To enter into life is our duetie, and wee muſt *ſtriue to enter*. To pray is our duetie, and wee muſt *wraſtle in prayer*, *Rom.* 15.30. *Ioſias* turned to God with all his heart. The law requires that we ſhould loue God

with

with all the powers of body and soule, and with all the strength of all the powers. In earthly things we must moderate our thoughts and cares, but spirituall duties must bee performed with all our might.

The accomplishment of persecution, is, that *Paul* wasted the Church, and made hauocke of it. Here I consider two points, *what is wasted?* and *who is the waster?* For the first, it is the church. Here two questions may be demanded, the first is, how the church can be wasted? *Answer.* In respect of the inward estate thereof, which standes in election, faith, iustification, glorification, it cannot be wasted. In respect of his outward estate, it may be wasted, that is in respect of mens bodies, and in regard of the publike assemblies, and the exercises of religion. The second question is, why God suffers his enemies to waste his owne church? *Answer.* Iudgement begins in Gods house: and his iudgements sometime are very sharpe, whether they be inflicted for triall or correction of sins past, or for the preuenting of sinnes to come. As in the body, sometime there is no hope of life, except armes, and legges be cut off: euen so is it in the church. Hence it appeares that there shall be a last iudgement, and that there is a life euerlasting in heauen: because the wicked man florisheth in this world, and the godly are often oppressed.

The waster of the church is *Paul.* By whom we learne that sinne where it takes place, giues a man no rest till it hath brought him to a height of wickednesse. Hatred hauing entred into *Cains* heart, leaues him not, till it haue caused him to imbrue his hands in his brothers blood. Couetousnesse makes *Iudas* at lenght to betray his master, and hang himselfe. Blind zeale makes *Paul* not onely to persecute, but also to wast the church. Therefore it is good to auoide the first beginnings, yea the very occasion of sinne.

The second part, and point in *Pauls* conuersion, is, that he profits in his religion. Thus should we profit in the Gospell of Christ. It is Gods commandement, *be yee perfect as your heauenly Father is perfect:* that is, indeauour to come to perfection. All the faith we haue or can obtaine is little enough in the time of temptation. *Iob* that said in his affliction, *though the Lord kill me I will still trust in him,* saith also that *God wrote bitter things against him and made him to possesse the sinnes of his youth.* It is a token that a man is dead in his sinnes, when he doth not grow, or increase in good. 1. *Pet.* 2. 2. In this regard great is the fault of our daies, for many are weary of the Gospell, many stand at a stay without profiting; many goe backward. The cause is this. Commonly men liue as it were without the law: and thinke

Math.5.48.

Iob.13.15. v.26.

it

ward. The cauſe is this. Commonly men liue, as it were without the law: and thinke it ſufficient, if they doe not groſſely offend: not conſidering that the law of God, is a law to our thoughts,and affections,and all the circumſtances of our actions. That we may hereafter make good proceedings in our religion,we muſt remember three caueats. One,that wee muſt indeuour to ſee,and feele in our ſelues the ſmalneſſe of our faith,repentance,feare of God, &c. and the great maſſe of corruption that is in vs. Thus with the beggar,we ſhal be alwaies peecing and mending our garment. The ſecond, that as trauailers,we muſt forget things paſt,and goe on to doe more good, *Phil.* 3. 14. The third, that wee muſt ſet before vs the crown of eternall glory,and ſeeke to apprehend it, 1.*Tim.*6.11. thus did *Moſes*, *Heb.*11.

In *Pauls* profiting, two things muſt be conſidered, the meaſure, and the thing in which he profited. The meaſure,in *that he profited aboue many others.* Hence wee learne, that in matters of religion there ſhould be an holy emulation,and contention among vs: and our fault is that we contend, who ſhall haue the moſt riches, and honour,or goe in the fineſt apparell, and ſtriue not to go one beyond another in good things. Againe,*Pauls* modeſtie muſt heere bee obſerued. Hee doeth not ſay that hee profited more then all, but *more then many:* and hee ſaith not, more then his ſuperiours, but *more then his equalls* for time: and hee ſaith not, more then all the world, but *more then they of his owne nation.* This modeſty of his muſt bee learned of vs,for it is the ornament of vs, for it is the ornament of our faith: and therefore muſt bee ioyned with our faith.

The matter or the thing in which *Paul* profited, is,that he was *abundantly zealous for the Traditions of the fathers.* Here I conſider three points. I. What zeale is. *Anſw.* It is a certaine feruency of ſpirit,ariſing of a mixture of loue and anger, cauſing men earneſtly to maintaine the worſhip of God, and all things pertaining thereto, and moouing them to griefe and anger, when God is any way diſhonoured. II. For what is *Paul* zealous? *Anſw.* For the outward obſeruation of the law, and withall,for Phariſaical vnwritten Traditions: which therefore he calles the Traditions of his fathers. III. What is the fault of his zeale? (for he condemnes it in himſelf) *Anſwer.* He had the zeale of God,but not according to knowledge. For his zeale was againſt the word, in that it tended to maintaine vnwritten Traditions,and Iuſtification by the workes of the law, out of Chriſt, *Rom.*10.2.

Hence wee learne ſundrie things. (For that which *Paul* did in his religion, are we to doe in the profeſſion of the Goſpell.) Firſt, we are to addict and ſet our ſelues earneſtly, to maintaine the trueth, and the trueth of the Goſpell. Chriſt was euen conſumed with the zeale of Gods houſe, *Iohn* 2. The Angel of the Church of Laodicea is blamed, becauſe he is *neither hote, nor cold, Reuel.* 3. He is accurſed of God, *that doeth the worke of God negligently, Ierem.* 48. Secondly, we are to be angrie in our ſelues, and grieued, when God is diſhonoured, and his word diſobeyed. When the Iſraelites worſhipped the golden calfe, *Moſes* in holy anger, burſt the tables of ſtone. *Dauid* wept, and *Paul* was humbled for the ſinnes of other men, *Pſal.* 119. 136. 2. *Cor.* 12. 21. Thirdly, we are here taught, not to giue libertie to the beſt of our naturall affections, as to zeale; but to mortifie them, and to rule them by the word, *Numb.* 15. 39. Otherwiſe they will cauſe vs to runne out of order, like wilde beaſts, as here we ſee in *Paul*. Laſtly, let it be obſerued, that *Paul* here condemnes zeale, for the maintenance of vnwritten Traditions. And let the Papiſts conſider this.

15 *But when it pleaſed God (which had ſeparated mee from my mothers wombe, and called me by his grace.)*

16 *To reueale his Sonne in me* (or to me) *that I ſhould preach him among the Gentiles, immediatly I communicated not with fleſh and blood.*

17 *Neither came I to Hieruſalem, to them which were Apoſtles before mee, but I went into Arabia, and turned againe to Damaſcus.*

Paul before prooued, that he learned not the Goſpel of any man before his conuerſion: here he further prooues, that he learned it of no man after his conuerſion. And the ſubſtance of his reaſon is this, becauſe immediatly vpon his conuerſion, hee conferred with no man; but went and preached in Arabia and Damaſcus.

In the words I conſider foure things. Firſt, the cauſes of *Pauls* conuerſion. And heere he ſets downe three degrees of cauſes, depending one vpon another. The firſt is, the good pleaſure of God, whereby he doth whatſoeuer he will, in heauen and earth, in theſe wordes [*when it pleaſed.*] The ſecond is, his ſeparation from the wombe: which is an act of Gods counſel, wherby he ſets men apart to bee members of Chriſt, and to be his ſeruants, in this, or that office. This ſeparation is ſaid to be *from the wombe*; not becauſe it began then, for it was appointed by God before all times, euen from eternitie, as all his counſels are. But the holy Ghoſt hereby ſignifies,

fies,that all our goodneſſe,and all our dexteritie, to this or that office,is meerely from God: becauſe we are ſanctified,dedicated,and ſet apart in the counſell of God,from all eternitie,& therfore from the wombe, or from our firſt conception & beginning. The third cauſe is,vocation by grace;the accompliſhment of both the former in the time which God hath appointed. The ſecond thing is, the manner or forme of *Pauls* vocation, in theſe words[*to reueale his Sonne to mee.*] The third is,the end of his vocation, to *preach Christ among the Gentiles.* The laſt is, his obedience to the calling of God, in the 16. and 17. verſes.

To begin with the efficient cauſes of *Pauls* conuerſion : heere we ſee the order and dependance of cauſes, in the conuerſion and ſaluation of euery ſinner. The beginning of our ſaluation, is in the good pleaſure of God : then followes ſeparation,or election to eternall life : then vocation by the word & Spirit : then obedience to the calling of God, and after obedience, euerlaſting life. This order *Paul* here ſets downe,and the conſideration of it, is of great vſe. Hence it appeares to be a doctrine erronious,which begins our ſaluation in the preuiſion of mans faith and good workes. For in *Pauls* order,workes haue the laſt place. And it muſt be Gods pleaſure,that man ſhall doe a good worke before he can doe it. And if ſeparation to eternall life, ſhould be according to faith, or workes, then we ſhould make ſeparation of our ſelues,as well as God. And vocation is not for works,but that we might doe good works, *Eph.* 1.4. Secondly,by this order it appeares,that the ſaluation of them that beleeue, is more ſure then the whole frame of heauen and earth : becauſe it is founded in the vocation of God,which is without repentance, in the counſell of ſeparation , and in the pleaſure of God. Thirdly, by obſeruing well this order, we may attaine to the aſſurance of our election. For if thou haſt bin called,and haſt in truth anſwered to the calling of God by obedience, thou maieſt aſſure thy ſelfe of thy ſeparation from the womb to euerlaſting life, becauſe this order is (as it were) a golden chaine, in which, all the linkes are inſeparably vnited. Laſtly, the conſideration of this order,ſerues to mortifie the pride and arrogancie of our hearts,in that it aſcribes all to God, and nothing to man in the cauſe of ſaluation. Reade *Ezek.* 16.63.

Againe,by the conſideration of theſe 3. cauſes, wee gather that God hath determined what he will doe with euery man, and that he hath in his eternall counſell aſſigned euery man his office and condition of life. For there is in God a pleaſure, whereby he may doe with euery man what hee will. And by his eternall counſell he ſeparates euery man from the very wombe to one calling, or other: and accordingly he calles them in time by giuing giftes, and will, to doe that, for which they were appointed. And this I vnderſtand of all lawfull callings, in the familie, Church, or common wealth. Thus Chriſt was called from the wombe, and ſet apart to be a mediatour. *Iſai*.47.1. and *Iohn*.6.27. *Ieremie* to bee a prophet, *Ieremie* 1.5. Chriſt is ſaid to giue Apoſtles, Prophets, Paſtors, teachers. *Eph*.4.11. God ſent *Ioſeph* vnto Egypt to be the gouernour thereof, and a releeuer of *Iacobs* familie. *Gen*.45. In this regard the Medes and Perſians are ſaid to be *the ſanctified ones of God* *Iſai*.13.3. and *the men of his counſell*, *Iſa*.46.11.

The vſe. Hence wee are all taught, to walke in our callings with diligence, and good conſcience: Becauſe they are aſſigned vs of God. Hence wee are taught to yeeld obedience to our rulers and teachers: becauſe they that are our rulers and teachers, were ſeparated from the wombe to bee ſo, and that by God himſelfe, without the will of man. Hence we may gather aſſurance of Gods protection, and aſſiſtance in our callings: for in that hee hath appointed vs our callings, he wil alſo defend vs in thē. 2.*Cor*.3.6. *Iſay*.49.2. Hence we may learne patience, and contentation in all miſeries, and troubles of our callings, for in what calling ſoeuer thou art, thou waſt ordained to it by God from thy mothers wombe. Thinke on this. Hence we learne thankfulnes to God, becauſe our callings, giftes, and the execution of our callings, is wholly of God: and this *Paul* ſignifies, when he ſaith that our ſeparation to our offices, and callings, was from our firſt conception. Hence wee learne to depend on Gods prouidence for the time to come. For if hee prouided our callings, when we were not, hee will much more aide, and bleſſe vs in them now while we haue a beeing. Reade *Pſalm*.22.8.9. Poore parents that cannot leaue landes, and liuings to their children after their deceaſe, let them comfort themſelues in this; that their children are from their mothers wombe, ſeparated to ſome good office and condition of life, by the wiſedome of God: and that a good office or calling, is better then land and liuing.

Thirdly, it appeares hence that the time of all euents is determined in the counſell of God. For God determines with himſelfe the time in which he will call, and conuert *Paul*. By this wee are taught, in our praiers not to limit God to any time for the accompliſhment of our requeſts: for the diſpoſition of time is his, & that is to be left to his wiſedome. Againe in our afflictions and temptations wee may not make haſte, for helpe and deliuerance before the time, but waite the leaſure of God, who hath decreede the time of deliuerance. *He that beleeues makes no haste*, *Isai.* 28.16. *Habacuk* must wait, *because the vision is for a time appointed*, *Hab.* 2.1. *Dauids* eyes and strength failed *in waiting on God*, *Psal.* 69.3. *Daniel* waites on God seuentie yeares, and then prayes for deliuerance out of captiuitie, the time beeing expired. This serues to discouer the wickednesse of them, that being in any kinde of miserie, cannot stay the leasure of God till hee deliuer them by good meanes, but they will haue present remedie, though it be from the diuell: and if helpe cannot bee had when they desire, they presently make away themselues.

The second point is, the forme of the calling, or conuersion of *Paul* in these words [*to reueale his Sonne in me*] that is, to teach me the doctrine of the redemption of mankinde by his Son Iesus Christ. Here I consider, to whom reuelation is made, and how?

For the first, reuelation of the Sonne is made to cruell and persecuting *Paul*, a desperate sinner. Hence euery man can gather, that God hath mercie for great and notorious offences, as for *Paul*, and such like: and the collection is good. For *God is much in sparing*, *Isai.* 55.7. And yet here it must be remembred, that all desperate offenders, shall not finde mercie, vnlesse they bee *great in their repentance*, as God is *great in mercie*. For Gods mercy hath a double effect in vs, one is, remission of sinne, by the imputation of the merit of Christ: the other, the mortification of originall sin, by his efficacy. And these two be inseparable, as we see in *Paul*, on whom God shewed great mercy, whose repentance also was notable. As the woman, *Luk.* 7. *had many sinnes forgiuen her, so she loued much*. v. 47. By this wee see the great and common abuse of the mercy of God. Men euery where presume vpon the greatnesse of Gods mercy, and they make Christ a pack-horse, lading him with their burdens, and there is little or no amendment of life.

The maner that God vsed in reuealing the Sonne to *Paul*, stands in two things: *Preparation*, and *Instruction*.

Preparation is a worke of God, whereby he humbled *Paul*, subdued the pride and stubburnnesse of his heart, and made him tractable, and teachable. This humiliation is outward, or inward. The outward was partly by lightening from heauen, that cast him to the earth, and made him blind: and partly by a voice reproouing him: *Saul, Saul, why persecutest thou me?* The inward humiliation was in a sight, and horrour for his sinnes. The sinnes that God reuealed to him, are these: the first was, an height of wickednesse, that in persecuting the Church, he made warre euen against God himselfe. Secondly, God made manifest vnto him the meaning of the tenth comman-

commandement, and that ſecret luſt without conſent of will, was ſinne, *Rom.*7.7. And thus the law killed him that was aliue, in his owne opinion, when he was a Phariſee.

The *inſtruction* whereby God taught the ſame to *Paul*, hath two parts. The firſt is, the cal of God, wherby he inuites *Paul* to become a member of the ſon of God. And this he did, firſt, by propounding vnto him the commandement of the Goſpel, which is to repent & beleeue in Chriſt. Secondly, by offering to him the promiſe of remiſſion of ſins, and life euerlaſting, when he beleeued. The ſecond part of inſtruction, is a reall and liuely teaching, when God made *Paul* in his heart to anſwer the calling, according to that, *Pſal.*27.5. *When thou ſaidſt, ſeeke ye my face, mine heart anſwered, I will ſeeke thy face, O Lord.* And in Zachary, 13.9. *He ſhall ſay, it is my people, and they ſhall ſay, the Lord is our God.* This is a ſpiritual Eccho, that is made in the heart. The ſound of Gods word goes through the world, and the hearts of men which be as rocks & ſtones, make anſwer. And this worke of God, that makes man yeeld to the calling of God, is in ſcripture, a kind of diuine teaching: thus the Father is ſaid to teach the Son, *by drawing, Ioh.*6.44. And God is ſaid to teach vs his waies, when he guides vs by his ſpirit in the land of righteouſnes, *Pſa.*143 That this reall, and heauenly kind of teaching may take place, God by his grace, puts a kind of ſoftnes into the heart, wherby it is made ſubiect, and obedient to the word. And it hath two parts. One is an acknowledgmēt by faith, that the Son is our redeemer. The ſecond is, regeneration, which is the putting off the old man, & the putting on of the new: which to do, by the vertue of Chriſt, is to learn Chriſt. *Eph.*4.20.23. Thus then God reueals the Son to *Paul*, by preparing him, & making him teachable, by propounding the doctrine of ſaluation to him, & by cauſing him inwardly to beleeue it, & to obey it. And thus we ſee the maner of the calling, & conuerſion of *Paul*.

For the better clearing of this doctrine, fiue queſtions are to bee anſwered. The firſt is, what was the preuenting grace in the conuerſion of *Paul? Anſwer.* Schoolemen, and Papiſts generally teach, that it was the inſpiration of good motions and deſires into the heart of *Paul.* But it is falſe which they teach: for the heart is vncapable of any good deſire or purpoſe, till it be regenerate. The trueth is this: that the preuenting grace, in the firſt conuerſion, is the grace of regeneration, & ſecondly, the inſpiration of good deſires & motions. When Chriſt preuents *Lazarus*, that he may reuiue againe, he firſt puts a ſoule into him, and then he cals vnto him, and ſaith, *Come forth, Lazarus*, becauſe he was dead: in like manner, wee are dead in ſinne, and therefore regeneration (which is the ſoule of our ſoules)

must

muſt bee put into vs, before any inſpiration of heauenly motions can take place. Yet after we are once borne anew, good motions and deſires put into our hearts, may bee the preuenting grace, for the doing of ſundrie good works.

The ſecond queſtion is, whether the will of *Paul* were an agent, or cauſe in the effecting of his firſt conuerſion? *Anſwer.* No: Scripture makes two ſorts of conuerſion: one *Paſſiue*, when man is conuerted by God. In this, man is but a ſubiect, to receiue the impreſſion of grace, and no agent at all. For in the creating, ſetting, or imprinting of righteouſneſſe and holineſſe in the heart, will can doe nothing. The ſecond conuerſion is *Actiue*, whereby man being conuerted by God, doth further turne & conuert himſelfe to God, in all his thoughts, words, and deeds. This conuerſion is not onely of grace, nor onely of will; but partly of grace, and partly of will: yet ſo as grace is the principall agent, and will but the inſtrument of grace. For beeing firſt turned by grace, we then can mooue, and and turne our ſelues. And thus there is a cooperation of mans will with Gods grace. And *Auſten* ſaid truly, *Hee that made thee without thee, doeth not ſaue thee without thee.*

Serm. 25. de verbis Apoſt.

The third queſtion is, whether God did offer any violence to *Pauls* minde and will in his conuerſion. *Anſwer.* There is a double violence, or coaction. One, which doeth aboliſh all conſent of will; and this he vſed not. The other drawes out a conſent from the wil, by cauſing it of an vnwilling will, to become willing. This coaction or violence, God offered to *Paul*, and in this ſenſe, they which come to Chriſt, are ſaid to be drawne, *Ioh.* 6.45.

The fourth queſtion is, wherein ſtands the efficacie of the preuenting grace, whereby *Paul* was effectually conuerted? *Anſwer.* The Councell of Trent, and ſundrie Papiſtes, incline to this opinion, to thinke that it ſtands *in the euent*, in that the will of man applies it ſelfe to the grace which God offereth. But then the efficacie of grace muſt bee from mans will: and then man hath ſomething whereof to boaſt, and hee is to thanke himſelfe for the grace of God. Other Papiſts place the efficacy of grace in the congruitie, or aptneſſe of motions, or heauenly perſwaſions, preſented to the mind of the man that is to be conuerted. But this opinion alſo is deuoid of truth. For there is no efficacie in any motions or perſwaſions, til there be a change, & new creation of the wil. The true anſwer is this. Outward meanes are effectual, becauſe they are ioyned with the inward operation of the ſpirit. Inward grace is effectuall, becauſe God addes to the firſt grace, the ſecond grace. For hauing giuen the power to beleeue, & repent, he giues alſo the will and the deed: and then faith and repentance muſt needs follow. And herein ſtands the efficacie of the firſt grace, that God addes vnto it, and *workes the will and the deed*, *Phil.* 2. 13.

The laſt queſtion is, whether it was in the power of *Pauls* will, to reſiſt the calling, or the grace of God? *Anſw.* The will for his condition is apt to reſiſt grace: neuertheleſſe, if we conſider the efficacie of Gods grace, and the will of God, hee could not reſiſt the calling of God. Euery one that hath heard and learned of the Father, comes to Chriſt, *Iohn* 6.45. Gods will determines and limits the will of man: and mans will is an inſtrument to effect the will of God. It may be here demanded, how the efficacie of grace may ſtand with the libertie of mans will, if it haue not libertie, to accept or refuſe the grace of God? *Anſw.* Libertie and freedome of will in God, is perfect libertie: now God cannot will either good or euill, but only that which is good. And mans will, the neerer it comes to this will of God, the greater libertie hath it. Therefore to will that onely which is good, ſo it bee freely without compulſion, is true libertie: to be able to will that which is euill, and to reſiſt the calling of God, is not liberty, but impotency. And he that can onely will that which is good, doeth more freely will good, and hath more libertie, then he that can will either good or euill.

The vſe. Miniſters of the Goſpell muſt learne Chriſt as *Paul* learned him. They may not content themſelues with that teaching which they finde in Schooles, but they muſt proceed further to a reall learning of Chriſt: and that is, to beleeue in the Sonne of God, to die to their ſinnes by the vertue of his death, and to liue to God by the vertue of his life. This is a reall and liuely learning of Chriſt. They that muſt conuert others, it is meete they ſhould bee effectually conuerted. *Iohn* muſt firſt eate the Booke, and then prophecie, *Reuel.* 10. 9. And they that would bee firſt Miniſters of the Goſpell, muſt firſt themſelues eate the booke of God. And this booke is indeed eaten, when they are not onely in their minds inlightned, but their hearts are mortified and brought in ſubiection to the word of Chriſt. Vnleſſe Chriſt be thus learned ſpiritually and really, Diuines ſhall ſpeake of the word of God, as men ſpeake of riddles, and as Prieſtes in former time ſaid their Mattens, when they hardly knew what they ſaid. Againe ſtudents in euery facultie, are with *Paul* to learne Chriſt, and that as hee learned him. Such perſons deſire and loue good learning: now this is the beſt learning of all, to learne to know, and to acknowledge Chriſt. The knowledge of Chriſt crucified is *Pauls* learning. The knowledge of the remiſſion of our ſins, is the learning

ning of *Dauid* that great Prophet. For this title he giues to the 32. Pſalme, The vnderſtanding of *Dauid*. Laſtly, all men are in this reall manner with *Paul* to learne the ſame. For he is an example to all that ſhall beleeue in him to life euerlaſting, 1.*Tim*.1.12. *Paul* biddes vs doe the good things which we haue ſeene in him, *Philip.* 5.9 *Hoc vrge.*

The third point is the end of *Pauls* conuerſion, in theſe words [that he might preach him among the gentiles.] Here I conſider what he muſt preach, namely the Sonne Chriſt: and to whom? namely among the nations. Againe of the preaching of Chriſt, I conſider two things: the firſt is, why Chriſt muſt be preached rather then *Moſes*? Anſwer, there be two cauſes. One is, becauſe Chriſt is the ſubſtance or ſubiect matter of the whole Bible. For the ſumme of the Scriptures may be thus gathered together. The Son of God made man, and working our redemption, is the Sauiour of mankind: but *Ieſus* the Sonne of *Marie* is the Sonne of God, made man, working our redemption: therefore *Ieſus* the Sonne of *Marie* is the Sauiour of mankind. The maior is the ſumme of the old Teſtament: the minor is the ſumme of the new: and the concluſion is the ſcope of both. The ſecond cauſe is. The law is the miniſtery of death: and the Goſpell (which is the doctrine of ſaluation by the Sonne) is the inſtrument of God to beginne and to confirme all graces of God in vs that are neceſſary to our ſaluation. Therefore the doctrine principally to be preached is the Goſpell, and not the law.

Secondly it may be demaunded, what it is to preach Chriſt? *Anſwer*: it is a great worke, and it containes foure miniſteriall actions. The firſt, generally to teach the doctrine of the incarnation of Chriſt, and of his three offices, his Kingly office, his Propheticall office, and his Prieſthood with the execution thereof. The ſecond, to teach that faith is an inſtrument ordained of God to apprehend and to apply Chriſt with his benefits. The third is, to certifie and to reueale to euery hearer, that it is the will of God to ſaue him by Chriſt in particular, ſo be it he will receiue Chriſt. For when the Goſpell is preached, God thereby ſignifies vnto vs, that his will is to giue vs life euerlaſting, 1.*Ioh*.5.11. The laſt is to certifie and to reueale to euery particular hearer, that he is to apply Chriſt with his benefits to himſelfe in particular, and that effectually by his faith, that a change and conuerſion may follow both in heart and life, 1.*Ioh*.3.23. And thus when theſe things are rightly performed, Chriſt is preached. Hence it appeares that to learne Chriſt, is not onely to know him generally, but alſo effectually to apply him to our selues by our faith,that there may be a change and renouation of the whole man. They which learne Christ,must thus learne him, els can they not be saued.

The second point is,that *Paul* must *preach to the gentiles*.there be two causes of it: one,that the prophecies of the calling of the gentiles might be fulfilled,*Psal.2.*and 110.*Isai.2.* The second,because at the death of Christ, the diuision which was betweene the Iewes and gentiles was quite abolished.*Eph.2.13.*Here I obserue the difference betweene Apostles and ordinary Ministers. Their charge is a set,and particular congregation; whereas the charge of an Apostle is the whole world.

The fourth and last point is the obedience of *Paul* to the calling of God, in that he *went and preached the Gospell.* Here a question may be demaunded: whether *Paul* performed his obedience, by vertue of the grace which he had formerly receiued without the helpe of new and speciall grace, no? *Answere.* No. His obedience proceedes from the first grace, helped or excited by speciall grace. In the regenerate, that haue power to doe good, God workes the will,and the deede,in euery good worke.*Phil.2.13.* And it is a certaine truth: we doe not that which we are able to doe, vnlesse God make vs doe it, as he made vs able to doe it. Therefore to the dooing of euery new act,there is new, and speciall grace required.

In *Pauls* obedience,I consider three points,1.When he obeyed? *Immediatly.* How? *without deliberation* or consultation. Where? *In Arabia and Damascus.*

For the first,in that he obeyed God in going to preach immediatly,we learne how we are to answer and obey the calling of God, that calles to amendment,and newnesse of life: namely in all hast, without deferring of time.*Hebr.3.8.To day if yee will heare his voyce, harden not your hearts*: and *v.13. exhort one another while it is called to day.Psal.119.60. I made haste and did not delay to keepe thy commandements.* And there be good reasons,why we should no longer deferre our conuersion to God. The end of our life is vncertaine: and looke as death leaues vs, so shall the last iudgement finde vs. Secondly, when we delay our repentance, we adde sinne to sinne, and so *treasure vp wrath against the day of wrath, Rom.2.* Thirdly, when we deferre to obey and turne to God, we grow to perfection in sinne: and *sinne beeing perfected bringes forth death. Iam.1.14.* Lastly, late repentance is seldome, or neuer, true repentance. For when men are dying, their sinnes forsake them, and they doe not commonly forsake their sinnes. God hath called vs in

England

England more then fourtie yeares together, and yet many of vs haue not liſtened to the call of God, but deferred to obey: let vs now preſently amend, and turne to God: leaſt if we ſtill deferre the time of our repentance, Gods iudgements come foorth in haſte vpon vs.

The manner of his obedience is, that *Paul did not communicate with men:* that is, conferre, and conſult with them, touching his doctrine, and calling. And this he amplifies by a compariſon, thus: *Hee did not conſult with any man, no not the Apoſtles of Hieruſalem.* And hee addes a reaſon of his doing: becauſe they were but *fleſh and blood* in reſpect of God: and indeede it is vnmeete to conſult with men, touching the matters of God.

Hence I gather, that Gods word, whether preached or written, doth not depend on the authoritie of any man, no not on the authoritie of the Apoſtles themſelues; it is ſufficient to authorize it ſelfe. Chriſt *receiues not the teſtimonie of man, Iohn.* 5.34. And it is an errour, to thinke that the Church doth authorize the word, and religion, in the conſciences of men. For the Church it ſelfe is founded on the word. The Church cannot conſiſt without faith, nor faith without the word.

Secondly, hence I gather, that there is no conſultation, or deliberation, to be vſed at any time, touching the holding, or not holding of our religion. Hee that will followe Chriſt, may not put his hand to the plough, and then looke backe againe to his friends, to ſee what they will ſay, *Luk.* 9.61. Hee that would bee wiſe, muſt denie his owne wiſedome, and become a foole, 1.*Cor.* 3. 18. The three children would not conſult, touching the worſhipping of the image, but ſaid: *be it knowen to thee, O king, that we will not worſhip thy gods, Dan.* 3. When the Iudge gaue *Cyprian* the Martyr leaue to deliberate awhile, whether hee would denie his religion: he anſwered, that *in diuine matters deliberation is not to be vſed.* By this I gather, that the Schoolemen haue done euill, which haue turned all diuinitie into queſtions, and haue made of the Articles of our faith, a queſtionary diuinitie. Secondly, by this we are taught, that in the day of triall we may not conſult of the change of religion: but wee muſt be reſolute, and tread vnder foot the perſwaſions of fleſh and blood.

Thirdly, our obedience to God muſt bee without conſultation. Wee muſt firſt trie what is the will of God, and then abſolutely put it in execution, leauing the iſſue to God. *Abram* is called of God to forſake his countrey and kinred, *Geneſis.* 12. hee directly then giues attendance to the commaundement, and goes as it

were

were blind-fold, hee knowes not whither. God promised him a child in his old age, he beleeues God without any reasoning, or disputing the case with himselfe, to or fro: *Rom.*4.20. But the common maner is, (though we know the wil of God) to dispute the case, and to consult with our friends, and to practise according to carnall counsell. *Eue* listens to the counsell of Satan, and neglects Gods commaundement. *Saul* being forbidden to offer sacrifice in Gilgal, till *Samuel* came to doe it; consults with himselfe, whether he may doe it or no: and followes his owne reason, against Gods commandement, and lost his Kingdome for it. And this kind of deliberation, whereby men consult what is to be done, is the cause of the manifold rebellions of men, in the world.

In that man is tearmed here, *flesh and blood*, we are taught, not to put confidence in man: we are taught to humble our selues before God: we are taught euery day, to prepare our selues against the day of death, and the day of iudgement: yea to account euery new day, as the day of death, because we are but flesh and blood.

The third point is, where *Paul* first preached? namely, *in Arabia and Damascus*. Arabia is a region of the world, where Mount Sinai standes, and where the children of Israel wandered 40. yeares. The inhabitants thereof, were of two sorts: some more ciuill, and some barbarous. Ciuill, as the Ismaelites, Amalechites, Madianites, &c. (Yet were they professed enemies of the people of God.) barbarous, as the Easterne part of Arabia, toward Babylon. For the inhabitants dwelt in Tents, and liued like wilde and sauage men, by robbing and stealing, and consequently by killing, *Isai.* 13. 20. *Ierem.*3.2.

Here we see *Pauls* estate and condition, when he first begins the execution of his Apostolicall function. God then layes vpon him a sharpe and weighty triall. For he goes alone into Arabia, and hee must become a teacher to his professed enemies, yea to a sauage generation, of whose conuersion he had no hope, in mans reason. And this hath beene an vsuall dealing of God with his owne seruants. When *Moses* was called to deliuer the Israelites, and was in the way, the Lord, for a defect in his family, comes against him, to destroy him, *Exod.*4.24. *Dauid* is annointed King of Israel: and withall *Saul* is raised vp, to persecute him, and to hunt him, as men hunt Partridges in the mountaines. *Ionas* is called to preach to Niniue, and withall God forsakes him, and leaues him to himselfe, so as he is cast into the sea, and deuoured of a fish: and after this, being deliuered, he must goe preach at Niniue. When Christ was in his baptisme (as it were inaugurated the Doctour of the Church)

presently

presently after, before he began to preach, he is caried into the wildernes, to be with wild beasts, and to be tempted of the diuel, *Mar.* 1.v.12. And the reasons of this dealing of God, are manifest: by this meanes sinful men are made fit for the office of teaching. For the saying is true, *Reading, prayer, & temptation, make a Diuine.* Again, by this meanes they are caused to depend on the prouidence and protection of God, and they are made fit for the assistance and presence of Gods spirit, who dwels onely with them that are of humble and contrite hearts. Now then let not them that in any notable change of their liues, find notable temptations, be discouraged; for this is a condition that befals them, by a wise & special prouidence of God. For it was the Spirit of God that led Christ into the wildernesse, to be tempted, after his baptisme.

Againe, heere wee are taught, to acknowledge three things in God. His power, in that he sets vp his kingdome, where it is most oppugned, and reignes in the midst of his owne enemies; namely, the wicked and sauage Arabians, according to that in the *Psalme* 110.v.2. His goodnesse, in that he sends *Paul* to preach repentance to the people that are in the snare of the diuell at his will, 2.*Tim.* 2. 26. His trueth, in that hee now fulfils things foretold by *Dauid, Psal.* 72. 10. *The Kings of Sheba and Saba shall bring gifts*: that is, Ethiopians and Arabians.

18 *Then after three yeeres, I came againe to Ierusalem, to visite Peter, and abode with him fifteene dayes.*

Paul hauing prooued before, that he learned not the Gospell of any man, no not of the Apostles at Hierusalem, goes about now to answer exceptions that might be made against his reason. And first of all, it might haue bene obiected, that hee was seene at Hierusalem sundrie times: and therefore in all likelihood, went thither to be instructed. To this hee answers three things: that hee went thither *three yeares after* his conuersion, and not before: that he went *to visite Peter*: that he *abode there fifteene dayes.* For the first, where he saith, he preached three yeares in Arabia and Damascus, and then after went to Hierusalem, and abode there fifteene daies (for some speciall causes:) we see *Paul* is readie, and able to make a good account of the spending of his time, both for daies and yeares. And good reason: for time is precious, and great care ought to be had of the expending of it. After *Pauls* example, we must so liue, that we may be able to giue a good account of the spending of our dayes. That this may bee done, wee must learne *to number our dayes*, and, *to redeeme the time. To number our dayes*, is to consider the

the ſhortneſſe of our liues, and that wee are euery day ſubiect to death: and withall ſeriouſly to bethinke our ſelues, of the cauſes of this our condition; namely, our ſinnes, both originall, and actuall. When this twofold conſideration takes place, wee then beginne to number our daies. The numbring of our time, and the parts thereof, brings vs to the redeeming of it. *To redeeme our time*, is to take time, while time ſerues, ſpecially for ſpirituall vſes, and for the amendement of our liues. When time is thus numbred and redeemed, then ſhall the good account bee made before God and men. Wherefore miſerable is the caſe of them, that ſpend their daies in idlenes, in riot, and ſporting, in chambering, and wontonneſſe. For they neither number time, nor redeeme it: and therefore they are farre from any good account.

The ſecond point is, that *Paul* goes vp to Hieruſalem *to viſit Peter*, that is, to ſee him, to be acquainted with him, to talke, and conferre with him. Hence it appeares, that there is a lawfull kinde of peregrination, or pilgrimage: in that *Paul* iourneies from Arabia to Ieruſalem, to ſee *Peter*. Thus the Queene of Saba, went vp to Ieruſalem, to heare the wiſedome of *Salomon*. The lawe of God, was, that all the males in Iſrael, ſhould thriſe in the yeare, goe vp to the place which God had appointed, *Deut.* 16. This law was practiſed by *Elkana* and *Hanna*, 1. *Samuel* 1. by *Ioſeph* and *Marie*, by the Steward of *Candaces* queene of Ethiopia. *Act.* 8. Neuertheleſſe, Popiſh pilgrimage is vtterly to bee condemned, for two cauſes. One is, becauſe it is made a part of Gods worſhip, whereas now in the new Teſtament, all religious diſtinction of places is aboliſhed, 1. *Tim.* 2. 8. Lift vp pure hands *in euery place* vnto God. Some alleadge, that vowes, which were not commanded, were neuertheleſſe parts of Gods worſhip, among the Iewes. I anſwer: though men were not commanded to vowe, yet the matter and forme of vowes was commanded. And in that God commanded the manner of vowing, he allowed the acte of vowe-making: let the Papiſts ſhew the like allowance for their pilgrimage. The ſecond reaſon is, becauſe Popiſh pilgrimage is not to liuing men, but to the reliques and images of dead men: which kind of pregrination, was neuer vſed in the world, till after the Apoſtles daies. For pilgrimage to reliques came in, 300. yeares after Chriſt, and pilgrimage to images, after 600. yeares.

In that *Paul* goes about to viſit *Peter*, the Papiſts gather the Primacie of *Peter*, ouer all the Apoſtles, but falſely. For this viſitation argues reuerence & reuerence is giuen, not only to ſuperious, but alſo to equalls. Again, primacie is twofold: *Primacie of order*, and *Primacie of power*. *Primacie of order*, was due vnto *Peter*, in that he was first called to be an Apostle, and hee was in the faith before *Paul*. And in this regard, he was reuerenced of him

The third point is, that *Paul* abides with *Peter* at Ierusalem, and that fifteene daies. His abode with *Peter*, was in token of mutuall consent, and fellowship. Like should be the consent of the Ministers of the Gospell. For their office is to publish and perswade peace betweene God and men, to which they are vnfit, that cannot maintaine peace among themselues. And all beleeuers should be of one mind, speaking and thinking the same things: and this cannot be, vnlesse there be a consent of them that are guides. This consent therefore is to be maintained, and greatly to be praied for. And when there cannot be consent of iudgment, by reason of humane frailtie, yet so long as the foundation is maintained, there must bee consent in affection. And iniuries offered may not dissolue this bond. Though the Church of Ierusalem suspected *Paul*, and would not at the first acknowledge him for a Disciple, *Actes* 9.26. yet did hee for his part, accept of their loue and fellowship.

Wheras he addes, that his abode with *Peter* was but for 15. daies: hereby he signifies, that he learned not the Gospel of him: for it could not be learned in so short a space: neither could *Paul* by the teaching of any man become an Apostle in so small a time.

19 *And none other of the Apostles saw I, saue Iames the Lords brother.*

It might haply bee obiected against the former verse, that *Paul* might bee taught of some other Apostle beside *Peter*, and that at Ierusalem: to this he answers two things. One, that there was none of the Apostles at Ierusalem, but *Iames:* (beside *Peter* beforenamed) the second, that he did but see *Iames*.

Heere I gather, that if there bee any mother Church in the world, it is rather Ierusalem then Rome, because the Gospel was first preached there, and went thence into the whole world: and Ierusalem was for a time guided by two of the cheefe Apostles, *Iames*, and *Peter*.

In that *Iames* is called our Lords brother, three things may bee demanded. One, which *Iames* this was? *Answere*. It was *Iames* the sonne of *Alpheus*: for he liued 14. yeares after this, *Galat*.2.9. whereas *Iames* the sonne of *Zebedeus* liued not so long, because hee was put to death by *Herod*. The second thing is, how *Iames* should bee the Lords brother? *Answer*. In Scripture, children of the

the ſame wombe, are brethren: men of the ſame bloud, are brethren; *Abraham* and *Lot. Gen.* 13.8. Men of the ſame countrie are brethren, thus *Sauls* countriemen are called his brethren. 1.*Chron*.12.2. And *Iames* is called our Lords brother, not becauſe he was of the ſame wombe, but becauſe he was of the ſame bloud or kindred: for *Elie* had two daughters, *Marie* eſpouſed to *Ioſeph*; and *Marie Cleophas*, who afterward was maried to *Alpheus* of whom came *Iames* here mentioned. *Iames* therfore was the coſin-german of Chriſt. Therefore *Heluidius* failed when he went about to infringe the perpetuall virginitie of the virgin *Marie* out of this place, as if ſhee had more ſonnes beſide Chriſt. The third thing is, what benefit *Iames* had by beeing the Lords brother? Anſwer. Hee is here called the Lords brother onely, for diſtinctions ſake in reſpect of the other *Iames* the ſonne of *Zedebeus*: and this brotherhood doth not make him the better Apoſtle, or the better man. Outward things doe not commende vs to God. And it is the ſpirituall kindred, by meanes of faith, and our new birth, that bringes vs into fauour with God, *Matthew* 12.49

20 *Nowe the things which I write, I ſpeake before God, I lie not.*

Before, *Paul* hath auouched ſundrie things of himſelfe: that hee preached in Arabia, and Damaſcus: that hee went thence to Ieruſalem: that hee did not learne the Goſpell there of *Peter*, *Iames*, or any other Apoſtle. Nowe ſome man might happely ſay, that theſe ſayings of his are but falſe and fabulous auouchments: therefore in this verſe *Paul* defends himſelfe, and iuſtifies his owne ſayings, by a diuine teſtimony.

The words containe 2. partes. An anſwer to an obiection concealed, on this manner; I may bee thought to lie, but indeede *I lie not*. The ſecond is, a confirmation by oath, *Before God I ſpeake it*. Touching the firſt part, there bee two points to bee handled: what is a lie? And whether it be a ſinne or no?

A lie is when wee ſpeake the contrarie to that we thinke with an intention to deceiue. More plainely, in a lie there bee foure things: the firſt is, *to auouch and affirme that which is falſe*. The ſecond is, *to ſpeake with a double heart, Pſal.* 12.2. That is, to ſpeake againſt knowledge, and conſcience, as when a man ſaith that is true which he knowes to be falſe, or that is falſe, which he knowes to bee true. This makes a lie, to be a lie, and this diſtinguiſheth an vntruth, from a lie. For here it muſt be obſerued, that a man may ſpeake that which is falſe, and not lie: namely if he ſpeake that which is falſe,

thinking

thinking it to be true. For then though he erre & is deceiued, yet he ſpeaks not againſt conſcience, and conſequently he ſpeakes no lie. Againe, a man may ſpeake that which is true, and yet lie: for if he ſpeake that which is true indeed, and ſpeake it as a trueth, and yet thinke it to be falſe, he lies indeed: becauſe hee ſpeakes the trueth againſt his conſcience. The third thing in a lie, is, *a mind or intention to deceiue or hurt.* For in the ninth commaundement that is a falſe teſtimony that is againſt our neighbor. The fourth point is, that *he which ſpeakes that which is falſe vpon a vanity of mind without reaſonable cauſe, is a liar.* Thus boaſters and flatterers are liers. And theſe are the things which concurre in the making of a lie.

For the better conceiuing of the nature of a lie, wee muſt put difference between it and ſundrie other things incident to ſpeech. Firſt, we muſt put difference betweene a lie and a *parable*, or *figure*. In a parable indeed there is ſomething ſuppoſed or fained; as for example, when the trees are brought in conferring, and conſulting about their king, *Iudg.* 9.8. neuertheleſſe a parable is farre from falſehood, or lying: for by things fained, it ſignifies and declares an vnfained truth.

Againe, difference muſt be put between a lie and *the concealement of a thing*: for it is one thing to ſpeake againſt our knowledge, and another to ſpeake that which wee know. And concealements, if there be a reaſonable cauſe, & if it be not neceſſary for vs to reueale the thing concealed, are not vnlawfull. Thus *Abram* ſpeakes the truth in part, calling *Sara* his ſiſter, & conceals it in part, not confeſſing her to be his wife, *Gen.* 12.10. Thus *Samuel* by Gods appointment reueals that he came to Bethlem to offer ſacrifice, & conceals the anointment of *Dauid*, that he might ſaue his life, 1.*Sam.* 16.5. *Ionas* preaches that Nineue ſhall be deſtroyed within fourtie daies, and he conceales the condition of repentance. The like did *Iſaie* to *Ezechias*, *Iſai.* 38.1.

Thirdly, a difference muſt be made betweene lying and *faining*: which ſome call *ſimulation*: not *diſſembling*, but rather *ſembling* (if I may ſo terme it.) And that is, when ſomething is ſpoken, not contrary, but beſide, or diuers to that which we think. And this kind of faining, if it bee not to the preiudice of trueth, againſt the glory of God, & the good of our neighbor, and haue ſome conuenient and reaſonable cauſe, is not vnlawfull. It was not the will and counſell of God to deſtroy the Iſraelites for their idolatry. And he doth not ſpeake vnto *Moſes* any thing contrary to his will, but ſomething that is beſide, or diuers vnto it, when he ſaith, *Let me alone, that my wrath may waxe hote, and I may deſtroy them*: *Exod.* 32.10. And this he ſpake, that he might ſtirre vp *Moſes* to feruency in praier for the Iſraelites, and the Iſraelites to vnfained repentance. *Ioſua* hauing beſieged Ai, meant not to flie, yet doeth he faine a flight, that hee might draw his enemies out of the citie, and deſtroy them, *Ioſ.*8.5. There is a kind of deceit called *dolus bonus*, that is, *a good deceit*, and of this kind was the act of *Ioſua*. Thus Phyſitians for their good, vſe to deceiue the ſenſes of their impotent patients. Thus parents inſinuate vnto their children, terrible things of the Beare, and bull-beggar, that they may keepe them from places of hurt and danger. And this may be done without fault, for it is one thing to contrary the truth, and an other to ſpeake or doe ſomething diuerſe vnto it without contrarietie.

The ſecond point is, *whether to lie, be a ſinne or no?* the anſwer is, Yea. For euen in this place, *Paul* puts lying from himſelfe, and that with an oath. The diuell is ſaid to be the authour of all lies, *Iohn* 8. And it is Gods commandement, that we ſhould *put away lying, Eph.* 4. 25. It is obiected, that *the ſporting*, and *officious lie*, is not againſt charitie, to the hurt of any, but for the good of men. I anſwer, firſt, though it be not to the hurt of our neighbour, yet is it to the hurt and preiudice of truth. Secondly, they are deceiued to whom theſe lies are told. Thirdly, he hurts himſelfe that tels a lie, though it be for the good of men: for when hee ſpeakes the truth indeed, he is leſſe beleeued. Laſtly, though theſe kind of lies ſeeme to be good in reſpect of their end, yet are they not good in reſpect of their nature and conſtitution. For in ſpeaking, there ſhould be a conformity and conſent between the tongue and the mind; which is not when any lie is vttered. Secondly, it is obiected, that the Egyptian Midwiues ſaued the male children of the Iſraelites: and *Rahab* the ſpies by lying, *Exod.*1.19. *Ioſ.*2.5. and that they are commended for this. I anſwer, we muſt diſtinguiſh the worke done, from the execution of the worke. The worke in ſauing the children, and the ſpies, was a fruit of faith, & the feare of God, and it is commended: but the manner of putting theſe workes in execution, by lying, is not approoued. If it bee ſaid, that faith and the feare of God cannot ſtand with a manifeſt ſinne: I ſay againe, that faith and the feare of God are imperfect in this life, and therfore they are ioyned with many frailties; and actions of faith are mixed with ſundrie defects and ſinnes.

Now then we are to be exhorted, to make a conſcience of lying, and to ſpeake the truth from our hearts. And there be many reaſons to induce vs to the practiſe of this dutie. Firſt, it is Gods commandement, *Iam.*3.14. Secondly, lying is a conformitie to the diuell,

uell, and by truth we are made conformable to God, who is truth it ſelfe. Thirdly, we are ſanctified by the word of truth, *Ioh.* 17.17. and guided by the ſpirit of truth: and therefore we are to deteſt lying, and deceit. Fourthly, truth is a fruit of Gods ſpirit, *Gal.* 5. & a mark of Gods child, *Pſal.* 32.v.2. he hath the pardon of his ſinnes *in whoſe ſpirit there is no guile*; and *Pſal.* 15.2. *he ſhall reſt in the mountaine of God, who ſpeakes the truth from his heart.* Laſtly, deſtruction is the liers reward, *Pſal.* 5.6. *God will deſtroy them that ſpeake lies*: and they muſt haue their portion in the lake that burnes with fire and brimſton, *Reuelation* 22.15.

Thus much of the anſwer to the obiection: now followes the confirmation by oath [*before God.*] Here it may be demanded, how theſe words can bee a forme of ſwearing? *Anſwer.* In an oath there be foure things. The firſt is, *an Aſſeueration of the truth.* The ſecond is, *Confeſſion*, whereby the partie that is to ſweare, acknowledgeth the power, preſence, and wiſdome of God, in ſearching the heart, and that he is both witneſſe & Iudge of all our doings. The third is, *Inuocation of God*, that he would bee a witneſſe with vs, and to vs, that we ſpeake the truth. The laſt is, *Imprecation*, that God would be a Iudge, to take reuenge vpon vs if we lie. Now then, the forme of an oath is a certain forme of words, in which not all, but ſome of the principall parts of an oath are expreſſed, and the reſt concealed, and yet to be vnderſtood. *Ierem.* 4.2. there is the forme of an oath, *The Lord liueth*, and here onely *confeſſion* is expreſſed. The forme of ſwearing, *I call God to witneſſe to my ſoule*, 2. *Cor.* 1.23. expreſſeth the third part, namely, Inuocation. The wordes, *Ruth.* 2.17. *The Lord doe thus and thus vnto mee*, is an *Imprecation.* The common forme, *The Lord thee helpe through Ieſus Chriſt*, is partly praier, and partly imprecation. And the forme in this place is directly a confeſſion, that God is preſent to witneſſe and iudge the truth. Thus commonly in all formes of oathes one part is expreſſed, and the reſt are infolded.

Here firſt we learne, that the forme of an oath, is to bee plaine, and direct in the Name of God, and not indirect, or oblique, in the name of the creatures, Gods name concealed. And it is the flat commandement of God, *Mat.* 5.34. It is alledged, that *Paul*, 1. *Cor.* 15.31. ſweares *by his reioycing in Chriſt.* I anſwer, the words of *Paul*, *by my reioycing*, are not an oath, but an obteſtation: for the meaning of his words is this, that his ſorrows and afflictions which he indured for Chriſt, would teſtifie (if they could ſpeake) that he died daily. Thus *Moſes* called heauen and earth to witneſſe, without ſwearing: for in an oath the thing by which he ſweares, is made not onely witneſſe, but alſo iudge. Neuertheleſſe, it is not vnlawfull to name the creatures in the forme of an oath, if they be conſidered as pledges preſented vnto God, that he ſhould puniſh vs in them if we lie. Thus *Paul* ſweareth, *I call God to witneſſe to (or vpon) my ſoule*. Here they are to bee blamed, whoſe common ſwearing is by the creatures, as by their faith, by their troth, by the Maſſe, Marie, by this bread, by this drinke, &c.

Secondly, here we learne to vſe an oath, onely in the caſe of extremitie, namely, when a neceſſary truth is to bee confirmed, and when this cannot be done by any reaſon, or proofe to be found among men vpon earth, then may wee flie vnto heauen for proofe, and make God our witnes. Thus *Paul* confirmes his owne calling, when all other proofes failed. And it muſt further be obſerued, that in extremities he vſeth an oath but ſeldome. This ſeemes to condemne their wickedneſſe, that crie at euery word in their common talke, *before God, before God*.

Thirdly, before we ſweare, we are to vſe great meditation, conſideration, and preparation: and therefore *Paul* in ſwearing vſeth a word of attention, and ſaith, *Behold, I ſpeake it before God*. This condemnes the raſh & cuſtomable ſwearing of men in their common talke: who alſo in that they commonly and raſhly ſweare, commonly forſweare themſelues.

In that *Paul* confirmes his writings by oath, it appeares that they are of God. For if he had ſworne falſly, God would haue taken reuenge vpon him, and his writings before this: which hee hath not done.

Whereas *Paul* ſaith, *Before God I ſpeake it*: he teacheth vs after his owne example, to bring our ſelues into the preſence of God, to walke before him as *Enoch* did, *Gene.5.22.* and as *Abraham* was commaunded, *Gene.17.1.* and to doe whatſoeuer we doe as in the ſight and preſence of God: and to be afraid to ſinne, becauſe of his preſence. This is the true feare of God, and this is the right practiſe of religion.

21 *After that I went into the coaſts of Syria and Cilicia: and I was vnknowne by face to the Churches of Iudea, which were in Chriſt.*

22 *But they had heard onely ſome ſay, Hee which perſecuted vs in times paſt, now preacheth the faith, which before hee had deſtroyed.*

23 *And they glorified God in mee.*

Heere *Paul* anſwers an other obiection, which may be framed thus: Though *Paul* learned not the Goſpell of the Apoſtles at Ieruſalem, yet might he haply learne it of them in other Churches of Iudea. To this *Paul* anſwers three things. The firſt is, that *hee went from Ieruſalem into Syria and Cilicia.* The ſecond, that *hee was not knowen in perſon to the Churches of Iudea,* but onely by heare ſay: and he ſets downe the report that went of him. The third is, that the Churches of Iudea did not diſgrace and ſlander him, but *they glorified God for him.* Of theſe in order. For the firſt, that *Paul* went from Ieruſalem ſtraight into Syria, and Cilicia, the regions of the Gentiles, there bee two cauſes. One, becauſe *Paul* was ordained ſpecially to be the Apoſtle of the Gentiles, *Act.* 9 15. *Rom* 15. 16. The ſecond, becauſe Cilicia was his owne countrey: for he was borne in Tarſus, a towne in Cilicia: and his loue to his countrey, no doubt, was great. For in the like caſe, hee could haue wiſhed himſelfe to be accurſed for his countreymen the Iewes. From this firſt anſwer I gather two things. Firſt, if any Apoſtle aboue the reſt, be the Paſtour and vniuerſall Biſhop of the Church ouer the whole world, it is *Paul,* and not *Peter*: becauſe he ſpecially was ordained to teach and conuert the nations. The ſecond is, that *Pauls* often and dangerous iourneys, muſt teach vs to attend on our callings with care and diligence, and not to bee diſmayed with the troubles that ſhall befall vs.

The ſecond anſwer, that *Paul* was known to the Chriſtian Iewes *not by face, but by hearesay*: this may ſeeme ſtrange, conſidering *Paul* was at Ieruſalem, & trauailed through Iurie, into Syria, and Cilicia: but it is the truth: and the reaſon of it is plaine. The office of an Apoſtle is not to build vpon the foundation of an other, or to ſucceed any man in his labors, but to plant & found the church of the new Teſtament, *where Chriſt had not bin preached or named, Rom.* 15. 20. In this the Apoſtles differ from all the Miniſters of the new Teſtamẽt whatſoeuer. And this is the cauſe why *Paul* was not known to the Churches of Iudea. And here we ſee, that ſucceſſion (which the Papiſts magnifie) is not alwaies a note of the true Church, and the true Miniſterie. For the true Miniſterie of the Apoſtles, and the Apoſtolicall Churches wanted it. And this is for the greater commendation of them.

Againe, it is ſaid, that *Paul* was not knowne to the Churches of Iudea, which were in Chriſt. Where let it be obſerued, that 4 yeares after the aſcenſion of Chriſt, the Apoſtles had gathered, & planted ſundrie Chriſtian Churches in Iudea. This greatly commends the efficacie and power of the Goſpel. For hardneſſe of heart had ouer-ſpread the nation of the Iewes, and they had reiected and crucified the Lord of life. And thus, that is verified whic Chriſt ſaith, that his Diſciples beleeuing in him, ſhould doe greater things, then hee had done, *Ioh.* 14. 12. for hee by preaching did not conuert multitudes of the Iewes, and range them into Churches, as the Apoſtles did. Here againe, we ſee that the Goſpel, by meanes of the corruption of man, is an occaſion of diuiſions. For after the Goſpel was preached by the Apoſtles, there aroſe a diuiſion of Churches among the Iewes. Some were Churches in Chriſt, and ſome out of Chriſt; namely, the Synagogues which refuſed Chriſt. We may not therefore nowe adaies take offence, if ſchiſmes and diſſentions followe, where the Goſpel is preached: it is not the fault of the Goſpel, it is the fault of men.

That *Paul* might the better ſhew, that hee was knowne to the Churches of the Iewes, onely by heare-ſay, he expreſſes the report that went of him. Hence I gather, it is not vnlawfull to tell and heare reports or newes, ſo be it, they bee not to the preiudice of the truth, of the glory of God, and the good name of men. Nay, it is commendable to report, and heare newes, that concernes the increaſe of Gods kingdome, and the conuerſion of wicked men.

In the report two things are ſet downe, what *Paul* did? *He once perſecuted vs, and deſtroyed the faith:* what hee now doth? *He preacheth the Goſpel.* By this we ſee that verified, which *Iſai* foretold, that the lyon, the wolfe, the lambe, &c. ſhould peaceably liue together. Againe, here we ſee, that all things vpon earth, are ſubiect to change and alteration: ſo as it may be ſaid, heretofore it was thus, and thus, but now it is otherwiſe. Therefore in miſeries, wee may not bee ouer-much grieued, for they are changeable: and in earthly things, we may not reioyce ouer much, becauſe they are mutable, and ſubiect to daily alterations. Our ſpeciall care muſt be, to auoide eternall and vnchangeable euils; as death, and the cauſe of death, namely, ſin; and to purchaſe to our ſelues, the good things which are euerlaſting; namely, the fauour of God, & euerlaſting life.

Furthermore, the thing, which *Paul* aimed at, in perſecuting the Church, is to be conſidered, and that was, *that hee might deſtroy the faith.* By *faith*, we are to vnderſtand the doctrine of the Goſpel, and withall, the vertue, or gift of faith, whereby it is beleeued: for the diuell and his inſtruments, ſeeke the ouerthrow of both. Chriſt ſaith, *Satan deſired to ſift his Diſciples,* that is, to ſift all their faith out of their hearts, and to leaue nothing in them, but chaffe, *Luk.* 22. 32. Here then, it may be demanded, whether faith may be loſt, ſpecially in the children of God, in the time of temptation, and

perſecution?

persecution? I answer thus. There bee three degrees of faith. The first consists in two things, *knowledge* of the Gospel, and *Assent* to the trueth of it. This faith the deuils haue, and it may be lost; and beleeuers by this faith, may quite fall away. The second kinde of faith, containes knowledge, assent, a taste, or ioy in the goodnesse of God, a zeale to the word of God, and apparent fruits of holinesse. This faith also (beeing better then the former) may bee lost in the daies of persecution: and beleeuers by this faith, may fall quite away. *Luk.* 8.13. The third faith, (called the faith of the elect) containes three parts, knowledge of the Gospel, assent to the truth of it, and apprehension, whereby wee doe receiue, and apply Christ with his benefits to our selues, or the promise of remission of sinnes, and life euerlasting. This faith may bee greatly wasted, for things appertaining to it, may be lost, as boldnesse to come vnto God, the sense or feeling of spiritual ioy, and such like. Againe, it may bee buried for a time in the heart, and not shew it selfe, either by fruits, or any profession: and in respect of the measure of it, it may be lessened and maimed: and if we respect the nature of it, it is as apt to be lost, as any other grace of God: for there is nothing by nature vnchangeable, but God. Neuerthelesse, where this faith is in truth, it is neuer by affliction and temptation put out or exitinguished: because God in mercie confirms it, by new grace. Christ saith to *Peter, I haue praied for thee, that thy faith faile not, Luk.* 22.32. And this priuiledge haue all the godly, for God promiseth that *they shal not be tepted aboue their strength,* 1.*Cor.* 10.13. Indeed, persecutors are said to destroy the faith: because this is their intent, & they indeauour to doe what they can; but God preuents their desires, by establishing true faith, that it may not vtterly faile.

It may be obiected to the contrarie, on this manner. The childe of God may fall into persecution, and denie Christ: by this fall, he is guiltie of a grieuous offence: beeing guiltie, hee hath not pardon of his offence, and beeing without pardon, hee is without faith. Touching guiltinesse, I answer thus, The child of God, when hee falls, is indeed guiltie: but how? Guiltie in respect of himselfe, or as much as in him lies: because he hath done that which is worthy of death, and he hath done all he can to make himselfe guiltie. But he is not guiltie to condemnation, because God on his part doth not breake off the purpose of adoption, and adiudge him to wrath.

Secondly, touching the pardon of his offence. I answer thus. In pardon there be foure degrees: the decree of pardon before all worlds: the promise of pardon in the beginning of the word. *The seede of the woman,* &c. The procurement of pardon vpon the crosse: and the donation, or the giuing of the pardon. This donation is an action of God, wherby he giues & communicates Christ vnto vs, and applies to our consciences the remission of our sinnes. In this donation, there is required a hand to giue, and a hand to receiue. The hand of God, whereby he giues, is the word preached, and the Sacraments: the hand to receiue, is our faith. The giuing of pardon is necessary: for though sinnes be pardoned in the decree of God, by his promise in the word, and by procurement vpon the crosse: yet pardon is no pardon to vs, till it bee giuen vnto vs by God. Furthermore, this giuing is not altogether at one instant, but it beginnes in the conuersion of a sinner, and is often iterated in the vse of the word and Sacraments, to the death. *Paul* wills the Corinthians reconciled to God, still to be reconciled, 2. *Cor.* 5.21. And we are taught euery day to pray to God, to giue vs the pardon of our sinnes. This giuing is twofold, conditionall, and absolute. Conditionall, when God giues the pardon of sin vpon condition. Thus in Baptisme, and in the first conuersion of a sinner, all sinnes without exception, are pardoned; yea future sinnes: yet not simply whether a man repent or no, but vpon condition of future repentance. The absolute donation is, when a man repents, or renewes his repentance: for then the pardon of sinne is simply and fully without condition, applied and reuealed to the conscience. When *David* confessed his sinne, *Nathan*, in the name of the Lord saith, *Thy sinne is forgiuen thee*. 2. *Sam*. 12.

Now then to come to the point, the child of God hath pardon of his fal, in respect of the decree to pardon, in respect of the generall promise of pardon, in respect of the procurement of pardon, in respect of the conditionall donation of pardon, which is made in baptisme: and he may be said to want pardon, in that the pardon of his offence is not fully and absolutely giuen him till he recouer himselfe, and renew his repentance. If it be here demanded, what the child of God askes when he praies for pardon day by day? I answer, he praies for two things. First, that God would continue to shew his fauour, & to impute the merits of Christ vnto him, wheras he for his part by his offence deserues to be depriued of all fauor. Secondly, he asks the giuing of the pardon, that is, that God would certifie his conscience thereof.

The vse. Seeing the intent of the diuell and wicked men, is to destroy the faith (as it appeares in this place, and in the first temptation wherwith Satan assaulted Christ, *Matth*. 4.) we must haue a speciall care of our faith. And first we must looke that our faith be a true faith, lest we be deceiued, as the foolish virgins. Secondly, we

must

muſt keepe and lock vp our faith in ſome ſafe and ſure place, namely in the ſtore-houſe or treaſury of a good conſcience, 1. *Tim.*1.19. Thirdly, our care muſt be to increaſe in faith, that our hearts may be rooted and grounded in the loue of God. And for this cauſe we are to make continuall experiences, and obſeruations of the loue of God toward vs, and to lay them all together, and to build a ioyfull concluſion thereupon.

The third anſwer of *Paul* is, *And they glorified God for me*: that is, the Churches of Iudea when they heard of my calling and conuerſion, they conſidered therein the power, the goodneſſe, and the mercy of God, and with ioy they gaue him thanks for it. In this practiſe of the Church, we learne that our dutie is to ſanctifie and glorifie the name of God in euery work of his. And this ſanctification hath 2. parts. The firſt is, the conſideration of the diuine vertues that ſhew themſelues in euery work of God, as his wiſdome, power, iuſtice, mercy, prouidence, preſence, &c. The ſecond is, praiſe and thankſgiuing to God for the ſame. And this practiſe muſt be inlarged to all his works without exception, to his iudgments, as well as to his works of mercy. Therefore we are commanded in perſecution *to ſanctifie God in our hearts*, 1. *Pet.*3.17. And *Moſes*, becauſe he failed in the doing of this dutie, was barred the land of Canaan, *Num.*20,12. In England God hath wrought his wondrous works among vs. He hath giuen vs peace and protection againſt our enemies, with the Goſpel, for the ſpace of fortie yeares and more. And our duty is to glorifie God in theſe works of his: but alas, we doe it not. For the Goſpel of ſaluation is little regarded of the moſt, and little obedience is yeelded to it. This neglect of ours in glorifying and praiſing of God, is a gteat ſinne: and it ſtands vs in hand to repent of it betime, leſt God take away his word from vs, and leaue vs to ſtrange illuſions, to beleeue lies.

Againe, here we ſee what is the right maner of honouring of the Saints, and that is, to glorifie God in them, and for them. As for religious worſhip of adoration and inuocation, it is proper to God, and the Saints deſire it not, *Reuel.*22.9.

CHAP.

CHAP. II.

1 *Then fourteene yeeres after I went vp againe to Ierusalem with Barnabas, and tooke with me Titus also.*

2 *And I went by reuelation, and communicated with them of the Gospel, which I preach among the Gentiles, but priuately with them that were the chiefe, least by any meanes I should runne, or had runne in vaine.*

N this Chapter, *Paul* proceeds to iustifie and defend his immediate and extraordinarie calling. And this whole Chapter seemes to depend on the last words of the former chapter, against which the aduersaries of *Paul* might haply obiect on this manner: Though the Churches of Iudea glorifie God for thee, yet will not the Apostles doe it; because thou teachest otherwise then they teach. To this obiection, *Paul* makes a double answer in this Chapter. The effect and summe of the first, is this: I went vp to Ierusalem: I conferred with the Apostles there: I had their consent and approbation. And the answer containes three parts. The first, of *Pauls* iourney to Ierusalem, in the first verse: the second, of his conference with the Apostles, in the second verse: the third, of the approbation which they gaue him, from the third verse to the eleuenth.

In his iourney, I consider foure things. The first is, the manner of his iourneying in these wordes, *I went vp*, or *ascended to Ierusalem.* And this he speakes, because Ierusalem was placed, and seated vpon a mountaine, and compassed with mountaines, *Psal.* 125. or againe, in respect of the dignitie and excellencie of the place: as wee in England are said to go vp to London, from all the parts of the land, because it is the chiefe citie.

The second thing to be considered in the iourney is, the time when, in these words, *Then after foureteene yeares.* Here two questions are to be demaunded. The first is, of which of his iourneyes must this be vnderstood? (for hee made fiue iourneyes to Ierusalem.) The first, from Arabia: the second, when he and *Barnabas* were sent by the Church of the Gentiles to carrie almes to Ierusalem: the third, when he went to the Councell at Ierusalem: the fourth, when he went vp for the keeping of his vow: the last, is mentioned *Acts* 19.21. *Answer.* These wordes are not spoken

of

of the firſt, for that was but three yeares after his conuerſion: neither can they well be vnderſtood of the ſecond, becauſe *Paul* then was ſent by the Church, and therefore he went not by reuelation. And they cannot well be vnderſtood of the third: for then *Paul* would here haue mentioned the Councell of Ieruſalem, whereof he was a principall member, ſpecially ſeeing he hath occaſion ſo to doe, and it ſerued much for his purpoſe The fourth and fifth iourneyes were after a longer time then foureteene yeares. It is likely therefore, that this iourney heere mentioned and deſcribed by *Paul*, is none of the fiue mentioned by *Luke*, but ſome other. The ſecond queſtion is, When theſe fourteene yeares muſt begin? *Anſwer*. It is vncertaine. Some thinke, they muſt begin at his conuerſion; ſome three yeares after, when *Paul* went firſt to Ieruſalem: and either may bee a trueth. None muſt heere take offence. For though circumſtances of time and place, beeing things of leſſe moment, cannot alwayes be certainly gathered, yet hiſtories for their ſubſtance and doctrines pertaining to ſaluation, are plainely ſet downe. And here we are put in minde, to be content to be ignorant in ſome things, becauſe the Spirit of God hath more darkly expreſſed them, or againe, becauſe wee cannot, by reaſon of our blindneſſe, gather them.

The third point is, concerning the companions of *Paul* in this iourney, namely *Barnabas and Titus*. And *Paul* takes them with him, that they might be witneſſes to the Iewes of the doctrine he taught among the Gentiles: and againe, to the Gentiles of the conſent that was betweene him and the reſt of the Apoſtles. For the Law of God is, that euery matter ſhall be eſtabliſhed by the teſtimonie of two or three witneſſes. Hence we learne, that if a queſtion ariſe of the doctrine which is deliuered in the publike miniſterie, then the hearers that are able to iudge, muſt bee witneſſes, and the triall is to be made by them. Thus ſaith Chriſt in the like caſe, *Why aske yee me? aske them that heard me*, *Iohn* 18.21. Therfore great care and circumſpection is to be had of things publikely deliuered. Againe, whereas *Paul* makes *Barnabas* a Iew, and *Titus* a Gentile, his companions, we are taught to imbrace with a brotherly loue, not only the men of our owne countrey, but alſo ſuch as be of other nations, ſpecially if they beleeue. For then they are all children of one Father, and pertaine all to one family: and there is no difference of nations now. It is a fault therfore, that men of one nation carrie in their hearts, a generall diſlike and hatred oftentimes of them with whom they deale and conuerſe, and that becauſe they are of ſuch or ſuch countries.

The

The fourth point is, the cauſe of his iourney, in theſe words, *and I went by reuelation.* Here we are taught, that for the iournies we make, we are to haue ſome good and ſufficient warrant: though not a reuelation, yet a commandement, or that which counteruailes a commandement: as when we trauaile by vertue of our callings. When *Noe* had made the Arke, hee enters into it at Gods commandement: he abides in it: and when the earth was in part dried, he preſumes not to goe out, till the Lord bade him. Here, three ſorts of men are to be blamed. Pilgrimes, that trauell to Ieruſalem, or other countries in the way of merite, or religion. For they haue no warrant. Secondly, trauellers, that goe from countrey to country, and out of the precincts of the Church, vpon vaine curioſitie, to ſee faſhions. Such when they trauell from their owne countries, yet they trauell not from their vices, but rather goe deeper into them, and come home againe, with many bad and corrupt faſhions. The laſt, are Beggers, and Rogues, that paſſe from place to place, that they may liue in idleneſſe and vpon the ſweate of other mens browes.

Thus much of the iourney: now followes the Conference, in theſe words; *and I communicated, &c.* Here generally I gather, that Conferences both priuate and publike, are laudable, and to bee maintained; ſpecially, when they tend to the maintenance of vnitie, and conſent in doctrine. The Papiſts blame vs Proteſtants for condemning Conferences (as they ſay) and Councels. But they doe vs wrong. Indeede the Councell of Trent we reiect, and condemne. For in it, againſt all equitie, the Pope was both partie, and iudge. In it there was no libertie to make triall of truth. For nothing was propounded but by the liking and conſent of the Pope. Againe, the whole Councell conſiſted of ſuch as were of the *Italian faction,* whoſe faith was pinned on the Popes ſleeue. Neuertheleſſe, we allow all Chriſtian Councells, lawfully gathered: and we deſire there might be a Generall Councell, for the triall of truth, and for the ſtaying of vnſetled minds: theſe three caueats beeing remembred. One, that the Councell be gathered by Chriſtian Princes, to whom the right of calling a Councell belongs. The other, that the Pope be no iudge, but a partie. The third, that Chriſt in his word be the iudge, and that the Delegates in the Councell be but as witneſſes, determining all things by the written word.

In this conference, we are firſt to conſider the manner of conferring, which was vſed. *Paul* ſaith, *he communicated with them,* that is, he laid downe vnto them, and expounded the Goſpel which preached;and this he did priuatly,that is,with the Apoſtles,one by one,in plaine and familiar maner,as one friend doeth with another. Therefore for the maintaining of this conference, there was no aſſembly made,neither was there any diſputation held. Onely *Paul* declares his doctrine,and they giue aſſent. Hence it appeares,that *Paul* doth not ſubmit the truth of his doctrine to triall. For he was reſolued of it,and he accurſed him that taught otherwiſe:but his intent was to ſeeke the approbation of the Apoſtles, that he might ſtop the mouth of his aduerſaries.

The ſecond point is,the matter of the conference, & that is the Goſpel which *Paul* preached. Here the Papiſt gathereth,that the Church is the iudge in all queſtions pertaining to religion,and the word: becauſe it is here the thing that is iudged. I anſwer,firſt,that they gather amiſſe. For *Paul* doeth not heere ſubmit the Goſpel which he preached,to the iudgement of the Church of Ieruſalem. And it is falſe which they teach : for the ſoueraigne Iudge of all queſtions and controuerſies in religion,is Chriſt alone. The power to determine and reſolue in caſes concerning faith and good life,is inſeparably annexed to his perſon; and in it are we to reſt. The principall voice of the iudge,& the definitiue ſentence,is the written word. And the office of the Church,is no more but to gather, declare,teſtifie & pronounce this ſentence. It is obiected,that when a queſtion is propounded, the Scripture cannot ſpeake,nor Chriſt in the Scripture,but the Church onely : I anſwer againe,that God aſcribes to the written word,a voice,or ſpeech,*Rom.*3.19. And the ſcripture ſpeakes ſufficiently,to the reſoluing of any mans conſcience, in all matters pertayning to ſaluation. Againe, they alledge, that the Church is before the ſcripture ; and therefore it beeing moſt auncient,muſt be the Iudge. I anſwer,that the Church was before the writing of the word, but not before the word which is written. For the Church preſuppoſeth faith, and faith preſuppoſeth a word of God. Vpon this our doctrine, they further vpbraid vs,that we will be tried by nothing,but by the Scriptures,euen as the malefactour, that will not bee tried by the Queſt, but by the euidence. I anſwer,for the ſatisfying of our aduerſaries, we ſubmit our ſelues to the triall of the Church and Councels, ſo bee it, the three cautions before remembred be duly obſerued : ſpecially,that all things be iudged,and tried by the written word,and by reaſons gathered thence.

Againe, the Papiſts hence gather,that the Scriptures are to bee approoued by the Church. *Anſw.* Thus much wee graunt : yet ſo as we hold, that the principall approbation of the word,(whereby wee we are mooued to beleeue and obey,) is in the word, and from the word, and not from the Church. For the ſcripture hath his euidence within it ſelfe, which is ſufficient to make vs to beleeue the word to be the word, though the Church ſhould ſay nothing.

The third point is, concerning the perſons, with whome *Paul* conferred: namely, *with them that were the chiefe*, that is, with them that were in price and account, as *Peter, Iames*, &c. Here we ſee, what is the honour and worſhippe that is due vnto excellent men, namely, a pretious and reuerend eſtimation. Thus the name of *Dauid* was in price in Iſrael for his vertues. 1.*Sam*.18. laſt. And thus with the Papiſts, are wee content to honour the Saints. Againe, here the Papiſts gather, that they are heretricks, that after *Pauls* example, will not goe vp to Rome, to *Peter*, and his ſucceſſour, to haue their doctrine and religion tried and examined. I anſwer, firſt, we are content to bee tried by the writings of *Peter, Iames, Iohn, Paul*, &c. And this is the commandement of God, in doubtfull caſes: *To the Law and the teſtimonie. Iſai*.8. Secondly, I anſwer, that we haue a commandement, not to goe vp to Rome at this day, to haue our religion tried. *Reuel*.18. *Come out of Babylon my people*. Thirdly, I anſwer, that the Biſhop of Rome is *Peters* ſucceſſour, not in teaching, but in denying Chriſt. And the learned Papiſts confeſſe, that for this ſucceſſion, they haue but a humane faith grounded vpon humaine hiſtorie.

The fourth point is, the Ende of the conference, *Leaſt I ſhould runne*, that is, leaſt I ſhould preach, or had preached in vaine. Theſe words of *Paul*, are not ſimply to be taken. For the Miniſterie of man, and euery ſermon, brings forth the fruite which God hath appointed. And whether it be vnto the hearers, the ſauour of life, or the ſauour of death, it is alwaies a ſweete ſauour vnto God. The words therefore carrie this meaning: Leaſt my preaching ſhould be of leſſe vſe, and profit: or againe, leaſt I ſhould preach in vaine, in reſpect of that good which is looked for at the hands of an Apoſtle. And this *Paul* ſpeakes, becauſe a rumor went abroad, that his doctrine in many things, was contrarie to the other Apoſtles. And by this meanes, many were kept from receiuing the Goſpel, and the faith of weake beleeuers was quenched. Now then the ende of the conference was, to ſtay this falſe report, that the Miniſterie of *Paul*, might haue paſſage, and that with greater profit.

Hence the Papiſts gather, that the doctrine of *Paul* was vncerten, and vnprofitable, till it was approoued by *Peter*. I anſwer, that *Paul* ſought the approbation of his doctrine, at the hands of *Peter*,

and

and the reſt: not becauſe it was vncerten, and vnprofitable; but becauſe it was ſlaundered: and the ſlander was, that he taught otherwiſe then *Peter* did. Now to cut off this ſlander, he vſeth meanes to maniſeſt his conſent with *Peter*, & therfore ſeekes approbation at his hand.

Againe, when *Paul* ſaith, *Leaſt I ſhould runne in vaine*, he giues vs to vnderſtand, that the Miniſterie of the word, is not a worke of eaſe, or pleaſure, but a labour: nay a continued labour, like to the running in a race. It were therefore to be wiſhed, that miniſters of the Goſpel, would ſo labour, and walke in this calling, that they might be able to ſay with *Paul*, *I haue fought a good fight, I haue finiſhed my courſe*, &c. 2. *Tim*. 4.

Thirdly, hence it appeares, that all beleeuers ſhould haue a certen knowledge of their faith and religion. The procuring of this, was the thing that *Paul* aimed at, in this conference with the Apoſtles at Ieruſalem. We muſt not *be as childrē, caried away with euery winde of doctrine*, *Eph*. 4. 14. Gods word requires faith in vs: and faith preſuppoſeth certen knowledge. The firſt, and ſecond commandements require, that we know God, and his will, diſtinguiſh him from falſe gods, and his worſhippe, from falſe worſhippe. Here comes the fault of our times to be conſidered: moſt men among vs, doe not know their religion, neither can they diſtinguiſh it from errour, and falſe religion. A foule negligence. Wee take paines to learne trades, and occupations, that wee may haue wherewith to preſerue this temporall life: what a ſhame then is it, that we learne no better to know the doctrine of true religion, whereby our ſoules are to be ſaued.

Laſtly, here we learne, that the office of the Miniſter is, not onely to teach and preach, but alſo to ſtudie, and to take care, how by preaching he may doe the moſt good.

3. *But neither yet Titus, which was with me, though he were a Grecian, was compelled to be circumciſed.*

After the Conference, followes the Approbation, which was giuen to *Paul*. It ſtands in foure things. The firſt, that the Apoſtles did not compell *Titus* to be circumciſed. v. 3. The ſecond, that they added nothing to his doctrine. v. 6. The third, that they gaue him the hands of fellowſhip. v. 7. The laſt, that at his departure, they required of him nothing, but the giuing of Almes, v. 16.

For the firſt; the words, *And Titus was not compelled to bee circumciſed*, carrie this ſenſe: I, for my part was readie to circumciſe *Titus*, if there had beene a meete occaſion: falſe brethren would haue impoſed

imposed a necessitie vpon vs: then I and *Titus* refused: and the Apostles did not vrge me to circumcise him.

Here it may be demanded, how this text can well stand with *Act.* 16.v.3. for there *Paul* circumciseth *Timothie*, a Grecian: and here he refuseth to circumcise *Titus*, though he were a Grecian. I answer thus. Circumcision was at this time, a thing indifferent. From the first institution, to the comming, and specially to the death of Christ, it was a thing commanded, a Sacrament, and a part of Gods worship. Again, after the planting of the Church of the new Testament, it was vtterly abolished, and a thing in respect of vse, vtterly vnlawfull. In the middle time, that is, while the Gospel was in publishing to the world, and the Church of the new Testament was yet in founding, it was a ceremonie free, or indifferent. It may bee obiected, that the whole Ceremoniall law was abolished in the death of Christ: I answer, it was so: and circumcision was abolished, in respect of faith, and conscience: yet so as the vse thereof was left to the libertie of the people of God for a while, Circumcision at this time was as a *corps that is dead, yet vnburied, and onely laid out*; and so it must remaine for a time, that it may bee buried with honour. It may againe be obiected, that baptisme was come in the roome of circumcision: and that therfore circumcision was but an idle and empty ceremonie. I answer, it was not vsed as a Sacrament at this time, or as a part of Gods worship, or as a matter of necessity, but onely as a free ceremonie, and that onely then, when it tended to the edification of men.

Beeing then a thing indifferent, it might as occasion serued bee vsed, or not vsed. Therefore *Paul* condescending to the weakenesse of the beleeuing Iewes, circumcised *Timothie*: and that hee might not offend the godly, and hinder Christian libertie, he refused to circumcise *Titus*.

Here a great question is answered, whether we may vse things indifferent, as oft as we wil, & how we wil? The answer is, No. Things are not called indifferent, because we may vse them indifferently, or not vse them when we will, and how wee will, but because in themselues, or in their own nature, they are neither good nor euill, and we may vse them well, or ill, and we may againe not vse them well, or euill. Furthermore, there bee two things which restraine the vse of things indifferent: the lawe of charitie, and the lawes of men. The lawe of charitie is this, *Things indifferent in the case of scandall, cease to bee indifferent, and are as things morall*, that is, either forbidden, or commanded. *Paul* saith, if to eate flesh, be to the offence of his brother, he wil eate no flesh while the world stãds, 1 *Cor.* 8.13.

And

And though he circumciſed *Timothie*, yet would he not circumciſe *Titus*, leſt hee ſhould offend the godly, and by his example hurt Chriſtian libertie.

Likewiſe, the good lawes of men, whether ciuill or Eccleſiaſticall, tending to the common good, and ſeruing for edification, reſtraine the vſe of things indifferenr, ſo that they which ſhall doe otherwiſe, then theſe lawes commaund, with a contemptuous, or diſloyall minde, are guiltie before God; yet heere two cautions muſt be remembred. One, that the lawes of men doe not change the nature of things indifferent: for it is the propertie of God, by willing this or that, to make it good, or euill. Neither doe they take away the vſe of things indifferent. For libertie granted by a ſoueraigne power cannnot bee reuerſed by an inferiour power. Therefore humane lawes doe no more but temper and moderate the ouercommon vſe of things indifferent. The ſecond caution is, That when the end of a law ceaſeth, when there is no contempt of the authoritie that made the law, when no offence is giuen: a thing indifferent remaines in his free vſe without ſinne, or breach of conſcience.

Againe, heere wee learne, that a thing indifferent, when it is made neceſſarie to ſaluation, (as Circumciſion was) is not to bee vſed. This concluſion ſerues to ouerthrow the Popiſh religion. For it ſtands in the obſeruation of things indifferent, as meates, drinks, apparell, times, &c. And the vſing, or the not vſing of them is made neceſſarie euen in regard of mans ſaluation. For the abſtinence from things that are by nature indifferent, is made a part of Gods worſhip, and meritorious of eternall life. For example: to marrie, or not to marrie, is for nature a thing indifferent: and therefore when abſtinence from marriage is made neceſſarie (as it is in diuers orders of men and women) the nature of the thing is changed, which God hath left free, and it is a doctrine of diuels, which is taught.

Here againe we learne to make a difference of perſons. Some are weake, ſome are obſtinate. Weake ones are ſuch, as hauing turned vnto God, and carrying in their hearts a purpoſe in all things to pleaſe God, neuertheleſſe do ſundry things amiſſe, vpon ſimple ignorance, or bad cuſtome, til they be better informed. Of theſe *Paul* ſaith, that *hee became all to all, that hee might ſaue ſome*, 1.*Cor*.9.22. and for their ſakes he condeſcended to circumciſe *Timothie*. And if we that haue ſcarce a drop of mercie in vs, muſt thus beare with them that are weake, much more will God doe it, who is mercie it ſelfe. The good ſhepheard *brings home the ſtray ſheepe vpon his* *ſhoulders: hee carries his lambes in his boſome, Iſai.*40.11. *Hee will not quench the ſmoaking flaxe, Iſai.*42. *He ſpares them that feare him, as a father ſpares his childe, Malach.* 3. 17. This beeing alwayes remembred, that weake ones truely turne to God, and carrie in their hearts an honeſt purpoſe not to ſinne againſt his lawes at any time, wittingly, and willingly. Obſtinate perſons, are ſuch as profeſſe the faith, and yet hold and practiſe bad things, of wilfull ignorance, and of malice. Theſe perſons are not to bee berne with, nor to bee reſpected: and in reſpect of them, *Paul* would not circumciſe *Titus.*

Laſtly, in that *Titus* was not compelled to bee circumciſed, it may bee demaunded, whether Recuſants may bee compelled to the exerciſes of religion? I anſwer, yea: for exerciſes of religion are not things indifferent, as Circumciſion was. *Ioſias* made a couenant with the Lord, and *hee cauſed all his ſubiects to ſtand to it,* 2. *Chron.*34 32. The King at the marriage feaſt of his ſonne, ſaith of the gueſtes, *Compell them to enter in, Luke* 14.23. It is obiected, that men may not bee compelled to beleeue. I anſwer: it is the commandement of God, *prooue the ſpirits,* 1, *Ioh.*4.1. and this commandement pertaines to all perſons. Therfore though men may not be compelled to beleeue: yet may they be compelled to come to the congregation, to heare our Sermons, and therein the reaſons and grounds of our doctrine, that they may trie what is the truth, and cleaue vnto it. For this is their dutie.

4 *For all the falſe brethren, that crept in: who came in priuily to ſpie out our libertie which wee haue in Chriſt Ieſus, that they might bring vs into bondage:*

5 *To whom we gaue not place by ſubiection for an houre, that the truth of the Goſpel might continue with you.*

Paul had ſaid before, that *Titus* was not compelled to be circumciſed: now hee addes: *For all the falſe brethren,* that is, though the falſe brethren did what they could to the contrary. Here then *Paul* ſets downe, who were the cauſe that *Titus* was not circumciſed, namely, certaine perſons at Ieruſalem, and them hee ſets forth by two properties, *they are falſe brethren,* and *they crept into the Church.* Touching the firſt, by it wee learne, that the Church of God vpon earth, euen when it is at the beſt, hath wicked men, and hypocrites in it. In *Adams* family, there is *Cain*: in the Arke, there is *Cham*: in Chriſts familie or ſchoole, there is *Iudas.* In the Church of Ieruſalem, planted and gouerned by the chiefe Apoſtles, there

bee

bee false brethren. The true sheepe be often without, and wolues within. Therefore we may not so much as dreame of a perfection of the Church of God vpon earth; so long as wicked men be mixed with true beleeuers.

Againe, these aduersaries of *Paul*, are called *false brethren*, because they ioyned circumcision with Christ, as a necessarie cause of iustification, and saluation. Hence it followes, that the Church of Rome, is *a false Church*: because it ioynes works with Christ, in the cause of our iustification, and that as meritorious causes.

Their second propertie is, that *they crept into the Church*, which I conceiue on this manner. The Church of God is as a sheepfold, or house, *Ioh.* 10.1. Christ is the onely doore. Now Pastors that teach Christ aright, are said *to enter in by this doore*: they which teach any other way of saluation, are said *to climbe in an other way*: and they which teach Christ, ioyning some other thing with him in the cause of saluation, are said *to creepe in*: because in appearance they maintaine Christ; and yet, because they adde something to Christ, they neither enter, nor continue in the true Church with any good warrant from God. In this they are like the serpent. Liuing creatures were all placed in Eden: and Man was placed in the garden of Eden, called Paradise, and so were not beasts. How then comes the serpent in? why, in all likelihood it crept in. And so doe false brethren into the Church. Hence I gather, that false brethren are not true and liuely members of the visible Chruch: though they be members in appearance. For if they were in their right place, they should not be said to creepe in. The true members of the Church creep not into the mistical body, but are built & set vpon the foundation by God. It may be alledged, that they are baptized, & therby made members of the Church. I answer: that faith makes vs members of Christ, & consequently of the true Church: and baptisme doth but seale our insition into Christ, and serues as a meanes of admission into the outward society of the congregation: and the outward washing doth not make any man a member of Christ. Againe, it followes hence, that false brethren are not members of the Catholike church. For the visible chruch is part of the Catholike: and therefore they which are not reall members of the true visible Church, are not members of the Catholike.

Againe, in that false brethren creepe into the Congregation, hence it appeares, that no man can set downe the precise time, when errours had their beginning. For the authours thereof enter in secretly, not obserued of men. *The enuious man sowes his tares when men be asleepe, Matth.* 13. It sufficeth therefore, if we can shew them to be errours by the word,though wee cannot deſigne the ſet time when they began. The time when a ſhip ſinketh,we often obſerue: but the time when it firſt drew water,we doe not. Let the Papiſts thinke vpon this.

Paul hauing thus declared who were the cauſes that *Titus* was not circumciſed,goes on, and ſhewes how they were cauſes. The effect and ſumme of his declaration,is this: They vrged the obſeruation of the Ceremoniall law,as neceſſary: and hereupon we refuſed to circumciſe *Titus*. Firſt therefore, *Paul* ſets downe how they vrged circumciſion,and that by three degrees. Firſt,*they come in priuily*. Secondly, *they ſpie out their libertie*. Thirdly, *they labour to bring them into bondage*. Againe, *Paul* ſets downe the manner of their refuſall in three things. *We gaue not place for an houre*. Wee gaue not place *by ſubiection*. We gaue no place,*that the truth of the Goſpel might continue with you*.

The firſt degree or ſtep in their vrging of circumciſion,was,that *they came in priuily*: that is, they ioyned themſelues in fellowſhip with the Apoſtles, and in ſhew pretended the furtherance of the Goſpel, & yet indeed meant nothing leſſe: though their fraud and wickednes was not perceiued. Here then the foundation they lay of all their naughty dealing,is their diſſembling, which *Paul* here notes and condemnes. On the contrary, our dutie is,to be indeed that which we profeſſe our ſelues to be: and to profeſſe no more outwardly,then we are inwardly: and to approoue our hearts to God,for that which we profeſſe before men.

The ſecond ſtep or degree is, that they *ſpie out the libertie which Paul and the reſt had by Chriſt*: that is, they conferre with the Apoſtles,and inquire of them what libertie they haue by Chriſt,in reſpect of the Ceremoniall law of God: and this they doe, not of a minde deſirous to learne, but for aduantage ſake. There bee two kindes of ſpying: one lawfull,the other vnlawfull. Lawfull, as when in iuſt and lawfull warre, wee inquire into the counſells and doings of our enemies, *Numbers* 13. 1. Vnlawfull, when men prie into any thing or matter, to find a fault. Thus hypocrites ſpie faults in the perſons and liues of men; that they may haue ſomewhat whereby to diſgrace them, *Mat*. 7.4. Thus Atheiſts prie into the Scriptures, that they may confute them. Thus ſundrie hearers come to Sermons,that they may carpe. Thus our enemies inquire into our religion, that they may finde (as they ſuppoſe) exceptions,vntruths,and contradictions. And in the Church of Ieruſalem, falſe brethren inquire how farre Chriſtian libertie extends, that they may ouerthrow it. This kinde of ſpying is a common

fault;

fault; we muſt take heed of it, and apply the eye of our minde to a better vſe. Firſt, we are to be ſpies, in reſpect of our owne ſinnes and corruptions, to ſpie them out, *Lament.* 3.40. *Let vs ſearch our wayes, and inquire, and turne againe vnto the Lord.* Againe, we are to play the ſpies, in reſpect of our ſpirituall enemies, that wee may finde out the temptations of the fleſh, the world, and the deuill. Thirdly, wee muſt bee as ſpies, in ſearching out thē Scriptures, *Iohn* 5.39. that we may vnderſtand the wordes of the Law of God, and finde comfort to our ſoules.

The third and laſt degree of vrging, is, that the falſe brethren ſeeke to *bring the Apoſtles in bondage,* that is, to binde them to a neceſſary obſeruation of the ceremoniall law. Here let vs marke the practiſe and pollicie of the diuell. Libertie from ſinne, death, and the ceremoniall law, is the treaſure of the Church: and therfore the diuell ſeekes to ouerthrow it, by holding men in bondage vnder aboliſhed ceremonies. Thus at this day, they of the Popiſh Church, are in bondage vnder an heape of humane Traditions, beeing indeed a yoke farre heauier then that of the ceremoniall law. Againe, when men profeſſe the name of Chriſt, the diuell is content with it: and hee indeauours with all his might, euery where to hold them vnder the bondage of ſinne, and to hold them in his ſnare at his will. Thus vnder the name of Chriſtianitie, there be ſwarmes of Atheiſts, Epicures, Libertines, worldlings, and prophane perſons. At this time, according to auncient cuſtome, we celebrate the memoriall of the birth of Chriſt: and yet no time ſo full of diſorder as this. For the moſt that profeſſe Chriſt, take and challenge to themſelues, a licentious libertie, to liue and doe as they liſt: and this kind of libertie, is flat bondage. But they that are ſeruants of Chriſt indeed, ſhould take heede of this bondage: *For beeing free from ſinne, they ſhould be ſeruants of* nothing but *righteouſneſſe, Romanes* 6. 18 They that be of a corporation, ſtand for their liberties: what a ſhame then is it, that men ſhould loue bondage, and neglect the ſpirituall libertie, which they haue by Chriſt.

Thus we ſee, how the falſe brethren vrged circumciſion: now let vs come to *Pauls* refuſall. The firſt point is, that *they would not giue place for an houre.* It ſeemes they were requeſted to vſe circumciſion but once; but they would not yeeld ſo much as once, becauſe their acte would haue tended to the preiudice of Chriſtian libertie in all places. Here we learne that we may not vſe the leaſt ceremonie that is in the caſe of confeſſion, before our aduerſaries, that is, when they ſeeke to oppreſſe the truth, by face, or by fraud, and make ceremonies, ſignes and tokens, of the confeſſion of any vntruth. *Iulian* the Emperour ſitting in a chaire of eſtate, gaue gold to his ſouldiers, one by one, withall commanding to caſt frankincenſe, ſo much as a graine into the fire, that lay vpon an heatheniſh altar, before him. Nowe Chriſtian ſouldiers refuſ to do it: and they which had not refuſed, afterward recalled their acte, and willingly ſuffered death.

Teodoret. hiſt.lib. 4.c.16.

Againe, here we learne, that we are not to yeeld from the leaſt part of the truth of the Goſpell, that God hath reuealed to vs. This truth is more pretious, then the whole world beſide: and heauen and earth ſhall rather paſſe, then the leaſt tittle of it ſhall not be accompliſhed. The commiſſion of the Apoſtles, was to teach them, to doe all things, which God had commanded. Therfore the vnion or mixture of our religiō with the Popiſh religion, is but a dreame of vnwiſe Politickes: for in this mixture, wee muſt yeeld, and they muſt yeeld ſomething: but we may not yeeld, a iot of the truth reuealed to vs. *There is no fellowſhip of light with darkeneſſe.* 2. *Cor.*6. Colaqinthus a naughtie pot hearbe marred a whole pot of pottage. 2. King. 4.40. Chriſt ſaith in the like caſe of the Phariſies; *Let them alone: they are the blinde leaders of the blind, Mat.* 15.14 Wee may yeeld in things indifferent, but not in points of religion. In matters of this world, we may be indifferent, and of neither ſide: but in matters of God, we may not. There is no halting betweene two religions.

Luk.10.16.

The ſecond point is, they gaue no place *by way of ſubiection.* The reaſon is, the Apoſtles were of higheſt authoritie, ſimply to be beleeued in their doctrine. And they had extraordinary authority, to puniſh them that rebelliouſly withſtood thē. *Act.*5.5.&10. & *Act.* 13.20.2. *Cor.*10 6. For this cauſe, they were not to ſtand ſubiect to the iudgement and cenſure of any man. They willingly ſuffered their doctrine to be tried; yet were they not bound to ſubiection, as other miniſters of the new Teſtament are, 1.*Cor.*14.32.1.*Ioh.* 4.1. It may be ſaid, if they would not giue place by ſubiection, how then gaue they place? *Anſwer.* There is two kinds of yeelding: one by tolleration without approbation, the other by ſubiection, which is the greateſt approbation that can be. By the firſt, it may be, *Paul* was content to giue place; but not by the ſecond. Here wee ſee, how we are to yeeld, to the corruptions of the times in which we liue, whether they be in manners, or in doctrine. We are to giue place by meeke and patient bearing of that which wee cannot mende, but we are not to giue place by ſubiection.

The third point is, the end of *Pauls* refuſall, *That the truth of the*

the Goſpel might continue: that is, that the Goſpel might bee preſerued in puritie, and integritie in all things. And by this *Paul* giues vs to vnderſtand, that if circumciſion bee made a neceſſarie cauſe of iuſtification and ſaluation, the truth of the Goſpel doeth not continue. Here let vs obſerue, that when iuſtification, or ſaluation is aſcribed to workes or Sacraments, the truth of the Goſpell giues place, and falſhood comes in the roome. Wherefore the religion of the Church of Rome, is a meere deprauation of the Goſpel, for it makes workes to be the meritorious cauſes of iuſtification, and ſaluation. Nay, which is more, it teacheth men to worſhip a peeece of bread, and to inuocate dead men, and to kneele downe to ſtockes, and ſtones.

6 *And of them that ſeemed to be great* *—: (*what they were in times paſt, it makes no matter to me: God accepteth no mans perſon:*) *for they that are the cheiſe, did not communicate any thing to me.*

*I learned nothing, or I was not taught.

Here *Paul* laies downe the ſecond ſigne of his approbation, namely, that in conference, he learned nothing of the chiefe Apoſtles. And this he expreſſeth in the firſt words: in which, the concealement which he vſeth, is to be obſerued. For hauing begun a ſentence, he breakes it off in the middle, and conceales the latter part, and leaues it to bee ſupplied by the reader thus; *Of them that ſeemed to be great, I was not taught*, or, *I learned nothing*. The like forme of ſpeaking, is vſed 1. *Chron*.4.10. Where *Iabez* ſaith, *If the Lord bleſſe me and be with me*; concealing the end of his ſentence, *I will bee thankefull, thus, and thus*,

In the roome of this concealement, *Paul* puts an anſwer to an obiection. For ſome man might take exception againſt his former ſpeech, thus: Thou calleſt the Apoſtles *Great*, but thou ſpeakeſt fainedly: for thou knoweſt, they were but poore fiſhermen. To this he makes anſwer thus: *What they were once, it makes no matter to me*. Then he renders a reaſon of his anſwer: *God accepth no mans perſon*. This done, he proceeds, and renders a reaſon of his firſt ſpeech: he learned nothing of the cheefe Apoſtles: becauſe, *they did not communicate any thing to him*, either in doctrine or counſell.

The vſe. This verſe ſerues to expound other places in Saint *Iohn*. Where Chriſt promiſeth to *giue his ſpirit to his Diſciples, to teach them all things, Ioh*.14.26 and *to leade them into all truth, Ioh*.16.13. Now theſe promiſes directly, and properly, concerne the Apoſtles: and they are here verified in *Paul*. Who was ſo farre forth taught by God, & led into al truth, that the chief Apoſtles could not teach, or communicate, any thing to him. For all this though, *Paul* and the rest, were led into all truth, that they could not erre, yet were they not led into all holinesse of life, that they could not sinne. *Paul* saith, *to will is present with me*, but he addes, *that he cannot doe the good he would.* Christ saith to all the Apostles, *He that is washed and is all cleane, must still haue his feete washed, Ioh.* 13.10. Wherefore they are to be rebuked, that thinke there must bee no want at all in them that are Preachers of the Gospell: and hereupon take occasion to despise their Ministerie, if they can spie any thing amisse in their doings. Vpon the same ground, they might reiect the Ministerie, of the Apostles. For though they could not erre in preaching, and writing, and though they had no neede to be taught of any man, yet were they not free from sinne in their liues; and the chiefe of them sundrie times failed.

Againe, here we learne, that there is a good, and lawfull kind of boasting: and that is, when a man is disgraced, & his disgrace is the dishonour of God, and the disgrace of the Gospel. This makes *Paul* here to say, that *he learned nothing of the chiefe Apostles.* For if hee had said otherwise, he should haue bin reputed to bee no more but an ordinary disciple: & the doctrine, which he taught before this conference, should haue bin called in question. For this cause, he stands vpon it, that they did not communicate any thing vnto him. Vpon the like occasion he professeth that he will boast. 2. *Cor.* 11.16. Here the saying of *Salomō* may be obiected, *Let an other mans mouth praise thee, and not thine owne, Prou.* 27.2. I answer, it sufficeth for the truth of sundry prouerbs, if they be commonly, ordinarily, and vsually true, though they be not generally true. Thus ordinarily, men are not to praise themselues: yet in a speciall & extraordinarie case, it may be otherwise. And the maner which *Paul* vseth in commending himselfe, is to be obserued. First, he doth it in great modestie: because in speaking of himselfe, hee concealeth that part of the sentence, which should haue serued to expresse his praise. Secondly, in praising of himselfe, he is not carried with enuie, but his care is, to maintaine the good name of the rest of the Apostles; when he saith, *What they haue bin, it is no matter to me.* Here then we see, that the Atheists doe *Paul* wrong, who challenge him for pride, & presumption, as though he could not brooke an equall, and withall skorned to learne of any. Againe, by *Pauls* example we are to take notice of a common sinne. Mens hearts are so possessed with selfe-loue, and they are so addictid to their own praise, that it is griefe to them, to heare any praised beside themselues: whereas loue binds vs as wel to take care for the good name of others, as of our owne.

When *Paul* ſaith, *What they were in times paſt, it matters not to mee*: wee learne, that wee are to eſteeme of men, not as they haue been, but as they are. *Peter, Iames*, and *Iohn*, though they had been fiſhermen, yet they are honoured of *Paul* as Apoſtles. Therfore when men haue repented, wee may not vpbraid them with their liues paſt. Neither may we take occaſion to contemne them that bee in authoritie; becauſe wee haue knowne what they haue bene heretofore: but euery man is to bee eſteemed according to his calling, and according to the grace of God giuen him. Like is Gods mercifull dealing toward vs. For he accepts men, not as they haue been, but as they are when they repent. Therefore if Sathan ſhall at any time obiect thy life paſt: ſay vnto him thus: *Tell me not what I haue been: but tell mee what I am, and what I will bee*. This ſufficeth when we repent.

God accepteth the perſon of no man] By perſon is meant, not the ſubſtance of a man, or the man himſelfe, but the outward qualitie, or condition of man, as country, ſexe, birth, condition of life, riches, pouertie, nobilitie, wiſdome, learning. &c. And God is ſaid, *not to accept the perſon*, becauſe he doth call men, beſtow his gifts, and giue iudgement, according to his owne wiſe and iuſt pleaſure, and not according to the outward appearance, and condition of the perſon. Reade *Iob* 34.19. It may bee obiected, that God deales not equally with them that are equall: becauſe all men are equall in *Adam*, and of them hee chooſeth ſome to eternall life, and refuſeth others. I anſwer: he is ſaid to accept perſons, that deales vnequally with men, being bound to deale equally: now God is not thus bound: becauſe he is a Soueraigne, and abſolute Lord ouer all his creatures, and may doe with his owne what hee will, *Matth*. 20.16. Secondly, it may be obiected, that *God had reſpect to Abel and his ſacrifice, Gen*. 4.4. *Anſw*. The condition of man is twofold, outward, inward. Outward, ſtands in worldly and ciuill reſpects. Inward, ſtands in a pure heart, good conſcience, and faith vnfained. For this only was *Abel* reſpected, *Heb*. 11.4. Though God accept not the outward perſon, *yet in euery nation hee that feareth God, is accepted of him, Actes* 10.34. Thirdly, it may be obiected, that God iudgeth euery man according to his works. *Anſw*. Though works appeare outwardly, yet the root and ground of them is in the heart. And the iudgement of God is according to them, as they are the fruits of the faith of the heart.

The vſe. All men are in this to bee like vnto God their heauenly Father: not accepting perſons in their dealings. As Magiſtrates in the execution of iuſtice, *Deuter*. 1.17. Miniſters in teaching, and in the reproouing of ſinne, *Marke* 12.14. and all beleeuers, who are not to haue religion in acceptation of perſons, *Iames* 12.1. This acceptation is the ruine of ſocieties. And it is the common fault. For vſually electiõs are made, offices beſtowed, and iuſtice executed with partialitie, and with blinde reſpects to countrey, kinred, friendſhip, money.

Secondly, wee are all taught to feare the iudgement of God, and to prepare our ſelues with all diligence, that wee may be found worthy to ſtand before God in that great day. For we muſt come naked before him, and hee will haue no reſpect to our birth, our riches, our learning. Therefore it is good for vs now to put on Chriſt, that in him we may be accepted. For with him the Father is well pleaſed.

Thirdly, we may not ſet our hearts vpon the outward things of this world: becauſe God doeth not reſpect vs for them. But wee are earneſtly to ſeeke after the things that make vs accepted with God; as true faith, righteouſneſſe, and good conſcience, *Rom*. 14.17.

Againe, ſuperiours muſt bee admoniſhed to deale moderately with their inferiours, *Coloſſ*. 2.11. Againe, inferiours are to comfort themſelues, if they be oppreſſed: in that God the Iudge of all accepts no perſons.

Laſtly, heere wee learne, that when wee ſhall haue immediate fellowſhip with God in heauen, all outward reſpect of perſons ſhall ceaſe. God himſelfe, and the Lambe Chriſt Ieſus ſhall bee all in all to the Elect.

In the ende of the verſe *Paul* addes: *For they communicated nothing to mee*: but to the contrary, *Rom*. 1.12. may bee obiected. Where *Paul* deſires to come to Rome, *that he might bee comforted by their mutuall faith, both his and theirs*. *Anſwer*. Though the Apoſtles did communicate nothing to *Paul*, in reſpect of doctrine, or iudgment; yet might they, or the meaneſt beleeuers conferre ſomething vnto him in reſpect of comfort, or the confirmation of his faith: and thus much hee ſignifieth to the Romanes. Heere is a good *Item* for them that come to no Sermons, becauſe they can learne nothing. Put the caſe they were as learned as the Apoſtles, yet might they profit in hearing, reſpect of comfort, of faith, and good affection.

7 *But on the contrary, when they ſaw that the Goſpell ouer the vncircumciſion was committed vnto me, as* the Goſpel *the circumciſion was to Peter:*

8 *(For he that was mightie by Peter in the Apoſtleſhip ouer*

the

the circumcision, was also mightie by me toward the Gentiles.)
9 *And when Iames, and Cephas, and Iohn knew the grace of God that was giuen to mee, which are accounted pillars, they gaue to me, and to Barnabas, the right hand of fellowship, that we should preach to the Gentiles, and they vnto the Circumcision.*

The wordes of more difficultie are thus to be explaned. [*Contrariwise*] that is, they did communicate nothing to mee in way of correction, but on the contrary they gaue me the hand of fellowship. Againe, the words [*Circumcision,* and *Vncircumcision*] signifie the nation of the Iewes, and the Gentiles, the one circumcised, the other vncircumcised. And when *Paul* saith, that *the grace of God was giuen to him,* hee meanes specially, the gift of an Apostle, *Rom.* 1.5. Lastly, *to giue the right hand of fellowship to Paul,* is to esteeme and acknowledge him for their collegue, or fellow Apostle, by giuing the right hand in token thereof.

The contents of the words are these. Here *Paul* sets downe the third signe of his approbation, namely, that the chiefe Apostles acknowledged him for their fellow Apostle, verse 9. Secondly, he sets downe the maner how the cheefe Apostles acknowledged this fellowship: and that was, by making a couenant with *Paul,* that he should preach to the Gentiles, and *Peter* to the Iewes. Thirdly, he sets downe the impulsiue cause that mooued the Apostles to receiue *Paul* to their fellowship: and that was the decree of God, whereby he ordained, that *Paul* should bee the cheefe Apostle to the Gentiles, and *Peter* the cheefe Apostle among the Iewes, ver. 7. Lastly, he sets downe the signes, whereby the Apostles knew, that *Paul* was ordained the Apostle of the Gentiles: and they are two, the grace of God giuen him, and the power of his Ministery among the Gentiles, v. 8, 9. Furthermore, the things here contained, are in a Syllogisme disposed thus:

When the Apostles saw that I was ordained the chiefe Apostle of the Gentiles, and Peter of the Iewes, they acknowledged me for their fellow Apostle, and made a couenant with me, that I should preach to the Gentiles, and Peter to the Iewes.

But when I was with them at Ierusalem, they saw that I was ordained the chiefe of the Apostles of the Gentiles, and Peter of the Iewes.

This *minor* is omitted, yet the proofe thereof is set downe thus. For they saw the efficacie of my ministery among the Gentiles, and the grace of God that was with me. Therfore they acknowledged me for their fellow Apostle, &c.

The vſe. This text makes notably againſt the primacie of *Peter*. Firſt therefore let vs obſerue the Ordinance of God here plainely expreſſed, that *Paul* ſhould be the chiefe Apoſtle of the Gentiles, and *Peter* the chiefe Apoſtle of the Iewes. And this may elſewhere bee gathered. For the Commiſſion of the twelue Apoſtles ranne thus, that *they muſt firſt preach to Ieruſalem and Iudea, then to Samaria: and in the laſt place, to the vttermoſt parts of the earth*, *Actes* 1.8. And *Pauls* Commiſſion was, that he ſhould firſt preach to the Gentiles, and in the ſecond place to the people of Iſrael, *Act.* 9. 16. It may be obiected, that the Commiſſion of all the Apoſtles, was to goe into all the world, and to preach to all men without exception. *Mar.* 16. 15. *Anſwer.* This power and liberty Chriſt gaue to all the Apoſtles, and he did not take it away afterward: neuertheleſſe, he ordered it by a ſecond decree, that *Paul* ſhould ſpecially haue care of the Gentiles, and *Peter* of the Iewes. And this the Lord did in great wiſedome, that confuſion and diſcord might be auoided, and a regard had of all prouinces through the world.

Hence it followes, that the primacy of *Peter* ouer Iewes & Gentiles is a ſuppoſed thing. For the ordinance of God is, that *Peter* ſhal be chiefe *ouer the Iewes*, and not *ouer the Gentiles*, which were almoſt all the world beſide. And thus the ſupremacie of the Pope goes to the ground, for if hee hold of *Peter*, and ſucceed him in authoritie and office, (as he pretends) hee muſt challenge a ſuperioritie ouer the Iewes, and he hath nothing to doe with vs. For *Paul* was chiefe ouer the Gentiles, and not *Peter*.

Secondly, this Ordinance of God giues vs to vnderſtand, that the place, *Matt.* 16.18. *Thou art Peter, and vpon this rocke will I build my Church, &c. and I will giue thee the keyes of the kingdome of heauen*: doeth not containe a promiſe made to *Peter*, of a Primacie ouer all the Apoſtles, and ouer the Catholique Church. If Chriſt had meant any ſuch thing, in theſe words, he would not haue aſſigned the Iewes to *Peter*, and all the nations of the world beſide to *Paul*. Thus we ſee how this text for many hundred yeares hath beene abuſed, and is ſtill at this day.

Thirdly, it is falſe which the Papiſts teach, that the place in Saint *Iohn*, *Feed my lambes*, and, *feed my ſheepe*, giues a primacie to *Peter*, ouer the whole world. For by the ordinance of God, this feeding of lambes and ſheepe, is limitted to the nation of the Iewes.

Laſtly, wheras *Euſebius* ſaith in his Chronicle, that *Peter* was Biſhop of Rome, & ſate 25. yeares, it hath no likelihood of truth: for then *Peter* liued in the breach of an expreſſe commaundement of God for a loong time: becauſe the Iewes were his ſpeciall charge.

Againe,

Againe, it is to bee obserued in this text, that *Iames, Peter, Iohn,* are made equall, all beeing pillars; and *Iames* is first named: and that not without cause. For not *Peter*, but *Iames* was the President of the Councell of Ierusalem: because hee spake the last, and concludeded all, *Actes*, 15.13. Therefore the first naming of *Peter*, in other places of Scripture, is no sufficient proofe of his supremacie.

Thirdly, *Peter* heere is said to make a couenant with *Paul, that hee shall bee the Apostle of the Gentiles, and Peter of the Iewes.* But if *Peter* had been head of the Church for fourteene yeares together, and had but knowen the primacie which the Papists giue to him, hee would not haue consented to this order. It is alleadged, that *Paul* was the chiefe Apostle ouer the Gentiles, in respect of paines and labour, and not in respect of iurisdiction. I answere, this distinction hath no ground in the word of God. Againe, *Paul* was an Apostle, and vsed his Apostolicall authoritie ouer the Gentiles: and there is no *Ecclesiasticall person* that is, or can bee aboue an Apostle. For hee was simply to be beleeued in preaching and writing, and had extraordinary power giuen him by God, to punish them that rebelled.

Againe, *Paul* here saith, that *the Gospel was committed to him and Peter*, that is, that they were put in trust with it. Hence we learne 3. things. The first, that the Gospel is not ours, but Gods; & that men are but the kepers of it. For this we are to praise God. The second is, that the ministers of the word are to keepe and maintaine the truth of it with all faithfulnesse and good conscience: and further, to apply it to the best vse, and to the greatest good of men. For this charge lies vpon them that are put in trust. The third is, that the Gospel is a special treasure. For this we in England are to giue vnto God all thankfulnesse, specially, by bringing forth the fruits of the Gospel. In this dutie the most of vs come short: and therefore we may iustly feare, lest God take from vs the Gospel of life, and giue it to a nation that will bring forth the fruit of it.

Moreouer, in that *Paul* saith, that *God was mighty by him and Peter to the Iewes and Gentiles*, we are to consider the efficacy of the Ministery. Of it three cautions are to be obserued. The first, that grace or power to regenerate, is not included in the word preached, as vertue to heale in a medicine. *Paul* saith, *He that planteth, and he that watereth, is not any thing*, 1. *Cor*.3 7. To regenerate is the proper work of God, not agreeing to Angels, no not to the flesh of Christ, exalted aboue men and Angels. For the vertue to renewe or regenerate, is not in it as in a subiect, but in the Godhead of the Sonne.

The

The ſecond caution is, that grace is not inſeparably annexed, and tyed, to the word preached; for to ſome it is the ſauour of death, to death. The third is, that the preaching of the word is an externall inſtrument of faith, and regeneration: and the proper effect of it, is to declare, or ſignifie. And it is an inſtrument: becauſe when the Miniſters of the word, doe by it ſignifie and declare, what is to be done, and what is the will of God, the ſpirit of God inwardly inlightens the minde, and inclines the heart to beleeue, and obey. Hence we learne that it is a magicall fiction, to ſuppoſe that fiue words, *For this is my bodie*, ſhould tranſubſtantiate the bread, into the bodie of Chriſt. Secondly we learne, that the Sacraments doe not conferre grace, *ex opere operato, by the worke done*. For the word and Sacraments, are both of one nature (Sacraments beeing a viſible word.) Now the word and the preaching of it, doth not conferre grace, but onely declare what God will conferre. Thirdly by this it appeares, that charmes or ſpels, haue not force in them to cure diſeaſes, and to worke wonders, but by ſatanicall operation. For the beſt word of all, euen the word preached, hath it not. Laſtly, we are here to bee put in mind, that wee looſe no time in hearing of the word; for it is a meanes whereby we are cleanſed and renewed. *Euery branch that bringeth forth fruite, God purgeth it* by his word and other meanes, *that it may bring forth more fruite, Ioh.15.*

It is a thing to be obſerued, that the Apoſtles at Ieruſalem acknowledged *Paul* to be an Apoſtle: becauſe he had the gifts of an Apoſtle, and becauſe his miniſterie was powerfull among the Gentiles. Therefore, they which haue the gift of teaching, by whome alſo God is powerfull in the conuerſion of ſinners, are Miniſters certenly called of God. Let them thinke on this, that vtterly condemne the miniſterie of the Church of England. For many teachers among vs, can ſhew both the gift of teaching, and the power, or efficacy of their miniſtery.

It is worth the marking alſo, that the Apoſtles are called *Pillars*. Here we ſee, what is the charge of the miniſters of the word, namely, to ſuſtaine and to vphold the Church, by doctrine, praier, counſel, good life. *Elizeus* is called of *Ioas*, *The charriots and horſemen of Iſrael*, 2 King.13.4. And the Church of God vpon earth, is called *the Pillar and ground of truth*, in reſpect of the Miniſterie of the word. 1.*Tim.*3.15,

Againe, in that all Miniſters in their places (according to the meaſure of gifts receiued) are *pillars*, they are admoniſhed hereby to be conſtant in the truth, againſt all enemies whatſoeuer. It is the praiſe of *Iohn* the Baptiſt, that he was *not as a reed ſhaken of the winde*,

Matth.

*Matth.*11.7. All beleeuers are to stand fast in temptation, against their spirituall enemies, *Eph.*6.13. and this they shal the better doe, if they bee directed by the good example of their teachers.

Thirdly, in that Ministers are *pillars*, we are taught to cleaue vnto them, and their Ministerie, at all times, in life and death. For wee are *liuing stones in the temple of God.* Christ is our *foundation*, and they be *pillars* to hold vs vp: & therefore not to be forsaken, *Deut.*12.16.

Furthermore, *Paul* at this time was not accounted a pillar; for he saith thus: *Iames, Cephas, Iohn, are accounted pillars*; as who shold say, I am accounted none. Thus *Paul* goes through good report, and euill report, and is content to be contemned.

Lastly, the example of concord among the Apostles is to be obserued: in that they giue the right hands of fellowship one to another.

10 *Warning onely that we should remember the poore: which thing also I was diligent to doe.*

In these words, *Paul* sets downe the fourth and last signe of his approbation at Ierusalem, on this manner. At my departing the Apostles warned me to remember the poore, and of no other thing did they giue me warning: therefore there was a full and perfect consent betweene vs.

In the wordes, two things are set downe, the Apostolicall warning, and the practise of it by *Paul.* The warning in these words, [*Warning only that we should remember the poore.*] In them three points are to be considered. The first, that the Church of Ierusalem was in extreame pouertie. And the causes of it may be two. The first, because the poorer sort receiued the Gospel: thus it was in Corinth, 1. *Cor.*1, 26. *Not many wise according to the flesh, not many noble.* The like haue we in experience at this day: the poorer sort among vs doe more heartily receiue it then they of the richer sort. By this we are taught, that wee may not fixe our loue, and our confidence vpon riches: and they that buie, must be as though they bought not, and they that possesse, as though they possessed not. Because riches steale away the heart. The second cause of their pouertie was, that *they were depriued of their riches for the profession of the name of Christ.* 1. *Thess.*2.14. *Heb.*10, 34. Here we are taught to sit downe, and to recken what the profession of Christ will cost vs to the vttermost: and we must put this in our account, that we must bee readie, and willing to part with the dearest things in the world, for the name of Christ. And this reckning and resolution must wee daily carrie about with vs.

The

The second point is, Why the Church of Ierusalem must bee releeued by the Gentiles, considering by Gods law *Deut.* 15.11. euery place must releeue his owne poore. *Ans.* We are first of all, debters to our owne poore, and they must first be releeued: this done (in the case of extreme necessitie) we are debters to the poore a thousand miles off. And in this case, did the Apostles craue releefe of the Gentiles, for them of Ierusalem.

The third point is, that the Apostles themselues are carefull for the gathering of releefe. Hence wee learne, that it is the office of Pastours and teachers, not only to preach and dispence the word, but also to haue care of the poore: and this care is to be shewed in exhortation, counsell, ouersight. As for the administration and execution of matters belonging to the poore, it belongs to others. If the Apostles at any time gathered, carried, and dispensed releefe, it was because the Church was not yet founded, and planted, and therefore there was no other to doe it.

Now I come to the practise of *Paul*, in these words; *Which thing also I was diligent to doe it.* Here first let vs marke, that *Paul* who had spoiled and made hauocke of the Church of Ierusalem, now gathers releefe, (and as we say) begges for it, and no doubt, the rather that hee may make some recompence for the wrong hee had done. By his example wee are taught to make Satisfaction for all iniuries and hurts done to others, and that to the vttermost. Hee that steales, according to the qualitie of his theft, must restore either twofold, or fourefold, *Exod.* 22.7. he that maimes a man must *pay for his healing, and for his resting*, that is, for the losse of his labour, *Exod.* 21.19. *Daniel* saith to *Nebuchadnezzar*, *O King, breake off thy sinnes with almes deedes*, *Dan.* 4.24. that is, whereas thou hast bin giuen to crueltie, and oppression, cease to doe so any more, and make some recompence by giuing of almes. *Dauid* saith, it is the property of a wicked man, *to borrow, and not to repay*, *Psal.* 37.21. Satisfaction, recompence, and restitution, is the way to life by the appointment of God. *Ezech.* 18.7. and 33.15. *If thou restore the pledge, and repay that which thou hast robbed, thou shalt liue, and not die.* The Lord saith, *Are the treasures of wickednes yet in the house of the wicked?* & he addes, *that he will not iustifie the false ballance. Mich.* 6.10, 11, *Zacheus* in his conuersion, for knowen wrongs restores fourefold: and for his vnknown wrongs he giues halfe his goods to the poore. *Luk.* 19.7.

Let vsurers, ingrossers, and all that oppresse, or deale deceitfully, remember this; and begin to make conscience of this duty of Satisfaction, or restitution. And that it may the better bee practised, I will further set downe fiue points.

The firſt is,who muſt ſatiſfie and reſtore? *Anſwer*. He that is the cauſe of any wrong or loſſe to others: and all they that are acceſſary. Men may be acceſſary many wayes, by commaundement,by counſel,by conſent, by partnerſhip,by receiuing,by ſilence when a man ought to ſpeake,by not hindring when he ought to hinder,by not manifeſting that which he ought to manifeſt.

The ſecond is, To whom muſt reſtitution be made? *Anſw*. To him that is wronged, and beares the loſſe,(if the party be knowne and aliue:) if he be dead,to his heires: if all be dead,to the poore. If the perſon wronged be not knowen to vs (as often it falles out) then reſtitution is to be made to the Church,or commonwealth, and reſtitution is to be turned into almes for the poore,*Dan*.4.24. Moreouer, if both the giuing and the receiuing of a thing bee vnlawfull, as in bribes, and Simoniacall gifts; reſtitution is not to be made to the giuer,but as before,it is to be applied to common vſe, ſpecially to reliefe.

The third point is,What muſt be reſtored? *Anſwer*. The things which are of vs vniuſtly receiued,or deteined,either knowen to vs or vnknowne. If they be knowne,they are in their owne kind to be reſtored,or in value,*Exod*.21.19. If the party,who is to reſtore, be in extreme pouerty,& haue not wherwith to make recompenſe, he muſt doe that which he can, that is, he muſt ſhew a ready and willing minde: and this is done by confeſſion, and by crauing of pardon. If goods to be reſtored, be for their value and qualitie vnknowne,then reſtitution muſt be made according to the iudgment and diſcretion of them that are wiſe.

The fourth point is,touching the time when? *Anſw*. In reſpect of preparation of mind,we muſt preſently ſatiſfie: yet not in reſpect of execution. For the act of reſtitution may be deferred,if there be ignorance of the right,or ignorance of the fact,if the reſtorer be in extreme need: if vpon preſent reſtitution, life, goods, or good name be indangered.

The laſt point is,in what order and manner reſtitution is to bee made? *Anſ*. Things certain muſt firſt be reſtored,and things vncertain after. Among things certaine,that is,which certainly belongs vnto another, things bought & not deliuered, are to bee reſtored, and *Depoſita*,things committed to our truſt. If things to be reſtored for their value and qualitie be vncertain,the order is this;Reſtitution muſt be made(according to the diſcretion of wiſe men)in ſome part: and for the reſt, pardon to be craued. Againe, in reſtitution warineſſe is to be vſed,leſt by the ſupplying the loſſes of other men, we make to our ſelues the loſſe of a good name.

Againe, in *Pauls* practise wee see an earnest care and diligence to prouide for the poore. And his diligence is further expressed, *Romanes* 15.25,28. where it is said, that *hee ministred to the Saints at Ierusalem*, and withall that he gaue himselfe no rest in this dutie, till he had *sealed this fruite vnto them*, that is, till hee saw it done according to his desire. His example must bee followed of vs. It is not enough for vs to giue good wordes, and to wish well, but wee must in our places and callings doe our endeauour, that reliefe may euen bee sealed to our poore. And there bee many reasons to mooue vs. First, let vs consider that the charge was very great, to maintaine the Altar of the Lord in the old Testament with sheepe, and oxen, and offrings of all kindes: and now in the new Testament the poore come in the roome of the Altar. Secondly, the poore represent the person of Christ; and in them he comes vnto vs, and saith, *I am hungrie, I am sicke, I am naked, I am harbourlesse:* therefore looke what wee would doe to Christ, the same must we doe to them. Thirdly, the poore haue title and interest to part of our goods: for God is the Lord of them, and wee are but stewards to dispose and vse them, according to his appointment. And his will is, that part of our goods bee giuen for the reliefe of the poore. If this bee not done, wee are theeues in respect of the goods we possesse. Lastly, mercie, or the bowels of compassion in vs, is a pledge or an impression of the mercie that is in God towards vs: and by it we may know, or feele in our selues, that mercie belongs vnto vs. Thus we see what is our dutie: now let vs consider what is our fault. Not to blame any person or persons, it is our common fault, that we are backward and slacke in this dutie. And the cause is, that we doe not heartily giue our selues to Christ: and this makes vs to be so slack in giuing our goods to the poore, 2. *Cor.* 9.5. Againe, we commonly liue (as it were) without a law. Wee doe not with *Dauid*, set the lawes of God before vs, *Psal.* 119. v. 168. Neither doe we apply our hearts to his statutes, v. 112. For then would we with *Dauid*, *make haste to keepe the commandements of God*, vers. 60. specially this great commandement of reliefe: and the rather, because the obseruing of it is the inriching of vs all.

Lastly, let vs marke, that *Paul* being warned of the Apostles, was diligent to doe that wherof he was warned. The like must we doe. It is not sufficient to heare, but besides this, there must be in vs a care and diligence to do and practise that which we heare. For this is to build vpon the rocke. And it is a common fault, to heare much, and doe little, *Ezech.* 33.24.

11. *And*

11 *And when Peter was come to Antioch, I withstood him to his face: for he was to be blamed.*

In these words *Paul* propounds the second answer, which hee makes to the obiection mentioned in the beginning of the chapter, to this effect. Though the Church glorifie God for thee: yet will not the Apostles doe it: because thou art contrary to them. Here *Paul* answers, that there was indeed a dissention between him and *Peter*, when he withstood *Peter* to his face at Antioch: but the fault was not his, but *Peters*, who was *wholly to be blamed.*

For the better vnderstanding of these words, three points are to be handled. The first is, who was resisted? The answer is, *Peter* the Apostle. For the intent of this chapter is to shew what agreement there was betweene *Paul* and the rest of the Apostles. And there was no Apostle of this name but one. Therefore they among the Ancient are greatly deceiued, who thinke that the Apostle *Peter* was not reprooued, but some other of that name. The second point is, who resisted? *Answer. Paul*: and that not for shew and fashion, but in truth and good earnest. And this appeares, because in the words following, he sets downe a weightie and vrgent cause of his reproofe. Therefore *Ierom* and others are deceiued, who thinke that *Paul* reprooued *Peter* * *in shew and appearance*, and not in good earnest. The third point is, what was *Pauls* mind and meaning in resisting of *Peter*? *Answer.* To doe his office. The kingdom of God, and all things pertaining thereto, must haue free passage without resistance. The second petition is, *Thy kingdome come. Iohn the Baptist* preached thus, *Prepare the way of the Lord, and make his paths straight, Mar.* 1. Saint *Paul* saith, *Pray that the word of God may haue free passage, & be glorified*, 2.*Thess.* 3.1. Contrariwise, such things as hinder the kingdome of God must bee withstood. Therefore *Peter* saith, *Resist your aduersarie the diuell, strong in faith*, 1.*Peter* 5.9. And thus men that are instruments of euill, are to bee withstood. And here *Paul*, by an holy reproofe, withstands *Peter* for his bad example.

* Simulatè, non verè.

In *Paul* here first we may behold an example of true vertue, in that he resists euil to the vttermost of his power, following his own rule, *Abhorre that which is euill, and cleaue vnto that which is good, Rom.* 12.9. *Haue no fellowship with the vnfruitfull werkes of darknesse, but rather reprooue them*, *Ephes.*5.11. In like manner must euery one of vs resist euill; first, in himselfe, and then in them that appertaine to him. Therfore *Paul* saith to all, *Put on the armour of God, that ye may resist, Ephes.*6.13. Here two things may be demanded: first, *what must*

must wee resist? *Paul* answers againe, *Principalities, and powers, and spirituall wickednesses:* that is, the diuell and all his angels. It may be said, we haue no dealing with them, for they vse not to appeare vnto vs. *Answ.* That the diuell comes not to vs visibly, but in the persons of euill men, and in the bad examples of all men. This made Christ say to *Peter*, *Mat.* 16, 23. *Come behind me, Satan, for thou art an offence vnto me*, when *Peter* would haue disswaded him from going to Ierusalem. Again, it may be said, *In what things must we resist them? Paul* answereth, *In heauenly things*, v. 12. that is, in things which pertaine to Gods kingdome, and concerne either the saluation of our soules, or the worship of God. For the diuel seeketh by all maner of euils, to hinder these good things. Moreouer, this dutie of resisting euill, is so necessary, that we must resist sinne, if need be, to the very shedding of our blood, *Heb.* 12.4.

Againe, we haue in *Paul* an example of boldnesse and libertie in reproouing of sin. This was a thing commanded to the Prophets and Apostles, *Isai.* 58.1. *Crie and spare not, lift vp thy voice like a trumpet, shew my people their transgression. Ierem.* 1.17. *Trusse vp thy loynes, arise and speake vnto them all that I command thee: be not afraid of their faces, lest I destroy thee before them.* Like libertie may the Ministers of the word vse, obseruing *Pauls* rule. 2. *Tim.* 1.7. *God hath not giuen vs the spirit of feare, but of power and of loue, and of a sound minde.* Where he sets downe *three caueats.* First, that this libertie in reproouing, is not the fruit of a bold and rash disposition, but it is a fruit of Gods spirit, and so to be acknowledged. Reade *Mich.* 3.8. The second, that the vse of this liberty is to be ordered by a sound mind, wherby wee are able to giue a good account of our reproofes, both for the matter, and manner of them. The third is, that all our admonitions must bee seasoned and tempered with loue: that they tend to the good and saluation of them that are reprooued. These caueats obserued, libertie in reprouing, shall neuer want his blessing, *Isai.* 50.7.

Thirdly, here is an example in *Paul*, of an ingenuous and honest mind. When he sees *Peter* do amisse, he reprooues him to his face. Contrary to this, is the common practise in backbiting, whispering and tale-bearing, whereby it comes to passe, that when a man is in fault, euery man knowes it, saue he which is in fault. This vice the law of God expresly forbids, *Leu.* 19.16. And it is the property of a good man, *not to take vp a false report*, *Psal.* 15. And *Dauid* reprooues *Saul*, because he did but lend the eare to tale-bearers, saying, *Wherefore giuest thou an eare to mens words that say, behold, Dauid seeketh euill against thee?* 1. *Sam.* 24.10.

In *Peter*, who when hee was reprooued, made no reply, wee ſee an example of patience and humilitie, whereby he humbled himſelfe before the reproouer, when he was conuicted of an offence. The like was in *Dauid*, when hee ſaid, *Let the righteous ſmite mee*, *Pſalm.* 141. v 5.

Whereas *Paul* ſaith, that *Peter* was to be blamed, or condemned, not in reſpect of his perſon, but of his example: we ſee that excellent men, euen the chiefe Apoſtles are ſubiect to erre, and be deceiued. It may be ſaid, how then may we truſt them in their writings? I anſwer, while they were in deliuering any thing to the Church, whether it were by Sermon, or writing, they were guided by the infallible aſſiſtance of the ſpirit, and could not erre. Otherwiſe they might erre, when they were out of this worke, in mind, will, affection, or action. Thus *Ionas*, when he ſaw that *Niniue* was not deſtroyed, was impotent in his anger. *Nathan* was deceiued in giuing aduice to *Dauid*, touching the building of the temple. 2. *Sam.* 7. The Apoſtles at the aſcenſion of Chriſt, ſtill dreamed of an earthly kingdome, ſaying, *When wilt thou reſtore the kingdome of Iſrael?* *Act.* 1. And *Peter* beeing bidden to ariſe, and eate of things forbidden by the ceremoniall law, ſaid, *Not ſo Lord*, *Act.* 10. 14.

Thus then, if *Peter* was ſubiect to errour, the pretended ſucceſſours of *Peter*, namely, the Biſhops of Rome, cannot bee free from errour. It is alleadged, that *Peter* erred in life; and not in doctrine. I anſwer, it was ſo indeed: yet did his bad example tend to the ruine of doctrine, if it had not bin preuented. Therefore the errour that was in acte, if we reſpect the euent, was in doctrine. Againe, I anſwer, that an errour in action, preſuppoſeth an errour in minde, or at the leaſt, ſome ignorance: becauſe the mind is the beginning of the thing done. Thus all ſinners are called *ignorant perſons*, *Hebr.* 5. 2. And it ſeemes that the errour of *Peter* was, that of two euils, it was the beſt to chooſe the leſſe: that is to chooſe rather to offend the Gentiles, then the Iewes, to whom he was an Apoſtle ſpecially appointed.

Here againe wee miſerable wretches are taught to watch and pray, that God would not leade vs into temptation: conſidering moſt excellent men are ſubiect to falling. And men muſt bee warned not to abuſe *Peters* example in boulſtering themſelues in their naughtie waies: by ſaying, wee are all ſinners, that the beſt man aliue is a ſinner, that the iuſt man falles ſeuen times a day. For the place in the *Prouerbes* 24. 16. is ſpoken of affliction, not of ſinne: the iuſt man falles ſeuen times a day, that is, he falles into manifold perills. And further, we ſhould not onely conſider the faults of iuſt men, but alſo their conuerſion and repentance. And againe, to ſinne, and to commit ſinne, are two diuers things. Though the godly ſinne, yet doe they not keepe a courſe in ſinning, and goe on from ſinne to ſinne.

12 *For before certaine came from Iames, hee ate with the Gentiles: but when they were come, he withdrew himſelfe, fearing them that were of the circumciſion.*

13 *And other Iewes diſſembled likewiſe with him: in ſo much that Barnabas was brought into their diſſimulation alſo.*

The Apoſtle hath propounded his ſecond anſwer in the former verſe: now he proceeds to make a declaration of it. And firſt he ſets downe the cauſe why *Peter* was reproued, and the maner of reproofe. The cauſe is in the 12.& 13. verſes, namely *Peters* ſin. And this ſinne is ſet forth by foure things. By the name of the ſin, the matter of the ſinne, the cauſe of the ſinne, the effects of the ſinne.

The name of the ſinne is noted, when *Paul* ſaith, *And other Iewes diſſembled likewiſe with him, verſe* 13. where I gather, that *Peters* ſin was *Simulation. Simulation* of it ſelfe is a thing indifferent, and according to circumſtances is either good or euill. Lawfull ſimulation is, when men conceit that which they may lawfully conceit, and ſignifie ſomething either by word or deed, that is onely beſide the truth, and not contrarie to it. This was the *Simulation* of *Ioſeph*, who carried himſelfe as a ſtranger to his brethren in Egypt, after he had examined them, and knew who they were, *Geneſis* 42. This was the *Simulation* of Chriſt, who when hee was come to Emaus, *made as though hee would haue gone further, Luke* 24.28. Thus *Paul* among the Iewes, plaid the Iew, 1. *Cor.* 9.20. Vnlawfull *Simulation* is that, when ſomething is ſignified, or fained againſt the truth, or to the preiudice of any. Of this kinde was the ſimulation of *Peter*, which tended to the preiudice of the Goſpel; and to the offence of the Gentiles.

The ſecond point is, the matter of the ſinne or the ſinne it ſelfe, which was on this maner. Firſt, among the Gentiles at Antioch, he vſeth Chriſtian libertie, in eating things forbidden by the ceremoniall law: yet after the coming of certaine Iewes from Ieruſalem, he ſeparates himſelf from the Gentiles, & plaies the Iew among the Iewes. Like to this was the halting of the Iſraelites betweene God and Baal, 1. *King.* 18.21. and the practiſe of ſundry men who are Proteſtants with vs; & yet in other countries go to Maſſe: and the practiſe of our people, who change their religion with the times.

Here

Heere wee ſee the great weakneſſe of *Peter*, in that vpon a very little occaſion, and that preſently, falles away from his profeſſion to his old courſe. In him we may behold our owne weakneſſe, and conſider what we are like to doe in like caſe. We now profeſſe the Goſpel of Chriſt: yet if any occaſion were offered, it is to be feared, that many of vs would be eaſily mooued to returne to our old prophanenеſſe, and to the ſuperſtition of Poperie. But for the ſtaying and the better eſtabliſhing of our minds, let vs alwaies remember, that they ſhal periſh who withdraw themſelues from their faith, profeſſion, and obedience, which they owe vnto God, *Hebr.* 10.38. *Pſal.* 73.27.

Againe, here it muſt bee obſerued, that *Paul* in deſcribing the ſinne, expreſſeth two actions, *his eating with the Gentiles*, and *his ſeparation from them*, the firſt good, and the latter euil. The beginning of his action was good, but the end of it was naught. The reaſon is this: the man regenerate is partly fleſh, and partly ſpirit: and herevpon it is, that when we wil that which is good, we cannot accompliſh it, and euill is preſent with vs. The child of God is like a lame man that goes the right way, but yet halts at euery ſtep. *Abraham* and *Sara* deſire iſſue, that is from the ſpirit: but they deſire iſſue by *Agar* their handmaid, that is from the fleſh. *Rebecca* ſeeks the bleſſing for *Iacob*, that is a worke of the ſpirit: but ſhe ſeekes it by lying, that is from the fleſh: *Peter* eates with the Gentiles, that is from Chriſtian libertie: hee afterwards ſeparates himſelfe, that is from corruption. Thus we ſee that the beſt works are imperfect, & mixed with corruption: and that for the beſt works we muſt humble our ſelues, and ſeeke pardon; not in reſpect of the goodneſſe of the worke, but in reſpect of the defect thereof.

It may be demanded, how the act of *Peter* ſhould be a ſin, conſidering he did onely abſtaine from certaine meats, that he might auoid the offence of certain Iewes? *Anſwer.* The fact of *Peter*, conſidered by it ſelfe, is not a ſinne: for *Paul* did the like in playing the Iew: but the circumſtance makes it a ſin. For firſt of all *Peter* doth not only abſtaine from meats forbidden by the ceremoniall law, but alſo he withdraws himſelfe from the company of the Gentiles, and keepes company apart with the Iewes. Secondly, he abſtaines not among the Iewes at Ieruſalem, but at Antioch among the Gentiles, where a little before he had openly done the contrary, in vſing his Chriſtian liberty. Thirdly, he vſed this abſtinence when certain Iewes came from Ieruſalem, to ſearch out the libertie of the Gentiles. Fourthly, while *Peter* ſeeks to auoid the ſmall offence of ſome Iewes, he incurres a greater offence of all the Gentiles. Laſtly, this act of *Peter* did tend to the ouerthrowing of *Pauls* miniſterie, and the ſuppreſſing of the truth of the Goſpel. Thus then the acte of *Peter* becomes vnlawfull, that was otherwiſe lawfull, being ſimply conſidered by it ſelfe. Here it may be demanded, what *Peter* ſhould haue done? *Anſwer*. He ſhould haue openly withſtood the Iewes that came from Ieruſalem: as *Paul* withſtood them that vrged the circumciſion of *Titus*: Or againe, before he had plaid the Iew, he ſhould haue aduertiſed the Gentiles, that for a time he was to yeeld to the infirmitie of ſome Iewes.

In *Peters* example we are taught, that we muſt not offend God, though all the world be offended. Leſſe offences muſt giue place, when the great offence is at hand: that is, when God is diſhonoured, and the very leaſt part of his truth is ſuppreſſed.

The third point to be conſidered, is, the cauſe of the ſinne of *Peter*: and that was the feare of the offence of the Iewes. Heere two queſtions are to be handled. The firſt, how *Peters* feare ſhould bee a ſinne? *Anſw*. There is a naturall feare created by God, and placed in the heart of man. This feare of it ſelfe is good. Neuertheleſſe by the corruption of nature it becomes euill. And it is made euill two waies. One is, when men feare without cauſe, as when the diſciples feare Chriſt walking vpon the ſea, & feare drowning when Chriſt was in the ſhip with them. The other is, when there is no meaſure in feare. As when men ſo feare the creature, that they neglect their dutie to God. This was *Peters* feare, and it was a ſinne in him. For God is to be feared, ſimply becauſe he is Lord of body and ſoule, and can deſtroy both: and he is to be feared for himſelfe, whereas euery creature is to be feared in part only, and for God, *Rom.* 13. 3, 4. By this wee are taught, daily to inure our ſelues in our hearts to feare God aboue all things.

The ſecond queſtion is, how *Peter* could haue the feare of God, conſidering he feared men more then God, at the leaſt in this one action? *Anſw*. There are three kinds of feare. One is, without all ſin: this was in *Adam*, and in Chriſt. The ſecond is altogether ſinfull in the wicked and vngodly, becauſe it is ſeuered from faith and obedience: as when there is a feare of men, without the feare of God. The third is a mixed feare in them that are regenerate, in whom the feare of God is ioyned with the corrupt feare of man. And in this mixture otherwhiles the one preuailes, otherwhiles the other. And this feare was in *Peter*: in whom at this time the carnall feare of man preuailed againſt the true feare of God.

Paul notes feare to bee the cauſe of *Peters* ſinne, that hee may thereby ſignifie vnto vs, what kinde of ſinne it was, namely, a

ſinne

ſinne,not of *malice*,but of *infirmitie*. A ſinne of infirmitie is,when there is a purpoſe in the heart not to ſinne: and yet for all this,the ſinne is committed, by reaſon the will is ouercarried by temptation,or by violence of affection,as by feare, anger, luſt. Thus *Peter* ſinned. And let it bee remembred, that to ſinne of infirmitie is properly incident to ſuch as bee regenerate, as *Peter* was. Euery wicked man makes his ſinne his infirmitie: fornication is the infirmitie of the fornicator,drunkenneſſe the infirmitie of the drunkard,&c.but it is falſe which they ſay. For they ſinne with all their hearts when they ſinne.

The fourth and laſt point is,the Effect of *Peters* ſinne,in drawing the Iewes,and *Barnabas*,to the like diſſimulation. Here we ſee the contagion of an euill example. And hence we learne, that Miniſters of the word muſt of neceſſity ioyne with good doctrine, the example of good life. For firſt of all,it is the expreſſe commandement of God, 1.*Pet*.5.3.*Be patternes of the flocke*, 1 *Tim*.4.12.*Be an example in word,conuerſation,loue,ſpirit,faith,puritie*,*Phil*.4.8.*What yee haue ſeene in me,that doe*. *Math*.5.16.*Let your light ſo ſhine before men, that they may ſee your good workes*. Secondly, practiſe in the Miniſter is a part of his teaching. For the multitude doe not marke ſo much what men ſay,as what men doe. *Herod* did many things, not becauſe *Iohn* the *Baptiſt* was *a good Miniſter*, but becauſe hee was *a good man*, *Marke* 6.20. Thirdly, Miniſters haue not the preſence and protection of God, vnleſſe their liues bee vertuous and godly. *If thou returne, thou ſhalt ſtand before me*, *Ierem*. 15.19. *God reueales his ſecrets to the Prophets his ſeruants*, *Amos* 3. 7. Laſtly, fearefull iudgements of God belong to Miniſters of wicked liues. Deſtruction befalles the ſonnes of *Eli*, and their families, becauſe they by leud example made the people of God to ſinne, 1 *Sam*. 2.24. The like beſell the ſonnes of Aaron for their preſumption.

Againe, all ſuperiours are warned to goe before their inferiours by good example. When *Moſes* went into Egypt to be the guide of the Iſraelites,the Lord would haue deſtroied him, by reaſon of the bad example in his owne family,namely,the vncircumciſion of his child. *Dauid*,for his euill example, whereby he cauſed the enemies of God to blaſpheme, is puniſhed, and that after his repentance,that men might ſee in him an example of Gods iudgement againſt ſinne, 2.*Sam*.12.14.

Heere againe we ſee, that the conſent of many together, is not a note of truth. *Peter*, *Barnabas*, and the Iewes, all together are deceiued, and *Paul* alone hath the trueth. *Ponormitane* ſayeth, that

that *a laie-man bringing Scripture, is to be preferred before a whole Councell.* *Paphnutius* alone had the truth, and the whole Councell of *Nice,* inclined to errour.

14 *But when I ſaw that they went not with a right foote to the truth of the Goſpel, I ſaid to Peter before all men: If thou beeing a Iew liueſt as the Gentiles, and not like the Ievves, vvhy conſtraineſt thou the Gentiles to doe like the Iewes?*

In theſe words, *Paul* ſets downe the reproofe of *Peter,* and the whole manner of it. In it, many points are to be conſidered. The firſt is, the time of this reproofe: and that was ſo ſoone as *Paul* ſaw the offence of *Peter.* Here we learne, that we muſt reſiſt, and cut off the firſt beginnings of temptation, of ſinne, and of ſuperſtition, becauſe we are prone to euill: and therefore if it once ſet footing in vs, it will take place.

The ſecond point is, the foundation of the reproofe in theſe wordes [*when I ſaw,*] and that is a certen knowledge of *Peters* offence. Here we are to take notice of the common fault, and that is, that we vſe to cenſure, and condemne men, ſpecially publike perſons, vpon ſuſpitions, and coniectures, and hereſay. Whereas we ſhould not open our mouthes to reprooue, till wee haue certen knowledge of the fault. Moreouer, publike perſons, as Magiſtrates and Miniſters, haue their priuiledge, that an accuſation is not to be receiued againſt them, without there bee a proofe by two or three witneſſes. 1. *Tim.* 5.20.

The third point is, the fault reprooued, which is here expreſſed by an other name, *not to walke with a right foote to the truth of the Goſpel:* that is, not to conuerſe with men, and to carrie himſelfe ſo as he may bee ſutable to the ſinceritie of the Goſpel, both in word, and deede.

Here is a notable dutie ſet downe for all men, *To walke with an euen foote according to the truth of the Goſpell:* and this is done, when in word and deede, and euery way, we aſcribe all the good we haue, or can doe, to grace, to mercie, and to Chriſt: when again, in word, and deede, and euery way, we giue all thanks to God for grace and mercie by Chriſt. Here two ſorts of men are to be condemned, as haulters in reſpect of the truth of the Goſpel. The firſt, are Papiſts, who ioyne Chriſt and workes in the cauſe of our iuſtification, and ſaluation. The ſecond, are carnall Proteſtants, and all other ſorts of men, that profeſſe the name of Chriſt, & withal challenge to themſelues a libertie to liue as they liſt. For they walke contrarie to the Goſpel, diſioyning Iuſtification and Sanctification, Faith and good

good life, remission of sinne, and mortification. This is the rife and common sinne of our daies.. We are light in the Lord, but wee walke not as children of light. We are content to come to the marriage of the Kings sonne, but we come not with the marriage garment. It is to be feared, this very sinne will banish the Gospel, and bring all the iudgements of God vpon vs. Let vs therefore, repent of our vneuen and haulting liues: and preuent the Lords anger, by walking worthie the Gospel of Christ.

It will be said, how must we performe this dutie? *Ans.* Two rules must be remembred. The first is, that we must haue and carrie in vs a right heart. For the want of this was *Simon Magus* condemned, *Act.*8.21. A right heart is an humble & an honest heart. The humble heart is, when in the estimation of our owne hearts, wee abase our selues vnder all creatures vpon earth, and that for our offences: when againe, in the affection of our hearts, we exalt the death, and blood of Christ, aboue all riches, aboue all honours, aboue all pleasures, aboue all ioyes, & aboue all that heart can thinke, or tongue can speake. The honest heart is, when we carrie, and cherish in our hearts the setled purpose of not sinning: so as if we sin at any time, we may in the testimonie of a good conscience say, that we sinned against our purpose. The second rule is, that we must make straight steppes to our feete, *Heb.*12.13. And that is done, when wee endeauour to obey God, according to all his commandements, *Psal.* 119. 6. and also, according to all the powers of the inward man, that is, not onely in action, but also in will, affection, and thought. Let vs also applie our hearts to the doing of this, least if we come to the marriage of the kings son without the garment of a right heart and life, we heare the sentence, *Binde them hand and foote, and cast them into vtter darknes, there shall be weeping and gnashing of teeth.*

The fourth point is, the place of reproofe [*before all men:*] for they that sinne openly to the offence of many, are openly to be reprooued. 1.*Tim.*5.20.

The fifth point is, concerning the reasons which *Paul* vseth for the restraining of the sinne of *Peter*. The first is set down in the 16. verse, *If thou beeing a Iew, &c.* Here the meaning of some words are to be opened. To *Iudaize*, or *to liue as a Iew*, is to obserue (and that necessarily,) a difference of meates, and times, according to the ceremonial law of *Moses*. To *Gentilize*, or *to liue as Gentile*, is to vse meates, and drinkes, and times, freely without difference. *Peter* is said, *to compell the Gentiles to Iudaize*, not by teaching of any doctrine (for the Apostles neuer erred, in teaching and deliuering any thing to the Church of God: this is a principle:) therefore hee

con-

constrained them by the authoritie of his example: wherby he caused them to thinke that the obseruation of the Cereremonial law was necessary.

The first reason then is framed thus: If thou beeing a Iew, vsest to liue as the Gentiles, thou maist not by thy example compel the Gentiles to Iudaize in the necessarie obseruation of ceremonies: but thou beeing a Iew, vsest to liue as the Gentiles: therefore thou maist not compell the Gentiles to liue as Iewes.

Here first, let vs obserue the force of euill example: it compells men to be euill. Therefore let all superiours, Magistrates, Ministers and all gouernours of families looke to their examples. For if they be euill, they constraine others also to be euill.

Here againe, we see what wonderfull subiection the ancient beleeuers yeelded to the ministery of the word. For if the actions of the Apostles compelled men to do this or that, what then did their doctrines, and heauenly exhortations doe? When *Iohn* the Math.11.12. Baptist preached, *the kingdome of heauen suffered violence, and the violent tooke it to themselues*. Luk.10.18. When the disciples preached in Iewrie, *they* 2.Cor.10.4. *saw Satan falling down from heauen like lightning*. The weapons of *Paul* were *spirituall, to cast downe holds, and to bring euery thought in subiection to God*. Here, the fault of our time is to be considered. We haue the forme of godlines, in hearing and in outward profession, but wee want the power of it. For we doe not in heart yeeld subiection by suffering our selues to be vrged, and compelled to obedience by the authoritie of the Ministrie.

Thirdly, here we see wherein stood *Peters* sinne: namely in that he constrained men to a necessarie obseruation of the Ceremonial law: by his example binding the Gentiles to the doing of that which the Gospel hath made free. Therefore great is the wickednes of the Romane religion: in that it placeth a necessitie in many things, in the vse whereof, Christ hath procured vs an holy, and Christian libertie. In this respect the vowes of perpetuall continencie, of pouerty, and regular obedience, are falsly tearmed *states of perfection*: and are indeede *estates of abomination*.

15 *We which are Iewes by nature, and not sinners of the Gentiles:*

16 *Know that a man is not iustified by the workes of the law, but by the faith of Iesus Christ: which (I say) haue beleeued in Iesus Christ, that we might be iustified by the faith of Iesus Christ, and not by the workes of the law: because by the workes of the law, no flesh shall be iustified.*

Here

Here *Paul* layes downe the ſecond reaſon of his reproofe: it is framed thus. That which we defend, both in iudgement and practiſe, that muſt we vrge, and not the contrary: but iuſtification by faith without works wee defend both in iudgement aud practiſe: therfore we muſt vrge it, and not the contrary, namely, the neceſſary obſeruation of the law.

The *maior* is wanting: the *minor* is expreſſed in the 16. verſe, and it is amplified by an argument of things diuers, thus: Though we be Iewes to whom the law was giuen; yet we forſake the law, and looke to be iuſtified by the faith of Chriſt. Secondly, the *minor* is confirmed by a teſtimony of the *Pſalme* v. 16. *By the works of the law no fleſh ſhall be iuſtified.*

Here two points are to bee handled. One, of the diſtinction of the Iewes and Gentiles: the other, of iuſtification.

Touching the diſtinction of Iewes and Gentiles, ſundry points are to be handled. The firſt, what is the cauſe of this diſtinction? *Anſwer*. The good will and pleaſure of God. *Moſes* ſaith, *God choſe the Iſraelites aboue all nations*, *Deut*. 7.6. *hee loued them*, *Deut*. 10.15. *when he diuided the nations, Iacob was his portion*; *Deut*. 32.8. *Hee knew them aboue all nations*, ſaith *Amos* 3.1. And he choſe them, becauſe *he loued their fathers*, *Deut*. 4.37. Hence we gather, the free election of God: and that they are deceiued, who thinke, that there was no difference of Iewes and Gentiles in reſpect of God, but in reſpect of themſelues: becauſe the one imbraced Chriſt, the other refuſed Chriſt. But there cannot be a refuſall where the Meſſias was not knowne: and among the Gentiles he was not ſo much as named, *Rom*. 15.20.

The ſecond point is, wherin ſtands the difference of Iewes and Gentiles. *Anſw*. Here the Iewes are oppoſed to ſinners of the Gentiles: and therfore by the Iewes are meant an holy & peculiar people. The diſtinction therfore lies in this, that the one was holy, the other prophane: the one in the couenant, the other out of the couenant, *Rom*. 9.4, 5. *Pſal*. 147.20. Here two errors muſt be auoyded. One, that the difference lay in earthly things: which is not true. For the law was giuen to the Iſraelites: and it was *a ſchoolemaſter to Chriſt*, *Gal*. 3. and *an introduction to a better hope*, *Heb*. 7.19. The ſecond errour is, that they differed only in this, that Chriſt was more plentifully and fully reuealed to the Iewes: more darkly and ſparingly to the Gentiles, But it was otherwiſe. For the Gentiles were *without God and Chriſt*, *Ephe*. 2.12. and they were left to themſelues, *to walke in their owne wayes*, *Act*. 14.16.

The third point is, how long this difference endured? *Anſwer*.

Till

Till the death of Chriſt. For the Diſciples were forbidden to goe into the way of the Gentiles,*Math.*10.5. And Chriſt ſaith,that *hee was not ſent, but to the loſt ſheepe of the houſe of Iſrael, Mat.*15.22. It may be obiected,that here we ſee the difference of Iewes and Gentiles,is ſtanding,long after the aſcenſion of Chriſt. *Anſ.* Chriſt in his death did fully merit the aboliſhment of this difference.*Eph*,2. Neuertheleſſe the execution of this aboliſhment was by degrees: and it was at this time begun by the miniſtery of the Apoſtles,yet not accompliſhed.

The laſt point is, that the Iewes are an holy people by nature: not becauſe holines is conueied to them by generation,but becauſe euen from their beginning, and birth, by vertue of the couenant, they are holy. *If the roote be holy,the branches are holy,Rom.*11.16. If either of their parents beleeue,*the children are holy*, 1.*Cor.*7.14. In a ciuill contract,the father and his heire make but one perſon,and the father couenants for himſelfe,and his poſterity: euen ſo,in the couenant of grace,he beleeues for himſelfe,and withall makes his poſterity partaker of the ſaid couenant: and thus the poſterity becomes holy. It may be obiected,that whatſoeuer is borne of fleſh is fleſh. *Anſwer* The parent ſuſtaines a double perſon. Firſt, he is to be conſidered as a childe of *Adam*, and thus he brings forth a childe, hauing with *Adams* nature,*Adams* corruption. Againe,he is to be conſidered as a beleeuer: and thus albeit he doth not propagate his faith and holineſſe to his child, yet by meanes of his faith, his childe is in the couenant, and conſequently is to be accounted holy in the iudgement of charitie, till God manifeſt the contrary. Againe,it may be obiected,that if the children of beleeuing parents be borne holy,they want originall ſinne.*Anſw.* The children alſo ſuſtaine two perſons. Firſt, they are conſidered as children of the firſt *Adam*: and thus they are conceiued and borne in ſinne, and are children of wrath. Againe,they are to be conſidered as children of beleeuing parents: and thus by meanes of the couenant, they are children of God; and originall ſin which is in them is couered from their firſt beginning, and not imputed to them.

The vſe. There was no abſolute neceſſity of circumciſion. For they which dyed before the eighth day,were borne holy,and conſequently,in the couenant: and therefore might be ſaued. And thus Baptiſme was not of abſolute neceſſity: for the children of beleeuers are borne holy and Chriſtian: and therefore dying in the want of Baptiſme,may for all that be ſaued. The ſeale of the couenant is not of like neceſſity,with the couenant it ſelfe.

Secondly, here we learne, that it is not the act of Baptiſme to conferre the firſt grace: but onely to confirme, and ſeale it vnto vs. Adoption, and life begins not in Baptiſme, but before. *If the roote be holy, the branches* ſpringing thence *are holy*. We are borne Chriſtians, if our parents beleeue, and not made ſo in Baptiſme.

Laſtly, if we be borne holy: it is our ſhame that we haue made no more proceeding in holineſſe, then we haue done: the moſt remaine ignorant, and vnreformed; and they of the better ſort, either ſtand at a ſtay, or goe backward.

The ſecond point is, concerning Iuſtification in the 16.v. of which ſundry things are there propounded. And firſt, I will begin with the name. The word, *Iuſtifie*, is borrowed from courts of iudgement, and ſignifies a iudiciall act. Otherwhiles it is put for the action of the iudge, and then it ſignifies to abſolue, or to pronounce innocent. Thus *Paul* ſaith, *Act.* 13.39. *That we are iuſtified from all things, from which we could not be iuſtified by the law of Moſes*, that is, abſolued, or cleered. Againe, he oppoſeth iuſtification to accuſation, and condemnation, *Rom.* 8.33. Now the contrary to condemnation, is abſolution. Sometimes againe, the word *Iuſtifie*, ſignifies the act of the party iudged, or of the witneſſes: and then it imports as much, as to giue teſtimony, or to declare and approoue. Thus *Iames* ſaith, *Abraham was iuſtified by workes*, chap.2.v.22. that is, declared, and approoued to be a iuſt man by workes. In the former ſignification is the word vſed, where the holy Ghoſt deliuereth the doctrine of iuſtification, as in this place.

The vſe. Here we ſee how to diſtinguiſh betweene Iuſtification, regeneration, and renouation. Regeneration is vſually in ſcripture, the change of the inward man, whereby we are borne anew. Renouation is, the change both of the inward and outward man, that is, both of heart and life. Iuſtification, is neither, but a certaine action in God applied vnto vs, or a certaine reſpect or relation, whereby we are acquit of our ſinnes, and accepted to life euerlaſting. Secondly, we muſt here note, that the Teachers of the Church of Rome, miſtake the word, *Iuſtification*. For by it, they vnderſtand nothing elſe, but a phyſicall tranſmutation of the quality, and diſpoſition of our hearts from euill, to good. And by this miſtaking, they haue made a mixture or rather confuſion, of the law and Goſpel. Thirdly, here we ſee, what is to be the diſpoſition of the party iuſtified: (for by the conſequent we may learne the antecedent.) A man therefore that would be iuſtified, muſt come before the iudgement ſeate of God, and there muſt he plead guilty, and be his owne aduerſary, condemning himſelfe: and being preſſed with the

terrours

terrours of the law, he muſt flie and make his appeale to the throne of grace, for pardon in Chriſt: and then he ſhall be acquit, or iuſtified from all ſinnes. Thus much doth the word, *iuſtifie*, import. Thus came the Publican before God, *Luk.* 18. when he ſaid, *Lord, be mercifull to me a ſinner*; and departed iuſtified. Thus in the fift petition, we are taught to come euery day into the preſence of God, and to acknowledge our debts, and to vſe the plea of mercie, ſaying, *Forgiue vs our debts*.

The ſecond thing to be conſidered, is the ſubiect of iuſtification, or the perſon to be iuſtified, and that is man generally, ſignifying that *a man is iuſtified.* The holy Ghoſt ſpeaketh thus generally, for two cauſes. The firſt is; becauſe all men without exception haue need of iuſtification, euen they which are regenerate, *Rom.* 3. 23. And in this place *Paul* ſaith, that he, and *Peter*, and the reſt, *haue beleeued in Chriſt, that they might be iuſtified by faith.* Here we are to take notice of the miſerable condition of prophane, and ſecure Epicures, who neuer ſo much as dreame of any iuſtification. The ſecond reaſon is; becauſe God communicates the benefit of iuſtification, generally to all ſorts of men: and this he doth in the Miniſtery of the word, in which he *beſeecheth men to be reconciled to God.* 2. *Corinth.* 5. v. 21. This muſt be an inducement vnto vs, to come vnto Chriſt, humbling, and iudging our ſelues, that wee may bee iuſtified. God himſelfe from heauen vſeth reaſons vnto vs daily, to mooue vs to the practiſe of this duetie. What meane theſe gracious and continuall preſeruations of Prince and people, Church and land? By them wee ſee, it is the good pleaſure of God, to giue vs a time to ſeeke his kingdome and righteouſneſſe: wherefore let vs not neglect the day of viſitation, but take the time while it ſerues, that wee may turne vnto God, and bee accepted of him, and eſcape the woe pronounced vpon Corazin and Bethſaida.

The third thing to bee conſidered, concernes things excluded from iuſtification, as falſe cauſes: namely the workes of the law. Here it may be demanded, what works are meant. I *anſwer*, firſt, not onely workes of the ceremoniall, but alſo of the morall law. For all men know, that ceremoniall actions are of no vſe, vnleſſe they be ioyned with moral duties of loue and mercy. And if *Paul* meant onely ceremoniall workes, hee needed not to haue made ſo long a diſcourſe againſt iuſtification by works: for he might haue ended the whole matter in a word or twaine, by ſhewing that the ceremoniall law, was abrogated by Chriſt. Secondly, I anſwer, that not onely workes done before faith, are excluded, but alſo workes that

that follow faith, and are done in the eſtate of grace. For *Paul* here reaſons thus: If no fleſh be iuſtified by workes, then not we beleeuers: but no fleſh at all is iuſtified by workes: therefore not we beleeuers. *Dauid. Pſal.* 143. reaſoneth of the ſame manner: *No fleſh ſhall be iuſtified in thy ſight*: therefore I cannot, though otherwiſe I be thy ſeruant, in keeping thy commandements. When *Abraham* was the father of all the faithfull, and was come to the higheſt degree of faith, and abounded in good workes, yet was he not then iuſtified by workes, *Rom.* 4. 1, 2. *Paul* kept *a good conſcience before God and men*, *Act.* 23. and yet was *he not iuſtified thereby*, 1. *Cor.* 4. 4. And he ſaith, that *wee are not ſaued by the workes which God hath ordained that wee ſhould walke in*, *Eph.* 2. 9, 10. And the workes that God hath ordained for vs to walke in, are the beſt workes of all, euen workes of grace. Againe, he ſaith, that *we are not ſaued by workes of mercy*, *Titus* 2. 5. It may be obiected, that there is a *Cooperation* of workes and faith, *Iam.* 2. 21. *I anſwer*, that this *Cooperation* is not in the act of iuſtification, nor in the worke of our ſaluation, but in the manifeſtation of the truth, and ſinceritie of our faith, without hypocriſie. And for the declaration and approbation of this, faith and workes ioyntly concurre. Here then we ſee it is a peſtilent and damnable doctrine of the Papiſts, when they teach iuſtification by the works of the law. Let vs here be warned to take heede of it.

The fourth point is, the Meritorious cauſe of our iuſtification: and that is Chriſt. Here it may be demanded, what is that thing in Chriſt, by and for which, we are iuſtified. I anſwer, *the Obedience of Chriſt*, *Rom.* 5. 19. And it ſtands in two things, *His Paſſion in life and death*, and *his Fulfilling of the law* ioyned therewith. For *by faith the law is eſtabliſhed*, *Rom.* 3. 31. *Chriſt was ſent in the ſimilitude of ſinfull fleſh, that the rigour of the law might bee fulfilled in vs*, *Rom.* 8. 4. and *Chriſt is the perfection of the law for righteouſneſſe to all that beleeue*, *Rom.* 10. 4. *He that doth not fulfill all things contained in the Law, is accurſed*, *Gal.* 3. 10. Seeing therefore we cannot performe the things contained therein, by our ſelues, we muſt performe them in the perſon of our Mediatour: who hath ſatisfied for the threatnings of the law by his paſſion; and hath fulfilled the precepts of the law by his obedience, in all duties of loue to God, and man. Wee owe to God a double debt. One is, that we are to fulfill the law euery moment, from our firſt beginning, both in regard of puritie of nature, and puritie of action. And this debt was laid vpon vs in the creation, and is exacted of vs in the law of God. The ſecond debt is, a ſatisfaction for the breach of the law. For this double debt, Chriſt is become our Suretie, and God accepts his obedience for vs, it being a full ſatisfaction, according to the tenour of the law.

For the better conceiuing of this obedience, foure queſtions may be demanded. The firſt is, when this obedience begins and ends? *Anſw.* Satisfactorie obedience performed by Chriſt, begins in his incarnation, & ends in his death. Chriſt ſaith, *Ioh.* 4. 34. *It is my meate to do my Fathers will, and to finiſh his worke.* But when was it indeede finiſhed? A little before his paſſion he ſaid, *Ioh.* 17. 4. *I haue finiſhed the worke which thou gaueſt me to doe.* Againe, in the ſurrendring of his ſoule, he ſaith, *It is finiſhed, Ioh.* 19. 30. *S. Paul* ſaith, *Chriſt was obedient to the death of the croſſe. Phil.* 2. 8. The triumph of Chriſt began vpon the croſſe, *Col.* 2. 15. and he could not triumph before he had made a full, and perfect ſatisfaction for vs. When Chriſt had procured deliuerance from hell, and Right to life euerlaſting, hee there made a perfect ſatisfaction for vs, to the iuſtice of God. And this he did in his death vpon the croſſe. For by the death of the Mediatour, *We receiue the promiſe of euerlaſting inheritance, Hebr.* 9. 15. and *with one oblation vpon the croſſe he perfected them that are ſanctified, Heb.* 10. 14. and they cannot be perfected, without the perfect obedience of Chriſt. Chriſt aroſe from death, and aſcended into heauen in our roome and ſtead: and this he could neuer haue done, vnleſſe he had made a perfect ſatisfaction in death. Here it may be asked, If ſatisfactorie obedience end in the death of Chriſt; to what vſe ſerue the reſurrection, and aſcenſion of Chriſt, and his ſitting at the right hand of the Father? *Anſ.* They ſerue alſo for our iuſtification, but after an other ſort. For they ſerue to apply and communicate to vs, and to put vs in poſſeſſion of the benefits, which Chriſt hath procured for vs, and purchaſed by his death. Saint *Paul* ſaith, *Hee aſcended to giue gifts to men, and to fill all things. Eph.* 4. 8. 10. And Chriſt ſaith, *When I am exalted, I will draw all men to me. Iohn* 12. 32. And *he liues for euer to make interceſſion for vs. Heb.* 5. 27.

The ſecond queſtion is, how Chriſt could obey beeing God, and ſatisfie for vs, being man? *Anſw.* Chriſt muſt be conſidered, not meerely as God, or as man, but as God-man, or Man-god. For the Godhead doth not redeeme vs without the manhood, nor the manhood without the Godhead. Neuertheleſſe, Chriſt as God and man, may both obey, and ſatisfie. For, as there are in Chriſt, two natures, ſo there are two diſtinct operations of the ſaid natures. And as the ſaid natures vnited make one Chriſt; ſo the operations of the natures concurring and beeing vnited in one, make the compound worke of a Mediatour. Therefore the Obedience of Chriſt, being the worke of a Mediatour, hath in it the operations of both natures. The practiſe, exerciſe, or execution of

obedience,

obedience, is from the manhood: therefore it is said, that *Christ bare our sinnes in his bodie vpon the crosse.* 1. *Pet.* 2. 24. that *he suffered in the flesh.* 1. *Pet.* 4. 1. that *he made a liuing way by the veile of his flesh. Heb.* 10. 20. that *we are reconciled in the bodie of his flesh. Coloss.* 1. 22. Obedience, is, properly a subiection of the will in reasonable creatures to the will of God: now the will of the Godhead of Christ, admits no subiection to the will of God: because the will of the Godhead (or of God,) is one and the same in all the persons. Christ therefore yeelds subiection onely in respect of the will of the manhood: in which he performes obedience. Moreouer, the operation of the Godhead is to make the said Obedience meritorious and satisfactorie for all that shall beleeue. In this respect *Paul* saith, *God was in Christ reconciling the world vnto himselfe,* 2. *Cor.* 5. 18. and that *God shed his blood, Act.* 20. 28. namely, in that nature which the Sonne of God assumed. Hence ariseth the value, price, and dignitie of the obedience of Christ.

The third question is, how the Obedience of Christ should bee made ours? *Answ.* By the free donation of God. For Christ is really giuen vnto vs in the word, and sacraments; and consequently the obedience of Christ is made ours: euen as when a peece of ground is made ours, the commoditie thereof is ours also.

The fourth question is, how the obedience of Christ should be our iustice? *Ans.* It is not our iustice in naturall manner: for then it should be in vs: but by a diuine and supernaturall manner, namely, by Gods Acceptation, in that he accounts it ours euen as truly as if it were in vs. And because God accepts it for ours, it is ours indeede: for his willing and approouing of any thing, is the doing of it: and he cals the things that are not, as if they were.

Thus we see what the Obedience of Christ is. And here two errours must be auoided. The one is of some Protestants, lesse dangerous, yet an vntruth; namely, that we are iustified, onely by the passion of Christ. But if this were so, wee should be iustified without fulfilling the law: for (as I haue said) we owe to God a double debt: one by creation, namely, the fulfilling of the law in all things, from our first beginning: the second, since the Fall of *Adam,* namely, a satisfaction for the breach of the law. Now the Passion of Christ, is a payment of the second debt, but not of the first; whereas both must be answered. For *Cursed is he that doth not continue in all things written in the law, to doe them.* The passion of Christ procureth deliuerance from hell, but alone by it selfe considered, it doth not purchase a Right to eternall life.

Obiection I. Christ fulfilled the law for himselfe; therefore his passion alone serues for our iustification. *Answ.* Christ as man, fulfilled the law for himselfe: that he might be in both natures an holy high Priest, and so continue. Neuerthelesse as Mediatour, God and man, he became subiect to the law: in this regard he did not fulfill the law for himselfe, neither was he bound so to doe.

Obiect. II. That which Christ did, we are not bound to doe: but Christ (say some) fulfilled the law for vs: therefore we are not bound to fulfill the law. *Answ.* That which Christ did, we are not bound to doe, for the same end, and in the same manner. Now he fulfilled the law in way of redemption, and satisfaction for vs: and so doe not we fulfill the law, but onely in way of thankfulnesse, for our redemption.

Obiect. III. The law doth exact both obedience, and the penaltie also. *Answ.* In the estate of innocencie the law threatned the penalty, and it onely exacted obedience. Since the fall, it exacteth both obedience, and the punishment. The threatning of the law, exacts the punishment; the precepts exact obedience.

Obiect. IV. Heb. 10. 19. By the blood of Christ wee haue entrance into the Holy place. Ans. By the *blood of Christ,* we are to vnderstand the Passion: and the passion may not be seuered from actiue, and voluntarie obedience. For Christ in suffering obeied, and in obeying, suffered. And (as *Chrysostome* saith) *the Passion is a kinde of action,* Christ in the oblation of himselfe did not onely offer to God his passion, but also praiers, which are no passions, *Heb. 5. 7.*

Humil. 2. in Act.

The second errour is of the Papists: who teach, that the thing by which, and for which, a sinner is formally iustified, is *remission of sinnes, with inherent iustice infused by the holy Ghost.* But this cannot be. For inherent iustice, and iustification, are made distinct gifts of God. *Paul* saith, *Christ is made vnto vs of God, wisedome, iustice, sanctification,* 1. *Cor.* 1. 30. Againe, *But ye are washed, ye are iustified, and sanctified.* 1. *Cor.* 6. 11. Secondly, the iustice whereby a sinner is iustified, is *reuealed without the law. Rom.* 3. 21. Now inherent iustice, or the habite of charitie, is reuealed by the law: and the obedience of Christ, is the onely iustice reuealed without the law. For it is a iustice imputed that the law neuer knew: and in this obedience, Christ performed the law, and more too. For he died for his enemies; and so loued his neighbour more then himselfe. Thirdly, God is not onely a iustifier, but also *iust in iustifying. Rom.* 3. 26. because he iustifieth none but such as bring vnto him a true and perfect iustice, either in themselues, or in their Mediatour. *Prou.* 17. 15. Now this inward, and inherent iustice is not such. For it is imperfect: because it is increased (as they teach) by a second iustifica-

iuſtification: and it is in this life mixed with the corruption of the fleſh. Fourthly, the righteouſnes of a good conſcience is an excellent grace, and gift God: but by it *we are not iuſtified*, 1. *Cor*. 4. 4. Laſtly, a cloſe errour is to be noted in this Popiſh doctrine of iuſtification. For in Popiſh learning, Remiſſion of ſinnes is not onely an aboliſhing of the guilt, and the puniſhment, but alſo of the corruption of ſinne: ſo as the partie pardoned, and iuſtified, hath nothing in him, that (as they ſay) God may iuſtly hate. And yet *Paul* iuſtified, and regenerate ſaith otherwiſe of himſelfe: that *ſinne dwelleth in him*; and that *the law of ſinne rebells in him againſt the law of his mind, and leades him captiue to ſinne. Rom*. 7.

The vſe of the doctrine. Firſt, in that we are iuſtified, by an obedience out of our ſelues, we are taught, vtterly to deny our ſelues, and to goe out of our ſelues, as hauing nothing in vs whereby we may be ſaued. Here is the foundation of the abnegation of our ſelues. Secondly, the obedience of Chriſt muſt be vnto vs the foundation of our obedience: for he performed all righteouſnes for vs, that we might be ſeruants not of ſinne, but ſeruants of righteouſnes in all duties of obedience. And in his obedience we muſt not onely reſpect the merit thereof, but alſo his holy example in loue, mercy, meekenes, patience, &c. and after it, are we to faſhion our liues. Thirdly, the obedience of Chriſt muſt bee the foundation of our comfort. In all daungers, & temptations, we that beleeue are to oppoſe the obedience of Chriſt againſt the fierce wrath of God, againſt hel, death, and condemnation. Certen beaſts, when they are purſued, flie the next way to their dennes, where they hold themſelues euen to death. Chriſt in reſpect of his obedience, is our hiding place: *Rom*. 3. 26. he is ſet forth vnto the world as *a Propitiatory*. For as the *Propitiatory* couered the Arke, and the decalogue, ſo he couereth our ſinnes, and he hides our bodies, and ſoules, from the furious indignation, and vengeance of God. Let vs therefore by our faith, flie to this our hiding place in the ſtorme & tempeſt of Gods wrath: and let vs there liue and die. Fourthly, this Obedience is the foundation of our happines. For true happines is, to be eaſed of our ſinnes, *Pſal*. 32. 1. and this eaſe we haue from Chriſt, *Math*. 11. 18. Laſtly, the conſideration of this obedience, is the foundation of our thankfulnes to God. For if we beleeue that Chriſt ſuffered, and fulfilled the law for vs, we are worſe then beaſts, if we doe not euery way ſhew our ſelues thankfull for this mercy.

The fifth point to be conſidered, is the meanes of iuſtification, namely, *the Faith of Chriſt*. Of which I conſider three things. The firſt, what faith is. The Papiſts define iuſtifying faith to be a gift of God, whereby we beleeue the articles of faith to be true, and the whole word of God. But this faith, the deuills haue. Here they alleadge, that *Abraham* was the father of all the faithfull, and that his faith was nothing els but a perswasion, that he was able to giue him a child in his old age. *Answ.* First, the obiect of *Abrahams* faith was double: one lesse principall, that he should haue issue in his old age: the second, more principall, that the Messias his Redeemer should descend of his loines. And this was the thing which his faith in the promise of God specially aimed at. I answer againe, that *Abraham* beleeued not onely the power of God, *Rom.*4.21. but also his will, which he had reuealed in the promise, *In thy seede all the nations of the earth shall be blessed.* Secondly, it is alleadged, that Christ in the curing of certaine blind men, required no more, but that they should beleeue his power, *Math.*9.28. I answer, that the ende of the miracles of Christ, was to confirme the certentie of doctrine, specially touching his natures, and offices. And therefore a generall faith touching the diuine power or Godhead of Christ was sufficient, for the obtaining of a miraculous cure. Thirdly, they obiect, that saluation is promised to generall faith. *Rom.*10.9. *If thou shalt confesse with thy mouth the Lord Iesus, and beleeue that God raised him from the dead, thou shalt be saued.* That *Peters* faith was generall, *Math.*16.10. *Thou art Iesus Christ, the sonne of the liuing God.* That the *Eunuchs* faith was of the same kind, *Act.*8.37. *I beleeue that Iesus Christ is the sonne of God. Ans.* It is a common rule in scripture, that *words signifying knowledge, signifie also the motions and good affections of the heart. Psal.* 1. *The Lord knowes the way of the righteous,* that is, knowes, and approoues it. 2. *Timothie* 2.29. *The Lord knowes who are his,* that is, hee knoweth and chooseth them. *Iohn* 17. 2. *This is eternall life to know thee the onely God,* that is, to know and acknowledge thee for our God. If this be true in wordes of knowledge, then much more wordes of beleeuing signifie the good motions, and the affiance of the heart. Thus to beleeue Christ to be the Sonne of God, in the places beforenamed, is to beleeue that he is God, and withall to fixe our affiance on him: otherwise the deuills beleeue thus much. When *Thomas* had put his finger in the side of Christ, he said, *My Lord, and my God, Iohn.* 20.28. And to this speech of his Christ saith, *Thou hast seene, and beleeued.* This then is true faith not onely to beleeue that Christ is God, but also that he is our God.

Iustifying faith in true manner is defined thus: *It is a gift, whereby wee apprehend Christ, and his benefits. Iohn* 1.12. To beleeue in Christ, and to receiue Christ, are put both for one. *Ioh.* 6. Faith is the mouth

mouth of the ſoule, whereby we eate the fleſh of Chriſt, and drinke his blood. *Iohn* 17.8. To receiue the word of Chriſt, to acknowledge it, and to beleeue it, are put all for one. *Paul* ſaith, that the Gentiles did apprehend *the iuſtice which is by faith*, *Rom.* 9.30. Againe, that *we receiue the promiſe of the ſpirit by faith*. *Gal.* 3.14.

This apprehenſion ſtands in two things. The firſt is, to know Chriſt, as he propounds himſelfe in the word, and ſacraments. The ſecond is, To applie him and his benefits vnto our ſelues. This application is made by a ſupernaturall act of the vnderſtanding, when we beleeue that Chriſt with his benefits is really ours. It may be obiected, that faith is a certen confidence whereby wee beleeue in Chriſt: & ſo it is deſcribed euen in this text. *Anſw.* I. Faith, and confidence, properly are diſtinct gifts of God: and confidence is the effect, or fruit of faith. For *Paul* ſaith, that *wee haue entrance to God with confidence by faith*, *Epheſians* 3.11. And reaſon declares as much; for a man can not put his confidence in Chriſt, till hee be aſſured that Chriſt with his benefits are his. We doe not reſt on his goodneſſe, of whoſe loue we doubt. Secondly, I anſwer that confidence, beeing a moſt notable effect of faith, is often in ſcripture, put for faith, and faith is deſcribed by it (as it is in this place) and yet for nature they are not one, but muſt bee diſtinguiſhed.

Furthermore, the grounds of apprehenſion muſt bee conſidered. For ſpeciall faith, muſt haue a ſpeciall, and infallible ground. The grounds are three. The firſt is this. In the Goſpel God hath propounded generall promiſes of remiſſion of ſinnes, and life euerlaſting by Chriſt: and withall hee hath giuen a commandement to apply the ſayd promiſes to our ſelues, 1. *Iohn* 3. 23. *This is the commandement of God, that we beleeue in the name of his Sonne Ieſus Chriſt:* And wee cannot beleeue in Chriſt, till wee beleeue Chriſt to bee our Chriſt. Now then, a generall promiſe, with a commandement to applie the ſame to our ſelues, is in effect as much as a ſpeciall promiſe. The ſecond ground is this. *Rom.* 8.16. *The ſpirit of God teſtifieth together with our ſpirit that we are the ſonnes of God.* In this teſtimony, foure things muſt be obſerued. The firſt, that it is ſufficiẽt to certifie & aſſure vs of our ſaluation. For if the teſtimony of two or three witneſſes eſtabliſh a truth among men, then much more the teſtimony of God. The ſecond is, that this teſtimony be certenly known; els it is no teſtimony vnto vs. The third is, that this teſtimonie is found and perceiued in the vſe of the word, praier, ſacraments. The laſt is, that it is eſpecially giuen and felt in the time of great danger and affliction. For when by reaſon of miſery and trouble, we know not to pray as we ought, then the *ſpirit makes requeſt for vs with groanes that cannot be vttered.* *Rom.* 8.26. And in afflictions, *Paul* ſaith, *The loue of God is ſhed abroad in our hearts.* Now then, if God giue to them that turne vnto him a teſtimonie that they are the children of God, they for their parts, are by ſpeciall faith to beleeue it. The third ground is this. A ſpeciall faith may be gathered, partly vpon things generally reuealed in the word of God, and partly vpon ſenſe, obſeruation, and experience: the ſame things being reuealed generally in the word, and particularly by experience. Vpon this ground may we truly conclude the forgiueneſſe of our ſinnes, and the ſaluation of our ſoules, on this manner: He which beleeueth, hath the forgiueneſſe of his ſinnes: but I beleeue in Chriſt (ſaith he which beleeueth:) therefore my ſinnes are forgiuen me. The *maior* or firſt part, is expreſſed in the Word; the *minor* or ſecond part is found true by experience, and by the teſtimony of the conſcience, which is a certen Teſtimonie. For *Paul* ſaith, *This is my reioycing, the teſtimonie of my conſcience.* 2. *Cor.* 1.12. And the concluſion, is the concluſion of ſpeciall faith. If this be not a good and ſufficient ground, there is almoſt no ſpeciall faith in the world.

Laſtly, wee are to conſider the degrees of Apprehenſion, and they are two: there is a *weake apprehenſion,* and there is a *ſtrong apprehenſion,* as there is a weake and a ſtrong faith. The weake faith, and apprehenſion is, when we endeauour to apprehend. This endeauour is, when we bewaile our vnbeleefe, ſtriue againſt our manifold doubtings, will to beleeue with an honeſt heart, deſire to be reconciled to God, and conſtantly vſe the good meanes to beleeue. For God accepts the will to beleeue for faith it ſelfe, and the will to repent for repentance. The reaſon hereof is plaine. Euery ſupernaturall act preſuppoſeth a ſupernaturall power, or gift: and therefore the will to beleeue and repent, preſuppoſeth the power and gift of faith, and repentance in the heart. It may be obiected, that in the mindes of them that beleeue in this manner, doubtings of Gods mercies abound. *Anſw.* Though doubtings abound neuer ſo, yet are they not of the nature of faith, but are contrarie to it. Secondly, we muſt put difference betweene true apprehenſion, and ſtrong apprehenſion. If we truly apprehend, though not ſtrongly, it ſufficeth. The palſie-hand is able to receiue a gift, though not ſo ſtrongly as an other. The man in the Goſpel ſaid, *Lord, I beleeue, helpe mine vnbeleefe.* *Marke* 9. 24. that is, helpe my faith which by reaſon of the ſmalneſſe thereof may rather bee called vnbeleefe, then faith. This is the common faith of true beleeuers. For in this world, wee rather liue by hungring and thirſting, then by full appre-

apprehending of Chriſt: and our comfort ſtands rather in this, that we are knowne of God, then that we know God.

The higheſt degree of faith is, a full perſwaſion of Gods mercy. Thus ſaith the holy Ghoſt, that *Abraham was not weake through vnbeleefe, but ſtrong in faith, Rom.*4.20. But wherein was this ſtrength? In that *he was fully perſwaded, that God, which had promiſed would alſo performe it*. This meaſure of faith is not incident to all beleeuers, but to the Prophets, Apoſtles, martyrs; and ſuch as haue bin long exerciſed in the ſchoole of Chriſt. And this appeares by the order, whereby we attaine to this degree of faith. Firſt, there muſt bee a knowledge of Chriſt: then followes a generall perſwaſion of the poſſibilitie of pardon, and mercie, whereby wee beleeue that our ſinnes are pardonable. An example whereof we haue in the prodigall childe, *Luke* 15.18. After this the holy Ghoſt worketh a will and deſire to beleeue, & ſtirs vp the heart to make humble and ſerious inuocation for pardon. After prayer inſtantly made, followes a ſetling and quieting of the conſcience, according to the promiſe, *Matth.7.7. Knocke, it ſhall be opened, ſeeke, ye ſhall finde, aske, ye ſhall receiue*. After all this, followes an experience in manifold obſeruations of the mercies of God, and loue in Chriſt: and after experience, followes a full perſwaſion. *Abraham* had not this ful perſwaſion, till God had ſundry times ſpoken to him. *Dauid*, vpon much triall of the mercie, and fauour of God, growes to reſolution, and faith, *Pſalm.*23.6. *Doubtleſſe kindneſſe and mercie ſhall follow me all the daies of my life*.

This diſtinction of the degrees of faith, muſt the rather be obſerued; becauſe the Papiſts ſuppoſe that we teach, that euery faith is a full perſwaſion, and that euery one among vs hath this perſwaſion. Which is otherwiſe. For, certentie we aſcribe to all faith, but not fulneſſe of certenty. Neither doe we teach, that all men muſt haue a full perſwaſion, at the firſt.

The vſe. If that be the right faith, which apprehends and applies Chriſt vnto vs, then is it a poore and miſerable faith of the Papiſt, to be baptized, and, withall to beleeue as the Church doth, when it is not knowne what the Church beleeues.

Of the ſame kinde is the faith of the multitude among vs, whoſe faith is their good meaning, that is, their fidelitie, and truth in their dealings.

Laſtly, if that be faith which truly apprehends Chriſt, there is little true faith in theſe laſt daies. For though the merit of Chriſt be apprehended by faith, yet is not the efficacie of his death: and that appeares by the badde and vnreformed liues of them that profeſſe

profeſſe the Goſpel. Indeede many ſay they haue and euer had, a ſtrong perſwaſion of Gods mercie: but in the moſt of them it is but a ſtrong imagination: for their faith was conceiued without the word, prayer, ſacraments: and it is ſeuered from good life. We are then all of vs carefully to ſeeke for this true and liuely faith. And the rather, becauſe faith and repentance are poſſible to all that by grace doe will it. Nay, they which will to beleeue and repent, haue begun to beleeue and repent: God accepting the will for the deede. *Luke* 11. 13. And hauing attained to a meaſure of true faith, we muſt goe on and ſeeke to iuſtifie our ſelues: but yet (as S. *Iames* teacheth, c.. 2.) iuſtifie our faith by good workes: and then ſhall our faith be a meanes to iuſtifie vs, in life and death.

The ſecond point to bee conſidered concerning faith, is the manner how it iuſtifieth. The Papiſts teach, that it iuſtifieth, becauſe it ſtirreth vp good motions and good affections in the heart, whereby it prepareth and diſpoſeth man, that he may be fit to receiue his iuſtification: againe, becauſe it being an excellent vertue meriteth that God ſhould iuſtifie. But this is falſe which they ſay. For if faith iuſtifieth by diſpoſing the heart, then there muſt be a ſpace of time betweene iuſtification and iuſtifying faith: but there is no ſpace of time betweene them. For ſo ſoone as a man beleeues, he is preſently iuſtified. For euery beleeuer hath the promiſe of remiſſion of ſinnes and life euerlaſting. Againe, in the caſe of iuſtification, *Paul* oppoſeth beleeuing and doing: faith, and workes of the law: faith therefore doth not iuſtifie as a worke, or as an excellent vertue, bringing forth many diuine and gracious operations in vs. Nay the proper action of faith, which is *Apprehenſion*, doth not iuſtifie of it ſelfe: for it is imperfect, and is to be increaſed to the end of our daies.

Faith therefore iuſtifieth, becauſe it is an inſtrument to apprehend, and apply that which iuſtifieth, namely, Chriſt and his obedience. As the Iſraelites ſtung of fierie ſerpents were cured, ſo are we ſaued: *Ioh*. 3. 16. the Iſraelites did nothing at all, but onely looke vpon the braſen ſerpent; ſo are we to doe nothing for our iuſtification and ſaluation, but to fixe the eye of our faith on Chriſt. The bankrupt paies his debt by accepting the paiment made by his ſuretie. It is the propertie of true religion to depreſſe nature, and to exalt grace: and this is done when we make God, the onely worker of our ſaluation, and make our ſelues to be no more but receiuers of the mercie and grace of God by faith, and receiuers not by nature, but by grace, reaching out the beggers hand, namely our faith in Chriſt, to receiue the gift or almes of mercie.

The last point is, that faith alone iustifieth. For here *Paul* saith, that *we are iustified by faith, without the workes of the law*: and that is as much as if he had said, *by faith alone*. Some Papists to helpe themselues translate the words of *Paul* thus, *Knowing that a man is not iustified by the workes of the law,* [ἐὰν μὴ] *if not by faith*, that is, except faith goe withall: then if faith be ioyned with workes, (say they) works iustifie. I answer, that this manner of translation corrupteth the text. For [ἐὰν μὴ] must here be translated, *but*: as appeares by the words following, *We haue beleeued in Christ, that we might be iustified by faith in Christ without the workes of the law*. We cannot doe more in the curing of our spirituall diseases, then in the curing of the diseases of our bodie: of which Christ saith, *Onely beleeue, Mark.* 5.36. When *Abraham* abounded both in faith and works, *Rom.* 4. it is said, that *he was iustified by faith without workes*.

This doctrine is of great vse. First, we learne hence, that a man is iustified by the meere mercie of God: and that there is excluded from iustification, all Merit of congruitie, all meritorious workes of preparation, wrought by vs, all Cooperation of mans will with Gods grace, in the effecting of our iustification.

Secondly, we learne, that a man is iustified by the meere merit of Christ: that is, by the meritorious obedience, which he wrought in himselfe, and not by any thing wrought by him in vs. Here then our merits, and satisfactions, and all inward iustice, is excluded from the iustification of a sinner. To this end *Paul* saith, that *we are iustified freely by the redemption that is in Christ, Rom.* 3.24. that *we are made the iustice of God in him* (and not in vs:) 2.*Cor.* 5.21. that *he gaue himselfe to deliuer vs, Gal.* 1. 4. that *he hath purged our sinnes by himselfe*; *Heb.* 1.3. and not by any thing in vs. Hence it appeares, that the Papists erre, and are deceiued, when they teach that Christ did merit, that we might merit, and satisfie for our selues: for then wee should not be iustified by our faith alone.

Thirdly, hence we learne, that a sinner is iustified by meere faith: that is, that nothing within vs concurres as a cause of our iustification, but faith; and that nothing apprehends Christs obedience for our iustification, but faith. This will more easily appeare, if we compare faith, hope, and loue. Faith is like an hand, that opens it selfe to receiue a gift, and so is neither loue, nor hope. Loue is also an hand, but yet an hand that giues out, communicates, and distributes. For as faith receiues Christ into our hearts, so loue opens the heart, and powres out praise and thankes to God, and all maner of goodnesse to men. Hope is no hand, but an eye that wishly looketh and waiteth for the good things which faith beleeueth. Therefore it is the

the onely propertie of faith to claſpe and lay hold of Chriſt, and his benefits.

It is obiected, that true faith is neuer alone. I anſwer thus. Faith is neuer alone in the perſon iuſtified, nor in godly conuerſation: but is ioyned with all other vertues. Yet in the act, and office of iuſtification, it is alone. The eye in the bodie is not alone: beeing ioyned with all other parts, hand, foote, &c. neuertheleſſe, the eye in ſeeing is alone. For no part of the body ſeeth, but the eye.

Secondly, it may be obiected, that being iuſtified by faith alone, we are ſaued by faith alone: and ſo may liue as we liſt. I anſwer, faith muſt be conſidered as an Inſtrument, or as a way. If it be conſidered as an inſtrument to apprehend Chriſt to our ſaluation, we are onely ſaued by faith, on this manner. Yet if faith be conſidered as a way, wee are not onely ſaued by faith. For all other vertues and workes are the way to life as well as faith, though they bee not cauſes of ſaluation.

Thirdly, it is obiected, that not onely faith, but alſo the ſacraments ſerue to apply Chriſt: I anſwer, they are ſaid to apply, in that they ſerue to confirme faith, whoſe office is to apply. And here let vs take notice of the errour of the Papiſts, who teach that our ſatisfactions ſerue to apply the ſatisfaction of Chriſt, and the ſacrifice of the Maſſe, to apply the ſacrifice of Chriſt vpon the croſſe: whereas nothing indeede applies but faith.

In the ſixt place, wee are to conſider the kinds of iuſtification. The Papiſts make two: one, when a man of an euill man is made a good man: the ſecond, when a good man is made better: and this, they ſay, is by workes. But it is falſe which they teach. For the Iewes which were borne an holy and peculiar people to God, by meanes of the couenant, *were iuſtified* (as *Paul* here ſaith) *by faith, without workes.* Againe, he ſaith, that the very end of our beleeuing is, *that we may bee iuſtified by faith without workes.* Therefore there is one onely iuſtification, and no more: and that by faith without workes.

The ſeuenth point is, the ground of this doctrine of iuſtification by faith without workes. And it is laid downe in the end of the 16. verſe, *No fleſh ſhall be iuſtified by the workes of the law.* And this ground is taken, as I ſuppoſe, from *Pſal.* 143 verſ. 2. It may be alleadged, that *David* ſaith thus, *No fleſh ſhall be iuſtified in thy ſight*, and that the other words, [*by the workes of the law,*] are not expreſſed. I anſwer, that the Apoſtles, and Chriſt, in citing places of the old Teſtament, applie them, and expound them, and hereupon ſometime adde words without adding to the ſenſe. *Moſes* ſaith,

Him

Him shalt thou serue, Deut. 6. 16. Christ alleadging the same words, saith, *Him onely shalt thou serue*, Matth. 4. 10. *Dauid* saith, *Sacrifice and burnt offering thou wouldest not, but mine eares hast thou pearced*, Psal. 40. 7. The author to the Hebrewes citing this text, saith, *Sacrifice and burnt offering thou wouldest not, but a bodie hast thou fitted me*, Heb. 10. 5. And thus the pearcing of the eare is explaned. For indeede it signifies to be made obedient: and to this end was a bodie giuen to Christ, that he might obey his Fathers will.

The eight, and last point is, the practise of them that are iustified; and that is to beleeue, or put their trust in Christ. *Trust in the Lord* (saith the Prophet) *and ye shall be assured*, 2. Chron. 20. 20. And *Salomon* saith, *Roll your care on the Lord*, Prou. 16. 2. By meanes of this faith the heart of the righteous is fixed and stablished. Psal. 112. 7, 8. For the better practise of this dutie, two rules must bee remembred. The one is, that faith and the practise thereof, must reigne in the heart, and haue all at command. We must not goe by sense, feeling, reason, but we must shut our eyes, and let faith keepe our hearts close to the promise of God. Nay, faith must ouerrule nature, and command nature, and the strongest affections thereof. Thus *Abraham* beleeued against hope, and by faith was content to offer his naturall and onely begotten sonne. Hebrewes 11. If faith ouerrule nature, then much more must it haue all the lusts, and corruptions of nature at command. The second rule is, that when we know not what to doe, by reason of the greatnesse of our distresse, we must then fixe our hearts on Christ without separation: as he that climes vp a ladder, or some steepe place, the higher hee goes, the faster he holds. 2. Chron. 20. 12. Iob 13. 12. Hence is true comfort. Psal. 27. 13.

17 *And if while we seeke to be made righteous by Christ, we our selues are found sinners, is Christ the minister of sinne? God forbid.*

For the better vnderstanding of the latter part of this chapter, it must be obserued, that *Paul* directs his speach not onely to *Peter*, but also to the Iewes that stood by, beeing maintainers of iustification by the law.

Some thinke, that in this verse *Paul* makes an obiection in the person of the false Apostles, on this manner: If wee be iustified by Christ alone, without the obseruation of the law, then there is no difference betweene vs Iewes and the Gentiles, but wee are as deepe sinners as they: and if this be so, then Christ is the minister

of

of sinne. And then they say, to this *Paul* answers, *God forbid.* But I somewhat doubt, whether this be the sense of the words, because *Paul* doth not make a direct confutation of this obiection in the words following.

Therfore I rather suppose, that *Paul* continues his former speech, euen to the ende of the chapter: and that in these words hee vseth a third reason, to disswade *Peter* from halting, betweene the Iewes and Gentiles. And the reason will the better appeare, if we search the meaning of the words. *If while we be iustified by Christ*, that is, by faith in Christ, without the workes of the law. *We are found sinners*, that is, found in our sinnes, not fully iustified, but are further to be iustified by the workes of the law. *Is Christ the Minister of sinne?* that is, doth it not hence follow, that Christ ministred vnto vs occasion of sinne, in that he hath caused vs to renounce the iustice of the law? *God forbid*, that is, ye doe all hold it with me as a blasphemie, that Christ should be the minister of sinne.

The argument then is framed thus. If beeing iustified by Christ, we remaine sinners, and are further to be iustified by the law, then Christ is the Minister of sinne: but Christ is no Minister of sinne: therefore they which are iustified, neede not further to be iustified by the law.

The vse. First, we learne hence, that it is a blasphemie to make Christ the Minister of sinne, who is the Minister of righteousnes, yea iustice it selfe. *Isa.* 53.11. *Dan.* 9.25. *He brings euerlasting righteousnes. Ioh.* 1. *He is the lambe of God that takes away the sinnes of the world.* Of this all the Prophets giue testimonie. *Act.* 10.43. Therefore Atheists are no better then diuells, that recken him among the false Prophets of the world. And many of them that professe Christ are greatly to be blamed, that make Christ the greatest sinner in the world: because Christ died for them: therefore they presume of mercie, and take libertie to liue as they list.

Again *Paul* here teacheth, that they which are iustified by Christ, are perfectly to be iustified; and neede not further to be iustified by any thing out of Christ, as by the workes of the law. It may be obiected, that they which are iustified feele themselues to be sinners, *Rom.* 7.14. *Ans.* The corruption of original sin, is in them that are iustified: yet it is not imputed to them by God, and withall, it hath receiued his deadly wound by the death of Christ. Therefore they which are iustified, are not reputed sinners before God. Againe, it may be obiected, that they which are iustified, must confesse themselues to bee sinners to the very death. *Answer.* Confession of sinne is not a cause, but a way for the obtaining of pardon.

Prou.

*Prou.*28.14. 1.*Ioh.*1.9.The vncouering of our sinnes is the way to couer them, before God.The sinnes therefore of men iustified,vpon their humble and serious confession, are not sinnes imputed, but couered.

Vpon this doctrine it followes, that there is not a second iustification, by workes, as the Papists teach. For he that is iustified by Christ, is fully iustified,and needes not further be iustified by any thing out of Christ, as by the law. Againe the same persons teach, that our sinnes are done away by the death of Christ, and wee iustified in our baptisme: and that if we fall, and sinne after baptisme, wee must doe workes of penance, that we may satisfie Gods iustice, and be further iustified by our workes and sufferings But then, by their leaues, after we are iustified by Christ, we are found sinners,and we are further to be iustified by our owne workes.Now this is the point, which *Paul* here confuteth.

Againe, by this doctrine we learne, that Christ alone is by himselfe sufficient,for our iustification. *In him* (saith *Paul*) *are wee complete, Col.*2.14.He is a Well of grace and life neuer dried vp. *Ioh.*4.14. Thirdly,we must content our selues with him alone,and with his obedience for our iustification, despising (in respect of him) all merits, and satisfactions done by man.

Lastly, here we see what must be the care of men in this world, namely,to seeke to be iustified by the faith of Christ. It was *Pauls* principall desire *to bee found in Christ, hauing not his owne righteousnes, but the righteousnesse which is by the faith of Christ. Phil.*3.10. The like desire should be in vs all.

18 *For if I build againe the things which I haue destroied, I make my selfe a transgressour.*

By *things destroyed, Paul* meanes the workes,or the iustice of the law, as appeares by the next verse following, where rendring a reason of this,he saith, *by the law I am dead to the law.*

These words, depend on the former thus. *Paul* had said before, that Christ was not a Minister of sinne vnto vs: and here he prooues it thus. He that builds the iustice of the law which he hath destroied, is a Minister of sinne, or makes himselfe a sinner: but the Iewes, and *Peter* by his example, build the iustice of the law, which they haue destroied, and so doth not Christ: therefore the Iewes, and *Peter*, make themselues sinners, and Christ doth not make vs sinners.

Here let vs obserue the modestie and meekenes of *Paul*. The things

things which he speakes, concerne *Peter*, and the Iewes: yet least he offend them, hee applies them to himselfe. This care, not to offend, was in Christ: who was rather willing to depart from his right, then to offend. *Matth.* 17. 27. And *Paul* bids vs *please all men in that which is good.*

Here againe it is *Pauls* doctrine, that we make our selues offenders, *When we build that which we haue lawfully destroyed.* Thus Teachers are great offenders, when good doctrine is ioyned with bad conuersation. For good doctrine destroyes the kingdome of darkenesse, and bad conuersation builds it vp againe. Thus rulers are great offenders when good counsell, and bad example goe together. For good counsell beats downe wickednesse, and bad example sets it vp againe. Thus beleeuers in Christ are great offenders, when reformed religion, and vnreformed life are ioyned together, as often they are. For then vnreformed life builds the kingdome of sinne, which Christ hath destroyed.

Further, wee are here taught to bee constant in that which is good. *Tit.* 1. 9. and to hold fast the Gospel which we professe. Wee haue put vnder foote the Popish religion for this many yeares: our duty is to bee constant herein, and no way to build either in word, or deede, that which wee haue to the vttermost of our power destroied.

19 *For I through the law, am dead to the law, that I may liue vnto God.*

In these words, *Paul* sets downe a second reason, to proue Christ to be no minister of sinne, in abolishing the iustice of the law. And the reason is framed thus: We Iewes, iustified by Christ, are dead to the law, not to liue as we list, but to liue to the honour of God. Therefore Christ in taking away the iustice of the law, is not the minister of sinne.

Here three points are propounded: the first is, that the person iustified, is dead to the law: the second, that he is dead to the law by the law: the third, that he is dead that he may liue vnto God.

For the better vnderstanding of the first point, we must search what is meant by *dying to the law.* Here the law is compared to an hard and cruell master: and wee to slaues, or bondmen: who so long as they are aliue, they are vnder the dominion, and at the command of their masters: yet when they are dead, they are free from that bondage, and their masters haue no more to doe with them. Here then, *to bee dead to the law*, is to bee free from the dominion

dominion of the law. And we are free, *in foure reſpects*. Firſt, in reſpect of the accuſing, and damnatorie ſentence of the law, *Rom.* 8.1. Secondly, in reſpect of the power of the law, whereby as an occaſion it prouoketh and ſtirreth vp the corruption of the heart in the vnregenerate, *Rom.*7.8. Thirdly, in reſpect of the rigor of the law, whereby it exacteth moſt perfect obedience for our iuſtification. Thus *Paul* here ſaith, that *hee is dead to the law.* Laſtly, in reſpect of the obligation of the conſcience, to the obſeruation of ceremonies, *Col.*2.20. Thus are all perſons iuſtified by the faith of Chriſt, free from the law.

Hence wee learne, that the Papiſts erre and are deceiued, when they teach, that the Law and the Goſpel are one for ſubſtance of doctrine. For then they which are iuſtified by Chriſt, ſhould not only be dead to the law, but alſo to the Goſpel. Now the Scripture ſaith not, that perſons iuſtified are dead to the Goſpel.

They erre againe, in that they teach, that perſons iuſtified by the merit of the death of Chriſt, are further to bee iuſtified by the workes of the law. For he that is iuſtified by the law, is dead to the law: but if wee be iuſtified by works, then are we by Chriſt made aliue to the law.

Thirdly, heere wee ſee how long the dominion of the law continueth, and when it endeth. The law reignes ouer all men without exception, till they bee iuſtified. When they once beginne to beleeue in Chriſt, and to amend their liues, then the dominion of the law ceaſſeth, and they then are no more vnder the law, but vnder grace. Here all ſuch perſons as liue in the ſecuritie and hardneſſe of their hearts, are to be admoniſhed to repent of their ſinnes, and to begin to turne vnto God. For they muſt know, that they liue vnder a moſt hard and cruell maſter, that will doe nothing but accuſe, terrifie, and condemne them, and cauſe them to runne headlong to vtter deſperation. And if they die being vnder the law, they muſt looke for nothing but death and deſtruction without mercie. For the law is mercileſſe. This conſideration ſerueth notably to awake them that are dead in their ſinnes. Againe, all ſuch as with true and honeſt hearts haue begun to repent and beleeue, let them bee of good comfort. For they are not vnder the dominion of the law, but they are dead to the law, and vnder grace, hauing a Lord, who is alſo their mercifull Sauiour, who will giue them protection againſt the terrours of the law, and ſpare them as a father ſpares his child that ſerues him, and not breake them, though they bee but as weake and bruiſed reeds, and as ſmoaking flaxe.

The ſecond point is, touching the meanes of our death to the law, and that is, the law. Here ſome by the law, vnderſtand *the law of faith*, that is, the Goſpel, *Rom.* 3.27. And they make this to be the meaning of the words, *By the law of Chriſt*, that is, by the Goſpel, *I am dead to the law of Moſes*. But this ſenſe, though it be a truth, yet wil it not ſtand in this place. For it is the queſtion, whether by the Goſpell wee be freed from the law? Now *Paul*, a learned diſputer, would not bring the queſtion to proue it ſelfe. Therfore I take the true meaning of the words to be this: *By the law* of *Moſes, I am dead to the law* of *Moſes*. It may be demanded how this can be, conſidering the law is the cauſe of no good thing in vs? For it is the miniſtery of death and condemnation, 2.*Cor*.3.7,9. Againe, that which the law cannot reueale, it cannot worke: but the law neither can, nor doth reueale faith in Chriſt, the death to the law, nor repentance, &c. therefore the law is no cauſe to worke them. It may peraduenture be ſaid, that the law workes repentance, and ſorrow for ſinne. I anſwer, there is a double repentance. One *Legall*, the other *Euangelicall*. *Legall* is, when men haue a ſight of their ſinnes, and withal are grieued for the puniſhment therof. This repentance is wrought by the miniſtery of the law: it was in *Iudas*: and it is no grace of God; but of it ſelfe it is the way to hell. *Euangelicall* repentance is, when being turned by grace, wee turne our ſelues to God. This repentance is a gift of grace, and is not wrought by the law, but by the miniſtery of the Goſpel. Againe, there is a *Legall ſorrow*, which is a ſorrow for ſinne, in reſpect of the puniſhment: this is no grace, and it is wrought by the law. *Euangelicall ſorrow*, is ſorrow for ſinne, becauſe it is ſinne. This indeed is a grace of God; but it is not wrought by the law, but by the preaching of mercy and reconciliation: and it followes in vs vpon the apprehenſion of Gods mercy by faith. The law then being the cauſe of no good thing in vs, it may be demanded (I ſay) how we ſhould bee dead to the law by the law? *Anſ*. Though the law bee not a cauſe of this death to the law, and ſo to ſinne: yet it is an occaſion thereof. For it accuſeth, and terrifieth, and condemneth vs: and therfore it occaſioneth or vrgeth vs to flee vnto Chriſt, who is the cauſe that wee die vnto the law. As the needle goes before, and drawes in the thred, which ſowes the cloth; ſo the law goes before, and makes a way that grace may follow after, and take place in the heart. Thus muſt this place bee vnderſtood, and all other places that ſpeake of the law in this manner: as *Rom*.7.8, &c.

The third point is, touching the end of our death to the law: and that is, that we *may liue to God*. It may bee demaunded, what life this is, whereby we liue to God? *Anſwer.* There is a naturall and a ſpirituall life. Naturall life is that which wee receiue from *Adam* by generation: and it is the function of naturall faculties, in liuing, moouing, vſe of ſenſes and reaſon. Spirituall life is that which we receiue from Chriſt by regeneration: and it is the action, motion, or operation of the Spirit in vs. This life is called by *Paul, the life of God, Epheſ.*4.18. And this is the life which he ſpeakes of in this place. And it is deſcribed by many things. Firſt, by the end and vſe of it. For it ſerues to make vs *to liue to God,* that is, to the honour and glory of God. And we liue to God by liuing *wiſely, godly, iuſtly, Tit.*3.12. *Wiſely,* in reſpect of our ſelues: *godly,* in reſpect of God: *iuſtly,* in reſpect of men.

That we may liue wiſely, we muſt obſerue *two rules.* The firſt: we muſt labour with all diligence, and with all ſpeed, that we may be worthy to ſtand before the Sonne of man at his comming. And therefore wee muſt labour to bee in Chriſt, hauing true faith and good conſcience, *Eph.*5.15. *Luke* 21.36. Conſider alſo the example of *Paul, Act.*24.16. It is true wiſdome to be wiſe for our ſoules, and for euerlaſting happineſſe: and it was the folly of the fooliſh virgins, that they did not furniſh themſelues with the oyle of grace in time conuenient. The ſecond rule: we muſt in this world come as neere heauen and the happineſſe of life euerlaſting, as may be, *Pſal.* 3.14. And for this cauſe we muſt ioyne our ſelues to the aſſemblies where the word is preached, prayer is made, and Sacraments adminiſtred: for there is the gate of heauen. Conſider the practiſe of *Moſes, Heb.*11.25,26. and of *Dauid, Pſal.* 84.10. Againe, being abſent from heauen both in body and ſoule, yet wee muſt haue our conuerſation there, by the cogitation of our minds, and by the affections of our hearts, *Phil.* 3.21.

That wee may liue godlily, *ſeuen rules* muſt bee remembred. The firſt: wee muſt bring our ſelues into the preſence of the inuiſible God: yea, we muſt ſet our thoughts, willes, affections, and all we doe in his ſight and preſence: and wee muſt euermore remember whatſoeuer wee doe, that wee haue to deale with God himſelfe. In this regard *Enoch* is ſaid *to walke with God, Gene.*5.24. *Abraham and Iſaac before God, Geneſ.* 17.1. and 48.15. and *Dauid, Pſalm.*116.9. and 139. all, and *Cornelius, Actes* 10.33. and *Paul,* 2.*Cor.*7.17.

The ſecond: we muſt take knowledge of the will of God in all things, whether it be reuealed in the word, or by any euent. It is not enough to know Gods will, but when time and place ſerues, we muſt acknowledge it, *Rom.*12.2. *Col.*1.10.

The third: we muſt bring our ſelues in ſubiection to the known will of God, and captiuate all our ſenſes vnto it: and ſuffer God to ſet vp his kingdome in vs, *Rom.* 12.1.

The fourth: when wee haue offended God, wee muſt inſtantly humble our ſelues before his Maieſty, confeſſing our offences, and making inſtant deprecation for mercy. Thus did *Ezra*, chap. 9. and *Daniel*, chap. 9. and *Dauid*, *Pſal.* 32.3.

The fifth: in all our miſeries and aduerſities we muſt bee ſilent in our hearts, by quieting our willes in the good will of God. *Pſal.* 4.4. *Examine your ſelues, and bee ſtill. Pſal.* 37.7. *Bee ſilent to Iehouah.* Conſider the example of *Aaron, Leuit.* 10.3. of *Dauid, Pſal.* 39.9. of the Iewes, *Actes* 11.18.

The ſixth: In all things wee doe or ſuffer, wee muſt depend on the goodneſſe, prouidence, and mercie of God, for the ſucceſſe of our labours, and for eaſe or deliuerance out of miſerie. This is *to liue by faith*: and, as *Peter* ſaith, 1.*Pet.* 3.17. *to ſanctifie God in our hearts.*

The laſt: In all things wee muſt giue praiſe and thankes to God: and that for our miſeries and afflictions, *Iob* 1.22. for in them God mingles his iuſtice with mercie, whereas hee might vtterly condemne vs.

That we may liue iuſtly in reſpect of men, *two rules* muſt be obſerued. The firſt: we muſt make God in Chriſt, our treaſure and our portion, and his fauour and bleſſing, our riches. Then ſhall not the vile ſinnes of auarice and ambition beare ſway in vs: and then ſhal we learne with *Paul, to be content in any eſtate, Phil.* 4.11. becauſe howſoeuer the world goe, wee haue our portion and treaſure. The ſecond, we muſt loue God in louing of man, and ſerue him in doing ſeruice to men by the offices & duties of our callings. They which labour in their callings for this end, to get riches, honors, and to ſet vp themſelues in this world, prophane their callings, and practiſe iniuſtice. For not ſelfe-loue, but loue to God, in duties of loue to men, muſt beare ſway in all our actions.

Thus we ſee what it is *to liue to God*. Now we are all to be exhorted, to order our ſelues in this manner. For firſt of all, wee are Gods: and therefore *we muſt glorifie God both in our bodies and ſoules*, 2.*Cor.* 6.20. Secondly, the end of our iuſtification and redemption is, that we may liue to God. And it is great wickedneſſe to peruert the order of God, by liuing to our ſelues and the luſtes of our hearts. Thirdly, there be 3. degrees of life: one is in this life, a ſpirituall and a renewed life: the ſecond in death, when the body goes to the earth, & the ſoule to heauen: the third, in the laſt iudgment,

when

when bodie and soule reunited, enter into the presence of God. Therefore that we may be saued, wee must liue vnto God in this life: for we can neuer come to the second degree of life, but by the first. And wee must not imagine, that we can step immediatly out of a lewd and wicked life, into euerlasting happinesse in heauen. Lastly, the grace of God in the ministery of the Gospel hath appeared and long taught vs, and called vpon vs to liue vnto God. Therfore vnlesse we be ashamed and confounded for our sinnes, and begin with all speed to liue vnto God, it will bee worse with vs, then with Sodom and Gomorrha, and many other natious.

20 *I am crucified with Christ: Thus I liue, yet not I any more, but Christ liues in mee. And in that I now liue in the flesh, I liue by the faith of the Sonne of God, who hath loued mee, and giuen himselfe for mee.*

Whereas *Paul* said before, *I am dead to the law*, heere he declares the reason of it, when hee saith, *I am crucified with Christ.* Againe, here *Paul* sets downe the true preparation to spirituall life. For God first kils, and then he makes aliue. And the measure of spiritual life, is according to the decay of originall sinne. This preparation stands in two things: the first is, fellowship with Christ in his crosse and passion, in these wordes, *I am crucified with Christ.* The second is Abnegation, or Annihilation (as some call it) in these words, *Not I any more.*

I am crucified with Christ.

For the better vnderstanding of these words, we must obserue, first, that *Paul* speakes not this of himselfe particularly, but he speakes in the person of the Christian Iewes, before whom he now reasoneth with *Peter*: nay in the person of all beleeuers. For all that beleeue *are buried into his death. Rom.6.* 4. Secondly, it must be obserued, that *Paul* speaketh of himselfe not as he is a man consisting of body and soule, but as he is a sinner carrying about him the body of sinne. *Rom.6.v.6.* Further it may be demanded, vpon what ground he should say, *I am crucified with Christ? Ans.* There be two reasons of this speach. One is, that Christ vpon the crosse, stood not as a priuate person, but as a publicke person, in the roome, place, and stead of all the Elect: and therefore when he was crucified, all beleeuers were crucified in him; as in the Parlament, when the Burgesse giues his voice, the whole corporation is said to consent by him, and in him. The 2. reason is this. In the conuerſion of a ſinner, there is a reall donation of Chriſt, and all his benefits vnto vs: and there is a reall vnion, whereby euery beleeuer is made one with Chriſt. And by vertue of this vnion, the croſſe and paſſion of Chriſt is as verily made ours, as if we had bin crucified in our owne perſons. Hereupon *Paul* ſaith in the time preſent, *I am crucified with Christ.* There are like phraſes in *Paul, Wee are dead with Christ: we are riſen with him: we ſit with him in heauenly places, Epheſ.2.6. Col.3.1.* and they are in the ſame manner to be expounded. Moreouer the benefits that ariſe of this communion with Chriſt in his paſſion, are two. One is, *Iuſtification* from all our ſinnes, *Rom.6.7.* The ſecond is, *Mortification* of ſinne by the vertue of the death of Chriſt, after we are ingrafted into him. Thus much of the meaning.

The vſe. Superſtitious perſons take occaſion by the paſſion of Chriſt, to ſtirre vp themſelues to ſorrow, compaſſion, and teares, by conſidering the pitifull handling of Chriſt, the ſorrow that pearced the heart of the Virgin *Marie*, and the crueltie of the Iewes. But this is a humane vſe, that may be made of euery hiſtorie.

The right vſe is this: wee are in minde and meditation to conſider Chriſt crucified: and firſt, we are to beleeue that he was crucified for vs. This being done, wee muſt goe yet further, and as it were ſpread our ſelues on the croſſe of Chriſt, beleeuing and withall beholding our ſelues crucified with him. Thou wilt ſay, this is a hard matter, I cannot doe it. I ſay againe, this is the right practiſe of faith: ſtriue therefore to bee ſetled in this, that the body of thy ſin is crucified with Chriſt. Pray inſtantly by asking, ſeeking, knocking, that thou maiſt thus beleeue. This faith and perſwaſion is of endleſſe vſe. Firſt, it is the foundation of thy comfort. If thou beleeue thy ſelfe to be crucified with Chriſt, thou ſhalt ſee thy ſelfe freed from the dominion of the law and ſinne, from hell, death, and condemnation; and to thy great comfort ſhalt ſee thy ſelfe to triumph ouer all thy ſpirituall enemies. For this Chriſt doeth, *Col.2.14.* and thou doſt the ſame, if thou be ſetled in this, that thou art crucified with him. Secondly, vpon this perſwaſion, thou ſhalt feele the vertue of the death of Chriſt to kill ſinne in thee, and to raiſe thy dead ſoule to ſpirituall life. When the *Shunamites* child was dead, *Eliſha* went and lay vpon him, applying face to face, hand to hand, foot to foot: and then his fleſh waxed warme, and reuiued, *1.King.4.34.* euen ſo apply thy ſelfe to Chriſt crucified, hand to hand, foot to foot, heart to heart; and thou ſhalt feele in thy ſelfe a death of ſinne, and the heat of ſpiritual life to warme and inflame

thy

thy dead heart. Thirdly, if thou beleeue thy ſelf to be crucified with Chriſt, thou ſhalt ſee the length, the breadth, the height, the depth of the loue of God in Chriſt. For thy ſinnes are the ſwords, & the ſpeares that crucified Chriſt: and yet thou haſt all the benefit of his paſſion. Laſtly, if thou canſt beleeue that thou art crucified with Chriſt, thou ſhalt further bee aſſured, that he is partner with thee in all thy miſeries and afflictions, to eaſe thee, and to make thee to beare them, 1.*Pet*.4.13. *Col*. 1.24.

The duties hence to be learned, are theſe. Firſt, if thou be crucified with Chriſt, then muſt thou apply thy heart to crucifie the body of corruption in thee, by prayer, faſting, by auoiding the occaſions, by abſtaining from the practiſe of ſinne, and by all good meanes. Behold, a man hanged vpon a gybbet. Thou ſeeſt hee hath ſatisfied the law: and there is no further iudiciall proceeding againſt him: and withall thou ſeeſt how he ceaſeth from his thefts, murders, blaſphemies: euen ſo, if thou canſt behold thy ſelfe ſpread vpon the croſſe of Christ, and crucified with him, there will be in thee a new minde and diſpoſition, and thou wilt ceaſe from thine olde offences. †Againe, beeing crucified with Chriſt, thou muſt bee conformable to Chriſt in thy ſufferings. Hee ſuffered in loue; and the more his paſſion increaſed, the more he ſhewed his loue: euen ſo in thine afflictions and ſufferings, thy loue to God and man muſt bee increaſed, though man bee the cauſe of thine afflictions. Secondly, Chriſt ſuffered in obedience: *Not my will, but thy will be done*: euen ſo in all thy ſufferings thou muſt reſigne thy ſelfe to God, and quiet thy ſelfe in his will. Thirdly, Chriſt ſuffered in all humilitie, humbling himſelfe to the death of the croſſe: euen ſo we, in, and vpon our afflictions, are to humble our ſelues vnder the mightie hand of God, confeſſing our ſinnes, and intreating for pardon. Fourthly, he ſuffered in faith as man depending on his fathers goodneſſe, euen in the middeſt of his paſſion: euen ſo are we to doe. Fifthly, he went on conſtantly in his ſufferings to the very death: euen ſo are we to ſuffer in the reſiſting of ſinne, euen vnto the ſhedding of our blood. Laſtly, the principall care of Chriſt was, to ſee the fruit of his ſufferings: ſo when we are diſtreſſed, our care muſt rather bee to ſee the fruit of our diſtreſſe, then to ſeeke deliuerance. This conformitie with Chriſt in his paſſion, is an infallible work and token of the child of God, and a ſigne that we are crucified with Chriſt.

Againe, heere wee are to take notice of the falſe faith of many men. They can bee content to beleeue that Chriſt was crucified for them: but there they make a pauſe: for they doe not beleeue that they are crucified with Chriſt. Their faith therfore is but halfe a faith: and their profeſſion is according. For they haue the forme of godlineſſe without the power thereof. They thinke that they beleeue the Articles of faith aright: but they are deceiued. For to beleeue in Chriſt crucified, is not onely to beleeue that he was crucified, but alſo to beleeue that *I am crucified with him*. And this is to know Chriſt crucified.

Laſtly, here we are to conſider the abomination of the Church of Rome. For it moſt abuſeth that which is the greateſt treaſure in the world, namely, *Chriſt crucified*. For they make a very Idol of him, in that they worſhip him in, at, and before painted and carued Crucifixes. For there is no ſuch Chriſt in heauen or in earth, that will be preſent when wee pray, and heare vs at crucifixes. Againe, they giue *Latria, diuine honor*, to deuiſed and framed crucifixes: and and thus they rob Chriſt of his honour.

Thus much of our communion with Chriſt in his paſſion: now followes the ſecond part of preparation, namely, *Abnegation, I liue, yet not I any more*: that is, I liue a ſpirituall life, yet not I as a naturall man. For in that regard, I carrie my ſelfe as a man crucified, or after the manner of a dead man, ſuffering nothing that is in me by nature to reigne in me, that Chriſt alone may liue & reigne in me. Here is a notable dutie to be learned: we beeing crucified with Chriſt, muſt carrie our ſelues as men crucified: and that in three reſpects. Firſt, in reſpect of corruption of ſinnefull nature. For in regard of our ſinnes, wee are to eſteeme our ſelues vnworthy of meat, drinke, ſleepe, breathing: yea, we are to eſteeme our ſelues to bee as vile as any of the creatures vpon earth: and we are to denie vngodlineſſe, and worldly luſts, not ſuffering any of them to reigne ouer vs. Secondly, we muſt carry our ſelues as dead men, in reſpect of the good things that belong to nature, as honours, riches, pleaſures, friends: all which in reſpect of preparation of minde, we muſt daily forſake for Chriſts ſake, not ſuffering any of them to take place in our hearts. Laſtly, we muſt bee as dead men in reſpect of our owne reaſon and will, and wee muſt tread them vnder foot, making Gods will our wiſedome, and will; and giuing it lordſhip and dominion ouer vs, our owne willes in the meane ſeaſon lying dead in vs. Thus are wee to carrie our ſelues as dead men: and we are to be carefull of it: that God may haue pleaſure in vs; *we muſt forget our owne people, and our fathers houſe, Pſal.* 45. 10. That we may buy the pearle, we muſt ſell all wee haue, our willes, our affections, and the deareſt things in the world. He that would liue when hee is dead, muſt die while he is aliue: and wee

muſt

muſt now lay out our ſelues as dead perſons. Corruption of nature, reaſon, and will, muſt be dead in vs, that Chriſt alone may liue and reigne in vs.

The third point concerning ſpirituall life is, touching the originall and well-ſpring thereof, in theſe wordes, *That Christ may liue in mee.* For the better conceiuing whereof, three points are to be obſerued. The firſt, that Chriſt is not onely the Author, with the Father and the holy Ghoſt, but alſo the root of life, hauing life in himſelfe, that hee may conuay it to all that beleeue in him. *He is the true vine, and wee are the branches, Iohn* 15.1. hee is *an appointed head to his Church, Epheſ.* 1.22. he is *the prince of life, Actes* 3.15. hee is *a quickening ſpirit*, 1.*Cor.* 15.45. And in this regard hee is ſaid *to liue in vs*, namely, as a root in the branch, or as the head in the members. The ſecond point is, that there muſt be an vnion with Chriſt, before we can receiue life from him, and he liue in vs. *If ye abide in me, and I in you, ye ſhall bring foorth much fruit, Iohn* 15.4. We muſt bee grafted with him, before we can be conformable to his death and reſurrection, *Rom.* 6.5. And againe, wee muſt be taken out of the wilde oliue, and ſet in the true oliue, *Rom.* 11.24. Thus much *Paul* ſignifieth, when he ſaith, *Chriſt liues in mee.* Of this coniunction two things muſt be noted. The firſt, that it is a ſubſtantiall vnion: in that the perſon of him that beleeueth, is vnited to the perſon of Chriſt. For we muſt *eate the fleſh of Christ, and drinke his blood*, before wee can haue life abiding in vs, *Iohn* 6.53. and *our bodies are members of Christ*, 1. *Cor.* 6.15. Againe, this vnion is ſpirituall, becauſe it is made by the bond of one Spirit, 1. *Cor.* 12.13. *By one ſpirit wee are baptized into one bodie.* And no man is to maruaile, that we on earth ſhould bee ioyned to Chriſt in heauen. By ciuill contract man and wife are one fleſh, though diſtant many miles aſunder: why then may not wee be ioyned to Chriſt by vertue of the couenant of grace? conſidering no diſtance of place can hinder the being of the Spirit of Chriſt in vs. The third point is, that after this vnion with Chriſt, he muſt further communicate himſelfe vnto vs, before we can liue by him, and he in vs. To this purpoſe S. *Iohn* ſaith, that *God hath giuen vs life:* that *this life is in the Sonne:* that *hee which hath the Sonne, hath life*, 1. *Iohn* 5.12. For the conceiuing of this truth, two queſtions may be demaunded. One, in what order Chriſt giues himſelfe vnto vs? *Anſwer.* Chriſt firſt of all giues his fleſh and blood, that is, himſelfe: and then ſecondly his gifts, namely, the efficacie and merit of his death. The inſtitution of the Lords Supper ſheweth plainly, that we are not partakers of the benefits of Chriſt, vnleſſe firſt of all Chriſt himſelfe be giuen vnto vs.

The

The ſecond queſtion is, how Chriſt can can be ſaid *to liue in vs?* *Anſwer* He is not in vs in reſpect of locall preſence,but by the ſupernaturall, and ſpeciall operation of his ſpirit, 1.*Corinth*.6.17.The operation of the ſpirit, is threefold. The firſt is, when God imputes the righteouſneſſe of Chriſt to them that beleeue, and withall giues the Right of Eternall life, and the Earneſt of this Right, namely, the firſt fruites of the ſpirit. Hereupon iuſtification is called *the Iuſtification of life*. *Rom*.5. The ſecond is, Viuification by the vertue of the reſurrection of Chriſt, *Phil*.3.10. And this vertue is the power of the God-head of Chriſt, or the power of the ſpirit,raiſing vs to newneſſe of life, as it raiſed Chriſt, from the death of ſinne. And by this power,Chriſt is ſaid to liue in them that beleeue. The third is,the Reſurrection of the dead body to euerlaſting glory,in the day of iudgement,*Rom*.8.11.

Thus then the meaning of the words is euident:that Chriſt as a roote,or head,liues in them that are vnited to him,and that by the operation of his ſpirit,cauſing them to dye vnto their ſinnes,and to liue vnto God.And againe,it muſt be remembred,that *Paul* ſpeakes this not priuately of himſelfe, but generally in the name of all beleeuers.For he ſaith,2.*Cor*.13.5.*Know ye not that Chriſt is in you,except ye be reprobates?*

The vſe. Hence it followes,that they which are true beleeuers, cannot make a practiſe of ſinne: and againe, that they ſinne not with the full conſent,or ſwinge of their wills. Becauſe,Chriſt liues in them,and reſtraines the will in part.When they ſinne therefore, they ſinne not of malice,but of ignorance,or infirmity.

Secondly,the true beleeuer,cannot wholly fal away from grace: becauſe the life of Chriſt cannot be aboliſhed. As Chriſt died but once,and for euer after liues to God: ſo they that are in Chriſt,dye once to ſinne,and liue eternally to God,*Rom*.6.10.The vertue and power of God,that was ſhewed in raiſing Chriſt to life, is likewiſe ſhewed in quickning them that doe beleeue.*Eph*.1.19.He therfore that is made aliue to God, dyes no more, but remaines aliue as Chriſt doth.

Thirdly,they which are true beleeuers, are a free and voluntary people obeying God,as if there were no law to compell them. For they haue Chriſt to liue in them.Reade *Pſal*.110.2.The ſpirit of life that is in Chriſt is alſo in them; and that is their law, *Rom*.8.2. It is the property of the child of God to obey God,as it is the nature,and quality of the fire to burne when matter is put to it.

It may be here demanded, how we may know that Chriſt liues in vs? *Anſ*. By the Spirit of God, 1.*Ioh*.3.24. And the Spirit is

knowne

knowne by the motions, and operations thereof. The firſt whereof, is a Purpoſe to obey God, according to all his commandements that concerne vs, with an inclination of our hearts to the ſaid commandements. *Paul* ſaith, *he was ſold vnder ſinne*: and yet withall he addes, that *he delighted in the law of God according to the inward man, Rom.*7.23. He that loues God, and keepes his commandements, hath the Father and the Sonne dwelling in him, *Ioh.*14 23. Let this be obſerued. *Pharaoh*, when Gods hand was vpon him, confeſſed he was a ſinner and his people, and requeſted *Moſes*, and *Aaron*, to let the plague goe. But after God had withdrawne his hand, he returned to his old courſe. The like doe ſicke men: they make promiſe to amend their liues, and they requeſt their friends to pray for them: but when they are recouered, they forget all their faire promiſes. The reaſon is this. There is conſcience in them; and by it they know themſelues to be miſerable ſinners: but they want this purpoſe to obey God, and the inclination to his lawes: and therefore indeede they hate not their ſinnes, but rather the commandements of God. The ſecond operation, & ſigne of the Spirit, is a mind and diſpoſition, like to the mind and diſpoſition of Chriſt: which is, to doe the will of God, to ſeeke his glory, and to apply himſelfe to the good of men in all duties of loue. The third and laſt (to omit many) is to loue Chriſt for himſelfe, and to loue them that loue Chriſt, and that becauſe they loue Chriſt. This is a true ſigne, that *we haue paſſed from death to life*, 1.*Ioh.*3.14. It may here be ſaid, how can Chriſt be ſaid to liue in vs, conſidering we are laden with afflictions and miſeries? Where Chriſt liues, there is no miſery. *Anſ.* In the midſt of all miſeries, the life of Chriſt doth moſt appeare. Where naturall life decayes, there ſpirituall life takes place, 2.*Cor.* 4. 10. *I beare in my bodie the mortification of our Lord Ieſus, that the life of Ieſus may bee made manifeſt in mee. Gods power is made manifeſt in weakneſſe*, 2. *Cor.* 12. Againe, it may be ſaid, if Chriſt liued in vs, wee ſhould not feele ſo many corruptions as wee doe. *Anſwer.* The life of Chriſt is conueyed vnto vs by little and little. God hauing *wounded and ſlaine vs*, firſt *bindes vs vp*, then *hee reuiues vs, and the third day he raiſeth vs vp. Hoſe.*6.1. Againe, nature feeles not nature, nor corruption feeles corruption, but grace: therefore it is the life of Chriſt in vs that makes vs feele the maſſe and bodie of corruption.

Furthermore, here we are to take notice of the common ſinne of our daies. Men will not ſuffer Chriſt to liue in them, and to rule ouer them. It is reputed a ſmall matter, but it is a grieuous offence. The Gentiles ſay, *Let vs break their bands, and caſt their cords from vs,*

Pſal.

Pſal.2.2. And it was the ſinne of the Iewes to ſay, *We will not haue this man to reigne ouer vs. Luke 19.14.* And therefore Chriſt ſaith, *bring them hither, and ſlay them before me.*

Laſtly, here we learne our duty: and that is, ſo to liue, that we may be able to ſay with good conſcience, that *Chriſt liues in vs*: we muſt ſeeke his kingdome aboue all things, and take his yoke on vs. It will be ſaid, what muſt we doe that Chriſt may liue in vs? *Anſw.* We muſt vſe the meanes appointed, meditation of the word, prayer, ſacraments: and withall we muſt ſpiritually *eate the fleſh of Chriſt, and drinke his blood, Ioh.6.57.* And that we may eate him, we muſt haue a ſtomacke in our ſoules like the ſtomacke of our bodies, and we muſt hunger and thirſt after Chriſt: and therefore we muſt feele our owne ſinnes, and our ſpirituall pouerty, and haue an earneſt luſt and appetite after Chriſt, as after meate and drinke. When *Siſera* was purſued by the army of the Iſraelites, he cried to *Iael* and ſaid, *Giue me drinke, I dye for thirſt, Iudg.4.19.* euen ſo we being purſued by the ſeutence of the law, by the terrours of hell, death, and condemnation; muſt flye to the throne of grace, and cry out, ſaying, *Giue me of the tree of life, giue me of the water of life: I periſh for thirſt*: Then ſhall our wretched ſoules be quickned, and reuiued to euerlaſting life, *Math.5.6. Reue.21.6.*

In the fourth place, here is ſet downe the Meanes of Spirituall life, in theſe words, *And in that I now liue in the fleſh, I liue by the faith of the Sonne of God, who hath loued me, and giuen himſelfe for me.* And that the doctrine may the better appeare, I will ſtand a while to ſhew the meaning of them. By *fleſh*, is meant the mortall body, or the fraile condition of this temporall life, *Heb.5.7.* & *1.Pet.4.2.* And therfore *to liue in the fleſh*, is to liue a naturall life by eating, drinking, ſleeping. Further, *Paul* ſaith that liuing in the fleſh, he liued *by faith*: and for the better conceiuing of this, two queſtions may be demanded. The firſt is, why a beleeuer is ſaid to liue by faith? *Anſ.* There be two cauſes. Firſt, faith is an Inſtrument to vnite vs to Chriſt: and by meanes of this vnion, we receiue life from Chriſt: for Chriſt dwells in our hearts by faith, *Eph.3.17.* Secondly, faith is a Guide, to order and gouerne temporall life, in all good manner according to the will of God. And this faith doth, by a diuine kind of reaſoning framed in the mind, whereby it vrgeth, and perſwadeth to good duties, *Rom.6.11.*

The ſecond queſtion is, How men liue by faith? *Anſwer.* The child of God liues a double life in this world: a *Spirituall*, and a *Temporall.* The *Spirituall* ſtands ſpecially in three things; Reconciliation with God,: renouation of life: and good workes. Now in our reconciliation with God, we liue in this world onely by faith. For wee haue, and enioy pardon of our ſinnes, imputation of iuſtice, and acception to life eternall, onely by meanes of our faith, *Rom.*4.4. and 5.1.

Againe, in the renouation and change of our liues, wee liue by faith. For our faith in Chriſt *purifieth our hearts, Actes* 15.9. partly, by deriuing holineſſe and puritie from Chriſt vnto vs, who is our ſanctification: and partly, by mouing and perſwading of vs to holineſſe and newneſſe of life, 1.*Iohn* 3.3.

Laſtly, in the doing of euery good worke, wee muſt liue by our faith. For firſt there muſt be a generall faith, that the worke in his kind pleaſeth God, *Rom.*14.25. Secondly, iuſtifying faith muſt giue a beginning to the worke. *I beleeued, therefore I ſpake, Pſal.*116.12. Thirdly, after the worke is done, faith muſt couer the defects thereof, that it may be acceptable to God, *Heb.*11.5.

Temporall life, ſtands in cares or miſeries: and miſeries are outward afflictions, or inward temptations. And in all our worldly cares, we are to liue by faith. For our care muſt be to doe our office, and the labour of our calling with all diligence. This being done, we muſt there make a pauſe: and for the ſucceſſe of all our praiers, and labours, we muſt caſt our care on God; 1.*Pet.*5.7.

Likewiſe, in our afflictions wee are to liue by faith. For our faith is to aſſure vs, that God according to his promiſe will giue a good iſſue, 1.*Corinthians,* 10.v.12. And though all temporall things faile vs, it makes vs retaine the hope of mercie, and of eternall life. Thirdly, it makes vs waite Gods leaſure for our deliuerance, *Iſai.*16.28.

Laſtly, in our temptations wee are not to liue by feeling, but by faith: yea againſt feeling, to reſt on the bare promiſe of God; when we feele and apprehend nothing but the wrath of God. And thus we ſee how the beleeuer liues by his faith in this world.

It may be ſaid, What is the faith wee liue by? Anſwer is heere made: *It is the faith of the Sonne of God.* And ſauing faith is ſo called; becauſe Chriſt is not onely the Authour of it, and the obiect or matter of it, but alſo the reuealer of it. For there was a certaine faith in God, which was put into the heart of man in the creation, which alſo the morall law requireth: but this faith in the Meſſias, was not knowen till after the fall; and then it was reuealed to the world by the Sonne of God.

Againe, it may be ſaid, What is this faith of the Sonne of God? Anſwer is here made: A faith whereby I beleeue that *Chriſt hath loued and giuen himſelfe for me.*

These

These words then thus explaned, are an answer to an obiection, which may be framed thus: Why shouldest thou say, that thou liuest not, but that Christ liueth in thee; considering thou liuest in the flesh, as other men doe? Answer is made, Though I liue in the flesh, yet I liue by faith in the Sonne of God.

The vse. Here first of all they are to be blamed, that liue by sense, like beasts: beleeuing no more then they see, and trusting God no further then they see him. For if a man whom we see and know, make a promise to vs, we are comforted: yet if God, who is inuisible, make in his word farre better promises (as he doth,) we are not in like sort comforted. Againe, we put too much confidence in meanes. If we haue good callings, house, land, liuing, we can then trust in God: but when meanes of comfort faile, we are confounded in our selues, as if there were no God. We are like the Vsurer, who will not trust the man, but his pawne: euen so we trust not God vpon his bare word, without a pawne. If he come to vs with a full hand, and with the pawne of his good gifts, and blessings, we trust him; else not.

Againe, they are to be blamed, that liue onely by the guidance of reason. For many dispute thus: I deale truly and iustly with all men, and liue peaceably with my neighbours: therefore God will haue me excused. But there must be a better guide to euerlasting life namely, faith in Christ: else shall we misse our marke.

Thirdly, they deceiue themselues, that thinke they may liue as they list: and call vpon God when they are a dying, and so dye by faith. It is well if they can dye by faith: but that they may so die, they must liue by faith.

Lastly, they are to be blamed, that spend their dayes in worldly cares, so as no good thing can take place. This is the life of infidels. And where true faith reignes, it cuts off the multitude of cares, and makes vs cast them on God.

Moreouer, here we see what we are to doe in perilous times, as in the time of plague, famine, sword, when present death is before our eyes: we must then liue by faith. When *Noah* heard of the flood, he prepared such meanes as faith would affoard for the sauing of himselfe, and his family. *Abraham, Isaac, Iacob*, by faith liued as pilgrimes in a strange land, and were content. *Moses* left *Pharaoes* court, and *feared not the wrath of the King: because by faith he saw him that was inuisible, Hebrew.* 11.27. *Dauid* in the feare of present death, *comforted himselfe in the Lord his God*, 1.*Sam*.30.6. When *Iehosaphat* knew not what in the world to doe, hee lift vp the eyes of his faith to the Lord, 2. *Chron*. 20.12. Christ in his agony and

passion

passion of the crosse, by faith commended his soule into the hands of his Father. Of the Saints of the new Nestament, some were racked, some were stoned to death, and that by faith, *Heb.* 11.36. We must therefore all of vs, learne to liue by faith: and for this cause we must acquaint our selues with the word, and promises of God; and mingle them with our faith: else shall the life of a man in the world bee worse then the life of a beast.

Againe, in these words [*who hath loued me, and giuen himselfe for me*] the nature and property of iustifying faith is set downe, which is, to apply the loue of God, and the merit of the passion of Christ vnto our selues. And therefore the Papists are deceiued, who say, that hope applieth, and not faith. It may be alleadged, that *Paul* speakes these words priuately of himselfe. *Ans.* He speakes them in the name of all beleeuers, Iewes and Gentiles. For (as we may see in the former verses) that which concerned *Peter*, and the rest of Christian Iewes, he applies to himselfe, least his speech should seeme odious.

☞ Againe, it may be obiected, that all beleeuers cannot say thus, *Christ hath loued me, and giuen himselfe for me. Ans.* If the minde be fixed on Christ: and there be also a will and indeauour to beleeue and apprehend Christ; there is faith indeede. For God accepts the true and earnest will to beleeue, for faith. We are not saued for the perfection of our faith, but for the perfection of the obedience of Christ, which faith apprehendeth. The Israelites which looked vpon the brasen Serpent with one eye, or with a squint-eye, with halfe an eye, or dimme sight, were healed, not for the goodnesse of their sight, but for the promise of God. The poore in spirit are blessed. Now they are poore in spirit, who finde themselues empty of all goodnesse, empty of true faith, full of vnbeleefe, and vnfeinedly desire to beleeue. So then if we grieue, because we cannot beleeue as we should, and earnestly desire to beleeue, God accepts vs for beleeuers.

Againe in these words [*who hath loued me, and giuen himselfe for me*] S. *Paul* sets downe the reason or argument, which faith vseth in the minde regenerate, to mooue men to liue to God. And the reason is framed thus: Christ loueth thee, and hath giuen himselfe for thee: therefore see thou liue to God, Reade the like, *Rom.* 12.1. and 2.4. and *Psal.* 116.12.

By this we are to take occasion, to consider and to bewaile the hardnesse of our hearts, who doe not relent from our euill waies, and turne vnto God vpon the consideration of his loue in Christ. The waters of the Sanctuary haue long flowed vnto vs: but they haue

haue not ſweetned vs,and made vs ſauoerie:therefore it is to be feared leaſt our habitations be at length turned to places of nettles and ſaltpits.*Eze*.47.11.

21 *I doe not abrogate the grace of God:for if righteouſneſſe be by the law,then Chriſt died without cauſe.*

The meaning.*Grace* in Scriptures ſignifieth two things:the free fauour of God; and the gifts of God in vs. And where the Holy Ghoſt intreates of iuſtification,grace in the firſt ſenſe,ſignifies the good will,and fauour of God, pardoning ſinnes, and accepting vs to life euerlaſting,for the merit of Chriſt.2.*Tim*.1.9.*Eph*.2.8.And in this ſenſe is the word vſed in this place. And when *Paul* ſaith,*I doe not abrogate the grace of God*;his meaning is,I doe not make void, or fruſtrate the grace of God in reſpect of my ſelfe , or in reſpect of other beleeuers, by teaching the iuſtification of a ſinner by faith alone. Hee addes , *If righteouſnes be by the law*; that is, if a ſinner be iuſtified by his owne obedience, in performing the law, then Chriſt died without cauſe. The word δωρεὰν, *freely*,tranſlated *without cauſe*, hath a double ſignification. One is, when it ſignifies as much as *without price, or merit*. *Math*. 10. 8. *Ye haue receiued freely, giue freely*. The ſecond is, when it ſignifies *raſhly, without iuſt,or ſufficient cauſe*:as *Pſal*.69.4. *Mine enemies hate me freely*,(as the Seuentie tranſlate)that is, wrongfully,or without iuſt cauſe. Thus heere is Chriſt ſaid to die *freely*,that is,in vaine, or without cauſe: becauſe if we be iuſtified by obedience to the law,then Chriſt died in vaine, to make any ſatisfaction to the law for vs.

Theſe words are an anſwer to an obiection.The obiection is this: If thou teach that a ſinner is iuſtified onely by his faith in Chriſt, then thou aboliſheſt the grace of God. The anſwer is negatiue: I doe not by this doctrine abrogate the grace of God. And there is a reaſon alſo of this anſwer: If wee bee iuſtified by our owne fulfilling of the law,then Chriſt died in vaine to fulfill the law for vs.

The vſe.Firſt, let vs marke that *Paul* ſaith,*he doth not abrogate the grace of God*: and why ? becauſe hee will ſuffer nothing in the cauſe of our iuſtification to be ioyned with the obedience of the death of Chriſt. And hence we learne, what is the nature of grace. It muſt ſtand wholly , and intirely in it ſelfe. Gods grace cannot ſtand with mans merit. Grace is no grace, vnleſſe it be freely giuen euery way *Rom*.4.4. *To him that worketh, the wages is giuen,not of grace, but of deſert*. *Romaines* 11.6.*If election bee of grace, then not of workes, elſe is grace no grace*.Grace, and workes of grace in the cauſing of iuſtification,

iustification, can no more stand together, then fire and water. By this we are admonished to be nothing in our selues, and to ascribe all that we are, or can doe, to the grace of God.

Againe, here wee see our duties, and that is to be carefull not to abrogate the grace of God vnto our selues. But how is that done? *Answ.* We must strip and emptie our selues of all righteousnesse, and goodnesse of our owne, euen to the death, and withall hunger and thirst after Christ and his righteousnesse. *Math.* 5.6. *Luke* 1.35.

Thirdly, *Paul* here sets downe a notable ground of true religion; That the death of Christ is made voide, if any thing bee ioyned with it in the worke of our iustification, as a meanes to satisfie Gods iustice, and to merit the fauour of God. Therefore the doctrine of iustification by workes, is a manifest errour. For if we be iustified by the workes of the law, then the iudgement of the holy Ghost is, that Christ died without cause. Againe, the doctrine of humane satisfactions is a deuice of mans braine. For if wee satisfie for our selues, then did Christ by death satisfie in vaine. Thirdly, it is a false and wicked (though a colourable inuention) to say, that Christ by his death merited, that wee should merit by our workes. For if wee merit by workes, Christ died in vaine to merit by his owne death. This is the sentence of God, who cannot erre. Lastly, here we see the Church of Rome erreth in the foundation of true religion: because it ioyneth the merit of mans workes, and the merit of the death of Christ, in the iustification of a sinner. And therefore, we may not so much as dreame of any reconciliation to bee made with that religion: for light and darkenesse cannot be reconciled, nor fire and water. Here the Papists answer, that *Paul* in this text speakes against them; that looked to be iustified by the naturall obseruation of the law, without the death of Christ. But it is false which they say. For *Paul* here speakes against Christian Iewes, who ioyned the law and the Gospel: and looked to bee iustified both by Christ, and by the workes of the law: and not by workes of the law, done by strength of nature, but by workes of grace.

CHAP. III.

1 *O foolish Galatians, who hath bewitched you, that ye should not obey the truth? to whom Iesus Christ before was described in your sight, and among you crucified.*

Hat we may see how this chapter depends on the former, we must repeate the principall argument of the Epistle: If I was called of God, and my doctrine be true, then ye should not haue reuolted to an other Gospel: but I was called of God, and my doctrine is true: therefore ye should not haue reuolted to an other Gospel.

The first part of the *minor*, that *Paul* was called of God, was handled in the first and second chapters. The second part: that his doctrine is true, is handled in the third, fourth, and fifth: and is propounded in this verse. Moreouer, the Conclusion of the argument set downe Chap. 1. v. 6. is here againe repeated, namely, that the Galatians should not haue reuolted to an other Gospel. And withall *Paul* here notes the causes of their Reuolt: and they are two. One, is follie, *O foolish Galatians.* The other is, the deceit of false teachers, *who hath bewitched you?*

Whereas *Paul* saith, *O foolish Galatians*, that we mistake not his example; three questions may be demanded. The first is, In what respect he giues this hard iudgement against them? *Answ.* Three things are subiected to Iudgement, the doctrines of men, the liues of men, and the persons of men. Doctrines are to be iudged by the word, and the liues of men: yet ordinarily, the persons of men are not to be iudged. For the saying is true, that *three things are not subiect to iudgement: the Counsels of God, the Scriptures, and the persons of men.* And in this place *Paul* giues iudgement, not against the Galatians themselues, or against their persons, but against their new conceiued doctrine, and against their practise in Reuolting.

The second question is, whether this iudgement be righteous and true iudgement? *Ans.* It is: because it is vpon good ground. For first of all, *Paul* giues this censure, by vertue of his calling: because his office was to reprooue and correct vice. *Tit.* 1. 9. and 2. 15. Secondly, it was in truth. For indeede they ouerturned the passion of Christ: and therefore he could not call them lesse then *fooles.* Thirdly, this iudgement was giuen in loue. For *Paul* intended, and desired

deſired nothing in this ſpeech, but their good and amendment. Vpon like grounds *Iſai* calles the Iſraelites, *People of Sodome and Gomorrha, Iſa.* 1. Chriſt cals the two diſciples, *fooliſh, and ſlow of heart to beleeue, Luk.* 24.25. *Paul* cals the Crecians *lyers and ſlow bellies, Tit.* 1.12. But *Mat.* 5.22. may be obiected, where he is ſaid to be in danger of a Councel, that ſaith, *Thou foole. Anſ.* The place is to be vnderſtood of them that charge men with folly, with a minde to reproch them, and in way of reuenge: which *Paul* in this place doth not.

The third queſtion is, whether wee may vſe like iudgement againſt men? *Anſ.* Vpon like grounds we may, if we haue a warrant, and calling from God ſo to do. For all iudgement is Gods, *Rom.* 14. 10, if this iudgement be in truth: if it be in charitie, for the amendment of the parties, and for the good of others. Otherwiſe, if theſe grounds faile vs, we may not giue iudgement againſt any man, but muſt follow the iudgement of charitie which thinks no euill, hopes the beſt, and conſtrues all things in the beſt part. 1. *Cor.* 13.

To come to the ſecond cauſe, *Paul* ſaith, *Who hath bewitched you?* that is, who hath deceiued you, as if ye were bewitched by ſome inchantments. Here *Paul* takes it for a confeſſed truth, that there is witchcraft, and witches. And that we may the better conceiue his meaning, two queſtions are to be propounded. The firſt is, what is the witchcraft here meant? *Anſw.* It is a Satanicall operation, whereby the ſenſes of men are deluded. For the diuell can by certaine meanes, delude and corrupt the phantaſie, or the imagination; and cauſe men to thinke that of themſelues, which is otherwiſe. There is a diſeaſe called *Lycanthropia*, in which, the braine beeing diſtempered, men thinke themſelues to be wolues, and carrie themſelues as wolues. And in this diſeaſe the diuell hath a great ſtroke. Againe, the diuell can delude the outward ſenſes, as the hearing, and the ſight. Thus *Iannes* and *Iambres* turned their rods into ſerpents, before *Pharaoh*, and brought frogges, by deceiuing the eye, and not in truth, *Exodus* 7. and 8. Thus the witch of Endor made a counterfeit of *Samuel* to riſe out of the earth, 1. *Sam.* 28.

The ſecond queſtion is, if this witchcraft bee an operation of Satan, how men ſhould be ſaid to doe it? for *Paul* ſaith, who, or what man hath bewitched you? *Anſ.* Men do it by league, and confederacie with the diuel. The inchanter charmes by *ioyning ſocieties. Pſal.* 58.5. The diuell ſeekes whom he may deuoure: and therefore, where he finds a fit perſon to worke vpon, he inſinuates and offers himſelfe. And after men be in league with him, he hath a word and ſacraments for them, as God hath: and he requireth faith, as

God doth. And looke as theeues, ſome lie in the way, ſome in the wood: and they in the way (when a bootie comes) giue a watch word to the reſt, and then all are at hand together: Euen ſo when men in league with the diuell vſe charmes, imprecations, curſes, praiers, ſuperſtitious inuocations, according to his appointment, and other Satanicall ceremonies, a watch word is likewiſe giuen vnto him, and he is ſtraight at hand to doe the intended feate. Thus, and no otherwiſe, are men ſaid to bewitch, or delude the eye.

That which *Paul* ſaith to the Galatians, if he were now liuing among vs, he would likewiſe ſay to vs, *O fooliſh nation, who hath bewitched you?* We are wiſe in matters of the world: but in matters concerning the kingdome of heauen, the moſt of vs are fooles, beſotted, and bewitched with worldly cares, aud pleaſures, without ſenſe in matters of religion, like a peece of waxe without all forme: fit to take the forme and print of any religion. And we muſt take heede, leſt this our fooliſhneſſe, and intoxication of our ſenſes, leade vs headlong to perdition. And therefore we muſt learne the way of life in humility. *Pſal*, 25.9. We muſt obey it, and in obedience we ſhall learne it. *Ioh*. 7.17. We muſt as heartily loue the word of God, as in minde we conceiue it; leſt by not louing of it, we be *giuen vp to ſtrong illuſions to beleeue lies*. 2. *Theſſ*. 2. 10. Laſtly, we muſt pray to God to be taught and guided by his word and ſpirit, in things pertaining to euerlaſting life.

To proceed further, the deluſion or bewitching of the Galatians, is ſet forth by two arguments. The firſt is, the end, in theſe words, *that ye ſhould not obey the truth*. Before I come to the conſideration of theſe words, a doubt muſt be reſolued. For ſome man may ſay, that this Epiſtle is corrupted: becauſe theſe words are wanting in ſundrie tranſlations, and editions of the Bible: and *Ierome* ſaith, that they were not found in the copies of the Bible in his daies. *Anſ*. In the Editions & tranſlations of the Bible, there are ſundry differences, and diuerſities of readings: and theſe differences are not the fault of the Scripture, but of the men which vſed to write out the Bible: for the Bible heretofore was ſpread abroad, not by printing, but by writing. Againe, though in the bookes of the Bible there bee ſundry varieties of reading, yet the prouidence of God hath ſo watched ouer the Bible, that the ſenſe thereof remaineth intire, ſound, and incorrupt, ſpecially in the grounds of religion. And not the words principally, but the ſenſe is the Scripture. And that which I ſay appeareth in this text: for whether theſe words be left in, or put out, the ſenſe of the verſe, is one and the ſame.

Theſe words, *that ye ſhould not obey the truth*, are meant of the obedience

obedience of faith. *Rom.* 1.5 and 16.28. And the obedience of faith is propounded vnto vs without adding, detracting, or changing. And this the Galatians did not: for they added iustification by workes, to the doctrine of *Paul*, touching iustification by faith alone: by which addition they depraued the truth, and shewed that indeede they beleeued not the truth. Here let vs obserue the scope of all the malice of the deuill: and that is, to hinder, or ouerthrow our faith. The first thing the deuil aimed at in our first parents, was to ouerthrow their faith, and to cause them to doubt of the truth of Gods word. The first temptation wherwith our Sauiour Christ was assaulted, was against his faith, as he was man: If thou bee the Sonne of God, thou canst cause these stones in thy hunger to bee made bread: but thou canst not cause these stones to bee made bread: therefore thou art not the child of God. The deuill desired to sift out all the faith of the Apostles, and to leaue in them nothing but the chaffe of vnbeleefe. *Luk.* 22. The deuill blindes the eyes of men, *that the light of the Gospell of Iesus Christ may not shine vnto them.* 2. *Cor.* 4.4. This must teach vs, that we must not onely holde and know the true religion for the time, but also build our selues vpon our faith, *Iud.* v.20. and bee rooted and stablished vpon our faith and religion, *Col.* 1.23. and the rather, because it hath bin the manner of this nation, wickedly to change religion with the times. And that we may indeed be rooted vpon our religion, we must not boast of the greatnes and strength of our faith, but rather labour to see in our selues a sea of vnbeleefe: heartily to bewaile it, and to striue to beleeue, and so to goe on from faith, to faith.

The truth here mentioned, is the heauenly doctrine of the Gospel: so called for two causes. First, because it is an absolute truth without errour. It is a principle not to be called in question, that *the Apostles and Prophets, in writing and preaching, could not erre.* It may be said, they were men, as we are: and therefore subiect to erre, and be deceiued in iudgement. *Ans.* Iudgement is twofold. One, conceiued by the discourse of naturall reason: the other, conceiued by the apprehension of things reuealed by God. In the first, the Apostles and Prophets might erre, and be deceiued; as *Nathan* and *Peter* were. In the second, they could not: because it was framed in them, by the inspiration, and instinct of the holy Ghost. And therefore, they neuer erred, either in preaching or writing. The second cause why the Gospel is called *the truth*, is, because it is a most worthy truth, namely, the truth which is according to godlinesse. *Tim.* 1. It may bee said, what is the truth? and how shall we know it, considering there be so many dissentions? *Ans.* First, make thy selfe fit to know, and then ſhalt thou know the truth. And thou ſhalt bee fitted to know the truth, if thou firſt of all giue thy ſelfe to obey it. Reade the golden text, *Ioh.*7.v.17. *Obey, and ye ſhall know.*

The ſecond thing, whereby the deluſion of the Galatians is expreſſed, is the ſigne thereof, in theſe words, *to whom Ieſus Chriſt was deſcribed, &c.* that is, to whom I haue preached the doctrine of ſaluation by Chriſt, in liuely and euident manner, euen as if Chriſt had bin painted before your eyes, and had bin crucified, in, or among you. And this is a manifeſt token that the Galatians were deluded, becauſe they could not acknowledge the truth, when it was ſet forth vnto them, (as it were) in orient colours. And where *Paul* ſaith, that *Chriſt was before deſcribed*, I referre it to the time before their reuolt.

Here firſt, we are to obſerue, the properties of the Miniſtrie of the word. The firſt, that it muſt be plaine, perſpicuous, and euident, as if the doctrine were pictured, and painted out before the eyes of men. Therefore the Church of Rome deales wickedly, in keeping the Scriptures in an vnknowne tongue. For this is to couer that from the people, which is to bee painted before the eyes of their minds. Againe, that kind of preaching is to be blamed, in which there is vſed, a mixed kind of variety of languages, before the vnlearned. For this is a ſigne to vnbeleeuers. 1. *Cor.* 14. 22. And in this kind of preaching we doe not paint Chriſt, but wee paint out our owne ſelues. It is a by-word among vs: *It was a very plaine ſermon.* And I ſay againe, *the plainer, the better.*

The ſecond propertie of the Miniſtery of the word, is, that it muſt be powerfull and liuely in operation, and as it were crucifying Chriſt within vs, and cauſing vs to feele the vertue of his paſſion. The word preached muſt pearce into the heart, like a two edged ſword, *Heb.*4.12. True prophecie iudgeth men, diſcouereth the things of the heart, and cauſeth men to ſay, *The Lord is within you*, 1. *Cor.*14.25. The ſcepter of Chriſt whereby he ſmiteth the nations, is in his mouth, *Iſa.*11.4. that is, in the Miniſterie of the word. *Ier.* 15.19. And it is the ſame Miniſterie, which ſhaketh heauen and earth. *Agg.*2.5. By this it appeareth, that to take a text, and to make a diſcourſe vpon ſomething in the ſaid text, ſhewing much inuention of wit, and much reading, and humane learning, is not to preach Chriſt in a liuely manner. It will bee ſaid: what then? I anſwer with *Paul*, *Who is ſufficient* either *for* the ſpeaking or doing of *theſe things*? yet ſomething may bee ſhewed. Know therefore that the effectuall and powerfull preaching of the word, ſtands in three things. The firſt is, true and proper interpretation of the

Scripture, and that by it ſelfe: for Scripture, is both the gloſſe, and the text. The ſecond is, ſauorie and wholeſome doctrine, gathered out of the Scriptures truely expounded. The third is, the Application of the ſaid doctrine, either to the information of the iudgement, or to the reformation of the life. This is the preaching that is of power. Let all the Sonnes of the Prophets thinke vpon theſe things, and ſtudie to be doers of them.

Furthermore, two queſtions are here reſolued. The firſt is, whether Images bee neceſſarie in the congregations of the people of God? *Anſ.* There are Chriſtian Images, and Pictures, and they are very neceſſarie. And theſe Images, are Sermons of Chriſt, and the right adminiſtration of the ſacraments. For in them Chriſt is deſcribed and painted out vnto vs. As for the painted and carued images of the Papiſts, we vtterly deteſt them, as Idols. They alleadge, that they are *lay-mens bookes:* but *Habakuk* ſaith, *they are doctours of lies, Hab.*2.18. And where the liuely preaching of the word is, there is no neede of them. And therefore Images were not eſtabliſhed in Churches in theſe Weſt parts, till after 700. yeares. As long as the Church had golden teachers, there were no wooden images: but when golden teachers did degenerate, and become wooden teachers, then came both golden and wooden Images. It is further ſaide, why may we not paint Chriſt in our Churches with colours, as with wordes in ſermons? *Anſwer.* The one, the Lord alloweth, namely, the deſcription of Chriſt in ſpeach. But the caruing or painting of images in Churches, and that for religious vſe, he condemneth. *Exod.*20.6.

The ſecond queſtion is, Whether there bee now in the Church of God, any ſacrifice or oblation of Chriſt? *Anſwer.* There is after a ſort. For there is a liuely repreſentation of the paſſion of Chriſt, in the Preaching of the word, and in the adminiſtration of the Lords ſupper, as if Chriſt were yet in crucifying, and as though his blood were now diſtilling from his hands, and ſides. As for the ſacrifice of the Maſſe, it is an abomination, and a meere mockerie, For there the Prieſt, when hee ſaith, *Accept theſe gifts,* &c. is become a Mediatour, betweene Chriſt and God: and the bodie and blood of Chriſt is offered in an vnbloodie manner; that is, blood is offered without blood: and the Prieſt, when hee hath offered Chriſt, eates vp that all hee hath offered. Yet for this damnable oblation many ſtand: and the reaſon is; becauſe they are bewitched, and inchanted with pretended ſhewes of Fathers, Councells, Antiquitie, Succeſſion, &c.

Laſtly, here we learne, what is the dutie of all beleeuers, namely, to behold Chriſt crucified. *Cant.* 3. 11. *O daughters of Sion, behold your king.* But where muſt we behold him? Not in Roodes, and Crucifixes, after the Popiſh manner; but we muſt looke on him, as hee propounds himſelfe vnto vs in the word, and Sacraments. For thus is he the true obiect of our faith. And how muſt we behold him? by the eye of faith, which makes vs both ſee him, and feele him, (as it were) crucified in vs. Here note, that implicit faith, (which is to beleeue as the Church beleeues,) is a blind faith: for by it we cannot contemplate and behold Chriſt. And the common fault is here to be noted, whereby men neglect and paſſe by this contemplation of Chriſt. There is among vs the euill eye that deuoureth all it ſeeth: there is the adulterous eye: but where is the eye of faith to behold Chriſt? where is the force of this eye to be ſeene, which maketh the thing which it beholdeth to be ours, and vs like vnto it? Wee loue to tricke and paint our bodies, and ſome to ſet fine complexions on their faces (and therefore complexions at this day are made a kinde of merchandiſe) but away with ſuch vanities. If ye loue to be painted, I will tell you what ye ſhall do. The office of the Miniſters is to deſcribe, and paint out Chriſt vnto vs: let them paint Chriſt crucified in the heart, and ſet vp his image there, and then ſhalt thou haue a fauourable complexion in the eye both of God, and man.

That this contemplation of Chriſt by faith, may take more place, and be the better practiſed, conſider the vſe of it. Firſt, by beholding Chriſt crucified, we ſee our miſerie and wickedneſſe. For our ſinnes are the ſwords and ſpeares which haue crucified him. *Zach.* 12. 10. Secondly, this ſight brings vs true and liuely comfort: for beholding Chriſt crucified, wee ſee Paradiſe as it were in the midſt of hell: we ſee the handwriting againſt vs, cancelled, *Coloſſ.* 2. 14. we ſee the remiſſion of our ſinnes, written with the heart blood of Chriſt, and ſealed with the ſame. Thirdly, this ſight of Chriſt makes a vniuerſall change of vs. The Camelion takes to it the colours of the things which it ſeeth, and are neere vnto it: and the beleeuing heart takes to it the diſpoſition, and minde that was in Chriſt crucified, by viewing, and beholding of Chriſt. This ſight makes vs mourne and bleede in our hearts for our offences, when wee conſider, that Chriſt was crucified for them: and it makes vs loue Chriſt, when we conſider the loue of God in Chriſt crucified.

Laſtly, this thing muſt be a terrour to all the vngodly. For they haue no care to behold Chriſt, but by their leud liues they crucifie him: and for this cauſe in the day of iudgement, they ſhall ſee with heauie hearts, Chriſt to be their iudge whom they haue pearced. *Reuel.* 1.7. Better therefore it is, now in the day of grace to behold him with the eye of faith to our comfort, then now to deſpiſe him, and then to behold him to our euerlaſting ſhame, with the eye of confuſion.

2 *This onely would I learne of you, Receiued ye the Spirit by*
the workes of the law, or by the hearing of faith?
3 *Are ye ſo fooliſh, that after ye haue begun in the Spirit, ye*
would now be made perfect by the fleſh?

The ſence of the words. When *Paul* ſaith, *This would I learne of you*, he meetes with the conceit of the Galatians, who thought themſelues wiſe: and the effect of his ſpeech is this: I haue called you fooles: but it may be, that you thinke your ſelues wiſe, and me fooliſh: well, let it be ſo: then with all your wiſedome teach me, and let me learne but one thing: and that is, by what meanes ye receiued the Spirit. Touching the phraſe, *Receiued ye the Spirit*, 3. things muſt be obſerued. The firſt, that the Spirit ſometimes ſignifies the eſſentiall ſpirit of the Father and the Sonne, as 1.*Cor.*12.4. *There is a diuerſitie of gifts, but one ſpirit.* Sometimes againe, it ſignifies the effects, operations, or gifts of the ſpirit, as namely when *fleſh* and *ſpirit* are oppoſed; as in this text. And further, when it ſignifies gifts, yet then the preſence of the ſpirit is not excluded, but included. The ſecond is, that here *the Spirit* ſignifies the ſpirit of adoption. *Eph.*1.13. *Rom.* 8.16. The third is, that to receiue the ſpirit, is not barely to receiue the gifts of the ſpirit, (as wee are ſaid to haue the Sunne in the houſe, when we receiue the beames of the body of the ſunne being in heauen:) but in this receiuing, there are two things. One is, that the ſpirit is preſent in vs; the other, that the ſame ſpirit teſtifieth his preſence, by his ſpeciall operation, and gifts of grace. *Paul* ſaith, *Eph.*4.30. *Grieue not the ſpirit.* Which is not meant of gifts, but of the very perſon of the ſpirit. And it muſt be remembred, that the effects and gifts of the ſpirit, preſuppoſe the preſence of the ſpirit. By *workes of the law*, we are to vnderſtand, the doctrine of iuſtification by the workes of the law. By *the hearing of faith*, is meant the doctrine of the Goſpel: *hearing* being put for the thing heard, namely, preaching: and *faith*, for the doctrine of iuſtification by faith in Chriſt crucified. For *faith* ſignifies not onely the gift whereby we beleeue, but alſo that which is beleeued.

In the third verſe, *ſpirit* ſignifies the operation of the ſpirit, whereby the inward man is renewed, and made like to God; or

againe,

againe, the Exerciſes of the inward man: and *fleſh* ſignifies outward things, or actions, that properly pertaine to the outward man, as circumciſion, and ſuch like. Thus 2. *Cor.* 5. 17. *fleſh*, and the *new creature* are oppoſed. And *Paul* ſaith, *Rom.* 2. 29. *He is a Iew, that is a Iew within, in the ſpirit, hauing the circumciſion of the heart. To begin in the ſpirit*, is to begin in godlines and religion, inwardly in the exerciſes of the renewed heart.

The Reſolution. In theſe words, is contained the firſt argument, whereby *Paul* prooues the truth of his doctrine. It is framed thus: If ye receiued the ſpirit by my doctrine, my doctrine is true, and ye fooliſh that adde vnto it, iuſtification by the workes of the law: but ye receiued the ſpirit by my doctrine: therefore it is true, and ye deale fooliſhly that haue added to it iuſtification by workes.

The *maior* or firſt propoſition, is not expreſſed, but the proofe thereof in the third verſe, thus: it is a point of extreame follie when ye haue begun in the ſpirit, to end in the fleſh: therefore it is folly in you hauing receiued the ſpirit by my doctrine, to adde any thing vnto it of your owne.

The vſe. When *Paul* ſaith, *Let me learne one thing of you*, he notes the fault of the Galatians, and of ſundrie others, who when they haue attained to a certaine meaſure of knowledge in Gods word, are preſently puffed vp with pride, and often thinke themſelues wiſer then their teachers. This was the fault of the Corinthians, 1. *Cor.* 8. 10. and of ſundry in our daies, who ſeparate wholly from all our congregations, preſuming to know that which they neuer learned of their teachers. That this ouerweening pride may not take place, we muſt ioyne the knowledge of our ſelues, with the knowledge of Gods word, and mixe our knowledge with loue. For *loue edifies*, and *bare knowledge ſwelles the heart*.

Againe, here when it is ſaid, *Receiued ye the ſpirit?* that is, ye did not receiue the ſpirit by the workes of the law, but by the hearing of faith. Here, I ſay, we ſee the difference betweene the law, and the Goſpel. The law doth not miniſter the ſpirit vnto vs: for it onely ſhewes our diſeaſe, and giues vs no remedie. The Goſpel miniſtreth the ſpirit. For it ſhewes what we are to doe: and withall the ſpirit is giuen, to make vs doe that which we are inioyned in the Goſpel.

Here alſo we learne, that the preaching of the Goſpel, is neceſſarie for all men, becauſe it is the Inſtrument of God to conferre the ſpirit. *While Peter was yet ſpeaking, the ſpirit of God fell vpon the Gentiles*, *Act.* 10. 44. *Paul* ſaith, *his miniſterie is the miniſterie of the ſpirit*, 2. *Cor.* 4. 5. ſauing the Miniſters and others. 1. *Tim.* 4. 16. And the moſt learned haue neede of this ordinance of God. For ſuppoſe they haue knowledge ſufficient, yet haue they neede of the ſpirit of God to guide, and gouerne them.

Further, let it be obſerued, what is the ſcope of all our hearing, and teaching: namely, that wee may receiue the ſpirit of God: without which ſpirit, we can doe nothing.

Moreouer, *Paul* here ſets downe an infallible argument, whereby we may be aſſured that the Scripture is the word of God. For the ſcriptures in their right vſe (which is in reading, hearing, meditation) haue the diuine and ſupernaturall operation of the ſpirit ioyned with them, to comfort in all diſtreſſes, and in the very pang of death, and to conuert the heart of man, making him in reſpect of righteouſneſſe and holineſſe, like vnto God. This priuiledge haue the Scriptures, *Iſa.* 59.21. and no word elſe.

Laſtly, let vs here obſerue the certen marke of true religion: and that is, that the preaching therof confers the ſpirit of adoption. This doth not the pretended Catholike Religion of the Papiſts: it doth not conferre vnto men the ſpirit to aſſure them that they are the children of God; becauſe it teacheth that we are to be in ſuſpence of our ſaluation. Againe, by teaching humane ſatisfactions, and merits, it miniſtreth the ſpirit of pride and preſumption, as alſo the ſpirit of crueltie, and not of meekeneſſe: for they of that religion, commonly delight in blood: and there haue bin no warres, or ſeditions, or rebellions in Europe, for many ages, but they of the Romiſh religion, haue bin at one end of them.

When *Paul* ſaith, v. 3. *Began ye in the ſpirit, &c.* he teacheth a diuine inſtruction, that true godlineſſe & Religion ſtands in the ſpirit, that is, the grace of the heart, or in the exerciſes of the inner man, whether we reſpect the beginning, the middle, or the accompliſhment thereof. *The kings daughter is all glorious within. Pſal.* 45.13. *True worſhippers worſhip God in the ſpirit. Ioh.* 4.25. *Rom.* 1.12. *He is a Iew, that is a Iew* not without, but *within in the ſpirit, in the circumciſion of the heart. Rom.* 2.29. Gods ſeruice and *kingdome, ſtands in iuſtice, peace of conſcience, and ioy in the holy Ghoſt, Romanes* 14. verſe 17. *Hee that is in Chriſt* muſt not know him in any carnall reſpects, but bee *a new creature.* 2.*Cor.* 5.17. *Gal.* 6.17. Baptiſme is not the waſhing of the ſpots of the fleſh, but the promiſe that a good conſcience makes to God. By this doctrine we ſee the fault of the world, which for the moſt part placeth religion in ceremoniall performance of ſome outward duties. The Iew vſed to come to God with ſacrifices, and to draw neere to him with his lip, his heart beeing farre from God. The Papiſt hath turned the Apoſtolike, and Catholike religion, into a maſſe of ceremonies, borrowed partly from the Iewes, and partly from the Gentiles. And the multitude among vs, place their religion, in comming to the Church; in outward hearing, in receiuing the ſacrament, in ſome kinde of formall praying. Theſe things may not be condemned, but the power and life of religion lies not in theſe things. Wherefore we muſt not ſtand vpon outward and painted ſhewes: but looke what thou art betweene God, and thy ſelfe; that onely art thou in religion. Thou praieſt in the church: but thou maiſt deceiue the world in this. Tell me, doſt thou pray at home? doſt thou pray in thine owne heart vnto God, by the ſpirit of praier? then thou praieſt indeede. If thou canſt approoue thy heart vnto God for any act of religion, then is it done indeede, elſe not. Remember this.

Furthermore, *Paul* here teacheth that our after proceedings in religion, muſt be anſwerable to our firſt beginnings in the ſpirit. And hence we may be aduertiſed of many things. Firſt, here wee muſt take notice of the follie of Popiſh religion. For it begins in Gods mercie, and the merit of Chriſt: and it ends in our merits and ſatisfactions. Secondly, we muſt take notice of the common ſinne of our times. For in the practiſe of our religion we are deceiued. We are not now that which we haue bin twentie or thirtie yeares ago. For now we ſee the world abounds with Atheiſts, Epicures, Libertines, Worldlings, Newters, that are of no religion: and ſundry that haue heretofore ſhewed ſome forwardneſſe, begin to faulter, and ſtagger, and to looke an other way. This is not to begin and end in the ſpirit: but to end in the fleſh. We are betime to amend this fault, leſt if our former zeale to be turned to preſent lukewarmes, God in his anger ſpue vs out.

Yong men muſt here be aduertiſed as they grow in yeares and ſtature, ſo to grow vp in good things, that both the firſt beginning, and the after proceedings may be in the ſpirit. Thus did Chriſt increaſe in grace as he increaſed in ſtature.

Laſtly, aged perſons that haue begun in the ſpirit, muſt looke that they grow vp in the graces of the ſpirit more then others, that they may end in the ſpirit. It is ſaid of the angel of *Thyatira*, that *his loue, ſeruice, and workes, were moe at the laſt then at the firſt*, Reu. 2. 19. the ſame ſhould be ſaid of al aged perſons. They which are planted in the houſe of God, *bring forth fruite in their old age*. *Pſal.* 91. 16. It is the commendation of the old man, that by reaſon of his manifold experience, he knowes the Father more then others. 1. *Ioh.* 2. 14. It is the praiſe of *Anna*, that ſhee continually ſerued God in faſting and praier beeing 80. yeares old. When the outward

man

man decaies, the inward man should be renewed. I speake all this the rather, because aged persons are much wanting in this duty. For none commonly are so ignorant in the things of God as they: they begin in the spirit, but the affections of their hearts vsually end in the loue of this present world. But they must bee warned, that as they goe before others in age, so must they also exceede in the graces of the spirit. We vse to say of children, *God make them good old men:* and it is well said. An old man is to be regarded: but specially, a Good old man, who is more to be respected then twentie of yonger yeares. Now aged persons when they grow in age, and not in the spirit, they lose their honour, for *age is a crowne of glory, when it is found in the way of righteousnes. Prou.* 16.31. Let them therefore pray with *Dauid, Forsake me not, O Lord, in mine old age. Psal.* 71. 9.

4 *Haue ye suffered so many things in vaine? if so be it be euen in vaine.*

The interrogation, *haue ye?* is as much as, *ye haue.* Because the question in this place counteruailes a speech affirmatiue. And the words carrie this sense: Ye haue professed the Gospel, and ye haue suffered many afflictions for the same: but now haue ye reuolted from the Gospel, and therefore all your former sufferings are voide, or in vaine.

The words [*if they be in vaine*] are a limitation or qualification of that which was said before: and they carrie this sense: Whereas I haue said that your sufferings are in vaine, I speake it not simply, but with some hope of your repentance: which if it be, then that which would be in vaine, shall not be in vaine.

In this verse, *Paul* sets downe a second reason, to prooue the proposition of his first argument, on this manner: If ye receiued the spirit by my doctrine, then is my doctrine true, and ye fooles in reuolting from it. For by this meanes the things which you suffered well, ye now suffer in vaine.

The vse. When *Paul* saith, *Haue ye suffered, &c.* he signifies vnto vs the estate and condition of all beleeuers in this life, that they must be bearers and sufferers. The reason. To this are we called, 1.*Pet.*2.21. for we are called to resigne all reuenge to God, & therefore of our selues to be bearers and sufferers. *Math.*5.39. *Resist not euill.* And we are called to imitate the passion of Christ, who suffered beeing innocent, and being reuiled, reuiled not againe. Moreouer, it is for our good that we should beare and suffer. 1. *Pet.* 1. 6. and *Psal.* 119. 71. It may be demanded. What if my cause be good, must I then suffer? *Ans.* Yea. The better thy cause is, the better are thy suffering: *They are blessed that suffer for righteousnes.* *Paul* commends himselfe by the multitude of his sufferings. 2. *Cor.* 11. 13. Againe, it may be demanded, how long we must suffer? *Ans.* Euen to the shedding of our blood, if it bee for the resisting of sinne, *Heb.* 12. 4. Lastly, it may be saide, how shall we be able to doe this? *Ans.* *God is faithfull, and will not lay on vs more then we shall be able to beare.* 1. *Cor.* 10. 3. By this we are admonished, not to make a reckoning in this world, of pleasures and delights, as though the Gospel were a Gospel of ease, and as we vse to say, *a Gospel made of veluet:* but euery one of vs must take vp his owne crosse. *Luk.* 9. 23. *If thou wilt be my disciple, denie thy selfe, take vp thy crosse:* that is, the particular affliction and miserie, which God laies on thee. Againe, if in this world we must be sufferers by condition, then in dissentions, and differences, we may neither giue nor take the chalenge, but must be content to beare and put vp wrongs, and abuses. Lastly, in these daies of our peace, we must looke for daies of triall and affliction. For as yet we haue suffered little for the name of Christ. The haruest of the Lord hath bin among vs, more then fourty yeares: therfore (no doubt) the time of threshing, fanning, and grinding comes on, that as the Martyr said, *we may be good bread to the Lord.* And that we may be able to suffer for the name of God, wee must pray for this gift at Gods hand. For power to suffer is the gift of Cod *Phil.* 1. 29. and we must obserue the commandement of God, *not to feare the terrour of men. Reu.* 2. 10. 1. *Pet.* 3. 14. And for this cause, *we must* (as *Peter* saith) *sanctifie God in our hearts:* beeing assured by our faith of the presence, protection, and prouidence of God.

VVen *Paul* saith, *Haue yee suffered so many things?* he shewes that wee must endure manifolde miseries in this life. *Iacob* saide to *Pharao*, *His dayes were fewe and euill. Many are the afflictions of the righteous, Psalme* 34. 20. Christ saith, *Take vp thy crosse euery day, Luke* 9. 23. and thereby hee signifies, that euery new day that comes ouer our heades, wee must looke for a newe crosse. And for this cause, it is not enough to bee patient for a fit, but we must shew all patience, and long suffering, and that with ioyfulnes. *Col.* 1. 11.

When *Paul* saith, *Haue ye suffered so many things in vaine?* he signifies, that our sufferings are of great vse, vnlesse our sinnes be the hinderance. It may then be demanded, what is the vse of our sufferings? The Papists answer, that in our baptisme or first conuersion Christ sufferings doe all: and abolish the whole fault and punishment: but if we sinne after our conuersion, then, say they, Christs sufferings abolish the fault, and the eternall punishment, and our owne sufferings, abolish the temporall punishment. But this doctrine lessens, and obscures the mercy of God: and it must bee obserued, that *Paul* hold all their sufferings to *be in vaine*, that seeke remission of sinnes, or iustification, in any thing, out of Christ.

Now we for our parts, make fiue other vses of our sufferings, First, they serue for triall of men, that it may appeare what is hidden in their hearts. *Deut.* 8.2. Secondly, they serue for the correction of things amisse in vs. 1. *Corin.* 11.23. Thirdly, they serue as documents, and warnings to others, specially in publike persons: thus *Dauid* suffers many things after repentance, for his murther and adultery. Fourthly, they are markes of adoption, if we be content to obey God in them. *Heb.* 12.7. Lastly, they are the troaden and beaten way to the kingdome of heauen. *Act.* 14.23.

When *Paul* saith, *If they be in vaine*, wee are to obserue his moderation. He reprooues and terrifies the Galatians, yet so as he is carefull to preserue the hope of mercy in them, and the hope of their amendment in himselfe. The like hath bin the practise of the Prophets. *Ionas* preacheth, *Yet fourtie daies and Niniue shall bee destroied*: but withall hee addes, *It may be the Lord will repent, and turne from his fierce wrath. Ion.* 3.9. *Peter* saith to *Simon Magus*, *Thou art in the gall of bitternes*: but withall he addes, *Pray God that the thought of thy heart may be forgiuen thee. Act.* 8.21. See the like, *Ioel* 2.14. and *Amos* 5.15. And thus are Ministers of the Gospel to delay and qualifie their reproofes, and censures.

5 *He therefore that ministreth to you the spirit, and worketh miracles among you, doth he it by the workes of the law, or by the hearing of faith?*

These wordes are a repetition of the second verse, whence the exposition must be fetched. The words [*and worketh miracles among you*] are added: and they carrie this meaning; That God gaue to the Galatians, not onely the spirit of adoption, but also other extraordinary gifts of the spirit, as to speake with strange tongues, to cure diseases, and such like.

Repetitions in Scripture are not idle, but of great vse, and signifie vnto vs the necessitie of the thing repeated, and the infallible certentie of it. The substance therefore of this verse must carefully be remembred, and that this. Ye receiued the spirit by my doctrine: therefore it is true, and of God. The argument is of great vse, For by it wee come to an infallible assurance of the Certentie of the Scriptures, and of true religion deriued thence.

The

The Galatians are now reuolted from *Pauls* doctrine, and they erre in the foundation: and yet *Paul* saith in the time present, *Hee that ministreth the spirit vnto you.* Hence it appeares, that falls of infirmitie in the child of God, doe not vtterly extinguish the spirit, but onely grieue, or make sadde the spirit.

Againe *Paul* here teacheth, that God is the onely and proper author of miracles. For he that ministreth the spirit, worketh miracles, namely God. A miracle is, a work aboue the strength of nature: therefore it can be effected of none but the author of nature. It may be obiected, the Apostles, Prophets, and others, had a gift to worke miracles. *Iosua* commanded the sunne to stand, *Iosua* 10. 12. & *Elias* commanded fire to come down from heauen, 2. *Kin.* 1. *Answer.* God neuer gaue to any man power to worke and effect a miracle, either mediately or immediately. The gift was the faith of miracles. The faith was grounded vpon reuelation: and the reuelation was, that God himselfe would worke such or such a miracle, when they praied, commanded, or imposed hands. Men therfore properly, are but the mouth of God, and messengers to signifie what he will doe. Againe, it may be obiected, that the diuell can worke miracles. *Answ.* He can worke a wonder, or things extraordinarie, in respect of the ordinarie course of nature. Thus he caused fire to fall from heauen: and he caused vlcers to arise in the bodie of *Iob*, and that true vlcers. And this he did by the force of nature; better knowne to him, then all the world. But as for a true miracle that exceedes the strength of nature, he cannot possibly doe it: no not Christ himselfe, as man, though he be exalted aboue all men and angels. By this we see that they are deceiued, who thinke that the diuell can make raine, thunder, and lightning. Indeede when the matter of raine and thunder is prepared by God, he can hasten it, and make it more terrible: but raine, and thunder he cannot make: for that is indeede as much as any miracle. Againe, it is a falsehood to thinke, that Alchimists are able to turne baser mettals into gold. For it is a worke of creation to turne a creature of one kind into a creature of an other kind. It is also as foolish to imagine that witches, by the power of the diuell, are able to to turne themselues, into catts and other creatures. None can doe this, but God that made the creature.

Here againe we see the vse of miracles, that is, to confirme doctrine in the Apostolike Churches. That their vse is further to confirme doctrine euen at this day, it cannot be prooued.

Lastly, here in the Galatians we see what an easie thing it is to fall from God, from our faith, and allegiance to him. They were

taught

taught by *Paul*: they had receiued the ſpirit of adoption: they were enabled to worke miracles: and yet for all this they fall away to an other Goſpel. They muſt be a looking glaſſe to vs. In peace we are now conſtant: but if triall ſhall come, our frailtie ſhall appeare. That our frailty and weaknes may not be hurtful to vs, we muſt remember two rules. One is, not to haue a conceit of any thing in vs, but to hold our faith & religion in feare, as in the preſence of God, *Rom.* 11.20. The ſecond, to take heed that there be not in vs an euill, corrupt, and diſſembling heart. For if our heart be naught, our faith cannot be good, *Heb.* 4.12.

6 As Abraham beleeued God, and it was imputed to him for righteouſneſſe:

7 Know yee therefore, that they which are of faith, are the children of Abraham.

The words, *Euen as Abraham, &c.* haue reference to that which went before, on this manner. Yee Galatians receiued the ſpirit by my doctrine: and my doctrine was the preaching of iuſtification by faith without workes: which doctrine is like and ſutable to the example of *Abraham, who beleeued God, and it was imputed for iuſtice.*

Heere *Paul* ſets downe the ſecond Argument, whereby hee prooues the truth of his doctrine. And it is framed thus: As *Abraham* was iuſtified, ſo are the children of *Abraham. Abraham* was iuſtified by iuſtice imputed, and apprehended by faith, verſe 6. Therefore the children of *Abraham* are thus iuſtified. This concluſion is the principall queſtion: it is not heere expreſſed, but in the roome thereof a declaration is made, who are the true children of God, namely, they that are of *Abraham*, in reſpect of faith.

That which is heere ſaid of *Abraham*, is a maine ground concerning the iuſtification of a ſinner, in the bookes of the old and new Teſtament: therefore I will more carefully ſearch the true interpretation of it.

Some expound the words thus: *Abraham* beleeued God, and the world reputed him for a good and vertuous man. But if this be the right ſenſe, then *Paul* is deceiued, who brings this text to proue the iuſtification of *Abraham*, not only before men, but alſo before God. Now vertue and goodneſſe, which is in eſtimation among men, is not ſufficient to acquit and iuſtifie vs before God.

The ſecond expoſition is of the Papiſts, who by *faith* here vnderſtand, a generall faith, wherby the articles of faith are beleeued. And by *imputation*, they vnderſtand *reputation*, whereby a thing is eſteemed as it is indeed. And they teach that faith is reputed for righteouſnes; becauſe (ſay they) faith formed with charitie, is indeed the iuſtice wherby a ſinner is iuſtified before God. But this expoſition hath his defects and errours. For firſt of all, charitie is not the forme, or life of faith, but the fruite and effect of it. 1.*Tim*.1.5. *The end of teaching is loue out of a pure heart, good conſcience, and faith vnfained.* It is obiected, that *as the body is dead without the ſoule, ſo is faith without workes, Iames* 2.26. and therefore that workes are the life of faith. *Anſw.* S.*Iames* by faith vnderſtands a pretended faith, or the profeſſion of faith, as appeares by the words, v.14. *though a man ſay he hath faith*: and v.18. *ſhew me thy faith.* Now of this profeſſion of faith, works are the life.

Secondly, this expoſition makes faith, or the act of beleeuing, to be our whole and intire iuſtice before God: whereas indeed if it be iuſtice, it is but one part thereof. And in the act of beleeuing, loue cannot be included.

Thirdly, faith ioyned with charitie, is not the iuſtice whereby a ſinner is iuſtified. For our faith and loue are both imperfect: and faith is imputed for righteouſnes without works, *Rom*.4.6. & therefore without charitie. For this is charitie, to keepe the commaundements of God, *Iohn* 15.10. *Paul* ſaith, that the righteouſneſſe wherby we are iuſtified, is *by*, or *through faith, Phil*.3.9. and therefore our iuſtice and our faith, are two diſtinct things.

The third expoſition is alſo from the Papiſts, that faith is reputed for righteouſnes: becauſe it is reputed to be a ſufficient meanes to prepare men to their iuſtification: but this cannot be the ſenſe of this place. For this was ſpoken of *Abraham* after he was iuſtified; and therefore needed no preparation to iuſtification.

Let vs now come to the true ſenſe of the wordes. In them I conſider two things, *Abrahams* faith, in theſe wordes, *Abraham beleeued God*: and the fruite of his faith, in theſe wordes, *and it was imputed to him for righteouſneſſe.* Touching his faith, I conſider three things. The firſt is, the occaſion, which was on this manner. After the conqueſt of the heathen Kings, *Abraham* was ſtil in ſome feare: In this regard the Lord comforts him, *Geneſ*.15.1. *I am thy buckler, and thy exceeding great reward.* But to this *Abraham* replies, *I want iſſue*: and the Lord anſwers, *I will make thy ſeede as the ſtarres of heauen, Geneſ*.15.5. Now then, looke as God renewes and inlarges his promiſe to *Abraham*, ſo *Abraham* renewes his faith: and hereupon *Moſes*, and *Paul*, ſay, *Abraham beleeued God.* God doeth

not

not now inlarge his promiſes to vs as to *Abraham*: neuertheleſſe, the promiſes recorded in the Bible, are renewed to vs partly by preaching, and partly by the vſe of the Sacraments: and wee accordingly are to renew our faith, ſpecially in the time of feare, and danger.

The ſecond thing is the obiect, or matter of his faith, and that is, the multiplication of his poſteritie. It may be ſaid, how could *Abraham* bee iuſtified by ſuch a faith? *Anſwer*. The promiſe of the multiplication of his ſeed, was a dependant of a more principall promiſe, *I am thy God all-ſufficient, Gene.*17.1. and, *I am thy exceeding great reward, Gen.*15.11. In this carnall ſeed, *Abraham* ſpecially reſpected (by the eye of faith) the bleſſed ſeed of the woman. Hee therefore beleeued the promiſe of a ſeed, as it was a pledge vnto him of a thing more principall; namely, the fauour of God, and as it was a meanes to effect the incarnation of the Sonne of God. In his example wee are taught how wee are to reſpect, and vſe earthly things: wee are to reſpect them as pledges of Gods fauour: and to vſe them as meanes to further vs to Chriſt, and to the attainment of our ſaluation.

The third point is, the propertie of *Abrahams* faith, which was a faith againſt hope. For he beleeued the promiſe of a ſeed, when his body was halfe dead, and *Sarai* was barren. In like ſort we keeping true religion and good conſcience, muſt in all our temptations, croſſes, miſeries, infirmities, againſt reaſon, ſenſe, and feeling, beleeue the promiſe of remiſſion of ſinnes, and life euerlaſting.

In the effect and fruite of *Abrahams* faith, three things muſt bee conſidered. The firſt is, what is meant by *Imputation*. To *impute* properly, is a ſpeech borrowed from merchants: and it ſignifies to reckon, or to keepe a reckoning of expences and receits. Thus *Paul* ſaith, *Philem.*18. *If he haue done thee any wrong, impute it to me*: that is, ſet it on my reckoning. And this word is here applied to the iudgment of God. Becauſe hee is our ſoueraigne Lord, and wee are his debters: and hee doeth adiudge vnto men for their ſinnes, either pardon, or puniſhment.

Imputation in God is twofold: one Legall: the other Euangelicall. Legal is, when God willeth and adiudgeth the reward to him that fulfilleth the law. Thus *Paul* ſaith, *Rom.*4.5. that *the wages is imputed to him that worketh*, and that *of debt*. Euangelical imputation is, when God accepts the ſatisfaction of Chriſt our ſurety as a paimēt for our ſinnes. In this ſenſe is the word, Impute, taken ten times in the 4. chapter to the *Romanes*, and in the ſame it is vſed in this place.

The ſecond point is, what is imputed? *And it was imputed*, that is, faith. *Faith* here muſt be conſidered two waies; firſt, as a qualitie in it ſelfe: and thus it is imperfect, and conſequently cannot be imputed to vs for our iuſtification. Againe, faith muſt be conſidered as an inſtrument, or hand holding and receiuing Chriſt: and in this regard beleeuing is put for the thing beleeued. And thus muſt this text bee vnderſtood. *It was imputed to him*, that is, the thing which his faith beleeued, was imputed to him by God: for the act of beleeuing is not our iuſtice, as I haue ſhewed.

The third point is, what is meant by *righteouſneſſe? Anſw.* That which is called in Scripture, the Iuſtice of God, which is ſufficient to acquit a ſinner at the barre of Gods iudgement. Thus then the ſenſe is manifeſt: *Abraham* beleeued the promiſe of God, ſpecially touching the bleſſed ſeed: and that which hee beleeued, namely, the obedience of the Mediatour (the bleſſed ſeed) was accepted of God as his obedience, for his iuſtification.

It is obiected, that the obedience of Chriſt is to be imputed to none, but to Chriſt, who was the doer of it. *Anſwer.* It is to be imputed, that is, aſcribed to him as to the Author therof: and withall becauſe he did performe it in our roome and ſtead, and that for vs, it is to be imputed to vs.

Secondly, it is obiected, that workes are alſo imputed, as well as faith, *Pſal.* 106. 31. *Phinees executed iudgement, and it was imputed to him for righteouſnes. Anſ.* There is *iuſtice of the perſon*, and *iuſtice of the act*. *Iuſtice of the perſon* is that, which makes the perſon of man iuſt. *Iuſtice of the act* is that, which makes the act of the perſon iuſt, and not the perſon it ſelfe. Now the *Pſalme* ſpeakes onely of the iuſtice of *Phinees* action: and the meaning of the words is this, that God reputed his action as a iuſt action, whereas men might haply condemne it. This place therefore proues not that works are imputed for the iuſtification of any man.

Thirdly, it is obiected, that imputed iuſtice was neuer known in the Church, till 1500. yeares after Chriſt. *Anſw.* It is falſe. *Bernard* ſaith expreſly, *Death is put to flight by the death of Chriſt, and the iuſtice of Chriſt is imputed to vs*: and againe, *the ſatisfaction of Chriſt is imputed to vs.* Againe, ſundry of the Fathers, as *Auguſtine, Hierome, Chryſoſtome, Theodoret, Anſelme*, entreating vpon the text of *Paul*, 2. *Cor* 5. 21. auouch, that the iuſtice whereby we are iuſtified, is not in vs, but in Chriſt. And it is a receiued doctrine with them, that *a ſinner is iuſtified by faith alone*: now faith alone preſuppoſeth an imputation of iuſtice.

Serm. ad mil. Temp. c. 11.
Epiſt. 190.

The vſe. Hence it followes, that there is no merit of mans workes, either in the beginning, or in the accompliſhment of our

iuſtifi-

iustification. For faith is imputed for iustice to him that beleeueth and worketh not, *Rom* 4. 5.

Againe, by this we see there is but one iustification; and that the second, by workes, whereby a man, of a good man, is made better, is a meere fiction. For iust *Abraham* is not iustified by his good works wherewith he abounded, but after his first iustification, faith still is imputed to him for righteousnesse.

Thirdly, here we see what is that very thing, whereby wee are to appeare iust before God, and to bee saued, and that is the obedience of Christ, imputed to vs of God, and apprehended by our faith.

Lastly, heere wee see our dutie. God sits as a Iudge ouer vs: he takes a reckoning of vs, for all our doings: the law is an handwriting against vs: to some hee imputes their sinnes, to some hee remits them. We therefore must come into the presence of God, pleade guiltie, and acknowledge our selues to be as bankrupts, and intreat him to graunt pardon to vs, and to accept the satisfaction of Christ for vs: then will God not impute our sinnes, but the obedience of Christ for our iustification: and accept him as our suretie in life and death.

The declaration of the conclusion followes in the 9. verse, and it shewes who are the children of *Abraham*. The meaning of the words must first be considered. *To be of faith*, is to be of *Abrahams* faith, *Rom*. 4. 16. And *to be of Abrahams faith*, is to beleeue, & applie the promise of righteousnes and life euerlasting by Christ, as *Abraham* did: and to rest in it for our iustification and saluation, vers. 10. they are said *to be of workes*, who do the works of the law, and looke to be iustified thereby: therefore they are of faith, who beleeue in Christ, and looke to be saued and iustified thereby.

And they which thus beleeue with *Abraham*, are said to bee *his children*. It may be demanded, how? *Answ*. Children of *Abraham* are of two sorts: some by nature, some by grace. By nature are they, which are of *Abraham* by the flesh, or naturall generation, as *Ismael* was. By grace, all beleeuers are children of *Abraham*: and that three wayes. First, by Imitation, in that *Abraham* is set foorth vnto vs as a paterne, in the steppes of whose faith all true beleeuers walke, *Rom*. 4. 12. Secondly, beleeuers are children of *Abraham*, by succession, in that they succeed in the inheritance of the same blessing. Thirdly, they are children to him by a kinde of spirituall generation. For *Abraham* by beleeuing the promise of a seed did after a sort beget them. Indeed properly the promise and election of God makes them children: and *Abraham* by his faith beleeuing the foresaid promise, receiues them of God as his children. In this regard beleeuers are called *children of the promise, Rom.* 9.8.and *the seede*,that is,of the faith of *Abraham, Rom.* 4.16. Now then the meaning of the text is,that beleeuers, though vncircumcised,are the children of *Abraham*. It may be said,what priuiledge is this? *Ans.*Great: for the children of *Abraham* are children of the couenant, *Act.*3.25.and children of God, *Rom.*9 8.

The vse. In this verse, *Paul* sets downe one thing,namely, the true marke of the child of *Abraham*,and that is,to be of the faith of *Abraham*.Here then marke,first of all the Iewes,though descending of *Isaac*, are no children of *Abraham*,because they follow not the faith of *Abraham*. Secondly, the Turks are no children, though they plead descent from *Agar* sometimes,and sometime from *Sara*, tearming themselues *Agarens*, and *Saracens*. For they tread vnder foote the faith of *Abraham*. Thirdly, the Papist will nothing helpe himselfe by the plea of Antiquity,Succession,and vniuersall consent, except he can shew some good euidence, that he is of the faith of *Abraham*, which he cannot. For this faith he hath corrupted, as I haue shewed. Lastly, our profession of *Abrahams* faith,partly in teaching,and partly in hearing,and in the vse of the Sacraments; is not sufficient to prooue vs the children of *Abraham*. For *not euery one that saith Lord, Lord, shall enter into the Kingdome of heauen*, *Math.*7.22.

Therefore we must labour to be indeed and in truth of the faith of *Abraham*, and to walke in the steppes of his faith. And to this end,we must doe three thrings. First,we must haue knowledge of the maine and principall promise,touching the blessing of God in Christ,and of all other promises depending on the principall: and we must know the scope and tenour of them, that we be not deceiued. Secondly,we must with *Abraham* beleeue the power,and truth of God, in the accomplishing of the said promises, or in the working of our vocation,iustification, sanctification, glorification. *Rom.*4.21. Thirdly,we must by faith obey God in all things,shutting our eyes, and suffering our selues(as it were)to be led blindfold,by the word of God. Thus did *Abraham* in all things,euen in actions against nature, *Heb.* 11.8. But this practise is rare among vs. For there are three things, which preuaile much among vs, the loue of worldly honour,the loue of pleasures, and the loue of riches: and where these beare a sway,there faith takes no place. It will be said,that faith is much professed. *Ans.*Faith was neuer more professed, yet there was neuer lesse true faith. For the common faith of men, is a false faith. For in some, it is conceiued without

the

the meanes of the word, prayer, ſacraments: and in others, it is ſeuered from the purpoſe of not ſinning. Now faith conceiued without the true meanes, and faith ioyned with the purpoſe to liue as we liſt, is nothing but preſumption. And ſurely, this is the faith, though not of all, yet of the moſt.

Moreouer, that which *Paul* hath ſaid of the children of *Abraham*, he prooues by the teſtimony of the Galatians, in theſe words, *Know ye therefore*, or *ye know*: that is, vpon the ſaying of *Moſes* in the former verſe, ye your ſelues know this to be a truth, which I ſaid. Marke here, *Paul* requires ſuch a meaſure of knowledge in beleeuers, that they muſt be able to iudge of the gathering of this or that doctrine, out of this or that place of Scripture. This ſhewes the contempt of knowledge in theſe our dayes to be great: for moſt men reiect the preaching of the Goſpel, and content themſelues with the teaching, and ſchooling of nature.

8. *For the Scripture fore-ſeeing that God would iuſtifie the Gentiles through faith, preached before the Goſpell vnto Abraham, ſaying, In thee ſhall all the Gentiles be bleſſed.*

9. *So then, they which are of faith, are bleſſed with faithfull Abraham.*

Againſt the argument in the two former verſes, a doubt, or exception might be mooued, on this manner. We grant, that they which are of the faith of *Abraham*, are iuſtified as he was, ſo they be Iewes, and not Gentiles. Now this doubt, exception, or obiection, *Paul* remooues in theſe verſes, thus. When God ſaid to *Abraham*, *In thee ſhall all the Gentiles be bleſſed*; he ſignified the iuſtification euen of the Gentiles by faith: therefore all that are of faith, euen the Gentiles, are bleſſed of God, as *Abraham* was.

In the 8. verſe, I conſider three things: the occaſion of the ſpeech of God to *Abraham*, namely, *Gods fore-knowledge*: the manner of his ſpeech, *the preaching of the Goſpel to Abraham*: and the teſtimony it ſelfe, *In thee, &c.*

Touching the occaſion; firſt it may be demanded, whether this fore-knowledge in God, be a bare fore-knowledge, ſeuered from the will of God, or no. *Anſw.* No: Gods fore-knowledge is in all things ioyned with his decree, or will. If God ſhould fore-ſee things to come, and in no ſort will or nill them, there ſhould be an idle prouidence. *Chriſt was deliuered by the will and fore-knowledge of God, Act.2 23.* And the Iewes for their parts *did nothing* in the crucifying of Chriſt, *but that which the hand, and counſell of*

God had determined to be done, *Act.*4 28. Neither is God by this doctrine made the author of ſinne. For ſinne comes to paſſe, not from the will of God, but according to his will: in that he foreſees euill, and withall wills not to hinder the being of it: and euill not hindred, comes to paſſe.

Againe, it may be demanded, in what order the fore-knowledge of God ſtands to his will. *Anſ.* The fore-knowledge of things that may poſſiby come to paſſe, goes before his will: the foreknowledge of things that ſhall certainly come to paſſe, followes the will, and decree of God. For things come not to paſſe, becauſe they are foreſeene; but becauſe they are to come to paſſe, according to the will of God; therefore they are foreſeene. Now then becauſe foreknowledge in God, is ioyned with his will, and is alwaies a conſequent of it, it is often put for the counſell, will, and decree of God as in this place.

In this text, two things are to be conſidered of Gods foreknowledge. The firſt is, who, or what foreſees? Anſwer here is made, *The Scripture foreſees*: that is, God foreſees, and the Scripture records things foreſeene by him. Hence it appeares, that the writings of *Moſes* are the word of God. For they fore-tell things to come 2000. yeares after, as the calling and benediction of the Gentiles in the ſeede of *Abraham*. In the ſame regard the writings of *Paul* are the word of God. For there he reueales and ſets down in writing, more then 2000. yeares after, what was the intention of God, when hee ſaid to *Abraham*: *In thee ſhall all the Gentiles be bleſſed.*

The ſecond point is, what is foreſeene? Anſwer is made, *that God iuſtifieth the Gentiles*, that is, God will as certainly iuſtifie them in time to come, as if he had then done it, when hee ſpake theſe words. Some teach that the Predeſtination of God, is his decree, in which he purpoſeth to redeeme, and iuſtifie all men, of all ages, and times, ſo be it, they will beleeue. But I finde no ſuch decree in the word. Here we ſee Gods decree, is onely to iuſtifie all Gentiles in the laſt age of the world. And thus the text of *Paul* muſt be vnderſtood, *God would haue all men to be ſaued*, 1.*Tim.*2. namely, all men, or all the Gentiles in the laſt age of the world, and not al the Gentiles, of all ages, and times.

In the next place, the manner of the ſpeech and teſtimony of God muſt be conſidered, in that he is ſaid *to preach the Goſpell to Abraham.* Here marke the Antiquity of the Goſpel: and the markes of true religion, which for his ſubſtance was knowne not onely to the Apoſtles, but alſo to the Prophets, and Patriarks. So ancient is the true way of life, and the doctrine of iuſtification by faith, without workes. Papistes pleade antiquitie for their religion: but in vaine: for the proper points and heads of their religion were taken vp since the dayes of Christ, some, two hundred yeares after, some foure hundred, some six hundred, some eight hundred, some a thousand, and some foureteene hundred yeares after.

The third poynt, is the speach, or testimony it selfe: *In thee shall all the Gentiles be blessed. In thee*, that is, in thy seed, *Christ*, *Gene.*22. 18. who is in thy loines: into whom the Gentiles are ingrafted by faith, and consequently into thee. For they are the seed of Christ, *Isai.*53.10. who is the seed of *Abraham*. Againe, here it is said, *All the Gentiles*: but *Gen.*17.4. *Abraham* is called *the father*, not of all, but *of many nations*. *Answ.* He is the father *of many*, in respect of his flesh; and he is a father *of all* the Gentiles in regard of his faith. Againe, it is vsuall in Scripture, to put the word *All*, for *many*, *Rom.* 5. 15.18. And the benediction heere mentioned, comprehends all the spirituall graces of God, as vocation, iustification, glorification, *Ephes.*1. v. 3.

The vse. In that the Lord saith, *All the nations shall bee blessed in Abraham*: Hence I gather, that the nation of the Iewes shall bee called, and conuerted to the participation of this blessing: when, and how, God knowes: but that it shall be done before the ende of the world, wee know. For if all nations shall bee called, then the Iewes.

Againe, that which was foretold to *Abraham*, is verified in our eyes. For this our English nation, and many other nations are at this day blessed in this seed of *Abraham*. Vpon the consideration of this, we are admonished of many things. First, wee are to giue to God great thanks and praise, that wee are borne in these dayes. For many Prophets and great Kings desired to see that which we see, and could not obtaine it. Secondly, we must euery one of vs in our hearts amend and turne to God, and vnfainedly beleeue in Christ, that wee may now in the acceptable day bee partakers of the promised blessing. The Lord saith, *Gene.* 22. 18. *In thy seed all the nations of the earth shall bee blessed*, or, *blesse themselues*: because they shall vse all good meanes, that they may bee filled with the blessings of God. Thirdly, we must blesse all, doe good to all, and hurt to none: for, *wee are heires of blessing*, 1. *Pet.* 3.8. Lastly, we must here marke our comfort: if we truly turne to God, and beleeue in the holy seed of *Abraham*, all things shall go well with vs: *God shall blesse them that blesse vs, and curse them that curse vs*, *Gen.*12.3.

The ninth verse, is the conclusion of *Pauls* answer: and it is in effect

effect and substance one and the same with verse 7. and it signifieth that all men that be of *Abrahams* faith, (though otherwise forrainers and Gentiles to *Abraham*) shall be partakers of the same blessing of God with him. It may be said: How shall we haue the same blessing, when we haue not the like faith? *Answ.* God respects not the greatnesse of our faith, so much as the truth of it. And if faith erre not in his obiect: that is, if we make Christ crucified our Redeemer, and ioyne nothing to him: if there be further a will to beleeue, and to apprehend Christ with care and constancie to increase in faith, and a purpose not to sinne, God will accept this true and honest will for deed.

10 *For as many as bee of the workes of the law, are vnder the curse. For it is written, Cursed is euery one that continues not in all things written in the Law, to doe them.*

In these wordes *Paul* sets downe a second reason, whereby hee prooues, that not only the Iewes, but also the Gentiles, are blessed as *Abraham* was, by faith. And the reason is drawne from the contraries, thus. *They that are of workes*, that is, that looke to be iustified by works, are vnder the curse. Therefore, they that are of faith, are blessed, or iustified with *Abraham*. Moreouer, *Paul* addes the proofe of this second reason in the next words, and it is framed thus: They which fulfill not the law, are cursed: they which are of works, fulfil not the law: therefore they are accursed.

Whereas *Paul* saith, *that they are vnder the curse, that will bee of workes*, wee see the whole world almost, walkes in the way of perdition: it is a conclusion of nature, that we must be saued, and iustified by our workes. The young Prince in the Gospel, said, *Good master, what must I doe to be saued? The Iewes would not bee subiect to the iustice of God, but they established their owne righteousnesse of the lawe, Rom.* 10.3. Our common people, and they that should bee wise, say, they looke to bee saued by faith: but indeed they turne their faith to workes. For what is their faith? surely nothing else (as they say) but their good meaning, or their good dealing, or their good seruing of God.

Hence againe it followes, that the Papacy, or Popish religion is the way to perdition, in that it prescribeth and teacheth iustification by workes. On the contrary, our religion is the safest and surest from danger, because it teacheth the free iustification of a sinner by the blood of Christ. And this makes the Papistes in the day of death, to renounce iustification by their workes. *Steuen Gardiner*, a

bloody

bloody perſecutor,being on his death-bed told of free iuſtification by the blood of Chriſt,ſaid;*You may tell this to me,but doe not open this gap to the people.* One of late in a publike execution of iuſtice,ſaid,he would die a Catholike,and withall he added, that he looked to be ſaued only by the paſſion of Chriſt.

In the proofe of the reaſon, three things are to bee conſidered: What the curſe is? who are curſed? and when?

The curſe is eternall woe and miſery: and it is either in this life, in the end of this life,or in the life to come.

The curſe in this life,is either within man,or without him. The curſe within man is manifold. In the minde there is ignorance of God,of our ſelues,of true happines,and of the meanes to attaine to it. Again,there is a great difficultie with much paine to learne,and retaine things to be learned & retained. And this is a curſe of God vpon our minds. In the conſcience there are manifold accuſations, terrors & feares,ariſing vpon euery occaſion,and they are flaſhings (as it were)of the fire of hell, vnleſſe they be quenched in this life by the blood of Chriſt. In the will there is an inclination to all maner of ſinnes without exception. Againe,there is hardnes of heart, whereby the will of man is vnpliable to that which is good,vnleſſe it be renewed. In the body there are more diſeaſes,then the Phyſicians bookes can expreſſe: and as many diſeaſes as there be in vs, ſo many fruits of ſinne there are,*Iohn* 5.4.

The curſe without vs is three-fold. The firſt is, a ſpirituall bondage vnder the power of the diuell: who by reaſon of ſinne, workes in the hearts of vnbeleeuers,*Ephe.*2.2. and hath the power of death,*Heb.*2.14.

The ſecond, is an enmitie of all the creatures with man, ſince the fall. And this appeares, becauſe when God receiues vs to bee his people, he makes a couenant with all creatures,in our behalfe, *Hoſea* 2.18.

The third containes all loſſes, calamities, miſeries, in goods, friends,good name, Reade *Deut.*28.

The curſe in the end of this life,is death,which is the ſeparation of body and ſoule, *Rom.* 5.13. and death in his owne nature is a fearefull curſe,and the very downfall to the pit of hell.

The curſe after this life,is the ſecond death: which is ſeparation of body and ſoule from God,with a full apprehenſion of the wrath of God. And if the paine of one tooth or finger,be oftentimes ſo great,that men rather deſire to die, then liue: how great then ſhall the paine be,when all the parts of body and ſoule ſhall be tormented? And the eternitie of this death increaſeth mans miſery. If a man might ſuffer ſo many yeares as there are drops in the ſea,and then haue an end,it were ſome comfort: but when that time is expired,man is as farre from the end of his woe,as euer he was.

Thus in ſumme and ſubſtance is the curſe here mentioned: and it were to be wiſhed,that men would more thinke and ſpeake of it then they doe: then would there be more conſcience of ſinne.

The next point is,who are curſed. *Anſ. They which do not all things written in the law.* Here is an *Item* for them that wil keep ſome commandements,but not all. *Herod* would do ſome things at the motion of *Iohn Baptiſt*, but hee would not leaue his inceſtuous mariage with his brothers wife, *Mar.*6.20. There be at this day that are very forward in good things: yet ſome of them will not leaue their ſwearing,ſome their lying,ſome their vncleanneſſe,ſome their vſury. But God will not part ſtakes with man: he will haue all or none. *He that breakes one commandement,is guiltie of all,Iam.*2. And there is good reaſon,that he which obeyes, ſhould obey in all. For where God renewes,he ſanctifies throughout,and fils them with the ſeed of all grace,that they may performe obedience,according to all the commandements of the law.

Againe, he is curſed that doth not all things which the law preſcribeth;or if he do them,yet doth not continue in all. So then he is curſed that breaks the law but once,and that only in one thought: for ſuch an one doth not continue in all things. Now then,O ſinful man,what wilt thou do to auoid the curſe? for thou haſt in thought, word,and deed, broken the law. Doeſt thou thinke to appeaſe the wrath of God with gold and ſiluer? the whole world and all things therein are the Lords. And thou maiſt not thinke to hide or withdraw thy ſelfe from the preſence of God: for all muſt come and appeare before his tribunall ſeate, in their owne perſons. Neither may we thinke to eſcape,becauſe God is mercifull: for he is as iuſt, as mercifull. What wilt thou then doe to eſcape this horrible curſe? when thou haſt done all thou canſt doe, thou canſt no way helpe or relieue thy ſelfe.

The onely way of helpe is this. Thou muſt flie from this ſentence of the law,to the throne of grace for mercy;inſtantly aſking, ſeeking,knocking at the gate of mercy for pardon of thy ſinnes. And that thou mayeſt be encouraged to this dutie,conſider with me,that at thy firſt purpoſe to amend,and to turne vnto God, thy ſinnes are pardoned in heauen. *Dauid* ſaith, *Pſal.*32.5. *I thought,I will confeſſe my ſinnes againſt my ſelfe, and thou forgaueſt me.* Marke the ſpeach, *I thought.* The prodigall child, *Luke* 15.vpon his purpoſe to returne to his father,(before hee had indeed humbled himſelfe in word) was receiued to mercy. When *Dauid* ſaid, *I haue ſinned, Nathan* in the name of God ſaid, *Thy ſin is forgiuen thee.* It may be thou wilt ſay, the curſe is abſolute. *Anſwer.* The threatnings of the law muſt bee vnderſtood with an exception which the Goſpell makes, on this manner: The law ſaith, Curſed is the tranſgreſſor: and the Goſpel ſaith, *Except he repent.* *Ionas* preached, yet fortie dayes, and Nineue ſhall be deſtroyed: yet withall hee addes an exception: *It may bee the Lord will repent of his fierce wrath, Ionas* 3.9. Againe, thou wilt ſay, my ſins are very grieuous, therfore I feare I ſhal not eſcape the curſe. *Anſ.* Forgiueneſſe is promiſed without any limitation to any number or kinds of ſinne, (only the ſin againſt the holy Ghoſt excepted.) Therefore appeale with boldneſſe in thy heart to the throne of grace, intreate for forgiueneſſe as for life and death, and thou ſhalt eſcape the curſe.

The third poynt is, when is a ſinner accurſed? *Anſw.* In preſent, in the time of this life. For the Lord ſaith not, *he ſhall bee accurſed*: but, *he is accurſed.* There bee among vs whom no Sermons or exhortations will amend: and ſuch perſons thinke themſelues without the reach of any danger. For they thinke the time is very long to the laſt iudgement. But they are deceiued touching themſelues. For God with his owne mouth hath giuen the ſentence, that they are accurſed, there remaines nothing but the execution. The halter is already about their neckes, and there remaines nothing but the turning of the ladder. Nay the execution is already in blindneſſe of mind, and hardneſſe of heart. He that beleeues not, is already condemned, *Iohn* 3.

Laſtly, a memorable concluſion of *Paul* is heere to bee obſerued. That it is impoſſible for any man within himſelfe, for the time of this life, to fulfill the law of God. For *Paul* here takes it for a confeſſed and graunted concluſion: otherwiſe his argument wil not hold: which muſt be framed on this manner. He which fulfils not the law, is curſed: hee which is of workes, fulfills not the law: therefore he is accurſed. I further prooue it thus. If wee could fulfill the law, wee might be iuſtified by the law: but no man can bee iuſtified by the law, or by workes: therefore no man can fulfill the law. Againe, *Paul* ſaith, *Rom.* 7.14. that *the law was ſpirituall*, requiring inward and ſpirituall obedience, and that *hee was carnall*, and therefore not conformable to the law: that *he was ſold vnder ſinne*: that *when he would doe good, euill was preſent*: that *he carried about him the body of death.* And all this hee ſaith of himſelfe, about twentie yeares after his owne conuerſion. Such as our knowledge is, ſuch is our loue to God and man. Now wee know God onely in part: there-

therefore we loue in part; and conſequently we doe not fulfill the law. Againe, the Scripture puts all men, euen the regenerate, vnder the name of ſinners to the very death: *Iſa.64. 4. All our righteouſneſſe is as a defiled cloth, Prouerbs 20.9. Who can ſay, my heart is cleane? Iob cannot anſwer God for one of a thouſand, Iob 9.* The righteous man ſhall pray for the pardon of his ſinnes *in a time when hee may be heard, Pſalm. 32.6. If we ſay wee haue no ſinne, wee deceiue our ſelues, 1.Ioh.1.9.* The Papiſts ſay, that all theſe places are meant of veniall ſins. *Anſw.* There are no veniall ſinnes, which in their owne nature, are not againſt the law of God, but onely beſide it. *The ſtipend of* euery *ſinne is death, Rom.6.23.* If we were perfectly ſanctified, and conſequently fulfillers of the law in this life, then Chriſt ſhould not bee a Sauiour, but an inſtrument of God, to make vs our owne Sauiours. And to ſay this, is blaſphemy. Laſtly, that which man could doe by creation, ſo much the law requires at our hands: but man by creation could loue God with all the powers of his ſoule, and with all the ſtrength of all the powers: which now (ſince the fall) no man can doe. It remaines then for an infallible concluſion, that it is impoſſible for any man in the time of this life, to fulfill the law.

The vſe. This point ſerues notably to condemne the folly of the world. The Iſraelites ſay at Mount Sinai, *that they will doe all things which the Lord ſhall command them, Exod.19.8.* The yong Prince ſaid, *that he had kept all the commandements from his youth, Mark.10.20.* Our common people ſay, *that they can loue God with all their hearts, and their neighbours as themſelues.*

Secondly, this doctrine ſerues to confute ſundry Errours of the Papiſts, who blaſphemouſly teach, that a man after iuſtification, may fulfill the law in this life: that a man may for a time be without all ſinne: that workes of the regenerate are perfect, and may be oppoſed to the iudgement of God: that men may ſupererogate, and doe more then the law requires. The ground of all theſe concluſions is this: They ſay, there is a double degree of fulfilling the law. The firſt is, in this life, and that is, to loue God truely, aboue all creatures, and to loue our neighbour as our ſelues, in truth. The ſecond is, to loue God with al the powers of the ſoule, and with al the ſtrength of all the powers: and this meaſure of fulfilling the law, is reſerued to the life to come. I will briefly conſider the reaſons and the ground of this blaſphemous doctrine.

Obiect. I. God promiſeth the Iſraelites, *that he will circumciſe their hearts, that they may loue him with all their hearts, with all their ſoules, and with all their ſtrength. Deutero.30.6.* And thus *Ioſias turned to*

God

God with all his heart, with all his soule, and with all his strength, according to all the law of Moses. 2.King.23.25. *Answ.* The phrase [*with all thy heart*] is taken in a double signification. Sometime it is opposed to a double heart, and then it signifies, a true vpright heart, without guile or dissimulation. Thus they of Zebulon are saide, *not to fight with a double heart*, 1.Chron.12.33. but *with a perfect heart*, v.38. Where, marke the opposition, of an whole or perfect heart, to a double heart. In this sense are the places before named, to be vnderstood. Neuerthelesse, the whole heart, soule, and strength, in the summe of the morall law, signifies all powers of the soule, and all the strength of al the powers. Thus doth *Paul*, *Rom.*7. expound the law, when he saith, *the law is spirituall*; and by the prohibition of lust, giues the meaning of the whole law. For concupiscence, or lust, comprehends the first thoughts, or motions.

Obiect. II. *Noah* is said to *be iust and perfect*, *Gen.*6. and God commands *Abraham to walke before him, and to be perfect*, *Gen.*17.1. *Paul* saith, *Let as many as be perfect, be thus minded*, *Phil.*3.15. *Answ.* There is a double perfection; *perfection of parts*, and *perfection of degrees*. *Perfection of parts is*, when a man hath in him, after he is regenerate, the beginnings of all vertues, and the seedes of all graces: by which he endeauours, to obey God in all his lawes and commandements. *Perfection of degrees*, is when the law is fulfilled both in matter, and manner, according to the rigour of the law. Now the former places speake onely of the perfection of parts: and that is, such a perfection in which wee are to acknowledge our imperfection, and it is no more but, a true and generall indeauour to obey God. *Isa.*38.1.

Obiect. III. Sundry holy men are saide to fulfill the law: *Dauid turned from nothing that God commanded him all the dayes of his life, saue in the matter of Vriah*, 1.*King.*15.5. *Zachary and Elizabeth walked in all the commandements of God, and that without reproofe before God.* *Luk.*1.6. *Answ.* There are two kinds of fulfilling the law: one *Legall*, the other *Euangelicall*. *Legall* is, when men doe all things required in the law, and that by themselues and in themselues. Thus none euer fulfilled the law, but Christ, and *Adam* before his fall. The *Euangelicall manner* of fulfilling the law, is to beleeue in Christ, who fulfilled the law for vs: and withall to indeauour in the whole man, to obey God in all his precepts. And this indeauour ioined with the purpose of not sinning, is called the righteousnesse of good conscience; and though it be not really a fulfilling of the law, yet it is accepted of God as a fulfilling of the law in al them that are in Christ. For God accepts the indeauour to obey,

for

for perfect obedience. Thus *Dauid, Zachary, Elizabeth*, and others are said to fulfill the law.

Obiect. IIII. We pray that we may fulfill the law, when we say, *Let thy will be done in earth, as it is in heauen. Answ.* Wee pray not that we may fulfill the law in this, but that we may striue as much as may be, to attaine to the fulfilling of the law. That is the scope of the petition. We desire not to be equall to the Angels, and Saints; but onely to imitate them more and more, and to be like to them.

Obiect. V. Romanes. 7. 18. *To will is present with mee*: therefore (say they) in will the lawe may bee kept, though the flesh relent. *Answer.* When *Paul* saith, *that to will was present*, hee doth not signifie that he could perfectly will that which is good. For his will beeing partly renewed, and partly vnrenewed, the good which he willed, hee partly nilled; and the euill which he nilled, hee partly willed.

Obiect. VI. Christ tooke our flesh, *that the righteousnesse of the lawe might be fulfilled in vs, Rom.* 8. 4. *Ans.* The righteousnes of the law is fulfilled in vs, not because we doe all things required in the law, but because we haue faith in vs, and by that faith wee apprehend the obedience of Christ in fulfilling of the law.

Obiect. VII. Rom. 13. 8. *Loue is the fulfilling of the law*: & the regenerate loue their neighbours. *Ans.* If we could loue our neighbour as our selues, perfectly, we should then fulfill the whole law. But our loue is imperfect.

Obiect. VIII. He that is borne of God sinnes not: 1. Ioh. 3. he that sins not, fulfills the law. *Ans. He that is borne of God sinnes not*, that is, hee doth not commit sinne, or make a practise of sinne. He may fall of frailtie, yet then he recouers himselfe, and doth not keepe a course in sinning. This is the meaning of Saint *Iohn.*

Obiect. IX. The commandements of God are not grieuous, 1. Ioh 5. *Ans.* They are not grieuous three wayes; first, in respect *of remission*: because they that beleeue in Christ, haue the transgression of the law pardoned. Secondly, in respect *of imputation*, because Christs obedience in fulfilling the law, is imputed to euery beleeuer. Thirdly in respect *of inchoation*. For they that beleeue receiue the spirit of God, whereby they are inabled to indeauour themselues to obey God in all his commandements. Otherwise in respect of our owne personall obedience, they are a yoke that no man can beare.

Obiection X. The workes of God are perfect, Deuter. 32. 4. Good workes, are workes of God: therefore they are perfect. *Answer.*

Workes,

Workes, that are meerely workes of God, which he worketh by himſelfe, and not by man, they are all perfect: and thus muſt the text in *Moſes* be vnderſtood. Now good workes, are workes of God in vs: and withall they are our workes, hauing their beginning in the minde, and will of man: and hence they are defiled. For when the firſt and ſecond cauſe concurre in a worke, the ſaid work takes vnto it the condition of the ſecond cauſe. Water pure in the fountaine, is defiled, when it paſſes by the filthy channell.

Obiect. XI. If God haue giuen vs an impoſſible law, he is more cruell then any tyrant. *Anſw.* When God firſt gaue the law, he alſo gaue power to fulfill the law. If the law be impoſſible, it is not Gods fault, but mans, who by his owne fault hath loſt this power of keeping the law.

The ground before named of the double fulfilling of the law, one for this life, the other for the life to come, is falſe. For there is onely one generall, and vnchangeable ſentence of the law, *Curſed is euery one that continues not in all things written in the law to doe them.*

I now come to other vſes of the former concluſion. If the law bee impoſſible, then muſt wee ſeeke for the fulfilling of it, forth of our ſelues in Chriſt, *who is the end of the law for righteouſneſſe, to them that beleeue.* Hence it followes neceſſarily, that our iuſtification muſt be by the imputation, or application of Chriſts iuſtice vnto vs.

Becauſe we cannot fulfill the law, wee muſt make it a glaſſe to ſee our impotencie, and what we cannot doe: and it muſt bee our ſchoolemaſter to driue vs to Chriſt. And by our impotencie wee muſt take occaſion to make praier to God for his ſpirit to inable vs to obey the lawes of God. Thus come wee to be doers of the law, and no otherwiſe.

Againe, it may be demanded, (conſidering we cannot fulfill the law,) how our workes can pleaſe God? *Anſ.* In euery good worke, there is ſomething that is Gods, and ſomething that is ours alone. The defect of the worke is ours alone, and that is pardoned to the beleeuer. That which is good in the worke, is from God, and that he approoueth as being his owne. And thus euery good worke, is ſaid to pleaſe God.

Laſtly, after that we haue begun to pleaſe God in obedience to his lawes, conſidering we fulfill them not, all boaſting of our goodneſſe muſt be laid aſide, and we muſt humble our ſelues vnder the hand of God euen to the death. Reade the practiſe of *Dauid, Pſal.* 143.2. and *Pſal.* 130.3. *Iob* 9.1.

11 *And that no man is iuſtified by the law in the ſight of God, it is manifeſt. For the iuſt liueth by faith.*

12 *And the law is not of faith: but he that ſhall doe theſe things, ſhall liue in them.*

The meaning. *By the law*] that is, the law not onely ceremoniall, but alſo iudiciall and morall. Indeede the occaſion of *Pauls* diſputation in this place, is taken from Circumciſion, pertaining to the ceremoniall law: but he inlarges his diſputation, from one part to the whole law. For they which thought Ceremonies neceſſarie to iuſtification, would much more thinke morall duties neceſſarie. And that *Paul* ſpeakes here of the morall, it appeares by the 10. verſe, where he alleadgeth a ſentence that ſpecially appertaines to the morall law: *Curſed is euery one, &c.* Againe, the law may bee conſidered, two waies, in the iuſtification of a ſinner: firſt, as it iuſtifieth without Chriſt. Secondly, as it iuſtifieth with Chriſt: and both waies it is excluded from iuſtification, and here ſpecially in the ſecond regard. For the intent of the Galatians was, to ioyne Chriſt and the law, in the worke of our iuſtification.

Before God] that is, in the iudgement of God, before whoſe iudgement ſeate we muſt all appeare, and be iudged.

The iuſt ſhall liue by faith] The ſcope of theſe words is this. The Iewes were oppreſſed by the Babylonians, and it was further told them by the Prophet, that they ſhould be led into captiuitie, by the ſaid Babylonians. Now in this diſtreſſe of theirs, the Lord ſets downe the duty of the faithfull Iewes, namely, that they muſt ſtay themſelues by their faith in the Meſſias, and conſequently, that they ſhall haue ſafetie in this life in the middeſt of all dangers, and in the end haue eternall life. And *Paul* applies this text to his purpoſe, thus. Life eternall comes by faith: and therefore true righteouſneſſe before God is by faith. For righteouſneſſe is the foundation of life eternall: and therefore it is called *iuſtification of life. Rom. 5. 17.*

The law is not of faith] The meaning of theſe words muſt be gathered, by the oppoſition in the latter part of the verſe: *but he that doth theſe things ſhall liue in them.* And the meaning is this. The law doth not preſcribe faith in the Meſſias: neither doth it promiſe life to him that beleeueth in the Meſſias, but to him that doth the things contained in the law.

In theſe wordes, *Paul* addes a new argument to the former, thus. Iuſtice is by faith: the law is not of faith: therefore the law is not our iuſtice. Or againe, thus. He that is iuſtified, is iuſtified by faith:

faith: the law iuſtifies no man by faith: therefore the law doth not iuſtifie. The concluſion is firſt, in the 11. verſe. The propoſition is expreſſed, and confirmed by the teſtimonie of the Prophet *Habacuk*. The aſſumption is in the 12. verſe.

The vſe, When *Paul* ſaith, *No man is iuſtified by the law in the ſight of God*: he makes a double iuſtification: one, before God: the other, before men. Iuſtification before God is, when God reputes a man iuſt, and that onely for the merit, and obedience of Chriſt. Iuſtification before men, is, when ſuch as profeſſe faith in Chriſt, are reputed iuſt of men. By this diſtinction, *Paul* who ſaith, *that a man is iuſtified by faith without workes*, *Rom.* 3.28. and *Iames*, who ſaith, *that Abraham was iuſtified by faith, and workes*, *Iam.* 2.24. are reconciled: for *Paul* ſpeakes of iuſtification before God, as hee himſelfe expreſſely teſtifieth, *Rom.* 4.2. and Saint *Iames* ſpeakes of iuſtification before men, which is not onely by the profeſſion of faith, but alſo by workes.

In the ſame ſort, there is a double Election. One ſpeciall, whereby *God knowes who are his*. The other, is more generall, whereby wee repute all men to be Elect, that profeſſe faith in Chriſt, leauing ſecret iudgements to God. Thus *Paul* writes to the Epheſians, Philippians, &c. as Elect. And the Miniſters of the word, are to ſpeake to their congregations, as to the Elect people of God.

In the ſame manner, there is a double ſanctification: one before God, in truth, *Eph.* 4.28 the other before men, in the iudgement of charitie. Thus men are ſaid, *to tread vnder foote the blood of Chriſt wherewith they were ſanctified*. *Heb.* 10.29. Thus all that are of right to be baptiſed, are holy and regenerate: not in the iudgement of certentie, which is Gods; but in the iudgement of charitie, which is mans: ſecrets alwaies reſerued to God.

Againe, when *Paul* ſaith, *in the ſight of God*, he giues vs to vnderſtand, that there is an vniuerſall iudgement of God, before whom we muſt all appeare, and be iudged. And when *Paul* ſaith in the time preſent, that *God iuſtifieth* (though not by workes) he ſignifies, that this iudgement is already begunne vpon vs, euen in this life. This muſt teach vs, to walke in godly and holy conuerſation, in the feare of God: and to watch and pray, that we may be found worthie, to ſtand before God. Malefactours, when they are going to iudgement, & when they ſee the Iudge ſet, lay aſide skorning, and bethinke themſelues what to ſay, or doe. Now we are theſe malefactours: and we know that God hath alreadie begunne to giue iudgement of vs: and therefore we muſt prepare our ſelues to make a good reckoning.

In the teſtimonie of the Prophet our dutie is ſet downe, and that is, that we muſt in this world liue by faith. That we may liue by faith, we muſt doe two things. One is, to chooſe the true God for our God: the ſecond is, in our hearts to cleaue vnto him, and that according to his word. Firſt therefore, wee muſt cleaue faſt to his commandements, by entring into the way of his precepts, and by walking in them. For this cauſe we muſt haue alwaies about vs the eye of knowledge, to direct our ſteps in the waies of God, that wee euer keepe our ſelues in our callings, that is the dutie wee owe to God and man. Secondly, while we ſtand in the waies of God, we ſhall be aſſailed with many Temptations on the right hand, and on the left: therefore we muſt further cleaue to the promiſes of God: beleeuing his preſence, protection, and aſſiſtance, in all temptations and dangers. And this our faith muſt be as it were a hand to ſtay vs. Here two caueats muſt be remembred. One, that we muſt not preſcribe vnto God the manner of his aſſiſtance: but leaue it, with other circumſtances of time, and place, to God. The ſecond is, when all earthly things faile vs, wee muſt reſt vpon the bare word of God, and beleeue the promiſe of remiſſion of ſinnes, and life euerlaſting. This is to liue by faith. And this dutie muſt be practiſed, when we are in the field to fight for our countrey: when we lie on our death beds: and when we are in any danger.

Marke further, *Paul* ſaith, *the iuſt man liues by faith*: he therefore that is iuſtified continues to be iuſtified by his faith: and therefore the ſecond iuſtification, that is ſaid to be by our workes, is a meere fiction. And in that none liues by faith, but he that is a iuſt man, we ſee that true faith is alwaies ioyned with the Purpoſe of not ſinning, or with the iuſtice of good conſcience: and where they are ſeuered, there is no more but a meere pretence of faith.

When *Paul* ſaith [*the Law is not of faith*] he ſets downe the maine difference betweene the Law and the Goſpel. The Law promiſeth life, to him that performes perfect obedience, and that for his workes. The Goſpel promiſeth life, to him that doth nothing in the cauſe of his ſaluation, but only beleeues in Chriſt: and it promiſeth ſaluation to him that beleeueth, yet not for his faith, or for any workes elſe, but for the merit of Chriſt. The law then requires doing to ſaluation, and the Goſpel beleeuing, and nothing elſe.

Obiect. 1. The Goſpel requires repentance, and the practiſe of it. *Anſ.* Indeede the law doth not teach true repentance; neither is it any cauſe of it, but onely an occaſion. The Goſpel onely preſcribes repentance, and the practiſe thereof: yet onely as it is a

fruite

fruite of our faith, and as it is the way to ſaluation in which we are to walke, and no otherwiſe.

Obiect. II. The law requires and commands faith. *Anſw.* The law requires faith in God, which is to put our affiance in him. But the Goſpel requires faith in Chriſt, the Mediatour, God-man: and this faith the law neuer knew.

Obiect. III. In the Goſpel there are promiſes of life, vpon condition of our obedience. *Rom.* 8.13. *If by the ſpirit ye mortifie the deedes of the fleſh, ye ſhall liue.* 1.*Ioh.*1.9. *If we confeſſe our ſinnes, God is faithfull to forgiue them. Anſ.* The promiſes of the Goſpel are not made to the worke, but to the worker: and to the worker not for his worke: but for Chriſts ſake, according to his worke. As for example: promiſe of life is made not to the worke of mortification, but to him that mortifieth his fleſh, and that not for his mortification, but becauſe he is in Chriſt, and his mortification is the token or euidence thereof. And therefore it muſt be remembred, that all promiſes of the Goſpel that mention workes, include in them Reconciliation with God in Chriſt.

Obiect. IV. Faith is a vertue, and to beleeue is a worke: therefore one is worke is commanded in the Goſpel, and is alſo neceſſarie to ſaluation. *Anſwer.* The Goſpel conſiders not faith as a vertue, or worke, but as an inſtrument, or hand, to apprehend Chriſt. For faith doth not cauſe, effect, or procure our iuſtification and ſaluation, but as the beggers hand, it receiues them, being wholly wrought and giuen of God.

This diſtinction of the law and the Goſpel, muſt be obſerued carefully. For by it we ſee that the Church of Rome hath erroniouſly confounded the law and the Goſpel, for this many hundred yeares. The law of *Moſes* (ſay they) written in tables of ſtone, is the law: the ſame law of *Moſes*, written in the hearts of men by the holy Ghoſt, is the Goſpel. But I ſay againe, that the law written in our hearts, is ſtill the law of *Moſes*. And this ouerſight in miſtaking the diſtinction of the Law and the Goſpel, is and hath bin, the ruine of the Goſpel.

We muſt here further obſerue, that * *beleeuing*, and *doing*, are oppoſed, in the article of our iuſtification. In our good conuerſation they agree: faith goes before, and doing followes: but in the worke of our iuſtification, they are as fire and water. Hence I gather, that to the iuſtification of a ſinner, there is required a ſpeciall and an applying faith, for generall faith is numbred among the workes of the law: and the diuels haue it. This kinde of beleeuing therefore, and doing, are not oppoſite. Againe, hence I gather, that workes of

* Credere, Facere.

 faith

faith and grace, are quite excluded from iuſtification ; becauſe the oppoſition doth not ſtand betweene beleeuing, and the workes of nature : but ſimply, betweene beleeuing, and doing.

Laſtly, it may be demanded, why the Lord ſaith, *Hee that doth the things of the law ſhall liue* ; conſidering no man ſince the fall, can doe the things of the law ? *Anſ.* The Lord ſince mans fall, repeates the law in his old tenour, not to mocke men, but for other weighty cauſes. The firſt is, to teach vs that the law is of a conſtant, and vnchangeable nature. The ſecond is, to aduertiſe vs, of our weakeneſſe: and to ſhew vs, what we cannot doe. The third is, to put vs in minde, that we muſt ſtill humble our ſelues vnder the hand of God, after we haue begun by grace to obey the law ; becauſe euen then wee come farre ſhort in doing the things which the law requires at our hands.

13 *Chriſt hath redeemed vs from the curſe of the law, when he was made a curſe for vs: (for it is written, Curſed is euery one that hangeth on the tree.)*

14 *That the bleſsing of Abraham might come to the Gentiles, through Chriſt Ieſus, that we might receiue the promiſe of the ſpirit by faith.*

Paul hauing prooued the truth of his doctrine by ſundrie arguments, in the former part of this chapter, he here anſwereth an obiection, the occaſion whereof is from the 10. verſe. It may be framed on this manner: If they be accurſed that continue not in all things written in the law to doe them, then all men are accurſed: and the Gentiles are not partakers of the bleſſing of *Abraham* (as you haue ſaid.) Anſwer is here made, that to them that beleeue there is full redemption, from the curſe of the law. And *Paul* for the better inlightning of his anſwer, here makes a deſcription of our redemption by foure arguments. The firſt is the author: *Chriſt hath redeemed vs from the curſe of the law.* The ſecond is the forme or manner of our Redemption, in theſe words, *When he was made a curſe for vs.* And this forme is further declared by the ſigne, in theſe words: *for it is written, Curſed is euery one that hangeth on the tree.* The third argument is the end, in theſe words, *that the bleſſing of Abraham might come on the Gentiles.* The laſt is alſo an other end, *that we might receiue the promiſe of the ſpirit.*

Touching the Author, in theſe words, *Chriſt hath redeemed vs from the curſe of the law*, ſundrie things may be learned. Firſt of all, comparing theſe words with the 10. verſ. or comparing the anſwer, and

and the obiection together, we ſee and are to obſerue, that the threatnings of the law, are to bee vnderſtood with an exception from the Goſpel. All are curſed, ſaith the law, that doe not continue to doe all things written therein, *Except they haue pardon,* and be redeemed by Chriſt, ſaith the Goſpel. And thus are all curſes of the law to be conceiued, with a limitation or qualification, from the Goſpel.

Againe, in that Chriſt hath redeemed vs from the curſe of the law, here is our comfort, that neither, hell, nor death, nor Satan, hath any right or power ouer vs, ſo be it we do vnfainedly beleeue in Chriſt. *For we are bought with a price.* And for this cauſe, we muſt be admoniſhed, not to feare any euill ouermuch, as the reuilings, & curſes of euill tongues, witchcraft, the plague, peſtilence, famine, the ſword, or death. For the curſe which makes all theſe, and many other things hurtfull vnto vs, is remooued from them that are in Chriſt. And therefore all immoderate feare ſhould be reſtrained.

Thirdly, our dutie is, to glorifie God and Chriſt, who hath redeemed vs, and that both in bodie and ſoule. The redeemed muſt liue according to the will of their redeemer. 1. *Cor.* 6. verſe 20. This is all the thankfulneſſe that we can ſhew to our Redeemer for his mercie.

Laſtly, here an obiection made by ſome, may be anſwered. If (ſay they) we were redeemed by Chriſt, beeing captiues to the diuell, the price of our Redemption was paid to him, and not to God. *Anſw.* We were captiues properly to the iuſtice of God in the law, to the order whereof we ſtand ſubiect: and by this meanes we are captiues to the curſe of the law, and conſequently to the diuell, who is the miniſter of God, for the Execution of the ſaid curſe. And being captiues to the diuell, no otherwiſe then as he is the miniſter of God, for the inflicting of puniſhment: the price muſt not bee paide to him, but to God, who is the principall, and hath a ſoueraigntie ouer him and vs.

I come now to the forme of our Redemption, *Who was made a curſe for vs.* For the better vnderſtanding of theſe words, foure points are to be handled. The firſt is, what is this curſe? *Anſ.* A double death: the firſt of the bodie, the ſecond of the ſoule. The firſt is, the ſeparation of the bodie and ſoule. The ſecond is, the ſeparation of the whole man from God: not in reſpect of his vniuerſall power and preſence (for the very damned haue their moouing and beeing from him,) but in reſpect of his fauour, and ſpeciall loue, whereby God ceaſeth to be their God. And this is death indeede, whereof the firſt, is but a ſhadow: and this is the curſe of the law.

The ſecond point is, How Chriſt was a curſe, or accurſed, who is the fountaine of bleſſedneſſe? *Anſw.* He is not ſo by nature: for he is the naturall Sonne of God: nor by his owne fault: for hee is the vnſpotted Lambe of God: but by voluntarie diſpenſation: and therefore *Paul* ſaith, *he was made a curſe.* And he was made a curſe, firſt, becauſe hee was ſet apart in the eternall counſell of the Father, Sonne, and holy Ghoſt, to be our redeemer, and conſequently to be a curſe. In this regard, the Father is ſaid *to haue ſealed him, Ioh.* 6.27. and he is ſaid againe to be *preordained before all worlds,* 1.*Peter* 1.20. and giuen *according to the counſell and foreknowledge of God. Act.* 3.22. Secondly, he was made a curſe, in that he was in time conſecrated to be our Mediatour and ſo a curſe. And this conſecration was firſt in his baptiſme, in which he put vpon him our guilt, as we put off the ſame in ours; and ſecondly on the croſſe and paſſion, in which he tooke vnto him the puniſhment of our ſinne. And thus was he made a curſe. It may be obiected, that he is the Son of God: and therefore no curſe. *Anſw.* Chriſt muſt be conſidered as the Son of God, and againe as our pledge and ſuretie. *Heb.* 7.22. In the firſt reſpect he was not accurſed, but in the ſecond.

The third point is, In what nature was Chriſt accurſed? *Anſw.* Whole Chriſt God-man, or Man-god, was accurſed. For *the Lord of life* (ſaith *Paul*) *was crucified*, and conſequently accurſed. 1. *Cor.* 2.8. Yet this limitation muſt be added, that the curſe was not vpon the Godhead of Chriſt, but onely in his fleſh, or manhood. For *he ſuffered* (ſaith *Peter*) *in the fleſh,* 1.*Peter* 4.1. Moreouer, the ſoule of Chriſt was the more principall ſeate of the curſe, as it was the principall ſeat of ſinne. Therefore the Prophet ſaith, *he made his ſoule an offering for ſinne, Iſa.* 53.10. and Chriſt ſaid, *My ſoule is heauie to the death.*

The fourth point is, How farre forth Chriſt was accurſed? *Anſ.* In the firſt death there are two degrees, *ſeparation* of the bodie and ſoule, and the *putrifaction* of the bodie ſeparated. And Chriſt entred onely into the firſt, and not into the ſecond. For his bodie beeing dead indured no corruption. Againe, in the ſecond death there are two degrees. The firſt is, a ſeparation from God in ſenſe and feeling: and the ſecond, is an abſolute ſeparation from God. Into this ſecond degree of death, Chriſt entred not, becauſe he ſaid in the middeſt of his paſſion, *My God, my God.* And this abſolute ſeparation could not be without the diſſolution of the perſonall vnion. Into the firſt degree of the ſecond death, he entred: namely, into the apprehenſion and feeling of the wrath & indignation of God due to mans ſin. And this appeares by his bloodie ſweat of thicke and clottered blood; by his complaint that he was forsaken: by his feares and sorrowes in the time of death, in which he comes short of sundry Martyrs, vnlesse we acknowledge that he indured further paines of death then euer they did: by his condition, in that hee takes vpon him the condition of the first *Adam*, who vpon his fall was to indure the first and second death. Here two questions are to be demanded: the first, How and in what manner Christ suffered the wrath of God? *Ans.* He indured it willingly of his owne accord: he did not onely in minde see it before his eyes, but also he felt it: it was laid and imposed on him, and he incountred with it: but it had no dominion or lordship ouer him. *Act.* 2.24. The second is, How much he suffered of the wrath of God? *Ans.* The punishment he suffered was in value and measure answerable to all the sinnes, of all the Elect past, present, and to come: the Godhead suppor-ting the manhood, that it might be able to beare, and ouercome the whole burden of the wrath of God. If it be said, that a creature cannot haue an infinite apprehension of the wrath of God: I an-swer, it sufficeth that God laid infinite wrath vpon him, and that he apprehended it according to the condition of a creature. For in so doing, he incountred with the whole wrath of God. One man in a breach, or at a bridge, may stand against an whole armie, and beare the brunt of it: why may not then the manhood of Christ supported by the Godhead, beare the stresse of the whole wrath of God? Against this doctrine, sundry things may be obiected.

Obiect.I. The Scripture ascribes all to the blood of Christ, and therefore to the death of the bodie. *Ans.* By blood, is meant a bloo-die death: by the bloodie death, the death of the crosse: by the death of the crosse, a death accursed, or the death of the bodie, ioy-ned with the malediction of the law.

Obiect.II. The suffering of the anger of God was not figured in Sacraments or Sacrifices. *Ans.* The beast, whereof the burnt offe-ring was made, was first tied to the hornes of the altar: his blood then was shed: and lastly hee was all burnt vpon the altar vnto God: and hereby was figured the fierie wrath of God.

Obiect.III. Temporall death, or the curse for halfe a day, can-not counteruaile eternall death. *Answ.* Yes, in Christ. For if man could suffer and ouercome punishment in measure infinite, hee should not suffer eternally: but this no man nor Angel can doe: and therefore man must suffer punishment for measure finite, for time infinite: because the punishment must be answerable to God, whose maiestie is infinite. Now Christ being God and man, suffe-red punishment indeede infinite: and therefore it was not necessary

that

that hee ſhould indure it eternally. Againe, here the dignitie of the perſon helpeth: for in that the Sonne of God ſuffered the curſe of the law for halfe a day, it is more then if all men had ſuffered eternall death. Therefore the death of Chriſt in reſpect of the meaſure of the puniſhment, as alſo in reſpect of the value, and dignitie therof, counteruailes death euerlaſting.

Obiect. IV. It is hard to ſay, that Chriſt ſuffered the paines of hell. *Anſw.* The Latin tranſlation (commonly receiued,) hath as much, that *he could not be holdē of the ſorrows of hel, Act.* 2.24. And there is no offence to ſay, he ſuffered the paines of hell, ſo farre forth as this ſuffering may ſtand with the puritie of his manhood, aud with the truth of the perſonall vnion.

The vſe. Friers teach, that if Chriſt had pricked his finger, and let fall but one droppe of blood, it had bin ſufficient to redeeme all the world. But they dreame. For *Paul* ſaith, *hee was made the curſe of the law, to redeeme vs.* This had bin a needleſſe work, if a pricke in the finger, or any puniſhment without death, would haue done the deede.

That Chriſt became a curſe for vs, it ſhewes the greatneſſe and horriblenes of our ſinnes, it ſhewes the grieuous hardneſſe of our hearts, that neuer almoſt mourne for them: it ſhews the vnſpeakable loue and mercy of God, for which we are to bee thankfull for euer, and that all manner of waies.

In that the Sonne of God became a curſe for our ſinnes, we are put in minde, to ſee, acknowledge, and conſider them, and withall to bewaile them, and to humble our ſelues for them: and to deteſt them more and more, vnto the very death. For what is more worthie of hatred, then that which cauſeth the Sonne of God to be accurſed. They which beleeue that Chriſt by beeing a curſe hath redeemed them from the curſe of the law, doe in truth die vnto all their ſinnes, and liue vnto God. Many indeede profeſſing Chriſt, make no change of life at all: and the reaſon is, becauſe a ſecret Atheiſme makes them ſay in their hearts, *There is no Chriſt, there is no curſe, that was endured by Chriſt.* Clenſe your hearts of this hidden Atheiſme, and looke that inwardly in your ſpirits, you die vnto your ſinnes, and liue to God.

In that Chriſt was obedient to his Father in bearing the curſe of the law, we are taught in all things to ſubiect our ſelues to the will of God. Our obedience muſt not onely bee in doing this or that, but alſo in ſuffering the miſeries laid on vs to the death: this is the beſt obedience of all, and the trueſt marke of Gods child, to obey in our ſufferings.

Moreouer,

Moreouer, that Chriſt was accurſed, it is confirmed by the ſentence and decree of God: *Curſed is euery one that hangeth on the tree.* *Deut.*21.23. The ground of this ſentence is the ſinne of the malefactour: for whom God curſeth, hee curſeth for his offence. And here it may bee demanded, why he that is ſtoned to death is not likewiſe accuſed? *Anſ.* Hee alſo is accurſed: but there are ſpeciall reaſons why the man hanged on the tree is curſed. Firſt, among the Iewes, they which were hanged, were moſt grieuous malefactours, as blaſphemers, and idolatours: and their puniſhment was accordingly, moſt grieuous. Secondly, hanging (as among all nations, ſo among the Iewes) was a moſt odious, and infamous death. Thirdly, God did foreſee that the Meſſias ſhould die on the croſſe, and therefore he accurſed this kinde of death. If it bee ſayd, that there was no fault or offence in Chriſt; and therefore he could not bee accurſed: I anſwer, that hee became ſinne for vs, in that our ſinne was applied and imputed to him. It may bee further obiected, that the theefe which repented, was not accurſed, though he were hanged on the tree. *Anſ.* As a theefe, he was accurſed; as he was a theefe, and repented, the curſe was remooued. For the lawe in the curſes thereof, giues place to the Goſpel: iudgment yeelds to mercy: and the Goſpel puts an exception to the law.

The vſe. If the malefactour hanged, be accurſed, and defile the earth: how vile and accurſed is the liuing malefactour, the blaſphemer, adulterer, murtherer, &c. who hath entred no degree of puniſhment? Let this be conſidered, to terrifie offenders.

Againe, let vs conſider the ſcope of this law. Becauſe he that hangs one the tree, is accurſed: therefore ſaith the law of God, *hee muſt be taken downe, and buried.* Marke the equity of the law: and that is, that things euill and accurſed, are to be remooued from the eye and ſenſe of man. This charge the Lord giues of leſſe matters, namely, of ſights vndecent, and vnſeemely. *Deut.*23.15. Againe, we are commanded not ſo much as to name fornication, vncleanenes, couetouſnes, ieſting, fooliſh talking, &c, *Eph.*5.3. Here we are to be put in minde, that the Plaies (commonly in vſe) are to be baniſhed out of all Chriſtian societies. For they doe nothing elſe but reuiue and repreſent the vile and wicked faſhions of the world, and the miſdemeanour of men, which are things accurſed, and therfore to be buried, and not once to be ſpoken of. Againe, all euill in our example, whether in word, or in deede, muſt bee buried, as much as may be: for it defileth, and is accurſed.

Here it may bee demanded, how this law of God, (*he is accurſed, therefore let him bee taken downe, and buried*) ſtandes with the

order

order vſed in this and other countries, in which men are hanged in chaines for the terrour of the world? *Anſ.* Iudiciall lawes, if they haue in them morall equitie, and ſerue directly to ſenſe in the precepts of the Decalogue, are perpetuall, and bind all men; elſe not. As for the iudiciall determinations of this or that manner of puniſhment, they concerne vs not, but God hath left euery nation free, though not in reſpect of puniſhment, yet in reſpect of the manner and order thereof.

The third point, whereby our redemption is deſcribed, is the ende thereof, *that the bleſſing of Abraham*, that is, righteouſneſſe and life euerlaſting, *may come vpon the Gentiles.* Here two things are to be conſidered. The firſt is, whence comes the benedictiō of *Abraham? Anſ.* From the curſed death of Chriſt. For thus are the words, *Hee was made a curſe for vs, that the benediction of Abraham might come on the Gentiles.* Marke here how God workes one contrarie by the other. In the creation, he made ſomething not of ſomething, but of nothing: he called light out of darkenes: he kills, and then makes aliue, *Hoſ.*6. he ſends men to heauen, by the gates of hell: hee gaue ſight by a temper of ſpittle and clay, a fit meanes to put out light. In the worke of our redemptiou he giues life, not by life but by death, and the bleſſing by the curſe. This ſhewes the wiſedome, and power of God: and it teacheth vs in the worke of our conuerſion and ſaluation, not to goe by ſenſe and feeling; becauſe God can, and doth worke one contrary, in, and by the other.

The ſecond point is, where this benediction of *Abraham* is to be found. *Anſ.* The text ſaith, *It is extant in Chriſt Ieſus,* who is as it were the ſtore-houſe of Gods bleſſing, and the diſpenſer of it to all nations. In him are hid all treaſures of wiſedome, and knowledge. *Col.*2. God and the Lambe are al things to all the Elect in the kingdome of heauen. *Reu.*21. Here wee ſee the right way to become rich: and that is, aboue all things to ſeeke to bee true and liuely members of Chriſt: for if he be ours, we can want nothing. *Rom.*8. 32. *Matth.*6.33. *Pſal.*34 10. This is a moſt ſure way to procure vnto vs all good things that he ſees to bee neceſſarie for vs. For Chriſt is the ſtore-houſe of the benediction of *Abraham.* Againe, this muſt teach them that beleeue in Chriſt, to be content in any eſtate, be it better or worſe, for true riches is the bleſſing of God; and this bleſſing is in Chriſt. This is the truth, if we could diſcerne of things that differ. Thirdly, in our pouertie, and in the middeſt of all our wants and loſſes, we muſt comfort our ſelues. For though we leeſe neuer ſo much, yet we retaine the principall, and that is Chriſt, who is the benediction of *Abraham.*

The

The fourth point is,an other end of our Redemption, *That wee might receiue the promiſe of the ſpirit by faith*.For the better vnderſtanding of this, foure queſtions may be demanded. The firſt is, what is meant by the promiſe? *Anſ.* The promiſe of God made in the old Teſtament, that he would powre out his ſpirit vpon all fleſh. *Iſa*.44.3.and *Ioel*.2.28.And here it is ſaid, that this promiſe is fulfilled to the nations,when they beleeue. Marke here how the promiſes of God lie as voide , dead,and of none effect, till the particular time of their accompliſhmēt.God promiſeth *Abrahā* that his poſterity ſhall be a great nation after 430 yeares:for which time they remaine in thrall and bondage ; but the very night after the former time was expired,nothing,no not the raging ſea could ſtoppe their deliuerance.*Exod*.12.41.God promiſeth deliuerance after 70 yeares captiuity to the Iſraelites in Babylon. When this time was expired.*Daniel* prayed,and at the very beginning of his ſupplications,the decree of God for deliuerance came forth.*Dan*.9.23.*The viſion of God*(ſaith the Prophet)*is for the appointed time*.*Hab*.2.1,and ſo is the promiſe.This muſt teach vs to be content,if after much praying,we finde not the fruit of our praiers:becauſe there is an appointed time for the accompliſhing of them.In this reſpect *Dauid* ſaith, that *his eyes failed*, and *he was hoarſe in praying*.*Pſalm*.69.4.

The ſecond queſtion is,what is meant by the giuing, or ſending of the ſpirit? *Anſ*.Without any alteration or change of place,it ſignifies two things. The firſt is,Order betweene the perſons,whereby the Father, and the Sonne worke mediately by the holy Ghoſt, and the Holy Ghoſt immediately from them.The ſecond is, that the Spirit doth maniſeſt his preſence by diuine effects in vs. In this reſpect hee is ſaide to be ſent,or giuen of the Father,and the Sonne.

The third point is,In what order is the ſpirit giuen?For it ſeemes, that we firſt of our ſelues beleeue, and then receiue the ſpirit? *Anſ*. Men are ſaid to receiue the ſpirit, when they receiue ſome new gift of the ſpirit, or the increaſe of ſome old gift.*Iohn* 20.22.Againe,to ſpeake properly, faith and the receiuing of the ſpirit, are for a time both together. For firſt of all, we heare the promiſe of God: then we beginne to meditate, and to applie the ſaide promiſe to our ſelues, to ſtriue againſt doubting, and to deſire to beleeue: and in doing of all this,we receiue the ſpirit. To beleeue, is the firſt grace in vs that concernes our ſaluation: and when we beginne to beleeue, we beginne to receiue the ſpirit: and when we firſt receiue Gods ſpirit, we beginne to beleeue. And thus by our faith receiue we the ſpirit: and thus alſo the ſpirit dwells in vs by faith.*Eph*.3.17.

And

And wee muſt not imagine, that we may, or can beleeue of our ſelues, without the operation of the ſpirit.

The fourth point is, for what end we receiue the ſpirit? *Anſw.* For ſixe. For illumination of our minds, 1.*Ioh*.2.27. 1.*Cor*.2.12. for regeneration, whereby the Image of God is reſtored in vs, *Ioh*.3. for the gouernment of our counſels, wils, affections, actions, *Iſa*. 11.1. *Rom*. 8.14. for the effecting of that coniunction, whereby we are vnited to Chriſt our head. 1.*Cor*.6.17. for conſolation, *Rom*. 8.16. laſtly, for confirmation in our faith, and euery good dutie. 2.*Cor*.1.22. *Eph*.1.13.

This receiuing of the ſpirit, is one ſpeciall end of our redemption: and therefore it is moſt neceſſarie for vs, to haue the ſpirit of God dwelling in vs. If we haue not the ſpirit, we are not Chriſts: and without it, we can doe nothing.

We muſt for this cauſe doe ſuch things, whereby we may obtaine and receiue a plentifull meaſure of Gods ſpirit. *Repent* (ſaith *Peter*) *and ye ſhall receiue the holy Ghoſt.*

Againe, we muſt carefully retaine and preſerue the grace of the ſpirit in vs; by meditation in the word of God; by earneſt and frequent prayer; by auoiding all ſuch acts, in word, or deede, that may make a breach in conſcience: for whatſoeuer offends conſcience, quenches the ſpirit. Laſtly, by ſauouring the thing of the ſpirit, *Rom*. 8.5. that is, by thinking on things ſpirituall, by affecting of them, and delighting in them.

15 *Brethren, I ſpeake as men doe: though it be but a mans couenant, when it is confirmed, no man doth abrogate it, or adde any thing thereto.*

16 *Now to Abraham and his ſeede were the promiſes made. He ſaith not, and to the ſeedes, as of many; but, and to thy ſeede, as of one, which is Chriſt.*

17 *And this I ſay, that the law which was* 430. *yeares after, cannot diſanull the couenant that was before confirmed of God in reſpect of Chriſt, that it ſhould make the promiſe of none effect.*

18 *For if the inheritance be of the law, it is no more by promiſe; but God gaue it vnto Abraham by promiſe.*

In theſe words, *Paul* meetes with a ſecond Exception, or obiection, made againſt that which he here principally ſtands vpon: namely, that the bleſſing of *Abraham* is conuaied to the Gentiles, and

and that by Christ. The obiection may be framed thus: The promise made to *Abraham*, cannot now pertaine to the Gentiles, because the law was added to it, and by the law it is abrogated: and therefore the Gentiles are to be iustified, and saued, by the obseruation of the law. To this obiection, *Paul* makes a double answer. One is, that the promise cannot be abrogated: the second, that if it might be abrogated, yet the law cannot doe it. The first he confirmes on this manner:

The Testament of God confirmed, cannot be abrogated:
The promises made to *Abraham* and his seede, which is Christ, are his Testament confirmed:
Therefore they cannot be abrogated.

The *proposition* is expressed in the 17. verse, and is confirmed, by comparison, thus. The testament of man after it is confirmed, may not be abrogated: much lesse the Testament of God. v. 15. The *minor* is propounded in the 16. and 17. verses. Now I come to speake of the words as they lie.

Brethren] *Paul* had before called them *fooles*; and that iustly, because they fell from the doctrine which he taught them, to an other Gospel. And yet here he calles them *brethren*. And hence let vs learne, that in diuision of iudgement and opinion, there must be no diuision but vnitie of affection. It is, and hath bin alwaies the plague of the Church, that diuision of heart and affection, there takes place, where any diuision is in iudgement, though men erre of infirmitie. This euill causeth more to be condemned for heretikes, then indeede ought to be: it maketh schismes where none should be: it maketh dissentions to be incurable: which otherwise might be cut off. And therefore if dissentions in iudgement arise, we must remember to suppresse, enuie, hatred, pride, selfe-loue, and let Christian loue beare sway.

Againe, here we see it is lawfull, to speake in Sermons as men doe, so it be done after the example of *Paul*, with these cautions. First, it must be done sparingly, and soberly, without ostentation. Secondly, it must be done vpon a iust cause, as when the sayings of men serue to conuince the hearers, and that in their consciences. Thirdly, a difference must be made betweene the word of man, and the word of God; least in adding one to the other, the word of God lose his grace, and excellencie. Lastly, Gods word onely must bee the foundation of the doctrine which is taught, and the word of man is to bee added, in respect of our infirmitie to giue light, or to conuince.

That which *Paul* speakes after the manner of men, is a principle of law, or a concluſion of the light of nature, namely, that a Couenant or teſtament confirmed, may not be abrogated. *Paul* ſaith, it is the propertie of them that are of reprobate mindes to bee *trucebreakers*. *Rom*.1.30. Hence ſundrie queſtions may be reſolued. The firſt is, whether Legacies giuen to the maintenance of the Maſſe, may be applied to the maintenance of the true worſhip of God? *Anſ.* The teſtator in the giuing of ſuch Legacies, hath a double intention: one is general, & that is to preſerue the worſhip of God: the other is ſpeciall, and that is to preſerue the idolatry of the Maſſe. In this he erreth, and therefore his will may be changed. For teſtaments vnlawfully made, may be abrogated. In the general he erred not: and therefore the goods may lawfully be applied to the maintenance of the true worſhip of God. But it may be ſayde, that the next heires may recall them when the Maſſe is aboliſhed. I anſwer, no. Becauſe they may ſtill bee applied to the publike good of the Church. The affection of the dead was good in this caſe, though their iudgement was naught: and therefore regard is to be had of their affection and intent.

The ſecond queſtion is, whether we are to keepe couenant with heretikes, and enemies? *Anſ.* Yea: for the principle, *A couenant confirmed, may not be abrogated*, is the concluſion of nature, which binds all men without exeption, at all times, if the couenant be lawfull.

The third queſtion is, what if damages and loſſes follow vpon the couenaut made and confirmed, muſt it then be obſerued? *Anſ.* Of couenants ſome are ſingle, that is, bare promiſes, not confirmed by oath; and ſome againe are with oath. Againe ſome couenants are meere ciuill, beeing made of man to man; and ſome are more then ciuill, beeing made of man to God, as contracts of marriage. Now if couenants be ſingle couenants, and meerely ciuil, then may they be changed by the makers, or by their ſucceſſours, if hurts and loſſes ariſe. Yet if couenants be confirmed by oath, and if they be made to God, they may not be changed, ſo long as they are lawfull, though great loſſes inſue. Reade the example of *Ioſua*.9.18. *A good man ſweareth, and changeth not, though he loſe thereby*, *Pſal*.15.4.

The fourth queſtion is, whether a contract may not be diſſolued, when one of the parties hath a diſeaſe contagious in deadly manner, and incurable? *Anſw.* If ſuch a diſeaſe follow the contract, the marriage not conſummate, we may preſume that God doth diſſolue the contract. And the couenant diſſolued by God, we may without daunger hold to be abrogated.

The laſt queſtion is, whether the Church of Rome hath not dealt wickedly in altering the laſt teſtament of Chriſt, when it miniſtreth

niſtreth

niſtreth the Lords ſupper vnder one kind? *Anſ.* They ſinne againſt the light of nature, which teacheth vs not to abrogate the teſtaments of men, much leſſe the teſtament of God. It is alleadged that we receiue whole Chriſt vnder the one kind. *Anſ.* True indeed. But we muſt conſider the end of the ſacraments is to ſignifie and repreſent perfect nouriſhment, in, and by Chriſt : now perfect nouriſhment is not in bread alone, but in bread & wine: and by them both ioyned together, is ſignified, that Chriſt is the bread and the water of life: now to aboliſh the cuppe, is to aboliſh the principall vſe of the ſacrament, and to leſſen our comfort.

In the 16. verſe *Paul* ſaith, *the promiſes were made to Abraham*, in the plurall number: becauſe they were ſometime made to *Abraham*, ſometime to his ſeede, and ſometime to both: and they were often repeated to *Abraham*, and therefore are called promiſes, though in ſubſtance they are but one. The ſeede of *Abraham* here mentioned, is the ſeede not of the fleſh, but of the promiſe, *Rom.* 9.7. and this ſeed is firſt Chriſt Ieſus, and then all that beleeue in Chriſt. For al theſe are giuen to *Abraham* as children by the promiſe & Election of God. Moreouer, this ſeed is not many, (as *Paul* obſerueth) but one: that is, one in number. It is obiected, that the word [*ſeede*] is a name *collectiue*, and ſignifies the whole poſteritie of *Abraham*. *Anſ.* It doth ſometime, but not alwaies: for *Eue* ſaith of *Seth*, *God hath giuen me an other ſeede*, *Gen.* 4.25. that is, an other ſonne.

Laſtly, it is ſaid, that this one particular ſeede of *Abraham* is Chriſt Ieſus. Here by the name Chriſt, firſt and principally the Mediatour is meant, and then ſecondly all Iewes and Gentiles beleeuing, that are ſet and grafted into Chriſt by their faith. For *Paul* ſaith, *Rom.* 9.8. *that the children of God*, or, *the children of the promiſe, are the ſeede of Abraham*: againe, *Gal.* 3.29. *They which are of Chriſt, are the ſeede of Abraham.* And the name, *Chriſt*, ſignifies not onely the head or Mediatour, God and man, but alſo the Church gathered partly of Iewes, and partly of Gentiles. *The body* (ſaith *Paul*) *is one, but the members are many : euen ſo is Chriſt.* 1. *Cor.* 11.12. that is, the Church of Chriſt. Againe, *I beare in my body the remainders of the ſufferings of Chriſt*, *Col.* 1.24 and the Church is called *the complement of Chriſt.* *Eph.* 1.23. It may be obiected, that by this meanes the ſeede of *Abraham*, is many, and not one: becauſe Chriſt and all beleeuers are the ſeede. *Anſ.* They are all one in reſpect of one and the ſame bleſſing of God, which is firſt giuen to Chriſt, and by Chriſt to all that beleeue in him. *All are one in Chriſt*, *Gal.* 3.28. and *he gathers things in heauen and earth into one head.* *Eph.* 1.10.

It is here to be obserued, that the promises made to *Abraham*, are first made to Christ, and then in Christ to all that beleeue in him, be they Iewes, or Gentiles. This Conclusion is of great vse. First, by it we learne the difference of the promises of the law and the Gospel. The promises of the law, are directed and made to the person of euery man particularly: the promises of the Gospel are first directed, and made to Christ, and then by consequent, to them that are by faith ingrafted into Christ.

Secondly, by this we learne to acknowledge the communion that is betweene Christ and vs. Christ as Mediatour, is first of all elected, and wee in him: Christ is first iustified, that is, acquit of our sinnes, and we iustified in him: he is heire of the world, and we heires in him: he died vpon the crosse, not as a priuate person, but as a publike person representing all the Elect, and all the Elect died in him, and with him. In the same manner they rise with him to life, and sit at the right hand of God with him in glory.

Thirdly, here we see the ground of the Certenty of perseuerance, of all them that are the true children of God. For the office of Christ to which he is set apart, is to receiue the promise of God for vs, and to apply it vnto vs. And this worke is done by Christ without impediment, and without repentance on his part. The seale & foundation of our saluation is this, that God accepts and knowes vs for his, 2.*Tim*.2.19. and that which concernes vs is, that we must worshippe God in Spirit and truth, and depart from iniquitie.

Lastly, here is comfort against the consideration of our vnworthines. Thou saiest thou art vnworthy of the mercy of God, and therefore hast no hope. And I say againe: dost thou truly exercise thy selfe in the spirituall exercises of faith, inuocation, repentance? be not discouraged: thou must not receiue the promise immediately of God, but Christ must doe it for thee. Though thou be vnworthy, yet there is dignity and worthines sufficient in him. If thou say, that thou must at the least receiue the promise at the hand of Christ: I adde further, that *he will not quench the flaxe that doth but smoake, neither will he breake the bruised reede*. He accepts the weake apprehension, if it be in truth. And our saluation stands in this, not that we know and apprehend him, but that he knowes and apprehends vs first of all.

v. 17. *This I say*] In the former verses *Paul* hath laid downe two grounds: one is, that Testaments of men confirmed, may not be abrogated: the other, that the promises were made to *Abraham* and his seede, which is Christ. Now, what of all this, may some man ſay? *Paul* therefore addes theſe words, *This I ſay*, that is, the ſcope and intent of all my ſpeech is, to ſhew, that the couenant or teſtament confirmed by God, cannot be abrogated: and ſecondly if it might ſo be; yet that the law could not abrogate the teſtamēt, becauſe it was giuen 403 yeares after the confirmation of the ſaide teſtament. And becauſe it might be doubtfull what *Paul* meanes, when he ſaith, *the couenant confirmed cannot be abrogated*, he explanes himſelfe in the end of the verſe by ſaying, *the promiſe cannot be made of no effect.*

It is here to be obſerued, that *Paul* ſaith, *the promiſe made to Abraham is a couenant*, or *teſtament*. It is a Couenant or compact, becauſe God for his part promiſeth remiſſion of ſinnes and life euerlaſting, and requireth faith on our part. In reſpect of this mutuall obligation, it hath in it the forme of a couenant. It is alſo a Will, or Teſtament in two reſpects. Firſt, becauſe the promiſe is confirmed by the death of the mediatour, *Heb*.9.15. Secondly, the things promiſed, as remiſſion of ſinnes, and life euerlaſting, are giuen after the manner of legacies, that is freely, without our deſert, or procurement. In this we ſee the great goodnes of God, who vouchſafeth to name them in his teſtament, that haue made couenant with the diuell, and are children of wrath by nature, as we all are.

Againe, in that the promiſe is *a teſtament*, remiſſion of ſinnes, and life euerlaſting is *a legacie*: and for the obtainment of them, wee muſt bring nothing vnto God, but hunger and thirſt after them, and make ſuite vnto God for them, by asking, ſeeking, knocking. Thus are all Legacies obtained, and there is no more required on our part, but to receiue and accept them. And though we bee neuer ſo vnworthy in our ſelues, yet ſhall it ſuffice for the hauing of the bleſſing of God, if our names bee found in the Teſtament of God.

Againe, *Paul* ſaith, that *the promiſe made to Abraham, is a couenant confirmed of God*. It may bee demaunded, by what meanes it was confirmed? *Anſwer*. By oath, *Heb*.6.17. Againe, it may be demanded, to whom it was confirmed? *Anſwer*. To *Abraham*, as beeing the Father of all the faithfull, and then to his *ſeed*, that is, firſt, to the Mediatour Chriſt, and conſequently, to euery beleeuer, whether Iewe, or Gentile. For *Abraham* in the firſt making, and in the confirmation thereof, muſt bee conſidered as a publike perſon, repreſenting all the faithfull.

Heere againe wee ſee Gods goodneſſe. Wee are bound ſimply to beleeue his bare word; yet in regard of our weakeneſſe, hee is content to ratifie his promiſe by oath,that there might bee no occaſion of vnbeleefe.

Againe, here we are admoniſhed to reſt by faith on the promiſe of God, as *Abraham* did, when there is no hope. Some may ſay, I could doe ſo,if God would ſpeake to me,as he did to *Abraham*, I anſwer againe, when God ſpake to *Abraham*, in him he ſpake to all his ſeed: and therefore to thee whoſoeuer thou art,that beleeueſt in Chriſt.

And hence we are to gather ſure hope of life euerlaſting. For in the perſon of *Abraham*,God hath ſpoken to vs: he hath made promiſe of bleſſing to vs: he hath made couenant with vs: and he hath ſworne vnto vs. What can wee more require of him? what better ground of true comfort? *Heb*.6.17.18.

Laſtly,in that God thus confirmes vnto vs the promiſe of life euerlaſting,it muſt incourage vs to all diligence in the vſe of al good meanes, whereby wee may attaine to the condition of *Abraham*: and it muſt arme vs to all patience in bearing the miſeries and calamities that fall out in the ſtrait way to eternall life.

Further,*Paul* ſaith, that *the promiſe is a couenant confirmed, and that in reſpect of Chriſt*: becauſe he is the ſcope and foundation of all the promiſes of God: partly by merit, and partly by efficacy. By merit; becauſe he hath procured by his death and paſſion,remiſſion of ſinnes and life euerlaſting. By his efficacy; becauſe he ſeales vp vnto vs in our conſciences,remiſſion of ſinnes,and withall reſtores in vs the image of God. The vſe. If Chriſt be the ground of the promiſe,then is he the ground & fountaine of all the bleſſings of God. And for this cauſe,the right way to obtaine any bleſſing of God,is firſt to receiue the promiſe,and in the promiſe Chriſt: and Chriſt beeing ours, in him,and from him,we ſhall receiue al things neceſſarie.

The ſecond anſwer of *Paul* to the former obiection, is, that if the promiſe made to *Abraham* might be diſanulled, yet the law could not doe it. And he giues a double reaſon. The firſt is drawn, from the circumſtance of time. Becauſe the promiſe or couenant was made with *Abraham*, and continued by God 430. *yeares before* the law was giuen: therefore ſaith *Paul*, *the law was not giuen to diſanull the promiſe*.

Againſt this reaſon,it may be obiected, that *Abrahams* ſeed, was but 400. *yeares* in a ſtrange land. *Gen*.15. 13. *Anſ*. *Moſes* ſpeakes of the time that was from the beginning of *Abrahams* ſeede, or from the birth of *Iſaac* to the giuing of the Lawe: and *Paul* heere ſpeaks of the time that was betweene the giuing of the promiſe to

Abraham,

Abraham, and the giuing of the law: and that was 30. yeares before the birth of *Isaac*.

Againe, it may bee obiected, that the Israelites were in Egypt 430. yeares, *Exod.* 12. 40. *The dwelling of the children of Israel, while they dwelled in Egypt, was* 430. *yeares*. Therefore it seemes there was more time betweene the promise, and the law. *Answ.* The meaning of *Moses* in this place, is thus much: that the dwelling of the children of Israel, while they dwelt as pilgrimes, was for the space of 430. yeares: and that in part of this time they dwelt in Egypt as strangers. The words may thus be translated, *The dwelling or Peregrination of the children of Israel, in which they dwelt in Egypt, was* 430. *yeares*. And this peregrination begins in the calling of *Abraham*, and ends at the giuing of the law.

In *Pauls* example, we see what it is to search the Scriptures, not onely to consider the scope of whole bookes, and the parts thereof; but to ponder and weigh, euery sentence, and euery part of euery sentence, and euery circumstance of time, place, person. This is the right forme of the studie of diuinitie to be vsed of the sonnes of the Prophets.

The second reason vsed by *Paul*, is in the 18. v. it may be framed thus. If the law abolish the promise, then the inheritance must come by the law: but that cannot be. He prooues it thus: If the inheritance of life eternall be by the law, it is no more by the promise: but it is by the promise: because God gaue it vnto *Abraham* freely by promise: therefore it comes not by the law.

The opposition betweene the law and the promise, shewes that *Paul* in this Epistle speakes not onely of the ceremoniall, but also of the morall. For the greatest opposition is betweene the morall law, and the free promise of God.

Let vs againe marke here the difference betweene the law and the Gospel. The law promiseth life, but to the worker, for his works, or vpon condition of obedience. The Gospel called by *Paul*, *the promise*, offers and giues life freely without the condition of any worke, and requires nothing but the receiuing of that which is offered. It may be obiected, that the Gospel promiseth life vpon the condition of our faith. *Ans.* The Gospel hath in it no moral condition of any thing to be done of vs. Indeede faith is mentioned after the forme & manner of a condition; but in truth it is the free gift of God, as well as life eternall: and it is to be considered not as a worke done of vs, but as an instrument to receiue things promised. This difference of the law and the Gospel must bee kept as a treasure: for it is the ground of many worthy conclusions in true religion.

And the ignorance of this point in the Church of Rome, hath bin the decay of religion, specially in the article of *Iustification.*

Thirdly, wee must here obserue, the opposition betweene the Law & the free promise of God, in the iustification of a sinner. *For if life come by the law, it comes by the promise*, saith *Paul.* And *Rom.* 4. 14. *If they which are of the law are heires, the promise is of none effect.* By this we see the Church of Rome ouerturnes and abrogates, the free promise of God. For they of that Church teach, that the first iustification is by meere mercie: and that the second, is by the workes of the law. But the law and the promise cannot be mixed together, more then fire and water: the law ioyned with the free promise, disanuls the said promise.

Lastly, in that *Paul* saith, God *gaue* and freely bestowed the *inheritance by the promise*, it must be considered, that this Giuing is no priuate, but a publike donation. For *Abraham* must be considered as a publike person: and that which was giuen to him, was in him giuen to all that should beleeue as he did. Art thou then a true beleeuer? doest thou truly turne vnto God? Here is thy comfort: the inheritance of eternall life is as surely thine, as it was *Abrahams*, when he beleeued. For thou art partaker of the same promise with him: and when God gaue him life, hee gaue thee also life in him. Againe, persons backward, and carelesse, must be stirred vp with all diligence to vse all good meanes that they may beleeue truly in Christ, and truly turne to God. For so soone as they begin to beleeue, and to turne vnto God, they are entred into the condition of *Abraham*, and if they continue, *they shall sit downe with Abraham, Isaac, and Iacob, in the kingdome of heauen:* and after this life, they shall rest in the bosome of *Abraham*. For that which was done to *Abraham*, shall be done to all that walke in his steps.

19 *Wherefore then serues the law? It was added because of transgressions, vntill the seede was come to which the promise was made: and it was ordained by Angels in the hand of a Mediatour.*

20 *Now a Mediatour is not of one: but God is one.*

Paul hath prooued before, that the law doth not abolish the promise: his last reason was, because then the inheritance should bee by the law: which cannot be. Against this reason in the 19. and 20. verses, there is an obiection made, and answered. The obiection is this. If life and iustice come not by the law, the law then is in vaine. And this obiection is expressed by way of interrogation,

Where-

Wherefore then ſerues the law? The anſwer is, in the next words, *It is added for tranſgreſſions*, that is, for the reuealing of ſinne, and the puniſhment thereof, and for the conuincing of men touching their ſinnes. *Rom.* 3. 19, 20. Moreouer, *Paul* ſets downe the time or continuance of this vſe of the law, when he ſaith, *till the ſeede came to which the promiſe was made*: that is, till Chriſt come and accompliſh the worke of mans redemption. Here two queſtions may be demanded. The firſt is, whether the law ſerue to reueale ſinne after the comming of Chriſt? For *Paul* ſaith, *it is added for tranſgreſſions, till Chriſt. Anſwer.* The law ſerues to reueale ſinne, euen to the ende of the world: yet in reſpect of the legall or Moſaicall manner of reuealing ſinne, it is added, *but till Chriſt.* For the law before Chriſt did conuince men of ſinne, not onely by precepts and threatnings, but alſo by Rites and Ceremonies. For Iewiſh waſhings, and ſacrifices, were reall confeſſions of ſinne. And they were an handwriting againſt vs, as *Paul* ſaith. And this manner of reuealing ſinne, ended in the death of Chriſt. *Col.* 2. 14 Againe, the Miniſtery of condemnation which was in force till Chriſt, at his comming is turned into the Miniſtery of the ſpirit, and of grace. 2. *Cor.* 3, 11. For vnder the law there was plentifull reuelation of ſinne, with darke and ſmall reuelation of grace: but at the comming of Chriſt, men ſaw heauen opened, and there was a plentifull reuelation of ſinne, with a more plentifull reuelation of grace, and mercie. And in this reſpect alſo the law is ſaid to be *till Chriſt.*

The ſecond queſtion is, whether the ſeede of *Abraham* were before Chriſt or no? *Anſ.* All that followed the ſteppes of *Abrahams* faith before Chriſt, were his ſeede. Yet were they not, that ſeed, that is, the principall ſeede, who is Chriſt, who is the ſeede bleſſed in himſelfe, and giuing bleſſedneſſe to all other. And the beleeuers that were before Chriſt or after him, are the ſeede of *Abraham*, in reſpect they are ſet into Chriſt, who is principally the ſeede mentioned in this text.

When *Paul* ſaith, *ordained by Angels in the hand of a Mediatour*, he makes a declaration of that which he had ſaid before by an euident ſigne, on this manner. That the law ſerues to diſcouer tranſgreſſions, it appeares by this, that the Iewes could not abide to receiue the law immediately from God, but it was deliuered by Angels, and receiued by the hand of a Mediatour: and this argues mans guiltineſſe, and his diſagreement with God, becauſe a Mediatour is of two, at the leaſt, and of two beeing at difference betweene themſelues.

The law is ſaid to be ordained or diſpoſed by Angels: becauſe

 they

they were attendants on God in the Mount, when the law was deliuered. Secondly, they were witnesses and approouers of the deliuerie. Thirdly it may be, the voice of God whereby the law was published in the hearing of all the Israelites, was vttered and pronounced by the ministerie of Angels: for the holy Ghost saith, *the word spoken by Angels was stedfast*, *Heb.*2.2. that is, the law. It may be said, all this prooues not, that Angels ordained the law. *Ans.* Often in Scripture, the worke or action of the principall Agent, is ascribed to the instrument, or minister. The Saints are said *to iudge the world*, 1. *Cor.*6. whereas indeede they are no more but witnesses and approouers of this iudgement. In the same manner *Timothie* is said *to saue himselfe and others*, 1. *Timothie*, 4.16. The last trumpet is sounded by Angels, *Matth.*24.31. and it is called the voice of an Archangel, and the trumpe of God. 1. *Thess.*4.

Moreouer *Paul* saith, *the law was deliuered by the hands of a Mediatour*, that is, of Christ, (as some thinke:) but that cannot be: for the hand of a Mediatour, signifies the ministerie and seruice of a Mediatour, and this seruice is inferiour to the seruice of Angels: because the law was deliuered by Angels, and receiued of them by a Mediatour. Therefore the Mediatour here mentioned, is *Moses*, who stood betweene the people and God, in the deliuerie of the law. *Deut.*5.5. It may be obiected, that there is but *one Mediatour Christ*, 1. *Tim.*2.8. *Ans.* Mediatour of reconciliation is onely one, and that is Christ: and *Moses* is a Mediatour onely in the relating and reporting the law from God to the Israelites.

Paul addes that a *Mediatour is not of one*, that is, that euery Mediatour is of two at the least, and of two at variance, and disagreement. And he saith further, that *God is one*: that is, alwaies the same and like himselfe without change. And the reason of the speech is this. *Paul* hath taught that the law was giuen by a Mediatour, and that this declared a differēce between God and man. Now it might be said, where is the fault in this difference, and who is the cause of it? *Paul* saith, not God but man: because *God is alwaies one and the same.*

The vse. In that the law is for transgressions, wee are taught to examine and search our hearts and liues by the law of God. *Zephan.* 2.1. *Fanne you, O nation, not worthie to be loued. Lam.*3.40. *Let vs search our hearts, and turne againe to the Lord.* That we may the better examine our selues, foure rules must be obserued.

1 The first, when any one sinne is forbidden in any commandement of the law, vnder it all sinnes of the same kind are forbidden, all causes of them, and all occasions.

The

The second, a commandement negatiue includes the affirmatiue, and bindes vs not onely to abstaine from euill, but also to doe the contrarie good.

The third is, that euery commandement must be vnderstood with a curse annexed to it, though the curse be not expressed.

The fourth is, that we must especially examine our selues by the first and last commandements. For the first forbids the first motions of our hearts against God, and the last forbiddes the first motions of our hearts against our neighbor, though there be no consent to doe the euill which wee thinke. *Paul* saith of himselfe, that the commandement, *Thou shalt not lust*, was it that especially humbled him. *Rom.*7.

According to these and other rules, (which now I omit) we must with speciall care examine our selues. The want of this dutie causeth men to rot away in their sinnes, without remorse or true repentance: and it is the cause that so many men profit so little in hearing the word preached; because they know not what sinne meanes, neither can they search aright their consciences and liues.

Moreouer, after we haue begunne to practise this dutie, we must often (as occasion shall be giuen) renue it to the end. Consider *Dauids* example. *Psal.*119.59.

When *Paul* saith, that *the law is added till Christ*, we see that the Legall ministerie of death is abolished now; and that we are vnder the Ministerie of the spirit and life. And for this cause wee in these last daies, that are Ministers of the word, must preach the doctrine of saluation plainly, to the very consciences of men. 2.*Cor.*4.1. Againe, the people of these daies ought to abound in knowledge, and their obedience should bee answerable to the measure of their knowledge. And, if after much preaching in these dayes of light, the Gospel be hid, (as it is to very many, who remayne still in ignorance, and disobedience) it is a fearefull signe vnto them of their condemnation. 2.*Cor.*4.4.

In that the law of God was ordained or deliuered by Angels, we are put in minde to reuerence it, and to esteeme it as a treasure. Secondly, we are to feare to breake the least commandement of the law: because the Angels that were ordayners of the law, doe no doubt, obserue the keepers & the breakers of it, and are ready prest to be witnesses and reuengers against them that offend. *Steuen* vpbraides the Iewes, that the law was giuen by the dispensation of Angels, and yet they brake it. *Act.*7.53. Thirdly, if thou offend and breake the law, repent with speede: for that is the desire ioy of Angels. They that deliuered the law, reioice to see the keeping of it.

Lastly,

Lastly, if thou sinne and repent not, looke for shame and confusion before God and his Angels.

Because *Moses* was a mediatour to the Iewes, Papists gather that therefore Angels and Saints, may be mediatours. *Answ.* It followes not. *Moses* was ordained a mediatour, so are not they. *Moses* was present with the Iewes, and had fellowship with them whose mediatour he was. Saints are absent in heauen, and Angels though they be about vs, haue no fellowship with vs. *Moses* was mediatour but once, and that onely in one thing: Saints are made continuall mediatours. Lastly, *Moses* was mediatour in relating and reporting the law from God to the people: Saints and Angels are made mediatours to relate and report our praiers, and the secrets of our hearts to God.

Whereas *Paul* saith; that *a Mediatour is not of one*, but a third, betweene two at the least: it may be demanded, how Christ can bee mediatour betweene man and God, considering he is God? *Answer.* Though Father, Sonne, and holy Spirit, be one and the same in respect of Godhead, yet are they distinct in respect of person, or in respect of the manner of subsisting; so as the Father is the Father, not the Sonne, or holy Ghost; the Sonne, the Sonne, and not the Father, or the holy Ghost; the holy Ghost, the holy Ghost, and not the Father, or the Sonne. The Sonne then, and the Father, beeing persons really distinct, the Sonne may be, and is Mediatour, first of all, in respect of order to the Father, and in him, to the Sonne, and the holy Ghost. For the three persons being of one nature and will, when the Father is appeased, in him also the Sonne, and the holy Ghost are appeased. Thus *Iohn* saith, *If any man sinne, we haue an aduocate with the Father*. It may be said, that Christ cannot be Mediatour to himselfe. *Ans.* In Christ consider his nature, and his Office. By nature, he is the Sonne of God: by office, he is Mediatour, and thus he is *God-man*, or *Man-god*: and as Mediatour by voluntarie dispensation, he is inferiour to himselfe as he is the essentiall Sonne of God. And in the same manner, Christ as God-man is Mediatour to himselfe as he is the Sonne of God. For as he is the Sonne of God, he is the partie offended; as he is Mediatour God-man, he is the partie that makes reconciliation.

Lastly, the propertie of God must be obserued, that he is vnchangeable, *Iam.* 1.17. *Mal.* 3.16. It may be obiected, that God is said in Scripture to repent. *Answ.* God is said to repent, not because hee changeth either nature or will: but because he changeth his actions of mercie and loue, into effects of anger after the maner of men. Againe, it may be obiected, that God changed the law and abolished

abolished ceremonies. *Answ.* This God did by an vnchangeable decree, before all worlds: and so the change is in the law, and not in God. For God can decree to change this or that, without change.

The vse. Gods vnchangeablenesse is the foundation of our comfort. Saint *Paul* saith, *If we loue God, we are knowne of him*, 1. Cor. 8. verse 3. Now the first wee may certenly finde in our selues, namely, the loue of God, and Christ: and for the second, God is vnchangeable. For they which are once knowne of God, are euer knowne of him; and that euen then when they feele nothing but Gods anger.

Againe, we are put in minde to be vnchangeable in good things, as in faith, hope, loue, good counsels, honest promises, and such like, specially in the maintenance of true religion. For we ought to bee like vnto God. It is the poesie of our gracious Queene, *Semper eadem, Alwaies one and the same*; no doubt in good things, specially in the religion established among vs. The same must be the minde of all good subiects and all good people. 1. Cor. 15. 58.

21 *Is the law then against the promise of God? God forbid: if there had beene a law giuen, which could haue giuen life, surely righteousnesse should haue beene by the law.*

22 *But the Scripture hath concluded all vnder sin, that the promise by the faith of Iesus Christ, should be giuen to them that beleeue.*

In these words, *Paul* propounds and answers an other obiection, in number the fourth. The occasion of the obiection, is taken out of the former words, in which *Paul* saith, *the law is for transgressions*. It may be framed on this manner: If the law serue to conuince and condemne vs of sinne, it serues not to giue life but to kill, and so it is contrarie to the promise which giueth life. The answer is made negatiuely, *God forbid*. And a double reason is rendered of the deniall. The first is this: If the law could giue life, it should also giue iustice, or iustifie, and so, it should be contrarie to the promise (because then there shold be two contrarie waies of iustification, one by faith alone, the other by faith with workes.) Therefore in that it kills and condemnes, it is not contrarie to the promise. The second reason, is in the 22. verse. Things subordinate, whereof one serues for the other, are not contrarie: the law and the promise are subordinate; for the law prepares the way for the accomplishing of the promise, in that it shuts all vnder sinne, that the promise may bee giuen to them that beleeue in Christ.

The vse. In that *Paul* reiects the blasphemous obiection, with, *God forbid:* wee are taught to auoide things said or done to the dishonour of God, with loathing and detestation. When it was related to *Ahab* and *Iezabel*, that *Naboth* had blasphemed God, they beeing idolaters, solemnise a fast, pretending danger by the sinne. 1. *King*. 21. 12. *Caiphas* supposing that Christ had blasphemed, rent his garments, *Matth*. 26. When *Iob* did but suspect his children of blaspheming God, he called them and sanctified them. *Iob* 1. 5. It is the fault of our daies, that many blaspheme by cursing, swearing, &c. without feare, and many doe it (as many dissolute souldiers) in a brauerie: and hearers thereof for the most part are nothing mooued thereat, so ordinarie is the offence. This shewes the wickednesse of our times.

In the first reason, *Paul* deliuers a notable conclusion, namely, that the thing which is the meanes to procure life vnto vs, is also the meanes of our iustice or iustification before God. And good reason. For iustice causeth life: and that which giueth life, first of all giueth iustice. Hence it followes that workes cannot meritoriously deserue eternall life. For if life be by the workes of the law, then iustice also: but that cannot be: for we must first of all be iustified, before we can doe a good worke. Let the Papists consider this. Againe, they which teach, that faith is alone in iustification, and that both faith and workes concurre as causes of saluation, are deceiued. For by the former conclusion of *Paul*, if workes be causes of saluation, then must they also haue a stroake in our iustification, which they haue not. And therefore they are the way of our saluation, but not any cause at all. Lastly, here we see that many among vs do not hold Christ, or beleeue in him aright, for their iustification: because they hold him without change of heart and life. For by *Pauls* conclusion, whom Christ quickneth, them hee iustifieth: and whom he doth not quicken, them he doth not iustifie. Examine thy selfe then: if Christ haue sanctified & renewed thy heart, thou art iustified: if thy heart be yet vnsanctified, and thy life vnreformed, deceiue not thy selfe with fond imaginations: thou art not yet iustified.

The 22. verse followeth, containing the second reason. And first let vs consider the meaning of the words. *The Scripture*] the words are in the Originall thus, *That Scripture*, namely, the Scripture before named, the written law in the bookes of the old Testament. And further, *by the law*, we must vnderstand, God in the law, *Rom*. 11. 32. God hath concluded all vnder vnbeleefe.

Concluded] The law is compared to a Iudge, or sergeant: sinne, to a priſon. And the law is ſaid to conclude, or incloſe men vnder ſinne: becauſe it doth to the full accuſe and conuince vs of ſinne, ſo as our mouthes are ſtopped, and we haue no way to eſcape.

All] All men that came of *Adam* by generation, with all that comes from them, their thoughts, deſires, words, and deeds.

The promiſe] The thing promiſed, which is remiſſion of ſinne, and life euerlaſting.

By the faith of Chriſt] That is, the faith whereof Chriſt is both the Authour, and matter. This is added, to ſignifie vnto vs, who are true beleeuers, namely, they which are beleeuers by the faith of Chriſt.

Againſt this text of *Paul* blind reaſon mooueth many queſtions, as namely why God created man, and then ſuffered him to fall? why God did not reſtraine the fall of *Adam* to his perſon, but ſuffers it to inlarge it ſelfe to all mankind, ſo as all be ſhut vp vnder ſin? why the promiſe is not giuen to all, but only to beleeuers? But there are two ſpeciall grounds, vpon which we are to ſtay our mindes. The firſt is, that God hath an abſolute ſoueraignetie and lordſhip ouer all his creatures. We may not therefore diſpute the caſe with God, *Rom.* 9.20. *He may doe with his owne what he will*, *Matt.* 20.15. The ſecond is, that the waies and iudgements of God are a gulfe, into which the more we ſearch, the more we plunge our ſelues: becauſe they are *vnſearchable*, *Rom.* 11.33.

Marke the phraſe of *Paul* [*the Scripture concludes all vnder ſinne*] if it conclude or ſhut vp, then it determines what is ſinne, what not. And if this be ſo: then it may alſo determine what is true, and what is falſe: and ſo be truly tearmed a Iudge of controuerſies in religion. If it ſhut vp ſinners vnder their ſin, then alſo it ſhuts them that erre vnder their errour, for errours be ſinnes and fruits of the fleſh. It is ſaid blaſphemouſly, that if the Scripture be a iudge, it is but a dumb iudge: and I ſay againe, that offenders may pleade for themſelues on this ſort, that the law is but a dumbe iudge, when it condemnes them, and ſhuts them vnder ſinne: but they ſhall find it hath a loud voyce in their conſciences, when they reade it ſeriouſly, & examine themſelues by it: euen ſo the Scripture ſpeakes ſufficiently for the determination of truth and falſhood, in matters of ſaluation, when it is ſearched with care and humilitie.

When *Paul* ſaith, *We are all ſhut vp vnder ſinne*, he puts vs in mind of our moſt miſerable condition, that wee are captiues of ſinne and Satan, incloſed in our ſinnes as in a priſon, like impriſoned malefactours that waite daily for the coming of the Iudge, and ſtand in continuall feare of execution. And ſeeing our condition is ſuch,

ſuch, wee muſt labour to ſee and feele by experience this our ſpirituall bondage, that wee may ſay with *Paul, Wee are ſold vnder ſinne,* and *that we know there is no goodneſſe dwelling in our fleſh, Rom.7.14,18.* This is one of the firſt leſſons that we muſt take out in the ſchoole of Chriſt. Againe, if we ſeriouſly bethinke our ſelues that we are captiues of ſinne, and worthy of death, it will make vs with contentation of minde to beare the miſeries of this life, ſickneſſe, pouertie, reproach, baniſhment, &c. conſidering they come farre ſhort of that wee haue deſerued; who are no better then ſlaues of ſinne and Satan.

Wheras *Paul* ſaith, that all men with all that proceeds from them, is ſhut vnder ſin, he teacheth that all actions of men vnregenerate are ſinnes. *The wiſdom of the fleſh*, that is, the wiſeſt cogitations, counſels, inclinations of the fleſh, *are enmitie with God, Rom.8.5. To the vncleane all things are vncleane, Tit. 1.15. An euill tree cannot bring forth good fruite, Matt.7.* It may be obiected, that naturall men may doe the works of the moral law, as to giue almes, & ſuch like, *Rom.2.14. Anſw.* Sinnes be of two ſorts. One is, when any thing is done flat againſt the commandement of God. The ſecond is, when the act or worke is done which the law preſcribes, yet not in the ſame maner which the law preſcribes, in faith, in obedience to the glory of God. In this ſecond regard, morall workes performed by naturall men, are ſinnes indeed. Hence it followes, that libertie of will in the doing of that which is truly good, is loſt by the fall of *Adam*: and that man cannot by the ſtrength of naturall will, helped by grace, apply himſelfe to the calling of God.

Whereas *Paul* ſaith, that *the promiſe is giuen to beleeuers*, it is manifeſt, that the promiſe is not vniuerſall in reſpect of all mankinde, but only indefinite, and vniuerſall in reſpect of beleeuers. Wherfore their doctrine is not ſound, that teach the redemption wrought by Chriſt, to bee as generall as the ſinne wrought by *Adam*. Indeed, if we regard the value and ſufficiencie of the death of Chriſt, it is ſo: but if we reſpect the communication and donation of this benefit, it is not. For though all be ſhut vnder ſinne, yet the promiſe is only giuen *to them that beleeue*. It is obiected, that *God was in Chriſt reconciling the world to himſelfe, 2. Cor.5.19. Anſw.* The text in hand ſhewes that by *the world*, we are to vnderſtand al beleeuers through the whole world. And whereas *Paul* ſaith, *God ſhut vp all vnder vnbeleefe, that hee might haue mercie vpon all, Rom. 11.32.* His meaning is here ſet downe, that he ſhut both Iewes and Gentiles vnder vnbeleefe, that hee might haue mercie vpon all that beleeue, both Iewes and Gentiles.

Marke further, the end of the law is conuiction: and the end of our conuiction is, that the promiſe of mercy may bee giuen to them that beleeue. Here is notable comfort, with encouragement to all good duties. Doth the law as it were in the name of God arreſt thee? doth it accuſe & conuince thee of manifold ſinnes? doth it arraigne thee at the barre of Gods iudgement, and fill thy ſoule with terrour? doeſt thou by the teſtimonies of the law and thine owne conſcience, ſee and feele thy ſelfe to be a moſt miſerable and wretched ſinner? Well. It may bee thou thinkeſt that all this is a preparation to thy damnation: but it is not. For it is contrariwiſe a preparation to thy ſaluation. For the law with a loud voice in thy heart, proclaimes thee a ſinner, and threatens thee with perdition: but the end of all this is, that Ieſus Chriſt may become a Sauiour vnto thee, ſo be it thou wilt come vnto him, and beleeue in him. For he ſaues no ſheepe, *but the loſt ſheepe*, and *he cals not iuſt men, but ſinners to repentance.* Let vs therfore with all our hearts come vnto Chriſt, and beleeue in him, and that by the faith of Chriſt, that is, with a faith ioyned with hope, loue, and new obedience. Then ſhall the promiſe of pardon and life euerlaſting bee giuen to vs. Vpon this ground, perſons in deſpaire, and grieuous offenders, may ſee a plain way to helpe and ſuccour themſelues. For the worke of the law concluding vs vnder ſinne, by the mercy of God, tends to our ſaluation, if we will vſe the good meanes.

Laſtly, *Paul* ſaith, the promiſe is made not to euery one that beleeueth according to any faith of his owne, but to them that are true beleeuers by the faith of Chriſt. Therefore euery man ſhal not bee ſaued in his owne faith and religion, but onely they that are of the faith of Chriſt.

23 *For before faith came, we were kept vnder the law, and ſhut vp vnto faith which ſhould afterward be reuealed.*

24 *Wherefore the law was our ſchoole-maſter to Chriſt, that we might be made righteous by faith.*

25 *But after that faith is come, wee are no more vnder the ſchoole-maſter.*

Paul in the 19. verſe had ſaid, that *the law was for trangreſſions, till the ſeede come, to which the promiſe was made.* And heere hee makes a more large declaration of his owne meaning. The ſumme of all that he ſaith may be reduced to a compariſon of things vnlike, on this manner. Before the comming of faith, we were vnder the dominion of *Moſes* law: but after faith was come, wee were free.

The firſt part of the cōpariſon is amplified by a double ſimilitude: the law was a guard vnto vs, v. 23. and the law was our ſchoolemaſter, v. 24. the ſecond part of the compariſon is in the 25. verſe.

Faith] That is, the Goſpel, or, the doctrine of remiſſion of ſinnes and life euerlaſting by Chriſt, exhibited in the fleſh.

Wee] We Iewes: I *Paul* a Iew, and the reſt of that nation.

Law] That is, the whole Oeconomie, Policie, and Regiment of *Moſes*, by lawes partly Morall, partly Ceremoniall, and partly Iudiciall.

Kept] Compaſſed or guarded. Becauſe the law before Chriſt was to the Iewes as a guard of armed men, to incloſe and keepe them, that they ſhould not depart from God, and from their allegiance to him, vnto the ſinnes, idolatries, and ſuperſtitions of the Gentiles.

Vnto the faith] That is, till the faith come.

Afterward reuealed] From the creation to the law, the Church of God was in one family; and the reſt of the world beſide was no people of God. From the law till Chriſt, the Church of God was incloſed in the nation of the Iewes, and all the world beſide no Church or people of God. And this diſtinction of a people and no people, ſtood ſome time after the comming of Chriſt. *Matth.* 10.5. *Go not into the way of the Gentiles, and into the cities of the Samaritans enter ye not.* After the aſcenſion of Chriſt, this diſtinction ended: becauſe the myſterie of mans redemption was then more plainely reuealed; and it began then to be reuealed to the whole world, *Coloſ.* 1.26, 27. and *Rom.* 16, 25.

Thus wee ſee that the law ſerued for tranſgreſſions: becauſe it was to the Iewes as a guard to keepe them in the compaſſe of their dutie, that they fell not away to ſundry tranſgreſſions.

The vſe. This ſhewes the greatneſſe of our corruption, and that the very frame of our heart is euill continually, that the Lord muſt be faine to ſet his lawes about vs as a guard of armed men, to keep vs that we ſinne not.

Againe, here wee ſee the vſe of Gods lawes, which ſerue to preuent, reſtraine, and cut off ſinne, into which otherwiſe men would fall, vnleſſe they were compaſſed and guarded by lawes. Some obiect for freedome of will, on this maner: If the lawes of God cannot be kept, they are in vaine: but they are not in vaine: therefore they may be kept. *Anſw.* The *maior* or firſt part of the reaſon, is not true. For there are other vſes of the lawes of God, thē the keeping of them: for they ſerue to reſtraine, and to preuent open offences: and to keepe men in order, at the leaſt outwardly.

An

An other vse of rhe Law of God, was to conclude and ſhut vp the Iewes into the vnitie of one faith and religion. For this cauſe the Iewes had but one Temple, on Mercy-ſeat, one high Prieſt, &c. Hence it followes, that in a godly and Chriſtian Common-wealth where true religion is eſtabliſhed, there may be no toleration of any other religion. For that which is the end of Gods laws, muſt alſo be the end of all good laws in all Common-wealths and kingdomes, namely, to ſhut vp the people into the vnity of one faith,

The Church of the Iewes, is called *a fountaine ſealed, a garden incloſed, Cant.*4.12. *a vineyard hedged in. Iſa.*5.5. *Pſal.*80.13. And here we ſee what is the hedge or wall of this garden, or vineyard: namely, the regiment or policy of *Moſes* by a threefold kind of law. This admoniſheth vs to reſpect and with care to obſerue good lawes: becauſe they are as it were hedges & fenſes of all good ſocieties: and the breaking of them is the pulling downe of our fenſe.

Where *Paul* ſaith, *till the faith be reuealed.* Note, that the faith, or the Goſpel, was not reuealed to the world, till the laſt age, after the comming of Chriſt. It may be ſaid, it was alwaies reuealed to all men, but not ſo cleerely as in theſe laſt daies. *Anſ.* It was not reuealed to all, either darkly or cleerely, before the comming of Chriſt. *Act.* 14.16. *God ſuffered the Gentiles to walke in their owne waies. Eph.* 2. 12. they were *without God, and without Chriſt. Rom.*15.20. *Paul* preached *where Chriſt was not ſo much as named.* Hence it followes, that the Vocation of men to life euerlaſting is not vniuerſall: becauſe Chriſt was neuer vniuerſally reuealed. Neither is mans Redemption vniuerſall in reſpect of the whole world. For Redemption by Chriſt was not reuealed to all nations before the comming of Chriſt: and a benefit to be apprehended by faith, if it be vnknown, is no benefit. Laſtly, it is erronious that ſome teach, namely, that grace ſupernaturall is vniuerſall: that is, that the power to beleeue in Chriſt, and the power to turne to God, if men will, is generally giuen to all. But this cannot be: becauſe it is not giuen to all men, ſo much as to heare of Chriſt, and to know him.

Seeing faith is now come, it may bee demaunded, what is the guard whereby we are kept now? *Anſw.* The precepts of the morall law. *The ſayings of the wiſe are as nailes* or *ſtakes faſtened* to range men in the compaſſe of their owne dueties, *Ecclеſ.* 12.11. Againe, the peace of God, or the aſſurance of our reconciliation with God, is a guard, to keepe our hearts and ſenſes in Chriſt, *Phil.* 4.7. If this will not doe the deed, God hath in ſtore his corrections and iudgements, to bee as an hedge to hedge vs in, *Hoſea* 2.6.

This beeing ſo, our duty is to guard and incloſe our ſelues, ſpecially our hearts, *Prou.*4.23. and all the ſenſes and powers of our ſoules, *Pſal.*141.3. by the wholeſome precepts, and counſells of God. Conſidering we lie open to ſo many enemies, we ſhould continually be armed and fenſed from the head to the foote, *Eph.*6.13. otherwiſe we ſhall vpon euery occaſion be ouerturned.

To come to the 24.v. the Iewes might haply ſay, Seeing we are thus kept and ſhut vp by the law, what meanes haue we of comfort and of ſaluation? The anſwer is made, *the law is* further *our ſchoolemaſter.* Here by *ſchoolemaſter*, vnderſtand one, that teacheth little children or Petits, the firſt rudiments or elements, A.B.C. And the law is *a ſchoolemaſter to Chriſt*, for two cauſes. One, becauſe it points out and ſhadowes forth vnto vs Chriſt, by bodily rudiments of ceremonies and ſacrifices. The ſecond is, becauſe the law, ſpecially the morall law, vrgeth and compelleth men to goe to Chriſt. For it ſhewes vs our ſinnes, and that without remedy: it ſhewes vs the damnation that is due vnto vs: and by this meanes, it makes vs deſpaire of ſaluation in reſpect of our ſelues: & thus it inforceth vs to ſeeke for helpe out of our ſelues in Chriſt. The law is then our ſchoolemaſter not by the plaine teaching, but by ſtripes and correction.

In this verſe, *Paul* ſets downe the manner and way of our ſaluation, which is on this manner; firſt, the law prepares vs by humbling vs: then comes the Goſpel, and it ſtirres vp faith. And faith wrought in the heart apprehends Chriſt for iuſtification, ſanctification, and glorification. *Paul* ſets this forth by a fit ſimilitude. They that would be the ſeruants and children of God, muſt come into the ſchoole of God, and be taught of him. In this ſchoole are two formes, and two maſters. In the firſt forme, the teacher and maſter is the law. And he teacheth men to know their ſinnes, and their deſerued damnatiō, & he cauſeth vs to deſpaire of our ſaluation in reſpect of our ſelues. And when men haue bin well ſchooled by the law, and are brought to acknowledge their ſinnes, and that they are ſlaues of ſinne and Satan; then muſt they be taken vp to an higher forme, and be taught by an other ſchoolemaſter, which is Faith, or the Goſpel. The leſſon of the Goſpel is, that men after they are humbled, muſt fly to the throne of grace, beleeue in Chriſt, and with all their hearts turne vnto God: that they may be iuſtified, and glorified. VVhen we haue by the teaching of this ſecond maſter, learned this good leſſon, we are become children and ſeruants of God.

By this then it is manifeſt, that there are two ſorts of badde

ſchol-

ſchollers in the ſchoole of Chriſt, among vs. One ſort are they, which come to the Lords table, & yet learne nothing, either from the law, or from the Goſpel: but content themſelues with the teaching of nature. The ſecond ſort are they, which learne ſomething, but in prepoſterous manner. For they haue learned that mercy & ſaluation comes by Chriſt: and with this they content themſelues, not ſuffering themſelues firſt of all to be ſchooled by the law, till they deſpaire in reſpect of themſelues: nor to bee ſchooled of the Goſpel, till they beleeue in Chriſt and repent of their ſinnes.

In a word, he is a good ſcholler in the ſchoole of Chriſt, that firſt learnes by the law to humble himſelfe, and to goe out of himſelfe: and beeing humbled, ſubiects his heart to the voice and precept of the Goſpel, which bids vs beleeue in Chriſt, turne to God, and teſtifie our faith by new obedience.

In the ſecond part of the compariſon 25. v. *Paul* ſets downe one point, that at the comming of the faith the Iewes were freed from the dominion of the law of *Moſes*, and conſequently that the ſaid law was abrogated. The lawgiuer, that is, the expounder of *Moſes* law was to laſt but till the coming of *Shilo.* *Gen.* 49. 10. The law of commandements ſtanding in ordinances, was abrogated by the fleſh of Chriſt. *Eph.* 2. 15. And the change of the prieſthood, brought the change of the law. *Heb.* 7. 12.

For the better cleering of this point, three queſtions are to be demanded. The firſt is, when was the policy, regiment, or law of *Moſes* abrogated, *Anſ.* At the comming of the faith, or when the Goſpel firſt beganne to be publiſhed to the world: which was at the Aſcenſion of Chriſt. And he in his death cancelled the ceremoniall law, and tooke it out of the way, *Col.* 2. 14. When the old Teſtament ended, and the new began, then was the abrogation of the law: now the ending of the old Teſtament, and the begin- of the new, was in the Reſurrection of Chriſt. For then was the beginning of the new world, as it were.

The ſecond queſtion is, how farre forth the law is abrogated? *Anſ.* The law is threefold: Morall, Ceremoniall, Iudiciall. Morall is the law of God, concerning manners, or duties to God and man. Now the morall law is abrogated, in reſpect of the Church, and them that beleeue three waies. Firſt, in reſpect of *iuſtification*: and this *Paul* prooues at large in this Epiſtle. And ſecondly, in reſpect of the *malediction*, or curſe. *There is no condemnation to them that are in Chriſt. Rom.* 8. 1. Thirdly, in reſpect of *rigour*. For in them that are in Chriſt, God accepts the indeauour to obay, for obedience it ſelfe. Neuertheleſſe, the law, as it is the rule of good life, is vnchangeable,and admits no abrogation. And Chriſt in this regard did by his death eſtabliſh it. *Rom*.3.31.

The Ceremoniall law, is that which preſcribed rites and geſtures in the worſhip of God,in the time of the old teſtament. Ceremonies are either of figure and ſignification, or of order. The firſt are abrogated at the comming of Chriſt,who was the accompliſhment of them all. *Col*.2. 17. The ſecond beeing ceremonies of particular order to the times of the old and new Teſtament, concerne not vs. For example: In the commandement of the Sabbath, ſome things are morall, ſome ceremoniall, ſome iudiciall. That in one day of ſeuen there ſhould be an holy reſt,it is morall. Reſt vpon the ſeuenth day from the creation, is Ceremoniall, in reſpect of order. Strictnes of reſt from all labour, is ceremoniall in reſpect of the ſignification of reſt from ſinne, and reſt in heauen. Therfore the particular day of reſt,and the manner of reſt,is abrogated:and Chriſt by his owne example,and by the example of the Apoſtles(examples not beeing contradicted in Scripture)appointed the eight day,or the day of Chriſts reſurrection,to be the Sabbath of the new Teſtament.

Iudiciall lawes are ſuch as concerne inheritances, lands, bargaines,controuerſies,cauſes criminall;and they pertaine to the regiment of the Common wealth. If the Common wealth of the Iewes were now ſtāding,they ſhould be gouerned by theſe lawes. For to them were they giuen.The caſe is not like with vs. Some are of minde, that all iudiciall lawes are abrogated: and ſome are of contrary minde, that all Common wealths are to be gouerned by them. But they are both deceiued: and the meane betweene both,is the truth.Know then that of Iudiciall lawes of *Moſes*,ſome are abrogated,ſome are not. Such lawes as are meerely Iudiciall, that is,iudiciall and not morall,and doe particularly concerne the nation of the Iewes,the land of Canaan, the times before Chriſt, the things of the old Teſtament,are abrogated.Of this kind is the law that commāds *the brother to raiſe vp ſeed to his brother.Deut*.25.5 The law of Tenths is partly ceremoniall,& partly iudiciall,& ſpecially concernes the land of Canaan.For as countries are richer or poorer then Canaan,ſo muſt their allowance to the Miniſtery be more or leſſe. The ſeuenths,the eights, the ninths,the eleuenths, the twelfths, and not the tenths. And the allowance of Tenths, ſtands not in force in this & other Common wealths by the Iudiciall law of God,but by poſitiue laws of countries.For if it did,then Miniſters ſhould not meddle with their Tenths,either for the gathering, or for the diſpoſing of them, but they ſhould be brought

into

into ſtore-houſes by certaine ouerſeers, and they ſhould diſpoſe of them according to the need of the Miniſter, 2.*Chron*.31. *Malac*.3. The law that the theefe muſt either reſtore fourefold,or be a bondman,concernes Canaan,and thoſe countreys. In Europe,(ſpecially in the Northern and Weſtern parts,) a ſtraighter law is required. For the people are much giuen to idleneſſe, and conſequently to robbing: and they are of fierce diſpoſition, & therefore with theft ioyne violence,& diſturbance of the common peace. And for this cauſe(excepting in ſome caſes)theft is puniſhed with death. And this muſt not ſeeme hard. For euen the Iewes, when the theft was aggrauated with other circumſtances, might puniſh it with death, 2.*Sam*.12.6. And it is in the power of the Magiſtrate, when ſinnes are increaſed,to increaſe the puniſhment.

Now iudiciall lawes,that are in foundation and ſubſtance moral, are not abrogated,but are perpetuall. For the better diſcerning of them,I giue two notes. The firſt is this: If a iudiciall law ſerue directly and immediatly,to guard and fenſe any one of the ten commandements,in the maine ſcope and end thereof, it is morall in equitie,and perpetuall: becauſe the end and vſe of it is perpetuall. I will giue ſundry examples. It is the law of God,that hee of the Iſraelites that ſhall intiſe them to goe and worſhip other gods,ſhal be put to death, *Deut*.13.6. This law ſerues to maintaine and vphold the firſt commandement,the end whereof is to inioyne vs to take the true God for our God: and this end is moſt neceſſarie both for Gods glory,and for the ſaluation of men: and therfore whatſoeuer thing or perſon ouerturneth or aboliſheth this end, it muſt bee cut off from the ſociety of men. Here note by the way,that they which haue beene borne, baptized,and brought vp among vs,and yet afterward become Maſſe-prieſts, and ſeeke maliciouſly and obſtinatly, without ceaſing to ſeduce our people, deſerue in this reſpect,to be put to death.

Example 2. *Thou ſhalt not ſuffer a witch to liue, Exodus* 22.18. This law againe is a fenſe to the firſt commandement. For Witches renounce God,and humane ſocietie: and therefore are worthily cut off, though they doe no hurt; euen becauſe they make a league with the deuill.

Example 3. *Hee that blaſphemeth the name of God, ſhall bee put to death,Leui*.24.16. Vnderſtand this law of manifeſt and notorious blaſphemies,that pearce through God,as the words import: and then it is a maine fenſe to the third commaundement. For Gods name may in no wiſe be abuſed,and troad vnder foot: and therefore blaſphemers pearcing God, are to be cut off. This is the very law of nature,as appeares by *Nabuchadnezzar*, who gaue in commandement to his people, that whoſoeuer blaſphemed the name of the true God ſhould be put to death,*Dan.3.29.* Here note, that manifeſt and conuicted Atheiſts, if they bee put to death,haue but their deſerts.

Example 4. *He that curſeth father or mother, ſhall die the death,Leuit.4.9.* This law is a neceſſary fenſe to the fift commaundement, and vpholds the honour that is due to parents.

Example 5. *Hee that ſmites a man that hee die,ſhall die the death, Exodus* 21.12. To this law there is no exception made, but one, and that is, when a man is killed at vnawares. And it is for his equitie perpetuall. For it is a maine and direct fenſe to the ſixth commaundement. Conſider an other reaſon, *Num.*35.33. *The whole land* (ſaith the Lord)*, ſhall bee defiled with blood, till his blood bee ſhed that killeth a man.*

Example 6. *The adulterer and the adultereſſe ſhall both be put to death, Leuit.*20. This Iudiciall ſerues to vphold and maintaine chaſtitie, which is the end of the ſeuenth commandement.Marke withal the reaſons,*Leuit.*20.22,23.*Leſt the land ſpue you out*: and,*for theſe things* that is,for ſuffering this and other ſinnes vnpuniſhed, *the Gentiles were caſt out.* It may be ſaid,that Chriſt did not condemne the woman to death,which was taken in adulterie. *Anſw.* He came to be a Mediatour,and not a Iudge or Magiſtrate.It is alledged that *Dauid* was not put to death for adultery. *Anſw.* He was the higheſt in the kingdom:there was none to iudge him.Againe,it may be ſaid,that if adultery be death,then innumerable perſons muſt die. *Anſw.* We muſt doe that which we find to be the will of God: and the euents of things muſt be left to God.

The ſecond note,whereby we may diſcerne a iudiciall law to be morall for his equitie,is this; If it follow neceſſarily and immediatly from the light,principles,and concluſions of nature. For example, *Deut.*22.5. *The man ſhall not put on the things that appertaine to the woman,nor the woman the things that appertaine to the man.* This law is more then Iudiciall: for it is a rule of common honeſtie, practiſed in thoſe countries by the light of nature,where the written law was neuer knowne. And things good and honeſt which nature teacheth,are morall and muſt be done. This is *Pauls* rule. *Doeth not nature teach this? 1.Cor.*11.14.

This I ſpeake,not to cenſure and condemne the lawes of this or any other common wealth: but onely to ſhew how farre Iudiciall lawes haue moralitie in them, and ſtand in force.

The third queſtion is, what is our guide now in the time of the

new

new Teſtament, ſeeing the regiment and law of *Moſes* is abrogated? *Anſw.* The outward guide is the doctrine of the morall law, and of the Goſpel. It is therefore called *the rod and the ſtaffe of God*, *Pſal.*23. and *the rod of his mouth*, *Iſai.* 11.4. The inward guide, is the Spirit of God, writing the lawes of God in our hearts, and by them guiding vs, and being a law vnto vs, *Rom.* 8.3,14. Thirdly, God by manifold afflictions nurtures and ſchooles vs, partly to preuent ſinnes to come, and partly to humble vs for that which is paſt, 1. *Cor.*11.32. *Iere.*31.18.

The vſe. Seeing the law is abrogated (as I haue ſaid) we muſt be a free and voluntary people, ſeruing God not of conſtraint but willingly, as if there were no law to compell vs. *All nations ſhall flow as waters to the mountaine of the Lord, Iſa.*2.2. *Thy people ſhall come willingly in the day of aſſembly, Pſal.*110.3. *In the dayes of Iohn Baptiſt, the kingdome of heauen ſuffered violence. Ieremie* ſaith, *They ſhall teach euery man his neighbour and his brother, Ierem.*31.31. becauſe men ſhall learne freely without compulſion, or calling vpon. Here is the fault of our times. Many ſay in heart to Chriſt, *Depart from vs, we will none of thy wayes*; and many againe are zealous for the things of this life, but for duties pertaining to Gods worſhip, and the ſaluation of their ſoules, they are neither hote nor colde. This negligence and ſlackneſſe is full of danger, and therfore with ſpeed to be amended. For *curſed is he that doeth the worke of God negligently*: and the Lord will ſpue out ſuch perſons.

26 *For yee are all the ſonnes of God by faith in Chriſt Ieſus.*

27 *For all yee that are baptized into Chriſt, haue put on Chriſt.*

28 *There is neither Iew nor Grecian: there is neither bond nor free: there is neither male nor female: yee are all one in Chriſt Ieſus.*

Paul had ſaid before, verſe 25. that the beleeuing Iewes, after the publiſhing of the Goſpel, were no more vnder the law as vnder a ſchoolemaſter: In this 26. verſe he renders a reaſon hereof: and it may be framed on this manner: If wee Iewes were ſtill vnder the law as vnder a Schoolemaſter, then we ſhould be ſtill after the manner of ſeruants: but we are not after the manner of ſeruants: becauſe wee are children: for euen ye Galatians, and that all of you are children of God, not by Circumciſion, or by the keeping of the law, but by faith in Chriſt. Againe, that they are children of

God, he prooues it thus: Ye are baptiſed into Chriſt, and in baptiſme ye haue put on Chriſt, in that ye are ioyned with him, and haue fellowſhippe with him, who is the naturall Sonne of God: therefore ye are ſonnes of God. It may be ſaide, All children of God? all baptized? all put on Chriſt? How can this be? ſeeing ſome are Iewes, ſome Gentiles; ſome bond; ſome free; ſome men, ſome women. The anſwer is made, v.27. there are differences of men indeede, but in Chriſt, all are as one.

In theſe words, I conſider two things. The firſt is, the benefit or gift beſtowed on the Galatians, which is ſonne-ſhip, Adoption, or the condition of Gods children. The ſecond is, the deſcription of this benefit by foure arguments. The firſt is, by the circumſtance of the perſons, *ye all are children of God.* The ſecond is, the inward meanes, namely, *faith in Chriſt Ieſus.* The third is, the outward meanes, or the pledge of adoption, *ye are all baptiſed into Chriſt.* The laſt is, the foundation of adoption, and that is, *to put on Chriſt*, or, *to be one with him.*

For the better conceiuing of the benefit, three queſtions may be mooued. The firſt is, whoſe ſonnes the Galatians were? *Anſwer.* The ſonnes of God. It may be ſaide, how the ſonnes of God? I anſwer againe, God is called a father, in two reſpects: firſt, he is a father in reſpect of Chriſt, the eſſentiall word: and then *God* ſignifies the firſt perſon. Againe, God is called a father in reſpect of men Elect to ſaluation; then the name of *God* is put indefinitly: and it comprehends not onely the firſt perſon, but alſo the ſonne, and holy Ghoſt. For all three doe equally regenerate them that are adopted. And *Paul* ſaith of the Godhead indefinitly: *there is one God and father of all. Eph.* 4.6. And when we pray, ſaying, *Our father*, &c. we inuocate not onely the firſt perſon, but alſo the Sonne, and holy Ghoſt. And the ſonne of God, is expreſſely called *the father of eternitie*, in reſpect of vs, *Iſa.9.6.* and he is ſaid *to haue his ſeede. Iſa.* 53.11.

The ſecond queſtion is, in what reſpect are the Galatians the children of God? *Anſwer.* A childe of God is two waies: *by nature*; *by grace.* The childe of God *by nature*, is Chriſt as he is the eternall ſonne of God. A childe *by grace*, is three waies. By *creation*: thus *Adam* before his fall, and the good Angels are the children of God. Secondly, by *the perſonall vnion*: thus Chriſt as he is man is the child of God. Thirdly, *by the grace of adoption*: thus are all true beleeuers, and in this text, the Galatians are ſaide to be *the children of God.* In this grace of adoption, there be two acts of God: one is *Acceptation*, wherby God accepts men for his children. The other

is

is *Regeneration*,whereby men are borne of God,when the image of God is reſtored in them,in righteouſnes,and true holines.

The third queſtion is,what is the excellency of this benefitte? *Anſwer*. Great euery way.*Ioh*.1.12.he which is the child of God is heire and fellowheire with Chriſt,*Rom*.8.17.and that of the kingdome of heauen; and of all things in heauen and earth. 1. *Cor*.3.22. he hath title in this life, and ſhall haue poſſeſſion in the life to come. Againe, he that is Gods child hath the angels of God to attend on him,and to miniſter vnto him for his good and ſaluation.*Heb*.1.14.

The firſt argument whereby the adoption of Gods children is ſet forth, is concerning the perſons to whom it belongs,in theſe wordes, *All ye are the children of God*, So *Paul* ſaith,all the Epheſians are *Elect*. *Eph*.1.3. And *Peter* calls all them to whom he writes, 1.*Pet*.1.1. *Elect*; and *Iohn* 1.epiſt.3.*the children of God* And herein they follow the iudgement of charity, leauing all ſecret iudgements to God.Here I obſerue one thing, that euery grieuous fall doth not aboliſh the fauour of God,and extinguiſh the grace of regeneration. For the Galatians erred in the foundation of religion, and had fallen away to an other Goſpel: and yet *Paul* ſaith, that *they were* (for all this) *the children of God*, and not ſome, but *all of them*. This truth may be ſeene by experience. The child of God before his fall, hath a purpoſe not to ſinne: in the time of temptation when he is in falling, he hath a ſtrife,after he is fallen, he lieth not in his fall, as wicked men doe,but he recouereth himſelfe by new repentance. And this ſhews,that the child of God by his fall doth not returne againe to the eſtate and condition of wicked men.When S. *Iohn* ſaith,*he that is borne of God ſinnes not*, his meaning is this;he that is borne of God,if he fall into any offence of frailty, yet doth he not make a practiſe of ſinne, as the wicked, and vngodly doe.

It may be ſaide, the Galatians, and all the Galatians, are the children of God:but what is that to vs? *Anſwer*. They among vs that profeſſe true faith in Chriſt, with care to keepe good conſcience,are likewiſe to hold themſelues to be children of God.He beleeues not the Goſpel,that doth not beleeue his owne adoption. For in the Goſpel there is a promiſe of all the bleſſings of God, to them that beleeue: and there is alſo a commandement to apply the ſaid promiſe to our ſelues; and conſequently,to apply the gift of adoption to our ſelues. When we are bidden to ſay,*Our Father*, we are bidden to beleeue our ſelues to be children of God,and ſo to come vnto him. Therefore with *Paul* I ſay,that al we that truly beleeue

leeue in Chriſt,and haue care to leade a good life, all I ſay, are indeed the children of God.

The vſe. Comforts ariſing by this benefit,are many. Firſt,if thou be Gods childe, ſurely he will prouide all things neceſſarie for thy ſoule and body, *Mat.*6.26. Our care muſt be to doe the office and dutie that belongs vnto vs: when this is done,our care is ended. As for the good ſucceſſe of our labors,we muſt caſt our care on God; who will prouide that no good thing bee wanting vnto vs, *Pſal.* 34.10. They that drowne themſelues in worldly cares, liue like fatherleſſe children.

Secondly,in that we are children,we haue libertie to come into the preſence of God,and to pray vnto him, *Epheſ.*3.12.

Thirdly,nothing ſhall hurt them that are the children of God. *The plague ſhall not come neere their tabernacle: they ſhall walke vpon the lyon and the aſpe,and tread them vnder feot,Pſal.*91.13. *All things ſhall turne to their good,Rom.*8.28. And the rather;becauſe the Angels of God pitch their tents about them.

Laſtly,God will beare with the infirmities and frailties of them that are his children,if there be in them a care to pleaſe him,with a purpoſe of not ſinning, *Mal.*3.7. If a childe be ſicke,the father or mother doe not caſt it out of doores: much leſſe will God.

The duties. Firſt,if ye be Gods childrē,then walk worthy of your profeſſion and calling. Be not vaſſals of ſin and Satan: carry your ſelues as kings ſonnes: bearing ſway ouer the luſtes of your owne hearts,the temptations of the deuill,and the leud cuſtomes and faſhions of the world. When *Dauid* kept his fathers ſheepe, he behaued himſelfe like a ſhepheard: but when hee was called from the ſheepfold,and choſen to be King, he carried himſelfe accordingly. So muſt we do,that of children of the diuell,are made the children of God. And if we liue according to the luſts of the fleſh,as the men of this world doe,whatſoeuer we profeſſe,wee are in truth the children of the deuill,*Iohn* 8.44. 1.*Iohn* 3.

Secondly, we muſt vſe euery day to bring our ſelues into the preſence of God, and wee muſt doe all things as in his ſight and preſence,preſenting our ſelues vnto him, as inſtruments of his glorie in doing of his will. This is the honour that the child of God owes vnto him, *Mal.*1.6.

Thirdly,our care muſt be (according to the meaſure of grace) to reſemble Chriſt in all good vertues,and holy conuerſation. For he is our eldeſt brother the firſt borne of many brethren: and therfore we ſhould be like vnto him. 1.*Ioh.*3.2,3.

Fourthly, we muſt haue a deſire and loue to the word of God, that

that we may grow by it, in knowledge, grace, and good life. For this is the milke and foode whereby God feedes his children, 1.*Pet.* 2.2. Such perſons then among vs, that haue no loue or liking of the word, but ſpend their daies in ignorance and ſecuritie, ſhew themſelues to be no children of God. The child in the armes of the mother or nurce, that neuer deſires the breſt, is certẽly a dead child.

Laſtly, we muſt put this in our accounts, that we muſt haue many afflictions, if we be Gods children: for he corrects all his children. And when we are vnder the rodde of correction, we muſt reſigne our ſelues to the will and good pleaſure of God. This is childlike obedience: and this muſt be done in ſilence, and with all quietnes: then God is beſt pleaſed.

The internall meanes of Adoption, is faith in Chriſt. And for the better conceiuing of it, three queſtions are to be propounded. The firſt, what a kind of faith is this? *Anſw.* A particular or ſpeciall faith: and it hath three acts, or effects. The firſt is, to beleeue Chriſt to be *Ieſus*, that is, a Sauiour: the ſecond is, to beleeue that Chriſt is my or thy Sauiour: the third is, to put the confidence of heart in him. When *Thomas* felt the wounds of Chriſt, he ſaid, *My Lord, and my God*: and thereupon Chriſt ſaid, *Becauſe thou haſt ſeene thou beleeueſt.* *Ioh.* 20.29. Here marke, that to beleeue Chriſt to be my Chriſt, is faith. Againſt this ſpeciall faith, the Papiſts obiect three arguments. The firſt is this: Euery ſpeciall faith muſt haue a ſpeciall word of God for his ground: but there is no ſpeciall word that thy ſinnes, or my ſinnes, are forgiuen by Chriſt: therefore there is no ſpeciall faith. *Anſwer.* We haue that which in force and value is equiualent to a ſpeciall word: namely, a generall promiſe, with a commãdement to apply the ſaid promiſe to our ſelues. Secondly, I anſwer, that the word and promiſe of God generally propounded in Scripture, is made particular in the publike Miniſtery, in which when the word is preached to any people, God reueales two things vnto them: one, that his will is to ſaue them by Chriſt: the other, that his will is that men ſhould beleeue in Chriſt. And the word thus applied in the publike Miniſtery in the name of God, is as much as if an Angel ſhould particularly ſpeake vnto vs from heauen.

The ſecond Argument. Speciall faith (ſay they) is abſurd; becauſe by it a ſinner muſt beleeue the pardon of his ſinnes, before he hath it: in as much as faith is the means to obtaine pardon. *Anſ.* The giuing and the receiuing of pardon and faith, are both at one moment of time: for when God giues the pardon of ſinne, at the ſame inſtant he cauſeth men to receiue the ſame pardõ by faith. For

order

order of nature,faith goes before the receiuing of the pardon (becauſe faith is giuen to them that are to be ingrafted into Chriſt,and pardon to them that are in Chriſt;)for time it doth not: and therefore this ſecond argument is abſurd.

The third argument. The full certaintie and perſwaſion of Gods mercie in Chriſt,followes good conſcience and good workes: and therefore faith followes after iuſtification. *Anſwer.* There be two degrees of faith. A weake faith, and a ſtrong faith. A weake faith is that, againſt which doubting much preuailes,in which there is a ſorrow for vnbeleefe, a will and deſire to beleeue in Chriſt, with care to vſe good meanes,& to increaſe in faith. Strong faith is that which preuailes againſt doubting,and it is a full perſwaſion or reſolution,of the loue and mercy of God in Chriſt. This ſecond degree of faith follows iuſtification,vpon the obſeruation and experience of the prouidence and goodnes of God: but the firſt degree of ſpeciall faith before named, for order goes before iuſtification, and for time is together with it.

The ſecond queſtion is,when faith begins firſt to breed in the heart? *Anſwer.* When a man begins to be touched in his conſcience for his ſinnes, and vpon feeling of his owne ſpirituall pouertie, earneſtly hungers and thirſts after Chriſt and his righteouſnes aboue all things in the world. Chriſt ſaith, *I will giue to him that thirſteth,of the well of the water of life freely,Reuel.*21.6. This promiſe declares that in thirſting there is a meaſure of faith. To eat & drink Chriſt the bread and water of life, is to beleeue in him: and to hunger and thirſt, hauing as it were a ſpirituall appetite to Chriſt, is the next ſtep to this eating and drinking. Therefore this muſt be remembred,that the profeſſours of the Goſpel, yea teachers of the ſame,that want this ſenſe of their vnworthineſſe, and this thirſting,are farre wide,what gifts ſoeuer they haue. For they are not yet come to the firſt ſtep of true faith.

The third queſtion is, how faith in Chriſt is conceiued in the heart? *Anſwer.* It is not faith to conceiue in mind a bare perſwaſion,that Chriſt is my Sauiour: and thereupon to thinke to bee ſaued. But faith in Chriſt is conceiued in the ſpirituall exerciſes of inuocation and repentance. When I ſee mine owne ſinnes and Gods anger againſt me for them by the law;when I ſee mine owne guiltineſſe,I draw my ſelfe into the preſence of God, making confeſſion of mine offences,and prayer for the pardon of them;and in this prayer I ſtriue againſt mine vnbeliefe, I will, deſire, and endeauour to aſſent to the promiſe of God touching forgiueneſſe: and withall I purpoſe with my ſelfe to ſinne no more. This is my

daily

daily practiſe: and thus is faith truly conceiued,and confirmed. Againe faith is conceiued in the vſe of holy meanes, namely, the preaching of the word and Sacraments. For in hearing and receiuing the Lords Supper to meditate vpon the promiſe of mercy,and in meditation to apply the ſaid promiſe to my ſelfe,is the right way to conceiue true faith. Therefore it muſt be remembred,that faith conceiued without the exerciſes of inuocation and repentance,or conceiued without the vſe of the word and Sacraments (as commonly it is) is not true faith, but an imagination or fiction of the braine,which will faile in the end.

The third point to bee conſidered, is the ſigne, or the outward meanes of Adoption, and that is Baptiſme. It may bee demanded, how Baptiſme can bee a marke or ſigne of the childe of God,conſidering all ſorts of men are partakers of it? *Anſwer.* Baptiſme alone is no marke of Gods childe, but baptiſme ioyned with faith: for ſo muſt the text be conceiued; *All ye Galatians that beleeue, are baptized into Chriſt.* For *Paul* had ſaid immediatly before, *Ye are the ſonnes of God by faith.* Againe, the Scripture ſpeaking of Baptiſme, comprehends both the outward and the inward baptiſme, which is the inward Baptiſme of the Spirit, *Matth.* 3.11. and 1. *Pet.*3.21. And thus is Baptiſme alwaies an infallible marke of the child of God.

It may further bee demaunded, what are the markes of the inward baptiſme? *Anſw.* The new birth, whereby a man is waſhed and cleanſed by the ſpirit of God,hath three ſpeciall markes. The firſt is,the ſpirit of grace and ſupplications, *Zach.*12.10. that is,the ſpirit of regeneration,cauſing men to turne to God, and withall to make inſtant praier and ſupplication for mercy and forgiueneſſe of ſinnes paſt. The ſecond is, to heare and obey the voice of God in all things, *Iohn* 8.47. & 10.27. The third is,not to ſinne,that is,not to liue in the practiſe of any ſinne after this new birth is begun, 1. *Iohn* 3. *He that is borne of God,doth not commit ſin.* He may faile in this or that ſpeach,or doe amiſſe in this or that action; but after his calling and conuerſion,the tenour and courſe of his life ſhall be according to the commandements of God. And this is a ſpeciall marke to diſcerne the inward baptiſme.

Some alledge, that hauing long agoe been baptized with water,yet they feele not the inward baptiſme: and therfore they feare that they are not the children of God. *Anſwer.* If there be in thee a ſorrow for thy corruptions and ſinnes paſt: if thou haſt a purpoſe to ſinne no more: if thou auoideſt the occaſions of ſinne, and feareſt to offend: if hauing ſinned, thou lieſt not in thy ſinne,

but

but recouereſt thy ſelfe by new repentance: thou art verily borne of God, and baptized with the baptiſme of the holy Ghoſt.

Others alleadge, that although they haue beene baptized, yet they feare they haue no faith: and therefore they thinke they are not the children of God. *Anſwer.* If there bee in thee a ſorrow for thine vnbeleefe, a will and deſire to beleeue, and a care to increaſe in faith by the vſe of good meanes, there is a meaſure of true faith in thee, and by it thou mayeſt aſſure thy ſelfe that thou art the child of God.

Others againe alleadge, that they haue long made prayer vnto God, and that according to his will, and yet their praiers haue not bin heard: and therefore they often doubt they are not Gods children. *Anſ.* If thou canſt pray, though thy praier be not heard according to thy deſire, content thy ſelfe. For the praier of the heart is the marke of the ſpirit of adoption, *Rom.* 8.16,26. And by it thou maiſt know that thou art the childe of God.

Thus then wee ſee what is the infallible marke of the childe of God; namely, Baptiſme ioyned with true faith in Chriſt, or the outward baptiſme ioyned with the inward baptiſme of the ſpirit. The vſe. Many auouch the preſent Church of Rome to bee the true Church of God: and that becauſe they ſay, in it there is true baptiſme, which is a marke of the Church of God. But they are deceiued: for baptiſme in the Church of Rome is ſeuered from true faith, or from the Apoſtolike doctrine: and the outward baptiſme is ſeuered from the inward baptiſme. For they of that Church, ouerturne iuſtification by the meere mercie of God, which is the principall part of the inward baptiſme. Againe, the ten Tribes retained circumciſion after their Apoſtaſie: yet for all that condemned to be no people of God, *Oſe.* 1.9. The light in the lanthorne pertaines not to the lanthorne, but to the paſſengers in the ſtreet: euen ſo the confeſſion of faith in the Symbole of the Apoſtles, and Baptiſme that are retained in the Papacie, pertaine not to the Papacie, but to another hidden Church, which by theſe and other meanes is gathered out of the middeſt of Romiſh Babylon. And therefore Baptiſme is rather a ſigne of this, then of the Romiſh Church.

Againe, wee muſt be warned to take heed that wee deceiue not our ſelues, thinking it a ſufficient matter that wee haue beene baptized. For except Chriſt inwardly waſh vs with his Spirit, *wee haue no part in him*, *Iohn* 13.8. *Circumciſion* (ſaith *Paul*) *auaileth not, vnleſſe thou bee a doer of the law*, *Romanes* 2.25. Baptiſme indeed faueth, 1.*Peter* 3.21, but that is not the baptiſme of water, *but the*

ſtipula-

ſtipulation of a good conſcience, by the reſurrection of Chriſt. The outward baptiſme without the inward, is not the marke of Gods childe,but the marke of the foole that makes a vow, and afterward breakes it, *Ecclef.*5.3.

Moreouer,baptiſme is not only a ſigne of our adoption,but alſo a ſeale thereof,and a meanes to conuay it vnto vs: and for the better vnderſtanding of this point, and for a further clearing of the 27. verſe,I wil ſpeake of the whole nature of baptiſme. That which is to be deliuered,I reduce to eight heads. I. the name of baptiſme and the phraſes. II. the matter. III. the forme. IV. the ende. V. the efficacie of baptiſme. VI. the neceſſitie thereof. VII. the circumſtances. VIII. the vſe.

Touching the name; Baptiſme is taken ſixe waies. Firſt,it ſignifies the ſuperſtitious waſhings of the Phariſies, who bound themſelues to the baptiſmes or waſhings of cups and pots, *Mark.* 7.4. Secondly,it ſignifies the waſhings appointed by God in the Ceremoniall law, *Hebr.*9.10. Thirdly,it ſignifies that waſhing by water, which ſerues to ſeale the couenant of the new Teſtament, *Mat.*28.19. Fourthly,it ſignifies by a metaphor,any grieuous croſſe or calamitie. Thus the paſſion of Chriſt is called his baptiſme, *Luk.* 12.50. Fiftly,it ſignifies the beſtowing of extraordinary gifts of the holy Ghoſt,and that by impoſition of hands of the Apoſtles, *Acts* 1.5. and 11.16. Laſtly, it ſignifies the whole Eccleſiaſticall Miniſterie. Thus *Apollos* is ſaid to teach the way of the Lord, *knowing nothing but the baptiſme*(that is, the doctrine)*of Iohn, Acts* 18.25. In the third ſenſe is baptiſme taken in this place,when *Paul* ſaith, *Yee are all baptized into Chriſt.*

The phraſes vſed in Scripture of baptiſme are ſtrange in reaſon: and therefore they are to bee explaned. Here it is ſaid, *Yee that are baptized into Chriſt,put on Chriſt.* The reaſon of this ſpeach is threefold. The firſt is this: the waſhing of the bodie with water,is an outward ſigne to repreſent to our eyes and minde the inward waſhing,and our vnion or coniunction with Chriſt: therefore they that are baptized,are ſaid *to put on Chriſt.* The ſecond reaſon is,becauſe the waſhing by water, ſeales vnto vs our inward ingrafting into Chriſt: for as certainly as the body is waſhed with water; ſo certainly are they that beleeue, ingrafted into Chriſt. The third reaſon of the ſpeech is, becauſe baptiſme is after a ſort an inſtrument whereby our inſition into Chriſt, and fellowſhip with him is effected. For in the right and lawfull vſe of baptiſme, God according to his owne promiſe, ingrafts them into Chriſt that beleeue: and the inward waſhing is conferred with the outward waſhing.

For

For theſe cauſes, they that are waſhed with water in baptiſme, are ſaid *to put on Chriſt*. In the ſame manner muſt other phraſes be vnderſtood; as when it is ſaid, that *baptiſme ſaueth*, 1.*Pet*.3.21. that *men muſt be baptized for the remiſſion of ſinnes*, *Acts* 22.6. that *we are buried by baptiſme into the death of Chriſt*, *Rom*.6.3.

The ſecond point concernes the matter of baptiſme. Here I conſider three things, the ſigne, the thing ſignified, the Analogie of both. The ſigne, is partly the element of water, *Actes* 8.36. and partly the rite by diuine inſtitution appertaining to the element, which is the ſacramental vſe of it in waſhing of the body: and theſe two, water, and externall waſhing of the body, are the full and complete ſigne of baptiſme.

Here a queſtion may be made, whether waſhing of the bodie in baptiſme, muſt be by dipping, or by ſprinkling? *Anſwer*. In hote countries, and in the baptiſme of men of yeares, dipping was vſed, and that by the Apoſtles: and to this *Paul* alludes, *Rom*.6.3. and dipping doeth more fully repreſent our ſpirituall waſhing, then ſprinkling. Neuertheleſſe in cold countries, and in the baptiſme of infants new borne, ſprinkling is to bee vſed, and not dipping, in reſpect of their health and life. For the rule is, *Neceſſitie and charitie, diſpenſe with the ceremoniall law*. Vpon this ground, *Dauid* did eate the ſhewbread: Circumciſion was not alwaies the eight day, as appeares by the Iſraelites in the wilderneſſe: and for the ſame cauſe in theſe countries, dipping may be omitted, though otherwiſe a ſacramental rite. And it muſt be remembred, that baptizing ſignifies not onely that waſhing which is by diuing of the bodie, but alſo that which is by ſprinkling.

The thing ſignified, or the ſubſtance of baptiſme, is Chriſt himſelfe our Mediatour, as hee gaue himſelfe to waſh and cleanſe vs. Thus *Paul* ſaith, that *hee cleanſeth his Church by the waſhing of water*, *Epheſ*.5.6.

The Analogie, or proportion of both is on this manner. Water reſembles Chriſt crucified, with all his merits. S. *Iohn* ſaith, *The blood of Chriſt cleanſeth vs from all our ſinnes*, 1.*Iohn* 1.7. that is, the merit and efficacy of Chriſt crucified, freeth vs from our ſinnes, and from the guilt and puniſhment thereof. Externall waſhing of the body, reſembles inward waſhing by the Spirit, which ſtands in iuſtification and ſanctification, 1.*Cor*. 6.11. *Titus*.3.5. The dipping of the body, ſignifies mortification, or fellowſhip with Chriſt in his death: the ſtaying vnder the water, ſignifies the burial of ſinne: and the comming out of the water, the reſurrection from ſinne to newneſſe of life, *Rom*.6.3,4.

The

The third point concernes the forme of Baptiſme, *Matt.*28.19. *Goe teach all nations, baptizing them in the Name of the Father, &c.* I explaine the words thus: Marke, firſt it is ſaid, *Teach them*, that is, make thẽ my diſciples, by calling them to beleeue & to repẽt. Here wee are to conſider the order which God obſerues in making with man the couenant in baptiſme. Firſt of all, hee calls men by his word, and commands them to beleeue and repent: when they begin to beleeue and repent, then in the ſecond place God makes his promiſe of mercy and forgiueneſſe: and thirdly, he ſeales his promiſe by baptiſme. This diuine order Chriſt ſignifieth when hee ſaith, *make them diſciples*: and it was alwaies obſerued of God. Before he made any couenant with *Abraham*, and before he ſealed it by circumciſion, he ſaith to him, *Walke before me, and be vpright, Gen.* 17.1. and of his ſeed, he ſaith, they muſt firſt *doe righteouſneſſe and iudgement, and then he will bring vpon them all that he hath ſpoken, Gen.* 18.19. to the Iſraelites hee ſaith, that they muſt *turne and obey, and then hee will make all his promiſes and couenants good, Deut.* 30.1,6. and *Iſa.*1.16,17,19. To the Iewes *Peter* ſaith, *Repent* firſt, *and then they ſhall bee baptized for the remiſſion of ſinnes, Actes* 2,38,42. And *Philip* ſaid to the Eunuch, *If thou beleeueſt with all thy heart, thou mayeſt bee baptized, Actes* 8.37.

The vſe. By this order we ſee, that the commandement to beleeue and to repent, is more large and generall, then the promiſe of mercy in Chriſt. For the commandement is giuen to all hearers, to turne and beleeue, and the promiſe made onely to ſuch hearers, as doe indeede turne and beleeue: therefore it is a falſhood to imagine, that the promiſe of ſaluation belongs generally to all mankind.

Againe, by this order it appeares, that Repentance belongs to baptiſme: and it is one of the firſt things that are required: & therfore it is follie to make Repentance a diſtinct meanes of ſaluation, and a diſtinct ſacrament from baptiſme.

Thirdly, if it be demanded, why ſo many perſons that haue bin baptized, liue for all this, as if they had not bin baptized, in the cõmon ſinnes of the world, like prophane *Eſaus*: and yet doe comfort themſelues in their baptiſme? *Anſ.* They doe not know and conſider the order which God vſed in couenanting with them in baptiſme: but they deale prepoſterouſly, ouerſlipping the commandement of repenting & beleeuing, and in the firſt place lay hold of Gods promiſe made to them in baptiſme. This is the cauſe of ſo much prophaneneſſe in the world.

Againe, there be many perſons that haue bin baptized, who

neuertheles cannot abide to heare and reade the word of God: and the reason is, because they obserue not the order of their baptisme, first of all to become disciples, and then to lay hold of the promises of God.

They likewise are to be blamed, that bring vp their youth in ignorance. For they are baptized vpon condition that they shall become disciples of Christ, when they come to yeares of discretion. And they are by this meanes barred from all the mercies of God: for we must as good disciples obey the commandement that bids vs turne and beleeue, before we can haue any benefit or profit by any of the promises of God.

Lastly, we are here taught in the working of our saluation to keepe the order of God which he hath set downe vnto vs in baptisme, which is, first of all to turne vnto God, according to all his lawes; and secondly vpon our conuersion to lay hold of the promises of God, and the confirmation thereof by the sacraments. Thus shall we find comfort in the promises of God, and haue true fellowship with God, if we beginne where he beginnes in making of his couenant with vs, and end where he ends. And this we must doe not onely in the time of our first conuersion, but also afterward in the time of distresse and affliction, and at such times as by frailty we fall and offend God. In a word, if for practise we alwaies keepe our selues to this order, we shall find true comfort in life and death.

It followes, *Baptizing them into the name*, or *in the name of the Father, Sonne, and holy Ghost*. These words signifie: first, to baptize by the commandement and authoritie of the Father, Sonne, and holy Ghost: secondly, to baptize by and with the inuocation of the name of the true God. *Whatsoeuer ye doe in word or deede, doe it in the name of our Lord Iesus Christ*, that is, by the inuocation of the name of Christ: *Col.* 3.17. Thirdly, *to baptize in the name, &c.* signifies to wash with water in token that the partie baptized hath the name of God named vpon him, and that he is receiued into the houshold or familie of God, as a child of God, a member of Christ, and the temple of the holy Ghost. Thus *Iacob* saith in the adoption of *Ephraim* and *Manasses*, *Let them be mine, and let my name be called vpon them. Gen* 48.5.16. And *Paul* saith, that the *Corinthians* might not be named and distinguished by *Paul, Cephas, Apollos*, because they were not baptized into their names, but into the name of Christ, 1.*Cor.* 1.13. And this I take to be the full sense of the phrase.

Here we see what is done in baptisme; the Couenant of

graces is ſolemniſed betweene God and the party baptiſed. And in this couenant ſome actions belong to God, and ſome to the parties baptiſed. Gods actions are two. The firſt is, the making of promiſe of reconciliation, that is, of remiſſion of ſinnes, & life euerlaſting to them that are baptiſed, and beleeue. The ſecond is, the obſignatiō or ſealing of this promiſe: and that is twofold, outward, or inward. The outward ſeale, is the waſhing by water: and this waſhing ſerues not to ſeale by nature, but by the inſtitution of God, in theſe words, *baptize them, &c.* and therefore *Paul* ſaith, *cleanſing the Church by the waſhing of water in the word. Eph.* 5.26. The inward ſealing is by the earneſt of Gods ſpirit, *Eph.* 1.13. The action of the party baptized, is a certaine ſtipulation, or obligation, whereby he binds himſelfe to giue homage to the Father, Son, and holy Ghoſt. This Homage ſtands in faith, whereby all the promiſes of God are beleeued, and in Obedience to all his commandements. The ſigne of this obligation is, that the party baptized willingly yeelds himſelfe to be waſhed with water.

It is not ſaide *in the name of God*, but *in the name of the Father Sonne, and holy Ghoſt*, to teach vs the right way to know and to acknowlege the true God. This knowledge ſtands in ſixe points, all here expreſſed, The firſt is, that there is one God, & no more. For though there be three that are named, yet there is but one name, that is, one in authority, will, and worſhip of all three. And elſwhere, men are ſaid to be baptized *into the name of the Lord, Act.* 10. 48. The ſecond is, that this one true God, is the Father, Sonne, and holy Ghoſt. A myſterie vnſearchable. The third, that theſe three are really diſtinct, ſo as the Father is firſt in order, the Sonne the ſecond, and the holy Ghoſt, not the firſt or ſecond, but the third. The fourth is, that they are al one in operation, *Ioh.* 5.19. and ſpecially in the act of reconciliation, or couenant making. For the Father ſends the ſonne to be our Redeemer: the Sonne workes in his owne perſon, the worke of redemption: and the holy Ghoſt applies the ſame by his efficacy. The fift is, that they are all one in worſhip: for the Father, Sonne, and holy Ghoſt, are ioyntly to be worſhipped together, and God in them. The laſt is, that we are to know God, not as he in himſelfe, but as he hath reuealed himſelfe vnto vs in the couenant of Grace: and therefore we muſt acknowledge the Father to be our father, the Son to be our Redeemer, the holy Ghoſt to be our comforter; and ſeeke to grow in the knowledge and experience of this.

It may bee demaunded, whether baptiſme may not be adminiſtred in the name of Chriſt alone, or in the name of God, without mention of the perſons in the Godhead? *Anſ.* No. For the true forme of baptiſme is here preſcribed. If it be ſaid, that *Peter* biddes them of Ieruſalem, *repent and be baptized into the name of Chriſt. Act.* 2.38. I anſwer, that *Peters* intẽt in that place is, to ſet down not the forme of baptiſme, but the end and ſcope thereof, which is, that we may attaine to true fellowſhip with Chriſt.

The fourth point is, concerning the endes of baptiſme, which are foure. The firſt is, that baptiſme ſerues to be a pledge vnto vs in reſpect of our weaknes, of all the graces and mercies of God, and ſpecially of our vnion with Chriſt, of remiſſion of ſins, and of mortification. Secondly, it ſerues to be a ſigne of Chriſtian profeſſion before the world: and therefore it is called *the ſtipulation or interrogation of a good conſcience.* 1. *Pet.* 3.21. Thirdly, it ſerues to be a meanes of our firſt entrance or admiſſion into the viſible Church. Laſtly, it is a meanes of vnity. Reade *Eph.* 4.5. 1. *Cor.* 12.13.

The fifth point concernes the efficacie of baptiſme. Of which there be foure neceſſarie queſtions. The firſt is, whether the Efficacie of baptiſme extend it ſelfe to all ſinnes, and to the whole life of man? For anſwer, I will ſet downe what we teach, and what the Papiſts. We teach, that the vſe of baptiſme inlargeth it ſelfe to the whole life of man, and that it takes away all ſins paſt, preſent, and to come: one caution remembred, that the partie baptiſed, ſtand to the order of baptiſme, which is, to turne vnto God, and to beleeue in Chriſt, and ſo to continue by a continuall renouation of faith and repentance, as occaſion ſhall be ſuffered. Reaſons may be theſe. Firſt, the ſcripture ſpeakes of them that bad long before bin baptiſed, and that in the time preſent, *Baptiſme ſaueth*, 1. *Pet.* 3. 21. and, *ye are buried by baptiſme, into the death of Chriſt, Rom.* 6, 4. And in the future tenſe it is ſaide, *he that beleeueth, and is baptiſed, ſhall be ſaued.* And *Paul* ſaith, that *the Church is cleanſed with the waſhing of water, that it may be preſented glorious and without ſpot vnto God, Eph.* 5. 26. And all this ſhewes that baptiſme hath the ſame efficacie after, which it had before the adminiſtration thereof. Secondly, the couenant of grace is euerlaſting, *Iſa.* 54.10. *Hoſ.* 2.19. and the couenant is the foundation or ſubſtance of baptiſme: therefore baptiſme is not to be tied to any time: but it muſt haue his force, ſo long as the couenant is of force. And this appeares by the example of the Galatians, who are now fallẽ away to an other goſpel after their baptiſme, and yet are inſtructed and directed by their baptiſme. Laſtly, it hath bin the doctrine of the ancient Church, that all ſins are done away by baptiſme, euen ſinnes to come.

Aug. de nupt. & concup. l. 1. c. 33. ad Bon. l. c. 13.

The doctrine of the Papiſts is, that baptiſme takes away all

ſinnes

ſinnes that goe before the adminiſtration thereof: and that ſinnes after baptiſme are not taken away by baptiſme, but by the Sacrament of penance. But the doctrine is erronious, as may appeare by the arguments which they vſe.

Argument 1. Circumciſion had no vſe after the adminiſtration thereof for the aboliſhing of ſinne. Therefore neither hath baptiſme. *Anſwer.* Circumciſion had. And this appeares, becauſe the Prophets put the Iewes in minde of their circumciſion, when they fell away from God, bidding them to circumciſe the foreskinne of their hearts, *Ierem.* 4.4.

Argum. 2. The Apoſtles vſed to call them that ſinned after baptiſme, to confeſſion of ſinne, and to repentance, or penance, *Acts* 8. 21. 1. *Iohn* 1.9. *Anſw.* This makes for vs: for in ſo doing they bring men to their baptiſme, and to the order ſet downe there, which is, that the partie baptized muſt firſt of all turne to God, and beleeue in Chriſt: and there is no new order ſet downe afterward, but only a renewing of this firſt baptiſmal order, both in the miniſtery of the word, and in the Supper of the Lord. And wheras they make a diſtinction of penance the vertue, and penance the Sacrament, placing the vertue before and after Baptiſme, and the Sacrament only after: for this they haue no word of God.

Arg. 3. *If a man bee inlightned,* that is, baptized; *and then fall againe, hee cannot bee renewed by repentance,* which is in baptiſme, *Hebr.* 6.6. *Anſw.* The text ſpeakes not of them that fall after baptiſme, but of them that fal* away by an vniuerſal apoſtaſie, denying Chriſt. For it is ſaid, v. 7. *that they crucifie Chriſt againe,* that is, crucifie Chriſt crucified, *and ſo make a mocke of him, and tread vnder foot the blood of Chriſt, Hebr.* 10.29. Againe, the text ſpeakes not particularly of repentance in baptiſme, but of all repentance whatſoeuer; yea of repentance after baptiſme. For there is no place for repentance where Chriſt is renounced.

* παραπεσόντας

Arg. 4. Penance (as *Hierome* ſaith) is a ſecond table after a ſhipwracke. *Anſwer.* Repentance in indeed is a ſecond table or boord, whereby a ſinner fallen from his baptiſme returnes againe to it, and ſo comes to the hauen of eternal happineſſe. Thus then we ſee that baptiſme is the true Sacrament of repentance: for repentance pertaines to the inward baptiſme.

The vſe. If baptiſme ſerue for the whole life of man: then if thou be in any miſery or diſtreſſe, haue recourſe to thy baptiſme, and there ſhalt thou finde thy comfort, namely, that God is thy God, if thou truly turne and beleeue in him. Secondly, remember euery day the obligation of homage, wherewith thou haſt bound thy ſelfe to God;ſpecially in thy temptations remember it: and ſee thou ſtand to it,and make it good.

The ſecond queſtion is, whether baptiſme aboliſh Originall ſinne,or no? The anſwer of the Papiſt is, that it doth: ſo as in the party baptiſed, there remaineth nothing that God may iuſtly hate: and therefore he ſaith, that Originall ſinne after baptiſme, ceaſeth to be ſinne properly. We teach,and are to hold, that the perfect and intire baptiſme(in which the outward and inward baptiſme are ioyned together)aboliſheth the puniſhment of ſinne, and the guilt, that is, the obligation to puniſhment,and the fault: yet not ſimply, but in two reſpects: firſt, in reſpect of *imputation*; becauſe God doth not impute Originall ſinne to them that are in Chriſt: ſecondly, in reſpect of *dominion*; becauſe Originall ſinne raigneth not in them that are regenerate. Neuertheleſſe, after baptiſme, it remaines in them that are baptiſed, and is ſtill, and that properly, ſinne. *Paul.* ſaith *Rom.*7.20.*If I doe that I would not, it is no more I that doe it, but ſinne that dwelleth in me doth it.* Here marke, *Paul* calls concupiſcence in himſelfe after regeneration, *ſinne*; and that properly: becauſe he ſaith it is the ſame that maketh men to ſinne. And *Col.*3. 5.he ſaith, *Mortifie your earthly members:* and amongſt the reſt he nameth, *euill concupiſcence.* And to the *Epheſians.*4.22.*Be ye renewed in the ſpirit of your mindes.* Therefore after baptiſme ſome portions remaine ſtill of the old man, or of originall ſinne. S. *Iohn* ſaith. 1. *Ioh.*1.8. *If we ſay we haue no ſinne, we deceiue our ſelues.* Anſwer is made,that this is ſpoken of veniall, or ſmall ſinnes:but how can they be ſmall ſinnes that are to be waſhed away with the blood of Chriſt,as he ſaith.v.7. And if theſe words be ſpoken of infants(as they are)then muſt Concupiſcence be a ſin in them:for they haue no actuall ſins.Laſtly,Chriſt ſaith, *Ioh.*13 10. *He that is all waſhed,muſt haue his feete*,that is, his carnall affections,*waſhed.* Here obſerue two things. One,that defilements of ſinne remaine in them that are waſhed. The ſecond, that they are after the firſt waſhing,to be done away by Chriſt,and not by the acts of our penance.

The grounds of Popiſh doctrine in this point,are two. The firſt is this. They make three degrees of Concupiſcence. The firſt is, the proneneſſe in the fleſh to rebell againſt the law of the minde, or the proneneſſe to euill. The ſecond, ſtands in the firſt motions to ſinne, which goe before conſent of will. The third, ſtands in acts of luſt ioyned with conſent of will. This third,they ſay,is forbidden in the moral law, which forbids and condemnes voluntarie concupiſcence: and the two firſt are not. Becauſe(as they ſpeake)

con-

concupiſcence it ſelfe with the firſt motions, are not in mans power: and therefore they are rather to be tearmed defects or infirmities, then ſinnes: and that men are no more to be blamed for them then for the diſeaſes of their bodies. *Anſ.* The doctrine is falſe: for it is an euident truth, that Concupiſcence with the firſt motions thereof to euill, is condemned in the morall law. It is a Principle in expounding the law: where any actuall ſinne is forbidden, there all cauſes, occaſions, and furtherances thereof, are likewiſe forbidden. Therfore conſidering actuall concupiſcence ioyned with conſent, is forbidden in the law, Originall concupiſcence with the firſt motions thereof, beeing cauſes of the former, are likewiſe forbidden. And *Paul* ſaith, he had not knowne Luſt to be ſinne, vnleſſe the law had ſaid, *Thou ſhalt not luſt. Rom.* 7.7. Now he was a Doctor of the law, & knew that luſt with conſent was a ſinne: for thus much the light of nature teacheth: therefore the law ſpeakes of an higher degree of luſt, namely, of luſt going before conſent.

The ſecond ground is this. When ſinne is remitted, it doth not make men guilty, but ceaſeth to be a fault: Originall ſinne therfore ceaſeth to be ſinne after baptiſme. *Anſ.* Though actuall guilt be taken away, yet potentiall guilt remaineth, namely, an aptnes in Originall ſinne, to make men guilty: and though it be not the fault of this or that perſon, yet it is a fault in nature, or as it is conſidered in it ſelfe.

The vſe. If Originall ſinne remaine after baptiſme to the death, then we muſt humble our ſelues, and vſe to the very death, the plea of mercy and pardon, denying our ſelues, and reſting on Chriſt.

Againe, if perſons baptiſed be ſinners to the death, it may be demaunded, what difference there is betweene the godly and vngodly? *Anſ.* In them that are regenerate, there is a ſorrow for their inward corruptions, and for their ſinnes paſt, with a deteſtation of them: and withall there is a purpoſe in them to ſinne no more, and with this purpoſe there is ioyned an endeauour to pleaſe God in all his commandements: ſo as if they doe ſin, they can ſay with good conſcience, that they ſinned againſt their purpoſe and reſolution. This cannot the vngodly man doe.

The third point is, how baptiſme conferres grace? *Anſwer.* It conferres grace: becauſe it is a meanes to giue and exhibite to the beleeuing minde, Chriſt with his benefits; and this it doth by his ſignification. For it ſerues as a particular and infallible certificate to aſſure the party baptiſed, of the forgiuenes of his ſinnes, and of his eternall ſaluation. And whereas the Miniſter, in the name of

God, applies the promise of mercy to him that is baptised, it is indeede as much as if God should haue made a particular promise to him. In this regard, baptisme may well be said to conferre grace, as the Kings letters are said to saue the life of the malefactour, when they doe but signifie to him and others, that the kings pleasure is to shew fauour. Againe, baptisme may be saide to conferre grace, because the outward washing of the body is a token or Pledge of the grace of God: and by this pledge faith is confirmed, which is an instrument to apprehend or receiue the grace of God. And this confirmation is made by a kind of reasoning in the minde, on this manner: He that vseth the signe aright, shall receiue the thing signified: I (saith the party baptised, beeing of yeares) vse the signe aright in faith and repentance: therefore I shall receiue the thing signified, remission of sinnes, and life euerlasting. A king saith to his subiect, He that brings the head of such a traytour, shall haue a thousand poundes. Well: the head of the foresaid traytour is cut off: and he that hath the head may say, Here is a thousand pound, or, this will bring me a thousand pounds, because it is vnto him as a pledge vpon the kings word of the reward of a thousand pounds. And so is the washing in baptisme an infallible pledge to him that beleeues, of the pardon of his sinnes. Thus doe the sacraments conferre grace, and no otherwise. One reason for many may be this. The word of God conferreth grace (for it is the power of God to saluation to them that beleeue) and this it doth by signifying the will of God, by the eare to the mind: now euery sacrament is the word of God made visible to the eye: the sacrament therefore confers grace by vertue of his signification, and by reason it is a pledge by the appointment of God, of his mercy and goodnes. It may be said, a sacrament is not only a signe and a seale, but also an instrument to conuay the grace of God to vs. Answer. It is not an instrument hauing the grace of God tyed vnto it or shut vp in it: but an instrument to which grace is present by assistance in the right vse therof: because in & with the right vse of the sacrament, God conferres grace: and thus it is an instrument, and no otherwise, that is, a morall, and not a physicall instrument.

The doctrine of the Papist is, that the Sacrament conferres grace by the worke done; that is, that the outward action of the Minister conferres grace by his owne force, when the Sacrament is administred. And that it may conferre grace, some say, that the said action hath vertue in it for this purpose, which passeth away when the action is ended: others say, it hath no vertue in it, but that Gods vsing of the action eleuates it, and makes it able to conferre grace.

Thom. Sum. p.3.q.62. art. 4. Bellar. de Sacr. l.2.c.11.

grace. But this doctrine is a fiction of the braine of man. *Iohn* the *Baptiſt, Matt.*3.11. makes two baptizers, himſelfe, and Chriſt; and hee diſtinguiſheth their actions: his owne action is, to waſh with water; & the action of Chriſt is, to waſh with the H.Ghoſt. This diſtinctiō he wold not haue made, if he by the waſhing of water had conferred the holy Ghoſt. *Paul* ſaith, *Chriſt ſanctifieth his Church by the waſhing of water through the word, Epheſ.*5.26. Baptiſme therfore doeth not conferre grace, becauſe the body is waſhed with water: but becauſe when it is waſhed, the word of promiſe is beleeued, and receiued. The Apoſtles are called, *fellow-workers with God,* 1. *Cor.*3.9. and yet in the worke of regeneration, and in giuing of life, they are not any thing, verſe 7. *Peter* ſaith directly, *that the waſhing away of the filth of the fleſh doeth not ſaue, but the ſtipulation that a good conſcience makes to God,* 1.*Pet.*3.21. The worke of creation is from God immediatly, and onely: now regeneration is a worke of creation: and therefore it is of God immediatly, and not immediatly from the Sacrament and mediatly from God. The fleſh of Chriſt is eleuated and exalted aboue the condition of all creatures: neuertheleſſe, vertue to giue life is not in the fleſh of Chriſt, but in the godhead: much leſſe then ſhal the Sacraments haue vertue in them to conferre grace. Faith is ſaid to iuſtifie, yet not by his owne vertue: for it doth not cauſe our iuſtification, but ſerue as a meanes to apprehend it, when it is cauſed by God: how then ſhall the ſacraments cauſe iuſtification? Laſtly, if the outward waſhing of the body bee eleuated aboue his naturall condition, in the adminiſtration of baptiſme, then ſo oft as the outward element is vſed in any Sacrament, there is a miracle wrought: and Miniſters of Sacraments are workers of miracles, which may not be ſaid.

Againe, their doctrine is erronious, in that they teach, that the outward act in the Sacrament performed by the Miniſter, confers grace, where there is no gift of faith to receiue that which is conferred: contrary to that ſaying, *Iohn* 1.12. *As many as receiued him, he gaue this power to be the ſonnes of God.* Indeed they ſay, there muſt bee faith and repentance to diſpoſe the party: but this diſpoſition ſerues onely to take away impediments, and not to inable vs to receiue that which God giueth.

The vſe. We muſt not thinke it ſufficient that wee come to the Church, heare Gods word, and pray, contenting our ſelues in the worke done. For thus ſhal we deceiue our ſelues: but in doing theſe acts of religion, we muſt in our hearts turne vnto God, and by faith imbrace his promiſes: otherwiſe the beſt actions we doe ſhall bee vnprofitable vnto vs, *Heb.*4.2.

Againe,

Againe, if the vſing of the element in the Sacrament do not conferre grace, then bee aſſured, that charmes, and ſpels, be the wordes neuer ſo good, haue no vertue in them to doe vs good, but by diabolicall operation.

The laſt queſtion is, whether baptiſme imprint a character or marke in the ſoule, which is neuer blotted out? *Anſwer.* In Scripture there is a two-fold marke of diſtinction, one viſible, the other inuiſible. Of the firſt kinde was the blood of the Paſchall Lambe, in the firſt Paſſeouer: for by it the firſt borne of the Iſraelites were marked, when the firſt borne of the Egyptians were ſlaine. Of this kinde is Baptiſme: for by it Chriſtian people are diſtinguiſhed from Iewes, Turkes, and Infidels. The inuiſible marke is two-folde. The firſt is, the eternall election of God, 2.*Timothie* 2. 19. *The foundation of God ſtands ſure, and hath this ſeale, The Lord knowes who are his.* By vertue of this, Chriſt ſaith, *I know my ſheepe, Iohn* 10. And by this the Elect of all nations are marked, *Apoc.* 7. and 9. The ſecond is the gift of regeneration, which is nothing elſe but the imprinting of the image of God in the ſoules of men: and by this beleeuers are ſaid to bee *ſealed, Epheſ.* 1. 13. 2.*Cor.* 1. 22. And baptiſme is a meanes to ſee this marke in vs; becauſe it is the lauer of regeneration.

The Papiſts haue deuiſed another worke, which they call the *Indeleble character*: and they make it to bee a diſtinct thing from regeneration: and they ſay it is imprinted in the ſoules of all men, good and bad, and remains with them when they are condemned. What this marke ſhould be they cannot tell; ſome make it a qualitie: ſome, a relation; but indeed there is no Scripture for it; the truth is, it is a meere fiction of the braine of man.

The ſixt point to bee handled, concernes the neceſſitie of Baptiſme. Here we muſt put difference between the couenant of grace and baptiſme, which is the confirmation or ſeale of the couenant. To make couenant with God, and to be in the ſaid couenant, is abſolutely neceſſary to ſaluation: for vnleſſe God be our God, and we the ſeruants of God, we cannot be ſaued.

Baptiſme it ſelfe is neceſſarie in part: firſt, in reſpect of the commaundement of God, who hath enioyned vs to vſe it: ſecondly, in reſpect of our weakeneſſe; who haue need of all helpes that may confirme our faith. Yet Baptiſme is not ſimply neceſſary to ſaluation; for the want of Baptiſme (when it cannot be had) doth not condemne; but the contempt of it when it may be had: and the contempt is pardonable, if men repent afterward: for the children of beleeuing parents are borne holy, 1.*Corinth.* 7. 14 and theirs is the Kingdome of God: and therefore if they die before baptisme, they are saued. The theefe vpon the crosse, and many holy Martyrs, haue died without baptisme, and are in the kingdome of heauen.

It is obiected, that the male childe, which is not circumcised, must (by Gods commaundement) bee cut off from the people of God, *Genesis* 17. 14. and therefore hee that is not baptized, must also bee cut off. *Answer.* The text is spoken and meant, not of infants, but of men of yeares, who beeing till then vncircumcised, despise the ordinance of God, and refuse to bee circumcised. And this appeares by the reason following: *for hee hath made my couenant voyd*: now infants doe not this, but their parents, or men of yeares.

Secondly, the speech of Christ is obiected, *Iohn* 3.5. *Except a man be borne of water and the holy Ghost, he cannot enter into the kingdome of God. Answer.* Christ alludes to the washings of the old Testament, *Ezech.*36.25. and withall giues an exposition of them on this manner. Thou art a Pharisee, and louest much washing: but if thou wouldest enter into the kingdome of heauen, thou must be washed with cleane water, that is, born anew by the holy Ghost. Againe I answer, that if the words be meant of baptisme, they carry this sense. The kingdome of heauen doeth not signifie life eternall, but the Church of the new Testament, and that in his visible estate, *Mark.*9.1. and baptisme makes men visible members of the Church, and regeneration by the spirit, makes them true and liuely members. Here then baptisme is made necessary, not in respect of eternall life, but in respect of our admission and entrance into the Church, whereof it is now the onely meanes.

The seuenth point is, touching the circumstances of Baptisme, which are fiue. The first, concernes the persons which are to administer baptisme, of whom I propound foure questions.

The first is, whether not onely Ministers of the word, but also lay-persons (as they are called) or meere priuate men, may administer Baptisme? *Answer.* Ministers of the word onely. For to baptize is a part of the publike Ministerie, *Matthew* 28. 18. *Goe teach all nations, baptizing them.* And marke how preaching, and baptizing are ioyned together: and things which God hath ioyned, no man may separate. Againe, hee that must performe any part of the publike Ministery, must haue a calling, *Rom.*10.14. *Heb.* 3.5. but meere priuate persons haue no calling to this businesse. And whatsoeuer is not of faith, is sinne: now the administration of baptisme by priuate persons, is without faith. For there is neither precept, nor fit example for it in the word of God.

The example of *Zippora* is alleadged, *Exod*.4.28. who circumciſed her child. *Anſwer*. The example is many waies diſcommendable. For ſhee did it in the preſence of her husband, when there was no need: ſhee did it haſte, that ſhee might haue preuented her husband: ſhe did it in anger: for ſhe caſt the foreskin at the feet of *Moſes*. And it ſeemes ſhe was no beleeuer, but a meere Midianite. For ſhee contemned circumciſion, when ſhee called her husband *a man of blood, by reaſon of the circumciſion of the child, verſe 26*. and in this reſpect it ſeemes, *Moſes* either put her away, or ſhee went away when he went downe to Egypt.

Againe, it is obiected, that priuate perſons may teach: and therfore baptize. *Anſwer*. Priuate teaching, and Miniſteriall teaching are diſtinct in kinde, as the authoritie of a maſter of a family, is diſtinct in kinde from the authoritie of a Magiſtrate. A priuate perſon, as a father or maſter, when hee teacheth the word of God, hee doeth it by right of a maſter or father, and hee is mooued to doe it by the law of charitie: but Miniſters when they teach, are mooued to teach by ſpeciall calling, and they doe it with authoritie, as Embaſſadours in the roome of Chriſt, 2. *Corinthians*, 5.21. Againe, though a priuate man might diſpenſe the word alone: yet doeth it not follow, that hee may adminiſter both the word and the ſeale thereof: both which are ioyned in baptiſme, and ioyntly adminiſtred.

The ſecond queſtion is, whether baptiſme adminiſtred by a wicked man or an heretike, be indeed true baptiſme? *Anſwer*. If the ſaid partie bee admitted to ſtand in the roome of a true paſtour, or miniſter, and keepe the right forme in baptizing, according to the inſtitution, it is true baptiſme. The Scribes and Phariſees the chiefeſt doctors of the Iewes, were not of the tribe of *Leui*, but of other tribes: and they were indeed euen the beſt of them, but heretikes and apoſtataes, and conſequently to be depoſed, and excommunicate: neuertheleſſe, becauſe they were in the place of good teachers, and ſate in *Moſes* chaire, that is, taught ſundry points of *Moſes* doctrine: therefore Chriſt ſaith, *Heare them, Matth*. 23.1. And to this effect was the concluſion of the Churches in Affrica, againſt *Cyprian*.

Vpon the ſame ground, the ſame anſwer is to be made, if it bee demaunded, whether baptiſme adminiſtred by him that cannot preach, bee of force or no? It were indeed to bee wiſhed, that all Miniſters of holy things, were preachers of the word: neuertheleſſe, if ſuch as preach not, ſtand in the roome of lawfull paſtours,

and

and keepe the forme of baptiſme, it is baptiſme indeed.

The third queſtion is, whether an Intention to baptize, be neceſſary in him that baptizeth? *Anſwer.* If the word of Inſtitution come to the Element, it is a Sacrament, whatſoeuer the Miniſter intend. *Paul* reioyced that Chriſt was preached, though many preached him of enuie or contention, intending no good, *Philip.* 1.16. And the Prieſt in the Maſſe pronouncing the wordes of conſecration, if hee intend not to conſecrate (in Popiſh learning) there is no conſecration: and thus the bread eleuated is meere bread, and not the bodie of Chriſt: and conſequently the people adore not Chriſt, but an Idoll. The intention therefore of the minde is not neceſſarie, ſo be it the Inſtitution be obſerued. And the efficacie of the Sacrament depends not on the will of man, but on the will of God.

The laſt queſtion is, what is the dutie of the Miniſter in baptizing? *Anſw.* He ſtands in the roome of God: and what he doth according to the Inſtitution, it is as much as if God himſelf had done it with his owne hand from heauen. And therefore, when the Miniſter applieth water, (which is the ſigne and pledge of grace,) to the body, hee doeth withall apply the promiſe of remiſſion of ſinnes, and life euerlaſting, to the partie baptized. And that is as much as if God ſhould ſay to the partie, calling him by his name, I freely giue vnto thee the pardon of thy ſinnes, and life euerlaſting, vpon condition thou keepe the order ſet downe in baptiſme, which is, to turne vnto mee, and to beleeue in Chriſt. Heere we ſee a ground of ſpeciall faith: for if God for his part by the hand of the Miniſter apply the promiſe of mercy vnto euery particular beleeuer: euery particular beleeuer is againe by a ſpeciall faith to receiue the promiſe. Againe, the conſideration of this which God hath done for vs in baptiſme, muſt mooue vs ſeriouſly to turne vnto him according to all his lawes, and by faith of our hearts to apprehend his mercifull promiſes, and to reſt on them. For when God ſhall ſpeake vnto vs particularly, and as it were, aſſure vs of his mercies with his owne hand and ſeale, we muſt needs be much moued and affected therewith.

The ſecond circumſtance is concerning the perſons to be baptized: and they are all ſuch as be in the Couenant, in likelihood, or in the iudgement of charitie. For the ſeale may not bee denied to them that bring the tables of the couenant. And they are of two ſorts, Men of yeares, and infants.

Men of yeares that ioyne themſelues to the true Church, are to be baptized: yet before their baptiſme, they are to make confeſſion of their faith, and to promiſe amendment of life, *Actes* 2.38. and 10.38. And thus places of Scripture that require actuall faith, and amendment of life in them that are baptized, are to be vnderſtood of men of yeares.

Infants of beleeuing parents are likewiſe to bee baptized. The grounds of their baptiſme are theſe. Firſt, the commaundement of God, *Matthew* 28.18. *Baptize all nations, &c.* in which wordes the baptiſme of infants is preſcribed. For the Apoſtles by vertue of this Commiſſion baptized whole families, *Actes* 16.31. and 38. Againe, circumciſion of infants was commaunded by God, *Geneſis* 17. 14. and Baptiſme in the new Teſtament, ſucceedes in the roome of Circumciſion, *Coloſſ.* 2. 11. therefore baptiſme of infants is likewiſe commanded. The ſecond ground is this: Infants of beleeuing parents, are in the couenant of grace: for this is the tenour of the couenant, *I will bee thy God, and the God of thy ſeede, Geneſis* 17.7. It may bee ſaid, that this promiſe was made in this ſort onely to *Abraham*, becauſe he was to be the the father of the faithfull. *Anſwer.* It pertaines to all beleeuing parents. *Exod.* 20. God promiſeth *to ſhew mercie to thouſands of them that loue him. Acts* 2.39. *Peter* ſaith to the Iewes that heard him preach, *The promiſes belong to you, and to your children. Paul* ſaith, *If the parents beleeue, the children are holy*, 1.*Cor*.7.14. If holy, then are they in the Couenant: now they are holy: becauſe wee are in the iudgement of Chriſtian charitie to eſteeme them all as regenerate and ſanctified, ſecret iudgements (in the meane ſeaſon) left to God. Now then becauſe infants are in the couenant, they are to bee baptized. For this is the reaſon of S. *Peter*: To whom the promiſes belong, to them belongeth baptiſme: but to you and your children belong the promiſes: therefore you and your children are to be baptized, *Actes* 2.38, 39.

It may bee obiected, that wee cannot tell, whether infants bee indeed the children of God, or no: and if they bee not children of God, wee may not baptize them. *Anſwer.* The ſame may be ſaid of men of yeares: for we know not whether they bee indeed the children of God. And therefore wee may by the like reaſon exclude them from all Sacraments. Againe, wee are to preſume (in all likelihood) that infants of beleeuing parents, are the children of God, becauſe in their conception and birth, God begins to maniſeſt his election: ſhewing himſelfe a God, not onely to the parents, but alſo to their ſeed.

Secondly, it is obiected, that infants haue no faith; and conſequently, that baptiſme is vnprofitable vnto them. *Anſwer.* Some

thinke

thinke they haue faith, as they haue regeneration, that is, the inclination, or seed, of faith. Others say, that the faith of the parents is also the faith of their children: because the parents by their faith, receiue the promise of God, both for themselues and their children: And thus to bee borne in the Church of beleeuing parents, is in stead of the profession of faith. To this second opinion I rather incline, because it is the ancient and receiued doctrine of the Church.

Thirdly, it is alleadged, that infants know not what is done, when they are baptized. *Answer.* For all this, baptisme hath his vse in them: for it is a seale of the Couenant, and a meanes to admit them into the fellowship of the visible Church, whereof for right they are members. A father makes a purchasse for himselfe and his children: at the time of the sealing, the children know not what is done; and yet the purchasse is not made in vaine for them.

It may bee demaunded, whether the children of Turkes and Iewes are to bee baptized? *Answer.* No: because the parents are foorth of the Couenant.

Secondly, it is demaunded, whether the children of professed Papists, are to be baptized? *Answer.* The parents are persons baptized in the name of the Father, Sonne, and Holy Ghost. And though the Papacie bee not the Church of God, yet is the Church of God hidden in the Papacie, and to bee gathered out of it: and for this cause baptisme remaines still in the Church of Rome. For this cause I thinke, that infants of professed Papists may be baptized, two cautions obserued: the first, that the foresaid parents desire this baptisme: the second, that there be sureties which promise the education of the child in the true faith.

Thirdly, it may bee demanded, whether the children of wicked Christians, that is, of such as hold in iudgement true religion, and denie it in their liues, may be baptized? *Answer.* They may: for all without exception, that were borne of circumcised Iewes (wherof many were wicked) were circumcised. And we must not onely regard the next parents, but also the ancestours: of whom it is said, *If the root be holy, the branches are holy, Rom* 11. Vpon this ground, children borne in fornication, may be baptized, so be it, there bee some to answer for them beside the parents. And there is no reason, that the wickednesse of the parent, should preiudice the child in things pertaining to life eternall.

Lastly, it may bee demaunded, whether the children of parents excommunicate, may be baptized? *Answer.* Yea, if there bee any beſide the parents to anſwer for the childe. For the parents after excommunication remaine ſtil (for right) members of the Church, hauing ſtill a right to the kingdome of heauen: out of which they are not caſt abſolutely, but with condition, vnleſſe they repent: and in part; that is, in reſpect of communion, or vſe of their libertie, but not in reſpect of right or title: euen as a freeman of a corporation impriſoned, remaines a free man, though for the time he hath no vſe of his libertie.

The third circumſtance concernes the time. Here one queſtion may be mooued: How oft baptiſme is to be adminiſtred? *Anſwer.* But once: for the efficacy of Baptiſme extends it ſelfe to the whole life of man: and we are but once borne againe, and once ingrafted into Chriſt. Here let it be obſerued, that the gift of regeneration is neuer vtterly extinguiſhed: for if a man be the ſecond time borne againe, he muſt be baptized againe and againe: becauſe baptiſme is the Sacrament of inſition. It may be ſaid, that a man may remaine ſtill ingrafted into Chriſt, and by his owne wickednes make himſelfe a dead member. I anſwer, that all the members of the myſtical body of Chriſt, are liuing members. *The ſpirituall temple is made of liuing ſtones,* 1.*Pet.*2.5. And marke what *Paul* ſaith, *All the body of Chriſt increaſeth with the increaſing of God,* *Col.*2.19. and *Epheſ.*2.21. Beleeuers are of the bone and fleſh of Chriſt: now there is no part of the bone and fleſh of Chriſt that dieth.

The laſt circumſtance is touching the place: and that is, the publike aſſembly or congregation of the people of God. Becauſe baptiſme is a part of the publike Miniſtery, and a dependance vpon the preaching of the word of God. Secondly, the whole congregation is to make profit by the enarration of the inſtitution of baptiſme: and laſtly, the ſaid congregation is by praier to preſent the infant baptized vnto God, and to intreate for the ſaluation thereof, the prayer of many being moſt effectuall.

The eighth and laſt point followes, concerning the vſe of Baptiſme. And firſt of all, our baptiſme muſt put vs in minde, that wee are admitted and receiued into the family of God: and conſequently, that wee muſt carrie our ſelues as the ſeruants of God. And that wee may doe ſo indeed, wee muſt diuide our liues into two parts; the life paſt, and life to come. Touching the life that is paſt, we muſt performe three things. The firſt is, *Examination,* whereby wee muſt call our ſelues to an account for all our ſinnes, euen from the cradle: the ſecond is, *Confeſſion,* whereby we muſt with ſorrowfull hearts bewaile and acknowledge the ſame ſinnes in the preſence of God, accuſing and condemning our ſelues

for

for them. The third is, *Deprecation*, whereby wee are to intreat the Lord in the name of Chriſt, and that moſt inſtantly from day to day, till wee receiue a comfortable anſwer, in the peace of conſcience, and ioy of the holy Ghoſt.

And for the life to come, there muſt be two things in vs: the firſt is, the purpoſe of not ſinning; and it muſt be a liuely and diſtinct purpoſe, daily renewed in vs, euen as we renew our dayes: ſo as wee may ſay, if wee ſinne, it is againſt our purpoſe and reſolution. The ſecond is, an endeauour to performe new obedience, according to all the commandements of God. Theſe things if we doe, we ſhall ſhew our ſelues to be the ſeruants of God. And of all theſe things, baptiſme muſt be (as it were) a daily Sermon vnto vs: and ſo oft to thinke on them, as oft as wee thinke or ſpeake of our names giuen vs in Baptiſme. This is the doctrine of *Paul*, who teacheth vs that we muſt bee conformable to the death and reſurrection of Chriſt, becauſe we haue been baptized, *Rom.*6.3,4.

Againe, our baptiſme into the name of the Father, &c. muſt teach vs, that we muſt learne to know & acknowledge God aright; that is, to acknowledge him to be our God, and Father in Chriſt: to acknowledge his preſence, and therefore to walke before him; to acknowledge his prouidence, and therfore to caſt our care on him; to acknowledge his goodneſſe and mercie, in the pardon and free forgiueneſſe of our ſinnes.

Thirdly, our baptiſme muſt bee vnto vs a ſtore-houſe of all comfort in the time of our need. If thou bee tempted of the diuell, oppoſe againſt him thy Baptiſme, in which God hath promiſed and ſealed vnto thee the pardon of thy ſinnes, and life euerlaſting. If thou bee troubled with doubtings, and weakeneſſe of faith, conſider that God hath giuen thee an earneſt and pledge of his louing kindneſſe to thee. Wee vſe often to looke vpon the willes of our fathers and grand-fathers, that wee may be reſolued in matters of doubt: and ſo, often looke vpon the will of thy heauenly Father ſealed and deliuered to thee in thy baptiſme, and thou ſhalt the better be reſolued in the middeſt of all thy doubts. If thou lie vnder any croſſe or calamitie, haue recourſe to thy baptiſme, in which God promiſed to be thy God, and of this promiſe hee will not faile thee.

Laſtly, if a man would bee a ſtudent in diuinitie, let him learne and practiſe his baptiſme. Commentaries are needfull to the ſtudie of the Scriptures: and the beſt Commentarie to a mans owne ſelfe is his owne baptiſme. For if a man haue learned to know ought and to practiſe his owne baptiſme, he ſhall the better be able to vnderſtand the whole: and without this helpe, the ſcriptures themſelues ſhall be as a riddle vnto vs.

The fourth point whereby the gift of adoption is deſcribed, is the ground thereof, in theſe words, *Ye haue put on Chriſt: and all are one in Chriſt.* The phraſe which *Paul* vſeth, is borrowed from the cuſtome of them which were baptiſed in the Apoſtles daies, who put off their garments, when they were to be baptiſed, and put on new garments after baptiſme. To put on a garment, is to apply it to the bodie, and to vſe or weare it. And to put on Chriſt, is to be ioyned neerely to Chriſt, and to haue ſpirituall fellowſhip with him. Here then the foundation of our adoption is in two things, our vnion with Chriſt, and our communion with him. Of which we are ſomewhat to be aduertiſed for the better vnderſtanding of the text.

The vnion with Chriſt, is a worke of God whereby all beleeuers are made one with Chriſt. Here two queſtions are to be demanded. The firſt in what reſpect, or for what cauſe are they ſaide to be one with Chriſt? *Anſwer.* They are not one with him in conceit or imagination: for this coniunction is in truth a reall coniunction. *Iohn.* 17.22. Chriſt prooues *that all beleeuers may be one with him, as he is one with the Father.* Secondly, they are not one barely by conſent of heart and affection: for thus all familiars and friends are one: and they of Ieruſalem are ſaid thus to be *of one heart & mind. Act.* 4.32. Thirdly, they are not one in ſubſtâce; for ſo many beleeuers as there are, ſo many diſtinct perſons are there: and euery one of them diſtinct from the perſon of Chriſt: And the ſubſtance of the godhead of Chriſt is incommunicable: & the fleſh of Chriſt is in heauen and ſhall there abide till the laſt iudgement: whereupon it cannot be mixed or compounded with our ſubſtances. Laſtly, beleeuers are not one with Chriſt by transfuſion of the propertes and qualities of the godhead, or manhood vnto vs. It may be ſaid, how then are they one with him? I anſwer, by one and the ſame ſpirit dwelling in Chriſt and in al the members of Chriſt. 1. *Cor.* 6.17. *He that cleaueth to the Lord, is one ſpirit.* *Paul* ſaith in this ſenſe, *Eph.* 2. 14. that Chriſt maketh the two diſtinct nations of Iewes and Gentiles *one new man.* S. *Iohn* ſaith, that *Chriſt dwells in vs and we in him by the ſpirit,* 1. *Iohn* 3.23. For the better conceiuing of this, ſuppoſe a man whoſe head lies in Italy, his armes in Germany, and Spaine, his feete in England: ſuppoſe further that one and the ſame ſoule extends it ſelfe to al the foreſaid parts, & quickens them all: they are all now become one in reſpect of one and the ſame ſoule, and all concurre as members to one and the ſame bodie:

euen

euen ſo, all the Saints in heauen, and all beleeuers vpon earth, hauing one and the ſame ſpirit of Chriſt dwelling in them, are all one in Chriſt.

The ſecond queſtion is, how are all beleeuers made one with Chriſt? *Anſ.* By a donation on Gods part whereby Chriſt is giuen vnto vs: and by a receiuing on our part. The donation is wherby Chriſt is made ours for right, ſo as a man may ſay truly, Chriſt is mine with all his benefits. Of this donation 4. things are to be obſerued. The firſt is, that Chriſt himſelfe and whole Chriſt is giuen to vs. For here we are ſaid to put on Chriſt. Here a diſtinction muſt be obſerued: the Godhead of Chriſt, is giuen to vs, not in reſpect of ſubſtance which is incommunicable, but onely in reſpect of operation. But the very fleſh or manhood of Chriſt is really giuen to the beleeuing heart. *Ioh.6.54.56.* By it we receiue eternal life from the godhead, and by it God is ioyned to man, & man to God. The ſecond is, that Chriſt giues his merit and ſatisfaction to them that beleeue. And this ſatisfaction imputed, is the couer whereby our ſinnes are couered, *Pſal.*32.1. and the white robes dipped in the blood of Chriſt. *Reu.*7.14. Thirdly, Chriſt giues the efficacie of his ſpirit to make vs conformable to himſelfe in holines and newnes of life: and thus *he makes vs put off the old man, and put on the new man, created after God in righteouſneſſe and holines, Eph.*4. 24. The fourth is, that the word preached and the ſacraments, are (as it were) the hand of God, whereby he exhibits and giues Chriſt vnto vs with al his benefits.

Of our receiuing of Chriſt giuen by God, two things muſt bee obſerued: one is, that wee muſt there receiue Chriſt, where God offers and giues him, that is, in the word and Sacraments. The ſecond is, that faith is our hand, whereby we receiue Chriſt; and this receiuing is done by a ſupernaturall act of the minde, whereby we beleeue Chriſt with his benefits to be ours, *Iohn* 1.12. Thus we ſee how we are one with Chriſt, and Chriſt with vs.

Communion with Chriſt is, when wee haue, poſſeſſe, and inioy Chriſt and his benefits: and that is partly in this life, and fully in the life to come. Of this communion ſpeaks *Salomon* at large in the Song of Songs, and *Dauid, Pſal.*45.

The vſe. In that we are to put on Chriſt, wee are put in mind to conſider our fearefull nakedneſſe. What is that? *Anſw.* There is a nakednes of creation, and a nakednes following the fall. The nakedneſſe of creation is, when the body without all couering, is in health, full of glory and maieſty, in reſpect of other creatures. Nakedneſſe ariſing of the fall of man, is either inward or outward. Inward, is the want of the image of God,the want of innocencie, of good conſcience,of the fauour of God,and affiance in him. For theſe are(as it were)the couerings of the ſoule. Outward nakednes is,when the bodie beeing vncouered is full of deformitie & ſhame. Now that inward nakednes of heart is noted as a ſpeciall euil, *Gen.* 3.7. *Exod.*32.15. *Prou.*29. *Reu.*3.17. We muſt labour to ſee & feele this nakednes in our ſelues.For by it, we are deformed and odious in the eye of God.

Secondly,we are here put in minde to haue a ſpeciall care of the trimming and garniſhing of our ſoule. And for this cauſe we muſt *put on the Lord Ieſus, Rom.*13.14. And that is done two waies.Firſt by vncouering our nakednes before God, and by praying him to couer it. To vncouer our ſhame, is the way to couer it. *Pſal.*32.1, 2.3. The ſecond way is,to ſubiect our ſelues to the word & ſpirit of God,and to be conformable to Chriſt both in his life and death. It ſtands vs in hand thus to put on Chriſt. For the king of heauen, hath long inuited vs to the marriage of his Sonne: we haue yeilded our ſelues to be his gueſts: and there is a time when the king will take a ſuruay of all his gueſts, whether they haue the wedding garment,which is Chriſt himſelfe: and they which are not cladde with this robe,ſhall be caſt into vtter darknes. We are as naked infants expoſed to death, *Ezech.*16.7. the merit and obedience of Chriſt is as ſwadling clothes and ſwadling bands. If we would then liue, we muſt lap and infold our ſelues in them. The rather I ſpeake this:becauſe in theſe daies men and women are intoxicated with a ſpirituall drunkennes,or rather madneſſe,whereby they are alwaies tempering and trifling about their bodies,& let their ſoules ly naked.It may be ſaid,we haue al put on Chriſt in baptiſme.I anſwer:we haue had in England peace & proſperity this 43.yeares:& we haue liued all this while,as it were in the warme ſun-ſhine: and therefore many of vs (no doubt) haue worne this garment very looſely.

Thirdly,there is a great temptation ariſing vpon the conſideration of our owne indignitie. For when our ſinnes come to our remembrance,they driue vs from the preſence of God,and make vs that we dare not pray.Now the remedy is this.We muſt come clothed with Chriſt into the preſence of God:we may not come in our names,but we muſt come in his name & preſent the merit of Chriſt vnto the Father, euen as if we were one and the ſame perſon with him.Thus ſhall we be accepted.

Fourthly, it may be demanded, what we muſt doe for our ſelues in the time of plague,famine, ſword? We muſt put on Chriſt,

Chriſt, then ſhall we walke in ſafetie in all dangers. This garment ſerues not onely for a couering of our ſhame, but alſo for protection. *Iſa.*4.6. And if we be taken away in any common iudgment, beeing clothed with Chriſt, there is no more hurt done to vs then to him: and he carrieth vs in his breſt, as if we were part of his bowels.

Laſtly, though we be clothed with Chriſt in baptiſme, yet we muſt further deſire to be clothed vpon. 2.*Cor.*5.4, In this life we are clad with the iuſtice of Chriſt, 1.*Cor.*1.30 this is one garment. In the life to come, we ſhall be clad with immortalitie. This is the ſecond garment to be vpon the former.

*Verſe.*28. *There is neither Iewe nor Grecian,&c.* Theſe words (as I haue ſaid) containe an anſwer to an obiection, which is this: If all beleeuers among the Gentiles be children of God, and all put on Chriſt, then there is no difference betweene Iewe and Gentile, and the prerogatiue of the Iewe is nothing. *Paul* anſwers thus: there be ſundry differences of men in reſpect of nation, condition, ſexe: yet in reſpect of Chriſt, all are one. Moreouer, I haue ſhewed, that theſe words containe the ground of the Adoption of the Galatians, which is an vnion with Chriſt, whereby all beleeuers are made one with him. There remaine other things to be added.

By occaſion of this text, two queſtions are mooued, the anſwer whereof ſerues much to cleare the meaning of *Paul*. The firſt is, whether Magiſtracie and gouernment be neceſſary in the ſocieties of Chriſtians? *Anſwer.* Yea: *Kings and Queenes ſhall bee nourcing fathers and nourcing mothers to the Church of God,* ſaith the Prophet, *Iſai.*49.23. *Paul* bids vs *pray for Kings and all in authoritie, that we may liue in peace and godlineſſe,* 1.*Tim.*2.1. The fift Commaundement, *Honour thy father, &c.* requires ſubiection to authoritie: and this commandement is eternall.

Obiection I. All beleeuers are one in Chriſt: therefore there is no ſubiection among them. *Anſwer.* Beleeuers are vnder a twofold Eſtate or Regiment: the firſt is, the Regiment of this world, in ciuill ſocietie: the ſecond is, the regiment of the Kingdome of heauen, which ſtands in *Iuſtice, peace of conſcience, ioy in the holy Ghoſt.* In the firſt eſtate, there are ſundrie differences of perſons that beleeue: ſome fathers and mothers, ſome children, ſome maſters and ſeruants, ſome Magiſtrates and ſubiects. In the ſecond eſtate, there are no outward differences of men, but all are members of Chriſt, and all one in him. Thus muſt the text bee vnderſtood.

Obiection II. Beleeuers are gouerned by Gods ſpirit, and therfore outward gouerment by magiſtrates is needleſſe. *Anſw.* In the viſible Church, hypocrites are mingled with true beleeuers, and they are not gouerned by Gods ſpirit, but by the ſpirit of the deuill: and therefore in reſpect of them, ciuill authority is requiſite. Againe, true beleeuers are but in part gouerned by the Spirit, for the time of this life. And for this cauſe, ciuill gouernmẽt is requiſite, for the ordering of the outward man, and for the protection of the Church.

Obiect. III. They that are in Chriſt, are freed from ſinne, and conſequently, from ſubiection which followes vpon ſinne. *Anſw.* Subiection is either politique, or ſeruile. Politicke is, when men are ſubiect for their owne good, and this was before the fall, yeilded by *Eue* to *Adam.* Seruile ſubiection, when they are ſubiect for the good of their maſters: and this onely comes of ſinne. Againe, ſubiection with ioy was before the fall: ſubiection ioyned with paine and miſery, followes vpon ſinne: *Gen.* 3.16.

The ſecond queſtion is, whether bondage, in which ſome are Lords, others bondmen, or ſlaues, may ſtand with Chriſtian religion? *Anſw.* It may, in the countries where it is eſtabliſhed by poſitiue lawes, if it be vſed with mercy and moderation. Righteous *Abraham* had in his owne houſe, bondſlaues: *Gen.* 17.13. God did permit the Iewes to buy the children of the *Canaanites, Leu.* 25.45. *Paul* ſaith, *If any man be called beeing a ſeruant* or *bondman, let him not care for it,* 1.*Cor.*7.21.

Obiection I. Be not ſeruants of men. 1.*Cor.*7.23. *Anſw.* That is, in reſpect of conſcience, the ſubiection whereof muſt be reſerued to God.

Obiection II. Chriſtians haue libertie by Chriſt: and where liberty is, there may be no bondage. *Anſwer* Chriſtians obtaine by Chriſt ſpirituall libertie in this life, and bodily libertie in the life to come.

Obiection III. Bondage is againſt the law of nature. *Anſwer.* Againſt the law of pure nature, created in innocencie, not againſt the lawe of corrupt nature, the fruite whereof is bondage,

Obiection IV. All are one in Chriſt: therefore the difference of bond men and free-men muſt ceaſe. *Anſw.* All are one in reſpect of the inward man, or in reſpect of faith & fellowſhip with Chriſt: but all are not one in reſpect of the outward man, and in regard of ciuill order.

The ſenſe then of the Text is this. There are diſtinctions

of

of men in reſpect of nation, ſome Iewes, ſome Gentiles : in reſpect of condition, ſome bonde, ſome free, ſome rich, ſome poore, ſome in authority, ſome in ſubiection, &c. in reſpect of ſexe, ſome men, ſome women: yet in Chriſt Ieſus, all are euen as one man.

The vſe. By this text we may expound another, 1. *Timothy.* 2. *God would haue all men to be ſaued*: that is, not all particular perſons vpon earth, but all kinds. For heere *Paul* ſaith, *All are one in Chriſt*: that is, men of all nations, of all conditions, and of all ſexes.

Againe, the name *(Iewe)* oppoſed to Gentiles, ſignifies not onely men of the tribe of *Iuda*, but all circumciſed perſons of all tribes, *Romanes* 2. 28. and thus it is all one with an Iſraelite. And thus we ſee how to expound the place of Scripture, 2. *Chronicles.* 21. 2. where *Iehoſaphat* king of *Iuda* is called *king of Iſrael.* The words *Iuda* and *Iſrael*, are ſometime oppoſed, *Iuda* ſignifying the kingdome of the two tribes, *Iuda* and *Beniamin* : and *Iſrael* ſignifying the tenne tribes. Sometimes againe, they are *Synonyma* and are put one for another, as *Pſalm.* 114. 1, 2. and in this text. And *Iuda* at this time was indeed the true *Iſrael* of God, and *Iehoſaphat* without any fault in the text (as ſome ſuppoſe) is called *king of Iſrael.*

Thirdly, they which are of great birth and of high condition, muſt bee put in minde not to be high minded, nor to diſpiſe them that are of lowe degree, for all are one in Chriſt: the obſcure and baſe perſon hath as good part in Chriſt, as the greateſt men that bee. Therefore wee may not ſwell in pride for outward things. *The king muſt not lift vp his heart against his brethren*, *Deut.* 17. 20. *Rich men* (ſaith *Paul*) *muſt not bee high minded*, 1. *Timothie* 6. 17. *Iob* would not deſpiſe the cauſe of his handmaid, *Iob* 31. 13. *Naaman*, a great man, reſpected the counſell of his ſeruants, 2. *Kings* 5. 13.

Fourthly, all beleeuers muſt bee of one heart and minde, 1. *Cor.* 1. 10. In the kingdome of Chriſt, the wolfe and the lambe dwell together, *Iſai.* 11. 6. And good reaſon: for all are one in Chriſt. And we haue great cauſe to bee humbled, when ſchiſmes, contentions, and differences ariſe in points of religion. For that ſhewes that hypocrites are mingled with true beleeuers, and that wee are but in part (as yet) vnited to Chriſt.

Laſtly, hence wee learne not to hate any man, but alwayes to carrie in minde a purpoſe to doe good to all by thought, word, and deede, and to doe good to men in reſpect of their names, their goods, their liues. And this holy minde and purpoſe, muſt alwayes beare ſway in vs. *There is no hurt in the Mount of the Lord, Iſai.*11.9. Men turne their ſwords and ſpeares into mattockes and ſithes, that are of the kingdome of Chriſt, *Iſai.* 2.4. becauſe they are one with Chriſt by the bond of one ſpirit.

29 *And if yee bee Chriſts, then are yee Abrahams ſeed, and heires by promiſe.*

Before, *Paul* had taught verſe 7,8,9. that all beleeuing Gentiles were the children of *Abraham*, and not the Iewes onely. Heere hee returnes to the ſame poynt againe, and prooues it by a new Argument, thus: Chriſt is the ſeed of Abraham, verſe 16. and all Gentiles beleeuing in Chriſt, are parts of him, and one with him: therefore they alſo are children of *Abraham*, and heires of all the bleſſings of God.

The intent of *Paul* in theſe words, is to eſtabliſh and confirme an argument which before hee had vrged in this chapter againſt patrons of works in the caſe of our iuſtification: it may be framed thus. As *Abraham* was iuſtified, ſo are all they that beleeue in Chriſt iuſtified: for they are *Abrahams* children and ſucceed him, verſ.29. but *Abraham* was iuſtified by faith without works; therefore all beleeuers in Chriſt are ſo iuſtified. Let the argument be obſerued: for it makes againſt the Papiſt, who if hee ſtudy till his head and heart ake, ſhall neuer anſwer it.

In this verſe, *Paul* ſets downe the fruite and benefit that comes by the gift of adoption, to them that beleeue: And that is, to bee children of *Abraham*, and heires of all the bleſſings of God. And therefore learne heere one golden leſſon; namely, that the baſeſt perſon that is, if he beleeue in Chriſt, is in the place of *Abraham*, and ſucceeds him in the inheritance of the kingdome of heauen. Some man may ſay; O this is excellent comfort, if I might know that I were in the caſe of *Abraham*. *Anſwer.* Thou mayeſt know it certainely, if thou wilt doe as *Abraham* did; namely, followe the calling of God, and obey the Goſpell; that is, ſubiect thy heart to the commandements of God, which bid thee repent, and beleeue in Chriſt: for then all the good things reuealed in the Goſpell ſhall be thine.

The vſe. Beleeuers in this world muſt bee content with any eſtate that God ſhall lay vpon them. For they are heires with *Abraham* of heauen and earth. In this regard, *Abraham* was content to forsake his countrie, and his fathers house, and as a pilgrime to dwell in tents to the death, *Heb.* 11.8,9.

Secondly, they that beleeue in Christ, must moderate their worldly cares, and not liue as drudges of the word. For they are heires of God, and haue a title or right to all good things promised in the Couenant. Therefore they shall neuer want any good thing that is needfull for them. Hee that hath made them heires, will carefully prouide for them. Therefore our care must bee, to doe the duties that belong vnto vs: and all other cares wee must cast vpon God. They in this world, that are borne to land and liuing, are content to liue sparingly, and oftentimes very barely with a little, vpon hope of further inlargement, after the deceasse of some friends.

Lastly, our speciall care must bee for heauen. For the things of this world are but trifles in respect of it. The citie of God in heauen is thy portion, or childs part. Seeke for the assurance of that aboue all thing. Thus did *Abraham*, *Heb.* 11.15,16.

CHAP. IIII.

1 *And I say, that the heire, as long as hee is a child, differeth nothing from a seruant, though he be Lord of all:*

2 *But is vnder Tutors and gouernors, till the time appointed of the father.*

3 *Euen so we, when we were children, were in bondage vnder the rudiments of the world*

4 *But when the fulnesse of time was come, God sent foorth his Sonne made of a woman, and made vnder the law,*

5 *That he might redeeme them that were vnder the law, that we might receiue the adoption of sonnes.*

6 *And because ye are sonnes, God hath sent forth the spirit of his Sonne into your hearts, which crieth, Abba, Father.*

7 *Wherefore thou art no more a seruant, but a sonne: and if thou be a sonne, thou art also an heire of God through Christ.*

THese wordes depend on the former Chapter, as an answer to an obiection, which may bee framed on this manner. *Paul*, thou saiest that the Iewes before Christ, *were vnder the law, as vnder a Schoolemaster*, c.3.v.24. and that *we are free from the same Schoolemaster*, v.25. *being children of God, and heires by Christ*, verse 29. but we for our parts thinke our selues seruants vnder the law, as well as the ancient Iewes, and that they are as well the children of God, as we. To this obiection *Paul* makes answer in these 7. verses, as the very first words import; *And I say*: that is, whatsoeuer you suppose, I say thus. And then hee propounds the reason of his answer, which may be framed thus: If the time of our bondage be ended, and the full time of our libertie come, then are wee sonnes, and not seruants: but the time of our bondage is ended, and the time of our libertie is come: therefore we are not seruants, but sonnes.

The *maior* is omitted, because it is manifest. The *minor* is in the sixe first verses: the *conclusion* is expressed in the 7. verse.

Againe, the *minor*, [*the time of our bondage is ended, and the time of our libertie is come*] is first of all declared by a similitude, and then confirmed. The similitude is borrowed from the Ciuill law; and it may be framed thus: Heires in their minoritie, liue in subiection to tutours and gouernours: but when they are of riper yeares, at the ap-

poincpointment of their parents, they are at their owne libertie. Euen so, the people of God before Christ, were in their infancie vnder the law as vnder a Tutour: but when the fulnesse of time was come, which God had appointed, they entred into the fruition of their libertie. The first part of the similitude is expressed in the two first verses, and the second in the 3. and 4.

Againe, the *minor* is confirmed by two reasons. The first is this: Your libertie is procured by Christ: therefore the time of your libertie is come. This reason is in the 4. and 5. verses. The second reason is taken from the signe, *You haue receiued the spirit of adoption*: therefore the time of your libertie is come, verse 6. Of these points in order.

First, where he signifies, that the father hath authoritie to dispose of his child. This is the law of nature, and the law of nations. *Paul* saith, *Col.* 3.20. that *children must obey their parents in all things*. When the diuell had obtained libertie to afflict *Iob* in all things that belonged to him, saue his person; hee destroyed his children, *Iob* 1.12, 18. And this shewes, that the children in respect of their bodies, are the goods of their parents. In this respect the Iewes were permitted to sell their children, *Exod.* 21.7. And so sacred a thing was the authoritie of the parent, that hee which rebelliously despised the same, was put to death, *Deut.* 21.21.

This authority shewes it selfe, specially in two things: in the mariage, and in the calling of the child. In the marriage of the child, the parent is the principall agent, and the disposer thereof, *Deut.* 7.3. *Exod.* 34.16. 1. *Cor.* 7.38. Where obserue, that the commaundement touching the mariage of the child, is giuen not to the child, but to the parent: and the parent hath authoritie by the said commandement to giue and bestow his childe, and to take wiues to his sonnes. Thus *Abraham* tooke a wife for *Isaac*, and *Isaac* suffred himselfe to be disposed at the appointment of his father. For a more ful declaration of this authoritie I propound these three questions.

The first is, whether the father may commaund his childe to marrie? *Answer.* Presuppose two things; one, that the commandement be without compulsion; the second, that the father knowes what is for the good of the child: then I answer, that he may command his child to marry, and to marry a person thus or thus qualified. Thus *Isaac* commanded *Iacob* to marry in the house of *Laban*, *Gen.* 28.1, 2. & *Iacob* obeied. Now whether a father may command his child to marry this or this person, I doubt, and therfore suspend.

The second question is, whether parents may make voyd the contract secretly made by their children, without or against their conſent? *Anſ.* The ſcripture giueth them authority either to ratifie ſuch contracts,or to make them void.*Num.*30.6.the father may make void the vow of the child pertaining to Gods worſhipppe: much more a matrimoniall promiſe. If a yong man deflowre a maide,and this be found,in equity he is to be compelled to marrie her,*Deut.*22.28.yet by Gods law this may not be,except the father conſent.*Exod.*22.17.

The third queſtion is, whether a marriage made without and againſt the conſent of parents, be a marriage or no? *Anſ.*It may be called a politicke, or ciuill marriage, becauſe it is ratified in the courts of men,according to humane lawes:and by this meanes the iſſue is freed from baſtardie.Neuertheleſſe it is not a diuine or ſpirituall coniunction, or marriage(as it ought to be)becauſe it is flat againſt the commandement of God.

Touching the callings of children, they are to be ordered and appointed at the diſcretion of parents. For if the parent may order the vowe and the marriage of the child, then much more the calling.

Here take notice of the impiety of the Romane religion. There are three eſpeciall eſtates whereby man liues in ſociety with man: the Church, the Common wealth, the Family. In the Church, that religion ſets vp an other head,beſide Chriſt:in the Commonwealth,it ſets vp an authority that ſerues to curb and reſtraine the Supremacy of Princes in cauſes Eccleſiaſticall.In the family,it puts downe the authority of the father:for it ratifieth clandeſtine contracts,& it giues liberty to children paſt twelue or fourteene yeares of age, to enter into any Order of religion againſt the conſent of their parents.

Againe, parents muſt be put in minde to know their authority, to mantaine it, and to vſe it aright,for the good of their children, ſpecially for their ſaluation. And children muſt be warned in all things honeſt and lawfull,to yeeld ſubiection to their parents:and in this ſubiection ſhall they find the bleſſing of God.

Againe, here is ſet downe the office of parents, and that is, to prouide meete ouerſeers and Tutors for their children after their departure. When Chriſt vpon the croſſe had the pangs of death vpon him, he commends his Mother to the tuition of *Iohn. Ioh.*19.26. When widdowes and Orphanes are wronged, God himſelfe takes vpon him the office of a Tutor in their behalfe. *Exod.* 22.22. And this ſhewes that it is a neceſſary duty to be thought vpon.

Thirdly, here the duty of children is ſet downe, and that is,

that

that they must be subiect to their Tutors and gouernors, as to their owne fathers and mothers. *Ruth loued Naomi, and claue vnto her as to her mother, Ruth.*1.16. Christ was subiect to *Ioseph* who was but a reputed father, *Luke* 2. last. The sonnes of the Prophets obey their master as their owne fathers, 2.*King.*2.12. and so doe the seruants to their master, 2.*King.*5.13.

Now I come to the second part of the similitude, v.3. *Euen so we*] that is, the Iewes, and all the people of God in the old Testament. *Were children*] were as children in respect of the Christian Church in the new Testament.

Were in bondage] The Iewes are said to be in bondage in respect of vs: because they were subiect to more lawes then we are, and they wanted the fruition of the libertie which we enioy. They had the right of sonnes, but they inioyed not their right as we do: and this is their bondage. For otherwise liberty in conscience from hel, death, and sinne, they had euen as we now haue.

Rudiments of the world] that is, the law or ministery of *Moses*; and it is so called, in respect of a more full and plentifull doctrine, in the Ministery of the new Testament. And it is called *the Rudiments of the world*, because Iewry was as it were, a little schoole set vp in a corner of the world; the law of *Moses* was as it were, an *a,b,c,* or *Primar*, in which Christ was reuealed to the world, in darke and obscure manner, specially to the Iewes.

The vse. Here we see, that the people of the old Testament, were for right, heires as well as we, and therefore they had right to all the blessings of God. The difference betweene vs and them, is onely in the manner which God vsed in dispensing the foresaid blessings to vs.

Againe, the Fathers of the olde Testament before Christ, were but as children in respect of vs now. Thus much saith *Paul* in expresse words. And they were so two waies. First, in respect of the Mosaicall regiment: because they were kept in subiection to more lawes then we. Secondly, they were so in respect of reuelation: because God hath reuealed more to vs, then to them. Reade *Luk.*10.24. It may be said, we now are (the best of vs) but children to *Abraham* & the Prophets, whether we respect knowledge, or faith. *Answ.* It is so if we compare person and person: but it is otherwise, if we compare body with body, & cōpare the Christian Church, with the Church of the Iewes before Christ: then we exceed them & they are but children to vs. This must teach vs al to be carefull, to increase in knowledge, & in the grace of God, that we may be answerable to our condition. And to liue in ignorance

as

(as the moſt doe) is the ſhame of vs all. For in reſpect of the time, we ſhould all be teachers, *Heb.5.12.* and yet God knowes, the moſt are very babes. For aske a man how he lookes to be ſaued, he will anſwer, by ſeruing God, and dealing truely. Now his ſeruing of God, is his ſaying of his prayers: and his prayers are the Beleefe, and the ten Commaundements. This is a poore ſeruing of God, fitter for babes, then for men of yeares. It is further to be obſerued, that *Paul* ſaith, the fathers of the old Teſtament *were in bondage vnder the law*, after the manner of ſeruants, ſpecially by reaſon of rites and ceremonies. And hence it followes, that the obſeruation of a religion, in which are manifold bodily rites and figures, is a kind of bondage, and pertaines to the Church, for the time of her infancie or minoritie. Let this bee remembred againſt the Romiſh religion: for it is like to that of the Iewes in the olde Teſtament; ſtanding for the greateſt part in bodily rites, in differences of meates and drinkes, in differences of times, places, garments; in exerciſes, and afflictions of the bodie, in locall ſucceſſion, in the collation of grace by the worke done, and ſuch like. This is manifeſt to them which know the *Maſſe*, which indeed is nothing but a *maſſe* of ceremonies. Therefore the Romane religion is a childiſh and babiſh religion: and if it were of God, yet is it not fit for the Church of the New Teſtament, that is come forth of her minoritie. Religion that ſtands in the afflicting of the body, is but a ſhadow, and an appearance of humilitie, *Coloſſ.2.23.* And *the true worſhippers of God* in the new Teſtament, *worſhip him in ſpirit and trueth*, *Iohn* 4.24.

The fulneſſe of time, or *the full time*, is that time in which the captiuitie of the Church endeth, and her libertie begins. This time was ended 4000. yeares from the creation: and it is called *a full time*, becauſe it was deſigned and appointed by the will and prouidence of the heauenly Father. For he is Lord of time, and all ſeaſons are in his hand: and his will or prouidence makes times fit or vnfit. Marke then, that is the onely full and fit time for the enioying of any bleſſing of God, which he by his prouidence appointeth. This muſt teach vs, when by prayer wee aske any good thing at Gods hand, not to preſcribe any time vnto God, but to leaue it to his prouidence. Againe, if thou liue in any miſery, waite on the Lord, and bee content. For that is the fit and beſt time of thy deliuerance, which God hath appoynted. Laſtly, thou muſt bee admoniſhed to pray to God for grace and mercie, and to turne to him this day before to morrow. For this is the time which God hath appoynted for theſe duties: *This is the day of grace,* and

and therefore the onely fit time, *Hebrewes* 3.7. *Pſalme* 32.6.

Thus much of the ſimilitude: now I come to the firſt reaſon, whereby *Paul* confirmes his maine argument. Chriſt hath purchaſed and procured your libertie: therfore the time thereof is come and paſt. For the better clearing of this reaſon, *Paul* ſets downe the way and order which was vſed in procuring this libertie. And it containes fiue degrees. The firſt is, the ſending of the Sonne; the ſecond, his incarnation; the third, his ſubiection to the law; the fourth, our redemption from the law; the fift, the fruition of our adoption, verſ.4,5.

The firſt, the ſending of the Sonne, in theſe words, *In the fulneſſe of time, God ſent forth his Sonne.* That we may attaine to the ſenſe of this great myſterie, ſixe queſtions are to be propounded.

The firſt is, what is meant by God? *Anſwer.* The Father, the firſt perſon. *Epheſ.*1.3. *Bleſſed be God the Father of our Lord Ieſus Chriſt*, 2. *Cor.*1.3. & *Ioh.*20.17. And he is called *God*, not becauſe he partakes more of the Godhead then the Son, or the holy Ghoſt: but becauſe he is the firſt in order of the three diuine perſons: and he is the beginning of the Sonne, and the holy Ghoſt; and hath no beginning of his owne perſon: becauſe he doth not receiue the Godhead by communication from any other. In this reſpect hee is called *God* more commonly then the Sonne, or the holy Ghoſt.

The ſecond queſtion is, How the Father ſends the Sonne? *Anſwer.* By his counſell and eternall decree, whereby the Sonne was deſigned to the office of a Mediatour, and conſequently to become man, *Actes* 2.23. And thus is hee ſaid to bee *ſealed of the Father, Iohn* 6,27. and to bee *ſanctified, and ſent into the world, Iohn* 10.36. And therefore this ſending implies no alteration or change of place.

The third queſtion is, whether the Sonne was ſent with his owne conſent or no? *Anſwer.* Yea, the decree of the Father is the decree of the Sonne, and the holy Ghoſt: becauſe as they are all one in nature, ſo are they all one in will. All the perſons then haue a ſtroke in this ſending, yet for orders ſake the Father is ſaid to ſend, becauſe he is firſt.

The fourth queſtion is, how the Father can ſend the Sonne, conſidering they are both one? *Anſwer.* In the doctrine touching the Trinitie, *Nature*, and *Perſon* muſt bee diſtinguiſhed. *Nature* is a ſubſtance common to many, as the Godhead. A *perſon* is that which ſubſiſteth of it ſelfe, and hath a proper manner of ſubſiſting, as the Father begetting, the Sonne begotten, the holy Ghoſt proceeding. Now the Father and the Sonne are one indeed for nature or Godhead, but they are not one for perſon. Nay thus they are really diſtinct. The Father is not the Sonne, nor the Son the Father. And thus doth the Father ſend the Sonne.

The fiſt queſtion is, why the Sonne is ſo called? *Anſwer.* Becauſe he was begotten of the Father, by a perfect & eternall generation, not to be vttered of man, or conceiued. And we muſt be warned, not to conceiue it in any carnall or humane maner. For an earthly father is in time before his ſonne, and the ſonne after: but God the Father and the Sonne are coeternall, and not one before or after the other for time. An earthly father is forth of the ſonne, and the ſonne forth of the father: but God the Father is in the Sonne, and the Son in the Father. An earthly child is from his father by propagation, but the Son is from the heauenly Father, not by propagation, but by communication of ſubſtance. Laſtly, the heauenly Father begets the Sonne by communication of his whole ſubſtance, and ſo doth no earthly father.

The laſt queſtion is, whether the Sonne bee God? For it is here ſaid, *God ſent his Sonne. Anſwer.* He is God. For he that is ſent foorth from God, was before hee was ſent foorth. And the Sonne is ſaid to bee ſent foorth; becauſe *hee was with God the Father before all worlds, Iohn* 1. 1. and becauſe *hee came from the boſome of his Father,* verſe 18.

Obiect. I. The Sonne is ſent of the Father: and he that is ſent, is inferiour to the Father: and he that is inferiour to God, is not God. *Anſwer.* Two equalles by common conſent may ſend each other: and therefore ſending alwayes implies not inequalitie. Againe, inferioritie is of two ſorts, inferioritie of nature, and inferioritie of condition. The firſt doth not befall Chriſt: becauſe for nature he is one and the ſame with the Father. The ſecond agrees vnto him, becauſe of his owne voluntary accord, hee abaſed himſelfe, and tooke vpon him the ſhape of a man, *Phil.* 2. 5.

Obiect. II. God hath his beginning of none: the Son hath his beginning of his Father: therefore he is not God. *Anſ.* The Sonne in reſpect of his perſon is of the Father: but in reſpect of his Godhead, he is of none. The Sonne of God conſidered as he is a Sonne, is of the Father, *God of very God.* But conſidered as he is God, he is God of himſelfe, becauſe the Godhead of the Sonne is not begotten, more then the Godhead of the Father.

Obiect. III. The Sonne was made Lord in time, *Actes* 2. 36. therefore no God. *Anſwer.* Chriſt, as he is the Sonne of God, was not made Lord in time, but is in nature an eternall Lord, as the Father. And he is ſaid to be *made Lord* in reſpect of his condition as he is God-man, and that in time, in respect of both his natures. In respect of his manhood, because it is receiued into the vnity of the second person, and exalted to the right hand of God in heauen. In respect of his Godhead, the Maiesty and Lordship whereof, he declared and made manifest in the flesh after his resurrection. Thus was he made Lord by declaring himselfe to be so indeede. *Rom.*1.4. 1.*Tim.*3.16.

Thus we see how God sent forth his Sonne: the vse followes. This act of God in sending, declares his infinite loue: for this sending was for their sakes that were the enemies of God. And it further signifies vnto vs the most free loue of God. For nothing in vs mooued him to send, but his owne goodnesse. This loue of God must mooue vs to loue God againe and to be thankfull.

The Sonne of God takes not to himselfe the office of a Mediatour, but he is called and sent forth of his Father: whereby two things are signified; one, that the office of a Mediatour was appointed of the Father: the other, that the Sonne was designed to this office in the eternall counsell of the blessed Trinity. And so, that we may please God in our callings aud places, we must haue a double assurance in our consciences: one, that the offices and callings which we performe, are good, and pleasing vnto God: the second, that we are designed and called of God to the said offices and callings. By this must we stay our minds in all our miseries.

The Sonne is *sent forth*, that is, he comes from his Father, layes aside his maiesty, and takes on him the condition of a seruant. The same minde must bee in vs to humble and abase our selues before God, to thinke better of others then of our selues, to be content with our condition, to be well pleased when we are despised and contemned, because we are worthy of it. This is to conforme our selues to Christ.

That the Sonne of God himselfe must be sent forth from the bosome of his Father, this shewes the greatnesse of our sinne and misery, which was the occasion of this sending. And this must teach vs with bitternesse to hate and detest our sinnes, which fetched the Sonne of God from heauen, and to humble selues with *Dauid* euen to the deepes, and thence to pray to God for his mercy. *Psal.*130.1.

The second point, namely, the Incarnation of the Sonne, is expressed in these words, *Made of a woman*: that is, made man, or made flesh of a woman. *The word was made flesh. Ioh.*1.14. Here three questions are to be handled. The first is, why the Sonne was made flesh? *Answer.* There be two speciall causes hereof. First, the order of diuine iustice requires that Gods wrath should be appeased, and a satisfaction made, in the same nature in which his Maiesty was offended. Now the offence was in mans nature: and therefore in it must satisfaction to God be performed. Secondly, the Mediatour betweene God and man, must be both for nature and condition in the meane betweene God and man, that is, both God and man: and thus the Sonne of God is a perfect Mediatour.

The second question is, how farre forth the Sonne of God was made flesh? I answer three things. The first, that he tooke vnto him the whole and perfect nature of man in respect of Essence, namely, the intire substance of a reasonable soule, and humane body. Here remember, that quantity, that is, length, breadth, and thicknesse, is not an accident, which may passe and repasse, but it is of the substance of euery body, & therefore of the body of Christ. And for this cause it is impossible that the body of Christ in his quantity, beeing foure or fiue foote in length, should be included in the compasse of a peece of bread that is but two or three inches in quantity. The second is, that the Sonne of God tooke vnto him the properties of mans nature, the powers of life, sense, motion, the facultie of reason, will, and affection. The third is, that he tooke to him the infirmities, and miseries of mans nature. Here two caueats must be remembred. The first, that he tooke to him onely such infirmities as are meere infirmities, and no sinnes. For example, vpon the words of Christ, *Let this cuppe passe, Mat.* 26. some say, that there was obliuion in Christ: but this may not be said. For obliuion is a sinne, namely, a forgetting of that which a man ought to remember: and there may be in Christ or other men, a suspending of the Memory, by some externall and violent cause, without obliuion. The second caueat is, that the Sonne of God tooke to him the infirmities which pertaine to the nature of man, and not such as pertaine to the persons of men, as dropsies, gouts, consumptions, and such like. For he tooke not the person of any man, but the nature of all men, with all the appurtenances thereof except sinne.

The third question is, How was he made flesh? *Answer.* The flesh or manhood of Christ, was first framed, then sanctified, and then vnited to the Godhead of the Sonne. And thus was he made man. Remember here that the forming of the flesh of Christ, the sanctifying of it, and the personall Vnion are all together for time: and I distinguish them in this sort, onely for doctrines sake.

In the framing of the manhood, I consider the matter, and the manner. The matter was the substance of the Virgin, signified in

these

theſe words, *made of a woman*. By this Chriſt is diſtinguiſhed from all men in the world: from *Adam*, becauſe hee was neither of man nor woman, but of red clay. From *Eue*, becauſe ſhee was made of man, and not of woman. From all that come of *Adam* and *Eue*, for they are both of man and woman; wheras Chriſt is of woman, and not of man. Againe, *Paul* addes theſe words, [*made of a woman*] to note the accompliſhment of the promiſe, *the ſeed of the woman ſhall breake the Serpents head, Gen.* 3.15.

The manner of framing is expreſſed, when *Paul* ſaith, *made*, not begotten of a woman. The manhood then of Chriſt, was framed without naturall generation, by an extraordinarie worke of the holy Ghoſt. Heere a doubt is anſwered. Some man may ſay, if hee were made of a woman, he comes of *Adam*, and conſequently hee is a ſinner. *Anſwer*. The order ſet downe by God with *Adam* in the creation is, that whatſoeuer hee loſeth, all his poſteritie ſhall loſe that comes of him by generation. Vpon this order, all that are begotten of *Adam*, with the nature of man, receiue the ſinne and corruption of nature. And ſo ſhould Chriſt haue done, if he had deſcended of *Adam* by generation. But conſidering his fleſh was made of the ſubſtance of a woman, and not begotten of any man: therefore he take the nature of man, and not the corruption of nature.

The ſanctifying of the manhood of Chriſt, is a worke of diuine power, whereby at the time of the framing thereof, it was filled with the gifts of the holy Ghoſt aboue meaſure, that he might in both natures be a perfect Sauiour. Here obſerue, that Chriſt by the actions of his life, did not merit for himſelfe glory, and eternall happineſſe: becauſe he was moſt worthy of all glory and honour at the very firſt moment of his conception. Againe, obſerue that Chriſt in his manhood increaſed in grace, as in age, and ſtature, *Luk.* 2. And this increaſe was without all imperfection: for in his infancy, Chriſt receiued a full meaſure of grace fitte for that age: when he was twelue yeares old, he receiued a further meaſure, fitte for that age: and ſo when he was thirty yeares old. And thus increaſe of grace, and the perfection thereof, ſtand both together. And this increaſe is not onely in reſpect of experience, and the manifeſtation of Grace before God and men, but alſo in reſpect of the habit or gift: though the *Schooles* for 400. yeares haue taught the contrary euer ſince the daies of *Lumbard*.

The third thing is, the Vniting of fleſh to the Godhead of the Sonne: and that is done, when the Sonne of God makes the fleſh, or nature of man, a part of himſelfe, and communicates vnto it his own ſubſiſtance. The like example to this is not to be found againe in the world: yet haue we ſome reſemblance of this myſterie in the plant called *Meſſelto*, which hath no roote of his owne, but growes in a tree of an other kinde, and thence receiues his ſappe. And ſo the manhood of the ſonne hath no perſonality or perſonal ſubſiſtance, but is receiued into the Vnitie of the ſecond perſon, and is ſuſtained of it. It muſt here be obſerued, that there is a difference betweene the manhood of Chriſt, and all other men. *Peter* is a perſon ſubſiſting of himſelfe, and ſo is *Paul*, and euery particular man: but ſo is not the manhood of Chriſt: and therefore it is to be tearmed a nature, and not a perſon. And it is no diſgrace, but an exaltation to the nature of man, that it ſubſiſts by the vncreated ſubſiſtance of the ſecond perſon.

It may be obiected, that all beleeuers are ioyned to the ſonne of God, as well as the fleſh of Chriſt: I anſwer, they are ſo, but in an other kinde, and in a lower degree, by communication of grace, and not by communication of perſonall ſubſiſtance.

Thus wee ſee how the ſonne was made fleſh: the vſe followes. Hence wee learne to vſe all meanes, that wee may become new creatures, and be borne of God. God becomes man, that we men might be partakers of the diuine nature. Chriſt is made bone of our bone, and fleſh of our fleſh by his incarnation, that we might be made bone of his bone, and fleſh of his fleſh by regeneration. The Sonne of God was made the ſonne of man, that we which are the ſonnes of men might be made the ſonnes of God.

To be made fleſh, is the abaſement of his Sonne: in this abaſement he goes on, till he become euen *as a worme of the earth*, *Pſalm.* 22.7. ſo muſt we abaſe our ſelues, till we be anihilated and brought to nothing: then ſhall wee bee like to Chriſt, and filled with the good things of God.

Our ſinnes are a wall of partition betweene God and vs: ſo as we are farre from God, and God from vs, *Iſai.* 59.2. and this partition is of our owne making: and by this meanes wee haue no acceſſe to God of our ſelues, though we pray vnto him, and fil heauen and earth with our crie. Now the Sonne of God made man, is *Emmanuel*, that is, *God with vs*, *Iſa.* 7.14. and his incarnation is a meanes whereby we haue acceſſe to God, *and hee is neere vnto vs, when wee pray vnto him in trueth*, 2. *Chronicles* 15.2. This muſt teach vs to draw neere to God, in the hearing and obeying of his word, in prayer, and in the vſe of the holy Sacraments. If this be not done, great is our wickedneſſe, and great ſhall bee the puniſhment, *Iob* 21.14. *Pſal.* 73.27.

The incarnation of Christ, is the foundation of all our comfort, and al good things which we inioy. By it God comforts *Adam, The seed of the woman, shall bruise the Serpents head. Iacob* is comforted by the vision of a ladder, reaching from heauen to earth: and this ladder is the Sonne of God made man, *Ioh.*1.51. *Iob* comforts himselfe, in this, *that his Redeemer of his owne flesh* (as the word signifieth) *liueth, Iob.*19.25. In the old Testament, they which sought vnto God, came to the Arke or Propitiatory, and there were they heard, and receiued the blessings of God. Now Christ, God and man, is in stead of the Arke, *Rom,*3.25. and therfore we must come to him if we would receiue any good thing of God. The godhead is the fountaine of all good things, and the flesh or manhood is a pipe or conduit to conuey the same vnto vs. If we would then receiue true comfort, we must hunger and thirst in our hearts after Christ, and by our faith eate his flesh and drinke his blood, *Ioh.* 6. 54.56.

The third point or degree, is the subiection of the Son of God to the law, expressed in these words, *made vnder the law.*

Here two questions are to be answered. The first is, who is made subiect to the law? I answer, the Sonne of God. And this may not seeme strange, that he which is Lord of the law, should be subiect to the law: for he must be considered, as he is our pledge and surety, *Heb.*5.22. and as one that standes in our place, roome, & stead; and before God represents the person of all the elect: and in this respect is he subiect to the law, not by nature, but by voluntary abasement and condition of will.

The second question is, how the Sonne of God was subiect to the law? *Answer.* By a twofold obedience: namely, by the obedience of his passion, and by his obedience in fulfilling the law. The obedience of his passion stands before God as a satisfaction for the breach of the law. In it consider two things, the foundation of the passion, and the passion it selfe. The foundation is, that *the Sonne of God was made sinne for vs,* 2.*Cor.*5.21. that is, all the sinnes of all the Elect were imputed to him, and he in our roome and place was recounted a sinner. The passion it selfe, is the curse of the law, laid on the Sonne of God, namely, the first death, and the paines of the second death, which is in effect and substance, the paines of hell, as I haue shewed in the 3. chap. v.13. of this Epistle.

By the second Obedience in fulfilling the law, the Sonne of God performed for vs, all things contained therein, that we might haue right to life euerlasting, and that according to the tenour of the law, *Leuit.* 18. 5. *Doe all these things and liue.* Of this obedience 2. questions are demanded. The first is, whether it be necessarie for the iustification of a sinner? *Answ.* It is. The summe of the law is, *Loue God with all thy heart, and thy neighbour as thy selfe*: Now euery iot and title of the lawe must necessarily be fulfilled, *Math.* 5. 18. Much more then the summe and substance of the lawe. And it cannot be fulfilled by vs, beeing sinners: therefore there must needs be a translation of the law from our persons, to the person of the Mediatour, who is to accomplish euery iot of the law for vs. Againe, *He that doth not all things contained in the law: is cursed. Gal.* 3. 13. He therefore that would eschewe the curse of the law, and come to life euerlasting, must by himselfe accomplish all things contained in the law: and if this cannot be done, the law and al the contents thereof, must needs be accomplished in the person of the Mediatour: otherwise the curse cannot be auoided. Lastly, we owe vnto God a double debt or tribute. The first is, homage or subiection to be performed with all the powers of the soule, and with all the strength of all the powers, and that from the first conception. The second is, a satisfaction by death for the breach of the law. And the law is the bond that binds vs to the paiment of this double debt. And till the iustice of God in the law be answered to the full, this bond cannot be cancelled. Therefore the Sonne of God, the Mediatour, must not only dy for vs, but also performe homage for vs to God, according to the tenour of the law. Therfore he saith, that *he must performe all righteousnesse, Math.* 3. 15. And *Paul*, that *Christ is the end of the law for righteousnesse. Rom.* 10. 4.

It is alledged, that Christ as man fulfilled the law for himselfe: and therefore not for vs. *Answer.* The flesh or manhood of Christ considered by it selfe apart from the godhead of the Sonne, is a creature that owes homage vnto God. Yet if it be considered as it is receiued into the vnity of the second person, & is become a part thereof, it is exempted from the common condition of all other men, and is not bound to performe subiection, as all men are. For if *the Sonne of man be Lord of the Sabboth*, then also is he Lord of the whole law. And *Paul* here saith, that the Sonne of God, is not borne but *made vnder the law.*

Againe, it is alleadged, *That the blood of Christ taketh away all sinne*, 1. *Ioh.* 1. 7. and when all sinne is taken away, the law is fulfilled, and the person iustified. *Answer.* When S. *Iohn* saith, *the blood of Christ purgeth vs from all sin*, he excludes the blood of beasts, and all meritorious meanes of saluation in man, out of Christ: and he excludes not the obedience which the Mediatour yeelded to the Father.

ther in all his ſufferings. Againe, it is not true that a ſinner is iuſtified, when all ſinne is aboliſhed: vnleſſe iuſtice be added. For iuſtification is an alteration of a ſinner from one contrary to another, from euill to good, from life to death: and therefore ſinne muſt depart, and iuſtice come in the roome thereof. That a darke houſe may be inlightned, darkenes muſt firſt be aboliſhed, and light muſt come in the ſtead thereof. And that a man may be iuſtified, ſinne muſt be couered, and righteouſneſſe imputed.

The ſecond queſtion is, how the Sonne of God performed this obedience? *Anſw.* He was obedient to his Father to the death, and that according to all the duties of loue in the firſt table: & for the ſecond table, he loued his enemie as himſelfe, becauſe he gaue his life for man. Marke then, he did all things contained in the law, and more too, in reſpect of the duties of the ſecond Table. For the law binds vs to loue our neighbours as our ſelues, and not more then our ſelues, This obedience therefore is truly to be tearmed *a worke of ſupererogatiō*: & there is none in the world beſide.

The vſe. That the Sonne of God was conformable to the law, it argues the goodneſſe, perfection, and excellencie thereof. Here againe marke the difference, betweene the man Chriſt, and all other men. He was not borne ſubiect to the law, but made ſubiect: not ſubiect by nature, but by will and by voluntary abaſement. All other men are ſubiect not by wil, but by nature, not made, but borne ſubiect. Therefore *Paul* ſaith, *the Gentiles doe by nature the things of the law.* The remainders of the law ſince the fall are naturall in all men: therefore the whole law was naturall before the fall. Man was at the firſt created in righteouſnes and holines, *Eph.* 4. 24. and therefore in a perfect ſubiection and conformity to the law. It is a naturall propertie of a reaſonable creature, to doe homage to the creator. It is an error then in the papiſt to teach, that the Image of God in our firſt parents was ſupernaturall.

The fourth point or degree is, the Redemption of man from vnder the law, in theſe words [*that he might redeeme them which were vnder the law.*] Here fiue things are to be conſidered. The firſt is, what is meant by beeing vnder the law? *Anſwer.* The law muſt be conſidered two waies: firſt, as the Rule of life. Thus angels are vnder the law, and *Adam* before his fall, and the Saints now in heauen. And none yeeld more ſubiection to the law then they: and this ſubiection is their libertie. Againe the law muſt be conſidered as a grieuous yoke which none can beare. It is a yoke three waies. firſt, becauſe it did bind the Church of the old Teſtament to the obſeruation of many and that very coſtly ceremonies, for the main-

maintenance of the altar at Hierusalem was a matter of great charges. Secondly, it is a yoke because it binds euery offendour to euerlasting death, *Gen.* 2.17. *Gal.* 1.3. Thirdly, it is a yoke as it increaseth sinne, and as it is the strength of it, 1. *Cor.* 15.56. *Rom.* 5.20. and 7.8. And it increaseth sinne, not as a cause, but as an occasion. For the wicked nature of man is, the more to doe a thing, the more he is forbidden. The Israelites are bidden to goe on to Canaan, then they like Egypt well. They are forbidden to goe to Canaan, and commanded to stay in the wildernesse, but then they will needs go to Canaan. Circumcision commanded, was lothed of all nations: when it was abolished, then men of sundry nations imbraced it as needfull to saluation. To be vnder the law then, is to be in subiection to it, as it is a burden and yoke in the three former respects, specially to be subiect to the curse of the law.

The second point is, who are vnder the law? *Answer.* The Iewes before the comming of Christ, were vnder the law in respect of Ceremonies: and all men naturally are vnder the law in respect of the malediction and curse thereof, all being borne children of wrath, *Ephesians* 2. 3. Heere comes a lamentable matter to bee considered. Very few in respect know themselues to bee in bondage to the curse of the law. For they thinke it an easie matter to obserue the law: and it is vsed for a forme of prayer whereby men vse to blesse themselues morning and euening. Learne therfore this one lesson, that thou art by nature in thy selfe vnder the curse of the law, and for thine offences by it bound ouer to euerlasting death. If thou shouldest be proclaimed an outlaw, or a writ of rebellion should bee serued on thee, it would make thee at thy wits ende. Now behold, the law proclaimes thee a traytour, and rebell against God through heauen and earth. The law shuts heauen against thee: it sets hell and death wide open for thee, and it armes all the creatures of God against thee. Therefore it stands thee in hand to looke about thee, and to flie from the sentence of the law to the throne of grace for mercie and forgiuenesse. It hath been the fashion of all holy men, to acquaint themselues with this one lesson, that they were by nature vnder the law, specially then when they were to humble themselues in the presence of God. *Daniel* in his praier, ascribes shame and confusion to himselfe, *Daniel* 9. according to the voice and cry of the law: and the prodigall sonne confesseth that he had sinned against his father, and against heauen, and that hee was vnworthy to bee accounted a child of God; according to the law iudging and condemning himselfe.

The

The third point is, what is the price wherby men are bought or redeemed from vnder the law? *Answer*. The obedience of the Son, whereby he stood in subiection to the Law for vs: as *Paul* signifies in the words immediatly going before. It may be said, how can the obedience of one man be a price of redemption for another? I answer, wee must consider Christ, not as a meere man, but as God-man, and by this meanes his obedience is of infinite merit and efficacie. Againe, we must consider him not as a priuate, but as a publike person, representing all the elect in his obedience to his Father. And by this meanes his obedience serues for all that beleeue in him. Againe, it may bee alleadged, that the law saith, *Thou shalt loue, thou shalt not lust, &c.* And, *the soule that sinnes, that soule shall die, Ezech.* 18. 20. And, *a man shall not redeeme the life of his brother, Psal.* 49. 7. *Answer*. The law requires that euery man performe obedience, and make satisfaction in his owne person, & the law knowes no other obedience. But this must be considered, that the law is but one part of the reuealed will of God: and that the Gospel is another distinct part, reuealing more then the law euer knew. And the Gospell teacheth a Translation of the law in respect of obedience, from our person to the person of the Mediatour, and thereby it addes an exception to the law.

The fourth point is, who are partakers of this redemption? *Ans.* They which see, and feele, and bewaile their condition that they are vnder the law, and flie from the sentence thereof to the throne of grace for mercy. *Christ came to saue sinners, Matth.* 9. that is, such as are conuicted by the law, and know themselues to be sinners. He offers ease *to them that trauell and are heauy laden, Matth.* 11. 28. *Hee preacheth deliuerance to captiues, Luke* 4. 18. Here wee are to bewaile the misery of our people, that know not themselues to be vnder the law: nay they loue and delight to be vnder it. For they alleadge for themselues, that they say their prayers duely and truely, that they meane well to God-ward, and deale truly with men: and therefore they thinke God will haue mercy on them, and haue them excused for all their offences.

The last poynt is, what benefits arise of this deliuerance from vnder the law? *Answer*. They which turne to God, and beleeue in Christ, reape foure benefits thereby. The first is, that no sinne shall haue dominion ouer them, *Romanes* 6. 14. Heere marke by the way, that they which are in Christ, cannot wholly fall from grace. For they which wholly fall away, are vnder the dominion of sinne.

The second is, that God will accept the indeauour to obay,

for obedience, because they are freed from the rigour of the law. Reade *Malach*.3.17.

The third is, that they haue libertie to liue and serue God without feare of damnation, or any other euill, *Luke* 1.74.

The last is, that afflictions cease to bee curses, and are turned to blessings: and for this cause they are delaied and qualified for the good of them which are afflicted. *Psalm*.89.32. *I will correct them that offend with a rodde, but I will not take my mercie from them.* *Prou*. 3.11. *Grieue not for the correction of the Lord: for hee loueth whom hee correcteth. Ierem*.10.24. *Correct vs in iudgement: and powre foorth thy wrath vpon the nations, that haue not knowen thee.* This must teach men that professe or teach Christ, not to be discouraged when they are abused, railed on, slaundered, or cursed. For if they bee from vnder the law, and from vnder the sting of a guiltie conscience, nothing shall hurt them. They must be content for a while to suffer the snatches and bitings of the diuell: for in the end his head shall be bruised in pieces.

To ende this poynt; it may bee said, if we that beleeue be not vnder the law, then we may liue and doe as we list. *Answer*. We are free from the law, as a yoke, but not free from it, as it is the rule of obedience, and good life. And because we are freed from the bondage of the law, therefore wee must bee a law to our selues: wee must bee *voluntaries*, *Psalm*.110.4. without constraint, freely yeelding subiection to the will of God, and not for feare of hell, and the last iudgement.

The third and last degree, is the fruition of adoption, in these words [*that wee might receiue the adoption of sonnes.*] Heere two questions are to be considered. The first is, How the Church of the new Testament is said to receiue the adoption which was before receiued in the old Testament? *Answer*. In Scripture a thing is often said to bee done, when it is done more fully, and plentifully. Christ tells *Nathanael* that *hee shall see heauen open*, *Iohn* 1.51. that is, more plainely opened. For it was not shut in the olde Testament. And, *the holy Ghost was not yet*, *Iohn* 7.39. that is, in the full measure. And, *the way into the Holiest, was not open while the Tabernacle was standing*: *Hebr*. 9.8. that is, plainly made manifest. And in this place, beleeuers of the New Testament *receiue the adoption* because they receiue it in a more full and plentifull manner, in that the spirit of children is powred foorth vpon them in larger measure, whether wee regard illumination, or the gifts of regeneration. This must teach vs that liue in these latter dayes, to put on the condition of sonnes and daughters of God, in reuerence, obedi-

obedience, and thankfulneſſe. But alas, among the multitude, it is farre otherwiſe. For the moſt liue euen as Atheiſts in ignorance, according to the luſtes of their owne hearts. The faith and repentance, which they profeſſe, is but ceremoniall Faith, and repentance.

The ſecond queſtion is, whence ſprings our adoption? The anſwer is plaine in the words: From the obedience of the Sonne, whereby he ſtood in ſubiection to the law. Here the queſtion of all queſtions is anſwered; namely, what is that thing, by which, and for which a ſinner is iuſtified before God, and ſaued? *Anſwer.* The obedience of the Sonne of God made man, and made vnder the law for vs. For this is it that frees vs from vnder the law, and giues vs the adoption of ſonnes. And this alone is it, whereby we ſtand before the tribunall ſeat of God, which alſo we are to oppoſe to the iudgement of God, to hell, death, and condemnation.

Therefore our common people erre, that looke to bee ſaued by their good deeds, that is, by their good meaning and dealing. They thus tread the blood of Chriſt vnder their owne feet, and become Ieſuſſes, or Sauiours to themſelues.

Secondly, they erre, that teach iuſtification by the eſſentiall iuſtice of the Godhead of the Sonne: for that it is incommunicable: and they which are iuſtified by it, are alſo deified.

Thirdly, the Papiſt erreth, which teacheth iuſtification partly by remiſſion of ſinnes, and partly by that which we call inward ſanctification: which is imperfect and mixed in this life with our corruption, and therefore vnfit to abſolue and acquit vs before God.

It may be ſaid, what muſt we doe that wee may bee iuſtified and ſaued by this obedience of the Mediatour? *Anſwer.* In the olde Teſtament, when a man had ſinned, he brought a ſheep, or an oxe to the doore of the Tabernacle, and when the Prieſt cut the throat of it, the partie laid his hand vpon the head of it, *Exod.* 29.10. And hereby he ſignified, that the beaſt had done no hurt, and that hee as a guiltie malefactor had deſerued death. Now all this was done in figure. And it teacheth vs that we miſerable ſinners muſt come to God; that wee muſt bring our ſacrifice with vs, namely, the Lambe of God, which is the Sonne of God, made man, and made vnder the law: that wee muſt preſent this Lambe, and the oblation thereof to the Father for vs, laying our handes on the head of it: that is, confeſſing our guiltineſſe, and that we haue iuſtly deſerued death and perdition from the preſence of God. In the laſt place, we muſt intreat the Lord to accept the blood of the Lambe

for

for vs, and the whole obedience of the Mediatour. Thus shall we be iustified and saued. Thou wilt say, I will therfore doe this when I am dying. I say again, let it be thy daily exercise to the very death. Thou wast seuen yeares in learning thy trade; thinke not therefore in an houre or two, to worke thy reconciliation with God. If thou art many yeares in learning such things as are done by the strength of nature, thinke not to attaine to things aboue nature, when, and how thou wilt. It is a rule receiued of al men, that they must blesse themselues: now the right way to blesse thy selfe, is to pleade guiltie before God, and to intreat him to accept the obedience of the Mediatour for thee.

Vers.6.

Sonnes] that is, such as inioy the libertie of sonnes. *Sent foorth*] a speech borrowed frō Embassadors, which are set forth with instructions, what they shall say or doe: and it signifies, that the spirit reueales nothing but that which is the will of the Father and Sonne, *Iohn* 16.14. *Crying*] making vs to crie, *Rom.* 8.26. For if the wordes bee taken properly, the spirit must pray to it selfe. *Abba*] the next word is the exposition, *Father.*

The sense. The Father hath sent foorth the spirit of his Sonne vnto you; this spirit sent foorth, dwells in your hearts: dwelling in your hearts, it makes you pray to God as to a father: and all this it doth, because you are indeed the sonnes of God.

The scope. The question is, whether beleeuers of the New Testament bee seruants to the law, or children? *Paul* answers, No: and hee giues two reasons. The first, was in the former verses: the second in this. And it is drawne from the signe, thus. Yee haue receiued the spirit crying, Abba, Father: therefore yee are sonnes indeed.

In the words, I consider fiue things: the person sent forth, *the spirit of the Sonne*: the person sending, *God*: the maner of sending: the place whither the spirit is sent, *your hearts*: the office of the spirit, *Crying, Abba.*

Of the first: *the spirit of the Sonne* it is, who is sent foorth. He is so called: first, because he proceeds by communication of substance, or Godhead, not onely from the Father, but also from the Sonne. Secondly, because in his manhood hee is annoynted and filled with the holy Ghost, aboue measure: Thirdly, because by his death, he hath merited the giuing and sending of the Holy Ghost vnto vs.

Moreouer, *the spirit of the Sonne* is here described. First, he is a person subsisting of himselfe, in that he is said to be sent forth: secondly, ly,hee is a diuine perſon, and no creature, becauſe he dwels in the hearts of all beleeuers: thirdly, hee proceeds from the Father and the Sonne: from the Father,becauſe hee is ſent of him: from the Sonne,becauſe he is the ſpirit of the Sonne.

The vſe. By this we learne,that the Interceſſion of Chriſt,is of force with God. For he praied for the ſending of the Spirit,and it is accompliſhed. Reade *Iohn* 14.16.

And it is a ſuperfluous doctrine, to teach the Reall preſence of the fleſh of Chriſt in the Sacrament. For Chriſt is departed from vs in reſpect of his manhood: becauſe the Spirit is ſent, *Iohn* 16.7.

Thirdly, that which the Spirit inwardly teacheth, is the ſame with that which the Sonne hath reuealed by the miniſterie of the Prophets and Apoſtles,becauſe the Spirit is the Spirit of the Son. Reade *Iohn* 16.14. Doctrines then concerning ſaluation,that are beſide,or contrary to the Scriptures (as a great part of the Romiſh religion is) are not reuealed by the Spirit of God, but are the fictions of the diuell.

The perſon ſending, is *God*, that is, the Father, in theſe words, *God ſent foorth the Spirit of his Sonne.* Where marke the diſtinction of the perſons in Trinitie. There is the Father, the Sonne, and the Spirit of the Sonne. And heere remember,that this action of ſending foorth, argues not ſuperioritie in the perſon ſending, nor inferioritie in the perſon ſent: (for equalls may ſend each other by common conſent;) but it argues order, and a diſtinction of perſons in reſpect of their beginning. For the Father is of none, the Sonne is of the Father, and the holy Ghoſt is of both: and hence it is that he is ſent of both.

The manner of this ſending foorth, was on this ſort. We may not imagine that in this ſending, there was any change of place: For the Holy Ghoſt is euery where. But hee is ſaid to bee ſent foorth, when hee manifeſts his preſence by his diuine operation, or by ſpeciall and ſupernaturall gifts in the hearts of beleeuers, as by the gift of illumination, faith, regeneration. Life, ſenſe and motion are the gifts of the Spirit, and ſo are ciuill vertues: but the ſending of the Spirit, is onely in reſpect of ſuch gifts as are beſtowed in the Church, in the receiuing of which, the Spirit is acknowledged.

The place or manſion of the Spirit is the heart, that is, the mind, will, and affection. The heart is the very ſinke of ſinne; yet that doth the Spirit chooſe for his abode. Hence we learne.

1. That the beginning of our new birth is in the heart, when a new

new light is put into the minde, a new and heauenly diſpoſition into the will and affection.

2. The moſt principall part of our change or renouation, is in the heart, where the ſpirit abides. The end of all teaching is *loue out of a pure heart, good conſcience, and faith vnfained*, 1. *Tim*. 1. 5.

3. The beginning and principall part of Gods worſhip is in the heart. Hee that ſerues God in the righteouſneſſe of his heart, in peace, and ioy in the holy Ghoſt, is accepted, *Rom*. 14. 17.

4. In our hearts no wicked or carnall thought, will, deſire, or luſt muſt reigne, but onely Gods word and Spirit. For thy heart is the houſe where the Spirit dwells, and hee muſt be Lord of his owne houſe.

5. Aboue all things keepe watch and ward about thy heart, and fil it with all good cogitations and deſires, that it may be a fit place of entertainment for the ſpirit, who is (as it were) an Embaſſadour ſent from the great God vnto thee.

The laſt thing is, the office of the ſpirit, which is, to make beleeuers crie, *Abba*. Here I conſider 4. things: 1. The meanes whereby this crie is cauſed. 2. The nature of it. 3. To whom it is directed. 4. The maner of direction.

For the firſt, in the effecting or cauſing of this crie, there are foure works of the Spirit. The firſt is, *Conuiction*, when a man in his iudgment and conſcience is conuicted, that the Scriptures of the Prophets and Apoſtles, are indeed the word of God. To this purpoſe there are many arguments which now I omit. This conuiction is a common worke of the ſpirit, yet neceſſary, becauſe much Atheiſme lies lurking in our hearts, which makes vs call into queſtion euery part of the word of God.

The ſecond worke is *Subiection*, whereby a man conuicted that the Scripture, and euery part of it, is the word of God, ſubiects himſelfe in his heart to the commandement of God, which bids him turne to God, and beleeue in Chriſt. And this ſecond is a worke of the ſpirit of grace proper to the elect.

The third is, the *Certificate* or teſtimony of the ſpirit, which is a diuine manner of reaſoning framed in the minds of them that beleeue and repent, on this manner:

He that beleeues and repents, is Gods child. Thus ſaith the Goſpel.

But I beleeue in Chriſt, and repent: at the leaſt I ſubiect my will to the commaundement which biddes mee repent and beleeue; I deteſt mine vnbeleefe, and all my ſinnes: and deſire the Lord to increaſe my faith.

Therefore I am the childe of God.

This is the practicall Syllogisme of the Holy Ghost. It is the testimonie of the spirit, that we are the sonnes of God: it is the earnest of the Spirit, and the seale whereby wee are sealed to the day of our redemption: and it containes the certaintie of speciall faith.

The fourth thing that followes vpon this testimonie, is peace of conscience, ioy and affiance in God. And from this affiance comes the crying heere mentioned, whereby euery true beleeuer with open throat (as it were) cries vnto God the Father. This doctrine is of great worth, it is the hinge vpon which the gate of heauen turnes: and therefore to be remembred.

The vse. By this we see a manifest errour in the Popish religion, which teacheth, that we can haue no other certaintie of our saluation in this life, but that which is probable or coniecturall, that is, a certaintie ioyned with feare, suspition, and some doubting. Certaintie in respect of God that promiseth: feare and doubting, in respect of our owne indisposition. But this doctrine is false. For they which are Gods children, receiue the spirit, crying, Abba: and this crying argues affiance or confidence in God. By faith wee haue confidence in God, and entrance with boldnesse, *Ephes.*3.11. and boldnes is opposite to feare, and excludes doubting in respect of ourselues.

Againe, by this doctrine we see it is ordinary & possible for all that beleeue & repent, to be certainly assured that they are the children of God. For if they haue the spirit of God crying in them (as al Gods children haue) they cannot but perceiue this crie, and withall they haue the testimony of the spirit in them, which is the groũd of this crie, *Rom.*8.16. And seeing this is so, we must be admonished to vse all means that we may be assured that we are the children of God. 2.*Pet.*1. *Giue all diligence to make your election sure. Paul* bids *rich men lay vp a good foundation against the time to come*, 1.*Tim.*6.18. And this foundation must be laid, not in heauen, but in the conscience. God of his mercy hath made a couenant or bargain with vs that beleeue and repent: in this bargaine he hath promised to vs pardon of our sinnes, & life euerlasting: let vs then neuer be at rest, till we haue receiued earnest from the hand of God, & haue his promise sealed vnto vs by the spirit in our hearts. You wil say, what shal I do to be assured that I am Gods child? *Ans.* Thou must examine thy selfe of two things. The first is, whether thou art conuicted in thy iudgement, that the Scripture is indeed the word of God: if thou art not yet conuicted, then enquire & vse meanes that thou maiest indeed be conuicted: otherwise all is in vaine. Secondly, inquire whether thou dost indeed and in good earnest, submit and subiect thy will

to

to the commandement of God, which bids thee beleeue in Christ, and turne vnto God. For if thou canst say, that thou doest will to beleeue, and will to repent, if thou shew this will indeed in the vse of good meanes, if thou condemne and detest thy vnbeleefe, and al other thy sins, thou hast receiued the earnest of the spirit, & thou art indeed the child of God. And this assurance shall be vnto thee of great vse. For it will make thee reioyce in afflictions: and it will worke patience, experience, hope, *Rom.* 5.5. It wil make thee despise this world, it will take away the feare of death, and kindle in thy heart a desire to be with Christ.

Touching the nature of this crie, it stands in the desires and groanes of the heart, directed vnto God. And these desires may be distinguished from all carnall desires, by three properties. First of all, they are in the hearts of them that are turned to God, or at the least beginne to turne vnto him. For God heareth no sinners. Secondly, they are conceiued in the minde according to the reuealed will of God, *Rom.* 8.27. 1.*Iohn* 5.14. Thirdly, they are diuine and spirituall, touching things which concerne the kingdome of God, *Rom.* 8.5.

Desires thus qualified, haue the force of a loud crie in the eares of God. *Psalm.* 10.17. *God heareth the desire of the poore. Psalm.* 38.9. *All my desires are before thee. Psal.* 145.19. *He fulfilleth the desire of them that feare him. Isai.* 64.24. *Before they crie, I will answer*: that is, so soone as a desire of my helpe is conceiued, and before it be vttered I will answer.

That the desires of our hearts are cries, it is by meanes of the intercession of Christ. This Intercession is not a *vocall*, but a *vertuall* prayer, in that the Sonne of God presents his manhood and his merits before the Father in heauen, willing as God, and desiring as man, that the Father should accept the said merits for vs. Now this will and desire of the Sonne, is of great force with the Father. It is a crie in which the Father is well pleased: and by it the desires of our hearts are cries in the eares of God.

Of these desires there bee two speciall examples in the Scriptures. The first is, when we are touched in our hearts for our sinnes, to flie to the throne of grace, & to desire reconciliation with God in Christ. When *Dauid* did but desire the pardon of his sinnes, and therefore purposed in his heart to humble himselfe, hee receiued pardon: *Psalme* 32.5. *I said, I will confesse my wickednesse against my selfe vnto the Lord, and thou forgauest the punishment of my sinne.* When the prodigall sonne conceiued a desire to bee reconciled to his father, with a purpose to confesse his offence, before he had vttered his desire, he is receiued to mercy, *Luke* 15. 21.

The second example is a desire of Gods presence and protection in common iudgements. When *Moses* stood at the red sea in great danger, hauing the sea before him, and *Pharaohs* chariots behinde him, no doubt he lifted vp his heart vnto God; but we reade not of any thing that he said, and yet the Lord saith, *Why criest thou to mee? Exod.* 14. 15. When *Iehosaphat* was in great distresse, by reason of the army of the Ammonites, confounded in himselfe, hee saith, *O Lord, we know not what to doe, but our eyes are towards thee*, 2. *Chron.* 20. 12. and hereupon he obtained deliuerance.

The vse. By this we learne to lay aside formall praying, and lip labour, and learne to lift vp our hearts to God in heauenly sighs and desires: for that is indeed to pray. It is the very first thing that the childe of God doeth, inwardly to sigh and desire reconciliation with God in Christ: and hee which cannot doe this, is not as yet borne of God.

Againe, many are cast downe in themselues, because they see their minds full of ignorance, their wils ful of rebellion, and subiect to many temptations; and they finde little goodnes in themselues, but they must be comforted by this: if they can but groane & sigh vnto God in their hearts for mercy and forgiuenesse, they haue the spirit of God crying in them, *Abba*; and they haue receiued the first fruits of the spirit. The desires and cries of our hearts are fruits of the intercession, or crie of the Sonne of God in heauen for vs.

Others are grieued, because they haue prayed long, and they finde not the fruite of their prayers: but if they can pray, sighing and groaning in their hearts for grace and mercy, let them be content: for it is the spirit of grace and praier, that makes them sigh and groane. And euery sigh of a contrite heart, hath a loude crie in the eares of God.

It falls out often, that men in extremitie of danger confounded in themselues, know not what in the world to say, or doe. *Ezechias* in his sickenesse could not say any thing, but chatter in his throat, and mourne like a doue, *Isa.* 38. 14. Some lie vnder the sword of the enemie, others in a tempest are cast ouer shipboard into the sea. Now this must be their comfort, if they can lift vp their hearts vnto God, if they can but sigh and groane for his presence & assistance, the Lord will heare the petition of their hearts: for the inward sobs, groanes, and sighs of repentant sinners, are loud and strong cries in the eares of God the Father.

The third point is, That the crie of the spirit is directed to God, because *it makes vs crie, Abba, Father*. Here first obserue, that prayer to Saints and Angels, is carnall prayer. For the prayer which is caused by the spirit, is direct to the Father. And good reason: for it is the propertie of God to heare the crie of the heart, *Romanes* 8.27. Some say, that the Saints in heauen are with God, and that in him they see the desires of our hearts: but it is false which they say. For the Scripture saith, that *God alone searcheth the heart*, 1. *Kings* 8.39. None knowes what is in man, but God, and the spirit of man, 1. *Cor*. 2.11. Though *Abraham* had the sight of God, yet is it said, *Thou art our Father, and Abraham knowes vs not*, *Isai*. 64.16. And for this cause, Inuocation of Saints, whether it be called *Latria*, or *Dulia*, is flat idolatrie.

Againe, Prayer is to bee made to God as he hath reuealed himselfe in the word; that is, to God, who is the Father of Christ, and in him our Father, who also sends his spirit into our hearts, crying, *Abba*. It is an heathenish practise (which is also the practise of many among vs) to pray to an absolute God, that is, to God out of the Father, Sonne, and holy Spirit.

Thirdly, here we see that true and spirituall Inuocation of God, is a marke of the Church of God: because it is a fruite of the spirit of God in them that are the children of God. And by this the people of God are noted, *Act*. 9.14. 1. *Cor*. 1.2. and on the contrary, it is the marke of an Atheist not to pray, *Psal*. 14.4.

The last poynt is, the manner of directing our cries to God. First of all, they are to bee directed to him with reuerence, as beeing present with vs: for to crie *Abba*, is not to speake words into the ayre, but to direct our hearts to one that is present with vs, in all dutifull and childlike manner. Thus did *Dauid*, *Psalme* 119. 58. and *Paul*, *Ephes*. 3.14. Secondly, our cries are to be directed to God with subiection to his will. Reade the example of Christ, *Marke* 14.36. and of *Dauid*, 2. *Samuel* 15.26. This condemnes the practise of many men. *Balaam* desired to die the death of the righteous, but without subiection to God: for hee would not liue the life of the righteous. And many among vs haue often good motions and desires in their minds, but there is no soundnesse in them: because they are not ioyned with a change and conuersion of heart and life. Thirdly, our desires are to be directed vnto God with importunitie and inconstancie. For the Spirit makes vs crie *Abba*, Father: that is, My Father, and thy Father. God requires this impotunitie of vs, *Luke* 18.1. It is practised by *Dauid*, *Psalme* 69.4. by the woman of Canaan, *Matth*. 15. We must doe as *Iacob* did, wrastle with God, and giue him no rest till he fulfill the desires of our hearts, and giue vs the blessing. And our constant desires

and

and groanes to heauen for mercie, ſhall neuer bee in vaine. For if wee aske any thing according to his will, hee heareth vs indeed, 1. *Iohn* 5. 14.

Verſe 7.

These words are the concluſion of the former doctrine of *Paul.* The time of your libertie is come, in that your libertie is procured and purchaſed by Chriſt, and ye haue receiued the ſpirit of ſonnes crying, *Abba*: therefore ye are not ſeruants to the law, but ſonnes of God. And from this concluſion *Paul* deriues a ſecond, which is the ſumme and ſubſtance of the whole diſputation, from the beginning of the third chapter to this place; namely, that they which are ſonnes, as alſo heires, not by the law and the workes thereof, but by Chriſt.

This verſe is a repetition of the 26. and 29. verſes of the third Chapter: therefore I will not ſtand any longer in the handling of it.

One thing is to bee obſerued, namely, the change of the number. *Paul* ſaid before, *yee are ſonnes*: here hee ſaith, *thou art a ſonne.* And this hee doeth, to teach vs, that they which turne to God, and beleeue in Chriſt, muſt bee aſſured that they are the ſonnes and heires of God. *Paul* hath ſet downe immediatly before, the infallible ſigne, whereby a man may know himſelfe to bee the childe of God: therefore in the next wordes hee ſaith; that thou art the ſonne of God. Saint *Iohn* ſaith, *Theſe things wee write vnto you that beleeue, that yee may know that yee haue life euerlaſting*, 1. *Iohn* 5. 13. Thus muſt euery beleeuer apply the Goſpel, and the benefits thereof to himſelfe.

The meditation of this point ſerues greatly to ſweeten all croſſes vnto vs: for if we know that we be Gods children, that is comfort enough; and wee may then aſſure our ſelues, that in euery croſſe, God comes vnto vs as a father. Againe, this meditation workes a contentation in euery loſſe. For if thou be the child of God, thou canſt haue no great loſſe. *For all things are thine, thou Chriſts, and Chriſt Gods*, 1. *Cor.* 3. 22. Laſtly, this meditation muſt ſtirre vp in vs a care to leade a heauenly and ſpiritual life, 1. *Iohn* 3. 3. that we may be like our eldeſt brother Chriſt Ieſus.

8 *But euen then when yee knew not God, ye did ſeruice vnto them, which by nature are not Gods.*

9 *But now ſeeing yee know God, or rather are knowne of*

God, how turne ye againe vnto impotent and beggarly rudiments,
whereunto as from the beginning, ye will be in bondage againe?
10 *Ye obserue dayes, and moneths, and times, and yeares.*
11 *I am in feare of you, lest I haue bestowed labour on you*
in vaine.

Heere *Paul* returnes againe to the principall conclusion of the whole Epistle, which is on this maner. If I *Paul* be called to teach, and my doctrine be true: yee haue done euill to reuolt from it to another Gospel: but I am called to teach, and my doctrine is true: this *Paul* prooued in the first, second, and third chapters. Therfore ye haue done euill to reuolt from my doctrine. This conclusion he propounded before, and heere againe he repeates it: and withall amplifies it two waies. First, by setting downe the particular matter of the reuolt and apostasie of the Galatians, v. 9. 10. *Yee returne to impotent rudiments: yee obserue daies and times.* Secondly, hee sets downe the greatnesse of their reuolt: first, by comparison thus: Once ye serued false gods: but there is some excuse of that offence: because ye did not know God: but that yee haue returned to the rudiments of the world, there is no excuse of it: for ye then knew God, or rather were known of God. Againe, he sets forth the greatnesse of their reuolt, by the effect, verse 11. It makes me feare lest I haue lost my labour among you.

Heere *Paul* sets downe a threefold estate of the Galatians: their estate in Gentilisme before their conuersion, their estate in their conuersion, and their estate in their apostasie.

Their estate in Gentilisme stands in two things: Ignorance of God [*then yee knew not God.*] Idolatry or superstition, *yee serued them which are not Gods by nature.*

Touching their ignorance of God, it may be demaunded, how they can bee said not to know God, whereas *Paul* saith, *that which may be knowen of God, is made manifest vnto the Gentiles? Rom.* 1. 20. and *that God did not leaue himselfe without witnesse? Actes* 14. 17. *Answer.* Knowledge of God is twofold, *Naturall*, or *reuealed knowledge. Naturall* is, that which all men haue in their mindes by the light of nature, which also they may gather by the view and obseruation of the creatures. This knowledge hath two properties. The first, it is imperfect: because by it wee know some few and generall things of God: as namely, that there is a God, and that he is to bee worshipped, &c. In this respect, this knowledge is like the ruines of a princely palace. Againe, it is weake: because it serues onely to cut off excuse, and it is not sufficient to direct vs in the worship

of

of God. Nay,when by it we beginne to set downe the worship of God, wee then runne headlong into superstition and vanitie. *Reuealed knowledge* is, that which is set downe in the written word, whereby wee may know what God is in himselfe, and what hee is to vs: namely,a Father in Christ,giuing pardon of sinne, and life euerlasting. This knowledge the Gentiles altogether want: nay, by reason of the blindnesse and impotency of their mindes, they iudge it foolishnesse. Thus then in effect, though the Gentiles by nature know some things of God, yet doe they not know God,as he will be knowen of vs.

Againe,it may be demanded,whether this ignorance be a sinne in the Galatians? *Answer.* Yea. For all men are bound to know God by the first Commandement. And this ignorance is a want of the image of God in the mind,*Col.* 3.10. And euery defect of the image of God,is a branch of originall sinne. And vengeance is the punishment of this sinne, 2.*Thess.*1.8.

It may bee obiected, that *Paul* heere excuseth the Galatians by their ignorance. *Answer.* It excuseth *à tanto, non à toto*, that is, the degree and measure of the sinne, and not the sinne it selfe, *Luke* 12.48.

Againe,it may be said,that this their ignorance is inuincible,because as the Gentiles doe not know God, so they cannot know him. *Answer.* That they cannot know him, it is not Gods fault, but the fault of their first parents, and consequently their fault: and this ignorance spreads it selfe ouer all mankind,as a punishment of the first offence.

The third point is,that this ignorance is a great and grieuous sinne: for here *Paul* makes it *the mother of superstition* and idolatry. This must teach vs all to detest this ignorance of God and his wil, and to seeke by all meanes to know God. God hath a controuersie with men,because they know him not, *Hosea* 4.1.6.

Againe,this serues to warne all Ministers of the word to be carefull to root out ignorance out of the mindes of the people, and to plant the knowledge of God. And by this we see,it is false which the Papist teacheth,that *Ignorance is the mother of deuotion.*

The second sinne of the Galatians is, that *they serued them,which are not Gods by nature*, that is, false gods, not gods indeed,but gods in opinion.

It may be obiected,that the wisest of the Gentiles worshipped the true God, creatour of heauen and earth. *Answer.* False gods are set vp two wayes. The first is, when that which is not God, is placed,and worshipped in the roome of the true God,as when the

Sunne, Moone, and Starres are worſhipped, &c. and this is the groſſeſt kinde of idolatrie. The ſecond is, when men acknowledge the true God, but doe not conceiue him, as he will bee conceiued, and as he hath reuealed himſelfe in the word. In this reſpect the Epheſians are ſaid to be *without God*, *Epheſ.* 3.12. and the Samaritanes to worſhip *they knew not what*, *Iohn* 4.22. For they conceiued the true God in a falſe manner, becauſe they conceiued him foorth of the Father, Sonne, and holy Ghoſt: and therefore they ſet vp a falſe god vnto themſelues. Falſe worſhip giuen to God, preſuppoſeth a falſe opinion of God: and a falſe opinion of God ſets vp an idole, or falſe god, in the roome of the true God. For it is not ſufficient to conceiue ſome true things of God, but wee muſt preciſely conceiue him, as hee hath reuealed himſelfe, without addition or detraction. And thus did the wiſeſt of the Galatians worſhip falſe gods.

This Idolatrie is a common ſinne, and bred (as it were) in the bone. The Turkes at this day worſhip a falſe and fained God. For they conceiue and worſhip a God creatour of heauen and earth, that is neither Father, Sonne, nor holy Ghoſt: and the Iewes worſhip God out of Chriſt: and ſo a fained God. For, *hee which hath not the Sonne, hath not the Father*, 1. *Iohn* 2. Likewiſe the religion of the Papiſt teacheth and maintaineth the worſhip of falſe gods. For it giues to Angels and Saints a facultie or power to know the deſires of our hearts, to heare and helpe vs in all places, at all times: and hereupon prayer is made to them: but all this is indeed the prerogatiue and priuiledge of the true God: and in as much as it is giuen to Angels and Saints departed, they are ſet vp in the roome of the true God.

Againe, that religion teacheth men to worſhip God, in, at, and before Images. And this worſhip preſuppoſeth an opinion or imagination that there is a God that will bee preſent to heare and helpe vs, in, at, and before Images: now this God is a God deuiſed by the braine of man. Papiſts alleadge, that their intention is to worſhip the true God, the Father, Sonne, and Holy Ghoſt. And I ſay againe, that the true God hath reuealed his will that hee doeth deteſt this manner of worſhip: and therefore the worſhip is directed either to the images themſelues, or to the god deuiſed in the braine.

Thirdly, they of the Popiſh religion worſhip a fained Chriſt of their owne deuiſing: namely, a Chriſt that ſits at the right hand of the Father in heauen, and is withall in the hands of euery Prieſt, after the words of conſecration. And they worſhip a God ſet vp by them-

themſelues,namely,a God that will bee appeaſed by humane ſatiſfactions,and at whoſe hands a ſinnefull man may merit euerlaſting life,that is to ſay,a God all of mercy,and little or no iuſtice.

Though our religion teach no Idolatrie, yet certaine it is, that many among vs practiſe a ſpirituall idolatrie in their hearts. For looke what a man loues moſt, and cares moſt for, and delights moſt in,that is his God; ſome therefore haue their riches for their God, ſome their pleaſures, ſome their beaſtly luſtes. For where the heart is,there is thy God. Againe,the ignorant multitude worſhip a God of their owne coyning,which is a God made all of mercie, and no iuſtice. For they perſwade themſelues, that there is mercie with God, though they repent not, but goe on in their ſinnes: whereas the true God is infinite,not onely in mercie, but alſo in iuſtice, *Exod.*34.

That this ſinne of Idolatrie may be rooted out of the minds of men,there muſt be firſt an *Illumination* of the mind,with the knowledge of the true God and his will: and there muſt alſo be a *renouation* of the heart and affections, that they ſet not vp ſomething elſe in the roome of God.

The eſtate of the Galatians after their conuerſion is in theſe words, *Ye know God,or rather are knowen of God.*

The knowledge wherby men know God, is either *literall knowledge*, or *ſpirituall knowledge*. *Literall*, is when the doctrine of God, and his will is knowen, without reformation of life. *Spiritual knowledge*, is when the minde is inlightened by the Spirit of God, with the knowledge of God, by the word, and according to the word; ſo as thereupon men are transformed into the image of God, 2. *Cor.* 3.18. And this kind of knowledge is here meant, when *Paul* ſaith, *Ye know God.*

The foundation of this knowledge is, that God is to be known in Chriſt, for in him God hath manifeſted his infinite wiſdome, iuſtice, mercy. Therefore is he called *the ingrauen image of the perſon of the Father*, *Heb.* 1.2. and *Paul* ſaith, that *we haue the knowledge of the glory of God, in the face of Ieſus Chriſt.* 2.*Cor.*3.6.

The properties of this knowledge are three. The firſt is, that it muſt be a ſpeciall knowledge, whereby we muſt acknowledge God to be our God in Chriſt. The firſt commandement of the law requires, that we take the true God for our God. The cõmandement of Chriſt is, *Beleeue the Goſpel.* Now the ſtipulation of the couenant of grace (which alſo is the ſubſtance of the Goſpel) is this, *I am thy God*, *Ier.*31.33. this therefore muſt we beleeue. And to this knowledge is the promiſe of life euerlaſting annexed, *Ioh.*17.3. *Iſa.*53.11.

The ſecond propertie is, that this knowledge muſt not bee confuſed, but diſtinct. Firſt, we muſt acknowledge the true God in reſpect of his preſence with vs in all places. Thus *Moſes* is ſaid *to know the inuiſible*, *Heb.* 11.27. Secondly, we muſt know and acknowledge God in reſpect of his particular prouidence ouer vs. Thus *Dauid* knew God, when hee ſaid that *hee numbred his flittings, and put his teares into his bottle*, *Pſal.* 56.8. Thirdly, wee muſt know God in reſpect of his will, in all things to bee done, and to bee ſuffered: and this is the right knowledge of God, to haue regard to his will, *Romanes* 12.2. *Epheſ.* 5.17. *Dauid* ſaith, *All thy lawes are before mee*, 2. *Samuel* 22.23. And when *Shimei* reuiled, hee ſpake thus, *Hee raileth, becauſe God biddes him raile*, 2. *Samuel.* 16.10. Laſtly, we muſt know, and acknowledge God in the power which hee ſhewed in the death and reſurrection of Chriſt. Reade and conſider *Epheſians* 1.17. where *Paul* placeth the knowledge of God in two things, in the knowledge of the riches of eternall life, and in an experimentall knowledge of the vertue of the reſurrection of Chriſt in our ſelues.

The third propertie is, that this knowledge muſt be an effectual and liuely knowledge, working in vs new affections and inclinations. *Hee that ſaith hee knowes God, and keepes not his commaundements, makes him a liar*, 1. *Iohn* 2.4. and 3.6. *Titus* 2. laſt.

The vſe. Seeing the conuerſion of a ſinner ſtands in this ſpirituall knowledge of God, wee muſt bee ſtirred vp to ſeeke to know God according as he will be knowen of vs. We deſire to ſerue God: and we cannot ſerue him, vnleſſe wee know him: nay, ſo long as we know him not, we doe nothing but ſerue the falſe gods of our owne hearts. Againe, we deſire life eternall: and this is life, in right maner to acknowledge God, *Iohn* 17.3. And the whole matter of our boaſting, muſt be the knowledge of God, *Iere.* 9.24. God himſelfe miniſtreth vnto me a further argument to mooue you to this deſire: namely, by the moouing of the earth yeſterday. For though Philoſophers aſcribe all to nature, yet the truth is, that the trembling and ſhogging of the earth, is a ſigne of the great and extraordinary anger of God. The cauſe of this anger is, that we know not God, neither doe we for the moſt part care to know him. We haue had the Goſpel long, but we bring forth but ſmall fruits. For this cauſe the earth in his trembling, doth as it were groane to bee diſburdened of ſo rebellious a nation; and it doeth after a ſort craue leaue of God, that it may deuoure a ſinfull people, as it once deuoured *Dathan*, and the company of *Abiram*. Now our dutie is, in this iudgement of God to acknowledge his maieſtie, his anger, and his

iuſtice,

iuſtice;and with feare and trembling to humble our ſelues for our ſinnes paſt,therby to preuent his anger to come. The earth a bruit and dumbe creature in his kind,is become a preacher vnto vs: and his trembling muſt teach vs to tremble in our hearts,and to ſinne no more.

Againe, if wee muſt know God, wee muſt remember God, and Chriſt: and as wee muſt know God,ſo muſt wee remember him. Now we muſt not know Chriſt according to the fleſh, 2.*Cor.*5.17. and therfore we may not remember Chriſt according to the fleſh, that is,in any worldly and carnall maner. This therefore is not to keepe a memory of Chriſt,to ſpend twelue daies in reuell and riot, in masking and mumming, in carding and dicing (as many doe:) this is rather to burie the memorie of Chriſt, and to doe homage to the god of pleaſure. Of them that ſaid, *Let vs eate, drinke, and ſleepe*, *Paul* ſaith thus: *Awake and doe righteouſly: for ſome of you do not know God*, 1.*Cor.*15.34.

Paul ſaith further, *But rather ye are knowne of God.* The knowledge whereby God knowes men, ſtands in two things; his election of them to his ſpeciall loue, 2.*Tim.* 1.19. and the execution of election, wherby he makes men his peculiar people, by calling, iuſtifying and ſanctifying of them, *Titus* 2.14.

Hence obſerue: firſt, that Gods Election is the root of all the gifts of God in vs. Wee know God, becauſe hee firſt knowes vs. *Paul* ſaith, that *wee were elected, that wee might bee holy*, *Epheſ.* 1.4. Therefore wee are not elected (as ſome teach) either for our faith, or according to our faith, but to our faith, that is, elected that wee might beleeue.

Secondly, hence we learne, that wee can neither thinke, will, or doe that which is good, vnleſſe God preuent vs with his grace. God muſt firſt vouchſafe to acknowledg vs, before we can acknowledg him, *Iohn* 10.14. Preuenting grace is twofold. The firſt, and the ſecond. The firſt, when God in our firſt conuerſion takes away the ſtony heart, and puts a fleſhy heart in the roome. The ſecond is, after we are regenerate: for then God ſtil preuents vs with good motions and deſires. Of both, reade *Ezech.*36.26. Some teach, that if we doe that which wee can, God will giue vs his grace: but this is falſe: for then we ſhould preuent God.

Thirdly, by this we ſee, that the workes of grace in God imprint their image in the hearts of them that belong to God. And this is worth the marking. There is a knowledge in God whereby hee knowes who are his: and this knowledge brings foorth another knowledge in vs, whereby wee know God for our God. There is

an

an Election in God which workes in the Elect an other Election, whereby they choose God for their God. The loue, whereby God loues vs, workes in vs an other loue whereby we loue God. 1. *Ioh.* 4. 19. Christ first apprehends vs: and this apprehension of his, works in vs the apprehension of faith, whereby we lay hold vpon him. *Phil.* 3. 12. When Christ makes intercession for vs in heauen, there is another intercession wrought in our hearts by the spirit, *whereby we crie Abba father, Rom.* 8. 26. The death of Christ hath a vertue in it, to worke in vs the death of sinne. Thus doth the Spirit of God seale vs to the day of our redemption. By this may we know that we belong to God, if we finde any impression of the grace of God in vs. The Sunne by his light shines vpon vs, and by the same light we view and behold the Sunne.

Lastly, here is the foundation of true comfort. Our faith doth not saue vs, because it is a perfect vertue: but because it apprehends a perfect obiect; namely, the perfect obedience of Christ. So then, if our faith erre not in his obiect, but be rightly fixed on the true causes of our saluation, though it be but a weake faith, and doe no more but cause vs to will, desire, and indeauour to apprehend Christ, it is true faith, and iustifieth: the weakenesse of it shall not hinder our saluation, which stands not in this, that we know God, but in this, that God knowes vs, whose knowledge is perfect and cannot faile. Againe, our saluation stands not in our apprehension of Christ, but in Christs apprehending of vs. *Phi.* 3. 12.

This knowledge of God whereby he knowes vs, hath two properties. Frist, it is speciall, whereby he knowes all the elect euen by name. *Exod.* 33. 17. Againe, it is a perpetuall and vnchangeable knowledge. For whom God once knowes, he neuer forgets, *Isai*, 49. 15.

The third estate of the Galatians is their estate in their reuolt or Apostasie, in these words, *How turne yee againe to impotent and beggarly rudiments, whereunto as from the beginning yee will bee in bondage againe?* or thus, *to which yee will doe seruice againe as from the beginning.*

The words carrie this sense: *How turne ye againe?* that is, it is an intollerable offence in you, hauing knowne God, to returne againe to the rudiments of the law. By *rudiments* we are to vnderstand Circumcision, the Iewish Sacrifices, and all the ceremonies of the law of *Moses*. And it may not seeme strange, that they are called impotent and beggarly rudiments. For they must bee considered three waies, with Christ, without Christ, and against Christ. With Christ, when they are consideredas types and figures of Christ to

come,

come,and as signes of grace by diuine institution for the time of the old Testament. Without Christ,when they are vsed onely for custome, whether before or after the death of Christ. Against Christ, when they are esteemed as meritorious causes of saluation, and the iustification of a sinner is placed in them,either in whole or in part : as though Christ alone were not sufficient. In this respect *Paul* calls them impotent and beggarly rudiments.

And *Paul* hauing said,that the Galatians returned againe to the rudiments of the law;in the next words he shewes how they doe it: namely, by *seruing them againe.* They serued or yeelded seruice to them three waies : In opinion,because they iudged them to be necessary parts of Gods worship, and meanes of their saluation. In Conscience : because they subiected their consciences to them. In affection, because they placed part of their affiance in them for their iustification and saluation.

It may be demanded, how the Galatians can be said to returne againe to the rudiments of the law, and serue them againe,that were neuer vsed to them before? *Answer.* In the speech of *Paul* there is that which is called *Catachresis*,that is,a kinde of speaking somewhat improper in respect of finenesse and elegancie. The like we haue,*Ruth* 1 22. when *Ruth* is said to returne to Iudea with *Naomi*;and yet she was neuer there before. Neuerthelesse,the speech in sense is most significant and proper. For *Paul* (no doubt) signifies hereby,that when the Galatians subiected themselues to the rudiments of the law,& placed their saluation in part euen in them, they did in effect and in trueth as much as returne againe to their old superstitions,and serue againe their false gods.

Heere then wee haue a description of the apostasie of the Galatians. It is a voluntarie sinne (for *Paul* saith,*yee will serue*)after the knowledge of the trueth, in which they returne againe to the rudiments of the law,by yeelding subiection, and seruice to them: which acte of theirs is indeed as much as if they had serued againe their false gods. Heere some may say, if this bee so, then they sinned against the Holy Ghost. *Answer.* The sinne against the holy Ghost,is indeed a voluntary sinne: but that is by reason of the obstinacy and malice of the will : and this offence in the Galatians was voluntary onely by infirmitie. Againe,the sinne against the holy Ghost, is an vniuersall apostasie, in respect of all the Articles of religion: for that sinne makes men crucifie Christ crucified, *Hebrewes* 6.5. and to tread vnder foot the Sonne of God: the apostasie of the Galatians was particular onely in the article of iustification.

The vſe. In that the Ceremonies of the law ſet vp againſt Chriſt,in the cauſe of our iuſtification and ſaluation, are called impotent and beggarly rudiments, *Paul* teacheth a weightie concluſion: That Chriſt ſtands alone in the worke of redemption, without collegue or partner, without deputie,or ſubſtitute,whether we reſpect the whole worke of redemption, or the leaſt part of it. Againe, that all the workes of mediation ſtand alone by themſelues, and admit nothing to be added and adioyned to them: *There is no other name whereby wee can bee ſaued beſide the name of Chriſt, Act.4.12. Chriſt ſaues them perfectly that come vnto him, Hebrew.7.25. In him wee are compleate, Coloſſ.2.10. Hee alone treads the wine preſſe of Gods wrath, and none with him, Iſai.* 63.3.If Chriſt be a Sauiour,he muſt be a perfect Sauiour, conſidering he is God and man: and being a perfect Sauiour in himſelfe,he needs no partner, and becauſe he is euery where at all times, therefore he needs no deputie in his ſtead. Againe, euery worke of redemption is acted by whole Chriſt,according to both his natures: and as there are in him two natures, ſo are there two operations of the ſaid natures: and as both natures concurre to make one perſon, ſo the operations of both natures concurre to make the compound worke of a Mediatour,which is an admirable worke,not meerely humane, but *theandricke*,that is,*humane-diuine*. For this cauſe no action pertaining to redemption,can be performed by a meere creature,whether man or Angel.

Obiection I. Ioh. 20. 23. The Apoſtles haue the power to remit and retaine ſinnes: therefore it is not proper to Chriſt. *Anſw.* To remit by meriting and by efficacie in the conferring of pardon, is proper to the Mediatour. The Apoſtles and other Miniſters remit by preaching and by declaring remiſſion. The Miniſters of the word doe not procure our reconciliation with God as Chriſt doth, but they exhort men to be reconciled to God. 2.*Cor.*5.20.

Obiect. II. 1.*Pet.* 3.18. *Baptiſme ſaueth*: therefore not Chriſt alone. *Anſw.* Baptiſme faueth by ſignifying and by ſealing vnto vs the grace and mercie of God: and the effecting of our ſaluation, is in the ſame place aſcribed to Chriſt and his reſurrection.

The concluſion then of *Paul* is to be remembred: for it ſerues as an engyne to ouerturne the maine grounds of poperie. The primacie of the Pope is a certen eſtate in which he is ſubſtituted into the place and roome of Chriſt: for hee takes vpon him to make lawes that properly and truly binde conſcience, euen as the lawes of God. Againe, he takes vnto him a proper and iudiciall power, to remit or retaine the ſinnes of men. Now theſe actions indeed, are

are the proper actions of God and Chriſt, no meere creature is capable of them. In this reſpect the primacy of the Pope is an impotent and beggarly inuention. Againe, the Romiſh religion beſide the all-ſufficient oblation of Chriſt vpon the croſſe, ſets vp the ſacrifice of the maſſe for the ſinnes of the quicke and the dead: beſides the Interceſſion of Chriſt, it ſets vp the Interceſſion of Saints and Angels: beſide the perfect ſatisfaction of Chriſt, it ſets vp humane ſatisfactions: beſide the infinite merit of Chriſt, it maintaines and magnifies the merit of humane workes. But all theſe are but impotent and beggarly deuices of men. For Chriſt in his Sacrifice, Satisfaction, Interceſſion, Merit, admits no corriuall or aſſociate. All actions of his are perfect in their kind, and need no ſupply.

This againe muſt teach vs, to content our ſelues with Chriſt alone, and not to ſet vp any thing with him, or againſt him. This is the ſafeſt and the ſureſt courſe. A certaine Papiſt writeth to this effect, that we Proteſtants in our iuſtification, cleaue onely to the body of the tree, and that the Papiſts cleaue both to the body and the branches. And I ſay againe, it is the ſafeſt with both the hands to cleaue to the body of the tree: and he that with on hand laies hold vpon the body of the tree, and with the other ſtaies himſelfe vpon the branches, is in great danger of falling.

The ſecond concluſion of *Paul* is, that to ſet vp any thing out of Chriſt, as a meritorious cauſe of ſaluation, and to place our iuſtification in it, either in whole or in part, is indeede the ſeruice of Idols. And the reaſon is plaine. For this is to ſet vp ſomething in the place and roome of Chriſt: and men put a confidence in that which they make a cauſe of their owne ſaluation.

The doctrine then of Iuſtification by workes, is a doctrine that maintaines idolatry: for if they iuſtifie, we may put our truſt in them: and if we put our confidence in them, we make idols of them. That works may merit at Gods hand, they muſt not onely be ſanctified, but alſo deified.

The diſtinction vſed of the Papiſts, of *Latria*, and *Dulia*, that is, of *worſhip, and ſeruice*, falls to the ground. They ſay they giue *worſhip* to God, and *ſeruice* to Angels and Saints. It is a toy. For here *Paul* condemnes the *very ſeruice* to the heathen Gods: and the ſeruice of the rudiments of the law, is the Apoſtaſie of the Galatians. And to giue ſeruice, or worſhip to any thing, are all one.

The third concluſion of *Paul* is, that they which haue giuen their names to God, and Chriſt, muſt not returne to any thing that they haue forſaken, or ought to forſake. He that puts his hand to the plough, muſt not looke backe: he that goes to the land of Canaan,muſt not looke backe to Egypt. Wee in England haue beene long deliuered from the ſuperſtition of Popery,and we muſt not ſo much as dreame of any returne. It is a common fault among vs,that in outward profeſſion we cleaue to the world, and walke after the luſts of our owne hearts. This is in ſhew to goe forward, but in deede to turne backe againe. But our duty is, in thought,conſcience,will,affection,word,and deede,to goe on forward,and no way to goe backe.

Verſe 10.

In the former verſe,*Paul* ſets downe the Apoſtaſie of the Galatians in generall tearmes,ſaying, *How turne you againe to the Elements of the world?* In the 10. verſe,he ſhewes,what theſe Elements be,*Yee obſerue daies,and moneths, and times, and yeares.* By *daies*, are meant Iewiſh Sabbaths: by *moneths*,the feaſts obſerued euery moneth in the day of the new moone. By *times*,ſome vnderſtand the feaſt of the Paſſeouer,the feaſt of Pentecoſt, and the feaſt of Tabernacles. But the word (καιροὺς) ſignifies,ſeaſons, or fit times for the doing of this or that buſines. So is it tranſlated, *Act.* 1.7. *It is not for you to know the times and ſeaſons.* It was the manner of the Gentiles to make difference of times in reſpect of good or bad ſucceſſe,and that according to the ſignes of heauen. And it is very likely,that the Galatians obſerued daies not onely in the Iewiſh, but alſo in the heatheniſh manner. By *yeares*,are meant euery ſeuenth yeare,& the Iubilie yeares, which the Galatians obſerued after the faſhion of the Iewes.

Againe, there is a fourefold kind of obſeruation of daies; one *Naturall*,the other *Ciuill*,the third *Eccleſiaſticall*,the fourth *Superſtitious*. *Naturall* is, when daies are obſerued according to the courſe of the Sunne and Moone, *Gen.* 1.14. Thus day followes night, and night followes day, and euery yeare hath foure ſeaſons, Spring,Sommer,Autumne,Winter. And the obſeruation of theſe times,is according to the law of nature. *Ciuill obſeruation* is, when ſet times are obſerued for husbandry,in planting, ſetting,reaping, ſowing: for houſhold affaires, and for the affaires of the common-wealth,in keeping of faires,and markets,&c. And thus to obſerue daies,is not vnlawfull. *Eccleſiaſticall obſeruation* of times is, when ſet daies are obſerued for orders ſake,that men may come together to worſhip God: theſe daies,are either daies of thankſgiuing or dayes of humiliation. Of daies of thankſgiuing,take the example of the Iewes,*Heſt.*9.26. who obſerued yearely the feaſt of *Purim*,for a memory of their deliuerance. In like manner they appointed and obſerued the feaſt of *Dedication*: and it ſeemes that Chriſt was preſent

at

at Ieruſalem, as an obſeruer of this feaſt, *Ioh.*10.22. And thus for orders ſake, to obſerue certaine daies of ſolemnity, is not forbidden. *Superſtitious obſeruation* of dayes is twofold, *Iewiſh, or Heatheniſh, Iewiſh,* when ſet dayes are obſerued with an opinion, that we are bound in conſcience to obſerue them, and when the worſhip of God is placed in the obſeruing of this or that time. *Heatheniſh,* when dayes are obſerued in reſpect of good or bad ſucceſſe. Now then to come to the point, the intent of *Paul* is onely to condemne the Iewiſh manner of obſeruing dayes, in theſe words. *Ye obſerue dayes, moneths, and yeares:* and the Heatheniſh manner in theſe words, *Ye obſerue ſeaſons.*

Againſt this interpretatiou, the place of *Paul* may be obiected *Rom.*14.6. *He that obſerues the day, obſerues it to the Lord. Anſ.* Indeede *Paul* in theſe words excuſeth the Romanes that obſerued daies, and ſaith, that their intention was to obſerue them to the honour of God: and this he ſaith, becauſe as yet they were not fully inſtructed touching Chriſtian libertie: but withall, let it be remembred, that in mild ſort he notes this to be a fault in them, when he ſaith, that *they were weake in faith.* Now the caſe was otherwiſe with the Galatians: becauſe they obſerued dayes after they had beene informed touching their libertie in Chriſt: and withall, they placed their ſaluation, in part, in the obſeruation of dayes: and thus they mixed the Goſpell with the law. And therefore they were iuſtly to be blamed.

Againe, it may be obiected, that now in the time of the new Teſtament, we in religious manner obſerue *the Lords day. Anſw.* Some men both godly and learned, are of opinion, that *the Lords day* was appointed by the Apoſtles for order ſake: and that it is in the libertie of the Church to appoint the Sabbath vpon any other day in the weeke, becauſe, they ſay, all daies without exception are equall: and they adde further, that when the publike worſhip of God is ended, men may then returne to their labours, or giue themſelues to recreation on the Lords day. But this doctrine ſeemes not to ſtand with the fourth commandement.

It ſeemes to bee a truth more probable, that euery ſeuenth day in the weeke, muſt bee ſet apart in holy reſt vnto God: for this is the ſubſtance of the fourth Commandement. And it is alſo very probable, that the Sabbath of the New Teſtament, is limited and determined by our Sauiour Chriſt to *the Lords day.* For *Paul* and the reſt of the Apoſtles obſerued the firſt day of the weeke for a Sabbath day, *Actes* 20.7. and he ſaith, *Whatſoeuer yee haue heard, and what yee haue ſeene in me, that doe, Phil.*4.9. Againe, it was the decree or constitution of *Paul*, that the collection for the poore should be *the first day of the weeke* at Corinth: now this collection in the Primitiue Church, followed preaching, praier, Sacraments, and it was the conclusion of all other exercises in the assembly. 1. *Cor.* 16.2. And this first day of the weeke is called *the Lords day*. *Apoc.* 1.11. and it is so called, because it was dedicated and consecrated to the honour of Christ our Lord. And who is the author of this Dedication but Christ himselfe the Lord of the Sabboth? It is alledged, that the Sabbath, and the commandement louching the Sabbath, is Ceremoniall: and vpon this ground, they take liberty, and keepe no Sabbath at all. But the truth is, that the commandement touching the Sabbath is not wholly Ceremoniall. It may be, the first words, *Remember the Sabbath day to sanctifie it*, and the words, *In it thou shalt doe no manner of worke*, *&c.* are spoken of the Iewes Sabbath: but the words, *Sixe daies shalt thou labour, and the seuenth day is the Sabbath of the Lord thy God*, are morall, and containe a perpetuall truth. Therefore the words of *Paul* must be conceiued with an exception of the Sabbath day, which is the seuenth day in euery weeke; which day Christ hath limited by his Apostles, *to the Lords day*.

The vse. This text of *Paul* discouers vnto vs a great part of the superstition of the Popish Church, in the obseruation of holy daies. First, beside *the Lords day*, they appoint many other Sabbaths: whereas it is the priuiledge of God to appoint an ordinary day of rest, and to sanctifie it to his owne honour. Secondly, they binde mens consciences to the obseruation of their holy daies, which *Paul* here forbids, and *Col.* 2.16. Thirdly, they place the worship of God in the obseruation of their holy daies: but God is worshipped in vaine by mens precepts. *Math.* 15. Fourthly, they place a great holinesse in their festiuall dayes, more then in other daies. Fiftly, they dedicate many of their holy daies to the honour of Saints and Angels: whereas the dedication of ordinary and set daies, is a part of diuine or religious worship. Lastly, their holy daies for number are more then the festiuall daies of the Iewes: and thus they bring people into their old bondage, nay to a greater bondage then euer the Iewes indured, in respect of daies and times. It may be said, that the Church of the Protestants obserues holy daies. *Answ.* Some Churches doe not: because the Church in the Apostles daies, had no holy day, beside the Lords day: and the fourth commandement inioynes the labour of sixe daies. Indeede the Church of England obserueth holy daies, but the Popish superstition is cut off. For we are not bound in conscience to the obseruation of these

daies:

daies: neither doe we place holines or the worſhip of God in them: but we keepe them onely for orders ſake, that men may come to Church to heare Gods word. And though we retaine the names of Saints daies, yet we giue no worſhip to Saints, but to God alone. And ſuch daies as contained nothing in them but ſuperſtition, as the conception and aſſumption of the Virgin *Mary*, we haue cut off. Thus doth the Church with vs obſerue holy daies, and no otherwiſe. Indeede the ignorant multitude among vs faile greatly in the obſeruing of daies. For they greatly ſolemniſe the time of the birth of Chriſt, and then they keepe few or no markets: but *the Lords day* is not accordingly reſpected: and men will not bee diſſwaded from following of faires on that day.

Againe, to obſerue daies of good and bad ſucceſſe, according to the conſtellations of the heauens, is an heatheniſh faſhion to bee auoided. For it is here condemned in the Galatians. Here therefore, we muſt be put in minde, not to obſerue the planetarie houres: for men ſuppoſe that the houres of the day are ruled by the planets, and hereupon, that ſome houres are good, and luckie (as they ſay) and ſome vnluckie: that men are taken with planets, and borne vnder vnluckie planets. But theſe are heatheniſh conceits. Neither muſt we reſpect our *Horoſcope* or the time of our birth, and the conſtellation of the heauens then, as though we could hereby know, what ſhould befall vs to the end of our daies. And we muſt not put difference of daies, as though ſome were luckie vnto vs, and ſome vnluckie, according to the courſe of the ſtarres. The like I ſay of the Criticall daies, that is, the 7. and the 14. day after that a man begins to be ſicke. For they are grounded vpon the aſpects of the moone, which are not to be regarded. And the *Climacterical* yeares are not to be obſerued as dangerous and diſmall. The obſeruation of the ſignes, is of the ſame nature. For the 12. ſignes are nothing elſe, but 12. parts of the firſt mooueable, which is but a ſuppoſed heauen. Therefore there is no danger in the thing, but in our conceit. We are to feare God, and not to feare the ſtarres: neither are we to make differences of daies in reſpect of them, as though the affaires we take in hand, ſhould proſper the better or the worſe, in reſpect of their different operation. Gods commandement is, *Feare not the ſignes of heauen, Ierem.* 10. 1. And good reaſon. For no man can by learning know the operation of the ſtarres: becauſe their lights and operations are all mixt togither in all places vpon earth: and therfore no obſeruation can be made of this or that ſtarre, more then of this or that hearbe, when all hearbes are mixed and compounded togither. Againe, the operation of the ſtarres is by their light, and light hath no operation but in heate or cold, moisture or drinesse. In this respect, (though we may well obserue the full and the change of the moone) it is foolishnesse to ascribe the regiment of our affaires to the starres, they being matters contingent, which depend on the wil and pleasure of man. Lastly, it is a great ouersight to hold sundrie of the starres to be malignant and infortunate, in respect of vs: whereas they are the creatures of God, and their light serues for the good of man. In a word, we are not to make difference of daies, neither in respect of holines, nor in respect of good or badde successe.

Vers. 11. *I am afraid, &c.*

In these words, the Apostle sets forth the greatnesse of the Apostasie of the Galatians, by the effect thereof, which was to cause him to feare, least he had bestowed labour in vaine among them.

First the occasion of the words must be considered, and that is expressed in the former words, *ye obserue daies and moneths.* And hereupon he saith, *I am in feare of you.* And thus *Paul* teacheth, that works set vp as causes of saluation with Christ, make void the Ministery and grace of God. It may be said, this is meant of ceremoniall workes, and so it is true. I answer, it is indeed spoken of ceremoniall workes, but it must be inlarged to all workes without exception. For *Paul* saith, c. 5. v. 3. *If ye be circumcised, ye are bound to fulfill the whole law.* Hence then it followes, that the doctrine of iustification by workes, is an errour in the foundation, and being distinctly, and obstinately maintained, there is no hope of saluation.

Againe, here we see the fidelity of the Apostle *Paul*, and it stands in two things: the first is, his painefull and wearisome labour, to gaine the Galatians to God. The second is, his care that the foresaid labour be not in vaine. And in this example of his, we learne three things. The first, that they which are, or desire to be dispensers of the word, must doe it not for the belly, or for lucres sake, or for the praise of men, but simply for this ende, that they may gaine soules to God. The Scribe that would haue followed Christ for gaine, was repelled with this answer, that Christ *had not so much as a place where to lay his head, Math,* 8. 20. and to preach for by-respects, is to make a merchandise of the word of God, 2. *Cor.* 2. 17. The second is, that Ministers after the example of *Paul*, must be labourers indeed, 1. *Cor.* 3. 9. and workemen, 2. *Tim.* 2. 15. And they must shew themselues to be so, by their care and industry in winning soules to

God. And it is not sufficient now and then to make a discourse vpon a text. Thirdly, Ministers of the word must be watchmen. *Ezech*.3.14. and *Heb*.13.17. Their office is not onely to gaine and call men to God, but also to preserue and keepe them in Christ, which are already called.

Thirdly, here we see the condition of the Church of Galatia, and of all other visible Churches vpon earth, that they are subiect to Apostasie. It may be said, how can this be, considering true beleeuers cannot fall away? *Ans.* In the visible Church on earth, there are foure kinds of beleeuers. The first are they which heare the word without zeale, and they are like the stony ground. The second are they, which heare, know, and approoue the word. The third are they, which heare, know, and approoue the word, and haue a taste of the power thereof, and accordingly yeeld some outward obedience. The fourth are they, which heare, know, approoue, and keepe the word, in that they beleeue it, and are turned into the obedience of it. The three first may fall quite away, the fourth cannot. And by this meanes it comes to passe, that visible Churches vpon earth may fall away: because of them that professe the faith, three to one may vtterly fall away.

The vse. This must teach vs that are members of the visible Church, to feare and to suspect our selues: and not to content our selues, because we haue some good things in vs: but we must labour *to be sealed vp to the day of our redemption, and to lay vp a good foundation against the time to come.* 1.*Tim*.6.18. By seeking to haue in vs such good things, as are proper to the Elect, as vnfained faith in Christ, and conuersion to God from all our sinnes.

It may be demanded, how *Pauls* labour should be in vaine? *Ans.* It was in vaine in respect of his owne desire and affection to saue all the Galatians: secondly, it was in vaine, in respect of the whole body of that Church, whereof many were hypocrites. It was not in vaine in respect of the elect, nor in respect of the counsell of God, *Isa*.55.11.

Againe, it may be demanded, what must be done when the labours of our callings are in vaine? *Ans.* We must follow the calling and commandement of God, whether we haue good successe or no, and whatsoeuer come of it. *Paul* feares least his labour is in vaine, and yet he still labours. When *Peter* had laboured all night and caught nothing, he saith, at the commaundement of Christ, *In thy word will I cast out my net*, *Luk*. 5. And thus to doe, (whatsoeuer followes) is true wisedome, and the feare of God. For it must suffice vs, that the worke we take in hand is pleasing vnto

God. And though it bee in vaine, in respect of men, it is not so before God, *Isai.* 49.4. and 2. *Corinth.* 2.18. This must euery man remember in his place and calling, for the establishing of his mind against all euents.

12 *Bee you as I, for I am euen as you: I beseech you brethren: ye haue not hurt me at all.*

The words in this verse, to the 16. verse, are an answer to an obiection. The obiection is this, wee see now by these reproofes, that *Paul* hath changed his minde toward vs, and that hee hath turned his loue into hatred. The answer is, *Be as I, I am as you*: the speech is very effectuall and significant; and it is like the common prouerbe, *Amicus, alter ego, alter idem*, that is, *a mans friend is all one with himselfe.* The sense of the words is, *Be as I:* looke that your minds be not estranged from me, but tender me euen as your owne selues: for I *Paul* am the same that euer I was, I respect and tender you euen as mine owne selfe. And lest the Galatians should say, see ye not how *Paul* commands imperiously, *bee yee as I?* therefore he addes, *I beseech you brethren,* I command you not. In the next words he addes a reason of his answer, thus: Hatred presupposeth a hurt or wrong to be done: ye haue done me no hurt or wrong: therefore ye may not thinke that I hate you.

When *Paul* saith, *Be as I, I am as you*: we learne, that there must bee a speciall and mutuall loue betweene the teachers and the people. *Paul* saith, that he did *inlarge his heart for the Corinthians*, and he requires the like of them, 2.*Cor.*6.11,13. Teachers must shew their loue, by tendering the saluation of the people by all meanes, euen as their owne soules. *Paul* could haue found in his heart to haue beene accursed for his countreymen the Iewes, *Rom.*9.1. Hee desired that he might be offered vp as a drinke offering vpon the sacrifice of the faith of the Philippians, *Philip.*2.18. When the Israelites had sinned, *Moses* stands in the breach, as it were in the face of the Cannon, betweene the wrath of God and them, by his prayer to stay the iudgement of God, *Psalm.* 106.23. Againe, the people must shew their loue to their teachers; first, by praying for them, as for themselues, *Rom.*15.30. Secondly, by hauing in singular price the worke of the ministerie, 2.*Thess.*5.13. and that is, by wholsome doctrine to repaire the image of God, and to erect the kingdom of God in the hearts of men. When this thing is loued & desired, then are Ministers loued. This mutual loue is of great vse, it incourageth people to obey, & the preachers of the word to labour in teaching.

When *Paul* saith, *I beseech you brethren*, hee shewes what moderation is to be vsed in all reproofes. He tells the Galatians his minde plainly to the full: and withall he indeauours to shew his owne loue to them, and to keepe theirs.

It may be asked, how *Paul* can say, *Yee haue done me no hurt at all.* For when a beleeuer in Corinth committed incest, *Paul* tooke it for a wrong to himselfe? 2.*Cor*.2.10. And no doubt, to call the doctrine of the Apostle into question, was a great wrong vnto him. I answer, the wrong was no wrong in his estimation and affection, who was content to put vp, and to forgiue the wrong. Here wee see the meeknesse of *Paul*, in that he quietly beares the crosses and wrongs laid vpon him. The like was in *Moses*, who 40. yeares together indured the bad manners of the Israelites, *Actes* 13.18. but the perfect example of this vertue is in Christ, who saued them that crucified him. We likewise are to exercise our selues in this vertue. And that we may indeed so doe, we must first of all haue a sense of our spirituall pouertie, and a faith in the mercie, presence, and protection of God.

Againe, mark the mind of the Apostle, that he may winne soules to God, he is content to suffer any wrong. The Priests and Iesuites among vs in England, are content to venter life and limme, that they may winne Proselites to the Church of Rome: much more then must the true Ministers of the Gospell bee content with any condition, so they may gaine men to God. In this case hurts and abuses, must be no hurts nor abuses.

13 *And yee know how through the infirmitie of the flesh, I preached the Gospel vnto you at the first:*

14 *And the triall of mee which was in my flesh, yee despised not, neither abhorred: but receiued me as an Angel of God, yea, as Christ Iesus.*

15 *What then was your felicitie? for I beare you record, that if it had beene possible, you would haue plucked out your eyes to haue giuen them to mee.*

16 *Am I therefore become your enemie, because I tell you the truth.*

The answer to the obiection in the former verse, was this: *Be ye as I: I am as you.* And the reason was this: hatred presupposeth an offence: ye haue done me no offence or hurt: therefore ye may not thinke that I hate you. The *minor* is in the 12.verſe;the *concluſion* in the 16.verſe.

Againe, the *minor* [*Yee haue done mee no hurt*] is confirmed in the thirteene,fourteene,fifteene verſes. The ſumme of the argument is this: Though my outward condition was ſubiect to contempt;yet did the Galatians ſhew loue and reuerence to me: therfore ye did me no hurt. Againe,*Paul* ſets foorth both the parts of his argument. And firſt of all he deſcribes his owne condition,by three things: that he preached *in weakneſſe of the fleſh*: that he preached *the firſt*: that he preached *hauing the triall of himſelfe in his owne fleſh*. Secondly,the loue and reuerence of the Galatians is ſet out by three ſignes, or effects: *They deſpiſed him not; they receiued him as an Angel, or as Chriſt himſelfe: they would haue plucked out their eyes to haue done him good.*

The firſt thing in *Pauls* condition is, that *hee publiſhed the Goſpel in the infirmitie of his fleſh*,that is,in a meane and baſe eſtate, without the ſhew of humane wiſedome,and authority,and ſubiect to many miſeries. In this ſenſe *Paul* oppoſeth *infirmitie* to the excellencie of humane wiſedome, 1.*Corinth*.2.1.3. and vnder it he comprehends all the calamities and troubles that befell vnto him. 2.*Cor*.12.10.

This was the condition of the reſt of the Apoſtles.For they were but fiſhers, and preached the word in their fiſher-like ſimplicity. Nay,this was the condition of Chriſt himſelfe. For he hid the Maieſty of his Godhead vnder the veile of his fleſh: and his outward man was ſubiect to reproch,and contempt.*Iſa*.53.3. And this is the order of God. The word muſt be diſpenſed in the infirmity of mans fleſh for ſundry cauſes. Firſt,that we might not exalt our teachers aboue their condition, who are no more but inſtruments of grace. When the men of Derbe, and Liſtra,would haue offered ſacrifice to *Paul*,and *Barnabas*.*Paul* forbids them,ſaying,*that they were men ſubiect to the ſame paſſions with themſelues*,*Act*.14.15.The ſecond cauſe,that we might aſcribe the whole worke of our conuerſion not to men,but to God alone. 2.*Cor*.4.7.The third is,that God might by this meanes confound the wiſdome of the world,and cauſe men that would be wiſe, to become fooles, that they might be wiſe. 1.*Cor*.3.18. The laſt is,that we might be aſſured, that the doctrine of the Apoſtles is of God: becauſe it preuailes in the world without the ſtrength and policy of man.

And as the word is preached in weakeneſſe, ſo it is beleeued of men; and the grace of God is conferred to vs,and continued in vs, in the weakeneſſe of the fleſh. Gods loue is ſhedde abroad in the

hearts

hearts of men: but when? euen then, when we are in the midſt of manifold afflictions. *Rom.*5.2.5. *Paul beares about him the mortification of our Lord Ieſus,* not for his damnation, but *that the life of God might be manifeſt in his mortall fleſh.* 2. *Cor.*4.10. And he ſaith plainely, that the grace of God is made *perfect through weakneſſe.* 2. *Cor.* 12.9. By this we are taught a high point of religion, and that is, not onely to be content with the miſeries and troubles of this life, but to reioyce therein: becauſe when we are weakeſt, we are ſtrongeſt: and when we thinke our ſelues forſaken of God in the time of diſtreſſe, we are not forſaken indeede, but haue his ſpeciall fauour and protection. 2. *Cor.* 12.10. Let this be thought vpon: for the workes of God in the cauſe of mans ſaluation, are in, and by their contraries. This is the manner of Gods dealing.

The ſecond thing is, that *Paul* preached the Goſpel to the Galatians *at the firſt,* as it were breaking the ice, where none had preached before. In this he claimes his priuiledge, that he was to be eſteemed as a Maiſter-builder, that laid the foundation of the Church of Galatia: and withall he giues a cloſe *Item* to the falſe Apoſtles, who did not plant Churches, but onely corrupt them after they were planted. Againe, *Paul* here notes the condition of Gods Church, or kingdome: in which firſt comes the husbandman and ſowes good ſeede, and then after comes the diuell with his tares, *Math.*13.24. and all this is euident in the Church of Galatia, firſt planted by *Paul*, and then ſeduced by falſe teachers.

The third thing is, that *Paul* preached *bearing about him the triall of God.* This *triall* is a worke of God whereby he diſcouers vnto vs, and to the world, either the grace or the corruption of our hearts. Thus God tried *Abraham, Heb.*11.17. the Iſraelites, *Deut.*6.1. and *Ezechias,* 2. *Chron.*32.31. and *Paul* in this place.

The vſe. We muſt not thinke it ſtrange, when we are afflicted any way. Nay, we muſt looke for trials, and be content when they come. 1. *Pet.*4.12. *Iam.*1.2. We are either gold indeede, or gold in ſhew; if indeede, we muſt be caſt into the furnace, that we may be purged: if we be gold in appearance, we muſt againe into the furnace, that we may be knowne what we are. The beſt vine in the vineyard muſt be lopped and cut with the pruning knife, that it may beare the more fruite. *Ioh.*15.

Againe, we muſt take heed leſt there be any hidden corruption reigning in our hearts: and we muſt labour to be indeed that which we appeare to be. For we muſt be tried by God: and then that which now lies hid, ſhall be diſcouered to our ſhame.

Laſtly, we muſt looke to it, that there be ſoundneſſe of grace in vs, that we may be able to beare the trialls of God, and shew forth some measure of faith, patience, obedience.

The first signe of Reuerence in the Galatians is, *that they did not despise Paul* in his base condition. This is a matter of commendation in them, and it is to be followed of vs. And he is a blessed man that is not offended at Christ, *Math.* 11.6.

The second signe of reuerence is, that *they receiued Paul as an Angel of God, or as Christ Iesus.* Here first we must distinguish betweene *Pauls* person, and his doctrine or ministery. And he is said *to be receiued as an Angel*, or *as Christ*: because his doctrine was receiued euen as if an Angel, or Christ had deliuered it. Secondly we must put a difference betweene an Apostle, and all ordinary Pastours and teachers. And to be receiued as an Angel, or as Christ, properly and simply concerns *Paul*, and the rest of the Apostles. For to them it was said, *It is not you that speake, but the spirit of the Father in you. Mat.* 10 20. Againe, *he that heareth you, heareth me, he that despiseth you, despiseth me, Luk.* 10.16. The Apostles were called of God immediatly, taught and inspired immediatly, and immediatly gouerned by the Spirit, both in preaching and writing, so as they could not erre in the things which they deliuered to the Church: and therefore they were to be heard euen as Christ himselfe.

As for other ordinary teachers, they are in part and in the second place to be heard as Angels, and as Christ, so farre forth as they follow the doctrine of the Apostles. Thus are they also called *the Angels of the couenant, Malac.* 2.7. *And Embassadours in the stead of Christ,* 2. *Cor.* 5.21.

Here *Paul* notably expresseth the Authority, and Honour of an Apostle, which is to be heard euen as Christ himselfe: because in preaching he is the mouth, and in writing the hand of God. This authority is to be maintained: and the consideration of it is of great vse. The Papists say, we know the scripture to be the word of God, by the testimony of the Church: but indeede the principall meanes whereby wee are assured touching the truth of Scripture, is, that the books of Scripture were penned by men, whose writings, and sayings, we are to receiue, euen as from Christ himselfe, because they had either Propheticall or Apostolicall authority, and were immediatly taught and inspired in writing: and all this may be discerned, by the matter, forme, and circumstances of the foresaid books.

De consid. ad Eugen.

Secondly, they are to be blamed that call the Pope *the spouse of the Church*, and *Christ by annointment* (as *Bernard* did,) for thus is he more then an Apostle.

Thirdly,

Thirdly, here we see the goodnesse of God, that doth not speake to vs in his Maiesty, but appoints men in his stead, who are his Embassadours to beseech vs to be reconciled to him.

Fourthly, there must be fidelity in teachers, because they stand in teaching, in the stead of Christ: and therefore must onely deliuer that which they know to be the will of Christ.

Fiftly, They must haue a speciall care of holinesse of life, because they speake in the name and roome of God. Reade *Leuit.* 10.2.

Sixtly, the people are to heare their teachers with all reuerence, euen as if they would heare the very Angels of God, or Christ himselfe.

Seauenthly, the comfort of the Ministery is as sure and certaine, as if an Angel came downe from heauen, or Christ himselfe to comfort vs: so be it we doe indeede truely turne to God and repent.

Verse 15.

What was your felicity?]that is, you esteemed it to be your felicity, that you receiued me and my doctrine. *Yee would haue plucked out your eyes, and haue giuen them to mee*]a prouerbiall speech, signifying the speciall loue of the Galatians to *Paul*, so as nothing which they had could be too deare for him. *If it had benne possible*] this he saith, because no man can plucke out his eye to doe another man good: or thus, no man can possibly giue his eye and the sight thereof to another.

In these words *Paul* sets downe the third signe of the loue and reuerence which the Galatians shewed to him: and that is, that they thought themselues happy by reason of *Pauls* Ministery, and would haue parted with their owne eyes for his good.

Hence we learne, that there is a felicity in the time of this life, and that is, to receiue and imbrace the doctrine of the Gospell. So saith Christ else-where. *Luk*, 8.21. and 11.18. *Math.* 7.26. True happinesse stands in our reconciliation with God in Christ. And this reconciliation is offered and giuen vs on Gods part by his word and promise, and it is receiued of vs, when we turne to God, and by faith rest on the said promise. To be in Gods kingdome is happinesse: and this is the kingdome of God, when we resigne our selues in subiection to his will and word. The preaching of the word is the key of this kingdome, *Math.* 16.19, and when it is receiued into our hearts by faith, heauen is set open vnto vs euen in this life, *Ioh.* 1.51.

The Philosophers therfore haue erred,that place our happinesse in honours,riches,pleasures,or in ciuill vertue.

Secondy,our common people are deceiued,who think because they deale truly and iustly before men, that they are in as good a case as they that heare all the Sermons in the world:as though true happinesse stood in ciuill conuersation.

Thirdly, this doctrine serues to beate downe a point of natural Atheisme in the heart of man,which makes many thinke it a vaine thing to serue God, and to heare his word,*Iob* 21. 15. *Malac.* 3.14. *Dauid* was troubled with this corruption, *Psalme* 73.15. Many of them which professe the name of Christ, will not bee brought to keepe the Sabbath day: and in their dealings they vse fraud, and lying as other men doe: and all is because they thinke they cannot liue by their religion.

Fourthly,the onely way to establish a kingdome or common-wealth, is to plant the Gospell there: for this makes an happy people. And this is the maine cause of our happinesse and successe in this Church and land. And the obedience of the Gospel it is that makes euery man in his trade,office,and calling whatsoeuer it be, to prosper. Reade *Psal.* 1.3.

Fiftly,on the contrary,they are wretched and miserable that liue without the Gospel, *Prou.* 29.18. 2.*Cor.* 4.3. 2.*Tim.* 3.7.

Sixtly,to receiue the doctrine of the Apostles, is an infallible marke of the Church of God. For this is it that makes a people blessed and happy.

Seuenthly,we may not despise the preaching of the word, 1.*Thes.* 5.20. If we doe,we despise our owne happinesse. If it be said,Preachers sometime are deceiued. *Answer.* Marke the addition of *Paul, Prooue all things,hold that which is good,* 2.*Thess.* 5.

Touching the speciall loue of the Galatians to *Paul,* first it may be demanded,what was the cause of it? *Answer.* The very ministerie of the Apostle,whose office it was to make disciples, *Matth.* 28.19. and so to plant the Church of the New Testament. And for this cause, hee had a priuiledge to preach the trueth, so as hee could not erre in things which he deliuered to the Church. Secondly,he preached with authoritie, as hauing power to correct rebellious offenders, 2.*Cor.* 10.6. and 1.*Cor.* 4. Thirdly,he preached with vnspeakeable diligence. Reade *Acts* 20.31. Fourthly,he had a prerogatiue,(as the rest of the Apostles had) after hee had made disciples,by imposition of hands to giue vnto them the extraordinary gifts of the holy Ghost, *Acts* 8:17. And these are the meanes wherby this speciall loue was procured.

Secondly,

Secondly, it may bee demaunded, whether the Galatians did not more then keepe the law, when they would haue plucked out their owne eyes, and haue giuen them to *Paul*? for thus they loue him more then their owne selues. *Answer.* The commandement [*Thou shalt loue thy neighbour as thy selfe*] doth not prescribe that we must in the first place loue our selues, and then in the second loue our neighbour: but it sets downe the right manner of louing our neighbour, and that is, to loue him, as heartily and vnfainedly, as our owne selues.

The measure of loue is expressed when Christ saith, *we must loue one another, as Christ loued vs, Iohn* 13.34.

There is a certaine case in which wee must consider our neighbour, not onely as a neighbour, but also as a speciall instrument of God: and thus are wee in some respects to loue, and to preferre him before our selues. Thus a subiect is more to loue the life of his Prince, then his owne life. Thus *Paul* was content to bee accursed for the Israelites, *Rom.* 9.1. And the Galatians would haue giuen their eyes to *Paul*, that was so worthy an instrument of the grace of God.

In their example we are taught to be willing to forsake the dearest things in the world for the Gospel of Christ, euen our eyes, hands, feete, yea and our life.

Verse 16.

Because I tell you the trueth.] We must after *Pauls* example speake the truth to all men, *Ephes.* 4.25. *Am I therefore your enemy*] the conclusion of the Apostles argument. Here we see a corruption of nature, which makes vs that wee cannot abide to heare the trueth in things that are against vs. Wee hate them that speake the trueth: selfe-loue makes vs conceiue the best things of our selues. Heere then learne.

1. To search thy heart and life, that thou mayest know the very worst by thy selfe: If thou wilt not know it now, thou shalt know it to thy shame in the day of iudgement.

2. Be vile and base in thine owne opinion, *Iob.* 34.last.

17 *They are iealous ouer you amisse: yea, they would exclude you, that ye should altogether loue them.*

18 *But it is good to loue earnestly alwayes in a good cause; and not onely when I am present with you.*

The word *zeale*, hath many significations; heere it is fitly translated iealousie. *Ye are iealous*] hereby much is signified; that there

is

is a ſpirituall mariage betweene Chriſt and his Church: that the Church is the Bride, Chriſt the Bridegroome, or husband, the Goſpel an inſtrument drawne touching the marriage: the Sacraments as ſeales, the graces of the Spirit as loue tokens, the Miniſters of Chriſt, as friends of the Bridegroome, and ſuters for him. In this reſpect they put on the affection of Chriſt, and are zealous for him. This iealouſie is twofold, *Pretended iealouſie*, and *true iealouſie*. *Pretended iealouſie*, is, when men falſely pretend the loue of the Church for Chriſtes ſake. Thus *Paul* ſaith, *They are iealous*, that is, they pretend a loue vnto you for Chriſtes ſake, but indeed they doe it *amiſſe*. And the reaſon followes, *They would exclude you*, namely, from louing of me. Others reade the words thus; they would exclude *ἡμᾶς, vs*: the difference in the originall is onely in one letter: and the ſenſe is the ſame, that the falſe apoſtles would exclude *Paul* from the loue of the Galatians, that they onely might bee honoured and loued.

It is good] Theſe words may be vnderſtood, either of the Galatians, or of *Paul*. I rather chooſe to apply them to *Paul*, that for ielouſie he may make an oppoſition betweene himſelfe and the falſe teachers. The ſenſe is this: that iealouſie is a good thing, if it be in a good cauſe; that is, if it be indeed for Chriſts ſake, and be alwayes the ſame. And *Paul* addes further, that this kinde of ielouſie is in himſelfe: becauſe he is ielous ouer the Galatians not only when he is preſent with them, but alſo when he is abſent: and this he further confirmes in the two next verſes.

The ſcope. In theſe words, *Paul* meets with a conceit of the Galatians: for they might haply ſay, that their new teachers loued them exceedingly, and were zealous for their ſaluation. *Paul* therfore anſwers by a compariſon, thus: they are ielous ouer you, but it is amiſſe: nay, ielouſie for you is good. The firſt part of the compariſon is in the 17. verſe, the ſecond in the 18.

The vſe. When *Paul* ſaith, that the falſe apoſtles were iealous ouer the Galatians amiſſe, hee ſets out the faſhion of men in the world, which is to doe things which are good in their kinde, but to doe them for wrong ends. It is an excellent office to preach the word, but ſome doe it of enuy and contention, *Phil.* 1.15. others make merchandiſe of the word. It is an excellent thing to imbrace the Goſpel: and yet many men doe it amiſſe for feare, or for honour, or for profit, or for other ſiniſter reſpect, and not for the Goſpels ſake. This temporall life is an excellent thing, yet few there are that know the ende of this life. For men commonly ſpend not their time to ſeeke the kingdome of heauen, and to ſerue God in seruing of men, but with all their might, they aime at honours, profites, pleasures: and thus they liue amisse, not for the honour of God, but for themselues. This must teach vs not onely to doe good, but to doe it well, and to propound good ends to our selues: and to seeke to bee vpright in the statutes of God, *Psalme* 119.80. To this ende, three things must bee done. First, wee must set before vs the will and commaundement of God, and this must mooue vs to doe the good we doe. Secondly, the outward action must be conformable to the inward motions of the inward man: and they must both go together. Thirdly, we must directly intend to obey God in all things wee doe, and to approoue our hearts and doings to him.

In that the false apostles are said to be *iealous*, or *zealous*, we see how nature can counterfeit the grace of God: and that which the child of God doth by grace, that the naturall man can doe by nature. Thus *Pharaoh* fained repentance, *Exod.*9.27. and *Ahab*, that *solde himselfe to worke wickednesse*, 1. *Kings* 21.27. and *Iudas* in the midst of his despaire, is said *to repent*, *Matth.*27.1. Daily experience shewes the like in such persons, who in their extremitie, with teares vse to bewaile their liues past, and with many vowes and protestations, promise amendment: and yet afterward when they are on foot againe, they returne to their old bias. In a word, there is nothing that the godly man doeth by the spirit of God spiritually, but an hypocrite may doe the like carnally. Nature can play the part of the ape, in imitating good things. Therefore it stands vs in hand to pray, and examine our hearts, lest we bee deceiued in our selues. For there may lie a depth of deceit and falshood lurking in the heart. And that we be not deceiued, two things must be obserued, One is, that wee must cherish in our hearts an vniuersall hatred of all and euery sinne; first in our selues, and then in others. The second is, that we must bee changed and renewed in our minds, consciences, and affections.

Thirdly, heere wee see the propertie of enuie, and ambition, in these false teachers. *Paul* must be excluded from the loue of the Galatians, that they alone may be loued. Thus *Iosua* would haue excluded *Eldad* and *Medad* from prophecying, and hee would haue *Moses* to be the only Prophet: but *Moses* saith, *I would to God all the people could prophesie*, *Numb.*11.29. *Iohns* disciples would haue excluded Christ baptizing: but *Iohn* saith, *He must increase, and I must decrease*, *Iohn* 3.30. The disciples of Christ would haue excluded one that cast out diuels in the name of Christ, but did not follow him, and Christ forbad them, *Luke* 9.49.

Lastly,

Laſtly, we here ſee the propertie of deceiuers is to make a diuiſion betweene the Paſtors and the people.

Beſide the former pretended ielouſie, there is a good iealouſie, which the Apoſtle takes to himſelfe, and elſewhere hee calls it *the iealouſie of God*, 2.*Cor*.11.2.

This ielouſie preſuppoſeth the office of the Apoſtles, and all Miniſters, which ſtands in three things. The firſt is, to become ſuiters to the Church, or to the ſoules of men, in the name of Chriſt, and to make the offer or motion in his name, of a ſpiritual mariage: and this is done in the miniſterie and diſpenſation of the Goſpell. The ſecond is, to make the contract betweene mens ſoules and Chriſt. Now to the making of a contract, the conſent of both the parties (at the leaſt) is required: Chriſt giues his conſent in the word, *Oſe*. 2.20. and we giue our conſent to him & chooſe him for our head, when we turne to God, and beleeue in Chriſt. And the miniſtery of the word, ſerues to ſignifie the will of Chriſt vnto vs, and to ſtirre vp our hearts to an holy conſent. The third is, after the contract, to preſerue them in true faith, and good life, that they may bee fit to be preſented to Chriſt in the day of iudgment, and ſo be maried to him eternally: for then, & not before, is the marriage of the lambe. Theſe dueties are all noted by *Paul*, when he ſaith, *that hee prepared the Corinthians that he might preſent them as a pure virgin vnto Chriſt*, 2. *Cor*.11.2. And becauſe this charge and office is laid vpon the Apoſtles and Miniſters: therefore they are ſaid to bee *iealous*.

This ielouſie ſtands in three things. The firſt is, to loue the Church, in deed and truth for Chriſts ſake. The ſecond is, to feare leaſt by reaſon of weakneſſe, and by meanes of the temptations of the diuell, the Church and they that beleeue, ſhould fall away from Chriſt. The third is, after the fall of the Church, to be angry with holy anger and indignation for Chriſts ſake. Thus *Moſes* was iealous, when the Iſraelites worſhipped the golden calfe: and *Elias* with like zeale ſlue the prieſts of *Baal*. Thus is *Paul* ſaid to be ielous in this place, *Actes* 14.

If the Apoſtle bee thus iealous, how much more then is Chriſt himſelfe ielous, who hath eſpouſed himſelfe to his Church? This plainly ſhewes, that hee cannot brooke either partner, or deputie. And therefore his ſacrifice on the croſſe muſt ſtand without the ſacrifice of the Maſſe, his interceſſion without the interceſſion of Saints, his merits without the merit of workes, his ſatisfaction without any ſatisfaction of ours. He will haue the heart alone, and all the heart, or nothing: and he will not giue any part of his honour to any other.

This ielousie in the Ministers must teach all faithfull seruants of God, that they keepe themselues as pure virgins for Christ, and set their hearts on nothing in the world, but on him. Therefore they must hunger after Christ: they must account all things dung for him: they must haue their conuersation in heauen with him: and loue his comming vnto them by death, *Psal.*45.10. Contrariwise they that set their hearts on any other thing beside him, are said *to goe a whoring from him*, and therfore they are accursed, *Psal.*73.27. Thus many Protestants doe in their practise, whatsoeuer they professe. Thus doth the Church of Rome both in word and deed. For beside Christ she hath many other louers: and she goes a whoring after them when shee worships Angels and Saints, the images of God and Christ, with religious worship.

Againe, by this we are put in minde to yeeld an vniuersall subiection to Christ: for this is the dutie of the espoused wife to her husband.

Lastly, that good things may be well done, good ends must bee propounded: and we must be constant in the good which we doe. And thus *Paul* saith, *it is good to be iealous.*

19 *My little children, of whom I trauell in birth againe, till Christ be formed in you.*

20 *I would I were now with you, that I might change my voice: for I am in feare of you.*

Paul hath said before, that *his icalousie ouer the Galatians was good*: because it was in a good cause, and it was constant, not only in his presence, but euen in his absence: and this he declares here by two signes: his loue now in his absence, in the 19. verse, and his desire in the second verse.

The word, ὠδίνω, translated, *I trauell in birth*, signifies not onely the trauell of the woman at the birth of the childe, but also the painefull bearing thereof, before the birth. And the wordes haue this sense, O ye Galatians, once heretofore I bare and brought you foorth, when I first preached Christ vnto you: and because now yee are reuolted from my doctrine, I am constrained once againe to beare you, and to trauell with you in my ministerie, till by the operation of the Holy Ghost, the right knowledge, and the true image of Christ defaced by the false apostles, bee once againe reformed and restored.

In these words (*my little children*) *Paul* takes to him the condi-

tion

tion of a mother, and hee ſignifies his moſt tender and motherly affection to the Galatians. It is the faſhion of mothers, when their children proſper and doe well, to reioyce; when they are ſicke, or die, to mourne exceedingly, and to bee mooued with pitie and compaſſion. The Galatians deſerued no loue at *Pauls* hand: for their apoſtaſie was very foule: yet becauſe there were ſome good things remaining in them, and there was hope of recouery, hee inlargeth his bowels towards them, and ſhewes his loue with compaſſion. If this bee the caſe with *Paul*, then great is the loue and compaſſion of God to his children. If the childe be ſicke and froward, the mother doeth not caſt it foorth of the doores, but ſhee tenders it, and carefully lookes vnto it: much more then will the Lord haue pitie and compaſſion. Heere then a maine comfort is to be remembred: if we be of the number of them that beleeue in Chriſt, hating vice, and hauing a care to pleaſe God, our weakeneſſes and falls of weakneſſe, doe not aboliſh the mercie of God, but are occaſions to illuſtrate the ſame. The weakeneſſe of the child, ſtirres vp the compaſſion in the mother: and *Dauid* ſaith, *As a father hath compaſſion on his children, ſo hath the Lord compaſſion on them that feare him*: and marke the reaſon: *for he knowes our frame, and that we are but duſt*, *Pſal.* 103.14.

When *Paul* ſaith, *I trauell*, hee ſignifies the meaſure of his miniſteriall paines, that they were as the trauell of a woman with child: and this he ſhewes plainely in the particulars, 2. *Cor.* 11.23. *Elias*, that was ſent in his time to reſtore religion, was at length ſo wearied in this buſineſſe, that he deſired the Lord to take him out of the world, 1. *King.* 19.4. The paines of the Prophet *Iſai*, made him crie, *My leanneſſe, my leanneſſe*; and *Ieremy* cries, *my belly, my belly*: ſignifying, that his griefs and his paines in the miniſtery, were as the paine of the *Cholicke*. By this we ſee, that they haue much to anſwer for before God, that are in this calling, and yet take little or no paines therein. And that they which take the moſt paines, come far ſhort of their dutie.

Againe, when hee ſaith, *I trauell*, hee ſignifies the dignitie of the miniſterie, that it is an inſtrument appointed of God for the worke of regeneration: for *Paul* compares himſelfe to a woman in trauell, and the worke of his miniſterie, to the trauell it ſelfe, whereby children are borne to God. This ſerues very well to ſtop their mouthes, that condemne the vocall and externall miniſterie.

When he ſaith, *I trauell gaine* he teacheth, that if men fall after their firſt initiall repentance, there is ſtill a poſſibilitie of mercie,

and

and place for a second repentance. We must *forgiue till seauenty seauen times, Mat.* 18.22. Much more will God doe it. The parable of the prodigall Sonne shewes, that they which fall from God after their calling and first conuersion, may againe by new repentance be recouered.

An obiection: *Pauls* second trauell presupposeth a second regeneration in the Galatians: and if they are borne againe the second time, then in their Apostasie they fell wholly from God. *Ans.* When *Paul* saith, *I trauell againe*, he doth not presuppose any second Spirituall generation: for the child of God is but once begotten to the Lord, and *Paul* here calls the Galatians, *little children*, because euen in the time of their fall, the seede of God still remained in their hearts. And because the image of Christ was againe to be reformed and restored in the Galatians, in this respect he saith, *I trauell againe with you.*

The end of *Pauls* ministery is expressed in the words, *till Christ be formed in you*: that is, till (as it were) the counterfeit or image of Christ be stamped and imprinted in your hearts. This image hath two parts. The first is, a Right knowledge of Christ in respect of his natures and offices, as they are set forth in the word. This knowledge was defaced in the Galatians, when they ioyned workes with Christ: for then they made him to be an imperfect Sauiour. The second part of this image, is a Conformity with Christ. *Rom.* 8.29. It is twofold, *conformitie in quality*, and *conformitie in practise.*

Conformity in quality is againe twofold. The first is a *Conformitie to the death of Christ*, when the vertue thereof works in vs a death of sinne, and when we suffer as Christ suffered, in silence, contentation, obedience, subiecting our selues to the will of God. The second is, *a conformity to the resurrection or life of Christ*, and that is, when we liue not onely a naturall, but also a Spirituall life, which is to submit our selues to be ruled by the word and Spirit of Christ.

Conformity in practise is, when we carry our selues as Prophets in the confession of the name of Christ, in teaching, exhorting, and admonishing one another: as Priests to offer our bodies and soules in sacrifice to God: as Spirituall Kings, bearing sway ouer the lusts and corruptions of our owne hearts. And thus is Christ to be framed in the hearts of men.

The vse. Here we see, the end of all preaching, is to make sinnefull men to become new creatures, like vnto Christ: this is the drift of the Ministery: and the doctrine that tends to this purpose, is sound and wholesome.

Againe, here we see, that in the new Testament, there is but one rule and order for all men, and that is the rule of Christ, *Take vp thy crosse and follow me*: and for this cause the Ministery serues to frame Christ in the hearts of all beleeuers: Therefore the seuerall rules and orders of Monks and Friars in the Church of Rome, are meere superstitions.

Furthermore, *Paul* here makes two degrees of Gods children; one is, when they are begottē of God, & Christ is formed in them. The second is, when they are begotten of God, yet so, as they are as yet vnformed. Such were the Apostles when they confessed Christ to bee the Sonne of the liuing God, *Math. 16*. for then they knew not the article of Christs death, resurrection, ascension, at that time, nor the manner of his kingdome. Of this sort was *Rahab*, when she receiued the spies, *Heb.* 11. for then she was not informed in the religion of the Iewes, but only acknowledged the God of Israel to be the true God, and had a resolution to ioyne her selfe to the people of God. Of this sort were the *Corinthians* at the first. For they were carnall more then spirituall, euen babes in Christ, 1. *Cor.* 3.3. This must teach vs, where we see any good thing in men, to cherish it. For though as yet they be not Christians formed, yet they may be Christians in forming.

When *Paul* saith, *vntill Christ be formed*, he shewes that the conuersion of a sinner is not wrought in one moment, but by little and little, in processe of time. In the generation of infants, first the braine, heart, and liuer are framed. then the bones, veines, arteries, nerues, membranes: and after this, flesh is added. And the infant first begins to liue the life of a plant, by growing and nourishing: then it liues the life of a beast, by sense and motion: and thirdly, the life of man, by the vse of reason. Euen so God outwardly preuents vs with his word, and inwardly he puts into vs knowledge of his wil, with the beginnings or seeds of faith and repentance, as it were a braine and a heart: from these beginnings of faith and repentance, arise heauenly desires: from these desires followes asking, seeking, knocking: and thus the beginnings of faith are increased, and men goe on from grace to grace, till they be tall men in Christ. And for this cause, we must with constancy vse the good meanes, in hearing, reading, praying.

Lastly, we are all here put in minde to study, and to vse all good meanes, that we may be like to Christ, specially in the disposition of the inward man. There is a spirituall madnes in the minds of many men: they thinke of nothing but of the fashion of their apparell, and of the trimming of their bodies: but let vs thinke

how

how to imprint the gracious image of Christ in our hearts: thus shall we be louely, and haue fauour in the eyes of God.

Thus much of *Pauls* loue: now follows his desire in the 20 verse. In which I consider three things: the desire it selfe, *I would I were with you now*: the end of his desire, *that I might change my voice*: the occasion thereof, *for I am in doubt of you.*

When *Paul* saith, *I would I were with you now*, he shewes, that the presence of Pastours with their people, is a thing most necessary. And there are two reasons thereof. One is, to preuent spirituall daungers, which are manifold and continuall, in that *the diuell seekes continually whome he may deuoure*: and *we fight against principalities and powers in heauenly things.* In this respect Pastours are called *watchmen*, and *ouerseers*. Secondly, the presence of Pastours with their people, serues to redresse things amisse, and to recouer them that be in Apostasie: as *Paul* saith in this place. Therfore it were to be wished that this mind of *Paul* were in all Pastors, that with one consent they might say to their people, *I would I were with you now.*

In the words, [*that I might change my voice*] *Paul* continues the allusion (which he made in the former verse) to a woman with child: and hereby he signifies two things. The first is, that he will leaue further disputing with the Galatians, and fall to lamenting and crying, as mothers doe in the time of their trauell, by reason of their paine. This is to change the voice. It was the maner of *Paul* to abase himselfe, and to mourne for the sinnes of others, 2.*Cor.* 12. 24. and hee reprooues the Corinthians, that they were puffed vp, and did not mourne for the incestuous person. Like was the practise of *Dauid*, *Psal.* 119.136. of *Lot*, 2.*Pet.* 2.7. of *Ieremie*, *Lam.* 2.11. of the friends of *Iob*, *Iob.* 2. last. of the godly in the daies of *Ezechiel*, c. 9 4 of Christ in respect of Ierusalem, *Luke* 19.41. And it hath bin alwayes the practise of holy men, when there was no other helpe, with teares to commend the case to God.

If sorrow for other mens offences make *Paul* change his voice, much more are men to doe it for their owne. *Peter*, in his repentance left his presumptuous speaking, and fell to bitter and secret teares: and so did the woman that stood at the feet of Christ weeping, and washed his feet with her teares, *Luke* 7 83. The like ought wee to doe for our offences and sinnes. The earth-quake this Winter past, must stirre vs vp to this dutie. For it is a matter full of terrour, 1.*Samuel* 14.15. and the sicknesse which hath taken hold of thousands as a gentle warning must bee respected. And it must bee considered, that the changes of the great world bring with them like changes in the little world, that is, in the bodies of men.

Againe, *to change the voice*, is to conferre with the Galatians, and vpon conference to temper his voice to their manners and condition, as nources stammer and lispe with children. For some are with pitie to be recouered: and some with terrour, *Iud.*22.23. Hence I gather,

That the conference of Pastours and people, is a thing very necessary. *Paul* heere ascribes more to it then to his Epistle. It is the life of preaching. For by it the teachers know better what to teach, and the people better to conceiue things that are taught. Here then we see a common fault. Men are content to heare, but they will not conferre with their teachers: and in the time of sicknesse, the first person that is conferred with, is the Physician: and the Minister is last sent for: whereas on the contrary, the cure of the soule, is the cure of the bodie, *Iob* 33.23,25.

Againe, here is set downe the way to attaine all good learning: and that is, that learners bee present with their teachers: and the teachers againe temper their voices to the capacitie of their learners. Thus *Samuel* was with *Eli* at the doore of the Tabernacle: thus Christ was in the Temple among the doctors, hearing them, and asking them questions, *Luke* 2,44.

Thirdly, *Paul* heere sets downe the way to make a pacification for religion in these last dayes: and the way is, that the Pastours of the Church bee assembled together by the authoritie of Princes: and being assembled, they temper their voices one to another according to the written word. Thus may they that lie now vnder the apostasie of Antichrist, be recouered, *Actes* 15.6. And the promise of God is, that *when two or three come together in his name, hee will be with them*, *Matt.* 18.

Lastly, the Ministers (as here wee see) are to temper their gifts and speach to the condition of their hearers. The Corinthians were babes in Christ, and *Paul* feeds them with milke, 1.*Cor.* 3.3. to the Iew he became a Iew, to the Gentile a Gentile, that he might winne some, 1.*Cor.* 9.18. For this cause it were to bee wished, that Catechising were more vsed then it is of our Ministers. For our people are for the most part rude and vncatechised: and therefore they profit little or nothing by Sermons. A sermon to such persons is like a great loafe set before a child. And it is no disgrace for learned Ministers, in plaine and familiar manner to catechise: for this is to lay the foundation, without which all labour in building is in vaine. Againe, our ignorant people should be content euen in

their

their olde age to learne the Catechisme: for by reason of their ignorance, they lie as a prey to the Atheist and Papist: and in much hearing, they learne little; because they know not the grounds of doctrine that are vsually in all Sermons. And it is a fault in many, that they loue to heare Sermons, which are beyond their reach, in which they stand & wonder at the preacher: and plaine preaching is little respected of such.

The occasion of *Pauls* desire is in these words, *I doubt of you*, or thus, *I am in perplexitie for you*: and this *Paul* speakes as a mother in some dangerous extremitie, in the time of her trauell; as *Rachel* was in the birth of *Beniamin*, *Gen.* 35. And the words carry this sense, I am troubled for your recouery; and I feare it will neuer be.

Heere wee learne, how dangerous a thing it is to fall from grace, though it bee but in part. For a man cannot recouer himselfe when hee will. Wee doe not the good wee can, vnlesse God make vs doe it, *Ezech.* 36. 27. *Cant.* 1.4. *Ierem.* 31.29. Therefore it is an errour to thinke that we may repent and turne to God when we will, as many suppose. And this must bee a warning vnto vs to preserue the good things that God hath put into vs, and not to quench the spirit.

And though *Paul* doubt of the recouery of the Galatians, yet he spares not to send his Epistle to them, and to vse meanes. And thus in desperate cases, we must vse the best meanes, & leaue the successe to God. Thus the Israelites when there was no other helpe, went into the sea, as into their deathbed, or graue, by faith staying themselues on the promise of God, *Heb.* 11. 29. 2. *Chron.* 20. 12.

That which *Paul* here saith, may bee said of many among vs, in whom Christ is not yet framed, whether we respect knowledge or good life: for they giue iust occasion of doubting, whether they will euer returne to God or no.

21 *Tell mee yee that will be vnder the law, doe yee not heare the law?*

22 *For it is written, that Abraham had two sonnes, one by a seruant, and another by a free woman.*

23 *But he which was of the seruant, was borne after the flesh: and he which was of the free woman, by promise.*

From the eight verse of this chapter to the 20. verse, *Paul* hath handled the conclusion of the principall argument of this Epistle touching the Apostasie of the Galatians: and here he returnes againe to his former doctrine touching the iustification of a sinner by faith, without the workes of the law: and he confirmes it by an other argument, the summe and substance whereof is this: Your libertie from the law, was prefigured in the family of *Abraham*: therefore ye are not bondmen to the law, but free men.

The argument is at large propounded, and it hath foure parts: a preface in the 21. verse: an history of *Abraham* and his family, ver. 22, 23. the application of the history from the 24. verse to the 30. the conclusion, verse 31.

And first of the Preface. *Law*] the word (*law*) in the first place, is taken properly for the moral and ceremoniall law of *Moses*: and in the second place, for the books of *Moses*, and namely, for the booke of *Genesis*. And in this sense the word is taken, when Christ is said *to expound the Law and the Prophets, Luke* 24. And sometime it signifies all the bookes of the old Testament, *Iohn* 15.15.

Vnder the law] to be vnder the law, is to hold our selues bound to the fulfilling of the law: and to looke for life eternall thereby.

Doe ye not heare the law?] that is, ye reade and heare in deed, but ye vnderstand not the scope and drift of that which you reade.

In this Preface, first *Paul* meetes with the pride of mans nature, whereby the Galatians went about to establish their owne righteousnesse by the law, when hee saith, *Yee that will bee vnder the law, &c.* With this pride were the Iewes tainted, *Romanes* 10. 3. and the young Prince that came to Christ, and said, *Good master, what must I doe to be saued?* And the Papists of our time, who will not bee subiect to the iustice of God, but set vp their owne iustice in the keeping of the law. The like doe the ignorant people among vs, who hold that they are able to fulfill the law, and that they are to be saued thereby. And when they say, they looke to be saued by their faith, they vnderstand thereby their fidelitie, that is, their good dealing.

Againe, *Paul* here notes the seruile disposition of men that loues rather to be in bondage vnder the law, then to be in perfect liberty vnder the grace of God. This we see in daily experience. All professe Christ among vs: yet is it euen a death to the most, to forsake the bondage of the flesh. Christ we professe, yet so as we take libertie to liue after the lusts of our owne hearts.

When *Paul* saith, *Doe ye not heare the law?* hee notes the cause of our spirituall pride, and of the seruile disposition before named, namely, ignorance in mistaking and misconceiuing the true scope of the law: for the Galatians did not consider that Christ was the scope of the law, but they supposed that the very obseruation of the law, euen ſince the fall of man, did giue life and iuſtice. This ignorance was to the Iewes as a veile before their eyes in the reading of the law, 2. *Corinthians* 3. 14. And this ignorance hath blinded the Papiſt at this day: for he ſuppoſeth that the Goſpel is nothing elſe but the law of *Moſes*: and that Chriſt indeed is but an inſtrument to make vs keepers of the law, and conſequently Sauiours of our ſelues.

In the hiſtory of *Abraham* I conſider three things, the fact of *Abraham* in taking two wiues: the euent vpon this fact, he had two ſonnes by them: the condition of theſe ſonnes.

Touching the fact of *Abraham*, it may bee demaunded, what is to bee iudged thereof? The ground to the anſwer ſhall bee this; that *marriage is the indiuiſible coniunction of one man and one woman only*. This Chriſt of purpoſe teacheth, *Matth*. 16. where he ſaith, that *God created them at the firſt man and woman*, and not women, v.4. *that a man muſt forſake father and mother, and cleaue to his wife*, not to his wiues, v.5. that *they twaine ſhall be one fleſh*, v.6. And in all this Chriſt makes no new law, but onely reuiues the firſt inſtitution of marriage made in Paradiſe. And *Moſes* hauing ſet downe this diuine inſtitution, addes withall, that *Lamech* was the firſt that brake it, by taking many wiues.

Now then, the anſwer to the queſtion, is two-fold. Some ſay, that *Abraham* and the reſt of the Patriarks had a diſpenſation from God to marrie many wiues, and therefore that it was no ſinne in them. Of this minde are ſundrie learned men, both Proteſtants and Papiſts. But the anſwer is only coniecturall, and hath no euidence in Scripture.

The ſecond anſwer is, that God did not approue the polygamie of the fathers, or commend it, but did onely tolerate it, as a leſſer euill, for the preuenting of a greater. This tolleration appeares, in that God commanded that *the king muſt not multiply his wiues*, *Deut*. 17.17. and that the child of the hated wife, (though ſhee be the ſecond wife,) if it bee firſt borne, ſhall be the heire, *Deut*. 21.15. The occaſions of this tolleration were two. One was, a deſire in the Patriarkes to multiply their poſterity, that if it were poſſible, the Meſſias might deſcend of their line. The ſecond was, the common cuſtome of men in the Eaſt countreyes, who made no matter of it, to marry many wiues: and a common cuſtome bred a common error, and a common error bred common ignorance, wherby that which was indeed a ſinne, was eſteemed no ſinne.

It may be obiected, if the hauing of many wiues were an offence, that *Abraham* and the reſt of the holy Patriarches liued and died in a sinne without repentance: because wee finde nothing in Scripture, touching their repentance for that sin. *Answer.* Knowne sinnes require particular repentance: but if sinnes be vnknowen, or vnconsidered, by reason that men are caried away with the sway of the times (as the Patriarches were) a generall repentance sufficeth, *Psalme* 19 12.

Againe, it may bee alleadged, that *Abraham* tooke *Agar* by the consent of *Sara. Answer.* That sufficeth not to make a full excuse for *Abraham.* For if marriage were a meere ciuill contract, as it is made by the consent of men and women, so it might be dissolued by like consent. But it is more then a ciuill contract: because in the making of it, beside the consent of the parties, the authoritie of God is interposed: and therefore *Saraes* consent (in giuing *Agar* to *Abraham*) is nothing, without the allowance of God: and wee may not thinke that God will allow of that which is directly against his owne ordinance.

Thirdly, it may be alledged, that if the hauing of many wiues be a fault, then *Abraham* and the rest were adulterers. *Answ.* Not so, the polygamie of the Fathers is to bee placed in the middle, betweene adulterie, and holy wedlocke. They tooke not wiues of a lewde minde, for the satisfying of their lust, but of a conscience not rightly informed in this point.

The euent vpon the fact of *Abraham* was, that his two wiues, bare him two sonnes. Hee had indeed more sonnes by *Ketura, Genesis* 25. 2. but these two, *Ishmael* and *Isaac* are onely here mentioned: because by the speciall appointment of God, they were ordained as types of true beleeuers and hypocrites. Reade *Rom.* 9. 7, 8.

The condition of children is set foorth by a double difference. The first is, that *one was borne of a bondwoman*, and therefore a bondman; *the other of a free woman*, and therefore a free man, & the heire. Here it may be demaunded, how the same person can bee both a wife, and a bond woman? *Answer.* Among the heathen (as also among the Iewes) there were two sorts of wiues. Of the first kinde were they, that were ioynt gouernours of the family with the husband, and they were called mistresses of the house. Of the second sort were they, that serued onely for propagation, and were in all other respects as seruants or strangers. Of the first kinde was *Sara*, and of the second, *Hagar*, and *Ketura*.

Vxor materfamilias.

Vxor vsuaria.

The second difference of the children was this. One, that is, *Ishmael was borne after the flesh*, that is, by the strength of nature, and according to the fleshly counsell of *Sara*, who did substitute *Hagar*

into

into her owne roome. The other, namely *Iſaac was borne by the promiſe*, that is, according to the order of nature, yet not by the ſtrength of nature, but by the vertue of the promiſe of God.

In the birth of *Iſhmael Saraes* deſires was good, that the promiſe of God might bee accompliſhed: but the meanes was carnall, the ſubſtitution of her handmaid. This is the condition of the godly: they intend and deſire the beſt things, but they faile in the maner of doing. The ſpirit ſtirres vp good motions, and the fleſh corrupteth them. *Paul* ſaith, *that to will was preſent with him, but he could not doe that which was good as hee ought.* This muſt cauſe vs alwaies to humble our ſelues for our beſt works.

Againe, we are here taught not to make haſte to accompliſh our deſires, but when God promiſeth any thing, to wait his leaſure, and in the meane ſeaſon to liue in ſubiection. *Sara* with all her haſte could not preuent Gods prouidence. Shee hath her deſire in the birth of *Iſhmael*, but yet hee is borne according to the fleſh, in bondage, and he is not the promiſed ſeed.

In the birth of *Iſaac* wee ſee the vertue of the promiſe of God, when it is mixed with our faith: for then it makes things poſſible, that are otherwiſe impoſſible, *Matt.* 17.20. If then we deſire any good things at the hands of God, our duetie is in ſilence and patience to reſt on the promiſes of God, and then our deſire ſhall indeed be accompliſhed.

24 *By the which things another thing is meant. For theſe mothers are the two Teſtaments, the one (which is Agar) of mount Sinai, which gendreth to bondage.*

25 *For Agar, or Sinai, is a mountaine in Arabia, and it anſwereth to Ieruſalem which now is, and ſhee is in bondage with her children.*

The application of the former here beginneth: and the ſenſe of the words is. *An other thing meant*] the words are thus. *Theſe things are ſpoken by allegorie*: that is, one thing is ſaid, and an other thing is meant. *Two mothers*] *Agar* and *Sara*. *Are two*] they repreſent or ſignifie the two Teſtaments. *Eſt* is put for *ſignificat*. Of the two Teſtaments I will ſpeake afterward.

The one] the one Teſtament, which is the couenant of workes, [*which is Agar*] which Teſtament is figured by *Agar* [*is of mount Sinai*] came from mount Sinai, where the law was deliuered to the Iſraelites. *And gendreth to bondage*] that is, it makes all them bondmen that looke to be iuſtified and ſaued by the works of the law.

For Agar or Sinai] here the tranſlatours are deceiued, ſuppoſing that mount Sinai had two names, *Agar* and *Sinai*: but this opinion of theirs hath no ground, and the words are thus to be read, *Agar is Sinai*. Here *Agar* ſignifies not ſo much the perſon of *Abrahams* handmaid, as that which is ſaid in the former hiſtory of *Agar*. For the words are, τὸ Ἀγάρ. And Sinai muſt be conſidered as a place where it pleaſed God to publiſh the law. And the words thus conſidered, haue this ſenſe, *Agar is Sinai*, that is, *Agar* figures Sinai, two waies. Firſt, in condition: for as *Agar* was a bodwoman, ſo Sinai in reſpect of the law, was a place of bondage: and in this reſpect alſo it is called Sinai of Arabia, which was a deſert out of the land of Canaan. Secondly, in effect: For as *Agar* bare *Iſhmael* a bondman to *Abraham*; ſo Sinai or the law, makes bondmen. *And it anſwereth*] Sinai anſwereth to Ieruſalem, that is, as *Agar* figures Sinai; ſo *Agar* figures Ieruſalem: and by this meanes, Sinai and Ieruſalem are alike, and ſtand both in one order. Now *Agar* figures Ieruſalem two waies, in condition, and effect. In condition: for as *Agar* was a bondwoman, ſo Ieruſalem, or the nation of the Iewes refuſing Chriſt, and looking to be ſaued by the law, are in Spirituall bondage. In effect: for as *Agar* brings forth *Iſhmael* a bondman; ſo Ieruſalem by teaching the law, makes bondmen. Therefore *Paul* ſaith in the laſt place, of Ieruſalem, *And ſhee is in bondage with her children*.

The vſe. *Theſe things are ſaid by allegory*.] Here the Papiſts make a double ſenſe of Scripture, one *literall*, the other *ſpirituall*. *Literall* is twofold. *Proper*, when the words are taken in their proper ſignification. *Figuratiue*, when the holy Ghoſt ſignifies his meaning in borrowed tearmes.

Spirituall ſenſes they make three. One *allegoricall*, when things in the old Teſtament are applied to ſignifie things in the new Teſtament. The ſecond, is *Tropological*; when ſcripture ſignifies ſomething touching maners. The third, is *Anagogicall*, when things are in Scripture applied to ſignifie the eſtate of euerlaſting life. Thus Ieruſalem properly is a citie: by allegorie, the Church of the new Teſtament: in a tropologicall ſenſe, a ſtate well ordered: in an anagogicall ſenſe, the eſtate of eternall life. Theſe ſenſes they vſe to applie to moſt places of the Scripture, ſpecially to the hiſtorie. But I ſay to the contrary, that there is but one full and intire ſenſe of euery place of Scripture, and that is alſo the literall ſenſe, ſometimes expreſſed in proper, and ſometimes in borrowed or figuratiue ſpeaches. To make many ſenſes of ſcripture, is to ouerturne al ſenſe, and to make nothing certen. As for the three ſpirituall ſenſes (ſo called)

called)they are not senses, but applications or vses of scripture. It may be said, that the historie of *Abrahams* familie here propounded,hath beside his proper and literall sense, a spiritual or mysticall sense. I answer,they are not two senses,but two parts of one ful and intire sense. For not onely the bare history, but also that which is thereby signified,is the full sense of the Holy Ghost.

Againe,here we see the Scripture is not only penned in the proper tearmes,but also in sundry diuine figures and allegories. The song of *Salomon* is an Allegory borrowed from the fellowship of man and wife,to signifie the Communion betweene Christ and his Church:& so is the 45.psalme. The booke of *Daniel*,and the Reuelation,is an allegoricall historie. The Parables of the old and new Testaments,are figures or allegories. When *Dauid* saith, *Psal.*45.4. *Ride on vpon the word of truth,meekenes,and iustice*,he describes a Princes charriot by allegory. The Guide is the word, the horses that draw it,are three, Truth,meekenes,iustice. And thus the throne of God is described by like allegorie. *Psal*.89.v.14. the foundation of the throne,are righteousnes,and equity:the maine bearers to goe before the throne,are mercy and truth.

It may be demanded, when doth the Scripture speake properly, and when by figure? *Answer.* If the proper signification of the words be against common reason, or against the analogie of faith,or against good manners, they are not then to bee taken properly,but by figure. The words of Christ. *Ioh.*15.1. *I am the true vine, and my Father is an husbandman*; If they be taken properly, they are absurd in common reason: therefore the wordes are figuratiue, and the sense is this: *I am as the true vine,and my Father as an husbandman.* The words of Christ, *Take,eate,this is my body*, 1.*Cor.*11.*v.*24. taken properly, are against the articles of faith, *He ascended into heauen, and sits at the right hand of God.* And they are against the sixth commandement, *Thou shalt not kill.* And therefore they must bee expounded by figure thus: *This bread is a signe of my body.* The like is to be said of other places: they must be taken properly, if it be possible: if not,by figure.

Here then they are to bee blamed, that make the vse of Rhetoricke in the Bible,to be a meere foppery. For to this purpose there is a booke in English heretofore published. As also they of the Family of loue are iustly to bee condemned, who in another extremity,turne all the Bible to an Allegorie, yea, euen that which is said of *Adam*,and of Christ.

They are two Testaments] *they are*,that is,they signifie:and so *Agar is Sinai a mountaine in Arabia*,that is,signifies Sinai. Thus *the rocke in*

the

the wilderneſſe is Chriſt, 1.*Cor.* 10.4. that is, figures Chriſt. Like to this is the Sacramentall phraſe, *This is my body*, that is to ſay, *this bread ſignifies my body*. Great is the madneſſe of men that hence gather Tranſſubſtantiation, or the reall conuerſion of bread into the body of Chriſt. They might as well gather hence the conuerſion of Agar into mount Sinai.

The two Teſtaments are the Couenant of workes, and the Couenant of grace, one promiſing life eternall to him that doth all things contained in the law: the other to him that turnes and beleeues in Chriſt. And it muſt be obſerued, that *Paul* ſaith, *they are two*, that is, two in ſubſtance, or kind. And they are two, ſundry waies. The law, or couenant of workes, propounds the bare iuſtice of God, without mercy: the couenant of grace, or the Goſpel, reueales both the iuſtice & mercy of God, or the iuſtice of God giuing place to his mercy. Secődly, the law requires of vs inward & perfect righteouſneſſe, both for nature and action: the Goſpel propounds vnto vs an imputed iuſtice reſient in the perſon of the Mediatour. Thirdly, the law promiſeth life vpon condition of works: the Goſpel promiſeth remiſſion of ſinnes and life euerlaſting vpon condition that we reſt our ſelues on Chriſt by faith. Fourthly, the law was written in tables of ſtone, the Goſpel in the fleſhy tables of our hearts. *Ier.* 31.33. 2.*Cor.* 3.3. Fiftly, the law was in nature by creation: the Goſpel is aboue nature, and was reuealed after the fall. Sixtly, the law hath *Moſes* for a Mediatour, *Deut.* 5.27. but Chriſt is the Mediatour of the new Teſtament. *Heb.* 8.6. Laſtly, the law was dedicated by the blood of beaſts, *Exod.* 24. 5. and the new Teſtament by the blood of Chriſt. *Heb.* 9 12.

Here then falls to the ground a maine pillar in Popiſh religion, which is, that the law of *Moſes*, and the Goſpel, are all one law for ſubſtance: and that the difference lies in this, that the law of *Moſes* is darke and imperfect, and the Goſpel or the law of Chriſt more perfect: becauſe he hath (as they ſay) added counſells to precepts. Againe, the law (they ſay) without the Spirit, is the law properly, and with the Spirit, it is the Goſpel. But all this is falſe which they teach. For the two Teſtaments the law and the Goſpel, are two in nature, ſubſtance, or kinde: and the difference lies not in the preſence or abſence of the ſpirit.

And whereas the Papiſts make two iuſtifications, the firſt meerely by grace, the ſecond by workes: beſides the two Teſtaments, they muſt eſtabliſh a third Teſtament compounded of both, and it muſt be partly legall, and partly Euangelicall; otherwiſe the twofold iuſtification cannot ſtand. For the law propounds onely one

way

way of iuſtification,and the Goſpel a ſecond. The doctrine therefore that propounds both,is compounded of both.

God did not approue the polygamy of *Abraham*, yet doth he vſe it to ſignifie the greateſt myſtery of our religion. Here we ſee a great point of the diuine prouidence of God, who ordereth and vſeth well the things which he doth not approoue. This is the foundation of our patience, and a meanes of true comfort. *Ioſeph* thus comforts himſelfe and his brethren, that God ordered and diſpoſed their bad enterpriſe, to his and their good. *Gen.*45.6,7.

Here againe *Paul* ſets downe two properties of the Teſtament of workes, or of the law. The firſt is, that *it came from mount Sinai.* And here lies the difference betweene the law and the Goſpel: the law is from Sinai,the Goſpel from Sion or Ieruſalem. For there it was firſt to be preached,and thence conueied to all nations. *Mich.* 4.1. *Ezech.*47.1.

The ſecond propertie of the law is,that it gendreth to bondage: becauſe it maketh them bondmen,that looke to be ſaued and iuſtified thereby. And this it doth, by reuealing ſinne and the puniſhment thereof, which is euerlaſting death; and by conuincing all men of their ſinnes,and of their deſerued condemnation. In this reſpect, it is called *the miniſterie of death*, 2.*Cor.*3.6.and *Paul* ſaith, that after he knew his ſinnes by the law, he died, and the law was the meanes of death vnto him, *Rom.*7.10. Here is another difference betweene the law and the Goſpel. The law genders to bondage: the Goſpel genders to life.For it is an inſtrument of the Spirit for the beginning and confirming of our regeneration and ſaluation: and ſo is not the law, which is no cauſe,but onely an occaſion of the grace of God in vs.

Whereas Ieruſalem that now is, is ſaid *to be in bondage, as Sinai and Hagar*: It is to bee obſerued, that there is no Church in the world,nor people, which is not ſubiect to apoſtaſie. For God had made great and large promiſes to Ieruſalem, *Pſalm.* 122. and 132. and yet for all this, Ieruſalem by refuſing Chriſt, and by eſtabliſhing the iuſtice of the law, is come into bondage, and depriues her ſelfe of the inheritance of eternall life. Therfore it is a falſhood which th Papiſts teach, that the infallible aſſiſtance of the Spirit is tyed to the Chaire and Conſiſtorie of the Pope, ſo as hee, and conſequently the church of Rome,cannot erre. Here againe,we ſee what may be the future condition of England. For it may be ſaid of it hereafter, England that now is,is not that which it hath bene, namely,a maintainer of the Goſpell of Chriſt. Therefore we muſt not be high minded but feare,and now take heed of the firſt beginning of apoſtaſie. The holy Ghoſt, *Hebr*.3.12,13. ſet downe the degrees thereof,and they are fiue in number. The firſt is, *the deceit of ſinne*: the ſecond is, *the hardening of the heart*, after men are deceiued by ſinne: the third is, *an euill heart*, which growes vpon hardneſſe of heart: the fourth is, *vnbeleefe*, whereby the word of God is called in queſtion, and the truth thereof: and after vnbeleefe followes *a departure from God and Chriſt*. That this may not bee,wee muſt carefully auoid all the deceits of ſinne, as namely, couetouſneſſe,ambition,luſt,&c.

Againe, as *Hagar* figures the law,ſo doeth *Iſhmael* all iuſticiaries, that looke to be ſaued by the law. Here then we ſee the condition of the world, the greateſt part whereof are *Iſhmaelites*. For the Turke, and the Iew, looke at this day to bee ſaued by their works. The Papiſt aſcribes his conuerſion not wholly to grace, but partly to grace, and partly to nature, or the ſtrength of mans will helped by grace. And thus are they borne after the fleſh as *Iſhmael* was. And our common people, though in ſhew they profeſſe reformed religion, yet indeed a great part of them are *Iſhmaelites*. For they looke to be ſaued by their good ſeruing of God, and by their good deeds: and they little thinke on Chriſt and his merits. And thus they depriue themſelues of all title to eternal life. Therfore it ſtands them in hand to condemne nature and the ſtrength therof, and to renounce their owne workes, and to reſt onely on the promiſe of mercy for eternall ſaluation: thus ſhall they be the children of the promiſe,and heires of God.

Laſtly,in that Ieruſalem is in bondage like *Agar*,or mount Sinai, wee ſee how vaine are the pilgrimages to the holy land, and how needleſſe were the warres made for the recouery thereof.

26 But Ieruſalem which is aboue, is free: which is the mother of vs all.

Heere *Paul* ſhewes what is figured by *Sara*, namely, the new Ieruſalem,which is the Catholike Church, *Hebr*.12.22,23. *Reuel*. 21.2. And it is heere ſo tearmed, becauſe Ieruſalem was a type thereof in ſixe reſpects. Firſt,God choſe Ieruſalem aboue all other places to dwell in, *Pſal*.132.13. And the Catholike Church is the company of predeſtinate, choſen to be a particular people to God. Secondly, Ieruſalem is a citie compact in it ſelfe, by reaſon of the bond of loue and order among the citizens, *Pſ*.122.3. In like ſort the members of the Catholike Church are linked together by the

bond

bond of one ſpirit. Thirdly, in Ieruſalem was the Sanctuarie, a place of Gods preſence, and of his worſhip, where alſo the promiſe of the ſeed of the woman was preſerued till the comming of the Meſſias: and now the Catholike Church is in the roome of the Sanctuarie: In it muſt wee ſeeke the preſence of God, and the word of life: therefore it is called *the pillar and ground of trueth*, 1. *Timothie* 3.15. Fourthly, in Ieruſalem was the throne of *Dauid*, *Pſalme* 122.5. and in the Catholike Church is the Throne or Scepter of Chriſt, figured by the kingdome of *Dauid*, *Reuelation* 3.7. Fiftly, the commendation of a citie (as Ieruſalem) is the ſubiection and obedience of the citizens: now in the Catholike Church all beleeuers are citizens, *Epheſians* 2.19. and they yeeld voluntarie obedience and ſubiection to Chriſt their King, *Pſalme* 110.2. *Iſai.* 2.5. Laſtly, as in Ieruſalem the names of the citizens were inrolled in a regiſter: ſo the names of all the members of the Catholike Church, are inrolled in the booke of life, *Reuelation* 20.15. *Hebr.* 12.23.

Againe, the Catholike Church dwelling here belowe, is ſaid to bee *aboue in heauen* for two cauſes. Firſt, in reſpect of her beginning, which is from the election and grace of God, and from Chriſt the Mediatour, of whoſe fleſh and bone we are that beleeue, *Epheſ.* 5.30. The iuſtice wherby we are iuſtified, is in Chriſt: our holineſſe and life, flowes from the holineſſe and life of Chriſt, as from a root. Secondly, the Church is ſaid to *bee aboue*, becauſe it dwels by faith in heauen with Chriſt: for the propertie of faith is to make vs preſent after a ſort, when we are abſent, *Heb.* 11.2.

The vſe. This being ſo, we are admoniſhed to liue in this world as pilgrimes and ſtrangers, 1. *Pet.* 2.11. and therfore we muſt not ſet our loue vpon any earthly thing, but our minds muſt be vpon the countrey to which we are trauelling. And whatſoeuer is an hinderance to vs in our iourney: we muſt caſt it from vs, that we may go lightly: and if we haue any wrongs done vs either in goods or good name, wee muſt the rather be content: becauſe wee are out of our countrey in a ſtrange place: and hereupon wee muſt take occaſion to make haſte to our iourneys end, to our own citie, and laſt abode. Thus did the Patriarches, *Heb.* 11.13,15.

Secondly, wee muſt carrie our ſelues as Burgeſſes of heauen, *Phil.* 3.20. And this we ſhall doe, by minding, ſeeking, affecting of heauenly things, by *ſpeaking the language of Canaan*, which is, to inuocate and praiſe the name of God. Laſtly, by leading a ſpirituall life, that may beſeeme the citizens of heauen. Many faile in this point, when they come to the Lords table, they profeſſe themſelues

ſelues to bee citizens of the citie of God, but in their common dealings in the world, they play the ſtarke rebels againſt God, and his word, and liue according to the luſts of their blinde and vnrepentant hearts.

Thirdly, when *Paul* ſaith, that *Ieruſalem which is aboue is free, &c.* he ſhewes that the Catholike Church is one in number, and no more, *Cant.* 6.8. *My doue is alone, and the onely daughter of her mother, Iohn* 10.16. *One ſheepefold. There be many members, but one bodie,* 1. *Cor.* 12.12.

Fourthly, hence we gather, that the Catholike Church is inuiſible. For the company of them that dwell in heauen by their faith cannot be diſcerned by the eye. *Iohn* ſaw the heauenly Ieruſalem deſcending from heauen, yet not with the bodily eye, but *in ſpirit, Reuelation* 21. 10. The things which make the Catholike Church to bee the Church, namely, election, vocation, iuſtification, glorification, are inuiſible. The Papiſt therefore erreth, when hee teacheth, that the Catholike Church is a viſible company vnder one Paſtour, namely the Pope. And the places which they bring to prooue the viſibilitie of the vniuerſall Church, concerne either particular Churches, or the Churches which were in the dayes of the Apoſtles, or againe, they ſpeake of the inward glory, and beautie of the Church.

Free] that is, redeemed from the bondage of death and ſinne: and ſo from the curſe of the law. Of this freedome I will ſpeake more afterward.

The mother of vs all] ſhee is called *a mother*, becauſe the word of God is committed to the keeping of the Church, which word is *ſeed*, 1. *Pet.* 1.23. and *milke*, 1. *Cor.* 3.2. and *ſtrong meat*, *Heb.* 5.14. And the Church as a mother, which by the miniſtery of the ſaid word, brings forth children to God, and after they are born, and brought foorth, ſhee feeds them with milke out of her owne breaſts, which are the Scriptures of the old and new Teſtament.

Here a great queſtion is to be propounded, namely, where wee ſhall find this our mother? For it is the dutie of all children to haue recourſe vnto their mother, and to liue vnder her wing. The aduocates of the Popiſh Church, Prieſts and Ieſuits, ſay, we muſt be reconciled to the Church and See of Rome, if we would bee of the Catholike Church. To this purpoſe they vſe many motiues, I will here propound ſeuen of them: becauſe heretofore they haue been ſcattered abroad among vs.

The firſt motiue. The Church of Rome hath meanes of ſure and certaine Interpretation, Tradition, Councels, Fathers: wee haue nothing

nothing but the priuate interpretation of *Luther*, *Melancthon*, *Caluin*, *&c.* *Answer.* Scripture is both the glosse and the text. And the principall meanes of the interpretation of Scripture, is Scripture it selfe. And it is a means, when places of Scripture are expounded by the analogie of faith, by the words, scope, and circumstances of the place. And the interpretation which is sutable to all these, is sure, certaine, and publike: for it is the interpretation of God. Contrariwise, the interpretation, which is not agreeable to these, though it bee from Chuch, Fathers, and Councels, is vncertaine, and it is priuate interpretations. Now this kind of interpretation we allow: and therefore it is false, that we haue only priuate interpretations: and that all the interpretations of the church of Rome are publike. Secondly, I answer, that we are able to iustifie our interpretation of Scriptqre for the maine points of religion, by the consent of Fathers, and Councels, as wel as they of the Church of Rome.

The second motiue. Wee haue no diuine and infallible authoritie to rest on in matter of religion: but they of the Church of Rome haue. *Answer.* In the Canonicall Scriptures of the Prophets and Apostles, there is diuine and infallible authoritie: for they are now in the new Testament, in stead of the liuely voyce of God. And this authoritie wee in our Church acknowledge. Secondly, I answer, that the Church hath no diuine and infallible authoritie distinct from the authoritie of Scriptures (as the Papists teach) but onely a Ministerie, which is, to speake in the name of God, according to the written word.

The third motiue. Wee haue no limitations of opinion, and affection, but they of the Church of Rome haue. I answer first: we suffer our selues to bee limitted for opinion, by the analogie of faith, and by the written word, and so doth not the Papist, which addes tradition to the Scripture. And for affection wee suffer our selues to be limited by the doctrine of repentance, and new obedience. Secondly, I answer, that the Church of Rome vseth false meanes of limitation. For it teacheth, that for opinion, we must captiuate our senses to the determination of the Church, by beleeuing as the Church beleeueth, though it be not knowne what the Church beleeueth. And it limits affection, by auricular confession, and by canonicall satisfactions, meere inuentions of men.

The 4. motiue. The Romane religion drawes the multitude. *Ans.* It draws them indeed, because it is a natual religion: but it doth not turn them frō darknes to light, frō death to life. Secondly, I answer, that Antichrist in his comming shal draw the multitude, 2. *Thes.* 2. 9

The fift motiue. There was neuer but two alterations of religion. One, in the dayes of *Elias*; the other, in the dayes of *Iohn* the *Baptist*. *Anſwer.* I will ſhew a third. *Paul* ſaith, that before the end there ſhall be a departure, *2. Theſſ. 2.* and this departure is generall in all nations, *Reuel. 13. 16.* and after a thouſand yeares there ſhall bee the firſt reſurrection, *Reuel. 20. 5.* and this reſurrection is the reuiuing and the reſtoring of the Goſpell, after long ignorance and ſuperſtition.

The ſixt motiue. The Church of Rome hath a Iudge to ende controuerſies: we haue none. *Anſwer.* Chriſt is our Iudge: and the Scripture is the voice of this Iudge, determining all things pertaining to ſaluation, fully, and plainly, to the contentation of any conſcience.

The ſeuenth motiue. The Romane religion is ſutable to ancient tradition. *Anſwer.* It is contrary. For it aboliſheth the ſecond commandement touching Images, and the tenth, touching luſt. And it ouerturneth ſundry articles of faith. For it aboliſheth one of the natures of Chriſt by the reall preſence, and his three offices, by ioyning partners and aſſociates with him.

To theſe ſeuen, I adde three other. *The eight motiue* then is this. Our Miniſters (ſay they) tooke vnto themſelues new callings: and conſequently, that we are but Schiſmatikes. *Anſw.* The offices of the firſt reſtorers of the Goſpell were ordinary: and their vocation to the ſaid offices was ordinary: for they were all either Prieſts, or Schoole-doctors. It may be ſaid, that they departed from their callings. I anſwer, they departed only from the common abuſe of their callings, which they reſtored to their right vſe.

The ninth motiue. The Church of Rome hath true baptiſme, and therfore it is a true Church. *Anſ.* Baptiſme in the Papacy pertaines not to it, but to another hidden church in the midſt of the Papacy: as the light in the lanthorne, pertains not to it, but to the paſſenger. Secondly, though the church of Rome hold the outward baptiſme, yet doth it ouerturne the inward, which ſtands in the iuſtification of a ſinner, by imputation of the obedience of Chriſt. Thirdly, baptiſme ſeuered from the preaching of the Goſpell, is no marke of a Church. Circumciſion was vſed in Samaria, and yet they were no people of God, *Hoſea* 1 9.

The tenth motiue. The Church of Rome hath antiquitie and ſucceſſion from the Apoſtles. *Anſw.* They are no marks of the church, vnleſſe they bee ioyned with Propheticall and Apoſtolicall doctrine. The kingdome of darkenes hath alſo antiquitie, ſucceſſion, vniuerſalitie, and vnitie.

Now

Now then we are to hold the church of Rome as a stepmother, nay, as a professed harlot: shee is no mother of ours. For the Lord saith, *Come out of her my people*, *Reuel.* 18. Let vs therefore come to the true answer.

The Catholike Church our Mother, is to bee sought for, and to be found in the true visible Churches, the certaine markes whereof are three. The preaching of the word of God, out of the writings of the Prophets and Apostles, with obedience, *Ioh.* 10.28. *Eph.* 2.20 True inuocation of God the Father, in the only name of Christ by the assistance of the Spirit, *Act.* 9.14. 1. *Cor.* 1.2. The right vse of the Sacraments, Baptisme, and the Lords Supper, *Matt.* 28.18. And by these shall wee finde the true Church of God in England, Ireland, Scotland, Germany, France, &c.

Againe, in that the Church is called our Mother, the Papist gathereth, that her commandements must bee obeyed, *Prou.* 1.8. and therfore in their Catechismes, beside the commandements of God, they propound the commandements of the Church. But I answer, that the precepts of the father and the mother must bee one: and then the mother must be obeyed.

The Church is called *the mother of vs all*: that is, of all true beleeuers. Hence it followes, that wicked men are not members of the Catholike Church, (as Popish doctors erroniously teach) for then the Church shall bee a mother, not onely to the children of God, but also to the children of the diuell.

Lastly, in that the Church is our mother, we are taught that wee must despise our first birth, and seeke to be borne againe vnto God, and suck the brest of our mother, feeding on the milke of the word, *Psal.* 45.11. 1. *Pet.* 2.2. Thus to be borne a member of the new Ierusalem, is a great priuiledge, *Psal.* 87.5. *Reuel.* 3.12.

27 *For it is written, Reioyce thou barren that bearest no children, breake foorth and crie, thou that trauellest not: for the desolate hath many more children, then shee which hath an husband.*

These words are the testimony of the Prophet *Isa.* c.54.1. and they are brought to proue that which *Paul* said in the former verse, that *the Catholike Church is the mother of vs all*, that is, not onely of the Iewes, but of all beleeuing Gentiles.

In the words, I consider the preface to the Testimonie, and the Testimony it selfe. The Preface, *It is written*: where two points are to bee considered. The first is, who saith, *It is written? Answer.*

The Apoſtle *Paul*, whoſe authoritie was diuine, and infallible, becauſe he was led into all trueth by the Spirit of God, ſo as he could not erre in deliuering doctrine to the Church. And yet for all this hee followes the rule of the written word. And his manner was ſo to doe, *Actes* 26.22. This ſhewes the ſhameleſſe impudencie of the Church of Rome, which takes to it ſelfe an abſolute power of iudgement in all matters, without, and beſide the Scripture, yea, a power to iudge of the Scripture it ſelfe, and of the ſenſe thereof, without the helpe of Scripture, vpon a ſuppoſed infallible aſſiſtance of the Spirit.

The ſecond point is, In what queſtion ſaith *Paul, It is written? Anſwer.* In a controuerſie betweene him and the falſe Apoſtles, touching the iuſtification of a ſinner. This ſhewes that the Scripture it ſelfe is the meanes to determine and decide controuerſies. There was for this purpoſe in the old Teſtament, the liuely voyce of God vttered in the Oracle at the Mercie ſeate: but in the new Teſtament there is no ſuch voyce of God, but the written word is in ſtead thereof, to the ende of the world. And therefore *Paul* ſaith, *It is written.*

In the Teſtimonie I conſider three things, the condition of two Churches, the change of the condition, the ioy that is vpon the change.

The condition of the Church of the new Teſtament, in theſe words, *Barren that beareſt no children: thou that trauelleſt not: the deſolate.*

Barren] The Chriſtian Church is ſo called, becauſe by the vertue and ſtrength of nature, it beares no children to God, no more then *Sara* did to *Abraham, Iohn* 1.13. 1. *Cor.*3.7. Secondly, it is ſo called in reſpect of the beginning therof, when the Iewiſh Church was yet ſtanding, till the ſpirit of God was powred foorth vpon all fleſh, after the aſcenſion of Chriſt: and before this, the number of them which were conuerted to God, was very ſmall: and therefore Chriſt himſelfe complained, that *he ſpent his ſtrength in vaine, Iſa.*49.1. Thirdly, it is ſo called in reſpect of the latter times of the Church, in which Chriſt ſhall ſcarce finde faith vpon the earth, *Luke* 18.8. Further, that the Church is barren, it is declared by the ſigne, becauſe ſhe neither brings forth child, nor beares.

Deſolate] that is, without husband in appearance, by reaſon of the croſſe and affliction, and without children: becauſe at the firſt the Chriſtian Church was conſtrained to hide her ſelfe in the wilderneſſe, *Reuel.*12.14. It may bee demanded how the Catholike Church ſhould be deſolate? *Anſwer.* The eſtate of the Church is twofold: inward, or outward. The inward eſtate ſtands in the true knowledge of God in Chriſt, in comfort touching remiſſion of ſinnes, and life euerlaſting, in the hearing of our praiers, in protection and deliuerance from all ſpirituall enemies, in the gifts of the Spirit, faith, hope, loue, &c. In reſpect of this eſtate, the Church is all glorious within, and neuer deſolate. *Pſal.* 45. 13. The outward eſtate of the Catholike Church, ſtands in viſible aſſemblies, in the publike Miniſtery of the word, and Sacraments, in a gouernement according to the word of God. In reſpect of this ſecond eſtate, the Church may be in deſolation. This was the condition of the Church in paradiſe vpon the fal of our firſt parents, of the Iſraelites at Mount *Horeb*, when they worſhipped the golden calfe, and in the daies of *Elias*, *Rom.* 11. 3. and afterward, 2. *Chron.* 15. 3. When Chriſt ſuffered, the Shepheard was ſmitten, and the ſheepe were ſcattered. After Chriſts aſcenſion, all the earth worſhipped the beaſt, *Reuel.* 13. 12.

Hence it followes, that the Catholike Church is not a viſible eſtate or company of men vnder one viſible head: becauſe in reſpect of her outward eſtate ſhe may be for a time in deſolation. And as this is the eſtate of the Church, ſo is it alſo of the members thereof. *They ſhall bee hated of all men*, *Luke* 21. 17. *Men ſhall thinke they doe God good ſeruice, when they kill them*, *Iohn* 16. 2. And Chriſt himſelfe was a man *without forme or beautie*, *Iſai.* 53. 2.

Hauing an husband] in theſe words the condition of the Iewiſh Church is ſet foorth, that ſhee is married or eſpouſed to God, who is her husband, *Ezech.* 16. 8, 9. *Oſea* 2. 19. The like may be ſaid of any other Church, and namely of the Church of England. The vſe.

This muſt teach vs, to dedicate our bodies and ſoules to God and Chriſt, and to giue the maine affections of our hearts vnto him, as our loue, and our ioy, &c.

Secondly, wee muſt adorne and trimme our ſelues with grace, that we may pleaſe our husband, *Pſal.* 45. 12.

Thirdly, we muſt be the glory of Chriſt, as the wife is to her husband, 1. *Cor.* 11. 7. and that is by ſubiecting our ſelues to Chriſt, and his lawes.

Againe, if we betroath our ſelues to Chriſt indeed, we may aſſure our ſelues that Chriſt is our Chriſt, and that hee hath giuen himſelfe vnto vs: and conſequently, that he wil ſanctifie vs, *Ezech.* 16. 9. protect vs as an husband doeth his wife, *Geneſis* 20. 16. and indow vs with all things needfull for this life, and the life to come, *Ezech.* 16. 10, 11.

The ſecond point is the change of the Church of the newe Teſtament, becauſe ſhe ſhall ceaſe to be barren, and bring forth many children.. This is the promiſe of God: and hereupon *Paul* concludes, that the Church is a Mother of all beleeuers, both Iewes and Gentiles. Obſerue, that the promiſe of God is of infinite vertue in his time and place. In the beginning God ſaid, *Let there be this or that, and it was ſo.* Of like vertue is Gods promiſe, if we can waite his leiſure. God promiſed that after 430. yeares, the Iſraelites ſhould be deliuered out of Egypt; preſently when the time was expired, nothing could hinder the promiſe. Reade *Exod.* 12. 41. Therefore our duty is, to reſt on Gods promiſes in all times, both in life and death.

The third point is the ioy vpon the change. *Reioyce.* Here are two things to be conſidered. The firſt, who muſt reioyce? *Anſw.* The Church. Gods kingdome is the place of ioy. *Rom.* 14. 17. Reioycing belongs to the people of God; *Pſal.* 68. 3. & 106. 5. The muſicke of the Temple was typicall, and figured the ioy of the Catholike Church, where is the aſſurance of remiſſion of ſinnes, and life eternall.

The ſecond point is, in what muſt the Church reioyce? *Anſ.* In the redemption of Chriſt and the fruit thereof, the conuerſion of ſinners to God. For the prophet had ſhewed at large the paſſion and ſufferings of Chriſt: *Iſa.* 53. and hereupon he ſaith, *Reioyce thou barren.* The Iſraelites were commanded to feaſt and to be merry *before the Lord*, *Leuit.* 23. 40. 1. *Chron.* 29. 32. that is, before the Lords Arke, which was the pledge of his preſence. Now this Arke was a figure of Chriſt: and the myrth before the Arke, ſignified, that the foundation of all our ioy, lies in our Reconciliation with God in Chriſt. The angels in heauen greatly reioyce at the conuerſion of a ſinner: and at the returne of the prodigall ſonne, the fat calfe is killed,

The vſe. It is falſe that religion breeds Melancholy, and cuts off all mirth. It doeth not aboliſh mirth, but rectifie it: nay it brings men to true and perfect ioy.

Our firſt and principall ioy muſt be, that we are in Gods fauour, reconciled to God by Chriſt, *Luk.* 10. 20. In *Dauid*, the head of his ioy, was the good eſtate of the Church, *Pſal.* 137. 6. And all other petty ioyes muſt flow from this, and be ſutable to it.

Breake foorth] this ſignifies, that the Church vpon earth is (as it were) pent in with preſent griefe. Our ioy in this life is mixed with ſorrow. The paſchall lambe was eaten *with ſowre hearbes*, to ſignifie, that we feele no ſweetneſſe in the blood of Chriſt, till

we

we feele the smart of our sinnes. We here must reioyce in trembling, *Psal.2.11. Ioy is sowne for them that are vpright in heart, Psal. 97.12.*

Crie] in our earthly ioyes, we must be moderate and sparing, we must not eate too much hony lest we surfet. Yet in spiritual ioyes the measure is to reioyce without measure, if we be rauished with ioy in Christ, that we cry againe, it is the best of all.

28. *Therefore brethren, we are after the manner of Isaac, children of the promise.*

Here *Paul* shewes, that as *Sara* figured the catholike Church: so *Isaac* was a figure of all true beleeuers the children of God.

Therefore[or thus, *And we brethren.*

We] not onely the Iewes, but also beleeuing Gentiles.

Promise] the promise made to *Abraham, I will be thy God and the God of thy seed:* or the promise made to the Church, that beeing barren shee shall beare many children.

Children of promise] beleeuers are so called: not because they beleeue the promise (though that be a truth) but because they are made children of God, by the vertue of Gods promise. For thus was *Isaac* the child of promise, in that he was borne to *Abraham*, not by the strength of nature, but by Gods promise. And *Paul* opposeth the children of the promise to the children of the flesh, which were borne by naturall strength, *Rom.*9.8.

Hence it followes, that the meere grace of God, is the cause of our election and adoption, & not any thing in vs. For the promise of God makes vs Gods children: and the promise is of the meere grace of God: & therfore we are Gods children by the meere grace of God. For the cause of the cause, is the cause of the thing caused. Therefore *Paul* saith, that *the Ephesians were predestinate to adoption, Eph.*1.5. And he saith, the 7000 that neuer bowed knee to *Baal, were reserued by the election of grace, Rom.*11.5. And it is a false Position, to teach, that Election and adoption, are according to Gods foreknowledge of our faith and obedience. For thus shall we elect our selues, and be children not of Gods promise, but of our owne freewill and faith. Moreouer God foresees our future faith and obedience, because he first decreed to giue the grace of faith vnto vs: because the foreknowledge of things which are to come to passe, depends vpon a precedent will in God.

Marke further, the children of God are called the children of the promise, and this promise is absolute and effectual. Here a queſtion may be reſolued: and that is, whether the child of God in his conuerſation, haue a libertie and power to reſiſt the inward calling of God? *Anſwer.* No. The abſolute will of God cannot be reſiſted: now the promiſe whereby men are made the children of God, is the abſolute will of God. Againe, with this promiſe is ioyned the infinite power of God, which without all reſiſtance brings that to paſſe which God hath promiſed. For hee makes men to doe that which he commands, *Ezech.* 36.26. he giues the will and the deed, *Phil.* 2.3. ſo as men effectually called, cannot but come, *Iohn* 6.45.

It may bee ſaid, that this is to aboliſh all freedome of will. *Anſwer.* It ſufficeth to the libertie of the will, that it bee free from compulſion: for conſtraint takes away the libertie of the will, and not neceſſitie. Secondly, the determination of mans will by the will of God, is the libertie of the will, and not the bondage thereof: for this is perfect libertie, when mans will is conformable to the will of God.

29 *But as he which was borne according to the fleſh, perſecuted him that was borne after the ſpirit, ſo is it now.*

Theſe words are an anſwer to an obiection, on this maner. We are hated of the Iewes: and therefore wee are not the children of promiſe. The anſwer is two-fold. One in this verſe, thus, No maruell: this is the olde faſhion: it was thus in *Abrahams* family. For *Iſhmael* (borne after the fleſh) perſecuted *Iſaac* (borne after the ſpirit:) and ſo it is at this day.

Obſerue, that there is a perpetuall enmitie and oppoſition betweene true beleeuers and hypocrites. *God put enmitie betweene the ſeed of the ſerpent, and the ſeed of the woman, Geneſ.* 13. 15. The world hates them that are choſen out of the world, *Iohn* 15.19. Carnall men cannot abide that their opinions & doings ſhould be iudged, and condemned of others, *Iohn* 3.20. And hence comes the oppoſition that is between beleeuers, and hypocrites, who cannot abide ſuch as are not like themſelues.

This hatred and oppoſition ſhewes it ſelfe in perſecution: of which three things are to be conſidered.

The firſt is, who perſecutes? *Anſwer.* Carnall Iſhmaelites, ſuch as are of the ſame religion and family with *Iſaac.* Thus the Iewes perſecuted their own Prophets, & the Theſſalonians were perſecuted of their owne countrymen, 1.*Theſſ.* 2.14. Thus Prieſts and Ieſuits, that haue bin heretofore borne, baptized, & brought vp among vs,

are

are the causes of many seditions, conspiracies, and seeke the subuersion of Church and land.

The second is, who are persecuted? *Ans,* Spirituall men, the children of the promise. They suffer wrong, but they doe none. *In the mount of the Lord there is no hurt done. Isa.* 11.9. they *turne their speares and swords, into mattocks and sithes. Isa.* 2.4. And they which doe no wrong, but are content to suffer wrong (and that for a good cause,) are in this respect blessed, *Matth.* 5.10.

The third point is, is, touching the kind of persecution: and that was skorning or mocking. *Gen.* 21.9. It may be demanded how mocking can be persecution? *Answer.* Mocking and derision, which riseth of the hatred and contempt of our brother, is a degreee of murder. *He which saith Raca to his brother, is guilty of a Councell. Matth.* 5.22. Here *Raca,* signifieth all signes & gestures that expresse contempt, as *snuffing, tushing, iering, gerning, &c. Cain* is rebuked of God, euen for the casting downe of his countenance. *Genes.* 4. verse 6.

Againe, the mocking wherewith *Ismael* mocked *Isaac,* proceeded from a contempt and hatred of rhe grace of God in *Isaac:* which *Paul* notes when he saith, that *he was persecuted which was borne after the spirit.* This hatred of Gods grace in men, is the beginning of all persecution, and the deriding of the grace of God, is as much as the spoiling of our goods, & the seeking of our liues. Thus *Cain* hated his brother, by reason of the grace of God: *because his deeds were good.* 1. *Ioh.* 3.12. A great part of the sufferings of Christ stood in this, that he was mocked for his confidence in God. *Psal.* 22.8. *Matth.* 27.43. The children of *Bethel* mocke *Elizeus:* first, for his person, calling him *bald pate:* Secondly, for the fauour of God shewed vpon *Elias* his master, in saying, *Ascend, bald pate:* that is, * ascend not to *Bethel,* but ascend to heauen as *Elias* did. And this prophane scorning he cursed in the name of God. 2. *King.* 2.23. The like skorning is vsed among vs at this day. For the practise of that religion which stands by the law of God, and the good lawes of this land, is nicknamed with tearmes of *precisenesse,* and *puritie.* A thing much to be lamented: for this bewraies that there is a great want of the grace of God among vs. Therfore take heede of it.

* Iustin. in quæst.

30. *But what saith the Scripture? Put out the bond-woman, and her sonne: for the sonne of the bondwoman shal not be heire with the sonne of the freewoman.*

The second answer to the former obiection, is in these wordes, that

that they which hate the children of promiſe, ſhall at length be caſt out of the houſe of God.

Obiect. I. Theſe words, *caſt out the bondwoman*, are the words of *Sara* to *Abraham*: therefore they are not the words of Scripture. *Anſwer.* The words were vttered by *Sara*, but they were afterward approoued by God, *Geneſis* 21.12. and thus they are the voice of Scripture.

Obiect. II. Sara is commended for her ſubiection to *Abraham*, 1.*Pet.*3.6. yet here ſhe ſpeakes imperiouſly, *Caſt out the bondwoman. Anſwer.* She ſpeakes this not as a priuate woman, but as the voice and mouth of God, and that (no doubt) by inſtinct from God. And therefore the words ſhee vttereth, are to be eſteemed as the commaundement of God. This her caſe is extraordinarie, and not to be followed.

The vſe. I. All carnall hypocrites, mockers of the grace of God, ſhall be caſt foorth of Gods family, though for a time they beare a ſway therein. This is the ſentence of God. Let vs therefore repent of our mocking, and hereafter become louers of the grace of God, as Chriſt was, *Marke* 10.21.

II. Conſolation: the perſecution of the people of God ſhal not be perpetual. For the perſecuting bondwoman and her ſonne, muſt be caſt out. *The rod of the wicked ſhall not reſt vpon the lot of the righteous, Pſal.* 125.3. This is our comfort.

III. All iuſticiary people, and perſons that looke to bee ſaued and iuſtified before God by the law, and the workes of the law, either in whole, or in part, are caſt out of the Church of God, and haue no part in the kingdome of heauen. The caſting out of *Agar* and *Iſhmael*, is a figure of the reiection of all ſuch. Behold here the voice of God caſting downe from heauen the greateſt part of the earth, the Turke, the Iew, the obſtinate Papiſt, with the ſtepmother, the Romiſh Church.

31 *Then brethren, wee are not children of the ſeruant, but of the free woman.*

The concluſion of the whole argument following directly from the 27. verſe. If we be children of the promiſe, then are we children of the free woman, and not of the bondwoman, and conſequently wee are iuſtified and ſaued without the workes of the law, by the meere grace of God, cauſing vs by faith to reſt on the promiſe of God, whoſe ſubſtance and foundation is Chriſt.

CHAP.

CHAP. V.

1 *Stand faſt therefore in the libertie wherewith Christ hath made vs free, & be not intangled again with the yoke of bondage.*

These words are a repetition of the principall concluſion of the whole Epiſtle. Which was on this manner: I *Paul* am called to teach, and my doctrine is true: therefore yee did euill to depart from it, and your dutie was to haue ſtood vnto it.

Further, they are collected and inferred vpon the concluſion of the laſt argument vſed in the laſt chapter, thus: Yee are children of the free woman: and therfore ye are free: and therefore ye ſhould hold faſt your libertie.

In the words, two maine points of doctrine are propounded. The firſt is, that by nature wee are all intangled with the yoke of bondage. For the better conceiuing of this, I will handle three points; the nature of this bondage, the ſigne of it, and the vſe.

Touching the nature of it. Our ſpirituall bondage ſtands in three things. The firſt, is bondage vnder ſinne, which *Paul* teacheth when he ſaith, *I am carnall ſold vnder ſinne*, Romanes 7.13. Heere remember, that by ſinne, is meant originall ſinne, which hath two parts: Guiltineſſe in the firſt offence of *Adam*, which is imputed to all mankinde; and the diſpoſition of all the powers of the ſoule to all manner of euill whatſoeuer. And this rebellious diſpoſition is like a leproſie infecting the whole man: and it reignes like a tyrant ouer the ſoule of man, by tempting, intiſing, and drawing him from one actuall ſinne to another, ſo as hee can doe nothing but ſinne, *Iames* 1.14.

The ſecond thing, is obligation or ſubiection to all puniſhment both temporall and eternall. And it hath three parts. The firſt is, Bondage vnder Satan, who keepes vnrepentant ſinners *in his ſnare according to his owne will*, 2.*Tim*.2.26. hee rules in their hearts like a God, 2.*Cor*.4.4. and hath power to blind them, and to harden their hearts, till he haue brought them to eternall death, *Heb*.2.14. The ſecond is, bondage vnder an euil conſcience, which ſits in the hearts of offendours as an accuſer and a terrible Iudge, and lies like a wilde beaſt at a mans doore, ready euer and anon to plucke out his throat, *Gen*.4.7. The third is, bondage vnder the wrath of God, and the feare of eternall death, *Heb*.2.15.

The

The third part of this bondage, is the obligation of the ceremoniall law. It pertaines not to all mankind, but onely concernes the Iewes, to whom it was a yoke of bondage, *Acts* 15.

The ſigne of this bondage, whereby it may bee diſcerned, is to keepe a courſe or practiſe in ſinning, *Iohn* 8. 34. *Hee that commits ſinne, is a ſeruant of ſinne:* or againe, a life led according to the cuſtome and faſhion of this world in the luſt of the fleſh, or the luſt of the eye, (which is couetouſneſſe,) or in the pride of life, *Epheſ.* 2.2. 1.*Iohn* 2.16.

The vſe. We muſt learne to ſee, feele, acknowledge, and bewaile this bondage in our ſelues. Deliuerance belongs onely to ſuch captiues as know themſelues to be captiues, *Luke* 4.18. and labour vnder this bondage, *Matt.* 11.28. Thus did *Paul* when he ſaith, *I am ſold vnder ſinne:* and, *O miſerable man, who ſhall deliuer me from this body of death?* To feele this bondage, is a ſtep out of it: and not to feele it, is to be plunged into it.

Secondly, we muſt pray earneſtly for deliuerance. The dumbe creatures ſigh and trauel till they be deliuered from their bondage: much more then muſt we doe it, *Rom.* 8.22.

Thirdly, wee muſt learne to deteſt whatſoeuer is of our ſelues: becauſe it wholly tends to bondage.

Laſtly, we muſt be content with any affliction that God laies on vs, though it be lingring ſickneſſe, pouertie, impriſonment, baniſhment. For God might worthily lay on vs all ſhame and confuſion: becauſe we are by nature ſlaues of ſinne and Satan.

The ſecond maine doctrine is, that by grace there is a libertie pertaining to the people of God. Heere I conſider foure things: Firſt, what this libertie is. Secondly, the authour of it. Thirdly, the perſons to whom it belongs. Fourthly, our duetie touching this libertie.

For the firſt: Chriſtian libertie is called, *the good, or commoditie of Chriſtians, Rom.* 14.16.

It is a ſpirituall right or condition, loſt by Adam, and reſtored by Chriſt. I ſay, *ſpirituall*, becauſe it pertaines to the conſcience. The vſe indeed of our liberty is in outward things, as meat, drinke, apparell, &c. but the liberty it ſelfe is in the conſcience. And thus it differs from *ciuill* libertie, which ſtands in the mouing of the body, in the choiſe of bodily actions, and in the free vſe of our goods.

Chriſtian libertie hath two parts, a *Deliuerance from miſerie*, and *Freedome in good things*.

Deliuerance hath foure parts. The firſt, is a deliuerance from the curſe of the law for the breach thereof, *Rom.* 8.1. *There is no*

condem-

condemnation to them that are in Chriſt. And this comes to paſſe: becauſe there is a tranſlation made of the curſe from our perſons to the perſon of Chriſt, *Gal.* 3.13.

The ſecond deliuerance is from the obligation of the law, whereby it binds vs to bring perfect righteouſnes in our own perſons for the attainement of euerlaſting life, according to the tenour thereof, *Doe this, and liue.* And this deliuerance is procured, becauſe there is a tranſlation made of the fulfilling of the law from our perſons to the perſon of our Sauiour Chriſt.

From theſe two deliuerances ariſeth the Pacification of the conſcience, partly for our Iuſtification, and partly for our conuerſation.

Touching iuſtification: A ſinner in his humiliation and conuerſion hath by his doctrine a Liberty without reſpect to his own workes, or to his owne fulfilling of the law, to reſt on the meere mercy of God for the forgiuenes of his ſinnes, and the ſaluation of his ſoule, and to appeale from the throne of diuine iuſtice, to the throne of grace, & to oppoſe the merit of Chriſt againſt the wrath and iudgement of God. And this hath alwaies bin the helpe of the godly in their diſtreſſe, Reade 2.*Chron.* 33.12. *Ezra.* 9. *Dan.* 9. *Pſal.* 32. 31.130.143. Conſider the example of the Publican, and the Prodigall ſonne, who condemne themſelues, and make their appeale to the court of mercy and grace.

Here ſome man may ſay, how ſhall I know that I am freed from the rigour of the law, and from the curſe thereof? *Anſ.* Thou muſt firſt ſet thy ſelfe at the barre of Gods iudgement: and there muſt thou arraigne, accuſe, and condemne thy ſelfe: this done, thou muſt vſe thy liberty, and make thine appeale to Gods mercy and grace for pardon, by aſking, ſeeking, knocking: and thus at length ſhalt thou be reſolued touching thy deliuerance.

Moreouer, touching conuerſation, our conſciences are ſetled thus: In what we are freed from the Rigour of the law, God in mercy accepts the will and indeauour to beleeue, repent, and obay, for faith, repentance, and obedience. He ſpares them that feare him, as a father ſpares his child when he indeauours to doe that which he can. *Mal.* 3.17. The law requires perfect obedience at our hands: yet God of his mercy lookes more at the will to obay, then the perfection of obedience. This muſt be a ſtay to our mindes, when we ſee more corruption, then grace in our ſelues, and our obedience tainted with many ſpots of diſobedience.

The third Deliuerance, is from the obſeruation of the Ceremoniall law of *Moſes.* *Col.* 2.16. And hence ariſeth another deliuerance

rance from the bondage of humane Traditions, as *Paul* saith, *If yee be dead with Christ from the Elements of the world, why are ye burdened with traditions? Col.2.20.*

The fourth Deliuerance, is from vnder the tyrannie and dominion of sinne. *Romanes. 6.14. Let not sinne haue dominion ouer you. For ye are not vnder the law, but vnder grace.* In the first conuersion of a sinner. Originall sinne receiues his deadly wound, and the dominion thereof is diminished according to the measure of grace receiued.

The second part of Christian liberty, is *a Freedome* in good things: and it is fourefold. The first, is a freedome in the voluntary seruice of God. *Luk. 1.74. We are deliuered from our enemies, that we may serue God in righteousnesse and holinesse before him all the daies of our liues without feare. Paul* saith, that *the law is not giuen to the righteous man, 1.Tim.1.9.* because he is a law to himselfe, and freely does good duties, as if there were no law to bind him, The cause of this freedome, is the Gift & donation of the free Spirit of God. Therfore *Dauid* praies, *Stablish me with thy free spirit. Psal.51.* And *Paul* saith, *Where the spirit is, there is libertie. 2.Cor.3.17.* And, *The spirit of life which is in Christ* (is a Law to vs, and) *frees vs from the power of sinne, and death. Rom.8.2.*

It may be obiected, that this freedome in the voluntary seruice of God, is bondage. For Christ saith, *Matth.11.29. Take my yoke vpon you.* And we are as streightly bound to the obedience of the law of God, as *Adam* was by creation, nay more streightly, by reason of our redemption by Christ. *Ans.* The more we are bound to obedience, the freer we are: because the seruice of God is not bondage, but perfect liberty.

The second freedome, is in the free vse of all the creatures of God. *Tit.1.15 To the pure, all things are pure. Rom.14.14.* And the reason is, because the dominion ouer the creatures, lost by *Adam*, is restored by Christ. *1.Cor.3.22.* And hence it is, that *Paul* calls the forbidding of marriage, and of meates, with obligation of conscience, *a doctrine of diuells. 1.Tim.4.1.*

The third freedome, is a Liberty to come vnto God the Father in the name of Christ, and in praier to be heard. *Rom.5.2. Eph.3.12.* Whereas according to our naturall condition, our sinnes are a wall of partition betweene vs and God, and cause vs to fly from the presence of God: and though we cry vnto God, and fill heauen and earth with our cries, so long as we are in our sins, we are not heard of him.

The fourth freedome, is a Liberty to enter into heauen in the

the day of our death: Chriſt by his blood hauing made a way, *Hebr.* 10.19.

Thus we ſee what Chriſtian libertie is. The vſe followes. The Anabaptiſts gather hence, that among Chriſtians there muſt be no magiſtrates, they muſt haue power to make lawes beſides the lawes of God: but this power they haue not, becauſe Chriſtians haue a free vſe of all the creatures of God by Chriſtian libertie. *Anſ.* We muſt diſtinguiſh betweene the liberty it ſelfe, and the vſe of it. And the magiſtrates authoritie deales not with the libertie which is in the conſcience, but with the vſe of it: and he doth neither diminiſh nor aboliſh the vſe of any of the creatures, but reſtraines the abuſe, and moderates the ouer common vſe for the common good. Thus Magiſtracie and Chriſtian libertie may ſtand together: and the rather, becauſe libertie is in the conſcience, and the Magiſtrates authoritie pertaines to the body.

Heere is further comfort for all the godly: for euen by Chriſtian libertie, their conſciences are exempted from the power of all creatures, men, and Angels, 1. *Corinth.* 7.23. *Yee are bought with a price, bee not ſeruants of men,* that is, let not your hearts and conſciences ſtand in ſubiection to the will of any man. Here then falles to the ground the opinion of the Papiſtes, namely, that the lawes and traditions of the Church bind conſcience as truly and certainly as the word of God. This doctrine is not of God, becauſe it is againſt Chriſtian libertie.

Obiect. I. Rom. 13.5. *Bee ſubiect to the higher powers for conſcience. Anſwer.* Conſcience here is not in reſpect of the lawes of the Magiſtrate; but in reſpect of the law of God, that binds vs in conſcience to obey the law of the Magiſtrate.

Obiect. II. Heb 13.17. *Obey them that haue the ouerſight of you, and be ſubiect. Anſw.* We muſt be ſubiect to them: becauſe as Miniſters of God, they deliuer the word of God in the name of God vnto vs, and that word binds conſcience. Againe, the lawes which they make touching order and comelineſſe in the ſeruice of God, are to be obeyed for the auoiding of ſcandall and contempt.

Obiect. III. A thing indifferent vpon the commandement of the Magiſtrate, becomes neceſſary. *Anſwer.* It is true. But it muſt be obſerued, that neceſſitie is twofold. Externall, Internall. And the law of the Magiſtrate makes a thing indifferent to be neceſſary onely in reſpect of externall neceſſitie, for the auoiding of the contempt of authoritie, and for the auoiding of ſcandall. Otherwiſe the thing in it ſelfe is not neceſſary, but remaines ſtill indifferent, and may be vſed or not vſed, if contempt and ſcandall be auoided.

auoided. The Apoſtles made a law that the Gentiles ſhould abſtaine from ſtrangled and blood,& things offered to Idols, *Act.*15. 28. yet *Paul* ſaith afterward to the *Corinthians*, *All things are lawfull*, 1.*Cor*.10.23. and *whatſoeuer is ſold in the ſhambles eate, and make no queſtion for conſcience ſake*, v.25. becauſe their intent was not, that the law ſhould ſimply binde, but onely in the caſe of offence: and therfore where there was no offence to be feared, they leaue all men to their liberty.

Againe, here is an other comfort to all that beleeue in Chriſt, that nothing can hurt them, and that no euill can be fall them, *Pſal.* 91.v.10. nay all things ſhall in the end turne to their good, though in reaſon and ſenſe, they ſeeme hurtfull. To beleeue this one thing, is a ground of all true comfort.

The conſideration of this benefit of Chriſtian liberty, teacheth three duties. The firſt is, from our hearts, to imbrace, loue, and mantaine Chriſtian religion: becauſe it is the meanes of this liberty. The ſecond is, carefully to ſearch the ſcriptures: for they are as it were the Charter in which our liberties are contained. Thirdly, our Chriſtian liberty puts vs in minde to become vnfained ſeruants of God in the duties of faith, repentance, new obedience. *Rom.*6.22. For this ſeruice is our liberty.

The ſecond point is, touching the Author of this libertie, in theſe words, *wherewith Chriſt hath made vs free.* Chriſt then is the worker of this liberty. *Ioh.*8.36. he diſſolues the works of the diuel. 1.*Ioh.*3.8. he binds the ſtrong man and caſts him out of his hold. *Matth.*12.29.

He procures this liberty by two meanes, by his merit, and by the efficacy of his ſpirit. The merit of his death, procures deliuerance from death, and it purchaſeth a right to life euerlaſting. The efficacy of his ſpirit aſſures vs of our adoption, and withall abates by little and little the ſtrength and power of ſinne. The vſe. Hence we learne the greatnes and grieuouſnes of our ſpirituall bondage, becauſe there was none that could deliuer vs from it, but Chriſt by his death and paſſion. Hence therefore we are to take occaſion to acknowledge and bewaile this our moſt miſerable condition in our ſelues.

Secondly, the price that was paid for the procurement of our liberty, namely, the pretious blood of the immaculate lambe of God, ſhewes that the liberty it ſelfe is a thing moſt pretious and excellent, and ſo to be eſteemed.

Thirdly, for this liberty we are to giue all praiſe and thankes to God. Thus did *Paul* at the remembrance of it. *Rom.* 7.25.

*1.Cor.*15.57. And not to be thankfull, is an height of wickedneſſe.

The third point is, concerning the perſons to whom this liberty belongs; and they are noted in theſe words, *Stand yee faſt; hee hath made vs free.* Whereby *Paul* ſignifies himſelfe and the Galatians that beleeued in Chriſt. Beleeuers then are the perſons to whom this libertie belongs, *Iohn* 1.12. 1.*Tim.*4.3. And true beleeuers are thus to be diſcerned. They vſe the ordinary meanes of grace and ſaluation, the word, and Sacraments: in the vſe of the meanes, they exerciſe themſelues in the ſpiritual exerciſes of inuocation and repentance: and in theſe exerciſes they bewaile their vnbeleefe, and ſtriue by all meanes to beleeue in Chriſt. As for them that conceiue a perſwaſion of Gods mercy without the meanes of ſaluation, and without the exerciſes of inuocation and repentance, they are not true beleeuers but hypocrites.

When *Paul* ſaith, *Chriſt hath made vs free*, that is, mee *Paul*, and you the Galatians, hee teacheth, that euery beleeuer muſt by his faith apply vnto himſelfe the benefit of Chriſtian liberty. But to doe this well, is a matter of great difficultie. The Papiſts in their writings report our doctrine to be this: that a man muſt conceiue a perſwaſion that hee is in the fauour of God the adopted child of God: and that vpon this perſwaſion hee hath the pardon of his ſins, and the benefit of Chriſtian liberty. But they abuſe vs in this, as in many other things. For wee teach, that the application of Chriſt and his benefits, is to bee made by certaine degrees. The firſt is, to vſe the meanes of ſaluation, prayer, Sacraments: the ſecond is, to conſider and to grow to ſome feeling of our ſpirituall bondage: the third is, to will and deſire to beleeue in Chriſt, and to teſtifie this deſire by asking, ſeeking, knocking: the fourth is, a certaine perſwaſion, or a certainty conceiued in mind of the mercy of God by meanes of the former deſire, according to the promiſe of God, *Aske, and it ſhall be giuen vnto you.* The fifth is, an experience of the goodneſſe of God after long vſe of the meanes of ſaluation, and then vpon this experience followes the full perſwaſion of mercy and forgiueneſſe.

The fourth poynt, concernes the office of beleeuers, and that is, to ſtand faſt in their Chriſtian libertie, and in the doctrine of the Goſpell, which reueales this libertie. And by this, wee in England are admoniſhed to ſtand faſt to the religion which is now by law eſtabliſhed among vs, and not to returne vnder the yoke of Popiſh bondage. For the Popiſh religion is flat againſt Chriſtian libertie, two wayes. For our libertie which we haue in Chriſt, frees vs from the law three wayes; in reſpect of *condemnation*, in reſpect of *compulſion* to obedience, and in reſpect of *iuſtification*, (as *Paul* ſhewes at large in this Epiſtle:) and yet the Popiſh doctrine is, that we are to be iuſtified by the workes of the law. Againe, Chriſtian libertie frees our conſciences from the Traditions of men, *Coloſ.* 2.20. and yet the Popiſh religion bindes vs in conſcience to the Traditions of men: nay, it is nothing elſe but a heape of Traditions.

Here two things are to be conſidered, the manner of ſtanding, and the time. The manner is ſignified in the very words. For *to ſtand faſt*, is to hold and maintaine our libertie with courage and conſtancy, whatſoeuer comes of it; as the ſouldier keepes his ſtanding, though it coſt him his life. Wee are readie to defend the libertie of our countrey, euen with the hazard of our liues: much more then are we to defend Chriſtian libertie with the loſſe of all that wee enioy: ſinne muſt be reſiſted euen vnto blood, *Heb.* 12.4. If men bee fearefull, they muſt pray to God for the ſpirit of boldneſſe and courage: and if God vouchſafe not this gift when opportunitie is offered, they may withdraw themſelues, and by flying, preſerue their libertie.

The time of ſtanding, is *the euill day*, that is, the day of triall, *Eph.* 6.13. And then to ſtand faſt, is a matter of great difficultie. And for this cauſe we are beforehand to prepare our ſelues by obſeruing theſe rules following. Firſt, wee muſt labour that religion be not onely in mind and memory, but alſo be rooted in the affection of our hearts, ſo as wee loue it, reioyce in it, and eſteeme it aboue all things. Secondly, we muſt not only be hearers of the word of God, but alſo doers of it in the exerciſes of faith, repentance, new obedience. Thirdly, we muſt ioyne with our religion, the ſoundneſſe of good conſcience: for if conſcience faile, we cannot be ſound in our religion. Laſtly, we muſt pray to God with all maner of prayer and ſupplication for all things needfull, *Eph.* 6.18.

2. *Behold, I Paul ſay vnto you, that if ye be circumciſed, Chriſt ſhall profit you nothing.*

Theſe words, are a reaſon of the former concluſion, thus. If ye be circumciſed, and go backe from your Chriſtian profeſſion, Chriſt ſhall profit you nothing: therefore ſtand faſt.

In the words, I conſider a ſentence, and the proofe of it. The ſentence, *If yee bee circumciſed, &c.* the proofe, *I Paul ſay vnto you.* For the better vnderſtanding of the ſentence, Circumciſion muſt here bee conſidered according to the circumſtance of time, three

wayes.

wayes. Before Chriſt it was a Sacrament, and a ſeale of the righteouſneſſe of faith, *Rom.* 4.11. after the death of Chriſt, till the deſtruction of the Temple, it was a dead ceremony, yet ſometime vſed as a thing indifferent. After the deſtruction of the Temple, when the Church of the new Teſtament was planted among the Gentiles, it was a deadly ceremonie, and ceaſed to be indifferent: and in this laſt reſpect *Paul* ſaith, *If ye be circumciſed, &c.* Againe, circumciſion muſt be conſidered according to the opinion which the falſe apoſtles had of it: now they put their confidence in it, and made it a meritorious cauſe of their ſaluation, and ioyned it with Chriſt. The words therefore carry this ſenſe: If yee will be circumciſed with this opinion, that circumciſion ſhall bee vnto you a meritorious cauſe of your ſaluation, *Chriſt ſhall profit you nothing.* The vſe. Hence it followes, that the doctrine of iuſtification by workes, is an errour ouerturning the foundation of religion, which whoſoeuer obſtinately maintaineth, cannot be ſaued. It will be ſaid, this is true of ceremoniall works, but not of morall works. *Anſwer.* Yea euen of morall. For that which *Paul* ſaith here of circumciſion, he ſpeakes generally of the whole law, verſe 4. *Yee are aboliſhed from Chriſt, whoſoeuer are iuſtified by the law.* And circumciſion muſt be conſidered as an obligation to the obedience of the whole law. Againe, it may be ſaid, this is true of the works of nature, but not of works of grace. *Anſ.* Yea, euen of workes of grace: for the Galatians were regenerate, and therfore looked not to be iuſtified, and ſaued by the works of nature, but by works of grace.

Secondly, hence we gather, that to adde any thing to the paſſion as a meritorious cauſe of our iuſtification and ſaluation, is to make Chriſt vnprofitable. For he muſt be a perfect Sauiour, or no Sauiour: he admits neither partner, nor deputie in the worke of our redemption. And the grace of God admits no mixture or compoſition with any thing that is of vs. Grace is no grace, vnleſſe it be freely giuen euery way. Therefore the Popiſh religion is a damnable religion: becauſe with the merit and ſatisfaction of Chriſt, it ioynes humane merits and ſatisfactions, in the caſe of our iuſtification. It may be alleadged, that the Popiſh religion maintaines all the articles concerning Chriſt, as we doe. *Anſwer.* It doeth ſo in word: but withall it addes to the foreſaid articles the doctrine of humane merites and ſatisfactions, which make void the death of Chriſt. Againe, Papiſts alledge that it is the glory of Chriſt, that he merits for vs, and withall makes vs to merit for our ſelues; as it is the glory of an Emperour to make other kings vnder him. *Anſwer.* It is not the glory of the Emperour to make kings as partners

 with

with him in his kingdome. And works set vp as meritorious causes of saluation, dishonour Christ; for they make him vnprofitable, as *Paul* here teacheth.

Popish religion therefore is in no wise, in any place to bee tollerated, where it may bee abolished: but it is to be wished that it were banished from towne and countrey: and students are to bee warned with great circumspection to reade Popish writers. For no good can be looked for of that religion that makes Christ vnprofitable.

Lastly, we are heere taught to content our selues with Christ alone, and with his workes, merits, and satisfactions. For *in him wee are complete, Col.* 2. 10.

The confirmation of the sentence followeth, *I Paul say it*: therefore it is so. This kind of reasoning may not seeme strange: for the Apostles in writing and preaching, had the diuine and infallible assistance of the spirit, so as they could not erre. This must bee held as a Principle in religion: and being denied, there is no certaintie of the Bible.

3 *For I testifie againe to euery man that is circumcised, that he is bound to keepe the whole law.*

4 *Ye are abolished from Christ, whosoeuer are iustified by the law, ye are fallen from grace.*

The meaning. *Paul* saith, *I testifie againe*: because hee hath spoken thus much in effect before, *Gal.* 3. 10.

That is circumcised] who is of opinion of the false apostles that will be circumcised, and looke for iustification thereby.

Bound to the whole law] that is, to the whole ceremoniall law, to the iudiciall law, and to the whole morall law. And further, bound in respect of iustification, and life, to doe all things in the law. For he that will be iustified by one act of the law, is bound to performe the rest for his iustification.

Abolished from Christ] that is, Christ is become an idle and empty Christ vnto you.

Whosoeuer are iustified by the law] that is, are of opinion that they are to bee iustified by the workes of the law. For indeed a sinner cannot bee iustified by the law, but onely in his owne false opinion.

Grace] that is, the loue, and fauour of God.

The resolution. The third verse is a confirmation of the reason in the ſecond verſe,and it may be framed thus:He which is bound to keepe the whole law, hath no part in Chriſt:he which is circumciſed,is bound to keepe the whole law: therefore he which is circumciſed, hath no part in Chriſt. The 4 verſe is a repetition of the ſecond verſe,with a declaration therof:for he ſhews what he means by circumciſion,namely,iuſtification by circumciſion, and conſequently by the whole law. And therefore when he had ſaid, *If ye be circumciſed,* he changeth his ſpeach, ſaying, *Whoſoeuer is iuſtified by the law.* Againe, leſt men might thinke it a ſmall matter to be aboliſhed from Chriſt, he ſhewes that it is indeede to fall from grace.

The vſe. Theſe verſes are as it were a thunderbolt againſt all Popery. And firſt of all, I vrge the argument of *Paul* againſt the Popiſh Church, and againſt the Popiſh religion: If ye be iuſtified by the law, ye are aboliſhed from Chriſt, and fallen from grace. Anſwer is made, that the words are to be vnderſtood of ſuch workes of the Law,as are from nature, and goe before faith: and not of ſuch workes as are from grace, and follow faith: for ſuch workes (they ſay) are from Chriſt, and ſtand with him. I anſwer,the words of *Paul* are to be vnderſtood of all workes of the law, whether they be from nature,or from grace. For this Epiſtle of *Paul* was written about fiue yeares after the conuerſion of the Galatians: therefore they were and had bin long regenerate perſons: now men regenerate looke not to be iuſtified by workes of nature, but by good workes, which are workes of grace. And *Paul* ſaith, *Epheſians* 2.10. *We are not ſaued by workes, which God hath ordained that we ſhould walke in:* and theſe are the beſt workes that are or can be. Againe, *Tit.* 3.5. *Of his mercy he ſaued vs, and not of works of righteouſneſſe.*

By this Text we further ſee,that we and the Papiſts differ not about circumſtances,vnleſſe Grace and Chriſt be circumſtances. Againe, we ſee that the Church of Rome is indeede no Church: becauſe by maintaining iuſtification by works, it is aboliſhed from Chriſt,and fallen from grace.

Againe, I vrge *Pauls* argument againſt them, on this manner. He which is debter to the whole law, hath no part in Chriſt: he which is iuſtified by workes,is debter to the whole law: therefore he which is iuſtified by workes hath no part in Chriſt. Let them anſwer,if they can.

I turne the ſame argument another way,thus: He which is iuſtified by workes,is bound to keepe the whole law: but no man can keepe the whole law: therefore no man can be iuſtified by workes.

They answer to the *minor*, by making a double fulfilling of the law, one for this life, the other for the life to come; and both in their kind perfect. The fulfilling of the law for the time of this life (they say) it is to loue God aboue all creatures in truth: and that he which doth thus much, fulfils the law, and is no offender. Hereupon they inferre, that works may be answerable to the law, and be opposed to the iudgement of God. And for this doctrine, they alleadge S. *Augustine*. I answer againe, that *Paul* in this place takes it for a confessed truth, that no man can fulfill the law: and he vrgeth it as a great inconuenience, that any should be bound to keepe the whole law. And before he hath said, *He which is of the workes of the law, is cursed*: *Gal.* 3.10. which could not be, if there were a fulfilling of the law for the time of this life. As for *Augustine*, it is true he makes two fulfillings of the law, and one of them for the time of this life: but this he saith is imperfect: and this imperfection he makes to be a sinne; whereas the Papists of our time teach, that men may fulfill the law for the time of this life without sinne.

Where *Paul* saith, *If ye be circumcised*: marke how the false Apostles abuse circumcision. It is by diuine institution a seale of the righteousnes of faith, and they make it a meritorious cause of saluation. It is indeede rather Gods worke, then our worke: and they make it their owne worke, and that meritorious before God. Like doe the Papists at this day. Baptisme is a signe and seale of Gods mercy, by diuine institution: and they turne it into a physicall cause which containes and conferres grace. In like sort they turne the workes of the spirit, almes, praier, fasting, contrition; yea their owne traditions, confession, satisfaction, and such like, into meritorious causes of iustification, and life. And this is the fashion of deceiuers, to retaine the names of holy things, but not to retaine the right vse of them.

As here we see Circumcision was an obligation to the keeping of the whole law in the old Testament: so is baptisme in the new, an obligation or bond, whereby we haue bound our selues to liue according to all the lawes of God. *Math.* 28.19, 20. This discouers the Atheisme and vnbeleefe of persons baptised in these our dayes: for few there be that thinke vpon, and performe this obligation.

We are further to obserue the condition of the law. *It is wholly copulatiue.* All the parts of it are linked one to another. He that is bound to one commandement, is bound to all: he that keepes one indeede, keepes all: he that breakes one, in respect of the disposition of his heart, is a breaker of all, *Iam.* 2.10. he that makes no conſcience to keepe ſome one commandement, if occaſion be offered,will breake any.Hence it followes, that true regeneration is that which is a reformation and change according to the whole law of God,and containes in it the ſeedes of all good duties. Chriſt ſaith,*He that is waſhed is all cleane, Ioh.*13.10. *Ioſias turned to God according to the whole law.Zachary* and *Elizabeth walked in all the commandements of God without reproofe.Luk.*1.*Dauid* ſaith,*He ſhall not be confounded,when he hath reſpect to all the commandements of God.Pſal.* 119.6.On the contrary, he which hath many excellent things in him,if he liue in the manifeſt breach of ſome one commandement, is ſound in none, nay indeede he is guilty of all. *Herod* did many good things : and yet all was nothing : becauſe he liued in inceſt. *Mark.*6.20. The diuell is able to bring a man to perdition as well by one ſinne,as by many.

Whereas *Paul* ſaith,*If ye be iuſtified by the law,ye are aboliſhed from Chriſt* : Firſt I gather, that the Law and the Goſpel are not one in ſubſtance of doctrine,as the Papiſts teach : for they ſay the Goſpel is nothing but the law made more perfect,and plaine : which if it were true, a man might be iuſtified both by Chriſt and the law, which *Paul* ſaith cannot be.Secondly,I gather hence, that it is a meere deuice of mans wit,to ſay that Chriſt by his death and paſſion merited,that we ſhould merit by our owne workes our iuſtification and ſaluation. For if this were true, that the merit of our workes,were the fruite of Chriſts paſſion,*Paul* would not haue ſaid that iuſtification by the law,ſhould aboliſh Chriſt vnto vs. For the cauſe and the effect, both ſtand together : whereas Chriſts merit, and the merit of our workes,agree euen as fire and water. And no maruell.For the reaſon why Chriſt meriteth,is the Perſonall vnion of the Godhead with the manhood : which vnion,becauſe it is not to be found in any meere man,neither is there any true and proper merit to be found.

Whereas *Paul* ſaith, *Yee are fallen from grace*, ſome gather, that the children of God may fall quite from the fauour of God. *Anſwer.* Men are ſaid to be vnder grace, two waies. Firſt,in the iudgement of infallibility : and thus onely the Elect are vnder the grace of God. Secondly,in the iudgement of Chriſtian charitie : and thus all that profeſſe Chriſt, (though indeede hypocrites)are vnder the grace of God. And in this ſenſe *Paul* ſaith,that the whole Church of Galatia is vnder the grace of God. And they are ſaid *to fall from grace*, not becauſe all were indeede vnder the fauour of God, and at length caſt out of it : but becauſe God makes it manifeſt to men,that they were neuer in the fauour of God.Thus Chriſts enemies are said *to bee blotted out of the booke of life, Psalme* 69.28. when God makes it manifest that their names were neuer written there. Secondly, I answer, that *Paul* speakes not this absolutely, but vpon condition, *If ye will be iustified by the law.* And therfore v.10. he saith, that *he is perswaded better things of them.*

Lastly, heere we see it is false, that euery man shall be saued by his religion: for he that is abolished from Christ, is quite out of the fauour of God. And therefore no religion, but that which is truely Christian, saueth.

5 *For wee in the spirit by faith, waite for the hope of righteousnesse.*

6 *For in Iesus Christ neither circumcision, nor vncircumcision auaileth any thing, but faith which worketh by loue.*

The meaning. *We*] I *Paul*, the rest of the Apostles, and all other Christian Churches. *In spirit*] that is, in the powers of the soule sanctified and renewed. In this sense *Paul* saith that the true circumcision is that which is in the heart, in spirit, *Rom.* 2.29. and Christ saith, that *true worship of God, is in spirit, Iohn* 4.24. And that *spirit* is here taken in this sense, it is manifest: because it is opposed to circumcision which is in the flesh.

By faith wee wait] Faith apprehends the promise, and thereby brings foorth hope: and faith by meanes of hope, makes them that beleeue to waite. *Hope of righteousnesse*] that is, saluation or life eternall, which is the fruite of righteousnesse, *Titus* 2.13. or againe, righteousnesse hoped for. Righteousnesse indeed is imputed to them that beleeue, and that in this life, yet the fruition and the full reuelation thereof is reserued to the life to come, when Christ our righteousnesse shall appeare, and when the effect of righteousnesse, namely sanctification, shall bee accomplished in vs, *Romanes* 8.23. 1.*Iohn* 3.2.

The sense then is this. All the Apostles and Christian Churches with one consent in spirit, by meanes of their faith, waite for the full reuelation of their imputed righteousnesse, and for euerlasting life: whereas the false apostles place their righteousnesse in the circumcision of the flesh, and looke to haue the fruition of it in this life.

Verse 6. *In Christ*] that is, in the Church, kingdome, or religion of Christ. 2.*Cor.* 5.17. *If any be in Christ*, that is, if any be a Christian, *he is a new creature.*

Vncircumcision.

Vncircumciſion] that is, the condition and workes of men vncircumciſed.

Auaileth any thing] is of no vſe, reſpect, or acceptation with God.
Faith working] faith effectuall in duties of loue.

The reſolution. Theſe words containe a ſecond reaſon, where *Paul* confirmes the former concluſion, and it may be framed thus. That thing which makes vs wait for the hope of righteouſneſſe, that iuſtifies: not circumciſion, but faith makes vs wait for the hope of righteouſnes: therefore not circumciſion but faith iuſtifies. The *propoſition* is omitted: the *minor* is in the 5. verſe. And it is confirmed by two arguments. The firſt, is the conſent of all Churches, *Wee wait*. The ſecond is taken from the property of faith in the 6. verſe, thus: It is faith, and not circumciſion that auailes before God: therefore faith and not circumciſion makes vs wait.

Again, in theſe two verſes, *Paul* meets with an obiection, which may be framed thus: If yee aboliſh circumciſion and the ceremoniall law, ye aboliſh the exerciſes of religion. The anſwer is: in ſtead of them we haue other exerciſes in our ſpirit, namely, the inward exerciſes of faith, hope, and loue. The vſe. In the 5. verſe, foure things are to be conſidered. The firſt is, who waites? *Paul* ſaith, *We wait*. Before he hath iuſtified his doctrine by the Scriptures, now he addes the conſent of the Churches. Here then wee ſee what is the office of all faithfull diſpenſers of the word, namely, to declare ſuch doctrines as are founded in the Scriptures, and approoued by the conſent of the true Church of God. *Paul* an Apoſtle that could not erre, reſpected conſent, much more are all ordinary Miniſters to doe it.

Againe, it is the office of all Chriſtian people to maintaine and defend all ſuch doctrines and opinions as are founded in the Scriptures, and ratified by the conſent of the true Churches of God, and no other. This to doe is to walke in the way of vnitie, and peace: and to doe otherwiſe is to walke in the way of ſchiſme and hereſie.

The ſecond point is, what is waited for? *Paul* ſaith, *the reuelation of righteouſnes, and eternall ſaluation*. Here I obſerue, that there is no iuſtification by the obſeruation of the law: and I prooue it thus: The righteouſnes whereby a ſinner is iuſtified, is apprehended by faith, and expected by hope: but if righteouſnes were by the law, men ſhould haue the fruition of their righteouſnes in this life, and conſequently the hope thereof ſhould ceaſe.

Secondly, heere is comfort for the godly. They complaine of the want of ſanctification: but they are to know, that in this life they

they ſhall neuer feele righteouſneſſe, as they feele ſinne: here they muſt hunger and thirſt after righteouſneſſe, liuing in ſome want of it. If wee haue the firſt fruites of the ſpirit, the hatred of our owne ſinne, the purpoſe of not ſinning, the feare of God, and ſuch like, wee muſt content our ſelues, and wait for the fruition of further grace till the life to come.

Thirdly, we muſt become waiters for the mercy of God, and for life euerlaſting, *Gen*. 49. 18. *Iud*. v. 21. For this cauſe we muſt doe as they which wait and attend for ſome great benefit: wee muſt daily ſtand with our ſupplications, knocking at the mercie gate to the death: and wee muſt daily prepare our ſelues againſt the day of death, and it muſt bee welcome vnto vs: for then is the end of all our waiting and attending.

The third point is, by what are we to wait? *Paul* ſaith, *We wait by faith*. Hence it followes, that faith brings with it a ſpeciall certaintie of the mercy of God, and of life euerlaſting. For men vſe not to wait for the things whereof they are vncertaine. Waiting preſuppoſeth certaintie. The Papiſts therefore that make ſpeciall hope, ſhould alſo make ſpeciall faith.

The laſt point is, where is this waiting? *Paul* ſaith, *in ſpirit*. Here obſerue, that all the exerciſes of Chriſtian religion, are to be in the ſpirit. *God muſt bee worſhipped in ſpirit*, *Iohn* 4. 24. *Rom*. 1. 9. The heart muſt be rent, and not the garment, *Ioel* 2. The inward motions of the ſpirit, are of themſelues the worſhip of God, whereas our words and deeds are not ſimply, but ſo farre forth as they are founded in the renewed motions of the heart. Men in our daies thinke they do God high ſeruice, if they come to Church, heare Gods word, and ſay ſome few praiers. Indeed theſe things are not to be condemned: yet are they not ſufficient, vnleſſe withall we bring vnto God, a renewed ſpirit indued with faith, hope, loue.

In the ſixth verſe, *Paul* propounds three concluſions. The firſt is this: that externall and bodily priuiledges are of no vſe and moment in the kingdome of Chriſt. *Paul* ſaith, 1. *Tim*. 4. 8. *Bodily exerciſe profiteth little*, and that *godlineſſe is profitable for all things*. It was a great priuiledge to bee familiarly acquainted with Chriſt, and to haue eaten and drunke with him: yet is it of no vſe in the kingdom of Chriſt. For of ſuch Chriſt ſaith, *Luke* 13. 26. *Depart from me, ye workers of iniquitie*. It was a great priuiledge to be allied to Chriſt in reſpect of blood, yet in the kingdome of Chriſt, it is of no vſe: and therefore Chriſt ſaith, *He that doth the will of my Father, is my brother, ſiſter, and mother*, *Marke* 3. 33. To conceiue and beare Chriſt, was a great honour to the virgin *Marie*: yet was ſhe not by this meanes a member of the kingdome of Chriſt, but by her faith in him. And if ſhe had not borne him in her heart, as well as ſhe bare him in her wombe, ſhe had not been ſaued. To propheſie or preach, and that in the name of Chriſt, is a great dignitie: and yet many hauing this prerogatiue, ſhall be condemned, *Matt.* 7.22. It may be alleadged, that ſome outward exerciſes, as Baptiſme, and the Lords Supper, are of great vſe in the Church of Chriſt. I anſwer, the outward baptiſme is nothing without the inward. *Not the waſhing of the fleſh, but the ſtipulation of a good conſcience ſaueth,* 1. *Pet.* 3. 18. *Circumciſion is profitable, if thou keepe the law, Rom.* 2. 35.

By this wee are taught, not to eſteeme of mens religion by their riches, and externall dignities. For the faſhion of the world is, if a man haue riches, and honour, to commend him for a wiſe, vertuous, and godly man. This is fooliſhly *to haue faith in reſpect of perſons, Iames* 2. 1.

Secondly, by this wee are taught to moderate our affections in reſpect of al outward things, neither ſorrowing too much for them, nor ioying too much in them, 1. *Cor.* 7. 30.

The ſecond concluſion. Faith is of great vſe and acceptation in the kingdome of Chriſt. By it firſt our perſons, and then our actions pleaſe God: and without it nothing pleaſeth God. It is the firſt and the greateſt honour we can doe to God, to giue credence to his word: and from this flowes all other obedience to all other commandements. Hence we learne,

Firſt, that we muſt labour to conceiue faith aright in our hearts, by the vſe of the right meanes, the word, praier, Sacraments: as alſo in, and by the exerciſes of ſpirituall inuocation, & repentance. This being done, wee muſt reſt vpon the bare word and teſtimonie of God, without, and againſt ſenſe and feeling: and quiet our hearts therein, both in life and death.

Secondly, faith in Chriſt muſt reigne and beare ſway in our hearts, and haue the command ouer reaſon, will, affection, luſt. And by it whatſoeuer we do or ſuffer, ſpecially the maine actions of our liues, are to be ordered and diſpoſed.

Laſtly, it is a thing to bee bewailed, that the common faith of our dayes is but a ceremoniall faith, conceiued without the ordinary meanes, and ſeuered from the exerciſes of inuocation, and repentance.

The third concluſion is; that true faith workes by loue. Hence the Papiſts gather, that loue is the forme and life of faith, not becauſe it makes faith to be faith; but becauſe it makes it to be a true faith, a good faith, a liuely faith. But this their doctrine is falſe and

and erronius. For faith is the cauſe of loue, and loue is the fruite of faith. 1. *Tim.* 1. 5. *Loue out of a pure heart, good conſcience, and faith vnfained.* Now euery cauſe as it is a cauſe, hath his force and efficacy in it ſelfe, and receiues no force or efficacie from his effect. Secondly, true faith is liuely and effectuall in it ſelfe, and hath a peculiar forme of his owne, and that is a certen power to apprehend Chriſt in the promiſe. For in faith, there are two things, *knowledge*, and *apprehenſion*, which ſome call application, or *ſpeciall affiance*, which affiance becauſe the Papiſts cut off, they are conſtrained to make a ſupply by loue. Thirdly, the operation of faith (according to the doctrine of the Papiſt) is to Prepare and diſpoſe a ſinner to his future iuſtification. Now, if this operation be from loue, then loue is before iuſtification: and that cannot be: becauſe (as they teach) iuſtification ſtands in loue. Loue therefore is not the forme of faith. They alleadge for themſelues this very Text in hand, where it is ſaid, *faith worketh by loue*: or (as they tranſlate it) *faith is acted and mooued by loue. Anſwer.* The meaning of the text is, that faith is effectuall in it ſelfe: and that it ſhewes and puts foorth his efficacy by loue, as by the fruite thereof. And it cannot hence bee gathered, that faith is acted and mooued by loue, as by a formall cauſe.

Againe, they alleadge, *Iames* 2. 26. *As the bodie is dead without the ſpirit: ſo is faith without workes. Anſwer* 1. The ſoule of man is not the forme of his body, but of the whole man. 2. *Spirit* may as well ſignifie breath, or breathing, as the ſoule. And ſo it carries a fit ſenſe. For as the body without breath, is dead, and it ſhewes it ſelfe to be aliue by breathing: ſo faith that is without workes, is dead, and it ſhewes it ſelfe to be aliue by works. 3. There is a falſe compoſition of the words to be conſidered: *faith that is without workes, is dead*: is true: but to ſay, *faith is dead without workes* (as though workes gaue life to faith) is falſe; and not the meaning of S. *Iames*, but the former onely.

Againe, the Papiſts hence gather, that faith and loue are ioynt cauſes in the iuſtification of a ſinner, and that faith worketh loue in iuſtifying men before God. But this interpretation is againſt the whole ſcope of this Epiſtle, in which *Paul* prooues that there is no iuſtification by the law, c. 5. v. 4. and therefore no iuſtification by loue. Againe, *Paul* ſaith, *Rom.* 3. 21. that *righteouſneſſe is reuealed without the law*: and therfore without loue. And againe, that *wee are made the righteouſneſſe of Chriſt, as Chriſt is made our ſinne,* namely, by imputation, and therefore not by infuſion of loue, 2. *Cor.* 5. 21. Thirdly, faith iuſtifies by apprehending Chriſt in the promiſe,

promiſe,and therefore not by loue. The conſequent I prooue thus. Faith and loue are two hands of our ſoule. Faith is an hand that laies hold of Chriſt,and it doth (as it were) pull him and his benefits into our ſoules. But loue is an hand of an other kind, for it ſerues not to receiue in,but to giue out the good it hath,and to communicate it ſelfe vnto others. Therefore faith cannot iuſtifie by loue. Laſtly,loue in order of nature followes iuſtification, and therefore it doth not iuſtifie. For firſt of all faith laies hold on Chriſt:then followes iuſtification: vpon iuſtification follows ſanctification, and loue is a part of ſanctification.

They vrge for themſelues the words of *Paul*,that *faith workes by faith. Anſ.Paul* doth not ſhew in this verſe,what iuſtifieth, but what are the exerciſes of Godlines in which Chriſtians muſt be occupied. And he doth not ſhew how faith iuſtifieth, but how it may be diſcerned to be true faith,namely,by loue.

Secondly, they obiect that faith and loue are alwayes ioyned: and therefore ioyntly worke in iuſtification. *Anſwer.* They are ioyned in one perſon or ſubiect: and they are ioyned in the exerciſe of Chriſtian life: but they are not ioyned in the article of iuſtification.

Thirdly, they vrge the 2. of S. *Iames*, where it is ſaide that *a man is iuſtified not onely by faith,but alſo by workes.* v.24. *Anſ. Faith in S. Iames* is put for an hiſtoricall knowledge of religion; or for the bare confeſſion and profeſſion of faith. Againe, *iuſtification* is twofold; one *of the perſon*,the other *of the faith of the perſon. Iuſtification of the perſon* is, when a ſinner is abſolued of his ſinnes, and accepted to life euerlaſting,for the merit of Chriſt. *Iuſtification of the faith of the perſon* is,when faith is approoued and found to be true faith: and a beleeuer iuſtifies himſelfe to be a true beleeuer. Of this ſecond iuſtification ſpeakes Saint *Iames*; and it is not onely by faith,but alſo by workes.

Laſtly,it may be obiected, that loue is of no vſe, if it doe not iuſtifie. *Anſw.* Iuſtification,and ſanctification,are two diſtinct benefits. 1. *Cor.* 1.30. and 6.11. Iuſtification miniſters vnto vs deliuerance from hell,and a right to life euerlaſting: Sanctification is a fruit of the former,and ſerues to make vs thankfull to God for our iuſtification: and loue ſerues for the ſame vſe, becauſe it is a ſpeciall part of Sanctification.

Thus much of the deprauation of the text by the Papiſts. Hence further I gather that many falſely in theſe laſt daies boaſt of faith: becauſe it is not ioyned with profiting in knowledg, with the true conuerſion vnto God, with fruits of loue to God and man: whereas all true faith is fruitfull in good workes.

7. *Ye did runne well: who did let you, that ye ſhould not obey the truth?*

The meaning. *Ye did runne well*] In theſe words, *Paul* alludes to the games of running, vſed among the heathen. And he compares the word and precepts of God, to a way or race; beleeuers to runners, life eternall to the price, God to the vmpire or iudge; the lookers on, are men and Angels, good and badde, and the Exerciſe of religion, is the running in this race. Reade of this, 1. *Corinth*. 9. 24. *Phil*. 3. 13, 14.

Who] the interrogation hath in it the force of a reproofe, or complaint. And the ſenſe is this: they did euill, which turned you forth of the way, and you haue done euill that you obeyed not the truth. The like is, *Pſal*. 2. 1. *Why doe the heathen rage*? that is, it is great wickednes for them to rage.

Let] ſtoppe, intercept your courſe, turne you out of the way.

That you ſhould not obey] that you ſhould not giue credence to the doctrine of *Paul*, and obey it.

The ſcope. Theſe words, are a repetition of the principall concluſion of the whole Epiſtle. And this repetition is not in vaine. For it ſerues to bring the Galatians to a conſideration of their offence, and to amendment of life. Hence I obſerue, that the often and ſerious conſideration of our ſinnes and liues paſt, is a meanes to worke in vs a deteſtation of our ſinnes, and a reformation of life. Thus *Dauid* ſaith, that vpon conſideration of his waies, *he turned his feete to Gods commandements*. *Pſal*. 119. 59. And the cauſe why there is ſo little amendment among vs, is, becauſe we neuer ſo much as thinke what we haue done.

In theſe words, *Paul* ſets downe three duties of Chriſtian people. The firſt is, that they muſt be runners in the race of God. Indeede the Sabbath of the Iewes figured a reſt, which is contrary to running: but this reſt is from ſinne, and not from good duties. This duty of running teacheth vs foure things. The firſt is, that we muſt make haſt without delay to keepe the commandements of God, ſpecially the commandements of faith, repentance, new obedience. *Pſal*. 119. 32, 60. Contrariwiſe it is a great fault for youth and others, to deferre amendment till old age, or till the laſt and deadly ſicknes. For that is the time to end our running, and not to begin.

The ſecond is, that we are to encreaſe and profit in all good duties

duties, specially in knowledge, faith, repentance. But we in this age doe otherwise. For either we stand at a stay, or goe backe, and very few of vs doe proceed forward in good duties. And there are two causes of this. One is blindnesse of mind, which makes vs that wee see not how little our faith and repentance is, and how great is the masse of our corruption: the second is our vnbeleefe in the article of life euerlasting.

The third dutie is, that wee must neither looke to the right or left hand, or look to things behind vs to set our affection on them, but wee must presse on forward to the price of eternall life, *Phil.* 3. 13. *Luke* 9. 62. Here comes a common fault to be considered: we in respect of profession go forward: yet we looke back in our course, and mind earthly things.

Lastly, we must not be mooued with the speaches of men which are giuen of vs either to or fro. They are lookers on, and must haue their speaches, and our care must be not to heed them, but to looke to our course.

The second dutie of Christian people is, that they must not onely be runners, but they must runne well. And that is done by beleeuing, and by obeying the true religion, or as *Paul* saith, by *hauing faith and good conscience*, 1. *Timoth.* 1. 18. These are as it were the two feet, by which we runne to life euerlasting. Vnder faith we are to comprehend the true acknowledgment of God, affiance in him, and inuocation, &c. Vnder good conscience, is comprised the purpose of not sinning, and the care to obey God in all his commandements. To apply this to our selues: runners wee are: but alas, few of vs are good runners. Wee haue one good foot, and that is our faith or religion, which is sound and good: but we halt on the other foot: our care to keepe conscience is not sutable to our religion. And three things cause a lamenesse or feeblenesse in this foot, the lust of the eye, that is couetousnesse; the lust of the flesh, and pride of life.

The third dutie is, that we must runne the race from the beginning to the end, and finish our course, so as wee may apprehend life euerlasting, 1. *Tim.* 6. 11. 2. *Tim* 4. 7. 1. *Cor.* 9. 24. And for this cause wee must cherish in our hearts a loue and feruent desire of eternall life, and by this meanes we shall be drawne on through all miseries, and ouerpasse them to the end. Secondly, we must hold and maintaine a constant and daily purpose of not sinning. And where wee are the weakest, there must our resolution bee the strongest. And thus shall we be constant to the death.

8. *It is not the perswasion of him that calleth you.*

The meaning. This opinion of iustification by the workes of the law, is not from God, who hath called you from bondage to liberty.

The scope. *Paul* here meetes with a conceit of the Galatians, which was this: Why dost thou so often and so sharpely reprooue vs? for we hold nothing against conscience, but are perswaded of the thing which we say. To this *Paul* answers here: *this perswasion is not of God*: because it is against the calling of God, for hee calls you to liberty: and this your opinion drawes you into bondage.

Here we see the cause of mens declining from God and his word, and that is this: Men deny credence to Gods word, and listen to plausible perswasions, and so fall away. Thus *Eue* fell in the estate of innocency by listning to the false perswasions of diuell. The Papists nussle themselues in their superstitions, by a presumption that the Church cannot erre, and that God will not leaue his Church destitute of the assistance of his Spirit. Our common people boulster themselues in their blind waies, by a presumption that God is all of mercy, and that if they doe their true intent, serue God, say their praiers, deale iustly, and doe as they would be done vnto, they shall certainly be saued. Tradesmen often vse many practises of fraud and iniustice, and that vpon a perswasion, that they haue a charge and family which must be maintained. If men now adaies will not blaspheame, drinke, and riot, as others doe, they shall be charged with precisenes: and that comes vpon a perswasion, that it sufficeth to auoid the outward and notorious crimes which are mentioned and condemned in the law. Thus the whole world is misled by blind perswasions.

Secondly, hence we learne to close vp our eyes (as it were) and absolutely to follow the calling of God, and to subiect all the powers of our soules vnto it. Thus did *Abraham* when he was called to goe he knew not whether, and *Paul* without vsing consultation went and preached in Arabia at the calling of Christ.

Thirdly, *Paul* here sets downe a note to discerne of false doctrines and opinions in religion. If they be sutable to the calling of God, they are good: if they be against the calling of God, they are naught. This is *Pauls* rule. God calls vs to liberty: therefore the doctrine of iustification by the workes of the law is naught: for it drawes vs into bondage. In like sort God calls vs to free iustification: and therefore the doctrine of humane satisfactions and of the

merit

merit of workes, is naught. Againe, God calles vs to an vtter deniall of our selues: and therefore the Popish doctrine of preparation, and of freedome of will in the conuersion of a sinner, is naught.

Lastly, it is to be obserued, that *Paul* saith in the time present [*of him that calleth you:*] for hence it appeares, that God continues to call the Galatians, euen after their fall, in which they fell away to another Gospel, and as much as in them lay, abolished themselues from Christ. This shewes Gods patience: and that there is a possibilitie of mercy after great and grieuous falls.

It may be said, how long doth God continue to call men vnto him? *Answer.* So long as he vouchsafeth them the benefit of the publike Ministery. Thus then more then fourtie yeares hath God called vs in England. And for this cause, it is our part to pray to God for hearing eares to be pearced in our hearts: and we must answer the calling of God, *Psalm.* 27.8. at the least in the desires and groanes of our hearts. And lastly, we must in life and conuersation be sutable to the calling of God.

9 *A little leauen, leaueneth the whole lumpe.*

The sense. As a little leauen, leaueneth and sauoureth the whole lumpe of dow: euen so, one errour or point of corrupt doctrine, corrupteth the whole body of Christian religion: because all the points of religion are linked and compounded together, so as if one be corrupt, the rest cannot remaine sound and incorrupt.

The scope. The obiection of the Galatians is: Put case, that we erre in ioyning Circumcision and Christ: yet there is no cause why thou shouldest so sharply reprooue vs: for it is no great errour to ioyne workes and Christ in the cause of our Iustification. *Paul* answers to this obiection by a Prouerbe, saying, that *a little leauen of false doctrine, corrupts the whole body of religion:* and one errour, though it seeme to bee of small moment at the first, may at length bring with it the corruption and deprauation of many other points.

The vse. In the example of the Galatians, we see what is the common fashion of men, namely, to extenuate their faults, and to make small matters of great offences. The Pharisies taught, that sundry of Gods commandements were *small* and *little commandements, Matth.* 5. 19. To them that make no conscience of sinne, great sinnes are little sinnes, and little sinnes are no sinnes. Pride is cleanlinesse; couetousnes is nothing but worldlinesse, drunkennes, good fellowſhip; fornication, a tricke of youth. Thus men put vizards vpon their vgly ſinnes. The polititian that is of no religion, ſaith, that wee and the Papiſts differ not in ſubſtance, but in ſmall circumſtances: and that if they erre, it is but in ſmall points. But on the contrary, wee are to eſteeme euery ſinne for a great ſinne, to humble our ſelues for the leaſt ſinnes, and to bring our ſelues in ſubiection to God in the leaſt of our actions.

Here wee are taught by all meanes to maintaine the puritie of ſound religion, whatſoeuer befall vs. And for this cauſe we are to reſiſt and withſtand euery erronious opinion that ſhall bee broched. For it is the policy of the diuell by foiſting in ſome one errour, to depraue & confound the whole body of truth. It may be ſaid, how may wee diſcerne errour from ſound doctrine, conſidering oftentimes they are like, as leauen is like dowe? *Anſ.* Leauen is diſcerned from dowe, not by colour, but by taſte: euen ſo they which are ſpirituall, and haue the gift of diſcerning, directed by the analogie of faith, diſcerne truth from falſhood. For whatſoeuer is againſt one article of faith, or againſt any of the commandements of the decalogue, is not ſound doctrine, but leauen.

Againe, that which is ſaid of falſe doctrine, may bee ſaid proportionally of bad manners. Heere therefore we muſt bee put in minde of three duties. The firſt, to reſiſt and withſtand euery particular ſinne. For euen one ſinne is able to defile the whole life of man. One flie is ſufficient to marre a whole boxe of ſweet oyntment. One offence in our firſt parents, brought corruption vpon them and all mankind, yea vpon heauen and earth. He that makes no conſcience of ſome one ſinne, is guilty of the whole law, *Iames* 2.

Secondy, wee muſt doe our endeauour to the vttermoſt, to cut off euery bad example in the ſocieties of men. For one bad example is ſufficient to corrupt a whole family, a whole towne, a whole countrey. The example of one inceſtuous man, was ſufficient to corrupt all Corinth. Therefore *Paul* ſaith, *Purge out the old leauen,* 1.*Cor.*5.6. The law of God is, that blaſphemers, murderers, adulterers, &c. ſhall be put to death: the reaſon is, *that euill may be taken out of Iſrael,* that is, the euill of wicked example, which being ſuffred, ſpreads abroad, and doth much hurt. The barren fig tree muſt be cut downe, leſt it make the whole ground barren, *Luke* 13.7.

Thirdly, wee are to withſtand and cut off the firſt beginnings, and the occaſions of euery ſin. We ſay of arrand theeues, that firſt they begin to practiſe their wickednes in pinnes, and points. For this cauſe, idleneſſe, fulneſſe of bread in exceſſiue eating, drinking, and swilling, riot, and vanitie in apparell, are to be suppressed in euery societie, as the breeders of many vices.

On the contrary, as one poynt of euill doctrine brings with it many other: so any one little grace of God, brings many other with it. *The entrance into Gods word giues light, Psalme* 119.130. In this respect Christ saith, *The kingdome of heauen is like leauen, hidde in three peckes of meale:* because Gods kingdome is set vp in the heart at the first vpon very small beginnings, *Matth.*13.33. This must teach vs to vse the meanes of our saluation, and not to bee discouraged, though wee haue in vs but some small beginnings of Gods grace.

10 *I haue an affiance in you in the Lord, that yee will bee no otherwise minded: but he that troubleth you, shall beare his iudgment, whosoeuer he bee.*

The sense. *In the Lord*] by the gracious assistance of God, who no doubt will giue a blessing to my Ministery.

No otherwise minded] that is, thinke no otherwise then ye haue done, and ought to thinke; and thinke no otherwise then I haue taught you.

He that troubleth you] the Church is troubled three wayes: 1. by false doctrine. Thus *Ahab troubled Israel,* 1.*Kings.*18.18. and the false apostles trouble Galatia. 2. By wicked example: thus *Achan troubled Israel, Iosua.* 7.25. 3. By force and crueltie: thus tyrants and persecutors trouble the Church.

Shall beare] shall haue his due and deserued punishment, partly in this life, and partly in eternall death. See this verified in the end of the booke of English Martyrs, in the desperate, horrible, and stinking ends of persecutors. But yet this threat must bee vnderstood with the exception of repentance.

The scope. The words are an answer to an obiection, which may be framed thus: It seemes by your former prouerb of leauen, that you hold vs to bee a people corrupted, and vnsauorie vnto God. To this *Paul* answers by a distinction: I hope better things of you: but the false Apostles for troubling the Church shal surely be punished.

The vse. When *Paul* saith, *I haue an affiance in you*, he teacheth in his owne example, that wee are to hope the best of men so long as they are curable. It may be said, they that hope the best, are sometimes deceiued. *Answer.* They are onely deceiued in their iudgement, and that in things wherof they haue no certain knowledge, and they are not deceiued in practiſe. For it is a dutie of loue to hope the beſt. And they which vſe to ſuſpect the worſe, are oftner deceiued. Againe, it may be ſaid, that wee muſt iudge of things as they are indeed. *Anſwer.* Iudgement of things, and iudgement of perſons muſt be diſtinguiſhed. Of things, vpright iudgement is to iudge of them as they are: and if they be doubtful, to ſuſpend. Now our iudgement of the perſons of men, muſt be to take things in the better part, as much as poſſibly may be. Laſtly, it may be alledged, that *wee muſt loue our neighbour as our ſelues:* and that we deſpaire in reſpect of our ſelues. *Anſwer.* We are to deſpaire in reſpect of our ſelues, becauſe we are priuy to our owne eſtate: but we are not priuy to the eſtate of any other man: and therfore we are to hope the beſt of them. This ſhewes the fault of our times: if any profeſſing the Goſpell fall vpon frailtie, there are numbers of men that will make no bones of it to condemne them to the pit of hell, for hypocrites: but ſuch perſons are not carried by the ſpirit of *Paul*, who hopes the beſt of them that fall.

Againe, here we ſee how we are to put affiance in men. We are to put affiance in God for all things whatſoeuer, whether concerning body or ſoule: but our affiance in men, muſt be onely for ſuch things as they are able to performe. Secondly, wee muſt put affiance in God abſolutely for himſelfe, and therefore wee ſay, *I beleeue in God, &c.* but all our affiance in men whatſoeuer, muſt be *in the Lord.*

When *Paul* ſaith, that he had *affiance of them in the Lord*, he ſhewes, that renewed repentance is the gift of God. And there are two graces required vnto it; Helping grace, and Exciting grace. Helping grace preſerues and confirmes the firſt and initiall repentance. Exciting grace giues the will and the deed. And without theſe graces the childe of God, if hee fall, cannot repent, and recouer himſelfe. They therefore are deceiued, who thinke that they may haue repentance at command, and that they may repent when they will.

It may be demanded, why *Paul* vſeth milde tearmes, and doeth not excommunicate the Galatians? *Anſw.* So long as men are curable, meanes muſt be vſed to recouer them. The ſheepe or oxe that goes aſtray, muſt be brought home againe, *Exod.* 23. 4. much more thy neighbour. Chriſt himſelfe brings home againe the loſt ſheep, and ſo muſt euery ſhepheard, *Ezech.* 34. 4. Now the Galatians were in all likelihood perſons curable: and therefore not to bee cut off. For the cenſure of Excommunication pertaines to them alone, of whoſe recouery there is no hope.

Some

Some there be that miſlike the preaching vſed in theſe daies; becauſe we vſe not ſeueritie, and perſonall reproofes, after the maner of *Iohn Baptiſt*. But theſe men are deceiued. We haue not the like calling that he had, nor like gifts: neither are we in the like times. For *Iohn* the *Baptiſt* was in the very time of the change betweene the old and the new Teſtament. Chriſt did not follow him in the ſame maner of teaching, neither doeth the Apoſtle in this place, when hee ſaith of the Galatians in Apoſtaſie, that *hee hoped better things of them*.

In the laſt place, the commination which the Apoſtle vſeth, is to be obſerued, that troublers of the Church ſhal beare their iudgment. Hence I gather,

1. That God watcheth ouer his Church with a ſpeciall prouidence. We in England haue found this by experience: and we are to be thankfull for it.

2. That the doctrine of the Apoſtles is of infallible certaintie: becauſe the oppugners of it are plagued by the iuſt iudgement of God.

3. On the contrarie, our dutie is, to pray for the good eſtate of the Church of God, and for the kingdomes where the Church is planted, and for the continuance of the Goſpell ſpecially in England. For what will all the things we haue doe vs good, if we bee forth of Gods kingdome, and loſe our ſoules?

11 *And brethren, if I yet preach Circumciſion, why doe I yet ſuffer perſecution? Then is the ſcandall of the croſſe aboliſhed.*

12 *Would to God they were cut off that trouble you.*

The ſenſe. *Yet preach*] now while I am an Apoſtle. Heere *Paul* takes it for graunted, that when he was a Phariſie, he taught and maintained Circumciſion: but he denies that he euer taught it after his Conuerſion in his Apoſtleſhip. *The croſſe*] the Goſpel, which is a doctrine teaching deliuerance from hell, and life euerlaſting, to be obtained by the death and paſſion of Chriſt crucified, 1. *Cor*. 1. 18, 23.

More plainly, the words are thus much in effect: It is reported, that I *Paul* an Apoſtle, preac[illegible] circumciſion: but the truth is, there is no ſuch matter. For if I taught circumciſion, the Iewes maintainers of circumciſion, would not perſecute me as they doe: neither would they take offence at the preaching of Chriſt crucified, if I ioyned circumciſion with Chriſt.

The drift. *Paul* here anſwers a new obiection, which is on this manner. There is no cauſe, *Paul*, why thou ſhouldeſt thus reprooue vs, for thou thy ſelfe art a teacher of circumciſion. To this *Paul* makes a double anſwer. Firſt, he denies the report, and proues his deniall by a double reaſon, one is, becauſe the Iewes ſtill perſecuted him; the other is, becauſe they tooke offence ſtill at his preaching of Chriſt crucified. Secondly, *Paul* anſwers by pronouncing a curſe vpon the falſe apoſtles.

The vſe. In the words I conſider two things, the report giuen foorth of *Paul*, and his Apologie. The report was, that *Paul* preached Circumciſion. In this wee ſee what is the condition of the Miniſters of the word, namely, to be ſubiect to ſlander and defamation, not onely in reſpect of their liues, but alſo in reſpect of their miniſterie and doctrine, as if they were heretikes. Thus the Papiſts at this day reproch the Miniſterie of the Church of England, charging it with ſundry foule hereſies. And many among vs ſpare not to charge it with the hereſie of *Puritaniſme*. And I doubt not to auouch it, that ſome are condemned for heretikes in the hiſtorie of the Church, who (if all were knowne) ſhould be found to be good ſeruants of God.

1. This verifies the ſaying of *Eccleſiaſtes*, Chapter 8. verſe 14. *There are righteous men to whom it befalles according to the worke of the wicked.*

2. Miniſters muſt hence be put in minde to vſe circumſpection both for the matter and the manner of their preaching.

3. Being defamed, and that wrongfully, they muſt hence take occaſion to be more carefull to pleaſe God, as *Dauid* did in the like caſe, *Pſal.* 119.69.

But how came this report of *Paul*? *Anſwer*. Sometime he tollerated circumciſion, as a thing indifferent for a time: and hereupon circumciſed *Timothie*. And vpon this occaſion a report is raiſed that *Paul* preached circumciſion. In this wee ſee the faſhion of the world; which is to raiſe fames, reports, and ſlanders of all perſons, ſpecially vpon magiſtrates and miniſters, and that vpon euery light and vniuſt occaſion. But good men will take no ſuch occaſions of raiſing reports, *Pſal.* 15.3.

But how did *Paul* take this report? *Anſwer*. Hee did not requite euill for euill (as the manner of men is,) but hee returnes loue and goodneſſe for euill: and for this cauſe (no doubt of purpoſe) he beginnes his ſpeech on this manner, *Brethren, if I yet preach Circumciſion.*

The Apologie and defence followes. And firſt hee denies the report. And this is: becauſe for his preaching he is perſecuted of

the

the Iewes. Here obſerue,that they which are called to teach, muſt preach the Goſpel, what trouble or danger ſoeuer follow, as *Paul* did. It may be demanded,whether a Miniſter may not in teaching conceale any part of the truth at any time without ſinne? *Anſw.* In the caſe of confeſſion when a man is called to giue an account of his faith,no truth,no not the leaſt truth may bee concealed. Againe,when the ſoules of men are to be releeued,and ſaued,all concealements are damnable. Yet in the planting, or in the reſtoring of the Church,doctrines moſt neceſſary may be concealed. *Paul* was about two yeares at Epheſus,and ſpake nothing againſt *Diana*, but in generall tearmes. If he had,he had planted no Chuch at Epheſus. Againe,when people be vncapable of doctrine, it may bee concealed,till they be prepared for it. Chriſt told his diſciples that *hee had many things to tell them, which they could not then learne.* Some beleeuers muſt haue no ſtrange meat,but milk only. Thirdly, when the teaching of a leſſer truth,hinders the teaching of a fundamentall truth,the leſſer truth may be concealed, that the fundamentall truth may be taught,and take place.

Here wee ſee the fidelitie of *Paul*: if he had ſought himſelfe, his honour,profit, or pleaſure, he would not haue taught any doctrine that ſhould haue cauſed perſecution. The like mind muſt be in all teachers,nay in all beleeuers,who are to receiue the Goſpell for it ſelfe, without reſpect to honour,profit,or pleaſure.

Paul addes further in way of defence, that the ſcandall of the croſſe was not aboliſhed. Hence it followes,that the Goſpell muſt be preached,though all men be offended.God muſt not be diſpleaſed,though all men be diſpleaſed, *Actes* 5.29. Indeed Chriſt pronounceth a woe againſt them by whom offences come: but that is meant of offences giuen, and not of offences taken: of which Chriſt hath an other rule, *Matth.* 15.14. *Let them alone, they are the blind leaders of the blind.*

Againe, by the offence of the Iewes, we ſee the mind of men, who cannot bee content with the death and paſſion of Chriſt, vnleſſe they may adde workes, or ſomething elſe of their owne, for their iuſtification and ſaluation. Thus doe the Papiſts at this day: and the like doe many of the ignorant people among vs, that will bee ſaued by their good dealing, and their good ſeruing of God.

Touching the imprecation in the 12. verſe, three queſtions are to be propounded. The firſt is, whether *Paul* did well thus to curſe his enemies? I anſwer, yea: for firſt wee muſt put a difference betweene the priuate cauſe of man, and the cauſe of God. Now

Paul accurseth the false Apostles, not in respect of his owne cause, but in respect of the cause of God; and not as his owne enemies, but as the enemies of God. Secondly, we must distinguish the persons of euill men. Some are curable, aud some againe are incurable, of whose saluation there is no hope. Now *Paul* directs his imprecation against persons incurable. And he knew them to be incurable by some extraordinary inspiration or instinct, (as the Prophets and the rest of the Apostles did in sundry cases) and hereupon he curseth sometime euen particular persons, *as Alexander the copper-smith*. 2.*Tim*.4.14. Thirdly, we must distinguish the affections of men. Some are carnall, as rash anger, hatred, desire of reuenge, &c. some againe are more spirituall and diuine, as a zeale of Gods glory, and of the safety of Gods Church. Now *Paul* in pronouncing the curse, is not carried with a carnall affection, but with a pure zeale of Gods glory, and with the same Spirit by which he penned this Epistle.

The second question is, whether we may not curse our enemies as *Paul* did? *Answ.* No: for we haue not the like Spirit to discerne the persons of men what they are: and our zeale of Gods glory is mixed with many corrupt affections, and therefore to be suspected. We in our ordinary dealings haue an other rule to follow; *Math.*5. *blesse and curse not.* If we dare goe beyond the limits of this rule, we must heare the speech of Christ, *Ye know not of what Spirit yee are*, *Luk*.9.55.

The third question is, how we should vse the imprecations that are in the Psalmes of *Dauid*, as *Psal.*109. and in other places of Scripture? *Ans.* They are to be directed generally against the kingdome of the diuell: and they are further to be vsed as Prophecies of the holy Ghost comforting his Church, and procuring a finall sentence vpon the enemies of God.

The word which is translated, *disquiet*, is to be considered: for it signifies to put men out of their estate, and to driue them out of house and home, as enemies doe when they sacke and spoile a towne.

By this we see that the doctrine of iustification by workes or by the law, is a doctrine full of danger and perrill, because it puts men out of their estate in Christ, and bereaues them of their saluation in heauen. Therefore let all men flye from the religion of the Papist, as if they would flye from an army of Spaniards or Turkes.

Contrariwise, they that would prouide well for themselues and their posterity, and plant themselues in a good estate, must take

this

this course. They must consider that there is a citie of God in heauen, the gates and suburbs wherof be vpon earth in the assemblies of the Church: that this citie hath many roomes and habitations, and many liberties: that the law whereby this citie is ruled, is the whole word of God, specially the doctrine of the Gospell. In this city there is all happinesse, and out of it there is nothing but woe and misery. Enter therfore into the suburbs of this city of God: as ye professe the Gospel, so subiect your minds and consciences, and all your affections to it, and bee doers of it in the exercise of faith, repentance, new obedience. Thus shall you haue a good estate in Christ, and ioyfull habitation in heauen.

13 *For brethren, yee haue beene called to libertie: onely vse not your libertie as an occasion to the flesh: but by loue serue one another.*

The first part of the Epistle touching the faith of the Galatians is ended: and here beginnes the second part touching good life, and it continues from this verse to the 11. verse of the 6. chapter. In it *Paul* doth two things: first, he propounds the summe of his doctrine, and then after makes a particular declaration of it. The summe of all is propounded in this 13. verse: in which *Paul* sets downe the ground of all good duties, and then two maine rules of good life. The ground is in these words, *Brethren, yee haue been called to libertie.* And it must be noted, that as these words are the foundation of that which followes, so are they also the reason of that which goes before, and therefore *Paul* saith, *For brethren, &c.* The two rules are in the words following: One in these, *vse not your libertie as an occasion to the flesh*: the other in these, *Doe seruice one to another by loue.*

In the ground of all good duties, namely, the calling to liberty, foure things are to be considered. First, who cals. Secondly, who are called. Thirdly, what is the calling of God. Fourthly, why it is here mentioned by *Paul.*

To the first, who calles? I answer, God the Father in Christ by the spirit, for he is absolute Lord of all his creatures: and therefore he may call out of the kingdome of darknesse into his owne kingdome whom he will. And it is God alone that *calleth the things that are not, as though they were, Rom. 4. 17.*

The second is, who are called? *Answer.* All they that any way answer the calling of God, for *Paul* saith indifferently of all the Galatians, that *they were called.* Now men answer the calling of

God,

God,some in profession,some in heart,and some in both. And all these are said to be called, yet with some difference. The calling of God is directed first of all and principally to the Elect: and then in the second place, it pertaines to them which are not Elect,because they are mixed in society with the Elect. And hence ariseth a distinction of the calling of God,sometime it is operatiue: because God signifies and withall workes his will in the Elect: sometimes againe in respect of others it is onely significatiue,when God reueales his will to men, but spares to worke it for iust causes knowne to himselfe.

The third point is,what is the calling to liberty? *Ans.* An action of God, translating men from the kingdome of darkenesse to his owne kingdome. It hath two parts,*inuitement* and *admission. Inuitement* is,when God offers remission of sinnes and life euerlasting to them that beleeue,outwardly by the preaching of the Gospel, inwardly by the inspiration of heauenly desires. *Admission* is, when men are entred into the kingdome of grace: and it is either outward or inward. Outward admission is made in baptisme. Inward admission is,when men are taken out of old *Adam*,and by faith ingrafted into Christ: for by this insition into Christ, men are made reall members of Gods kingdome.

The last question is,why *Paul* mentions the calling to liberty in this place? *Ans.* It is the ground of all comfort,by it *Paul* comforts the Corinthians, 1.*Cor*.1.9. Againe, it is the ground of good life. Therefore *Peter* saith,*Be ye holy,as he that hath called you is holy*. 1.*Pet*. 1.15. And *Paul, Walke worthy the calling wherewith he hath called you*. *Eph*.4.1. If the calling of God doe not mooue vs to amendment of life,nothing will doe it.

Wee in England haue heard the calling of God more then forty yeares: and yet very few of vs are mooued to change and amend our liues. This shewes our Atheisme and vnbeleefe: here is almost nothing but heauing, shouing, and lifting for the world. Some are held captiues of their couetousnesse, some of their pride,some of their damnable and fleshly lusts: and all this shewes that few or none,so much as dreame of a calling to spirituall liberty.

The first Rule followes: *Only vse not your liberty, as an occasion to the flesh.*

The sense. *Flesh*] hereby the Papists vnderstand Sensuality or carnall appetites: but hereby is meant the corruption of all the powers of the soule, euen of reason and conscience. *Paul* saith, that *the wisedom or vnderstanding of the flesh is enmity to God*. *Rom*.8.7.

fleshlines

fleſhlineſſe therefore pertaines to the vnderſtanding. Againe, he ſaith of ſome that *they are puffed vp in the mind of the fleſh, Coloſſ.* 2.18. and he willes the Epheſians *to be renewed in the ſpirit of their minds. Eph.*4.23.

The meaning then of the rule is this, vſe not the benefit of ſpirituall liberty as an occaſion to the fleſh to liue according to the fleſh. Here I conſider three things, what is the abuſe of liberty? where is this abuſe to be found? and what is the right vſe thereof?

The firſt queſtion is, what is the abuſe of Chriſtian liberty? *Anſwer.* To vſe it as an occaſion of fleſhly and carnall liberty: and that is done 3. waies. The firſt is, when men make more things indifferent then God euer made. Thus the Corinthians vſed fornication as a thing indifferent. 1.*Cor.*6. To many in theſe dayes drunkenneſſe and ſurfeiting is but a thing indifferent. Men vſe not to diſtinguiſh a thing indifferent, and the vſe of it: but they commonly thinke, that if the thing be indifferent in it ſelfe, then alſo the vſe of it is indifferent. Thus all abuſes of meat, drinke, apparell, all rioting and gaming, dicing and carding, &c. are excuſed by the names of things indifferent.

Secondly, our liberty is abuſed by an immoderate vſe of the gifts of God. The vſe of them is immoderate three waies, firſt in reſpect of time, as when *Diues fared deliciouſly, and was araied in rich attire euery day.* Thus many gentlemen and others offend, when they turne recreation into an occupation. Secondly, the gifts of God are immoderately vſed in reſpect of themſelues; as when men exceed in eating and drinking, as the Prophet ſaith, *Deut.*29.19. *adding drunkennes to thirſt.* Thirdly, in reſpect of the callings and conditions of men: for euery man is to vſe the gifts of God according to his place and condition. They then offend, that being but meane perſons, and liuing by trades, yet for their diet and apparel, are as great gentlemen and gentlewomen.

Thirdly, libertie is abuſed when the bleſſings of God are made inſtruments, and (as it were) flags and banners to diſplay our riot, vanity, oſtentation, pride: for this cauſe ſundry things, wherof ſome are indifferent in themſelues, are condemned, *Iſa.*3.16.

The ſecond queſtion is, where is this abuſe? *Anſwer.* Euen among vs in England. It is the faſhion of men to take vnto themſelues a tolleration of ſinning, ſome vpon the patience of God, others vpon the doctrine of the gracious election of God, ſaying, that they will liue as they liſt: becauſe, if they be elected to ſaluation, they ſhall certainly be ſaued whatſoeuer they doe. And ſome there

there be that take occaſion to continue in their ſinnes, vpon the mercy of God in the death and paſſion of Chriſt. A certaine dweller in this towne of Cambridge made away himſelfe. In his boſome was found a writing to this effect, that God did ſhew mercy on great, grieuous, and deſperate ſinners: and therefore he ſaid that he hoped of mercy though he hanged himſelfe. Of this mind are many ignorant perſons who perſeuering in their ſinnes, yet perſwade themſelues of mercy: becauſe they haue heard that Chriſt dyed for mankind. And thus the death of Chriſt is as it were a licence or letters patents to commit ſinne. Againe, great is the abuſe of meate, drinke, and apparell. To *Elias* there came an Angell and ſaid, *ariſe and eate*. 1.*King*.19.7. but to the men of our dayes, there had need come an Angell and ſay, Ceaſe to eate, ceaſe to drinke, ceaſe to game.

The third queſtion is, what is the right vſe of Chriſtian liberty? *Anſw*. It ſtands in two things: firſt of all, we our ſelues muſt be renewed and ſanctified. *To the pure all things are pure*. 1.*Tit*.1.15. The perſon muſt firſt pleaſe God before the action can pleaſe him. The ſecond is, that beſide the lawfull vſe of the creatures we muſt haue a ſpirituall and holy vſe of them. The lawfull vſe of the creature I call the politicke vſe thereof commonly allowed and taken vp among men. The ſpirituall vſe is whereby we receiue and vſe the creature as from the hand of God the Father in Chriſt according to his will and word. And the godly are not to ſeparate the one vſe from the other, but are bound by vertue of the third commandement to take vp an holy vſe of euery gift of God. When *Noe* came out of the Arke, ſo ſoone as he ſet foote vpon the earth hee built an altar, offered ſacrifice, and called on the name of God: not onely for this end to worſhip God, but alſo to ſanctifie the earth and all the creatures of God vnto his vſe. The like did *Abraham* when he came into the land of Canaan. And to this end we muſt obſerue fiue rules. The firſt, that the creatures of God muſt be ſanctified by the word and prayer. 1.*Tim*.4. the word muſt, ſhewes vs what we may doe: and prayer obtaines the doing of it. The ſecond rule: we muſt be circumſpect leſt we ſinne in the vſe of the creatures. In this reſpect *Iob* ſends for his children after they had feaſted together, and he ſanctifies them. *Iob*.1.5. The third rule: we muſt vſe the gifts of God with thankſgiuing. *Rom*.14.6. Commonly in theſe dayes there is no feaſting or reioycing, vnleſſe all memory of God be buried: for that is ſaid to breed melancholy. The fourth rule: We muſt ſuffer our ſelues to be limited and moderated in the vſe of our liberty, partly by the law of the Magiſtrate

ſtrate, and partly by the law of charity, in the caſe of offence. I ſay in the vſe: becauſe liberty it ſelfe is inwardly in the conſcience: and the vſe of it is often in the outward action: and therefore vnder the order of humane law. The 5. rule: Our liberty muſt be vſed for right ends; as namely the glory of God. 1.*Cor.* 10.31. the preſeruation of nature, and not the pampering of the fleſh. *Rom.* 13.13. and the good of our neighbour. *Rom.* 12.13.

Make conſcience to obſerue this rule: and the rather, becauſe the holy and ſpirituall vſe of Chriſtian liberty, is a ſigne and token that thou art in the kingdome of God, and a true member thereof: as on the contrary, the abuſe of Gods bleſſings ſhewes thee to be ſtill in the kingdome of darknes. When men ſell things of great worth for a little value, and then afterward giue themſelues to rioting and ſpending, we commonly ſay that they are theeues, and no right owners of the goods which they ſolde. The like may be ſaid of them that abuſe ſpirituall liberty, that they are but vſurpers, and no right owners of it.

Laſtly, it muſt be obſerued, that this rule hath two branches. The firſt is, that we muſt not miniſter to the fleſh any occaſion of ſinning. The ſecond is, that we muſt giue no occaſion of ſinning by meanes of Chriſtian liberty.

The ſecond maine rule followes, *Serue one an other by loue*: For the right conceiuing of it, I will propound three queſtions. The firſt is, why is this rule propounded in this place? *Anſwer.* It ſets downe the end of all Apoſtolike doctrine, as *Paul* ſheweth, 1.*Tim.* 1.5. *The end of the commandement is loue out of a pure heart, good conſcience, faith vnfained.* Here men commonly vnderſtand by the commandement, the morall law. That is indeed a truth, but it is not the meaning of the place. In the third verſe *Paul* ſets downe a commaundement or a denunciation vnto *Timothy*, that hee and the Paſtors of Epheſus, teach no other doctrine, but the doctrine of the Apoſtles: then in the 5. verſe he propounds the ſumme and ſubſtance or end of the foreſaid commandement: in the 18. verſe after a long *anantapodaton*, he inioynes *Timothie* to obſerue it carefully. So then the end of all ſound doctrine is loue out of a pure heart: and all our preaching muſt tend to this.

The ſecond queſtion is, what is the loue of our neighbour ſpecified in this rule? *Anſwer. It is an affection renewed, whereby wee are mooued to wiſh well to our neighbour in the Lord.* I ſay, *an affection*, to confute *Lombard*, who ſaith, that loue is not an habit in vs (as other vertues are,) but the H. Ghoſt. I ſay, it is an affection *renewed*, to confute the Papiſt, who teacheth that we haue the true loue of God, and our neighbour by nature, and that we want nothing but the ſecond acte or the exerciſe of loue, which they ſay is from grace. Further, I adde that loue *inclines vs to wiſh well to our neighbour*: for this is the formall and proper effect of loue, and all this is done when we thinke well, ſpeake and doe well, and that in reſpect not onely of the body, but alſo in reſpect of the ſoule of our neighbour. Laſtly I ſay, that loue to our neighbour muſt be *in the Lord*. Becauſe we are to loue him in reſpect that he is a creature of God, and beares his image: and not in reſpect of honour, profit, or pleaſure, which we receiue from him. Loue for ſuch ends, is ſelfeloue.

The third queſtion is, what is the vſe of loue? *Anſ.* It ſerues to make vs ſeruiceable to our neighbour. *Loue ſeekes not her owne things.* 1.*Cor.*13. Chriſt was ſeruant to his enemies in bearing their ſinnes vpon the croſſe. *Paul that was free from all, became a ſeruant to all, to win ſome.* 1.*Cor.*9.19. To Chriſt we are to doe ſeruice: and he hath put our neighbor in his ſtead, ſo as that which is done to our neighbour, ſhall be done to him: our neighbour therfore muſt be ſerued of vs; and this is not againſt our liberty. For wee are free inwardly in conſcience, yet in the outward vſe of our liberty, we muſt be ſeruants to men.

The vſe. If we examine our liues by this rule, we ſhall find that there is very little power of religion among men. There are ſixe ſorts of men that liue in the breach of this rule. The firſt are vſurers, who lend for aduantage, when they ſhould lend freely to them that are in need; theſe ſerue themſelues and make a prey of all. The ſecond ſort are ingroſſers, who gather in commodities to inrich themſelues. The third ſort are idle perſons of what degree ſoeuer, that ſpend their time in eating, drinking, ſleeping, gaming: ſuch are but vnprofitable burdens of the earth. To this ſort I referre beggars and vagabonds. The fourth ſort are Riotous perſons that vſe to go from alehouſe to alehouſe, from tauerne to tauerne, and miſpend that whereby they ſhould maintaine their families, and be ſeruiceable to their country. The fift ſort are Tradeſmen, who in their dealings vſe lying, diſſembling, fraud, iniuſtice. They ſeeke nothing but their priuate aduantage. And this kind of men abounds in the world. The laſt ſort are drowſie and carnall Proteſtants, who onely ſeeke the things of this world, and neuer ſo much as giue good example to ſeruants or children, or any good counſell. Beſide all this, it is the common fault of the world, for men to ſerue themſelues, according to the common ſaying, *Euery man for himſelfe, and God for vs all.* And the beſt men that are, if they examine themſelues, ſhall find that they faile many waies,and come ſhort in the duties of loue to men with whom they liue.

This being ſo, we are to acknowledge before God this maine offence of ours: and to intreat for pardon of it for Chriſts ſake. And euer hereafter to change our liues, and to reforme them according to this rule. Aud that is done on this manner. Euery man hath,or ought to haue two callings, a generall, and a particular. The generall is, whereby wee are called to bee Chriſtians. In this calling wee are to doe good to all men by teaching, admoniſhing, exhorting, and by example of good life. A particular calling, whereby men are called to ſome eſtate of life in the family, Church or Commonwealth. And according to the ſeuerall conditions of particular callings, muſt euery man in his place doe the beſt good hee can. The Magiſtrate muſt vſe his office, firſt for the maintenance of the Goſpell, and then for the execution of iuſtice. The Miniſter muſt preach ſound religion in loue of the ſoules of men. The maſter of the family muſt cauſe his houſhold to imbrace the Goſpell, and frequent the exerciſes of religion. Laſtly, euery man that is in a trade or office, muſt apply himſelfe to the vttermoſt of his power, to doe all he can for the good of his countrey: and he muſt ſo deale, that he may bee helpfull to all with whom he deales, and hurtfull to none. Wee are, or ſhould be, *trees of righteouſneſſe:* our fruite muſt bee meate for others, and our leaues for medicines. We muſt be as candles, that ſpend themſelues to giue light to others.

14 *For all the law is fulfilled in one word, which is this, thou ſhalt loue thy neighbour as thy ſelfe.*

Fulfilled] compriſed, *Rom.* 13.9. *One word*] One precept: for the holy Ghoſt calls precepts, *words*. It may bee demaunded, how the whole law ſhould be fulfilled in the loue of our neighbour? *Anſwer.* The loue of God, and the loue of our neighbour are ioyned together, as the cauſe and the effect: and the loue of God is practiſed in the loue of our neighbour. For God that is inuiſible, will be loued in the perſon of our neighbour whom wee ſee, and with whom wee conuerſe. And the firſt Commaundement of the law, muſt be included in all the Commandements following: and thus the loue of God is preſuppoſed in euery Commaundement of the ſecond Table: he therefore that loues his neighbour, loues God alſo.

Thou ſhalt loue] vnderſtand both the affection, and the duties of

loue.

loue. *Thy neighbour*] any one that is neare vnto vs in reſpect of mans nature. *Iſa.*38.7. though he be our enemy, yet if by any occaſion he be offered vnto vs of God, he is our neighbour.

As thy ſelfe] theſe words ſignifie not the meaſure of our loue: as though we ſhould loue our ſelues in the firſt place; and then our neighbour in the ſecond place, for there are ſome caſes in which we are to loue our neighbour more then our ſelues. As for example, we are more to loue the ſoule of our brother, then our temporal life, and a good ſubiect is more to loue the life of his Prince then his owne life: here then the Holy Ghoſt ſignifies, what muſt be the manner of our loue; the word (*as*) ſignifies not *quantity*, but *quality*: and that we are as truly and earneſtly with loue to imbrace our neighbour, as our ſelues.

The ſcope. The words containe a reaſon of the ſecond Rule, which may be framed thus: to ſerue our neighbor in duties of loue, is the keeping of the whole law: therefore this ſeruice muſt carefully be performed.

The vſe. Here we ſee that the end of a mans life is to ſerue God in ſeruing of man, for this is the ſumme of the whole law. Seruants are commanded in ſeruing their Maſters, to ſerue God, and to do whatſoeuer they doe, as vnto God. *Col.*3.23. And ſo euery man in his place, in dealing with men, muſt ſo deale as if he were to deale with God himſelfe. Therefore moſt men prophane their liues, when they make the ſcope and drift thereof, to be the getting of riches, and honours. And though they haue great charges, that is no excuſe, for the principall end of our liuing here is to performe ſeruice to men, and in this ſeruice to do homage to God, for which homage God will giue the honour and riches, which he ſees conuenient for vs.

Secondly, here we may obſerue what is true religion and godlines, namely to loue and ſerue God in ſeruing of man. *He that ſaith hee loues God, and yet hates his brother, is a lyer.* 1. *Ioh.*4. 20. And hence it followes, that to liue out of all ſociety of men, though it be in prayer and faſting, (after Monkiſh faſhion) is no ſtate of perfection, but meere ſuperſtition: for that is true and perfect loue of God, that is ſhewed in duties of loue, and in the edification of our neighbour. Againe, the hypocriſie of ſundry Proteſtants is here diſcouered. If they come to the Church, & heare ſermons, and frequent the Lords table, they thinke they may do afterward what they will; and many ſuch are frequenters of tauerns, and alehouſes, and are giuen to riot, and licenciouſnes. But it is not enough for thee to be holy in the Church: thou maieſt be a Saint in the Church, and a diuell at home. True religion is that which shewes it selfe in thy priuate house, priuate dealings, & in the course of thine owne life: such as thou art in thy particular calling, such art thou indeed and trueth, what showes soeuer thou makest before men.

15 *If ye bite and deuoure one another, take heed that ye be not consumed one of another.*

The sense. *If yee bite*] Here *Paul* alludes to the fashion of wilde beastes, as lions, wolues, &c. And by *biting* wee are to vnderstand all iniuries in words, as railing, cursing, slandering, backbiting, &c. *Deuoure*] Here *Paul* vnderstands all iniuries in deed, or violence, euen to the shedding of blood. *Take heed lest*] Here *Paul* signifies, that contentions and dissentions, breed the destruction and desolation of the Church.

The scope. These words are a second reason of the second rule, drawne from the dangerous effect of the contrary, thus. Contentions breed the desolation of the Church: therefore doe seruice one to another by loue.

The contents. In the words *Paul* deliuers three things. The first is, that there were greeuous contentions in the Church of Galatia. The like also were in the Church of Corinth, 1.*Cor*.3. The cause of the former contentions were differences in points of religion. Some of the Galatians (no doubt) withstanding circumcision, and the most of them standing for it. For hereupon great were the dissentions of the Churches in Iudea, *Act*.15.2. Obserue then, that vnity is not an infallible and an inseparable marke of the Church of God. Vnity may be out of the church, & dissention in the Church, as here we see. It may be obiected, that there is peace in the kingdome of God, and that there the wolfe and the lambe dwell together, *Isa*.11. *Answer*. This is but in part verified in the kingdome of grace vpon earth: and it is fully accomplished in the kingdome of glory in heauen. Againe, it may be alledged, that the Church is the company of them that truly consent in one & the same faith. *Answ*. That is properly meant of the Catholike Church: but the case is otherwise in particular Churches, where true beleeuers are mixed with hypocrites, whereupon ariseth much dissention. And of true beleeuers, some are more carnall then spirituall: and that is another cause of dissention, 1.*Cor*.3.3.

The second point, concernes the qualitie of these dissentions. When *Paul* saith, *If yee bite and deuoure, &c.* he signifies that they were fierce, and violent. And such commonly are dissentions for religion, as appeares by the persecution in Queene *Maries* dayes, the heate whereof nothing could slake but mans blood. Againe, he signifies in these very words, that they were brutish, and beastlike, more beseeming wolues, lions, dogges, then men. This must teach vs to detest railing cursing, euill speaking, fighting, vnles it be in the case of necessary defence, for by these actions we degenerate to the condition of beasts, and repell from vs the worke of grace: for Christ of lyons, wolues, beares, hath made vs his sheepe and lambes. *Isai.* 11.

The third point is touching the effect of contention, and that is the ruine and desolation of the Church. The diuision of the members among themselues is the dissolution of the whole body. Differences in points of religion, breede doubting: doubting hinders faith and inuocation, and the free course of the Gospel: and where these be hindered, the Church goes to decay. And by reason of the dissentions that be in these last dayes, many liue as Atheists, and will be of no religion.

By this we are to be admonished to study and to vse all meanes to maintaine Christian peace and concord. *Ephesians* 4.3. To this end we must remember one generall rule. *Rom.* 12.18. *Haue peace with all men.* And withall we must obserue the cautions which *Paul* addes; one is, *if it may be* with good conscience, for there are some, with whom there is no peace, vnlesse we sooth them in their vices, or deny our religion, either in whole or in part. The second is, *If it lye in you,* for sometime men are accused, and must of necessity defend themselues. These two cautions obserued, *peace must bee had with all men.*

It may then be demanded, why do not the Protestants make a Pacification with the Papists? *Ans.* We are content so to do in respect of ciuill society, but not in respect of religion. We haue a commandement to the contrary. *Reuel.* 18.4. *Come out of Babylon my people, and touch no vncleane thing.* where a pacification is made, both the partes must yeeld somewhat: but we may not yeeld in any point of our religion, to the Papists. In an Instrument of musicke, the stringes out of tune are set vp, or set downe, to the rest: and the strings that are in tune are not stirred: Euen so the Papists are to turne to vs, we are not to turne to them: our religion being the doctrine of the Prophets, and Apostles.

Peace, is threefold, *Church peace, Ciuill peace,* and *Houshold peace.* All these are to be maintained. Touching *Church peace* I giue three rules. The first is, that *for the ending of differences in religion there must*

be

bee conferences in a free or chriſtian Councell: the ſpirit of the Prophets, is ſubiect to the Prophets, 1. *Cor.* 14.32. When there aroſe differences in the Churches of Iudea, *the Apoſtles and Elders came together to inquire of the matter*, *Actes* 15.6. And this is a thing much to bee deſired in theſe dayes, ſpecially in theſe Weſterne parts of the world. It may be demaunded, why did not the Proteſtants ioyne with the Papiſts at the Councell of Trent? *Anſwer.* From the firſt Seſſion it was more then ſixe yeares before any ſafe conduct was giuen to the Proteſtants: and at their appearing in the Councel, exception was taken againſt their letters, and they diſmiſſed. And when they appeared the ſecond time vpon new ſafe conduct, the Councell was the next day reiourned for two yeares. And when ſafe conduct was giuen the third time, the Proteſtant Princes refuſed to ſend their Diuines: becauſe they had bin twiſe mocked. Moreouer, the Councell was not a free Councell: becauſe the Pope himſelfe was both partie, and iudge.

The ſecond rule. *There muſt be a Chriſtian toleration one of another*, *Epheſ.* 4.2. Heere that wee miſtake not, I propound two queſtions. One is, in what there muſt be a toleration? *Anſwer.* A toleration preſuppoſeth an errour or defect in our brother. An errour is either in iudgement, or manners. An errour in iudgement, is either in the foundation of religion, or beſide the foundation, in lighter matters: if the errour be in the foundation, there is no toleration of it. If it bee in ſome leſſer matter, a toleration is to bee vſed according to the rule of the Apoſtle, *If yee bee otherwiſe minded, God will reueale it*, *Philip.* 3.15. When others ſee not that which we ſee, we muſt not preſently condemne them, but tolerate their ignorance, till God reueale his trueth vnto them. Againe, errours in manners bee of two ſorts, ſome without offence, as haſtineſſe, frowardneſſe, vaineglorioufneſſe, &c. theſe we muſt tolerate, *Prou.* 19.11. and others with open offence, and ſuch admit no toleration, 1. *Cor.* 5.11.

The ſecond queſtion is, to what end we muſt tolerate the infirmities and ignorances of our brethren? *Anſwer.* Toleration muſt tend to the good and edification of men, *Rom.* 15.2. We muſt not ſo tolerate, as that we approoue of the leaſt vice, or betray the leaſt part of Gods truth.

It may here be demanded, whether there may not be a toleration for Popery? *Anſ.* No. The toleration of two religions in one kingdome, is the ouerthrow of peace. Againe, Popery is a religion both heretical and ſchiſmaticall. It may be ſaid, that faith and conſcience is free. I anſwer, though faith in the heart, and conſcience in it ſelfe be free in reſpect of mans authoritie: yet is not the publiſhing of faith, and the profeſſion of conſcience free in like ſort, but it ſtands ſubiect to the power of the Magiſtrate.

The third rule. *Euery man in his place, ſpecially teachers muſt ſet themſelues to build the Church, Iud.* 5.20. *Epheſ.* 4.12. Indeed the truth is to be defended: but marke how. The truth muſt be confeſſed, when time and occaſion ſerues, without oppoſition: this done, all contentions laid aſide, we muſt ſet our ſelues to build the Church. And the rather Miniſters of Gods word in England muſt remember this: becauſe while wee are ſtriuing among our ſelues in ſundry points of difference, the Papiſt our common enemy, gets ground.

Touching *ciuill peace*, it muſt be remembred, that the peace and good eſtate of Ieruſalem ſtood in this, that it was made the ſeat of Gods Sanctuary, and the throne of iuſtice, *Pſalm.* 122. When the arke was in the houſe of *Obed-Edom*, all things proſpered with him. Now in the New Teſtament, the preaching of the Goſpell, inuocation of Gods name, with the vſe of the Sacraments, come in the roome of the Sanctuary. *Ciuill peace* then is maintained, when men yeeld ſubiection to the Goſpel of Chriſt, which brings peace to all that receiue it.

Touching *houſhold peace*, I giue two rules. One is, that *gouernours of families muſt vrge and compell all vnder them to admit, (at the leaſt outwardly,) the practiſe of religion in the exerciſes of faith, repentance, new obedience.* Thus did *Abraham, Gen.* 17. and *Ioſua* c.24. They that doe not firſt of al conſent in Chriſt, cannot conſent among themſelues. Secondly, it muſt be obſerued, that a family is the ſchoole of God, in which hee will exerciſe our faith, inuocation, loue, patience, long ſuffering, &c. And there is more vertue to bee ſeene in the well ordering of a family, then in the pretended holineſſe of Monkiſh cloiſters.

Thus we ſee how we are to maintaine the vnitie of the ſpirit in the bond of peace. For the better inforcing of this dutie, *Paul, Eph.* 4.4. giues ſeuen reaſons: One body, one ſpirit, one hope of eternall life, one Lord, one faith, one baptiſme, one Father of all. It may be ſaid, we are at peace, what needs all this adoe? *Anſwer.* The peace of many, is peace in drunkenneſſe, (called good fellowſhip,) peace in prophaneneſſe, & wickednes. This is the diuels peace, where he beares the ſway. The peace of which I now ſpeake, is *in the Lord*, and in the true worſhip of God: of which reade *Iſa.* 2. where men are ſaid hand in hand to goe vp to the Mountaine of the Lord, that they may heare his will, and ioyntly obey it.

16 *Then I ſay, walke in the Spirit, and ye ſhall not fulfill the luſts of the fleſh.*

The ſcope. Here *Paul* returnes to the firſt rule v.13.and ſhewes the way, how it is to be obſerued, thus, *If ye walke in the Spirit, ye ſhall not fulfill the luſts of the fleſh:* and when the luſts of the fleſh are not fulfilled, there ſhall no occaſion be giuen to the fleſh, by the vſe of Chriſtian liberty.

The words containe two parts: a Rule, *walke in the Spirit*: and the benefit that comes by the rule, *Yee ſhall not fulfill the luſtes of the fleſh.*

In the rule I conſider two things, what is the Spirit, and what is walking. *The Spirit is the gift of regeneration, loſt by Adam, reſtored by Chriſt.* I ſay *it is a gift*: and this gift is tearmed by the name of *the Spirit*: becauſe the Spirit worketh it immediatly in vs, from the Father and the Sonne. Againe, I ſay it is *a gift of regeneration*, to make a diſtinction betweene it, and ciuill vertue. For there is a gift of regeneration, which mortifies corruption, and a gift of reſtraint, which ſerues onely to keepe in corruption. Of this ſecond kind, are all ciuill vertues, in naturall and heathen men, and not of the firſt. *Ioſeph* is chaſt, and ſo was *Xenocrates*. *Ioſephs* chaſtity is a part of regeneration, and proceedes from the Spirit here mentioned, but the chaſtity of *Xenocrates* is not ſo, proceeding onely from the generall prouidence of God, and not from the Spirit of Sanctification. The like I ſay of all other ciuill vertues.

More plainely, The Spirit is a Diuine nature, quality, or condition, whereby we are made conformable to Chriſt, in righteouſnes, and holines.

The Spirit hath fiue properties. The firſt, that it is a rich and liberall grace of God. For it containes in it the ſeede of all vertues, and all neceſſary graces of God: becauſe it comes in the roome of originall ſinne, which containes in it, the ſeedes of all vices or ſinnes.

The ſecond is the largenes of it, for this Spirit is in all the powers of them that are regenerate, that is, in the mind, conſcience, wil, affections, and in the ſenſuall appetite. 1.*Theſ*.5.23. And he that is ſanctified in one part, is ſanctified in all. Hence it follows, that they which haue plenty of illumination, without change of affection, and life, are indeed carnall, and not ſpirituall.

The third property is ſincerity, for the grace of God is without falſhood or guile. *Pſalm*.32.1. Hence ariſeth the difference betweene the godly man, and an hypocrite: betweene the workes of nature,and the workes of grace. There are men that in diſtreſſe deſire the aſſiſtance and fauour of God:and they do it without the ſpirit of God: for they do it deceitfully, deſiring Gods fauour not for it ſelfe, but in reſpect of ſome euill from which they would be deliuered,as the Mariners in *Ionas*,and *Pharao* did. Againe, there are men, that mourne for their ſinnes without the Spirit of God. For there is much falſhood in their mourning:becauſe they mourn for ſinne in reſpect of the puniſhment thereof, and not in reſpect of the offence of God. Laſtly, there are that pretend a loue to God,and yet want the Spirit; for they loue God in reſpect of his benefits,as *Saul* loued God for a kingdome: ſuch loue is mercenary, and a worke of nature, whereas the loue which is from the Spirit, makes vs loue God for himſelfe.

The fourth property is excellency, for the Spirit of grace in Chriſtians is more excellent then the grace of creation, in two reſpects. Firſt, in reſpect of the beginning thereof. For the Spirit is from Chriſt the ſecond *Adam*, both God and man: the grace of creation ſhould haue beene conueyed vnto vs from the firſt *Adam*, but a meere man, if he had ſtood. Secondly,in reſpect of conſtancy, for God gaue to *Adam* the will to perſeuere if he would: he giueth further to beleeuers, both the will to perſeuere, and the deed.

The fift property is liuelineſſe, whereby the Spirit is effectuall in operation, *Elihu* ſaith that the Spirit compelled him, and was in him as a veſſell of new wine which muſt haue a vent. *Iob* 32.19. Of the operation of the Spirit, I deliuer three things. The firſt, that the Spirit workes in and by the word of God: which therefore is called *the Miniſtery of the Spirit*. 2.*Corin*.3.6. The ſecond, that the Spirit worketh by certaine degrees. The firſt degree and the very firſt beginning of his diuine operation, is, to make vs feele in what great need we ſtand of Chriſt, and to deſire to be reconciled and turned vnto God. This is the firſt motion of the Spirit in vs: and they which want this,haue nothing as yet of the grace of God in them. The third,that the whole worke of the Spirit may be reduced to three actions,The firſt is,to caſt downe euery thing in vs,that exalts it ſelfe againſt God, 2.*Cor*.10.as namely, to beate downe erronious reaſon, and rebellious affection, and to put a man out of heart with his chiefe delights,and with his owne ſelfe. The ſecond action is,to kindle in our hearts a care and deſire of reconciliation with God in Chriſt: hence the Spirit is called *the Spirit of grace and ſupplication*. *Zach*.12. The third action is,to write the law in our hearts: and that is done by putting a new light of know-

knowledge into the minde, and new inclinations into the will, and affections.

Thus much of the Spirit. *Walking in the Spirit*, is, to Order our liues according to the direction, and motion of the Spirit. For, as the Spirit renewes our nature within, so it makes vs to change and renew our actions, in three respects. First, it makes vs put a further beginning to our actions, then nature can afford, causing vs to doe them in faith, whereby we beleeue, that our persons please God in Christ, that our worke to be done pleaseth God, that the defect of the worke is pardoned. Secondly, the Spirit makes vs doe our actions in a new manner, namely, in obedience to the written word. Thirdly, it makes vs put a new end to our actions, that is, to intend and desire to honour God in the things that we doe. For example. A man is wronged by his neighbour: and nature tells him that *he must requite euill with euill*: yet he resolues to doe otherwise: for (saith he) God in Christ hath forgiuen me many sinnes: therefore must I forgiue my neighbour. And he remembreth that *vengeance is Gods*: and that he is taught *so to aske pardon as he forgiueth others.* And hereupon he sets himselfe to requite euill with goodnesse. This is to liue in the Spirit.

The vse. By this rule we see that most of vs faile in our duties. For many of vs professing Christ, liue not according to the lawes of nature, in our common dealings. We minde earthly things: and therefore we are carnall. It is a principle with many, that if we keepe the Church, obserue the Queenes laws (which are indeed to be obserued) and auoid open and grosse sinnes, we doe all that God requires at our hands. Hereupon to walke in the Spirit, is thought to be a worke of precisenes, more then needes. And they which deeme it to be a worke of precisenesse, walke not in the Spirit. And indeede they which haue receiued the greatest measure of the Spirit, must say with *Paul*, that they are *carnall, sold vnder sinne, Rom.7.14.*

Secondly, this rule telleth vs, that we must become spirituall men, such as make conscience of euery sinne, and doe things lawfull in spirituall manner, in faith, and obedience, and not as carnall men doe them carnally. It may be said, that Ministers of the word must be spirituall men. I answer, if thou whatsoeuer thou art, be not spirituall, thou hast no part in Christ. *Rom.8.* And the rather, thou must be spirituall, because a naturall man may doe the outward duties of religion in a carnall sort.

Thirdly, we must not iudge any mans estate before God, by any one, or some few actiosn, either good or badde, but by his walking, or by the course of his life, which, if it bee carnall, it shewes the partie to be carnall: if it be spirituall, it shewes him to be spirituall.

The benefit that ariseth by the keeping of the rule, followes in these words, *Yee shall not fulfill the lusts of the flesh.*

Flesh] The corruption of nature, the root of all sinnes.

Lusts] Inordinate motions in the mind, wil, and affections. Thus largely is lust taken in the tenth commandement, which condemneth the first motions to euill.

Fulfill] Fulfilling, is not a simple doing of euill, but the accomplishing of lust with loue, pleasure, and full consent of will: as also perseuerance in euill, by adding sinne to sinne.

A question. How farre doeth the childe of God proceed in the lust of the flesh? *Answer.* He is assaulted by the lusts of the flesh: but he doth not accomplish them. More plainly: there are fiue degrees of lust, *Suggestion, delight, consent, the act, perseuerance in the act. Suggestion,* and *delight,* whereby the mind is drawne away, are incident to the child of God: *Consent* is not, ordinarily: and if at any time the child of God consent to the lustes of his flesh, it is but in part, and against his purpose, because he is ouercarried. Likewise the *act*, or *execution of lust,* is not ordinarily and vsually in the child of God: If at any time hee fall, he may say with *Paul, I doe that which I hate.* Lastly, perseuerance in euill doth not befall the child of God: because vpon his fall he recouers himselfe by new repentance. In this sense S. *Iohn* saith, *Hee that is borne of God, sinnes not,* 1. *Iohn* 3.9.

The vse. Hence it followes, that the lust of the flesh is in the childe of God to the death: and consequently they doe not fulfill the law, neither can they bee iustified thereby, as Popish doctrine is.

Secondly, our dutie is not to accomplish the lusts of the flesh, but to resist them to the vttermost, *Rom.* 13.14.

Thirdly, heere is comfort for the seruants of God. Some man may say, I am vexed and turmoiled with wicked thoughts and desires, so as I feare I am not Gods child. I answer againe, for all this despaire not. For, if thou hate and detest the lusts, that are in thee: if thou resist them, and wage battell against them: if being ouertaken at any time, thou recouer thy selfe by new repentance, they shall neuer be laid to thy charge to condemnation, *Rom.* 8.1. It is heere made a prerogatiue of Gods childe, when the lusts of the flesh are in him, not to accomplish them, or to liue in subiection to them.

17 *For the fleſh luſteth againſt the ſpirit, and the ſpirit againſt the fleſh, and they are contrary one to another, ſo that ye cannot doe the things which yee would.*

Theſe words are a reaſon of the former verſe, thus: If ye walke in the ſpirit, ye ſhall not fulfill the luſts of the fleſh: for the fleſh and ſpirit being contrary, mutually reſiſt and withſtand one another, ſo as ye can neither doe the good, nor the euill, which ye would.

Paul here ſets forth a ſpirituall combate, of which ſixe things are to be conſidered. The firſt is, concerning the parties by whom the combate is made: namely, *the fleſh*, and *the ſpirit*. *The fleſh* ſignifies the corruption of the whole nature of man: and *the ſpirit* is the gift of regeneration, (as hath bene ſhewed.) It may be demanded, how theſe twaine being but qualities, can be ſaid to fight together? *Anſwer.* The fleſh and the ſpirit are mixed together in the whole man regenerate, and in all the powers of the ſoule of man. Fire and water are ſaid to be mixed in compound bodies: light and darknes are mixed in the aire at the dawning of the day. In a veſſell of luke warme water, heate and cold are mixed together, wee cannot ſay, that the water is in one part hot, and in another cold, but the whole quantity of water is hot in part, and cold in part. Euen ſo the man regenerate, is not in one part fleſh, and in another part ſpirit, but the whole mind is partly fleſh, and partly ſpirit, and ſo are the will and affections throughout, partly ſpirituall, and partly carnall. Now vpon this mixture it comes to paſſe that the powers of the ſoule are carried and diſpoſed diuers wayes: and heereupon followes the combate.

The ſecond point concernes the meanes whereby this combate is made: and that is, a twofold concupiſcence, expreſſed in theſe words, *the fleſh luſteth againſt the ſpirit, and the ſpirit againſt the fleſh*. The luſt of the fleſh ſhewes it ſelfe in two actions. The firſt is, to defile and repreſſe the good motions of the ſpirit. In this reſpect *Paul* ſaith, *When I would doe good, euill is preſent*, and *the law of the fleſh rebells againſt the law of the mind, Rom.7.21,23.* Hereupon the fleſh is fitly reſembled by the diſeaſe called *Ephialtes*, or *the mare*, in which men in their ſlumber, thinke they feele a thing as heauy as a mountaine lying on their breſts, which they can no way remooue. The ſecond action of the fleſh, is, to bring foorth, and to fill the minde with wicked cogitations, and rebellious inclinations. In this reſpect concupiſcence is ſaid to tempt, intice, & draw away the minde of man, *Iames* 1.14. Againe, the luſt of the ſpirit hath two

other

other actions. The firſt is,to curbe and reſtraine the fleſh. Thus S. *Iohn* ſaith,that the *ſeed of grace keepes the regenerate that they cannot ſin*, 1.*Iohn* 3.9. The ſecond action of the ſpirit is,to ingender good motions, cogitations,and inclinations, agreeable to the will of God. Thus *Dauid* ſaith, that *his reines did teach him in the night ſeaſon*, *Pſal.* 16. And the Prophet *Iſai* ſaith, *Thine eare ſhall heare a voice, ſaying, Heere is the way, walke in it, when thou turneſt to the right hand, or to the left*, c.30.v.21. And this voice,(no doubt)is not onely the voice of ſuch as be teachers, but alſo the inward voice of the ſpirit of God in vs. And thus by the concurrence of theſe contrary actions in one and the ſame man,is this combate made.

The third point is,concerning the cauſe of this combate,in theſe words (*and theſe are contrary one to another.*) The contrarietie of the fleſh and the ſpirit makes the combate. And the contrarietie is very great,for the ſpirit is the gift of righteouſnes: and the fleſh ſtands in a double oppoſition to it, for it is firſt of all the want of righteouſnes,and ſecondly,a proneneſſe to all vnrighteouſnes: that is to ſay,not a ſingle,but a double priuation or want of the grace, or gift of God. Hence I gather, that man hath no freedome of will in good duties, before his conuerſion, becauſe hee is then wholly fleſh,and wants the ſpirit of God: and the ſpirit is flat contrary to the ſpirit: and one contrary hath no power at all to bring forth the effect of his contrary. And hence it followes, that there are no ſuch workes whereby a man may prepare himſelfe to his owne iuſtification; for though the mind be inlightned with a general faith, yet man before he be iuſtified,is nothing but fleſh: and fleſh being in nature oppoſite to the ſpirit, can make no preparation for the ſpirit, no more then darkeneſſe can make preparation for the entrance of light.

The fourth point,is,concerning the perſons in whom this combate is to bee found. And they are beleeuers,(not vnbeleeuers or wicked men:) ſuch as the Galatians were, to whom this combat is ſaid to belong. It may be alledged, that naturall men haue a combate in them. For they can ſay, *I ſee and approoue that which is good, but I doe that which is naught. Anſwer.* This combate is betweene the naturall conſcience,and rebellious affection: and it is incident to all men, that haue in them any conſcience,or light of reaſon. But the combate of the fleſh and the ſpirit is of an other kinde, for in it the minde is carried againſt it ſelfe, the will againſt it ſelfe, and the affections againſt themſelues: by reaſon they are partly ſpirituall, and partly carnall. Secondly, not all beleeuers haue this combate in them, but onely ſuch as bee of yeares: for infants,though they haue

haue the ſeed of grace in them, yet doe they want the act or exerciſe thereof: and therefore they feele not this combate, becauſe it ſtands in action. Thirdly, this combate is in the godly for the time of this life onely, becauſe in death the fleſh is aboliſhed, and conſequently the combate it ſelfe.

The fift poynt is, in what things doeth this combate ſhew it ſelfe. *Anſwer.* In all the actions of men regenerate, which *Paul* ſignifies, when he ſaith, *Yee cannot doe the things which ye would.* For example: in prayer, ſometime wee feele feruent deſires, and ſometime againe deadneſſe of ſpirit; ſometimes faith, ſometimes doubting. This combate is in all the actions of the godly, ſpecially in good actions. Thus much *Paul* teacheth, when hee ſaith, *I finde by the Law of God, that when I would doe good, euill is preſent, Rom.*7.21. And, *I doe not the good which I would, but the euill which I would not, that doe I*, verſe 19. And that we miſtake not, it muſt bee remembred, that *Paul* ſpeakes all this of himſelfe, as being regenerate: that hee ſpeakes it not of this or that action, but of the courſe of his life, in which he willed and indeauoured to do that which was good and acceptable to God. And that appeares by the very words, when he ſaith, *To will is preſent with mee.* And, *I would doe good, but I doe it not.* Marke further, while *Paul* willes and indeauours to doe that which is good, if he faile and doe amiſſe, hee may well ſay, *It is not I that doe it, but the fleſh that dwells in mee.* And vngodly men, for the couering of their wickedneſſe, if they ſay (as they doe) that *it is their fleſh that ſinneth, and not they*, they abuſe the holy doctrine and example of *Paul.*

The laſt point, concernes the effect of the combate, which is to hinder the godly, that they cannot doe that which they would, and that three wayes. Firſt, it makes them that they cannot ſinne, that is, liue in practiſe of any one ſinne, 1.*Iohn* 3.9. Secondly, if at any time they fall, it ſtayes and keepes them, that they ſinne not with full conſent of will. For they ſay when they ſinne, *The euill which I hate, that doe I.* Thirdly, though in the ordinarie courſe of their liues they doe that which is good, yet by reaſon of this combate, they faile in the doing of it. *Romanes* 7.18. *To will is preſent with mee, but I finde no meanes to fulfill or accompliſh that which is good.* Euen as a ſicke man that is in recouerie, for his affection, thinkes hee is able to walke a mile or twaine, and yet by reaſon of faintneſſe and weakeneſſe, is ſcarce able to walke once or twiſe about his chamber. So the regenerate man, for affection inclines to the beſt things: and yet by reaſon of the fleſh, failes in the doing of them.

Thus

Thus much of the combate, the vſe followes. Hence I gather, that concupiſcence or luſt after baptiſme, in the regenerate, is a ſinne. For the luſt of the Spirit, is the thing that God requireth and approoueth: now the luſt of the fleſh is directly contrary to it, as a defect or priuation thereof: and therefore the luſt of the fleſh is properly a ſinne, whether conſent of will goe with it, or no.

Againe, hence it followes, that workes of the regenerate, are mixed workes, that is, good workes indeed, yet not perfectly good, but partly euill: for ſuch as the cauſe is, ſuch is the effect: now the minde and will of man, are the cauſe of his workes, and the mind is partly carnall, and partly ſpirituall: ſo alſo is the will: and therefore the workes that proceed from them, are partly ſpirituall, and in part carnall. Vpon this ground it followes, that all the workes of regenerate men, are ſinfull, and in the rigour of iuſtice deſerue damnation. *Obiect.* Sinne is the tranſgreſſion of the law: good works are no tranſgreſſion of the law: therefore good works are no ſinnes. I anſwer to the *minor*. The tranſgreſſion of the law is two fold: One, which is directly againſt the law, both for matter, and manner: the ſecond is, when that is done which the law requires, but not in that maner it ſhould be done. And thus good works become ſinfull. The dutie which the law requires, is done, but it is not done perfectly as it ought to be done, by reaſon of the fleſh. Secondly, it is alledged that good workes are from the ſpirit of God: and that nothing proceeding from the ſpirit of God is ſin. *Anſwer.* Things proceeding from the ſpirit of God alone, or from the ſpirit immediatly, are no ſinnes: now good works proceed not only from the ſpirit, but alſo from the mind and will of man, as inſtruments of the ſpirit. And when an effect proceeds from ſundry cauſes that are ſubordinate, it takes vnto it the nature of the ſecond cauſe: hereupon works are partly ſpirituall, and partly carnall, as the mind and will of the doer is. Thirdly, it is alledged, that good workes pleaſe God: and that things pleaſing God, are no ſinnes. *Anſw.* They pleaſe God; becauſe the doer is in Chriſt, and ſo pleaſeth God. Againe, they pleaſe not God before, or without pardon: for they are accepted, becauſe God approoues his owne work in vs, and pardons the defect therof. Laſtly, ſome obect on this manner. No ſinnes are to be done: good workes are ſinnes: therefore not to be done. *Anſwer.* They are not ſimply ſinnes, but onely by accident. For as God commands them, they are good: and as godly men doe them, they are good in part. Now the reaſon holds onely thus: That which is ſinne, ſo farre forth as it is a ſinne, or if it

be

be ſimply a ſinne,is not to be done. Now then vpon this doctrine it followes,that there is no iuſtification by workes, nor no fulfilling of the law,for the time of this life.

Thirdly,hence it followes,that the grace of God for the time of this life,is mixed with his contrary,the corruption of the fleſh. This mixture the godly feele in themſelues to the great griefe of their hearts. When they would beleeue,their mindes are oppreſſed with vnbeleefe. They ſee more ignorance in themſelues, then light of knowledge. There are a number amongſt vs,that ſay, they know as much as all the world can teach them, that they doe perfectly beleeue in Chriſt, and euer did, that they loue God with all their hearts,and did neuer ſo much as doubt of the mercy of God. But theſe men are void of the grace of God: they are like empty barrels that make a great ſound: they neuer knew what is meant by the combate of the fleſh,and Spirit.

Fourthly,we are here to be admoniſhed, in all duties of religion to vſe induſtry,and paines,by willing,ſtriuing,and indeuouring to the vttermoſt, to doe that which we ought to doe. We muſt vſe *asking,ſeeking,knocking*, *Math.*7.7. We muſt with *Paul* vſe *wraſtling in our prayers to God.Rom.*15.30. They that would haue knowledge in the booke of God,muſt doe more then heare a Sermon: they muſt ſtriue againſt their ignorance, and blindneſſe, and laboriouſly exerciſe their ſenſes in the diſcerning of good and euill. They that would beleeue, muſt ſtriue againſt their naturall vnbeleefe, and indeauour to beleeue. *Bleſſed* (ſaith *Salomon,Prou.*28.) *is the man that feareth himſelfe,* or *inures himſelfe to feare. Paul* ſaith of himſelfe, that *hee laboured and tooke paines to keepe a good conſcience. Act.*24.16.

Laſtly,by reaſon of this combate,we are put in minde to vſe ſobriety,and watchfulnes ouer our owne corruptions,with much and inſtant prayer, leſt we fall into temptation. *Math.*26.41. We ſhould practiſe theſe more then we doe: for beſide the enemies without, we haue an enemie within,that ſeekes our perdition.

18 *And if ye be led by the Spirit,ye are not vnder the law.*

In the 13.verſe *Paul* propounds a maine rule of good life, *Giue no occaſion to the fleſh*: and for the better keeping of this,he giues a ſecond rule,v.16. *Walke in the ſpirit.* Of this ſecond rule he giues two reaſons. The firſt is taken from the contrariety of the fleſh and the ſpirit,v.17. The ſecond is in theſe words: *they that walke according to the ſpirit,are freed from the curſe of the law.*

In

In theſe words, *Paul* ſets downe three things. The firſt is, the office of the ſpirit, which is, firſt of all, to regenerate and renew all the powers of the ſoule; and ſecondly, to guide and conduct them that are regenerate, *Pſal.* 143.10. In this guidance or conduction, there are foure actions of the ſpirit. The firſt is, *Preſeruation*, whereby the holy Ghoſt maintains the gift of regeneration in them that are regenerate. The ſecond is, *Cooperation*, whereby the will of God as the firſt cauſe, workes together with the regenerate will of man, as the ſecond cauſe. And without this cooperation, mans will brings forth no good action: no more then the tree which is apt to bring foorth fruite, yeeldes fruite indeed, till it haue the preſence and cooperation of the Sunne, and that in the ſeaſon of the yeare. The third is, *Direction*, whereby the ſpirit of God ordereth and eſtabliſheth the minde, will, and affections in good duties, 2. *Theſſ.* 3.5. The laſt is, *Excitation*, whereby the ſpirit ſtirres, and ſtil moues the will and minde, after they are regenerate: becauſe for the time of this life, the grace of God is hindred and oppreſſed by the fleſh. Hereupon after regeneration, there muſt ſtill bee new *inclining*, *Pſalm.* 119 36. new *drawing*, *Cant.* 1.3. new *working* of the will and the deed, *Phil.* 2.13.

Hence it follows, that beſide the antecedent, and firſt grace, there is neceſſary a ſubſequent, or ſecond grace. For we do not that good which we can doe, vnleſſe God by a ſecond grace make vs doe it, as he made vs able to doe it by the firſt grace.

The ſecond thing is, the Office of all true beleeuers: and that is, to reſigne themſelues in ſubiection to the worke of Gods ſpirit. Now Gods ſpirit workes in and by by the word of God. And heereupon this ſubiection hath two parts. The firſt is, to make triall, inquirie, and examination, what is the good will of God in euery thing, *Romanes* 12.2. Thus did *Dauid*, *Pſalm.* 119.94. *I am thine, ſaue me, for I ſeeke thy commandements.* The ſecond part is, to denie our ſelues, and to conforme our mindes, conſciences, willes, affections in all things to the aforeſaid will of God, *Rom.* 12.2. Let all ſuch as deſire to be ſpirituall, remember and make conſcience to practiſe this.

The third is, the priuiledge of beleeuers, in the laſt words, *Ye are not vnder the law.* Vnderſtand this, in reſpect of the curſe and condemnation of the law: for otherwiſe wee are all vnder the law, as it is the rule of good life. The priuiledge then is, that God doth not impute the defects of obedience to ſuch as truly beleeue and repent, but hee accepts their imperfect obedience, as perfect and abſolute. This ſerues to comfort them that grieue, becauſe they feele the want of sanctification in themselues. For if they can and doe will that which is good, & indeauour themselues in the course of their liues according to their will, let them not feare ouermuch, when their obedience is defectiue: because they are not vnder the rigour of the law: and therefore God accepts the will and indeauour to obey, for obedience. And the consideration of Gods mercifull acceptation, must stir vs vp to an earnest care and conscience of good duties.

19 *Moreouer, the workes of the flesh are manifest, which are*
adultery, fornication, vncleannesse, wantonnesse,
20 *Idolatrie, witchcraft, hatred, debate, emulations, wrath,*
contentions, seditions, heresies,
21 *Enuie, murthers, drunkennesse, gluttony, and such like:*
whereof I tell you before (as I also haue told you before) that they
which doe such things, shall not inherite the kingdome of God.

Paul before deliuered his rule in generall tearmes, *Giue no occasion to the flesh:* and, *fulfill not the lusts of the flesh.* Now he proceeds further in way of declaration, to make a Catalogue or rehearsall of the particular workes of the flesh, which were in vse, and knowne to the Galatians. And this hee doeth for weightie cause. For we are full of blindnesse, and see not our corruption: and wee are full of hypocrisie, and therefore ready to esteeme our selues spirituall, when we are carnall. And therefore this Catalogue serues fitly as a table, or glasse, to discouer the corruption of mans heart, by the fruits thereof.

After *Pauls* example, euery man shall doe well to make a catalogue of the sinnes of his whole life. By this meanes shall we better know our selues, and take a manifest view of our sinnefull condition.

In this Catalogue, I consider three things: the condition of the works of the flesh: the kinds of them: and the punishment thereof. The condition is, that the workes of the flesh are said to bee *manifest*, not onely to God, but euen to men that haue the light of reason, and natural conscience. Hence it followes, that there is matter sufficient for the condemnation of them that neuer knew the Gospell. For though the flesh it selfe be secret and hidden, yet the works of the flesh are manifest to the naturall man. And this must further admonish vs, neuer to hide or excuse our sinnes, but freely to confesse them before God, and before men also, when need requires.

quires. Whether we confeſſe them or no, they are manifeſt : and the ingenuous confeſſing or vncouering of them,is the way to couer them.*Pſal.*32.1.4.

Touching the kinds or ſorts of the workes of the fleſh,they are in number ſeuenteene: and I may reduce them to foure heads. The firſt ſort,are againſt chaſtity;the ſecond, againſt religion; the third,againſt charitie;the laſt,againſt temperance.

The workes of the fleſh againſt chaſtitie,are foure; and they are placed in the firſt ranke,for iuſt cauſe:for by them,men are brought to reprobate mindes.*Rom.*1.28. and to be without ſenſe or feeling. *Eph.*4.19.and the body which ſhould be the Temple of the Holy Ghoſt,is made a ſtable and a ſtie for the diuell.

Adulterie] *it is the incontinency of perſons married, or of perſons whereof one at the leaſt is married,or betrothed.* I ſay betrothed: becauſe one and the ſame puniſhment is deſigned to married, and betrothed perſons: and therefore the ſinne is alike in both.

If adultery,which is the breach of wedlocke, be a worke of the fleſh,then damnable is the decretall of Pope *Syricius*,that marriage it ſelfe was the pollution of the fleſh. It may be obiected,that yong widdowes by marrying *haue damnation, and breake the faith of baptiſme.*1. *Timoth.*5.12. *Anſwer.* They are not ſaid to breake the faith of baptiſme,becauſe they marry: but becauſe they waxe wanton againſt Chriſt,and ſo marry: that is, caſt off the reines of obedience, by committing fornication, and then to couer their offence, they marry. This I take to be the right ſenſe of that place.

Adultery is named in the firſt place, and that for ſpeciall cauſe. For as it is a common,ſo it is alſo a great ſinne.For it is the breach of the couenant of marriage,made in the preſence of God, and vnto God: and therefore it is called *the couenant of God. Pro.*2.17.It is the puniſhment of Idolatry.*Rom.*1. 24. It is a ſinne greater then theft. *Prou.*6.30.32.The committers of this ſinne cut off themſelues from humane ſociety, and become men of death, and women of death, according to Gods law.And it will neuer be well with humane ſociety,till adulterers be made fellons, their liues taken from them, and their goods confiſcate.Laſtly,this ſinne brings the ruine of the families of adulterous perſons: and it ſets a fire in them that burnes to deſtruction.

Fornication] *it is the incontinencie of ſingle perſons.* Marke how it is made a manifeſt worke of the fleſh. Hence it followes, that *fornication* is no light matter, or a thing indifferent, as ſome haue taught.It may be obiected,that it is numbred among things indifferent,

indifferent, *Act.*15.29. for with ſtrangled, and blood, is ioyned *fornication. Anſ.* The Gentils indeed eſteemed it as a thing indifferent: and hereupon it may be, it is ioyned with things indifferent. But the iudgment of the Church was otherwiſe: & this opinion of the Gentiles is confuted by *Paul*, 1.*Cor.*6. Againe, it may be obiected, that the Lord commaunded the Prophet *Oſe* to take vnto him an harlot, *Oſe* 1.2. *Anſwer.* It was done in type or figure: and then the words of the Lord cary this ſenſe, *Take vnto thee a wife of fornications*, that is, propheſie and publiſh, that thou art like one that takes a wife of fornication. Againe, if the thing were done indeed, yet did not the Prophet take an harlot, to liue in fornication with her, but at Gods commandement, to liue with her according to Gods ordinance, namely, in marriage.

Againe, hence I gather, that there is no warrant for the toleration of fornication. For it is a foule & manifeſt work of the fleſh. Magiſtrates may *not do euill, that good may come thereof*, *Rom.*3.8. Whoſoeuer doeth euill, muſt feare: becauſe the Magiſtrate beares the ſword to puniſh, *Rom.*13.4. And the commandement of God was, that *there muſt be no whore in Iſrael*, *Deut.*23. Therefore the permiſſion of the ſtewes in Rome is without warrant: & the rather, becauſe there the prohibition of marriage (in ſundry orders of men) beares ſway.

Vncleanneſſe] The incontinencie againſt nature, as inceſt, the ſinne of Sodom, and ſuch like. Marke, where theſe ſinnes were knowne, there they are named particularly by *Paul*, as among the Romanes, *Rom.*1.27,28. and to the Corinthians, 1.*Cor.*6.9,10. but where they were not knowne, as in Galatia, there they are onely mentioned generally, leſt by the naming of them, he ſhould after a ſort teach them.

Wantonneſſe] That is, the open profeſſion and oſtentation of incontinency, by vnchaſt words, wanton geſtures, and wanton apparell. Hence it appeares, that wee are to deteſt all ſignes of incontinencie: and that we are to be chaſt not only in deed, but alſo in our words, geſtures, and behauiours.

The puniſhment of theſe ſinnes is in v.21. in theſe words, *They which doe theſe things, ſhall not inherit the kingdome of God.* And it muſt be remembred, that this threat or curſe muſt bee applied to euery one of theſe ſinnes particularly.

The vſe. There are a number of men that liue ſecretly in theſe ſinnes, adultery, fornication, &c. And becauſe they profeſſe Chriſtian religion, and ſometime come to the Church, and to the Lords Table, they thinke all is well, and they ſuppoſe there is no danger. Thus *make they a couenant with hell and death*, *Iſai.*28. But they deceiue themſelues; for God is vnchangeable, and all his threats ſhall be accompliſhed. And no adulterer, no fornicatour, no vncleane perſon ſhall enter into the kingdome of God, whatſoeuer men ſuppoſe, or dreame.

Secondly, by the conſideration of this threat, we are admoniſhed to flye adultery, fornication, wantonneſſe, &c. They ſay, theſe are but tricks of youth. Belike then it is but a tricke, to loſe the kingdome of heauen. *Salomon* ſaith, *Bleſſed is the man that feareth, or cauſeth himſelfe to feare. Prou.* 28. 14. Now that ſhall be done, when we terrifie our ſelues from theſe offences by ſetting Gods iudgements before vs.

Laſtly ſome man may ſay, what ſhall they doe that are ouertaken with theſe ſinnes, if the doers thereof cannot enter into the kingdome of God? *Anſwer*. Their caſe is dangerous: and there is but one way to helpe them in the world: and that is, to ceaſe from adultery, fornication, vncleannes, wantonnes, and to doe the contrary. *Pſal.* 34. 14. And this will doe the deede: for the promiſe of God is, *he that confeſſeth his ſinnes, and forſaketh them, ſhall haue mercie. Prou.* 28. 14. And this promiſe of God is not contrary to his threat. For ſo long as men are doers of theſe ſinnes, or of any one of them, they are out of Gods kingdome: and when they ceaſe to be doers of them, and contrariwiſe exerciſe themſelues in the workes of chaſtity, poſſeſſing their veſſels, that is, their bodies, in ſanctification and honour, the caſe is altered, and they muſt no more be reputed doers of theſe ſinnes. For God accepts men not as they haue bin, but as they are.

In that theſe foure ſinnes, *adultery, fornication*, &c. are *manifeſt workes of the fleſh*, we are taught three things. The firſt is, that wee muſt ſtocke vp the roote of theſe things, that is, mortifie the paſſion of concupiſcence, *Col.* 3. 5. 1. *Theſſ.* 4. 5. which is nothing elſe but an inordinate inclination to theſe vices. And it is mortified in vs, if wee learne to feare God in his word, and in the commandement that forbids adulterie. For the feare of God clenſeth both heart and life. *Ioſeph* tempted by his miſtris to folly, by this meanes eſchewed the offence, ſaying, *ſhall I doe this, and ſinne againſt God?* Further, it muſt be remembred, that without holineſſe, no man can ſee God, or haue fellowſhip with him. *Heb.* 12. 14 And while the luſt of concupiſcence beares the ſway, there is no holineſſe: and therefore no fellowſhip with God.

The ſecond rule is, that all occaſions of theſe ſinnes muſt bee cut off, two ſpecially, *Idleneſſe*, and the *pampering of the bodie*. For Idleneſſe, conſider *Dauid*, who when he was out of ciuill warres,

and

and free from banishment, at peace in his owne house, his wandring affection carried him to commit adulterie. And the Israelites, when they were stored and pampered with all the blessings of God, gaue themselues to the committing of these offences, *Ierem.* 5.7. 1.*Cor.* 10.7. and the people of Sodom and Gomorrha, *Ezech.* 16.49.

The third rule is, that all signes of these vices must bee auoided and detested, that is, any speach or action, that may signifie or giue suspition of an incontinent disposition, as light talke, wanton behauiour, curiousnes and excesse in trimming of the body, suspected company, or company that may in likelihood be suspected. For it is Gods will, that not only the vice it selfe, but also the appearance of euery vice should be auoided, 1.*Thess.* 5.22.

Idolatry] The second sort of sins follow, which are against godlinesse: and they are three, *Idolatry, witchcraft, heresie. Idolatry* is the worship of Idol-gods. An Idol is taken two wayes. First of all, a fiction, or a thing meerely deuised, is an Idol: againe, when we conceiue a thing that is otherwise then it is, it is an Idol. So likewise Idolatry is twofold. One is, when something that is not God, is set vp in the roome of God: and that is done three waies. One is, when the Godhead is ascribed to a creature, as when it was said to *Herod, The voyce of a God, and not of a man.* The second is, when any pro- Acts 12.22.
pertie of the Godhead is ascribed to the creature. The third is, when the affections of our hearts are giuen to the creature. Thus couetousnesse is called idolatry, *Col.* 3.5. because it makes men put their affiance in riches.

The second kinde of *Idolatry*, is to worship the true God with deuised worship, as namely with, in, and at images, set vp to the honour of God. This *Idolatry* is forbidden in the second commandement, as *Moses* hath expounded the law, *Deut.* 4.16. *Thou sawest no image in the day that I appeared in mount Sinai: therefore thou shalt make no image, namely of God.* It is alledged, that the commandement only forbids the making of the images of false gods. I answer, and of the true God also. *Aarons* calfe was an image of the true God, *Exod.* 32.5. And it must be obserued, that *Iehu* destroied the idols of *Baal*, 2.*Kings* 10.26. and withall remained still in the sinne of *Ieroboam*, verse 31. which was to worship the calues in Dan and Bethel, which were images of *Iehouah.* And for this he is discommended.

The vse. By this wee see that the Romish religion is a carnall religion: for it teacheth Idolatie foure wayes. First, it inioyneth men to giue to the *Consecrated Hoste*, the name and honour of God.

God. And thus they set vp vnto themselues a breaden God made with mans hand. An Idol, as abominable as euer was among the Gentiles. Secondly, it teacheth men to inuocate Angels, & Saints departed: and thereby it giues vnto them the searching of the heart, the hearing and helping of all men, at all times, and places according to their seuerall necessities: and these things are the properties of the Godhead: and therefore, whether they call this inuocation, *Latria*, or *Doulia*, it matters not: it is flat idolatry, because the honour of God is giuen to the creature. Thirdly, it teacheth that we may put confidence in workes, so it be done in sobriety. Lastly, it adoreth God, in, at, and before Images: and so it binds the presence, grace, and operation of God to them, without his word. Papists alleadge for themselues, that they intend to worship none in images but the true God. I answer, it is nothing that they say. Not mans intention, but Gods will makes Gods worship. Let thē shew Gods will, if they can. If they cannot, then they must know that it is but an Idol-god, which they worship. For there is no such God in nature that will be worshipped in Images, but an Idol of their owne braines. They alleadge againe, that God may as well be worshipped in Images, as a Prince in the chaire of Estate. I answer, the reason is not like. The worship of Images is religious, the reuerence to the chaire of Estate, is meerely ciuill, and in ciuill respect, and according to the Princes will, and so is not the bowing to Images according to Gods will. Let them prooue it if they can. That God was worshipped before the Arke, we approue of it. For it was his word and will. Let vs heare the like word for Images of God and Christ, and then we are ready to reuoke the charge of Idolatry.

Again, by this we see that many of vs are very carnal. For though we detest *outward Idolatry*, yet the *inward idolatrie* of the heart abounds among vs. For looke where the heart is, there is the God. Now the hearts of men are vpon the world, and vpon the riches, and pleasures thereof. For them we take the most care, and in them we place our chiefe delight, whereas God in Christ should haue all the affections of our hearts.

Witchcraft] The word φαρμακεία, properly signifies, *poisoning*: but here it is fitly translated, *witchcraft*: because al poisoning is comprehended vnder murther which followeth. And the Magitians of Egypt, *Exod.7.* are called φαρμακοῖς, in the translation of the Seuentie: as also the wise men. *Dan.2.* Now if they had bin but poisoners, they had not bin fit for *Pharaos* & *Nabuchadnezars* turne, neither would they haue desired their presence, and helpe.

Witchcraft, ſignifies all curious arts, wrought by the operation of the diuell. For the better conceiuing of it, I will conſider two things. *The ground* thereof, and *the kinds* of witchcraft.

The ground, is a league or compact with the diuell. It is twofold, an *Expreſſe* or *open league*, and *a ſecret league*. *The open league* is, when men inuocate the diuell in expreſſe words, or otherwiſe make any manifeſt couenant with him. *The ſecret league* is, when men vſe meanes, which they know haue no force, but by the operation of the diuell. And the very vſing of ſuch meanes in earneſt, is an implicit couenanting with the diuell. If by true faith, we make a couenant with God; then a falſe faith, in the vſe of Satanicall ceremonies makes a couenant with the deuill. And without this, there is no practiſe of witchcraft.

There are three kindes of witchcraft. The firſt is, *Superstitious diuination*, which ſerues to tell men their fortunes, or to reueale ſecrets by the flying of foules, by the intrals of beaſts, by the obſeruation of ſtarres, by conſulting with familiar ſpirits, and ſuch like, *Deuteron.* 18. 11. The ſecond, is *Iuggling*, which is to worke wonders, or feates beyond the order of nature, as did the Magicians of Egypt. The third is, *Charming*, or *inchanting*, which is by the pronouncing of words, to procure ſpeedie hurt, or ſpeedie helpe.

The vſe. By this wee ſee that wee are a carnall people. For in the time of diſtreſſe vpon extremitie, figure-caſting, and charming, are ouermuch vſed. And yet both of them are full of ſuperſtition, and folly. For the reuealing of things to come is Gods: and the ſtarres are vniuerſall cauſes, working vpon all things alike: and therefore it is not poſſible by them to foretell euents that are contingent, or caſuall. And words haue no force in them but to ſignifie. And therefore when they are aplied to cure diſeaſes, they are abuſed to a wrong end, and their operation is from the deuill. And for this cauſe they are to be auoyded of Chriſtian people. It may bee ſaid, how may wee diſcerne of charmes, that wee may the better auoyd them? *Anſwer.* Keepe this rule in memory alwaies. Such obſeruations, of whoſe force and efficacie, there is no reaſon or cauſe either in the thing done, or in the inſtitution of God, haue their operation, and efficacie, from ſome compact and ſocietie with the diuel. As for example, ſcratching of the ſuſpected witch, is ſaid to bee a meanes to cure witchcraft: but indeede it is a charme, and a practiſe of witchcraft. For it hath no ſuch force from the inſtitution of God, becauſe it is againſt the ſixt commandement: and no naturall reaſon can bee rendred, why drawing of blood, ſhould cure witchcraft. The action therefore is a ſacrifice to the diuell: and in way of recompence, the cure is done by him.

It may be ſaid, what ſhould we doe in diſtreſſe, if ſuch helps may not be vſed? *Anſ.* We are to vſe approoued and ordinary meanes: and for the reſt, namely the euent, to leaue it vnto God, liuing by faith, and caſting our care on God, and quieting our hearts in his will, whatſoeuer comes to paſſe. It is a want of faith thus *to make haſt* for the deliuerie before the appointed time. And whereas it is thought that ſome perſons haue a gift of God, by words preſently to cure any diſeaſe, whereupon they are called *wiſe*, or *cunning men* & *women*, it is falſe: it is no gift of God, but rather a curſe, that leaues them to be deluded dy the diuell, who is the worker of theſe cures, when Satanical and ſuperſtitious meanes, and that in a falſe faith, are vſed.

For the better conceiuing of the ſinne, it may be demanded what is a witch? *Anſw. One that wittingly, and willingly, vſeth the aſſiſtance of the diuell himſelfe for the reuealing of ſecrets, for the working of ſome miſchiefe, or for the effecting of ſome ſtrange cure.* I ſay *wittingly*, to put a difference betweene witches, and ſome ſuperſtitious perſons, who vſe charming, and by it doe many cures, perſwading themſelues, that the wordes which they vſe, haue force in them, or that God hath giuen them a gift, to doe ſtrange things. Such people in a naturall honeſtie, deteſt all knowne ſocietie with the diuell; in that reſpect they are not the witches which the Scripture adiudgeth to death, yet are they at the next dore to them: and therefore they are to bee admoniſhed by Magiſtrates and Miniſters to relinquiſh their ſuperſtitious practiſes, and that vpon a double ground. I. Nothing hath efficacie but by the Ordinance of God. And this efficacie was either put into the thing in the creation, or ſince by ſome new Inſtitution in the word. And the efficacie of things that comes by any other meanes, is by Satanicall operation. II. Charmes, inchantments, and ſpells whatſoeuer, haue no force vnleſſe wee beleeue that they can doe vs good. Now this faith is falſe faith, and the ſeruice of the diuell. For wee muſt beleeue nothing, hope nothing, doe nothing, without, or againſt the word of God. If theſe two rules bee obſerued, not onely charming, but all witchcraft ſhall be baniſhed out of the world.

Againe, it may be demanded, what are the ſignes that ſerue to diſcouer a witch? *Anſwer.* This diſcouerie is verie hard. For witches doe their feates in cloſe manner, not onely by foule and open

curſing,

curſing, but alſo by faire ſpeaking, and by praiſing of things. And hereupon wee haue a faſhion in England, when wee praiſe any thing, withall to bleſſe it, (as to ſay, *it is a goodly childe, God ſaue it*) that our ſpeach may not be ſuſpected of witchcraft. Neuertheleſſe, there are fiue ſpeciall things that ſerue to diſcouer a witch. One is, the free confeſſion of the accuſed, or ſuſpected witch. The ſecond is, the confeſſion of the aſſociats with the witch. The third is, Inuocation of the diuell. For that is to renounce baptiſme, and to make a league with the diuell. The fourth is, Euidence, that the partie hath entertained a familiar ſpirit, in the forme or likeneſſe of ſome viſible creature. The fift is, Euidence of any action or actions, that neceſſarily preſuppoſe a league made with the diuell. As for example: if the partie ſhew a mans face in a glaſſe: though he profeſſe angelical holineſſe, he is in league with the diuel, by whoſe meanes the feate is wrought.

There are beſides theſe, other ſignes, but they are either falſe, or vncertaine. A man is ſicke, hee ſuſpects that he is bewitched: hee takes it on his death, that ſuch a partie hath bewitched him. All this is nothing, but the ſuſpition of one man, and therefore no proofe. Likewiſe the teſtimonie of ſome wizzard, is but the teſtimonie of one, and it is the diuells teſtimonie, and therefore not to be receiued. Againe, neighbours fall out, threatnings are vſed in anger: afterward the partie threatned, is either ſicke, or hee dies: heereupon the partie that vſed threatning words, is accuſed of witchcraft. And this is the common courſe. But great circumſpection muſt bee vſed, for ſickeneſſe and death may ariſe of any other cauſes. Laſtly, markes in the bodies of men and women, are vncertaine ſignes of witches. All this I note the rather: becauſe if a iudgement befall a man in his family, preſently (according to the common faſhion) hee ſaith he is hurt by euill tongues, and challengeth ſome one or other of witchcraft: wheras his owne ignorance, vnbeliefe, contempt of Gods word and Sacraments, &c. are the onely witches that hurt him, and pull downe Gods iudgements vpon him.

Hereſies] The word hereſie, generally ſignifies any opinion, either good or bad. More eſpecially it ſignifies any errour in religion. Thus Eccleſiaſticall writers take it. For they condemne for heretikes ſuch as erred in ſmaller points, holding the foundation, as *Vigilantius, Nouatus, &c.* And the very opinion that there are *Antipodes*, was condemned for hereſie, though it bee a matter of ſmall moment. Yet moſt properly, Hereſie may be thus defined: *It is an errour in the foundation of Chriſtian religion, taught and defended with obſtinacy.* Thus *Paul* ſaith, *Tit.* 3.11. that *an hereticke is peruerted,* that is, put beſide the foundation: and *condemned of himſelfe* in his ſinne, that is to ſay, he erres obſtinatly euen againſt his owne conſcience.

I ſay that hereſie is *an errour in religion,* to put a difference betweene an errour in Diuinity, and an errour in Philoſophy, which is not tearmed hereſie: and againe, to put a difference betweene ſchiſme, and hereſie: for hereſie is in doctrine, ſchiſme in manners, order, regiment. Againe, I ſay hereſie is an errour, *in the foundation of religion,* to diſtinguiſh it from errours that are in ſmaller points of Diuinity. Some teach that *Abraham* was borne the 70. of *Terah,* ſome the 130. of *Terah.* Both cannot be true: yet neither of them are hereſie. Some teach that *Daniels* weekes begin ſtraight after the returne out of captiuity: others teach that they muſt begin 80. yeares after: both cannot be true: yet neither opinion is hereſie. So there are ſundry opinions touching *Ophir, Tarſhiſh,* (to which Ionah fled) and *Decapolis* in the Goſpel: and all cannot be true: yet they are not hereſies, becauſe they concerne onely times, and places, and other circumſtances of the Bible. Laſtly, I ſay that hereſie is *maintained with obſtinacy,* to diſtinguiſh hereſie, and a ſingle errour. For there are three things in hereſie, *an errour* in the maine doctrine, *conuiction* of the party touching his errour, and *obſtinacy* after conuiction.

The vſe. In that hereſie, an errour in the minde or vnderſtanding, is made a worke of the fleſh: hence it followes, that the word *fleſh,* ſignifies more then *ſenſuality*: namely, the corruption of the higher powers, euen of the minde and conſcience: though Papiſts teach otherwiſe.

Againe, if hereſie be a worke of the fleſh, our duty is, to deteſt and eſchew hereſies. And that we may for euer preſerue our ſelues from them, three rules muſt be obſerued.

I. We muſt propound vnto our ſelues the right Principles of religion. For as euery Art hath his confeſſed principles, ſo hath Diuinity. The head and chiefe Principle whereof, is this. *All Scripture of the Prophets, and Apoſtles, is giuen by inſpiration of God.* This is the foundation of all true faith: here is the higheſt ſtay and ſtop. This principle is the demonſtration of all doctrines, and concluſions: and it hath no principle aboue it ſelfe, whereby it is to be confirmed. As for humane reaſon, it is no principle of religion. For it is imperfect and erronious, and ſerues onely to make men without excuſe. Indeede in the minde of man, there are certaine naturall concluſions, that there is a God, and that he is to be worshipped, &c. but the certentie of these is in the written word. We can by reason dispute of the creation of the world, but a full certentie we haue not by reason, but by faith in the world. *Hebrewes*. 11.3. Againe, the Papists makes the authoritie of the Church, a principle. For that is the first ground which they lay downe, that we must captiuate our senses, to the authoritie of the Church. But this is no principle in religion. For we cannot imagine a Church without faith: and faith cannot be without the word of God. It may be saide, that Scripture is the sense of the written word: and this sense must be from the Church. *Ans*. Scripture it selfe is both *the glosse*, and *the text*. Scripture is the best interpreter of it selfe. And the sense which is agreeable to the words of the text, to the scope of the place, to other circumstances, and to the analogy of faith: in the plainer places of Scripture, is the proper and infallible sense of Scripture. Thus fetching the sense of Scripture from it selfe, we shall keepe our selues within the limits of Scripture, and in the matter of our saluation haue certentie of faith, which we shall neuer haue, if we listen to reason, tradition, and the authority of men.

II. Reade the Scriptures, and be a doer of them in the exercises of inuocation, faith, repentance; then shalt thou neuer be a heretike. It is Gods promise. *Ioh*. 7.17. *If ye will obey, ye shall know whether my doctrine be of God or no*. *Psal*. 25.14. *The secret of the Lord is reuealed to them that feare him*. Marke them, that make Apostasie, and become Papists: they are such as neuer had a minde to loue and obay the religion, in which they haue beene baptized, and brought vp.

III. *Col*. 2.8. *Let no man spoile you through Philosophie*. *Paul* doth not condemne the Philosophie of the Gentiles, but he puts a caueat, that it be vsed with circumspection, as Merchants vse the sea, to wit, in eschewing rockes, and sands, and Pirates. So students may vse the Philosophy of the Gentiles, but they must take heede, lest their mindes be corrupted with the errors thereof, which are to be considered. Naturall Philosophy giues too much to nature, or to second causes; and too little to God. It puts downe principles flat against the word, as the eternity of the world, and the mortality of the soule. Morall Philosophy, placeth happines in ciuill vertue, out of Christ: it teacheth, that vertue is a meane or mediocrity of affection, whereas in true vertue there is not onely a restraint or moderation of affections, but also the renouation of them by regeneration. It teacheth that Vrbanity in iesting and frumping, is a vertue: *Paul* saith no, *Eph*. 5.4. It teacheth that Magnani-

Magnanimitie, whereby a man thinkes himselfe worthy of great honour, is a vertue: but it is contrary to Christian humilitie, *Psalm.* 131.1,2. Lastly, it teacheth that man hath a freedome of will in good actions: which doctrine applied by the Schoolemen to matters of religion, is false and erronious.

The third head of sinnes, are such as are against *Charity*, and they are in number eight.

The first is, *Enmitie*: of it I consider three things. The first is, whether it be a sinne, or no? for somewhat may be obiected to the contrary.

Obiect. I. Psal. 139.21. *Doe I not hate them that hate thee? Answer. Dauid* here speakes of the hatred, wherby he hated Gods enemies, not in respect of their persons, but in respect of their sinnes, whereby they were enemies of God. And this hatred is commendable, and not here to be vnderstood.

Obiect. II. Luke 14.26. *Hee that will bee a disciple of Christ, must hate father, and mother, and his owne soule. Answer.* This hatred is not simply commanded, but onely in a certaine respect, namely, as father, and mother, and a mans owne soule, are in comparison opposed to God, and Christ, in regard of whom they are vtterly to be despised.

Obiect. III. Romanes 9. *God chose Iacob, and hated Esau*: and wee must be like vnto God. *Answer.* We are to be like vnto God in holinesse, and the duties thereof, and not in the soueraigntie and Lordship ouer the creatures, whereby he either loues or hates them.

Obiect. IV. It is the vniuersall nature of all creatures to flie their contrary: therefore men may hate their enemies. *Answer.* Man, and man are not contrary in nature, or naturall properties: but are all one flesh: the contrarietie that is, is by reason of the corruption of nature.

The second point is, what is this *Enmitie? Ans.* It is a peruerse disposition of minde, whereby men remember iniuries, discourtesies, and vnkindnesses, and carry about them a purpose, and desire to requite like for like, when time and place shall serue. Thus did *Esau* hate *Iacob, Genes.* 27.41. and *Absolom* his brother *Amnon*, 2. *Samuel* 13.

The third point, where is this *Enmitie? Answer.* Euery where among vs. For wee daily see person diuided against person, family against family, and corporation against corporation. This shewes that wee are carnall: and that Gods kingdome takes no place among vs as it should. For in it the lambe and the wolfe quietly dwell together, *Iſa.*11. The remedy of this enmity is, That all be of one minde, deſire, and affection, in the receiuing and furthering of the Goſpel of Chriſt, 1.*Cor.*1.11. If in the maine point there be a concord, in leſſer matters the agreement will be eaſie.

Debate] It is a contention in words, whereby men ſtriue, who ſhall ſhew moſt courage, who ſhall get the victorie, and who ſhall carry away the laſt word, no reſpect had of equitie, or trueth. In this reſpect, *crying*, or *lifting vp the voyce* in reaſoning, is condemned, *Epheſ.*4.31.

Emulations] There is *a good emulation*, and that is when men ſtriue to bee like to them that excell in vertue, or to goe beyond them. And it is commaunded by the holy Ghoſt, 1 *Corinth.*14.12. Beſide this, there is a *carnall emulation*, whereby men that excell in any thing, grieue that any ſhould be equall to them, or goe beyond them.

The vſe. If to grieue at another mans Excellencie, bee a worke of the fleſh, then it is our duetie to reioyce in the excellencie of others. Thus did *Moſes, when Eldad and Medad propheſied, Numbers* 11.29. And *Iohn* the *Baptiſt, when Chriſt increaſed, and hee decreaſed, Iohn* 3.29, 30. And *Paul* gaue thankes as well for the graces beſtowed on the Churches, as for gifts beſtowed on himſelfe.

Anger] Of it I conſider three points. The firſt is, whether there be any lawfull anger? *Anſw.* Yea. Chriſt (in whom was no ſinne) was angry, *Marke* 3.5. When there is a iuſt cauſe of anger, then is anger iuſt. When there is a manifeſt offence of God, there is a iuſt cauſe of anger: therefore anger is then iuſt.

The ſecond is, when is anger a ſinne? *Anſwer.* When men are haſtie to bee angry, *Eccleſ.*7.11. and are offended at euery thing that goes againſt their minds. Or againe, hauing a iuſt cauſe to be angry, yet they keepe no meaſure in their anger.

The third poynt, is the remedie. And that is here ſet downe. Haſtineſſe is a worke of the fleſh, or of corrupt nature, and it barres men from the kingdome of heauen: and therefore it is to be auoyded.

Contention] There are ſundry kindes of lawfull contention: as contention with the enemie in iuſt warre: contention at the barre with an aduerſary in a iuſt cauſe: contention in diſputation with an heretike: contention in Schoole-diſputation for exerciſe, and triall ſake.

Contention is carnall, and ſinnefull, in reſpect of matter, and manner. In matter, when men contend for things for which they ſhould

ſhould not contend,as the diſciples for primacie,*Luke* 22. or when contention is without forgiuing,forbearing or ſuffering; and that in trifling matters,1.*Cor*.6.7. Contention likewiſe is faultie, in reſpect of maner, when men wilfully defend their owne priuate cauſes,no regard had, whether they bee right or wrong, true or falſe: and by this meanes they often oppugne truth, or iuſtice, or both. Of this kinde are the warres of the rebell in Ireland: the warres of the Spanyard in the low Countries: and the ſuits of many quarrelſome and contentious perſons among vs.

The vſe. *Doe nothing by contention, Philip*.2.2. And therefore wee muſt forgiue,put vp,as much as may bee, and yeeld of our right.

διχοστασίαι. *Seditions*] The originall word ſignifies ſuch diſſentions in which men ſeparate one from another: and that is done two waies, either by ſchiſme in the Church,or by faction in the Commonwealth.

Queſtion. Why are not we Schiſmatikes in England, Scotland, Germanie: conſidering wee haue diſſented and ſeparated our ſelues,from the Church of Rome? *Anſwer*. We indeed haue ſeparated our ſelues,but they of the Church of Rome are ſchiſmatikes: becauſe the cauſe of our ſeparation is in them: namely, their Idolatry,and their manifold hereſies. The caſe is the like: A man threatens death to his wife: hereupon ſhe ſeparates. Yet not ſhe, but he makes the ſeparation: becauſe the cauſe of ſeparation, and the fault is in him.

For the auoiding of ſchiſme, and ſedition, remember two rules. I. So long as a Church, or people doe not ſeparate from Chriſt, wee may not ſeparate from them. II. *Prou*.24.21. *Feare the King, and meddle not with them that vary*, that is, make alterations againſt the lawes of God,and the King. Indeed,ſubiects may ſignifie what is good for the State, and what is amiſſe: but to make any alteration in the eſtate, either Ciuill,or Eccleſiaſticall, belongs to the ſupreme Magiſtrate.

Enuy] It is a compound of carnall griefe and hatred. For it makes men grieue and repine at the good things of others, and to hate the good things themſelues. Thus the high Prieſts of enuy hated Chriſt, and all his moſt excellent ſayings, and doings, *Matthew* 27. 18. At this day, they which haue any good things in them, are commonly condemned for hypocrites, and their Religion for hypocriſie. All this is but the cenſure of Enuie.

The vſe. That we may depart from Enuy, wee muſt loue them

that

that feare God: and loue the gifts and graces of God wheresoeuer they be: euen in our enemies.

Murthers] *Obiect. I.* A plant liues, a beast liues, and man liues: the cropping of a plant, and the killing of a beast, is no sinne: why is it then a sinne to kill a man? *Ans.* God hath giuen liberty for the two first, and hath restrained vs in the latter. Againe, the life of a plant is but the vigour in the iuice, and the life of a beast is but the vigour in the blood, *Gen.*9.4. but the life of man is a spirit and spirituall substance. Thirdly, man is of the same flesh with man, and so is neither plant, nor beast.

Obiection II. The Magistrate kills without sinne. *Answer.* The killing which is in the name of God, by publike reuenge, is not murther. And *Paul* onely condemnes that killing, when men take the sword, and vpon their owne wills slay and kill by priuate reuenge.

Obiect. III. *Sampson* is saide to kill himselfe, *Iudg.* 16.13. and he sinned not in so doing. *Ans. Sampson* was a Iudge in *Israel*, and tooke publike reuenge of his enemies: and in this reuenge he hazzarded his life, and lost his life. Though he died in the execution, yet his intent was not to kill himselfe, but onely to take reuenge. Secondly, his example is speciall. For he was in his death a figure of Christ. The words, *Matt.2. he shall be called a Nazarite*, are first spoken of *Sampson*, and then applied to Christ, in whom was verified that which *Sampson* figured. For as *Sampson* conquered his enemies more in his death, then in his life: euen so did Christ.

Obiect. IV. For the auoiding of some great danger, or some great sinne, as the deniall of Christ in persecution, men may make away themselues: so said the Donatists. *Answer.* Death is no remedie in this case, but faith in the promise of God: which is, that he wil giue an issue in euery temptation, 1.*Cor.* 10.13.

The vse. Seeing *murther* is a worke of the flesh: our dutie is by all meanes to preserue both our owne, and our neighbours liues. Life is a treasure. For by it wee haue time and libertie to glorifie God, to doe good to our neighbours, and to saue our owne soules.

The sinnes of the fourth sort, are against *Temperance*: and they are two: *drunkennesse, gluttony.* For the better conceiuing of the nature of these sinnes, we are first of all to consider the right manner and measure of eating and drinking; of which I deliuer two rules. I. Wee may vse meat and drinke, not onely for necessitie, but also for delight, *Psal.*104.15. II. That measure of meat and

drinke,

drinke, which in our experience makes vs fit both in body and mind for the seruice of God, and for the duties of our callings, that measure (I say) is fit, conuenient, and lawfull. This is a confessed principle in the light of nature.

Drunkennesse then is, when men drinke, either in wine, or strong drinke, beyond this measure: so as there follows an intoxication of the powers of the soule. And in the sinne there are two things: excessiue drinking, and the distempering of the powers of the soule.

Gluttonie, is, when men in eating, goe beyond the measure before prescribed. This gluttony, is that which now adayes is called *reuelling, rioting, swaggering*. And it is fitly ioyned with drunkennesse. For there are men that vse to drinke exceedingly, and will not be drunke: and for all this, they are not free from blame: because they drinke out of measure. To bee giuen to drinking, and to loue to sit by the cup, when there is no drunkennesse, is a sinne, 1.*Tim*.3.3.

These sinnes are said to be rife among vs. The maner of many is, to meet together, and to fill themselues with wine or strong drink, while their skinnes will hold. Afterward, they giue themselues to dicing, carding, dancing, singing of ribauld songs: and thus they passe the day, the night, the weeke, the yeare.

But we must be put in mind, to detest, and to flie these vices. Inducements to this dutie are many.

I. Gods commandement. *Keepe not company with drunkards, and gluttonous persons, Prouerb*.23.20. *Bee not drunke with wine, in which is excesse, Ephes*.5.18.

II. The punishment of drunkennesse, is plague, pestilence, famine, captiuitie, *Isai*.5.11,12,13.

III. The example of the bruite beast, that in eating and drinking, keepes measure, and takes no more then will suffice nature. The horse and the asse may bee schoolemasters to many of vs.

IV. If wee cannot forsake a cup of wine, or beere, which is not needfull for vs, wee shall neuer bee able to forsake wife, and children, house, and land for Christs sake. If we haue not the command of our selues in a trifle, we may neuer hope for it in weightie matters.

V. There are dangerous effects of drunkennesse. First, it destroies the body. For it inflames the blood with an vnnatural heat: and this vnnaturall heat, ingenders vnnaturall thirst, which ingenders immoderate drinking, whence comes dropsies, consumptions, all cold diſeaſes,and death. Secondly,it hurts the minde: for the ſpirits of the heart and braine (being the immediate inſtruments of the ſoule) are by drinking diſtempered and inflamed: and hereupon ariſe wicked imaginations, and diſordered affections. And thus the diuel in the roome of Gods image,ſets vp his own image: and makes the minde a ſhop of all wickedneſſe. Thirdly,the vile imaginations and affections that are in men when they are drunk, remaine ſtill in men when they are ſober: ſo as being ſober they are drunke in affection.

In fauour of drunkeneſſe, it is alleadged that *Noahs* drunkenneſſe is remembred in Scripture,but no where condemned. *Anſw.* While *Moſes* ſets downe the foule effects that followed *Noahs* drunkenneſſe,he doeth indeed condemne it. Secondly,his example is noted in Scripture,as a warning to all ages following. Thirdly, his ſinne may be leſſened, though not excuſed,becauſe hee had no experience of wine.

Obiect. II. Ioſeph and his brethren did drinke and *were drunke together, Geneſis* 43. ver. laſt. *Anſwer.* The meaning of the text is, that they dranke liberally, or that they dranke of the beſt together. For the word *(ſhakar)* ſignifies not only to be drunke in drinking, but alſo to drinke liberally, or to drinke of the beſt drinke, *Hag.*1.6.

Obiect. III. Learned Phiſitians, as *Raſis, Auicenna,* and others teach,that it is greatly for health,to bee drunke once or twice in a moneth. *Anſwer.* As learned as they teach the contrary. And wee may not doe any euill, or ſinne againſt God, for any good to our ſelues.

Obiect. IV. It is ſaid to be neighbourhood and good fellowſhip. *Anſwer.* It is drunken fellowſhip. The right fellowſhip is in the doctrine of the Apoſtles, Prayer, Sacraments, and the workes of mercie.

Thus much of the workes of the fleſh. Now followes the puniſhment of them, of which I conſider three things. Firſt, a Premonition in theſe words, *whereof I tell you before, as I alſo haue told you before.* Secondly, the deſignement of the puniſhment in theſe words, *ſhall not inherite the kingdome of God.* Thirdly, the deſignement of the perſons, in theſe words, *They which doe ſuch things.*

In the Premonition,is ſet downe the office of all Miniſters: and that is, often to forewarne the people of the future iudgements of God for their ſinnes, *Mich.*3.8. *Iſa.*58.1. And this may eaſily bee done. For they may know the ſinnes of men by experience, and the

the iudgements of God due to euery ſinne, they may finde in the word of God.

Againe, all people are warned by this, often to meditate of the future iudgements of God. Thus did *Dauid*, *Pſal.* 119.120. and *Paul*, who knowing the terrour of the Lord, was mooued to doe his dutie, 2. *Cor.* 5.11. The old world neuer ſo much as dreamed of Gods iudgements, before they came vpon them, and ſo they periſhed, *Matt.* 24.39.

The puniſhment of theſe ſinnes is, *not to inherite Gods kingdome*. Gods kingdome ſometime ſignifies the regiment of God, wherby he rules all things in heauen and earth. More ſpecially, it ſignifies a ſtate or condition in heauen, whereby God and Chriſt is all things to all the Elect, 1. *Cor.* 15.28. And thus it is taken in this place. And an entrance or beginning to this happy eſtate, is in this life, when men in their conſciences and liues are ruled by Gods word, and ſpirit. It muſt here further be obſerued, that not to inioy the kingdome of God, is to be in torment in hel: becauſe there are no more but two eſtates after this life: and therefore to be out of heauen, is to be in hell.

The vſe. I. This muſt teach vs aboue all things to ſeeke Gods kingdome, and to eſtabliſh it in our hearts: and that we ſhall doe, if we know the will of God, and yeeld ſubiection to it, in the duties of repentance, new obedience, &c.

II. The kingdome of God comes by inheritance: therefore there is no merit of good works.

The perſons which are puniſhed, are ſuch as are doers and practiſers of the works of the fleſh. Marke the words, not ſuch as haue bin doers, but ſuch as are doers. The word ſignifies a preſent and a continued act of doing amiſſe.

The vſe. Hence is the difference betweene the godly man, and the vngodly. The godly man falls into the works of the fleſh, and being admoniſhed thereof, he repents and recouers himſelfe: hee doth not ſtand in the way of ſinners, though ſometime he enter into it, *Pſal.* 1.1. The vngodly man, when he fals, he lies ſtill in his ſin, and heaps ſinne vpon ſinne, and makes a practiſe of euill.

I. *Warning*. They which are priuy to themſelues of any of the former works of the fleſh, muſt bewaile their offences, and vtterly forſake them. For if we be found doers of any one worke of the fleſh, there is no hope of ſaluation.

II. *Warning*. They which haue turned vnto God from the works of the fleſh muſt bee conſtant, and take heede of going backe, leſt they loſe the kingdome of God.

22 *But*

22 *But the fruite of the spirit, is loue, ioy, peace, long suffering, gentlenesse, goodnesse, loue.*
23 *Meeknesse, temperance: against such there is no law.*

For the better obseruing, and the more easie vnderstanding of the rule in the 16. verse. *Walke in the spirit, Paul* here sets downe a Catalogue of the workes of the spirit. In the Catalogue I consider three things, the propertie of the works of the spirit, in these words, *The fruite of the spirit:* the kindes of works, and they are nine: the benefit that comes by them, in these words, *Against such there is no law.*

The fruite of the spirit] It is the propertie of the works of Gods Spirit in vs, to be called *the fruites of the Spirit.* And by this, much is signified: namely, that the Church is the garden of God, *Cant.*4.16. that teachers are planters and setters, 1.*Cor.*3.9. that beleeuers are trees of righteousnesse, *Isai.* 61.3. that the Spirit of God is the sappe and life of them: and good works and vertues are the fruits which they beare.

In that the workes of the spirit, are called *fruites* thereof, hence it followes, that there are no true vertues, and good affections, without the grace of regeneration. The vertues of the heathen, how excellent soeuer they seemed to bee, were but shadowes of vertue, and serued onely to restraine the outward man, and no further.

Againe, here we see the efficacy of the Spirit, which makes men fruitfull, or bearing trees of righteousnesse, *Psal.*1.3. yea, trees that beare fruite in their old age, *Psal.*92.14. Here we haue cause to cast downe our selues. For the most of vs are barren trees, that beare no fruite, but the bad fruits of the flesh: and therefore wee may iustly feare the curse that God laid vpon the figtree, *Luke* 13.7. and looke euery day to be stocked vp, *Matt.*3.16.

Againe, good workes are made acceptable to God euen by his grace; and therefore they are called *the fruits of the spirit*: and hence it is that they are acceptable to God, *Rom.*15.16. Wee that are by nature wild branches, must be taken out of old *Adam*, and set into Christ: and after our insition draw a new sappe and life from Christ, namely, his spirit, and then our actions shall be fruits of the spirit, and consequently acceptable to God.

Lastly, hence it followes, that free will of it selfe, is like a dead or rotten piece of wood, and that it beares no fruit, but as it is quickned by the Spirit, *Iohn* 15.5.

Thus much of the property: now follow the kinds of the works of the spirit.

Loue] It may be demanded, how it is a fruit of the spirit? *Answ.* First, the Spirit of God workes faith, then regeneration, then loue, 1.*Tim.*1.5. Loue followes faith: because we must know first that we are loued of God, before that wee loue God, 1.*Iohn* 4.19. And loue followes regeneration: because till the will and the affections be changed, there is no place for loue. The Papists then erre, who teach, that the first act of loue, that is, the inclination to loue God and man aright, is in nature; and that the second act, namely, the exercise of loue, is from the Spirit. Againe, they erre in that they teach, that charitie or loue, is the formall righteousnes of a Christian. For it is a fruit that followes regeneration.

The loue here mentioned, is either of God, or of man. The loue of God, is an holy affection, whereby wee loue God in Christ for himselfe. There are three speciall signes whereby it is discerned, I. A desire of fellowship with God, and Christ, and the holy Spirit: and therefore to be much and frequent in the vse of the word, and prayer: because in the word, God speakes to vs, and in prayer, wee speake to him. II. To loue the word of God aboue all earthly treasure: and to tread our owne wills vnder foot, and to desire that Gods will may be preferred in all things, 1.*Iohn* 2.5. There are many houses among vs, where the cards and tables are walking, but the Bible is seldome or neuer seene. And this argues the want of loue. III. The loue of them that loue God and Christ.

The loue of our neighbour, is to loue him simply, in, and for the Lord, and for no other by-respect. The signe of this loue is, to loue, *not in word*, but *indeed.* And this is *to loue indeed*, to shew loue, and to do good (when we are wronged and abused) to them that wrong vs and abuse vs.

Ioy] Ioy is twofold; ioy of glory after this life, and the ioy of grace in this life: and it stands in three things. The first is, to reioyce in the true acknowledgement of God, that he is our God, and reconciled to vs in Christ. The second is, to reioyce in the worke of our regeneration. The third is, to reioyce in the hope of eternall glory.

This ioy of grace hath a double fruite. First, it moderates all our sorrowes, which makes vs reioyce in the middest of our afflictions, 1.*Thess.*5.16. Secondly, it causeth men to reioyce at the good of their neighbours, *Romanes* 12.15. And this ioy is heere meant specially. For ioy is heere opposed to enuie, and emulation.

This fruite ſhewes, that wee are moſt of vs bad trees. For the ioyes of the world be for the moſt part in iniquitie, and in the workes of the fleſh. And it is our common ſinne not to reioyce, but to pine away with griefe, as *Cain* did, when we ſee Gods bleſſing vpon our brother.

Peace] It is a care and deſire to mainetaine concord, as much as may be, if it lie in vs. *Rom.* 12.18. It is an excellent vertue. For the kingdome of God ſtands partly in peace. *Rom.* 14.17. For the maintenance of peace, obſerue two rules. I. Neither take offence, nor giue offence. *Abraham* choſe rather to loſe his right, then to offend *Lot. Gen.* 13. and ſo did Chriſt. *Matth.* 17.27. II. Seeke to edifie one another, either doe good, or take good. *Rom.* 14.19.

Long-ſuffering] is to moderate our anger, and deſire of reuenge, when many and great wrongs are done to vs. It is an excellent fruit, but it takes very hardly in theſe parts. For our manner is, *a word and a blow: a word and a ſtabb: a word and a writte.*

Set and ſow this plant in the furrowes of your hearts, and that the weede of reuenge ouergrow it not, vſe theſe remedies. I. Gods commandement forbids raſh anger, *Iam.* 1.19. for it is a degree of murder. II. The example of God, who is ſlow to anger, and of Chriſt, who is meeke and lowly, *Matth.* 11. III. All wrongs done to vs by men, come by Gods prouidence, to which we are to ſubiect our ſelues. IV. The goodneſſe of God, who forgiues more to vs, then wee can forgiue. V. There is daunger of Gods anger. For vnleſſe wee forgiue, wee are not forgiuen. And wee craue forgiueneſſe, as wee forgiue. VI. It is the dutie of loue to ſuffer and beare, 1. *Corinth.* 13. VII. It is a point of iniuſtice to reuenge our ſelues, for then we take to our ſelues the honour of God, and againſt all equitie, we are both the parties, and iudge, and witneſſe and all. VIII. Wee are often ignorant of the minds of men, in their actions, and of the true circumſtances thereof: and ſo may eaſily be deceiued.

Obiect. I. Anger is a ſudden affection: therefore it cannot bee ruled. *Anſwer.* Meanes are to be vſed before hand, when wee are quiet: then ſhall we better reſtraine it.

Obiect. II. It is hard for fleſh and blood to doe this. *Anſw.* We are more then fleſh and blood. For we haue the Spirit of God, elſe we are but hypocrites.

Gentleneſſe] Gentleneſſe, is to giue good ſpeach, and to ſhew good countenances, euen to them that wrong vs, and abuſe vs, without any minde, or deſire to reuenge, *Romanes* 12.14. *Epheſ.* 4.32.

The curtesie of the world, in the cappe and the knee, and all the complements of humanity, is commonly seuered from good affection: and it is often the maske of enmity: and therefore it is but a worke of the flesh. Right curtesie is with an honest heart, to blesse when we are wronged.

Goodnesse] It is vertue, whereby we communicate to others, the good things that are in vs, for their good and benefit. It is prescribed by *Paul* in other tearmes, when he saith, *Communicating to the necessitie of the Saints, Rom.* 12.13.

Question. I. What are we to communicate? *Answ.* The gifts of our minde, our temporall goods, yea our liues too, if neede be, 1.*Ioh.*3.16.

Question. II. Why are we so to doe? *Answ.* We are members all of one body; and we are members one of another, *Eph.*4.25. And it is Gods pleasure, that men shall be instruments of good mutually one to another.

Goodnesse, respects either the body, or the minde. Goodnesse concerning the body, hath many actions: as to feede the hungry, to giue drinke to the thirsty, to harbour the harbourlesse, to cloath the naked, to visit the sicke, and them that are in prison, *Math.*25.35, 36. to bury the dead, 2. *Samuel* 2. 5. Lastly, to lend freely and liberally, to such as be decayed and impouerished. *Deuteronomy* 15.7.

Goodnesse concerning the soule, is to indeuour, partly by counsell, and partly by example, to gaine the soule of our neighbour to God: and it stands in foure actions: to admonish the vnruly, to comfort the distressed, to beare with them that are weake, and to be patient towards all, 1.*Thess.*5.14.

Goodnesse is hard to be found in these dayes among men. The common practise is according to the common prouerbe, *Euery man for himselfe, and God for vs all.* The study of men is, how to gather goods, honours, riches, for themselues, and for their children: and the common good is not aymed at. Good orders hardly take place, as namely, the order for the poore; and the reason is, the want of goodnesse in vs. If any professe any shew of goodnesse more then the rest, they are sure to be despised and reproched at euery hand: and this shewes that there is little goodnesse among men.

Faith] First, we are here to vnderstand faith towards God, which is to beleeue the remission of our sinnes, and our reconciliation with God in Christ.

This faith is common to all among vs: yet is it but a false,

dead,

dead,& ceremoniall faith,in many men. Reaſon. I. Faith comes by the hearing of the word of God preached,*Rom.*10.14.but this faith in many is conceiued without preaching:for they ſay,they beleeue their ſaluation by Chriſt, and withall they liue in the perpetuall neglect or contempt of the publike Miniſtery. II. True faith is ioyned alwaies with the exerciſes of inuocation,and repentance : yet in many among vs, this faith is without any conuerſion or change of heart and life: and therfore it is but a dead faith.III. True faith is mixed with cõtrary vnbeleefe,ſo as they that beleeue,feele in themſelues a want of faith,and much vnbeleefe. But there are many among vs that ſay,they perfectly beleeue, and that they neuer ſo much as doubted in all their liues. Now ſuch a faith,is a vaine perſwaſion. IV. Many that boaſt of their faith in Chriſt,want faith in the prouidence of God, touching food and raiment. And that is manifeſt, becauſe they vſe any lawfull meanes to helpe themſelues : now if their faith faile them in a ſmaller point,it cannot be ſound in the greateſt of all.

Secondly, by faith is meant faith towards men, and that ſtands in two things. One is, to ſpeake the trueth from the heart : the other is,to be faithfull and iuſt in the keeping of our honeſt promiſe, and word.

This faith is a rare vertue in theſe dayes. For the common faſhion of them that liue by bargaining, is, to vſe gloſing, facing, ſoothing, lying, diſſembling, and all manner of ſhifts. And with many it is a confeſſed principle,that *there is no liuing in the world,vnleſſe we lie and diſſemble.* They that deale with chapmen, ſhal hardly know what is trueth, they haue ſo many words, and ſo many ſhifts. In this reſpect,Chriſtians come ſhort of the Turks,who are ſaid to be equall,open,and plaine dealing men, without fraud, or deceit.

Our care therefore muſt bee to cheriſh, and maintaine among vs,the vertue of faith, and truth. Reaſons. I. Gods commandement,*Put away lying,and let euery man ſpeake the truth to his neighbour. Epheſ.*4.15 II. By *truth* wee are like to God,whoſe waies are all truth : who hates a lying tongue,*Prou.*6.17. whoſe ſpirit is the ſpirit of truth. III. Lyars beare the image of the diuell. Hee is the father of lies,*Iohn* 8.44. So oft then as thou lieſt, thou makeſt thy tongue the inſtrument of the diuell. IV. Eternall puniſhment in the lake that burnes with fire and brimſtone, *Reuel.*22.15. Here marke, that liars are entertained at the ſame table with murderers and theeues : and the liar neuer goes vnpuniſhed, *Prou.*19.5. V. To ſpeake the trueth from the heart, is a marke of Gods child,*Pſal.*15.2. And he whoſe faith failes towards men,ſhal much more faile towards God.

Meekeneſſe] The ſame in effect with long ſuffering. The difference is,that *meekenes* is more generall,and *long ſuffering* is the higheſt degree of meekneſſe.

Temperance] It is the moderation of luſt and appetite, in the vſe of the gifts and creatures of God. For the better practiſing of this vertue,remember theſe foure rules.

I. We muſt vſe moderation in meats and drinks. This moderation is to eat and drink with perpetual abſtinence. And abſtinence is to take leſſe then that which nature deſires,and not more. And that meaſure of meat and drinke, which ſerues to refreſh nature, and to make vs fit for the ſeruice of God and man, is allowed vs of God,and no more.

II. Wee muſt vſe moderation in our apparell. And that is,to apparell our ſelues according to our ſexe,according to the receiued faſhion of our countrey,according to our place and degree,and according to our abilitie. Here the common fault is,to be out of all order: for none almoſt know any meaſure. Euery meane perſon now adayes will be a gentleman,or gentlewoman.

III. We muſt vſe moderation in getting of goods: and that is, to reſt content if we haue food & raiment for our ſelues, and them that belong vnto vs, 1.*Tim.*6.8. Here is our ſlint;we may not deſire to be rich,verſe 9. The King himſelfe muſt not multiply his golde and ſiluer,*Deut.*17.17. and yet hath he more need of gold and ſiluer,then any priuate man.

IV. There muſt bee a moderation in the ſpending of our goods: contrary to the faſhion of many,that ſpend their ſubſtance in feaſting,and company,and keepe their wiues and children bare at home.

Againſt ſuch there is no law] Heere *Paul* ſets downe the benefite that comes by the former vertues. The words carrie this ſenſe: Againſt ſuch vertues, and againſt perſons indued with ſuch vertues there is no law. And that for two cauſes. One, there is no law to condemne ſuch. Secondly,there is no law to compell them to obey: becauſe they freely obey God, as if there were no law.

Marke then the condition of ſpirituall men. They are a voluntary and free people,ſeruing God freely without conſtraint. So as if Chriſt would not giue vnto them life euerlaſting, yet would they loue him,and deſire the aduancement of his kingdome. On the contrary,if there were no hel,and God would not puniſh adultery, drunken-

drunkenneſſe, blaſphemy, &c. with eternall death, yet would a Chriſtian man abſtaine from theſe things: becauſe he knowes that they diſpleaſe Chriſt, and hee is gouerned with another ſpirit, to which they are contrary.

Alſo theſe words are a reaſon of verſe 16. *There is no law against them that doe theſe things:* therefore *walke in the ſpirit.*

24 *For they that are Chriſts, haue crucified the fleſh, with the affections, and luſts.*

The ſcope. In theſe words, *Paul* prooues that which he ſaid immediatly before, namely, that there is no law againſt ſpiritual men. And of this he giues a double reaſon. One is, ſpirituall men are Chriſts: therefore there is no law againſt them. The ſecond is this: That is crucified in ſpirituall men, which the law condemneth, namely, the fleſh, with the affections and luſts: therfore there is no law to condemne the ſpirituall man.

In the words, I conſider three poynts. The firſt is, What is a Chriſtian? *Anſw.* A Chriſtian is one that is Chriſts, (ſaith *Paul.*) And he is Chriſts fiue wayes. I. By the right of creation. And ſo are all men. II. By right of redemption, 1. *Cor.* 6. 19. III. By the free gift and donation of God the Father, *Iohn* 17. 11. This donation is begun in the eternall Election of God, and it is accompliſhed in our effectuall vocation. IV. By propagation. For all true beleeuers ſpring out of the blood of Chriſt: and are of his bone, and of his fleſh, as *Eue* was of the bone and fleſh of *Adam.* V. By our donation in Baptiſme, in which wee conſecrate our ſelues to God, and to Chriſt.

The vſe. This muſt teach vs to reſigne our ſelues to Chriſt, and to ſuffer him to reigne in our hearts: and to take the yoke of the Goſpel vpon vs. But alas, it is farre otherwiſe with many of vs. For ſome liue in the tranſgreſſion of the very law of nature, ſo farre are they from obſeruing the Goſpel. Others thinke it ſufficient to follow the teaching of nature. If they worſhip God in ſome generall maner, if they liue peaceably, and hurt no man, and meane well (as they ſay) then all is wel: and the doing of further duties, is reputed curious preciſeneſſe. And ſuch perſons vſually reduce religion to the practiſe of nature. They will be ſaued by faith: but their faith is nothing elſe but fidelity. They ſay they worſhip God, but this worſhip is nothing elſe but their good meaning, and their good dealing. Theſe men are content that Chriſt ſhall bee theirs: but they will not be Chriſts, and ſuffer him to haue a lordſhip ouer them.

II. If thou be Christs, then commend thy soule, and life, and all that thou hast into the hands of Christ. This was the practise of *Dauid, Psal.* 22. of Christ vpon the crosse: of *Paul, 2.Tim.* 1.12. And this practise is the only way to obtaine safetie and protection. For Christ no doubt will keepe his owne.

III. Comfort. If thou be Christs, he will care for thee, and nothing shall be wanting vnto thee that is for thy good, *Iohn* 17.24. *Rom.* 8.33. Therefore remember this lesson, Neuer grieue ouermuch, neuer care ouermuch, neuer reioyce ouermuch in the things of this world. If thou werest at thine owne disposing and finding, it were somewhat: but there is one that cares for thee, namely Christ.

The second poynt to be considered, is, what is the flesh? *Answer.* It is the corruption of the whole nature of man. For the right conceiuing of this, wee must make a distinction of three things, Mans nature, the faculties of nature, and the corruption of both, which corruption hath two parts: the losse of the image of God, and a pronenesse to all wickednes. Moreouer, this distinction must be without separation of nature from faculties, or of corruption from either: so as wee may say truly, that the nature, and the powers of the soule of man, are corrupted.

In the flesh are two things: *Affections*, and *Lustes*. By *affections* vnderstand inordinate affections, which shew themselues, and beare sway in carnall men, as anger in *Cain*, loue of pleasures more then of God, in the men of the last times, 2.*Tim* 3.3. immoderate sorrow in *Ahab*, when hee could not obtaine *Naboths* vineyard, 1. *Kings* 21.4.

Lusts, are inordinate and insatiable desires after the things of this world, as riches, honors, pleasures, &c. of this sort are couetousnes, gluttony, pride, the lust of the flesh, &c.

The vse. By this we see what a carnall man is, namely, one that is carried away with some inordinate affection, or some inordinate lust. *Herod* did many good things at the aduice and motion of *Iohn Baptist*, whom he reuerenced: yet was hee a carnall man. For hee was possessed with an inordinate loue of his brothers wife. *Iudas* a disciple of Christ, yet a carnall man: because hee was carried away with the inordinate lust of couetousnesse.

The third point, is touching the office of a Christian man. And that is, to crucifie the flesh, with the affections and lusts. For the better conceiuing of this, Crucifying must be distinguished. It is either the action of Christ, or our action. Crucifying, which is the action of Christ, is threefold. The first is, vpon the crosse, where

where Chriſt ſtood in our roome, and bare the burden of our ſins, and made an expiation of them. In this reſpect we are ſaid to bee crucified with him, *Gal.*2.19. The ſecond is in vs, when Chriſt conueies the vertue of his death into the hearts of them that are ioined to him, for the cauſing and effecting of the death of ſin. The third is, in baptiſme, whereby Chriſt ſeales the two former to them that beleeue, *Rom.*6.6.

The crucifying, which is our action, is nothing elſe but the imitation of Chriſt crucified, on this manner. He was firſt attached: ſo muſt we bring our ſelues into the preſence of God. He was arraigned: ſo muſt we ſet our ſelues at the barre of Gods iudgement. He was accuſed: ſo muſt wee indite and accuſe our ſelues of our owne ſinnes at the barre of Gods iudgement. He was condemned: and ſo muſt we iudge our ſelues, that wee bee not iudged of the Lord. After iudgement, we muſt proceed to execution of the fleſh: and that is, to vſe meanes to crucifie it: and they are three. The firſt is, by faith to apply to our ſelues Chriſt crucified: and that is to beleeue, not onely that Chriſt was crucified for vs, but that wee alſo were crucified with him. Where this faith is, ſinne ſhall no more haue dominion. The ſecond is, to beat down the fleſh by the ſword of the ſpirit: and that is done by a ſerious application of the commandements and the threatnings of God, to our ſeueral affections and luſts. The third is, to flie the occaſions of euery ſinne, and to cut off the firſt beginnings of euill.

The vſe. This doctrine ſerues to condemne the drowſie Proteſtants of our time, who profeſſe Chriſt without making any change in life and conuerſation. For they are Saints in the Church, but in their common dealings they are as worldlings.

II. Secondly, they are heere reprooued, that haue many good gifts of God in them, and yet neuer proceed to a through reformation. For they vſe to cheriſh in themſelues naughtie affections, and damnable luſts. There is ſome one ſweet ſinne or other, that they cannot abide to crucifie.

III. They alſo are to bee blamed, that cannot abide to heare their owne particular ſinnes to be noted, and reprooued. They are vncrucified and vnmortified perſons. And the word of God is the ſword of the ſpirit, that ſerues to kill and deſtroy the fleſh.

IV. In afflictions be content and quiet. For we ought to crucifie the affections and luſts of our fleſh: and becauſe we faile in this dutie, therefore God himſelfe takes the worke in hand: and he will crucifie our corruption by his chaſtiſements.

Further, of this duty of crucifying the fleſh, there are three points to to be considered. I. The time when this action must begin; namely, in our baptisme, or first conuersion. Therefore *Paul* saith, they that are Christs, *haue crucified, &c.* II. What must be crucified? *Ans.* The whole flesh, with euery inordinate affection and lust. This makes against them that fly and detest some fewe sinnes, and runne headlong into others. III. What is crucifying? *Ans.* In it are two things, the restraint of the exercise of sinne, (which is in part in ciuill men,) and the killing of Originall corruption, in al the parts and branches thereof. And that is done, when we doe not only mourne for our corruptions, but also hate and detest them in our selues.

25. *If we liue in the Spirit, let vs also walke in the Spirit.*

In these words is contained, the last reason of the rule of good life before mentioned, in the 16. verse. For the vnderstanding whereof, two things are to be considered, what it is to liue in the Spirit; and what to walke in the Spirit; Touching the first, Life is twofold: created, or vncreated. Vncreated life, is the life of God. Created is that which pertaineth to the creature. And this is either naturall, or spirituall. Naturall life, is led by naturall causes and means, as by meat, drinke, cloathing, breathing, &c. Spirituall life, is by, and from the Spirit. Of this there be two degrees. The first is, when the Spirit of God takes vp his habitation in man, and withall gouerneth all the powers of his soule, by putting into the minde, a new light of knowledge, into the will and affections, new motions, and inclinations, whereby they are made conformable to the will of God. The second degree of spirituall life is, when the Spirit dwelleth in man, and gouerneth the powers of the soule, and further doth sustaine the body, immediatly without naturall means. 1. *Cor.* 15. 44. *It riseth againe a spirituall body*, that is, a body liuing in the second degree of spirituall life, not being sustained by meanes, but immediately by the eternall sustentation of the Spirit. The first of these degrees is in this life, the second after this life, in, and after the last iudgement, when body and soule shall be reunited. And of the former, this place is to be vnderstood.

To walke in the Spirit, is, first to sauour the things of the Spirit, *Rom.* 8. 5. 7. And that is, to minde, wish, like, desire, and affect them; or in a word, to subiect a mans selfe to the law of God, in all the powers and faculties of the soule. For the things reuealed in the Law, are the things of the Spirit, which Spirit must at no hand be seuered from the word. Secondly, to walke in the path of

righteous-

righteouſneſſe, without offence either of God or man, *Pſal.*143.10. Thirdly, to walke not ſtragglingly, but orderly by rule, by line, and by meaſure. For ſo much the word [*walke*] importeth, in the originall; as if *Paul* ſhould haue ſaid, Let vs, (whilſt we liue in this world) not onely indeauour to doe ſome one, or ſome few good actions, but in the courſe of our liues and callings, order our ſelues according to the rule and line of the word of God. στοιχῶμ.

The vſe. This text in the firſt place, cuts off the ſhiftes and excuſes of ſundry perſons in theſe daies, who profeſſe themſelues to be the children of God, and yet for their liues, are much to be blamed, becauſe they leade them not according to the Spirit, but according to the fleſh. And theſe perſons, whatſoeuer they ſay, doe indeed and in truth, deceiue themſelues, and are quite deſtitute of Gods Spirit. For if they liued in the Spirit, they would alſo walke in the Spirit; It is not an idle ſpirit in any, but it will ſhew and maniſeſt it ſelfe, in a holy and orderly conuerſation. You will ſay; If ſuch perſons haue not the Spirit of God, what other Spirit haue they? *Anſ.* If their life be naught, they haue an vncleane Spirit dwelling in them: and the god of this world hath blinded their eies, and makes them that they cannot ſee the right way wherein they ſhould walke, 1.*Cor.*4.4.

Againe, we learne from hence, a true and pregnant ſigne, wherby to diſcerne, whether any man hath in his heart the Spirit of God or no? The life of a man will diſcouer and proclaime to all the world, before God, men, and Angels, what himſelfe is. If a man in the courſe of his life and calling be godly and vertuous, leading his life according to the will & word of God, in an honeſt and carefull indeauour, though he faile in ſome particulars: what euer the world thinkes of him, he is the man that is indued with the Spirit of God.

Laſtly, this teacheth, what is the office of all Chriſtian people, namely, *to walke in the ſpirit,* that is, to frame and order the whole courſe and tenour of their liues, according to the line and ſquare of Gods word and Spirit. A motiue to which dutie, may be that fearefull threat pronounced vpon thoſe that turne aſide, and walke in their owne crooked wayes, *Pſal.*125.5.

26 Let vs not be deſirous of vaine glorie, prouoking one another, enuying one another.

The ſcope. From this 26. verſe, to the 11. verſe of the chapter following, S. *Paul* handles the ſecond Rule, which he had propounpounded in the 13. verse of this chapter: *By loue serue one another*. In the handling whereof, he first laboureth to take away the impediments of Loue. and then he sets downe the manner, how the rule is to be obserued. This 26. verse is a rule, the ende whereof, is to remooue the impediments of loue.

In this verse foure points are especially to be considered. First, what the desire of vaineglory is? *Answ.* It is a branch of pride, which makes men to referre all they haue, or can do, to their owne priuate glory, and aduancement. For better vnderstanding whereof, consider a little the excuses that men haue, for the defence, or excuse of this sinne.

I. Excuse. Vaine-glory in effect is no more, but the seeking of mens approbation, which may lawfully be done. *Answ.* To seeke the approbation of men, is no fault, so that it be sought in a good manner. The right manner of seeking the praise of men, is this: A man must in this life passe through three iudgements; the iudgment of God, of his owne conscience, and of his neighbour: and the order of going through them, is; in the first place, he must seeke for the iudgement and approbation of God: in the next, his owne: and in the last, his neighbours. Now the vaine-glorious man takes another course, first and principally ayming at the glory and good liking of man, hauing small or no regard of the two other.

II. Excuse. There is a good boasting, which *Dauid* vsed, and that we may lawfully vse. *Psal.* 7.8. *Ans.* Boasting is either lawfull, or vnlawfull. Lawfull boasting is in the Lord, when, beeing vrged and compelled, we confesse the good things that are in vs, to Gods glory. Of this read at large, 2. *Cor.* 11. Vnlawfull is, when men ascribe the gifts that they haue of God, vnto themselues: or hauing gifts, do arrogate more vnto themselues, then indeed they haue: or in a word, doe so esteeme of their gifts as if they had not receiued them from God. And this is a damnable boasting.

III. Excuse. Gods blessings we may seeke for: and what are glory and honour, but the blessings and gifts of God? *Answer.* There are two degrees of honour. The first is, the honour that euery man hath in his place and calling. For euery calling ordained by God, hath a glory annexed vnto it: which beeing the gift of God, it may be both sought for, and enioyed. The other degree, is that which is aboue a mans place and calling, and that ought not to be sought for. Euery person must content himselfe with the honour which is sorted vnto his calling. Neuerthelesse, if God giue greater honour, he may accept it, but where God giues it not,

there

there it muſt not bee deſired. It remaineth therefore, that vaine-glory is a branch of pride, wherin men principally referre all their ſtudies, counſels, indeauours, and gifts, to the honouring and aduancing of themſelues.

The next point to bee conſidered, is, why hee admoniſheth the Galatians of vaine glory? *Anſwer.* The Galatians were men of vnderſtanding and knowledge, and were adorned with many excellent gifts. Now, they that haue receiued good gifts of God, many times are moſt vaine-glorious, 2. *Cor.* 12.7. *Matt.* 6.5. And whereas all other vices feed vpon that which is euill, this vice of vaine glory feeds vpon good things. For a man ſometimes will be proud, euen becauſe he is not proud.

A third point to be conſidered, is, where vaine glorie is to bee found? *Anſwer.* It is no rare matter, but it is a common vice, and ſpreads it ſelfe farre and wide. Some there are, which neuer lift vp heart nor hand vnto God at home, and yet the ſame perſons in the publike aſſemblies, will make as though they prayed with great deuotion. And what is the reaſon hereof, but this, that they are carried with a ſpirit of pride & arrogancy, ſeeking the commendation of men that behold them, rather then to approoue their hearts and conſciences vnto God. Of another ſort are thoſe, that haue bin old and ancient hearers of the word, who notwithſtanding, do little, or not at all profit, either in knowledge or good life: and the cauſe is not in the Goſpel, or in the diſpenſers of it, but in themſelues: becauſe they receiue not the Goſpel for it ſelfe, but for the praiſe and commendation of men, and for the credit and account they are in, by reaſon of Chriſtian profeſſion.

The laſt thing is, the remedy of pride and vaine glory; which is the rather to be thought vpon, becauſe it is a great impediment of Chriſtian loue. This remedie conſiſts partly in *meditation*, and partly in *practiſe*.

Remedies in *meditation*, are theſe. 1. God reſiſteth all proud perſons, and giues grace to the humble, 1. *Pet.* 5.5. the reaſon is, becauſe the vaine-glorious man, ſeeking himſelfe and not God, robs God of his honour. Thus the proud Phariſie exalting himſelfe aboue the poore Publican, went away leſſe iuſtified, that is, not approoued of God, as the Publican was. 2. It is the worke of the diuell, to puffe vp the minde with ſelfe-liking, and conceit, that therby he may worke mans perdition, *Gen.* 3.5. But God worketh contrarily: for he therfore abaſeth men, that he might in his good time the more exalt them. 3. There is no religion in that heart, that is wholly bent to ſeeke the praiſe of men, *Iohn* 5 44. And the

man

man that desires to be talked of, and admired by others, doth therby in effect giue notice vnto all the world, that his heart is not sound in the sight of God.

Remedies consisting in *practise*, are: first, an indeauour to acknowledge the great Maiestie of God, and withall our owne basenesse, and vilenesse before him. 2. Wee ought to ascribe all good things we haue, or can do, to God alone, and nothing to our selues. For in all that befall vs, God is the principall agent, our selues are but tooles and instruments in his hand; by right therfore the commendation belongs vnto him, and not to vs. 3. In all actions and duties of religion, first we must endeauour to approoue our selues to God, and the next place is to be giuen to man, not contrariwise. 4. When we are reuiled we must rest content; when wee are praised to our faces, or otherwise we must take heed. For then Satan stands at our right hand to puffe vs vp, and consequently to ouerthrow vs. It is a true saying, that temptations on the right hand, are far more dangerous, then those on the left. In the fift place, *Pauls* reason to disswade from this sinne, is taken from two euill fruits of it, *Contention*, and *Enuy*, *prouoking one another*, *enuying one another*. Men that are ambitious, if they bee crossed in their courses, grow contentious, if they prosper in the world, then are they enuied by others. Reade for this purpose the history of *Samuel* and *Saul*, 1. *Sam.* 15. Seeing then vaine glory hath so bad fruits issuing from it, it must teach vs to abhorre and detest it with all our hearts, and on the contrary to seeke by all meanes possible to preserue and maintaine loue in the whole course of our liues.

FINIS.

THE SVPPLEMENT, OR, CONTINVATION OF THE COMMENTARIE VPON THE SIXTH *Chapter.*

LONDON,
Printed by IOHN LEGATT, Printer to the Vniuersitie of CAMBRIDGE. 1617.

TO THE RIGHT WOR-shipfull Sir BASSINGBVRNE CAVDY, *Knight*.

R*Ight Worshipfull, hauing beene licenced some yeare agoe, (according to the ancient laudable custome of the Vniuersitie) to interpret* S. Pauls *Epistles: and then earnestly intreated by* M. Perkins *his Executour, and others his friends, (which had some interest in me) to supply that which was defectiue in his Commentary vpon the* Galatians*: ouercome at the last by their importunitie, I vndertooke the businesse, making triall of my simple facultie in this short Chapter, which I haue here according to my poore talent, finished: Yet not daring to publish it to the view of the world, without premising somewhat in way of excuse for my boldnesse. For if* Hirtius*, or (as others thinke)* Oppius*, beeing importuned by his friend, to continue the Commentaries which* Cæsar *left vnfinished, durst not presume to make a Supplie, without making first an Apologie for himselfe, for attempting to take in hand so great a taske, seeming therein to compare with him, who was incomparable: Iust cause haue I to excuse my selfe for this my bold attempt, in vndertaking to equall him, who in the iudgement of all, (saue such as esteeme of Writers by tale, and not by touch)* is so substantiall, concise, exact, methodicall, *that (as it is said of* Cæsar*)* hee hath discouraged wise men from writing. *But seeing I doe not in the vaine confidence of mine owne sufficiencie, or exactnesse of the worke, proclaime a chalenge to all mens censures: nor yet take vpon me (as * some haue done in other writers) so to carry the Authour along, that the Reader shall not perceiue but that he is still reading him, nor know where he endeth, or where I beginne (for that beeing impossible to attaine, were folly to attempt:) but onely to finish that which otherwise should haue beene imperfect, to satisfie the request of my friends, and to help forward the Lords building, though not as a master builder with hewen stones, or polished Saphirs: yet as a seruer, and vnderlabourer, as it were with a handfull of rubbish. I hope I shall obtaine (at least) this fauourable construction, to bee thought as farre from vanitie herein, as my conscience doth witnesse with me, I did it in simplicitie, and without affectation*

Præf. lib. 8. de bello Gall.

Sanos homines à scribendo deterruit. Cic ad Brut. Suet. in Cæs. cap. 56.

*Michael de Montaign. in his Essayes.

fectation of singularitie. And if it were no presumption in Gillebertus *to finish* Bernards *Sermons vpon the Canticles, nor in* Clichtoueus *to supply*
*the 5,6,7,8. **foure books which were wanting in* Cyrils *Commentaries vpon* Iohn, *nor in* Wolfius, Reuterus, *and other moderne writers, to continue the Commentaries of* Martyr, Zanchius, &c. *but rather workes worthy great commendation, and deseruing well of the Church of God: I trust it will not bee imputed to me as a vice, which in others is accounted as a vertue. Further, if I shall seeme to any with the vnskilfull limmer to haue ioyned* humano capiti, ceruicem equinam, *in that I exceed as much the other part in prolixitie, as I come short of it in dexteritie, I hope I shal the more easily obtaine pardon, considering it was my first draught, not hauing taken pensill in hand before: and seeing the worke which I was to finish, was* caput Veneris, *the faire face of* Venus, *I chose rather (because I could not hit of the iust proportion which I aimed at) to exceed measure a little, then to be defectiue: thinking therby to sute them the better, seeing beauty or fairenesse (to speake*
Ethic. lib. 4. cap. 3. *more properly) consists onely in greatnesse, as the Philosopher saith. And some perhaps may thinke that it falleth out well, in that I haue giuen it more body, because it had lesse spirit. But what others thinke or say (for as in other things, so in this, lookers on will haue their wordes) it skilleth not, so I may haue the approbation of the godly and well affected Reader: especially your Worshipful Patronage, to whom I humbly commend it, as the first fruits of my labours, a simple floure growing in a Schollers garden: desiring it may be suffered to grow either in the shadow, or Sunne shine of your protection, that so of the godly it may be better accepted, and of the caterpiller the lesse touched: (those I meane which will correct the Verbe before they vnderstand the Nowne, condemning that which they ought rather to commend, at least which they cannot amend.) Vouchsafe therfore Right Worshipfull, to receiue this poore present, as a pledge of my vnfained loue, & humble dutie: and a testimony of my thankefulnesse to God for his manifold graces of prudence, iustice, sobrietie, meeknesse, humilitie, liberalitie bestowed vpon you, especially, your loue of his trueth, and continuall meditation in his word: which was the thing that mooued mee, (all by-respects set aside) to offer this Commentary to your view, & to haue it graced with your countenance: that by this meanes I might the more stirre vp and kindle (if it be possible) your loue and liking of the word, by adding fewel to the fire, and oyle to the flame. It is recorded of* Theodosius *the second, that he writ the New Testament ouer with his owne hand: and of* Alphonsus *King of Spaine and Naples, that hee read the Bible* 14. *times ouer with the ordinarie Glosse, (the best helpe that he had in those dayes.) And I doubt not but that you will peruse this Exposition at your leasure, and still continue to reade the holy Scripture as hitherto you haue done, and so bee answerable to that which is voiced of you, and to that extraordinary commendation which your faithfull Pastour*

hath

hath often giuen of your diligence and dexteritie in that behalfe. Now let mee adde this one thing, that though there bee not the like efficacie in a dead letter, that is in a liuely voice, yet the bare reading of the Scripture is of great and ſingular vſe, which may appeare by this, that it is ſo often commanded by precept, and ſo highly commended by the practiſe of the Saints: and ſo ſtraightly forbidden, as by cruell Antiochus, *ſo by the Romane Antichriſt:* 1.Macc.1.60. *neither dare I deny but that God hath and doeth vſe it, not onely as a meanes of edification, but alſo of working the conuerſion of many of his ſeruants, as* Auguſtine *confeſſeth of himſelfe, that he was conuerted by reading that place in* Paul, Rom. 13.14. *conuerted (I ſay) not as an heretike* Confeſſ.lib.8. cap.12. *only which is reclaimed from his erronious opinions, but as a loſt ſheep which is reduced and brought home from the errour of his way. Notwithſtanding, in reading the Scripture, to goe alone is not ſo ſafe: a guide therefore is neceſſary (as the Eunuch confeſſeth) which may be as the* Mercurialis ſtatua, Actes 8.31. *to point a man to the right way. And this guide is either the outward, or the inward guide: the outward guide (I ſpeake of reading onely) is a* Commentarie, *eſpecially ſuch a one as a ſanctified ſpirit hath much breathed vpon: ſeeing it is the beſt learning the* Theorick *of him which is skilfull in the* Practicke. *The inward guide, is the ſpirit of Reuelation, which dwelleth only in an humble, docible, & obedient heart, which whoſoeuer bringeth, hath a promiſe that he ſhall know the truth,* Iohn 7.17. *and vnderſtand the ſecrets of God,* Pſal.25.14. *and without which the Scriptures are but as a* riddle, *or* claſped booke. *For the full and perfect knowledge of the word conſiſteth (as* Epiphanius *ſaith) in* vnderſtanding, *and* feeling, *that is,* νῷ καὶ αἰσθήσει in Anchorat. *not in bare ſpeculation onely ſwimming in the braine, but in a ſenſible ſauing knowledge ſinking into the affections of the heart: and by this latter, the comfortable meaning of the Scripture is better vnderſtood, then by all the ſpeculations of the moſt curious Skeptikes: as the ſweetneſſe of hony is better knowne in a moment by him that taſteth it, then by thoſe that ſpend many houres in the contemplation and diſcourſe of it.*

But I forget myſelfe very much, in taking vpon me to reade a lecture to ſuch an exerciſed ſcholler in the booke of God. Therefore without further inſinuation, either for pardon of my boldnes or acceptance of my paines, I commend you to God, and to the word of his grace, which is able to builde you further, and giue you an inheritance among all them which are ſanctified. From Emmanuel *Colledge.* Auguſt. 13. 1604.

A louer of your Worſhips vertues

in all duties to command,

Ralfe Cvdvvorth.

CHAP. VI.

1 *Brethren, if a man be fallen by occasion into any fault, yee which are spirituall, restore such a one with the spirit of meekenes, considering thy selfe, lest thou also be tempted.*

THE Apostle hauing finished the first part of *the Instruction,* touching the faith of the Galatians in the 12. verse of the 5 Chapter. In the 13. verse hee comes to the second part, touching good life, which continues to the 11. verse of the 6. Chap. in which he first propounds the summe of his doctrine, verse 13. Secondly, hee makes particular declaration therof. In the summe of his doctrine, first, he sets downe the ground of all good duties, which is, *their calling to Christian libertie.* Secondly, two rules of good life. The first, that *we must not vse our libertie as an occasion to the flesh;* which is illustrated and handled in particular, from the 16. verse to the 26. The second, that *wee must serue one another in loue,* which is amplified from the 26. to the 11. verse of this Chap. In handling whereof, he first remooues the impediments of loue, as vaine-glory, enuy, &c. verse 26. Secondly, he prescribes the manner, how it is to bee obserued, and practised by sundry speciall rules: the first wherof is contained in this first verse: where we may obserue these two generall points. First, the dutie prescribed. Secondly, the reasons to vrge the performance thereof. The dutie is, the restoring of our brethren: where wee are to consider foure things. First, the dutie it selfe, *restore.* Secondly, the persons who are to be restored, *they that are ouertaken by any offence.* Thirdly, the persons that must restore, *those that are spirituall.* Fourthly, the manner how, *in the spirit of meeknesse.*

For the first, the dutie is set downe in the word, *restore,* which in καταρτίζειν. the originall signifies, to set a ioynt, or bone that is broken; so as it may become as strong and sound, as euer it was: so the word is vsed, *Matth.* 21.16.

By this wee learne sundry things. First, that it is the nature of sinne, to set all things out of order. It was the sinne of *Achan* that *troubled the Iewes, Ios.* 7.25. It was the sinne of *Ahab* that *troubled*

Israel. 1, *King.* 18. 18. the sinne of false Apostles that *troubled the Galatians.Gal.*5.10. Nay, it driues men beside themselues, as appeares in the example of the prodigall sonne, who repenting of his sinnes, is said *to haue come to himselfe. Luk.* 15.17. Small sins are like to slipps and slidings, whereby men fall and hurt themselues, but great sinnes are like downefalls: for as they wound, lame, disioynt, or breake some member of the body; so these doe wound and waste the conscience. Therefore as we are carefull for our bodies, to auoid downefalls; so ought we to be as carefull, nay a thousand times more carefull for our soules, to take heed of the downefall of sinne, or falling away from grace. And as we shunne an yce or slippery place, for feare of sliding and falling: so ought we to shunne the smallest sinnes, and the least occasions of sinne, for feare of making a breach in conscience. Secondly, I gather hence, that sinners are not to deferre their repentance: nor those that are to admonish, their reproofes: for sinning, is the breaking of a bone, or disioynting of a member: and reproofe is the setting of it in order againe. Now the sooner a bone newly broken, or out of ioynt, is set, the sooner it is restored to his right frame, and cured: So, the sooner a man after his fall is admonished, the sooner and more easily shal he be able to recouer himselfe. Thirdly, this shews, that it is a point of great skill, to bring a soule in order and frame againe. There is great dexterity required in setting of a bone, and Chirurgians finde it a matter of great difficulty, to set a ioynt; much more difficulty is there in the soule: and therfore as it is not for euery horsleach to meddle with setting of bones: no more it is for vnskilfull workmen to temper with mens soules. This is one speciall reason why *Paul* saith, *they that are spirituall ought to restore them that are fallen.* Fourthly, hence we are taught, not to wonder, though sinners be so loath to be reproued, and account it so painefull a thing to be restored, and thinke those offensiue vnto them, and skarse their friends, which labour to reclaime them: considering the same is to be seene in the body: for he that hath a bone broken, or out of ioynt, can hardly endure to haue it touched, or pointed at. Lastly, in that S. *Paul* commands those that are spirituall to restore them that are fallen, and prescribes not how often, but speakes indefinitely: we learne, that as often, as our brother falleth, we must restore him: for as we are not to forgiue our brother once or twise, or seauen times (which *Peter* thought very much) but euen *seauentie times seauen times*, that is, as often as he sinneth against vs. *Matthew* 18. so we may not restore our brother, twise, or thrise onely, but *toties, quoties*: as often as he shall sinne against vs.

Matth.18. If he ſinne againſt thee, goe and tell him of his fault, &c. Therefore it were to be wiſhed, that as men haue a care to reſtore their decaied limmes, ſo they would reſtore their brethren being fallen into any ſinne, euen becauſe they are fellow members of the ſame myſticall body.

The ſecond thing to be conſidered, is the perſon to be reſtored, and that is, euery one that is preuented and ouertaken, either by the ſleight of Sathan, or allurement of the world, or ſuggeſtions of his owne fleſh: (ſo he ſinne not againſt the holy Ghoſt, nor openly ſkorne religion, and diſcipline.) as *Peter* who fell beeing ouertaken with ouermuch feare, and *Dauid* with ouermuch pleaſure. Hence we ſee the ſubtilty of Sathan, who is alwaies tripping at the heele, labouring to ſupplant vs; as alſo the deceitfulnes of ſinne, preuenting and ouertaking vs, before we be aware. We are therefore to be circumſpect and carefull, leſt we be ſupplanted. The Apoſtle admoniſheth vs *to take heede leſt we be hardened through the deceitfulnes of ſinne. Hebr.* 3.3. and, *that we walke circumſpectly, not as fooles, but as wiſe. Eph.*5.15. that we *walke with a right foote. Gal.* 2.14. and, *make ſtraight ſteppes vnto our feete, leſt that which is halting be turned out of the way. Hebr.*12.13. For as thoſe that wraſtle and try maſteries, looke warily to themſelues, leſt they be ſupplanted by their aduerſaries: ſo ought we much more, conſidering, *we wraſtle not againſt fleſh and blood, but againſt principalities and powers. Eph.*6.22.

Againe, whereas it is ſaid, *if a man be ouertaken by any ſin,* he teacheth, that no man is exempted from falling, or being ouertaken and ſupplanted by ſinne: for he ſpeakes indefinitely, *if a man,* as S. *Iohn* doth: *if any man ſinne, we haue an aduocate.* 1. *Ioh.*2.1. This makes againſt the *Catharists* or *Puritanes,* who auouch, they neither haue ſinne, nor can ſinne: becauſe they be trees of righteouſnes; and *a good tree cannot bring forth euill fruite.*

Further, hence I gather, that pardon and reſtitution, is not to be denied to them that fall, after their conuerſion, as though there were no place for repentance, or hope of ſaluation. For *Paul* would haue ſuch to be reſtored, as are ouertaken by any ſinne, except they be incorrigible, and incurable. Therefore the *Nouatians* doe erre, in teaching, that ſinnes committed after a mans conuerſion, are vnpardonable, conſidering there is hope in ſtore, for great and hainous ſinners. For though a man in perſecution deny Chriſt, and renounce his religion, yet he may be reſtored, and repent as *Peter* did. *Luk.*22.32. (for that ſaying of Chriſt, *Whoſoeuer ſhall denie me before men, him will I deny before my father which is in heauen*

*uen, Mat.*10.33. is meant only of a *totall*,and *finall deniall.*) Though a man be a grieuous Idolater, a ſorcerer, and giuen to witchcraft, yet he may be reſtored and find mercy, as *Manaſſes* did, 2. *Chron.* 33. Though a man be defiled and polluted with ſinnes againſt nature, yet he may be clenſed and waſhed from them. Some among the *Corinthians* were fornicators, adulterers, wantons, buggerers; *but yet were waſhed, ſanctified, iuſtified.* 1. *Cor.*6 9.11. It may be ſaide, that *it is impoſſible, that they which haue beene once inlightned, and taſted of the heauenly gift, &c. if they fall away, ſhould be renued againe by repentance, Heb.*6,4,5,6. *Anſ.* That text is to be vnderſtood of a vniuerſall, totall, and finall Apoſtaſie. And that text, *Hebr.* 10. 26. *If we ſinne willingly, after that we haue receiued the knowledge of the truth, there remaineth no more ſacrifice for ſinne*, is to be vnderſtood, of a wilfull, and malicious renouncing of the knowne truth, as the circumſtances of the place, and collation of it with others, doe manifeſtly euict. Againe, if all ſinne committed voluntarily, and willingly, were ſimply inexpiable, euery mans caſe were damnable. And though the word ἑκουσίως, ſignifie *willinglie*, as *Ariſtotle* takes it, *Eth.l.*3.*c.* 2. yet ſometime it ſignifieth, *ſpitefully*, and *maliciouſly*, as it is vſed by the Seuentie, *Exod.*21 13. 14. *Obiect.* παραπτώματα, or *delicta*, may be reſtored, not ἁμαρτήματα, or *peccata. Anſw.* They are vſed indifferently one for the other, as might be ſhewed, if it were needfull. But it is a confeſſed truth, auouched by *Anſelme*, and others, vpon this text. Laſtly, whereas the Apoſtle ſpeaketh indefinitely; *if any man be ouertaken, reſtore him*, I gather, that the gifts and graces of God, beſtowed vpon vs, ought to be vſed in reſtoring thoſe that are fallen, without reſpect of perſons: for herein ſpiritual men are debters, to the wiſe, & fooliſh, as the Apoſtle ſaith of himſelfe, *Rom.* 1.14.

The third thing to be conſidered, is, the perſons that are to reſtore their brethren, laid downe in theſe words, *yee that are ſpirituall.*

Spirituall men are oppoſed to *carnall*, as 1. *Cor.* 3.1. *I could not ſpeake vnto you brethren, as vnto ſpirituall men, but as vnto carnall*: and to *naturall* men. 1.*Cor.*2.14.15. *The naturall man perceiueth not the things of the Spirit of God: but he that is ſpirituall diſcerneth all things.* Now carnall and naturall men, are of two ſorts: either they are ſuch as are altogether fleſhly, deſtitute of grace and godlines, beeing in their pure (or rather corrupt) naturalls, of whome S.*Paul* ſaith, *They that are of the fleſh, ſauour the things of the fleſh, Rom.*8.5. and verſe the 8. *They that are in the fleſh, cannot pleaſe God.* or ſuch as are regenerate, yet are weak, as being but babes in Chriſt; the fleſh being far ſtronger in them, then the ſpirit: ſuch were moſt

in

in the Church of Corinth: for *Paul* saith, *he could not speake vnto thẽ, as vnto spirituall men, but as vnto carnall.* 1. *Cor.* 3. 1. *for yet ye are carnal; for when there is among you enuying, are ye not carnall?* vers. 40. So *spirituall men*, opposed to *carnall*, are of two sorts. First, those that haue receiued the spirit of regeneration, and doe begin to sauour the things of the spirit, *Rom.* 8. Secondly, those that haue receiued a greater portion of the spirit, and greater measure of spiritual graces. of whom *Paul* speakes, 1. *Cor.* 14. 37. *If any man thinke himselfe to be a prophet or spirituall*——, Of the latter, the words are to be vnderstood, and by them he meaneth those, whome he called *perfect men, Philip.* 3. 13. *Ebr.* 5. 4. Now spirituall men are more fit to restore those that are falne, then any other, first, because they are les tainted with sinne, then others, and so may more freely reprooue. Secondly, because they haue more knowledge & loue, both knowing how to restore, and willing to doe it with greater compassion, and fellow feeling. He that must speake in season a word to the wearie, must *haue a tongue of the learned, Isay.* 50. 4. *When Peter is conuerted, he must strengthen his brethren, Luke* 32. 22. Hence it followes, the more excellent gifts any man hath receiued, the more he is bound to be seruiceable vnto others. For if spirituall men must restore them that are fallen, the more a man is indued with spirituall graces, the more he ought to restore. For the Apostle saith, *As euery man hath receiued a gift, so let him minister it vnto others,* 1. *Pet.* 4. 10. This dutie was practised by our Sauiour Christ, *Ioh.* 13. 12. And it meetes with the sinne of many, who hauing receiued great gifts and graces of the spirit, are so far from restoring those that sinne against them, that they scorne and disdaine to speake vnto them: for if they be at variance with any, the common saying is, *I am as good a man as he, why should I go to him? let him come to me, &c.* These men are farre vnlike *Abraham*, who though hee exceeded *Lot* as well in outward gifts, as inward graces, yet stood not vpon his priuiledge, but was the first man in making the league of vnitie, *Gen.* 14. 8. Further, in that spirituall men must restore their brethren, wee learne, that we haue not the gifts of God bestowed vpon vs for our selues alone, but for the good of others: the possession of them belongs to vs, the vse of them to others. Lastly, in that spirituall men, especially the holy men of God, and ministers of his word, are the Lords surgeons, to bind vp the broken, and raise vp those that are fallen: as also his physitians, to restore those that are in a spiritual consumption of grace: wee ought to make great account of them and *haue them in singular loue for their works sake,* 1. *Thess.* 5. 19. For if we must honor the bodily physician (as *Syradices* saith) *Eccles.* 38. 1. who cureth but the diseases of the bodie: how much more ought wee to honour spirituall Physicians, which cure the spirituall maladies of our soules?

The fourth and last point, is, the manner how wee must restore, laid downe in these words, *in the spirit of meeknesse.*

Arist.Rhet.ad Theod.lib.2. cap. 3.

Meeknesse is, the setling or quieting of the mind, freeing it from perturbation, especially in repressing the reuengefull affection. *A meeke and quiet spirit* are ioyned together, 1.*Pet.*3.4. A notable example heereof we haue in *Moses*, who being prouoked, in stead of anger, shewed meekenesse. It further makes a man to yeeld of his right, and not to prosecute the matter in rigour and extremity, and so it is opposed to *seueritie*, 1. *Corinth.*4.21. *Shall I come vnto you with a rodde, or in loue, and the spirit of meeknesse?* Hence ariseth another propertie; it bridleth the tongue, and the outward man, either by silence, as Christ beeing prouoked, *was dumbe, and opened not his mouth, Isai.*53.7. *was silent, and answered not a word, Luke* 23.9. or by a soft and gentle answer, which *asswageth wrath, Prou.* 15.1. There is great reason why men should restore their brethren in all meekenesse: for without it there is nothing but swelling, and faction, but troubles and tragedies. Againe, as meeknesse is necessary for euery Christian, *Coloss.* 2.12. *Titus* 3.2. so is it most necessary for him that would fruitfully, and effectually reprooue. Hence it is that the Apostle commaunds vs, to *instruct them in meeknesse, that are contrary minded,* 2.*Tim.*2.25.

Motiues to inforce this dutie, are these.

First, the exhortation and example of Christ, *to bee followers of him,* 1.*Cor.*11.1. who was *lowly and meeke, Matt.*11.29. for *he was led as a sheepe to the slaughter, and like a lambe dumbe before his shearer, so opened he not his mouth, Isa.*53.7. *When he was reuiled, reuiled not againe; when he suffred, he threatned not,* 1.*Pet.*2.23. as it may appeare by that meeke answer, *If I haue euill spoken, beare witnesse of the euill; but if I haue well spoken, why smitest thou me? Iohn* 18.23. *Paul* hath no stronger argument to exhort the Corinthians, then *by meeknesse and gentlenesse of Christ,* 2.*Cor.*10.1.

Secondly, it is a vertue which God doeth make great account of, 1. *Peter* 3.4. *A meeke and quiet spirit, is before God, a thing much set by.*

Thirdly, God hath made excellent promises to them that are of a meeke and humble spirit, that *he will guide them in iudgement, and teach them in his wayes, Psalm* 25.9. That *they shall bee hid in the day of the Lords wrath, Zeph.* 2.3. That *they shall inherite the earth, Matth.*5.5.

Fourthly,

Fourthly, consider the comfortable effects, and the good that comes thereby. A soft, meeke, and mild answer, *turneth away wrath*, *Prou.* 15.1. Meeke, and gentle behauiour, *heapeth coales of fire vpon our enemies head, Rom.* 12 20. *A soft tongue breaketh the bones, Prou.* 25. 15. See the example of *Gideon* appeasing the Midianites, *Iudg.* 8.1. &c. and *Abigail* pacifying *Dauid*, 1 *Sam.* 25.

Fiftly, without meeknesse, we cannot sauingly heare the word, either read, or preached, *Iames* 1.21.

ἐν πνεύματι πραότητος. i. ἐν πραότητι ἥτις ἐστ χάρισμα τοῦ ἁγίου πνεύματος. Ocumen.

It is further said, wee must restore *in the spirit of meeknesse.* The word *spirit* is added, because it proceeds from the spirit of God, who is both the worker and contriuer thereof: as on the contrarie, *the spirit of Iealousie, Numb* 5.14 *the spirit of errour*, 1. *Ioh.* 4 6. *the spirit of vncleanesse, Zach.* 13.2. *the spirit of giddines, Isa.* 19.14. *the spirit of slumber, Isa.* 29.14 are so tearmed, because they proceed from a wicked spirit. So quicke motions, sudden perturbations, strong affections, proceeding either from the Spirit of God, or of Sathan, are termed by the name of *spirit*. Hence we learne that the holy Ghost is authour not onely of *meekenes*, but of all sanctifying graces, and therefore is called *the spirit of wisdome, and vnderstanding; the spirit of counsel and strength; the spirit of knowledge, and of the feare of the Lord, Isa.* 11. *verse* 2. Secondly, this teacheth vs, that all true vertues are wrought onely by the operation of Gods spirit in vs: for though there be diuersities of gifts, yet it is the same spirit, 1. *Corinthians* 12. *verse* 4. and therefore the vertues of the Heathen are but glittering sinnes.

Thirdly, that when wee see the gifts or graces of God in our selues or others, we returne all the praise and glory to God, from whom they proceede, ascribing nothing to our selues.

Fourthly, this shewes, to whom we must haue recourse in our neede, namely, not to the virgin *Mary*, nor any Saint (who stand in as great need of the fauour of God, as our selues) but to God alone, who is the fountaine of grace, *Ierem.* 2.13.

Lastly, in that the spirit is set before meeknesse, it shewes that the spirit of God is present with his graces, to inspire them, to cherish and increase them. Therefore the commandement, *Quench not the spirit*, 1. *Thess.* 5.19. is to be obeyed, if we will retaine the graces of God.

Thus much of the dutie. The reasons vsed by the Apostle, to enforce this dutie follow, to be considered, and they are two. The first is implied in the word *Brethren*] which is of great force to perswade vs to vse moderation, lenitie, and gentlenesse. *Abraham* could vse no stronger argument to pacifie *Lot*, then this, *Let there*

*there be no ſtriſe betweene thee and me,for we are brethren,Gen.*13.8.*Moſes* vſed it as a motiue to accord two Ebrewes : *Sirs, ye are brethren ; why doe you wrong one to another? Act.*7.26.For it is a ſhame that thoſe whom nature hath ſo neerely conioyned, ſhould be ſo farre diſioyned in affection. But the reaſon beeing taken from ſpirituall brethren, ſuch as are not onely *brethren in the fleſh* but alſo *in the Lord*, hauing the ſame God for their Father, the ſame Church for their mother, Chriſt for their elder brother, being begotten by the ſame immortal ſeed, waſhed by the lauer of one new birth, conglutinate by the ſinewes of the ſame faith, nouriſhed by the milke of the ſame word ; is ſo much the ſtronger, by how much grace is a ſtraiter bond, then nature: therefore *Paul* would haue vs reſtore one another in the ſpirit of meekenes, becauſe we are *brethren.* Nay, perſons excommunicate, are not to be accounted as enemies, but to be admoniſhed as brethren, 2.*Theſſ.*3.15. The reaſon why men vſe no more mildneſſe in their reproofes, is, becauſe they forgette themſelues to be brethren, or conſider not that they haue to deale with their brethren: as *Ioſephs* brethren, who conſidering him as an enemie, ſaid one to another, *Behold, this dreamer commeth, come therefore, let vs kill him, Gen.* 37.v.19.20. But when they conſider him as their brother, they ſay, *Come, and let vs ſell him vnto the Iſhmaelites, and let not our hands be vpon him: for he is our brother, and our fleſh*.v.27.

The ſecond reaſon, is in theſe words, *Conſidering thy ſelfe, leſt thou alſo be tempted.* And it is taken from the conſideration of our owne eſtate, that we are ſubiect to fall, and to fall into temptation, as well as others: and therefore we ought to deale with them in all meekenes, as we would be dealt withall in the like caſe. The words are laide downe by way of admonition or aduiſe, and they carrie a double ſenſe: either thus, *Conſidering thy ſelfe*, that is, looking to thy ſelfe: *leaſt thou alſo be tempted*, that is, leaſt thou offend, and ſin in beeing too ſeuere a cenſurer of thy brother, in reproouing ſinne with ſinne. Or thus, *Conſider thy ſelfe*, that is, thine owne frailtie, how thou maieſt eaſily be ouertaken with the ſame, the like, or a greater ſinne, ſeeing thou maieſt be taken in the diuells ſnare, and deceiued with his pleaſant baites, as well as he was : therefore deale as mildly with him, as thou wouldeſt other ſhould deale mercifully with thee. Here *Paul* forbiddeth vs not to conſider the actions of our brethren, for we are to conſider one another; Firſt, that we may auoid the contagion of euill example, *Marke them diligently which cauſe diuiſion and offences, and auoid them. Rom.*16.17.Secondly, that we may be able to reprooue and cenſure them. *Conſider the matter, conſult, and giue ſentence. Iudg.*19.30. Thirdly, that we may follow their

their good example. *Looke on them which walke ſo, as yee haue vs for example, Philip.* 3.17. *Let vs conſider one another, to prouoke vnto loue, and to good workes, Hebr.* 10,24. But he would haue vs, eſpecially to conſider our ſelues, that by the conſideration of our owne weakeneſſe, wee might learne more mildneſſe towards others in our reproofes: for ſeeing we ſtand in need of mercy, we ought to deale mercifully: and ſeeing God forgiueth vs innumerable ſinnes, wee ought to forgiue ſeuen times, yea, ſeuentie times ſeuen times: ſeeing he forgiueth vs ten thouſand talents, wee ought to forgiue an hundreth pence, *Matth.* 18.32,33. *Obiect.* The Phariſie conſidered himſelfe, when as hee ſaid, *Lord, I thanke thee, that I am not as other men, thus and thus, or like this Publican, Luke* 18.11. and yet he is reprooued by our Sauiour Chriſt. *Anſwer.* True it is: for he onely conſidered his owne ſuppoſed vertues, which hee ſhould not haue conſidered, but forgotten, though they had bene true vertues indeed, according to Chriſts precept, *Matth.* 6.3. *Let not thy left hand know what thy right hand doeth:* and *Pauls* practiſe, *Philip.* 3.13. *I forget that which is behind*: and neuer ſo much as lightly conſidered his owne ſinnes, which *Paul* would haue vs to conſider, and therefore he is reprooued.

Paul would haue vs conſider our ſelues, becauſe the ſerious conſideration of our owne weakenes, wil mooue vs to practiſe this duty of meekenes: for as we helpe vp thoſe that are fallen, releeue the diſtreſſed, pitie the afflicted, burie the dead, &c. becauſe we conſider our ſelues in them, that their caſe may be ours: So we ought to reſtore thoſe that are fallen, in all meeknes; becauſe we may fall, and be ouertaken as well as they: the rather, becauſe God himſelfe in correcting and reproouing vs, doth deſcend to our weakenes, *and conſider that we are but fleſh, and a winde that paſſeth, and commeth not againe, Pſalm.* 78.39. and Chriſt became like vnto vs in all things, and was tempted in like ſort (yet without ſinne) that he might be a mercifull, and a faithfull high Prieſt, and might be touched with a ſenſe of our infirmities, *Hebr.* 2.17,18. and 4.15. *Obiect.* He therfore that knowes aſſuredly he cannot be ouercome by temptation, is not to reprooue in the ſpirit of meekenes. *Anſ.* No man is ſure, and therefore no man can be ſecure. Againe, though a man know he cannot totally nor finally fall away, yet ſeeing he doth finde by experience, that he cannot ouercome without much adoe, without much ſtriuing and wraſtling, nay oftentimes not without reſiſting vnto blood: he ought to vſe more meekenes and mildneſſe, conſidering with what difficultie he ouercame: Our Sauiour Chriſt learned by experience how hard a thing it was to ouercome temptations,

tations, that he might haue a fellow-feeling of our infirmities. Therefore spirituall men must remember, that they were once carnal, euen babes in Christ: those that are strong must consider that they were once weake: old men that are graue and staied, must call to mind that once they were in the heate of their youth, and what difficulties encountred them, and with that contention they passed the vanitie of that age: and so they shall the better reprooue others in the spirit of meekenes, if they looke themselues in the glasse of their example: this is *Pauls* reason, why we should *shew all meeekenes to all men, because we our selues were in times past, vnwise, disobedient, &c.* *Tit.* 3. 1. 3.

Lastly, marke here how *Paul* changes the number: for hauing said, *Ye that are spirituall, restore &c.* in the plurall number, here he saith, *considering thy selfe*, in the singular, and not *your selues*: *lest thou also be tempted*, and not *you*: which he doth not through rudenesse of speech, as some of the ancient Diuines haue thought: but with great iudgment he vseth a familiar Hebraisme, changing the number. First to giue the greater force and to set the sharper edge vpon his admonition. For that which is spoken to all, is spoken to none. Secondly, to shew how hard a thing it is for a man to consider him selfe. It is naturall for men to spie motes in other mens eyes, and not to perceiue beames in their owne, *Mat*, 7. 3. to looke outward at others, not inward at themselues. Like *Plutarchs Lamiæ*, or *fayries* which carried their eies in their heads when they went abroad, but when they came home put them vp in a boxe. In doing good and being beneficial, we must not so much consider our selues, *Phil.* 2. 4. but in iudgeing and reproouing, we ought to begin with our selues.

Hierom in hunc locum.

For the better vnderstanding of the doctrine of brotherly correction, and christian reproofe, I will handle these foure questions: I. who are to be reprooued? II. for what? III. by whome? IIII. in what manner?

I. Who are to be reprooued?

Ans. All that are *brethren*: for so our Sauiour Christ saith, *If thy brother sinne against thee, reproove him betweene thee and him*, *Math.* 18. 16. And S. *Paul* saith. *Brethren of any man &c.* The name *Brethren* is taken foure waies in Scripture, as *Ierome* hath well obserued against *Heluidius*. I. for those that are brethren by nature, as *Iacob* and *Esau*; the 12. Patriarkes; *Andrew & Peter*; *Iames* and *Iohn*. II. for those that are of affinity. Thus the kinsemen of Christ, are called *his brethren*: which the *Helvidians* not obseruing, thought they had beene his naturall brethren, by the virgin *Mary*: Thus *Abraham* and *Lot* are

cal-

called *brethren*, *Gen.*13.v.8. 14. though *Lot* was but his brothers sonne, *Gen.*14.12. Thus *Iacob* the nephew of *Laban*, calleth himselfe *his brother*, *Gen.*29.12. and so *Laban* calleth him, verse. 15. III. for men of the same countrey. Thus all the Iewes are called brethren one to another. *Deut.* 17 verse 15. *From among thy brethren shalt thou make a king ouer thee:* and, *Deut.*23,19. *Thou shalt not giue to vsury to thy brother*, and, *Rom.*9.1. *Paul* saith, *he could wish himselfe anathema, or accursed, for his brethren*, that is, the Iewes. IIII. for those of the same religion. 1. *Ioh.*3.16. *We must lay downe our liues for our brethren*, *Math.*23.8. *One is your Doctor*, to wit Christ, *and all ye are brethren.* 1. *Cor.*5.11. *If any that is called a brother be a fornicatour, with such a one eate not.* To these we may adde a fift acception: for all those that are confederate, or otherwise ioyned together by the bond of nature, humanitie, societie, or friendship. Thus *Ahab* calleth *Benhadad his brother*, that is, his friend, 1. *Kings* 20.32, 33. Thus *Simeon* and *Leui* are called *brethren in wickednesse*, that is, Gen.49.5.
confederate in euil. Thus all men are called *brethren* one to another by reason of the bond of nature, *Genes.*9.5. *at the hand of a mans brother, will I require the life of man.* In all countries, those that associate themselues together in warre, after a speciall manner are called *sworne brethren.* Now wee must not restraine the word *brethren*, to those that are brethren by nature, or by affinitie, or by countrey: neither inlarge it to all those that are brethren by the bond of nature; but onely to those that are brethren in the fourth acception, that is to say, *brethren in religion*, or *brethren in the Lord*, (though they be *false brethren*) if they be brethren at least in outward profession: for reproofe being a part of *Ecclesiasticall discipline*, belongeth not to those that are out of the visible Church, as to Iewes, Turkes, Pagans: because our Sauiour Christ saith, *If hee heare them not, tell the Church: and if hee will not heare the Church, let him bee vnto thee as an heathen man, and a Publican.* Which cannot be vnderstood of him that is a heathen or Pagan already. And *Paul* saith, 1. *Cor.* 5.11. *If any that is called a brother*, that is, a Christian, *bee a fornicator, &c.* and then he addes in the next verse, *what haue I to doe to iudge them that are without?* that is, such as are no members of the church, to whom *Ecclesiasticall Discipline* reacheth not; *Doe not ye iudge them that are within?* that is, such as are of the visible Church, such as doe subiect themselues to the censure and discipline of the Church. It belongs therfore to those that are of the Church, at least in shew; but specially to those that are of the same particular Church, liuing vnder the same particular gouernement. Albeit the case may so fall out, that those of another Church, professing the

same religion with vs, may bee reprooued, and censured: yea one Church may admonish another, for they being members one of another, are to procure the good one of another, as *Paul* teacheth by the similitude of *the head* and *the members* of the same bodie, 1. *Cor.* 12. Therefore all that are in the bosome of the Church, euen the mightie Princes and Potentates of the earth, are subiect to reproofe, if they offend: thus *Nathan* the Prophet, reprooued *Dauid*, 2.*Sam.* 12. and *Azarias* the Priest rebuked *Vzziah*, 2.*Chron.* 26.18. and *Paul* reproued *Peter* to his face, *Gal.* 2.11. Therfore those men, yea, those Magistrates, or Monarchs, that cannot endure the least reproofe, and wil not yeeld their necks to Christ his yoke, and their backs to the rod of *Ecclesiasticall censure*, are greatly to be censured: for herein they contemne the ordinance of God. Let them consider, that they are not better then King *Dauid*, who hauing sinned, patiently endured reproofe by *Nathan*. Let them remember how king *Vzziah* was stricken with leprosie for resisting God in the ministery. And heere the Popish sort come to be taxed, who exempt their cleargy men (as they call them) from reproofes, and Ecclesiasticall proceedings, in thrusting them into some one monastery or other, lest their exemplary punishment should be a blemish or disparagement to their order and profession: whereas *Paul* would haue the Ministers and Elders, yea all superiours, to be reprooued as well as others, so it be done in order, and with due respect (as after I will shew.) Thus *Paul* biddeth the *Colossians*, that they should say to *Archippus*, *Take heed to thy ministery, that thou hast receiued in the Lord, that thou fulfill it*, *Col.* 4.17.

II. Wee are bound to reprooue all that are in the Church, to whom we owe dutie of loue: but we are to loue our superiours, as much, if not more then others: therefore we are bound to reproue them as well as others. III. There is greater reason wee should reproue them then others. 1. Because they being in higher place, are in greater danger of falling then others, and therefore haue more need of admonitions and reproofes. 2. Because they haue many that will flatter them, but few or none that will, or dare reprooue them.

It will be said, all are not to bee reprooued which liue in the Church; for some be scorners, who (as *Salomon* saith) must not bee reprooued. And our Sauiour Christ forbiddeth vs, *to cast pearles before swine*, *Matth.* 7.6. I answer, that onely open scorners, contemners, persecuters of the word, are to be excepted: otherwise all wicked men are to bee censured and rebuked. For first, Christ speaketh of manifest contemners of religion, when he saith that *they are like swine, which trample precious pearles vnder their feete:* and of persecutours, when he saith, that *like dogges they returne againe, and all to rend them.* Secondly, Christ being here vpon earth, did not hinder the Pharisies, Sadducees, Publicanes, and harlots, from comming to his Sermons: much lesse would he debarre them of this censure of the Church. Thirdly, the woman of Syrophenissa (though called *a dog) yet eateth of the crummes that fall from the childrens table, Matth. 15.27.* Fourthly, *Paul* did often admonish and rebuke the Corinthians, though they were carnall and fleshly minded: therefore all men, though neuer so publike and notorious offenders, (if they bee not open scorners, or persecutours of the knowne truth) are to be reprooued.

Obiect. Profane men, which notoriously offend and scandalize the Church by their wicked liues, haue no fellowship with Christ, but are to be accounted as dogs out of the Church.

I answer, 1. They are not to be accounted dogs, which doe acknowledge their faults, the greatnesse of their sinne, and the merit of Christ: for such a dog was the Canaanitish woman, who was a true beleeuer. 2. This is agreeable to S. *Pauls* practise, who did admonish those among the Corinthians, that were carnall, and did not at the very first excommunicate them, or yet suspend them: and so answerably he commands *Titus*, that he should rebuke the *Cretians sharpely, or precisely*, for their notable lying and idlenesse, *Titus* 1.12. ἀποτόμως. 3. Christ denieth not pardon to them that fall by *recidiuation*, but would haue them forgiuen, not onely till seuen times, but till seuentie times seuen times; and *Paul* speakes indefinitely in this place, that we should *restore him that falleth by occasion into any offence*, not specifying how often we should forgiue. 4. We must distinguish betwixt the Magistrates sword, and the keyes of the Church: notorious offendours when they repent, are to be receiued into the bosome of the Church, as sonnes of the Church: yet for all that they may, nay they ought to be punished by the magistrate: as the good thiefe (albeit a member of Christ) yet iustly punished for his offence.

II. For what faults are men to be reproued?

Men are to be reprooued for euery knowne sinne: This is manifest from the end of reproofes, which is the gaining of our brother, that he perish not in his sinne: but euery sinne is of this nature and quality, that it bringeth death, being not repented of: therfore for euery sinne a man is to bee reprooued. Secondly, our Sauiour doeth not restraine this precept to priuate iniuries, because in that case, we are to follow another rule. *Resist not euill. Blesse, and curse not. Doe good to them that hate you, &c.* Thirdly, it is extended to euery ſinne, becauſe hee which ſinneth againſt God, or the whole Church, ſinneth alſo againſt thee, and euery particular member of the Church. For euery Chriſtian ought more to be affected for the ſinnes committed againſt God, or the body of the Church, then for thoſe that are perſonally, and directly intended or done againſt himſelfe: therefore Chriſt ſpeaketh not onely of ſinnes, as they are priuate wrongs, iniuries, or damages; but as they are diſhonorable to the maieſtie of God, ſcandalous to the Church, pernitious to him that committed them; not onely as they offend him againſt whom they are committed. It will be obiected, that Chriſts commandement is to be vnderſtood of thoſe that wrong vs, when he ſaith, *If thy brother ſin againſt thee.* I anſwer, that phraſe and forme of ſpeach *(againſt thee)* is not meant only of priuate wrongs offered vs, (as I haue ſaid) but of any ſinne committed againſt God: for in euery knowne ſin, we are in a ſort wronged: 1. Becauſe we ought to be ſo zealous of the glory of God, that wee ought to be more grieued when men ſinne againſt God, then when they ſin againſt vs: yea, we muſt make Gods quarel, our owne quarell. 2. Becauſe he which ſinnes in our preſence, doth, or at leaſt ought to offend vs. As *Hezechiah* was offended when he heard the blaſphemies of *Rabſhekah*, 2. *King.* 19. 1. and *Dauid*, whoſe eyes powred out riuers of waters, becauſe men kept not Gods law, *Pſal.* 119. verſe 136. and *Lot*, who vexed his righteous ſoule, in ſeeing and hearing the abhominations of the Sodomites, 2. *Pet.* 2. 8. For to expound theſe words [*againſt thee*] thou being priuie to it, is farre from the meaning of the text, neither can the phraſe be ſhewed in that ſenſe.

Now that men are to be reprooued for knowne ſinnes committed againſt God, of what nature, quality, and condition ſoeuer they be, beſides the former reaſons, it is manifeſt *Leuiticus* 19. 17. *Thou ſhalt not hate thy brother in thine heart, but thou ſhalt plainely rebuke him, and ſhalt not ſuffer ſinne to reſt vpon him.* Therefore a man is to bee rebuked for euery ſinne. The Apoſtle whereſoeuer hee ſpeaketh of reproofes, neuer reſtraines it to one kinde, but extends it to all knowne ſinnes. 1. *Cor.* 5. he reprooues the inceſtuous perſon for his inceſt, and excommunicateth him being impenitent. So in this place, *if a man be fallen by occaſion into any offence*, he ſaith not, this or that offence, but in generall, *into any offence*, whether in life or doctrine, by euill example, or otherwiſe, againſt the firſt, or ſecond Table. Yet this is ſo to bee vnderſtood, as that iniuries and wrongs offred vs, are not to be excluded: for euen for them alſo, are

men

men to be reprooued. I. It is the purpose of our Sauiour Christ, *Matthew* 18. to teach this very point, for hauing taught, *Matt.* 18. verse 6. that none should offend or scandalize his brother; in the 10. verse, he shewes what is to be done, if any man did offend his brother, by iniuring or wronging him: to wit, that hee is to reprooue him. II. Hee maketh him that suffered the wrong, a witnesse, not an accuser, when he saith, *If hee heare thee not, take yet with thee one or two, that by the mouth of two or three witnesses, euery word may be confirmed*, *Matth.* 18. 16. He biddeth him take *one or two*, that so it may bee confirmed *by the testimonie*, not of one or two, but *of two or three*: therefore the partie offended is one of the witnesses. III. If it were lawfull to reprooue men for iniuries offered vs, what course should hee take that is secretly wronged, none being priuie to the wrong but himselfe, and the partie offending? Thus men would be imboldned to sinne, seeing they could by no meanes be controlled, and so men might frustrate the commandement of Christ. I adde further, that he which is iniured, is fitter to reproue him that offered the iniury then any other. I. Because the offence, both for substance and circumstance, is better knowne vnto him, then to any other. II. Because the reproofe (in all likelihood) will take the better place, when as the offender shall haue coales of fire heaped vpon his head, when he shal see, that the partie wronged, is desirous of his good, and ready to requite good for euil, in seeking his amendment, whereas hee sought his hurt. And whereas it might seeme, that it sauoureth of reuenge, to reproue those that wrong vs, I answer, though many in reprouing reuenge themselues, yet the one may bee done without the other; and the right vse of a thing is not to be neglected, because of the abuse thereof.

Obiect. Authors of heresies, schismes, dissentions are to be auoided *Rom.* 16. 17, therefore not to be reprooued, *Ans.* Generall places of Scripture, are to be expounded, according to particular limitation in other places: now that general text, *Rom.* 16. 15 is restrained and limited, *Tit.* 3. 10. *Auoid an heretike after once or twise admonition.*

Obiection. *Paul* commands the *Corinthians*, that without any more adoe, they should proceede forthwith to the publike censure of excommunication against the incestuous person: and as it may seeme, without any former reproofe, 1. *Cor.* 5. Besides, hee commaunds that wee should not eat, that is, familiarly conuerse with notorious persons of scandalous life, 1. *Cor.* 5 11. and that wee should *withdraw our selues from euery brother that walketh inordinately,*

2.*Theſſ.*3.6. *Anſwer.* *Pauls* practiſe is not contrary to Chriſts precept. He purpoſed indeed to excommunicate the inceſtuous perſon, if he perſiſted in his ſinne, yet marke how; *in the name, and by the power of our Lord Ieſus Chriſt*, 1.*Cor.*5.4. in which words the forme of proceeding againſt him is limited, and that according to Chriſts inſtitution, *Matth.*18. *the name and power of Chriſt*, ſignifying the word and inſtitution of Chriſt. 2. *Paul* doeth plainely expound himſelfe in other places, what his practiſe was in that behalfe, as 2. *Corinth.*13.1,2. where hee ſignifieth, that hee did not excommunicate vncleane perſons, fornicatours, wantons (mentioned chap.12.21.) before the third admonition; making his third comming vnto them, in ſtead of three admonitions, or witneſſes againſt them.

It will be ſaid, that *Paul* threatneth, when hee commeth he will not ſpare *the reſt*, 2.*Cor.*13.2. therefore it ſeemeth hee was reſolued to excommunicate them without any former proceeding againſt them. *Anſwer.* When *Paul* ſaith, *I write to them which haue ſinned, and to all others, that if I come againe, I will not ſpare.* By *all others*, he meaneth not ſome which he purpoſed to excommunicate without former admonition, (for in writing this Epiſtle to them, hee admoniſheth them all to repent, leſt when he came he ſhould vſe ſeueritie) but thoſe which liued ſecurely in the open breach of the law, to whom he threatned to come with a rod, if they did not amend, 1.*Cor.*4.21. and when hee now againe admoniſheth, threatning that if he come the third time, he wil not ſpare. Beſides this, *Paul* ſhould be vnconſtant and vnlike himſelfe, if he ſhould admoniſh vncleane perſons, fornicatours, wantons, and that three times before excommunication: and ſhould at the firſt excommunicate certain others without any precedent admonition.

Ἐπιτιμία. 3. The word there vſed, ſignifieth reproofe in word, as it is taken, *Luke* 17. *If thy brother ſinne againſt thee, rebuke him*: therefore *the reproofe by many, or of many* mentioned, 2.*Cor.*2.6. may ſignifie as well the graue, ſerious, and effectuall reproofe of the Church, by which the inceſtuous perſon was reclaimed from his ſinne, and ſo preuented the thunderbolt of excommunication; as the reall eiection out of the Church: and thoſe words, verſe 10. *if you forgiue any thing*, may as well ſignifie receiuing into fauour and familiaritie before excommunication, vpon his repentance, as reſtitution after excommunication.

4. Be it granted, hee were indeed excommunicate (as it is moſt probable he was) yet hence it cannot be inferred, that they did proceed againſt him without precedent admonition. The Scripture is ſilent

ſilent in this point. Therefore the reaſon is not good; it is not recorded, therefore it was not practiſed.

5. Though the Apoſtle command that we ſhould haue no familiaritie with inordinate liuers, 2.*Theſſ*.3.6. but that wee withdraw our ſelues from them, yet hee addes withall, that if there were any amongſt them that would not obey his ſayings, they ſhould note him by a letter, verſe 14. and he expreſſely commandeth that they ſhould *admoniſh the inordinate*, 1.*Theſſ*.5.14. for that was his practiſe, as it may appeare, 2.*Theſſ*.3. *Thoſe that are ſuch*, that is, inordinate liuers, *wee exhort and commaund by our Lord Ieſus Chriſt, that they worke with quietneſſe, and eat their owne bread.*

III. Who are to reproove?

It is a dutie which concerneth all men; our Sauiour Chriſt ſaith, *If thy brother ſinne againſt thee, reproove him*: and the commandement is generall, *Leuit*. 19.17. *Thou ſhalt not hate thy brother in thy heart, but ſhalt rebuke him plainely*: now all Chriſtians are brethren, (as I haue ſhewed,) therefore all men are bound to reproove their brethren, as occaſion ſhall ſerue. Secondly, all Chriſtans are members of the ſame bodie whereof Chriſt is the head, therefore they are to helpe and further one another, as members of the naturall body do: and this is done by admonition and reprehenſion. Thirdly, the bond of charitie tieth all men to help their brethren, in what they can for their good, and therefore (if need be) to reproue them. And albeit ſome may ſeeme to bee vnfit or vnworthy reproouers of others, being tainted with as great, or greater ſinnes themſelues, and ſo cannot caſt out motes out of other mens eyes, they hauing beames in their owne; yet wee muſt know, that ſinne freeth none from this dutie: Indeed none ought to reproove, either with ſcandall to others, or with hurt and hinderance of him that is reprooued; yet no man is exempted from this dutie. For euery man ought to be cleare and blameleſſe, ſpecially of open crimes, that ſo hee may more freely and fruitfully reproove his neighbour; but though he be not, yet he remaineth ſtill bound to the performance of this dutie. Our Sauiour ſaith not, that hee which hath a beame in his eye, is therefore freed from pulling foorth the mote out of his brothers eye; but, *firſt caſt out the beame out of thine owne eye, and then ſhalt thou ſee to pull out the mote out of thy brothers eye.* They therefore are ſeuerely to bee cenſured, nay deepely to bee condemned, who ſay with *Cain, Am I my brothers keeper?* [Geneſ.4.9.] as though it concerned them not a whit whether hee ſinke or ſwim; as though euery man were to looke to himſelfe alone, for his owne behoofe and benefit, and not vpon the things of his brethren, for their [Philip.2.4.]

good? or as though God had not made euery man a guardian to his brother? The dimme candle light of corrupt nature, condemneth these men, which teacheth that he which may saue, and doth not, doeth in effect as much as kill, or destroy. The dutie therefore lieth vpon all, but chiefly vpon the Pastours and Ministers of the word: for they are to inquire into the liues of men, specially of those that are committed and commended to their charge: for which cause they are called the Lords ouerseers, or watchmen, *Ezech.* 33. and 34. *And if they doe not strengthen the weake, heale the sicke, binde vp the broken, bring againe that which was driuen away, nor seeke that which is lost, &c. he will require his sheepe at their hands. Ezech.* 34. verse 4.10. *Paul* inioynes the Pastours of the Church of Ephesus, that *they should take heed to themselues, and to the flocke whereof the holy Ghost had made them ouerseers, Actes* 20.28. and hee commaundeth *Timothie*, that hee *should bee instant in season, and out of season; that hee should improoue, rebuke, exhort with all long suffering and doctrine, 2.Tim.* 4.2. and *Titus*, that *hee rebuke and exhort with all authoritie, Titus* 2,15.

Further, it is to be obserued, that though all men are bound to reprooue their neighbours if they offend, yet in fiue cases they are not bound.

I. If a man be ignorant of the offence. For a man that reproo-ueth another, must be certaine of the fault, otherwise he doth purchase to himselfe a blot: and priuate persons are not to prie into other mens actions, that so they may haue matter to reproue, *Prou.* 24.15. For wee are bound to reproooue, as wee are bound to giue almes: now wee are not bound in giuing almes, to seeke some, to whom we may giue; if we giue to those whom we meet, that stand in need of our almes, wee haue done our dutie. The like is in reproofes. And although reproofe bee a debt which wee owe our neighbour; yet it is no debt due to any priuate person (for then we were bound to search out the partie, and discharge the debt) but it is a publike debt which we owe to all: and therefore it is not necessary we should seeke them out. If we discharge it to those we meet withall, it is sufficient. S. *Augustine* saith well, *Admonet Dominus non negligere inuicem peccata nostra, non quaerendo quod reprehendas, sed videndo quod corrigas.*

De verb. Dom. Serm. 16.

II. If hee haue repented of his fact, he is not to be reprooued, for the end of reproofe, is to reclaime him; therefore if he be reclaimed already, there is no place left for reproofe: although the Magistrate may punish and correct him in regard of the common good.

III. A man is not to reproove, if hee be certaine his reproofe will doe no good: for when the end ceaſeth, all things tending to the end, doe likewiſe ceaſe; therefore if there be no hope of amendment (which is the end of reproofe) reproofe is to be omitted; ſpecially if it bee ſo farre from bettering the partie, that it make him much worſe. *Salomon* ſaith, *Hee which inſtructeth a ſcorner, getteth himſelfe reproach, and he that reprooueth a wicked man, purchaſeth to himſelfe a blot, Prou.9.7.* And then he addes in the next verſe, *Rebuke not a ſcorner, leſt he hate thee; rebuke a wiſe man, and hee will loue thee.* And verily it were great folly to ſpend labour in vaine, in telling them of their faults, when our ſchooling wil not better them, but incenſe them more and more: It were better to bee ſilent, or to ſeparate from them, then to ſtirre vp hornets, or to thruſt our hands into a waſpes neaſt. It is well ſaid of one, that he which ſhall beſtow the Muſcul. ſeeds of wholſome admonitions on ſuch curſed and vnprofitable ground, ſhall reap nothing for his paines, but the thornes of mocks and reproaches.

It will bee ſaid, the Iudge ceaſeth not to puniſh malefactours, though they bee not bettered by their puniſhment; therefore ſeeing brotherly correction is commaunded, it muſt not be omitted, though the partie reprooued be not bettered, but offended therby, and made worſe. I anſwer. The reaſon is nothing alike; for the Iudge in puniſhing, doth principally intend the good of the Common wealth, which commeth by chaſtiſing, or by cutting off malefactors, though they themſelues be nothing bettered: but the end of reproofe, is the amendment, and good of him that is reprooued: therefore a man may not be reprooued, except it be for his priuate good, though the Magiſtrate may puniſh him in regard of the common good.

IV. Reproofe may be omitted, if it be certaine that the partie will either preſently redreſſe his fault without reproofe: or that ſome others wil admoniſh him therof, whom it doth more neerely concerne. As the giuing of almes may be omitted, if it bee certaine that the partie that is in want, will prouide for himſelfe, or that he will be ſufficienly relieued by others.

V. If it may bee done more conueniently and profitably another time, it may be omitted for the time. Except in theſe fiue caſes, he that doeth not reprooue his brother, is guilty of his ſinne, *Leuit.5.1.*

IIII. Point. *In what manner are men to be reprooued?*

The manner to be obſerued in reproouing, I will lay downe in ten rules.

I. A

I. A man muſt ſo reprooue his brother, as that it may be moſt for the aduancement of Gods glory, beſt for the winning of him to God, and leaſt to the defaming of him abroad in the world: and that it may appeare vnto him, that he doth it of loue (aiming at nothing but his good) not of any malicious humour, or ſiniſter affection of reuenge, or vaine-glory, &c. and that this may be done, two things muſt be practiſed. Firſt, he that reprooueth another, muſt pray that God would ſo guide his tongue, and mooue the others heart, that his reproofe may be profitable vnto him: for without Gods bleſſing our admonitions are but words ſpoken in the wind, 1. *Iohn*, 5. v. 16. *If any ſee his brother ſin a ſin that is not vnto death, let him pray, &c.* Secondly, we may not traduce him to others, either before or after our reproofe, 1. *Pet.* 4. 8. This rule is generall: the reſt following are more ſpeciall.

II. Euery reproofe muſt be grounded vpon a certaine knowledge of the fault committed. For we may not goe vpon priuate ſurmiſes and ſuppoſes, or flying reports or and rumours blazed abroad: no nor vpon vehement ſuſpitions, or ſtrong preſumptions, *Deut.* 13. v. 14. for in ſo doing, we ſhall but offend the party, who knowes himſelfe to be innocent of the crime obiected, & purchaſe to our ſelues a blot of indiſcretiō, in being zealous without knowledge. Therefore for ſecret ſinnes, men are not to be reproou ed. *Secret* I call thoſe that are knowne onely to God, and the conſcience of the doer: or onely to others, but not to vs. This was practiſed by S. *Paul*, *Gal.* 2. 14. who reprooued not *Peter*, till he was throughly informed of his offence: which condemnes the common practiſe of the multitude, who cenſure and reprooue others, ſpecially publike perſons, as agiſtrates and Miniſters, vpon falſe reports, or wicked ſurmiſes, when as no accuſation may be admitted againſt ſuch, vnder two or three witneſſes. 1. *Tim.* 5. 20. Yet a man may reprooue vpon credible informatiō, as *Paul* did the *Corinthians* for their contentions, grounding his reproofe vpon the report of the houſe of *Cloe*, 1. *Cor.* 1. 11. which he beleeued to be in true part, 1. *Cor.* 11. 18. If the report be not certaine, we muſt onely reproou e hypothetically, and not peremptorily.

III. In reproouing others, we muſt conſider our ſelues, ſpecially our owne weakenes, and beginne the reproofe in our ſelues, if not for the ſame fault we reprooue in our neighbour, yet for as great as that (if not a greater) in another kind: this maner of reproouing is inioyned by S. *Paul*, when he ſaith, *conſidering thy ſelfe, leſt thou alſo be tempted*: and a man is to conſider himſelfe in three reſpects: in regard of the *time paſt*, *preſent*, and *to come*: in regard of the *time paſt*, that he was as wicked,prophane,& graceleſſe as another: yea that he was (as the Apoſtle ſpeaketh) *darkeneſſe,and the child of wrath as wel as others*: *Paul* ſhewes the force of this conſideration, when he perſwades men to be ſoft and gentle,ſhewing all meekenes to all men: a reaſon taken from the conſideration of our owne frailties and ſins in time paſt. *for* (ſaith he) *we our ſelues alſo were in times paſt vnwiſe,diſobedient,deceiued,ſeruing the luſts and diuers pleaſures,liuing in maliciousneſſe and enuy,hatefull and hating one another,Tit*.3.v.2.3. In regard of the *time preſent*,that he is but a fraile man,ready to fall euery moment,that he is not able of himſelfe to thinke the leaſt good thought,much leſſe to reſiſt the leaſt temptation,and that whatſoeuer he is,he is it out of himſelfe,by grace in Chriſt,as *Paul* ſaith, *By the grace of God I am that I am.* So that were it not for this preuenting and cooperating grace, he would fall into as great enormities as other men. In regard of *the time to come, Conſider thy ſelfe, leſt thou alſo be tempted*: remember *Pauls* Item, 1.*Cor.* 10.v.12. *Let him that thinketh he ſtandeth,take heed leſt he fall*: for if thou haſt not bin ouertaken with the like ſinne, yet thou maieſt be hereafter: therefore as thou wouldeſt haue others to be compaſſionate towards thee, if thou were in the like caſe,ſo be thou to them. The not obſeruance of this rule,is the cauſe that there are ſo many cenſorious *Catoes*, ſo many ſeuere *Ariſtarchi* of others mens actions, ſo many that are ſharpe ſighted and Eagle eied,in ſpying motes in other mens eies: and as blind as moles or beetles,in diſcerning the great beams that are in their owne eies.

Aut ſumus, aut fuimus, vel poſtumus eſſe quod hic eſt.

IIII. It is very requiſite and expedient,that the reproouer be not tainted with the ſame,or the like fault which he reproueth in an other, leaſt it be ſaid vnto him, *Phyſitian cure thy ſelfe. Luk*.4. 13. *In that thou iudgeſt another, thou condemneſt thy ſelfe,Rom*.2.v.1. Therfore *Dauid* ſaith not, Let the wicked ſmite me,or let him that is as deep in fault as my ſelfe reprooue me: but *Let the righteous ſmite me, for that is a benefit, and let him reprooue mee, that ſhall be as pretious oile: that ſhall not be wanting to my head, Pſal.*141.v.5. For albeit in regard of the reproofe it ſelfe,it be not greatly materiall, yet it si not ſo expedient, nor ſo profitable in regard of the reproouer, 1. becauſe he ſeemeth vnworthy to reprooue another, who is to be reprooued himſelſelfe, beeing as deepe in fault as any: 2. becauſe it will be thought, that he which maketh no conſcience to redreſſe himſelfe, will not be ſo ready to reclaime others, of loue to their perſons,or hatred of their ſinnes,or zeale of Gods glory; but for pride, or buſineſſe in other mens matters, or vanity, or ſome ſuch ſiniſter ends.

V. All

V. All reproofes muſt be ſo miniſtred, as that the party reprooued may be brought to a true ſight of his ſinne: as alſo to a liuely ſenſe and feeling thereof, and ſo to a compunction of heart, by reaſon of it, and of the wrath of God, which attendeth vpon him for his ſinne; For the performance of this rule, we haue the example of God himſelfe, *Pſal.* 50. v. 21. *I will reprooue thee, and ſet thy ſinnes in order before thee*; as alſo the Prophet *Nathan*, who by the parable conuicted *Dauids* conſcience, and ſo made him condemne himſelf, 2. *Sam*, 12. And the precept of Saint *Paul*, commanding *Timothy*, that he ſhould ſo reprooue, as that he conuict the conſcience of the ſinne, when he ſaith, *Reprooue, rebuke, exhort with all long ſuffering & DOCTRINE*: now this is done by ſhewing the true meaning of the law, and the curſe of God annexed to euery breach thereof, and ſo by vnfolding the horrible greatneſſe of ſinne, to the conſcience of him whom we doe reprooue. For reproofes which are not thus qualified, are but cold and perfunctory, ſuch as was that of *Elie*, in reproouing his lewd ſonnes, *Why doe ye ſuch things? for of all this people, I heare euill reports of you: doe noe more my ſonnes; for it is no good report that I heare*, 1. *Sam.* 2. v. 23. 24. beeing a meanes rather to cheriſh ſinne in them, then to reclaime them from it. Theſe kinds of reproofes, not vnfitly may be compared to hot or haſty healing ſalues, which draw a faire ſkin one a fowle wound; which becauſe it is not ſoundly cured from the bottome, but ouerly healed vp, doth afterward apoſtemate or fiſtulate, and becometh more dangerous and deſperate then euer before.

2. Tim 4.2.

VI. The vineger of ſharpe reprehenſion, muſt be allaied and tempered with the oyle of milde and gentle exhortation; we may not onely vſe the *corraſiues of the law*, but withall we muſt apply the *cordialls of the Goſpell*: bitter pilles of reproofe, muſt bee ſugered ouer with louing & affectionate perſwaſion: leſt the patient abhor the phyſicke: euery man in this caſe is to follow the ſkilfull Chirurgeon, who doth not alway vſe *ſection* and *vſtion* in launcing the wound with ſharp inſtrumẽts, but mollifying ointments, mundifying waters, to clenſe and ſupple the wound, and heale the ſore. *Paul* ſaith *that the ſeruant of the Lord muſt be gentle toward all men: and that he muſt inſtruct with meekenes them that are contrary minded.* 2. *Tim.* 2. 25. 26. & in this place he commands the Galatians that they ſhold *reſtore their brethren with the Spirit of meekenes*. The word tranſlated [*reſtore*] is very emphatical: for it ſignifieth to ſet a bone that is broken, or any member of the body that is out of ioynt: and therefore we are to deale with a man that is fallen, and by his fal hath diſioynted ſome member of the new man, as the Chirurgeon doth with an arme or a leg that is broken,or out of ioynt,to handle it tenderly,and gently, so as it may bee most for his good, and least for his paine. More particularly,this may be done foure wayes.

1. When a man doeth propound the reproofe in his owne person, as *Paul* did, 1. *Corinth.* 4. 6. *Now these things, brethren, I haue figuratiuely applied vnto mine owne selfe and Apollos, for your sakes, that yee might learne by vs, that no man presume aboue that which is written, &c.*

2. When a man doeth not directly reprooue another in plaine tearmes,but closely shewes a mislike of the fact, and conuayeth a reproofe in an exhortation,and so lappeth vp pils (as it were) in sugar: as when a man sweares;not alwaies to say,*thou,&c.*but *yea and nay shall serue betwixt vs: what needs this vehemency betwixt vs two? I will as soone take your word,as your oath,&c.*

3. When the reproofe is propounded in a parable: as *Nathan* dealt with *Dauid*, 2.*Samuel* 12. and as our Sauiour Christ by the parable of the two sonnes reprooued the Pharisies, *Matthew* 21.28.

4. When we reprooue a man directly (as at the length *Nathan* did *Dauid, Thou art the man,* 2.*Sam.*12.7.) wee must so carrie our selues, as that the partie may see himselfe rather reproued by God, then by vs: and not to proceed bluntly to worke, to rebuke and censure at the very first: but to vse some preface before hand; as, that we doe that which we doe in loue of his person, for his good, wishing him well, both temporally, the reputation of his name, and eternally the saluation of his soule; and that wee consider our selues heerein, how that we may easily be ouertaken,as he was. These cautions obserued, the inferiour may reproue his superiour, as 2.*Kings* 5.13.

VII. Euery reproofe must bee fitted to the qualitie and condition of him whom we reprooue; and to the nature of the offence for which he is reprooued; we shall fit the reproofe to the person reprooued,if wee consider that a man may reprooue another foure waies. First,by *friendly admonition*: and thus one equall is to reproue another. Secondly, by *reuerent and submisse exhortation*: thus the yonger must reprooue the elder, the inferiour their superiours. It is Gods commandement that wee should *not rebuke an Elder, but exhort him as a father*, 1.*Tim.*5.1. And thus Kings and great Potentates are to bee reprooued, they being *Patres Patriæ*. That saying of the Philosopher, ἢ ἤκουσα, ἢ ᾔδεσα, hath place in this case. Thirdly, by *sharpe reprehension*: thus Elders or superiours are to reprooue their inferiours, specially, if the fact bee notorious, scandalous,

or

or dangerous. *Paul* commandeth *Titus* that he should *rebuke the Cretians,* ἀποτόμως, *sharpely, that they might be sound in the faith. Tit.* 1. 13. Fourthly, by *due chastisement and correction*: thus the superiours must reprooue their inferiours ouer whom they are set, as the father the child, the master the seruant, the Magistrate the subiect, &c. and thus the inferiour cannot reprooue his superiour, nor one equall another, though he doe it with neuer so great mildnes.

Secondly, we shall fit our reproofe to the offence committed, if in spirituall wisedome and discretion we put a difference betwixt sinne and sinne, as the Apostle teacheth vs, *Iud.*v.22,23. *Haue compassion on some putting difference: and other saue with feare, pulling them out of the fire.* Sinnes committed of humane frailty, or through ignorance, must be distinguished from those of malice, of pride, and presumption; both must be reprooued, yet after a different manner: for the one must be wonne with gentlenesse, the other with sharpnesse: the one with lenity, the other with seuerity; to the one we must come with the pleasant pipe of *Christ*, to the other with the lamentation of *Iohn Baptist.* To the one in the Spirit of *Elias*: to the other in the Spirit of *Moses*. When gentle admonition would take no place, Christ thundreth out threats against Corazin and Bethsaida. And *Paul* threatens seuerity, when lenity will doe no good. 2.*Cor.*13.

VIII. Euery reproofe must be administred in fitte time when we may doe the most good: therefore if in wisedome we shall foresee fitter opportunity to winne our brother, we are to take that time, and to omit the present: not to tell him of his fault beeing drunke, or in the heate of his passion, but after, when he commeth to himselfe, as *Abigail* dealt with *Nabal*. 1.*Samu.*25. For the commandement of God touching reproofe, being affirmatiue, bindeth not to all times, but onely to that which in spirituall discretion we shall iudge the fittest, both to reclaime him, and saue his credit. *Salomon* saith, *that a word spoken in due time, is like apples of gold, with pictures of siluer. Prou.*25.11. Now if this be true of a word spoken in due time, it is much more true of a reproofe deliuered in due season. *There is a time for all things. Ecclesiast.*3.1. And surely if euery thing that commeth to passe in the world, haue his set time, and opportunity, reproofe must needes haue his time and season.

IX. Secret sinnes knowne onely to thee or to a few, must bee reprooued secretly, betwixt thee and the party alone: they must not be divulged, but concealed in loue, which couereth a multitude

of

of sinnes. For if thou hast offended, or *if thy brother hath ought against thee, goe thy way, and be reconciled to thy brother. Math.* 5.23,24. If he haue trespassed against thee, or *thou hast ought against him, goe and tell him his fault betweene him and thee alone. Math.* 18.15. And albeit *Salomon* say, *That open rebuke is better then secret loue, Prou.* 27.5. yet it makes nothing against this rule: for hee vnderstandeth not that reproofe which is vttered before witnesses, but that priuate reproofe which is giuen to his face, and not behind his backe, betwixt them two alone. But open sinnes are reprooued openly. 1. *Tim.* 5.20. *Them that sinne, rebuke openly, that the rest also may feare.* Which text of Scripture must rightly be conceiued: for it is not a generall commandement giuen to all, (as some haue thought, in alleadging it to prooue that they may lawfully reprooue open swearers, and offenders, and that openly:) but it is a speciall commandement giuen to the Pastours, or gouernours of the Church, that they should reprooue those elders, and so consequently all such as were conuicted of any crime, by witnesses, and that before all men, that is, before the whole Church, and not before all men, in euery place and assembly, where they offend. For we haue no warrant in Scripture so to doe. Secondly, this open disgracefull rebuking of men will rather harden them in their sinnes, then any way reclaime them from sinne. *Augustine* saith well, *Præ pudore incipiet defendere peccatum suum, & quem vis correctiorem, facis peiorem.* (De verb. Dom. serm. 16.) Thirdly, they might as well say, a man is to be reprooued for euery sinne, and that openly before all men, as for open sinnes, because *Paul* saith not, *Them that sinne openly, rebuke before all men,* but *them that sinne, rebuke openly.* Fourthly, the wordes depend vpon the former verse, where it is said, *Receiue not an accusation against an Elder, vnder two or three witnesses*: and then it followes, *Those that sinne, rebuke openly*: that is, those elders that sinne, and haue been first priuatly admonished, and after that before witnesses, if they be accused by two or three witnesses; then reprooue them openly before all men: that is, before the whole Church.

X. We must carefully obserue the order set downe by our Sauiour Christ, *Matth.* 18.15. First, we must trie, whether by priuate reproofe our brother will be reclaimed, or not; if he be, wee must proceed no further, for then we haue attained the maine end of all reproofes, *If hee heare thee, thou hast wonne thy brother*: If not, we must take one or two, which may witnesse the fact, and that for sundry causes: the first is giuen by Saint *Hierom*, vpon the place, That they may witnesse that to be a sinne, for which hee

is

is reprooued,and that he is worthily reproued for the ſame. The ſecond is laid downe by Saint *Auguſt.Epiſt.*109.to conuince the party offending,of the act committed,if he ſhould iterate the ſame again. The third,by *Chryſoſtome.Hom.6*.in *Matth.*to witneſſe that he which reprooues,hath diſcharged his duty,and done what in him lay to win his brother. If he be reclaimed at the ſecond reproofe before witneſſes,we muſt proceede no further,but reſt there, as before:if not,we muſt relate it to the Church:if he heare the Church, there is no further proceedings to be vſed : if he heare not the Church,he is to be excommunicated,and holden as a heathen. Offenders therefore are not to be excommunicated at the very firſt, but orderly to be proceeded againſt,and louingly to be dealt withall,and patiently to be endured,according as the Apoſtle commandeth. 2.*Tim.*4 2.*reproone with all long ſuffering.* It may be obiected that *Paul* biddeth *Titus* he ſhould *auoid an hereticke after once or twiſe admonition.Tit.*3.10. Therfore we are not to proceed againſt offenders according to Chriſts commandement. *Anſ.* That Text makes nothing againſt this orderly proceeding commended vnto vs by our Sauiour Chriſt. For firſt this commandement is not giuen to all,but only to the Paſtors(as here to *Titus*)or Biſhops,who repreſenting the whole Church,are to giue ſentence of excommunication. Secondly, it is to be vnderſtood of publike admonition in the face of the Church,after that the partie hath bene priuately dealt withall;and if after this admonition,he doe no recant his errours, and reforme himſelfe,then is he to be reiected as an hereticke, that is,*αυτοκατάκριτος,condemned of his owne ſelfe,Tit.*3.11.

Neuertheleſſe,there be certaine caſes,in which we are not bound to follow this order or manner of proceeding in our reproofes, and they are principally three.

I. When the ſin committed tendeth to the hurt of the Church, or common wealth,and there be danger in delay,as alſo danger to the partie that is priuie to it, and doth not detect it;and ſmall hope of hindering of it,(as when a man doth plot treaſon, or intermedleth in treaſonable practiſes;)in this caſe the partie offending is not firſt priuately to be reprooued,but publikely to be detected,and ſo to be dealt withall of the Magiſtrate,according to the nature and quality of his offence: for the common good is to be preferred before any one mans priuate good:*better it is that one man periſh, then that the bond of vnity ſhould be broken.*

Melius eſt vt pereat vnus quam vnitas. Hieron.

II. When the fault is greater if it be committed,then the loſſe of his credit that committed it,though it be publiſhed. For example,if one intend to ſlay another, and lie in wait for him; in this caſe

case, we are not bound priuately to admonish the party intending murther, or blood shed, but to detect him to the Magistrate: for his life is to be preferred before the mans credit that sought his life. When *Pauls* kinsman (to wit his sisters sonne) heard that aboue 40. men, had conspired together, and bound themselues with an oath, that they would neither eate nor drinke, till they had killed *Paul*, he doeth not goe and reprooue them for this fact, but relates it to *Paul*: and *Paul* hearing of it, doth not counsell him to goe and reprooue them first, and if they would harken to him, to take two or three witnesses, &c. but sent him straight, to the chiefe captaine, that he might take order to preuent their bloody attempt.

Act.24.19,17.

III. When a man is assured priuate reproofe will doe no good, and that the party offending will not brooke it, nor take reproofe at his hand, he is not to follow that order, and manner of reproofe, but to acquaint them with it, that can and will redresse it. Thus *Ioseph* (as it may seeme,) did not reprooue his brethren, because he knew well they would not be bettered by him, (seeing they hated him) but *he brought vnto his father their euill sayings*, *Gen.* 38.2. Albeit others say, that their sinne was publike, and therfore needed no priuate admonition: and others, that he did admonish them secretly, before he did relate it to his father; (although it be not expressely set downe in the text.) Howsoeuer this example be vnderstood, the rule is certaine, that priuate reproofe is to be omitted, when it will either doe hurt, or no good.

2. *Beare ye one anothers burdens, and so fulfill the lawe of Christ.*

In this verse, the Apostle propounds another rule, touching brotherly loue, and it dependeth vpon the former, as an answer, to a secret obiectiō, which might be made vpon the former doctrine, in the 1. verse, in this manner: Thou enioynest vs we should restore our brother, if he fall by occasion into any sinne, in the Spirit of meekenesse: but there are some infirmities in our brethren which cannot be amended nor redressed by brotherly correction: what is to be done in such a case? The Apostle answereth, such infirmities must be borne and tollerated, in these words, *Beare ye one anothers burdens*: And this rule is enforced by an argument taken from the excellency thereof, in that the practising of it, is the keeping and fulfilling of the whole law, in these words, *And so fulfill the Law of Christ.*

First, for the rule: The Apostle calleth slippes, infirmities, and sinnes, by the name of *burdens*, taking his metaphor from trauellers, who vse to ease one another, by carrying one anothers burden, either wholly, or in part: that so they may more cheerefully, and speedily goe on in their iourney. Mens burdens are of two sorts: either such as euery man is to beare by himselfe alone, without shifting them off his owne shoulder, and laying them vpon other men (Of which we are to intreate, when we come to the fift verse.) Or such as may be borne of others, as well as of our selues: of these the Apostle speaketh in this place, when he saith, *Beare yee one anothers burdens*: and there are foure sorts of them: First, those whereof our brethren may either be wholly disburdened, or in part eased, such is the heauy burden of pouertie, sickenesse, nakednesse, hunger, thirst, banishment, imprisonment, &c. Secondly, the outward and bodily wants, that are in sundrie persons, as blindnesse, deafenesse, maimednesse, lamenesse, &c. Thirdly, personall or actuall sins of men, as anger, hatred, iealousie, enuie, &c. Lastly, outward frailties, in the actions of mens liues, (which are not felt oftentimes of those that are subiect vnto them, but are heauie burdens to others with whom they conuerse) as curiousnesse, nicenesse, slownesse, selfe conceitednesse, frowardnesse, hastinesse, and such like: The two first sorts, are to be borne three waies. First, by hauing a holy sympathie, and fellow feeling of them, *in weeping with those that weepe*: and *in remembring those that are in bonds, as though we were bound with them; those that are in affliction, as if we were also afflicted in the body, Ebr.* 13.v.3. This was *Pauls* practise, 2. *Cor.* 11.29. *Who is weake, and I am not weake? who is offended and I burne not?* Secondly, by bearing with them in their wants and infirmities, according to that of the Apostle. *Beare with the weake,* 1.*Thess.*5.14. Thirdly, by putting vnder our shoulders, and bearing part of the burden with them; in helping and easing of them in their necessities. *Rom.*12 v.13. *Distributing vnto the necessities of the Saints.* The two latter sorts (beeing principally meant in this place) are not to be borne by dissembling of them, or yeelding to them, much lesse by bolstering men vp in them, or by partaking with them; For albeit the adulterer and vncleane person would gladly make Christ a baud, the thiefe would make him his receiuer: and many there are who would be content to shift off their sinnes, in whole, or in part, and lay them vpon the shoulders of others: yet in Gods cause and quarrell, in matters of faith, we are not to yeeld a haire bredth; *Moses* told *Pharao,* that he would *not leaue so much as a hoofe behind him, Exod.*10.26. And *Paul would not giue place to Peter and them that* *were with him, no not for a moment, that the truth of the Gospel might continue with them, Gal.*2.5. They must therefore be borne by disburdening them of them, by gentle and mild admonition, or if they cannot be redressed, by bearing and tollerating of them, in passing by them, as though we did not perceiue them, for as *Salomon* saith, *It is the glory of man to passe by infirmitie* : or Lastly, by praying for them. For if we shall breake the bond of brotherly loue, and Christian societie, by reason of these or such like infirmities, which we see to be in our brethren : we walke not in loue, in that we beare not their *burdens*, as the Apostle commandeth in this place, and *Ephesians* 4.*verse* 4. *Support one another, through loue.* And surely, this is a most necessarie precept, of great vse and consequence, in the life of man ; for except we beare and tolerate the frailties of men, in passing by them in such sort, as I haue said, it is impossible we should lead a quiet, or comfortable life in any societie. We must seeke for a new world, or leauing the fellowship of men, betake our selues to some solitarie desert, as sundry *Eremites*, and *Anchorites* haue done, because they could not (by reason of their froward and wayward natures) digest the manifold inconueniences which they saw to be amongst men in publike societies.

Rom.14.1. and 15.1.

Prou.19 21.

This dutie therefore of bearing one anothers burdens, albeit it be difficult, yet it must be practised, specially of those that are strong men in Christ : for as in architecture, all stones are not fit to be laid in euery place of the building, but some below, as the fundamentall and chiefe corner stones, to beare vp the weight and burden of the building ; others aboue in the wall, that so the whole building may be firme and compact in it selfe : So in the Church, which is the house of God, (where all beleeuers are liuely stones, built vpon Christ Iesus the chiefe corner stone, bearing vp the whole burden, euen all the infirmities of the Church:) those that are strong must support the infirmities of the weake, that so the whole building beeing compact and knit together, may grow vp to a holy Temple in the Lord. For otherwise the whole frame of the building must needs be dissolued, and come to ruine. It is a common prouerbe among the Italians, that *Hard with hard, neuer makes a good wall.* By which is signified, that as stones cobbled vp one vpon another, without morter to combine thẽ, make but a tottering wall, that may easily be shaken ; but if there be morter bewixt them, yeelding to the hardnes of the stones, it makes the whole like a solide continued body, strong and stable; able to endure the shocke of the ramme, or the shot of the cannon : So that society, where all are as stiffe as stones, which wil not yeeld a haire,

1.Pet.2.5.

Duro con duro non fa bon muro.

one vnto another, one being as faſt, as froward, as haſtie, as another; cannot be firme and durable. But where men are of a ſoft, a yeelding, and relenting nature, giuing place to the ſtiffeneſſe of others, and yeelding to the tempeſt for a time, that ſocietie is compact in it ſelfe, and ſo cannot but continue, becauſe one doth beare the infirmities of another. Doſt thou therefore ſee thy brother to be ouertaken with ſome ſinne, or to be ouer curious, very froward, too ſelfe-conceited, abounding in his owne ſenſe, exceeding haſtie, &c. beare this his infirmitie now; and ſo he (perhaps) may beare with thee in the like caſe, another time: or beare thou with his curiouſneſſe, he will beare with thy dulneſſe: beare with his fickleneſſe, hee will beare with thy frowardneſſe: beare with his haſtineſſe, hee will beare with thy ſelfe-conceitedneſſe. For it is to bee obſerued, that the Apoſtle ſaith not, that thoſe onely which are ſtrong, ſhould beare the fraileties of the weake, but that both ſtrong and weake, ſhould beare one anothers burdens, it beeing a mutuall and reciprocall dutie impoſed vpon all, becauſe there is none ſo ſtrong, but one time or other hee may ſlippe, and fall; and ſo may ſtand in need to bee ſupported euen of the weake: the palſie man being ſicke, had his burthen (to wit, his bedde) borne, but beeing reſtored, could helpe to beare another mans burden: ſo if thou beare another mans burthen that is weake, when hee is ſtrong, hee will be ready to beare thine, if need require. God commands, that if we find our neighbours beaſt lying vnder his burthen, wee muſt lift him vp: how much more ought we to helpe our brethren, lying vnder the burden of ſinne? Therefore the ſtrong, are to ſupport the weake, and the weake muſt (vpon occaſion) ſupport the ſtrong: as in the arch of a building, one ſtone doeth beare mutually, though not equally, the burthen of the reſt: or as harts ſwimming ouer a great water, doe eaſe one another, in laying their heads one vpon the backe of another: the foremoſt that hath none to ſupport him, changing his place, and reſting his head vpon the hindermoſt. Thus in a family, the husband muſt beare with the niceneſſe, and frowardneſſe of his wife: the wife with the faſtneſſe or haſtineſſe of her husband. Thoſe Magiſtrates, and Miniſters, which are too colde and backeward in good things, muſt beare with the ouer great heat and forwardneſſe of their fellow-Magiſtrates, or fellow-Miniſters: and thoſe muſt beare with them againe, ſeeing both aime at the ſame end, the edification of the Church, and the good of the Commonwealth. Thus in Gods prouidence, *Luther* and *Melancthon* were happily ioyned together, and did beare

August. Ser. 21. de verbis Apoſt. Beda in hunc locū ex Auguſt.

with

with one another, *Luther* with his softnesse, *Melancthon* with his hastinesse; he with his boldnesse, he with his timorousnesse: *Melancthon* did wel temper the heat and zeale of *Luther* with his mildnesse, beeing as oyle to his vineger; and *Luther* on the other side, did warme his coldnesse, being as a fire to his frozennesse. Thus the Apostle commaundeth, that *wee should beare with the infirmities of those that are weake*, and not sufficiently catechized in the doctrine of our spirituall libertie purchased vnto vs by Christ, *and not to please our selues* too much, *but rather to please our neighbour in that which is good to edification, Rom.* 15. ver. 1, 2. For amongst other properties of loue reckned vp by S. *Paul*, 1. *Cor.* 13. this is not the least, that *it suffereth all things*, verse 7. that is, all such things as may bee borne and suffered with good conscience, for the good of our brother. For looke as a louer doth suffer all things in regard of his loue, in three respects. First, in vndergoing any labour that may be for her good, as *Hercules* did for the loue of *Omphale*. Secondly, in bearing patiently all hard measure that is offered him for her sake, as *Iacob* did for the loue of *Rachel*. Thirdly, in induring any thing that is imposed vpon him, and putting vp what wrong soeuer is done vnto him by her, as *Sampson* did for the loue of *Dalilah*. So Christian charity causeth vs to suffer all things. First, *pro fratribus*, to indure any labour, cost, or trauell, for their good. Secondly, *propter fratres*, to beare all afflictions for their sakes, as *Paul* saith he did for the Church. 2. *Tim.* 2. 10. Thirdly, *à fratribus*, to beare wrongs, and put vp iniuries at their hands, as he did, being shamefully entreated at Philippi, stoned, scourged, &c. This must be considered of vs all, but specially of such as will giue a man as good as he bringeth, who are but a word and a blow: a lie, and a stab: a word, and a writ: such as cannot beare coales, (as they say) nor brooke any little wrong, nor indure any small frailtie in their brethren. These men must remember, that *in bearing coales*, that is, in suffering and forbearing, *they heape vp coales of fire vpon their heads*, (as *Paul* speaketh, *Rom.* 12. 20.) as also that God doeth beare with them in greater matters, euen when they wound him with their oathes, *Leuit.* 24. 11. and giue him the lie through vnbeleefe, 1. *Iohn* 5. 10. as hee bare the manners of the Israelites in the wildernesse. ἐτροποφόρησεν. Acts 13. 8. That Christ, whose example wee are to follow, *hath borne our infirmities, Esay* 53. *and doeth ease them that trauell, and are heauie laden, Matthew* 11. 28. and therefore wee treading in his steppes, *must forbeare one another, and forgiue one another, if any man haue a quarrell against another, euen as Christ forgaue vs, Coloss.* 3. 13. Thus, if when wee see any sinne in our brother, wee reclaime him from it by reproofes, exhortations,admonitions,we are Gods instruments,to *saue a soule from death,and so doe couer a multitude of sinnes*,euen before God. *Iam.* 5 20. And if,when we perceiue common frailties in our brethren, we shall not stand too much vpon our right, but shall yeeld vnto them in bearing,forbearing,and forgiuing,we *shal couer a multitude of sinnes* before men. 1.*Pet*.4.8.

Thus much touching the rule. Now I proceede to the reason, whereby the Apostle vrgeth the practise of this precept, in these words, *And so fulfill the law of Christ*. The reason standeth thus: That which is the fulfilling of the law of Christ,must be practised of vs: but the bearing of one anothers burdens, is the fulfilling of the law of Christ: therefore we ought to beare one anothers burdens. For the clearing of this Text, sundry things are to be considered.

I. It may be demanded, what the Apostle vnderstandeth by *the law of Christ*? *Answer.* Nothing els but the doctrine, precept, or commandement of Christ,enioyning the loue of our brethren. *Ioh.*13.34.35. *A new commandement giue I vnto you, that ye loue one another, as I haue loued you, &c.* And it is all one, as if he had saide, Beare ye one anothers burdens, and so fulfill the *commandement* of Christ, who hath after a speciall manner commanded the loue of your brethren. Now the Apostle rather vseth the word *Law*, then *Commandement*, because he would make a clearer *Antithesis* betwixt the *Law of Christ*,& the *Law of Moses*,so vehemently vrged by the false Apostles: as if he should haue said, You Galatians are taught to obserue the Law of *Moses*,circumcision,daies, and times,moneths, and yeares, and so ye doe indeede. Well, if ye will needs be obseruing of Lawes, here is a Law for you to obserue,beare with the frailties one of another,& so you shal fulfill the most excellent law that euer was, the law of Christ, which is necessary to be kept,wheras the keeping of the Ceremoniall law is but in vaine.

II. *Question.* Why doth *Paul* call the loue of our brethren, the Law of Christ,rather then the law of nature, or the Law of God, or the Law of *Moses*? seeing it was written in the minde of man in the creation,was giuen by God himselfe in Mount Sinai,was written by *Moses*, the reliques whereof are yet remaining in the mind of man? *Answer.* It is so called, because it is a new commandement giuen by Christ himselfe, after a speciall manner. But it is hereupon further demanded, why this commandement of louing our brethren, should be called a new commandement? To which some make answer, that it is so called,only because it shews

a new

a new manner of louing our brethren, after the example of Christ; *as he hath loued vs.* Now this maner of louing our brethren (as *Chrysostome* expounds it) is this; that as Christ loued vs freely, not mooued by any amiable thing in vs, nor for any profite that should redound vnto himselfe therby: so we should freely loue one another, not for any benefit receiued, or expected. But as *Cyril* of *Alexand.* vpō *Iohn*, expounds it, it stands in this, that as Christ loued vs more then himselfe, so we should loue our brethren more then our selues. But this cannot be the meaning. For S. *Iohn* in his 1. Epist. 2. and Epist. 2. repeating this new commandement, saith onely, *this is a new commandement, that ye loue one another*, and neuer ads, *as Christ loued vs*: the which he should haue done, if these words [*as I haue loued you*] be an essentiall part of the new commandement, which he enioyneth vs to obserue.

Besides, our Sauiour himselfe saith, a little after, *By this shal al men knowe, that ye are my Disciples, if ye loue one another*, not adding, *as I haue loued you*: therefore, the new commandement is laid downe in these words, *Loue one another*, not respecting those that follow, as a modification or limitation, *as I haue loued you.* Besides, this exposition takes it for granted, that the moral law, *Loue thy neighbour as thy selfe*, is a certaine rule, by which we are to square our loue, that is, that we must begin at our selues, and looke how much we loue our selues, so much we ought to loue our neighbour, and no more, and that therefore Christ should giue a new commandement of greater perfection, then that in the law, to wit, that we loue one another as he loued vs, that is, more then our selues. But this is a flat mistaking of the Scripture: for the commandement, *Loue thy neighbour as thy selfe*, is no exact rule whereby we are to try and examine our loue, (as the Popish doctors, and some others teach.) For then *Paul* and diuers of the Saints of God, should haue done workes of supererogation, more then the law requires, in louing their neighbours more then themselues, *Rom.* 9. 1. And if it were a rule it were but a leaden and false rule: for we are in some cases bound to loue our neighbour, more then our selues, especially if he be a greater instrument of Gods glorie, in procuring the good of the Church or Common wealth, as to loue our godly king more then our selues, and preferre his safety and life before our owne, as the Israelites did *Dauids*: *Thou art worth tenne thousand of vs*, 2. *Sam.* 18. 3. for *ὡς*, is a note of similitude, and not of equality, signifying, that as we loue our selues heartily, and earnestly, and inwardly, wishing all good to our selues: with the like sincerity of affection we should loue our brethren. So that Christ hath added nothing to the lawe, in

* ὡς ὁμοιότητος, ἰσότητος.

Theophylact. Sic Hugo de S.Victor lib. quæst. in Epist. ad Rom. q. 308.

in commanding to loue one another, as he loued vs. Others say, it is called a new commandement, because it ought to be kept with as great care and diligence, as though it were new, and had beene now first giuen: for new lawes (we know) are commonly precisely kept at the first, but after a while, they begin to be neglected: and men doe (as it were) antiquate them, accounting them as though they were not.

Others, by a new commandement, vnderstand another diuers or different commandement; for Christ in the beginning of the Chapter, had giuen them a cōmandement to fly pride, to be humble, to liue at peace, and concord one with another: and then he saith, *But I giue you a new commandement*, i. a commandement differing from the former, *that ye loue one another.*

The word *New* is often taken in scripture in this sense, as *Exod.* 1. 8. *There arose vp a new king which knew not Ioseph:* that is, (as the 70. interpreters, and S. *Luke*, *Act.* 7. 18, translate it) *another king*, *Mar.* 16 17. *they shall speake with new tongues*, that is, *other*, *diuers*, or *different* languages, from their vsuall tongue: for the meaning is not, that they inuented a new language, which was neuer spoken before, but that they spake in a language diuers from that which they vsed before: for it is said, *Act.* 2. 4. *They beganne to speake with other tongues*: Thus our Sauiour Christ telleth his Apostles, *that he will not drinke any more of the fruit of the vine, till he drinke it new with them in the kingdome of God*, *Matth.* 26. 29. Where by *new wine*, he meaneth not the liquor or iuyce of the Grape, to preserue animall life: but another different drinke, wherewith he would entertaine all that were inuited, and came vnto his table. But these expositions are not so fitte.

γλώσσαις καιναῖς.

ἑτέραις γλώσσαις.

I take it therefore to be called *a new commandement*, either in respect of Christ, or of vs: in respect of Christ two waies: First, Because he renued it, not onely by freeing it from the false glosses and interpretations of the Scribes & Pharises, the Iewish Rabbins: but also in fulfilling it most perfectly, whereas it was obliterated, and almost antiquated, by the great corruption of man: for none did neuer so perfectly obserue and keepe the law, as he did. Therefore in regard of the new manner of fulfilling it, it is called *a new commandement*. Secondly, because he abrogating the ceremoniall Law, and many iudicialls, onely renued this precept of the morall law, in commanding it as his law to the Church. *Ioh.* 15. *This is my commandement, that ye loue one another*, as if he should say, Though I haue abrogated the ceremoniall law, and antiquated the iudiciall, yet this commandement shall neuer be abrogated: and this I commend

mend vnto you againe and againe, as my commandement, which aboue all others, I would haue you carefully to obserue, as that whereby ye shall be knowne to be my Disciples. In regard of vs it is called *a new commaundement*, and that in two respects: 1. Because it beeing defaced, and almost cleane blotted out of the mind of man by originall sinne, is renued againe in the hearts of beleeuers, by the powerfull operation of the Spirit of God, both in their mindes, and affections: In their mindes, because they are daily inlightened with the true knowledge thereof, in beeing taught whom they ought to loue: *viz.* not onely their friends, but euen their enemies: with what kind of loue, to wit, with a feruent loue, not in word, or tongue onely, but in deed, and truth: and that with free, sincere, and constant loue: in their wills, and affections: in that they are perswaded by the inward working of the Spirit, to loue: and are inclined thereto, being turned by grace. Secondly, because it doth after a peculiar manner belong vnto vs, who are vnder the New Testament, in the kingdome of grace, seeing that this commandement onely is renued by Christ, as his owne proper commandement, many others being abrogated: as also because it is daily written by the Spirit of Christ, after a new manner, in the hearts of new conuerts: so that they haue not onely a new, that is, a true knowledge thereof, but also a new, that is, a true sense and feeling of the power of it in their hearts: in that they are become new creatures in Christ Iesus. For in him *all olde things passe away, and all things become new, 2.Cor.5.* For to them the law is no killing letter, written in tables of stone; but a quickening spirit, as being written in the fleshy tables of their hearts. This seemeth to be the true, ful, and proper meaning of these places: for thus S. *Iohn* 1. Epistle 2.8. doeth expound it, when hee saith, that *it is true in him and in you*, in the sense before specified: both in regard of Christ, and the beleeuers in Christ.

III. Quest. Seeing the commandement of louing our brethren, is called the law of Christ and a new commandement, is not the Gospel a new law? *Answer.* In no wise: for albeit the Law and the Gospel agree in sundrie things, as first in the Authour, God being the Authour of them both; of the Gospell, *Rom.* 1.1. of the Law, *Rom.*7.22. Secondly, in that both of them were preached, knowne, and vnderstood in both Testaments: the law being written in the heart of man in the creation: the Gospell preached to our first parents in Paradise, immediately after the fall, and repeated againe and againe to the Patriarkes and Prophets, from time to time. Thirdly, in the generall matter, and end of them both, in that

both

both the Law and the Goſpell, require righteouſneſſe in him that would come to life eternall. Fourthly, in this, that they confirme and eſtabliſh one another, in that the law commanding iuſtice, and iuſtifying none, ſhewes that a man is iuſtified by the free gift and grace of God, and that Chriſt is the end of the Law to euery one that beleeueth. In that the Goſpel iuſtifieth not by workes, but by faith, and yet ſo, as that we doe not by our faith abrogate the law, or make it of none effect, but rather eſtabliſh it, and that in two reſpects. Firſt, becauſe by faith wee apprehend the righteouſneſſe of Chriſt, and ſo in him (who hath fulfilled the Law for vs) wee fulfill it, and ſo eſtabliſh it. Secondly, becauſe hauing our hearts purified by faith, we liue no more according to the fleſh, but according to the Spirit, and ſo by inchoate obedience wee fulfill the law.

Laſtly, in the end, in that both the Law and the Goſpel tend directly to the manifeſtation of the glory of God.

Yet they differ in fiue things. Firſt, in the manner of reuealing: the law before the fall was perfectly knowen by nature, and ſince the fall in part, *Rom.* 2.15. The Goſpel is not knowne by nature, neither was it euer written in mans heart, before, or after the fall, as *Paul* ſaith, 1.*Cor.* 2.9. *Thoſe things which the eye hath not ſeene, nor the eare heard, nor the heart of man conceiued, are they which God hath prepared for them that loue him*: therefore the Goſpell is called *a myſterie*, *Rom.* 16.v.25,26. Firſt, becauſe the doctrine of the Goſpell was made knowne to men and Angels by the reuelation of God, *Eph.* 3.5. and 9. Secondly, becauſe there is required a ſpeciall reuelation, and worke of Gods Spirit, before a man can yeeld aſſent vnto it. Therefore *Paul* ſaith, *Wee haue not receiued the ſpirit of the world, but the Spirit of God, that we might know the things that are giuen to vs of God*, 1.*Cor.* 2.12. Secondly, in the ſubiect or doctrine it ſelfe, and that in two reſpects. Firſt, the law preacheth nothing, but abſolute iuſtice to the tranſgreſſors therof: the Goſpel ſheweth how iuſtice is qualified with mercy: *from all things from which ye could not be abſolued by the law of Moſes, by him euery one that beleeueth is iuſtified*, *Actes* 13.39. Secondly, the Law teacheth what maner of men we ought to be, and what we ought to doe, that we may come to eternal life, but ſhewes not how we may become ſo indeed: the Goſpel teacheth, that by faith in Chriſt, we may be ſuch as the law requires. *God hath made him to be ſinne for vs, who knew no ſinne, that we might be made the righteouſneſſe of God in him*, 2.*Cor.* 5.21.

Thirdly, in the obiect, *The law is giuen to the vniuſt and lawleſſe, vngodly, and prophane*, 1.*Tim.* 1.9, 10. that it may ſhew them their

ſinnes,

sinnes, and the punishment thereby deserued, and so may accuse and condemne them: the Gospel is to be published and dispensed onely to the penitent, which are contrite and broken in heart, and mourne for their sinnes, *Matth.* 11. *Isa* 57. *Luke* 4.

IIII. The Law promiseth eternall life, vpon condition of workes: *Doe this, and liue: If thou wilt enter into life, keepe the Commaundements.* The Gospell promiseth eternall life freely without any condition of workes. *Romanes* 4. 5. *To him that worketh not, but beleeueth in him that iustifieth the vngodly, his faith is counted to him for righteousnesse. Rom.* 3. 21, 22. *The righteousnesse of God is made manifest without the Law, by the faith of Iesus Christ, vnto all, and vpon all that beleeue.*

V. In the effects. The Law is no instrumentall cause of faith, repentance, or any sauing grace: it is *the minister of death,* 2. *Cor.* 3. 7. *causing wrath, Rom.* 3. 15. But the Gospell causeth life: it is *the grace of God which bringeth saluation, Titus* 2. 11. For this cause *Paul* calleth the Law, *a dead,* or *killing letter*: the Gospell, *a quickening spirit,* 2. *Cor.* 3.

Fourthly, it may be demaunded, whether any man bee able to fulfill the Law, considering that *Paul* biddeth vs beare one anothers burdens, *and so fulfill the Law of Christ? Answer.* No meere man can perfectly fulfill the Law in this life. This conclusion S. *Paul* prooueth in sundrie of his Epistles, specially by these arguments.

First, by the great and generall deprauation of nature, which remaineth in part euen in the regenerate, staining their best actions, and making them like a menstruous cloath: confessing withal, that his best workes are not answerable to the law, by reason of the remainders of originall corruption, *Rom.* 7. Now perfect fulfilling of the law, cannot stand with corruption of nature, and transgression in life. For a corrupt fountaine cannot send foorth sweet waters: neither can a corrupt tree beare good fruit. Saint *Iames* saith, *Hee that offendeth in one, is guiltie of all*: and the Scripture pronounceth him accursed, *that abideth not in all things written in the booke of the law to doe them.* Popish Doctours answer, first, that originall corruption (which they call the fewell of sinne) and the first motions to euill, preuenting all consent of will, are indeed in the regenerate; but they are no sinnes properly. But it is false which they teach. For euery transgression of the Law, is a sinne, as Saint *Iohn* defines it, 1. *Iohn* 3. 4. but these are transgressions of the tenth Commandement: For it either forbiddeth these first motions, whether they bee *primò prima,* or *secundò prima,* (as Schoole-men speake) or

Fomes peccati.

or it forbiddeth nothing but the motions, which are with conſent of will, which were forbidden in the former commandements, and ſo in effect there are but nine commandements, the tenth forbidding no ſpeciall ſinne.

Rom.7.23.

Againe, *Paul* teacheth, that theſe motions preuenting all conſent of will, are formally oppoſed to the law, *I ſee another law in my mẽbers, rebelling againſt the law of my mind.* Secondly, they anſwer, that *Paul, Rom.* 7. ſpeakes not of himſelfe, but in the perſon of the vnregenerate, according to the opinion of S. *Auguſtine. Anſwer. Auguſtine* indeed was once of that iudgement, but hee after retracted that opinion, (as it is manifeſt out of his booke of *Retractations*, and the 6. Booke, againſt *Iulian* the Pelagian,) and that for theſe reaſons. Firſt, becauſe *Paul* ſaith, *To will is preſent with mee:* and, *I doe not the good I would:* and, *I delight in the law of God concerning the inward man:* all which are proper to the regenerate, and cannot bee affirmed of the wicked. Secondly, becauſe he makes mention of *the inward man*, which is all one with the new man, or the new creature: which agreeth onely to the regenerate. Thirdly, becauſe he ſaith, *He is led captiue to ſinne*, verſe 23. whereas the wicked are not drawne to ſinne by force, againſt their willes, but runne riot of their owne accord into all wickedneſſe, as the horſe ruſheth into the battell, *Ierem.* 8.6. Laſtly, in that he cries out in a ſenſe and ſorrow for his ſinnes, *O wretched man that I am, who ſhall deliuer mee from the bodie of this death?* verſe 25. which can not bee the voice of the vnregenerate, for they feele not the burden of their ſin, nor deſire to be eaſed of it, but take delight and pleaſure in it. His ſecond reaſon is this: ſuch as our knowledge is, ſuch is our loue of God and man: but our knowledge is onely in part: therfore our loue is but in part, and therefore there is no perfect fulfilling of the law. The aduocates of the Romiſh Church anſwer, that our knowledge, loue, and obedience, are perfect for the condition and eſtate of this life, as we are *viatores*, which is ſufficient: though they be not perfect for the condition of the life to come, when we ſhall be *comprehenſores*, which is not required at our hands in this life: for they make a double perfect fulfilling of the law: one, for the tearme of this life, which is to loue God aboue all things, and our neighbor as our ſelues. The other after this life, and that is to loue God with all the ſoule, with all the powers and faculties of the ſoule, and with all the ſtrength and vigor of all theſe powers.

And this diſtinction they make to be the ground of their opinion, touching the fulfilling of the law, and iuſtification by workes, &c. But it is a ſandy foundation, and therefore that which is built

vpon

vpon it, cannot stand. For besides that it is a fond and friuolous distinction forged by Schoolemen, without warrant of Scripture, or consent of Antiquitie; it is manifestly false. For there is one onely rule of righteousnesse, and not two: one onely generall sentence of the Law, more vnchangeable then the Lawes of the Medes and Persians, euen as vnchangeable as God himselfe: which is, that, *He which continueth not in all things written in the Law to doe them, is accursed.* So that he which loueth not God with all his soule, minde, and might, with all his *valde suo,* that is, with all the faculties of his soule, and all the powers of all these faculties, and that in this life, is accursed. And it is absurd which they teach, that a man is not bound for the tearme of this life, thus to loue God, but onely in the life to come. For looke what man could doe by creation, in the estate of innocency, the same and so much the Law requires at his hands in the state of Apostasie. But *Adam* by creation could loue God with all his soule, with all the faculties of his soule, and all the powers of all these faculties: therefore the same perfect, absolute, and entire obedience is now required at his hands. For the sentence of the law, *Cursed is he that continueth not in all things, &c,* is not onely giuen to men glorified, but to those that are in the state of grace. And S. *Paul* doth so apply this sentence to men euen in this life, that he pronounceth all that are of the workes of the Law, to be vnder the curse. Againe, if this were so, the Iewes had no cause to feare the seueritie and strictnesse of the Law, as they did: when they said, *If we heare the voice of the* Exod.20.19.
Lord any more, we shall die: considering they were able to keepe and Deut.18.16.
fulfill it, according to this Popish opinion. Neither would God haue
promised them a Messias or Mediatour to redeeme them from the Deut.18.18.
curse of the law: but wold rather haue comforted them in that their so great feare and astonishment, by giuing them to vnderstand that they were not bound to the full and perfect fulfilling of the law for the time of this life,

Besides, the patheticall exclamation of *Paul, O miserable man that I am, &c. Rom.* 7.24. and that saying of *Peter,* in calling the law. *a yoke,* which neither we nor our fathers were able to beare, *Act.* 15. Rom.8.3.
should be childish and ridiculous, if *that which is impossible in the law* (as *Paul* speakes) did not appertaine vnto vs.

The third argument. If a man could fulfill the Law, he should not stand in need of a Mediatour. *For if righteousnesse be by the Law, Christ died in vaine, Gal.* 2.21. It is answered, that Christ dyed in vaine, if men by the strength of nature could fulfill the Law: but the fulfilling of the Law is by grace, and so his death is not in vaine: for by vertue of the obedience of Chriſt, wee are enabled to fulfill the law. But this were to make Chriſt no Sauiour, but onely an inſtrument, whereby we fulfill the Law, and are our owne Sauiours; whereas the Scripture ſaith, that *hee is made vnto vs righteouſneſſe*, 1.*Corinth.* 1.30. not that wee are made righteouſneſſe by him. That *wee are made the righteouſneſſe of God in him*, 2.*Corinth.* 5.21. not *by him*, as an inſtrument. That *we are complete in him*, *Coloſſ.* 2.10. and not complete of our ſelues, by him.

Laſtly, the Scripture ſhutteth vp all men vnder ſinne, euen the moſt ſanctified, *Prou.* 20.9. 1.*Iohn* 1.9. *Iob* confeſſeth he cannot anſwer one of a thouſand, *Iob* 9.3. and *Dauid* ſaith, *If thou, Lord, ſhalt marke what is done amiſſe, who can abide it?* *Pſalm.* 130.3. and *Paul* ſaith of himſelfe, that *hee found no meanes to performe that which is good*, *Rom.* 7.18. Hee ſaith further, that *it is impoſſible* to bee kept, by reaſon of originall corruption, *Rom.* 8.3. It is anſwered, that all theſe places and examples muſt bee vnderſtood of veniall ſinnes, which make men ſinners indeed, yet are not *againſt*, but *beſide the Law*; and therefore though a man commit them, yet he may fulfill the lawe for all that. *Anſwer.* The common receiued opinion in Schooles, that ſome ſinnes are mortall, others veniall of their owne nature, is a witleſſe diſtinction. For if all ſinnes deſerue death, as *Paul* teacheth, *Romanes* 6.23. either veniall ſinnes are no ſinnes, or they muſt needs deſerue death. *Moſes* ſaith, that *hee that abideth not in all things written in the Law, is accurſed*, *Deuter.* 27.26. where the wordes, *this Law*, may not be reſtrained, onely to the Catalogue of great and hainous ſinnes, which are there reckoned vp, but extended to all ſinnes, as *Paul* applies it, *Galat.* 3.10. pronouncing him accurſed, *that continueth not in all things written in the Lawe*, not *this Lawe*. So that euery ſinne, euen the leaſt ſinne in thought, makes a man ſubiect to the curſe, and ſo in rigour of diuine Iuſtice, deſerues eternall death. And it is but a poore ſhift, to ſay that ſome ſinnes are *againſt the Lawe*, as all mortall ſinnes, and others *beſides the Law*, as veniall. For the doing of that which God forbiddeth, is a ſinne, not *beſide*, but *againſt the Lawe*. But idle words, ieſting, and gybing, &c. (which the Popiſh Doctours account veniall ſinnes,) are expreſſely forbidden in the word, *Matthew* 12. verſe 36. *Of euery idle word that men ſhall ſpeake, they ſhall giue account at the day of iudgement.* And *Paul* forbiddeth *all fooliſh talking, and ieſting*, as things vncomely, *Epheſians* 5.4. Therefore they are not *beſide*, but *flat againſt the Lawe*. Secondly, they anſwer, that theſe places and the like are to be vnderſtood of ſeue-

rall

rall workes, and actions of the Saints, whereof some were good, as *Dauids* sparing of *Saul*, &c. Some euill, as his adultery, murther, and numbring of the people: and not of the same particular workes. *Answer.* It is false. For *Paul* speaking of the same indiuiduall worke, saith, that it is partly good, and partly euill, *I finde, when I would doe good, that euill is present with mee, Rom.* 7. 21. *In my minde I serue the lawe of God, in my body the lawe of sinne*, verse 25. And the Prophet saith, that *all our righteousnesse is as a menstruous cloath, Isai.* 64 4. Therefore euery good worke is stained with sinne.

Thus much shal suffice to shew, that it is impossible for any man in the time of this life to fulfill the Law. The reasons alleadged to the contrary, are sufficiently answered before, Page 164. &c. To which place I referre the Reader.

It may further be said, if we cannot perfectly fulfill the law, why doth *Paul* command vs to beare one anothers burthens, and *so to fulfill the law of Christ?*

Answer. The law is said to bee fulfilled three wayes. First, by *personall obedience*, and thus Christ onely fulfilled it. Secondly, by *imputed obedience*, thus the regenerate fulfill it in Christ, hee being *their righteousnesse*, 1. *Cor.* 1.30. and they *complete in him, Coloss.* 2.10. Thirdly, by *inchoate obedience*, thus *Zacharie* and *Elizabeth* are said to walk in all the commandements of the Lord, without reproofe, *Luke* 1.6. And thus all the faithfull fulfill the Law, in labouring to obey God in all the Commandements; according to the measure of grace receiued: and thus wee are said to fulfill the Law in this place, God accepting the will for the deed. Wee are further to consider, that *fulfilling of the Law* is sometime opposed to the transgression of the Law, as *Iames* 2.10. in which sense no man euer did, or can fulfill it, except Christ, God and man, who for this cause is said to bee *the ende of the law for righteousnesse, to euery one that beleeueth, Romanes* 10.4. Sometime it is opposed to hypocrisie, and dissimulation, as 1. *Iohn* 2.4,5. and thus all the Saints fulfill it, in that they indeauour to mortifie their corruptions, and in all things to approoue their hearts and liues to God, in keeping faith and a good conscience. In which sense, *Paul* heere biddeth vs to fulfill the Law of Christ, in performing duties of loue, and bearing one anothers burthens. It will be said, if the law can no otherwise bee fulfilled, then by *inchoate obedience*, to what end serueth it? *Answ.* It hath a threefold vse euen since the fall. First, it serues to restraine the outward man, by keeping men in order, through the feare of punishment, of which vse *Paul* speaketh, when he saith, that *the law is not giuen to a righteous man, but to the lawlesse and disobedient, &c.* 1. *Tim.* 1.9. Secondly, to arouse the drousie conscience: and this it doth many waies. 1. By reuealing sinne; *for by the law* commeth *the knowledge of sinne, Rom.* 3.20. 2. By reuealing the wrath and anger of God for sinne, for *the law causeth wrath, Rom.* 4.15. 3. By conuicting the conscience of sinne. *When the commandement came, sinne reuiued, Rom.* 7.9. 4. By arraigning and condemning vs for sinne, for *the law is the minister of death,* 2.*Cor.* 3.7. and so putting vs out of all heart in our selues, it causeth vs to flie to the throne of grace, and so is *our schoolemaster* to bring vs *to Christ, Gal.* 3.24. Thirdly, it serues as a rule of good life: *Dauid* saith, that *the word of God* (specially the law) *is a lanterne to his feet, and a light to his paths, Psa.* 119.105. So that though a regenerate man be not vnder the law, in regard of iustification, or accusation, or coaction, or condemnation: yet he is vnder it, in regard of direction, and instruction, for it shewes what is good, what is euil, what we ought to do, and what to leaue vndone. Lastly, wheras *Paul* saith, *Beare ye one anothers burdens, and so fulfill the law of Christ.* The word *SO* hath great emphasis, for it implies the manner how the Galatians, and all men are to fulfill the law, not by obseruing circumcision, daies, or times, moneths, or yeares, as the false apostles taught: but by bearing, forbearing, and tolerating the infirmities of their brethren. It may not vnfitly bee applied to the religious orders of *Franciscans, Dominicans, Carthusians, &c.* Let them not thinke that they keepe the law, by abstaining from flesh, by whipping themselues, by single life, counterfeit fasts, voluntary pouertie, regular obedience, &c. But let them comfort the afflicted, relieue the distressed, beare with the weake, support one another in loue, and *SO* they shall fulfill the law of Christ.

3 *For if any man seeme to himselfe, that hee is somewhat, when he is nothing, he deceiueth himselfe in his imagination.*

In this verse the Apostle remooues an impediment, which hindereth most from performing the former dutie of bearing other mens burthens, and that is, a vaine conceit and imagination they haue of their owne excellency, farre aboue their brethren: in thinking themselues too good to doe any dutie or seruice vnto them, to be their packhorses to beare their burthens. This vaine imagination and swelling conceit (which puffeth vp the most) the Apostle laboureth to purge in this place, when he saith, *Hee that seemeth to himselfe, &c.* where by the way wee may obserue the method of the Apostle, first, to giue rules of direction; after to remoue impediments

diments which may hinder our obedience. 2. Wee see here the force of the word, which *searcheth the secrets of the heart, Hebr.*4. 12. *in that it casteth downe the imaginations, and euery high thing that is exalted against the knowledge of God: and bringeth into captiuitie euery thought to the obedience of Christ,* 2 *Cor.*10.4. In the words we may obserue these foure things: 1. That men are nothing of themselues. 2. That though they be nothing, yet they seeme to themselues to be somewhat, and that of themselues. 3. That in so doing, they deceiue themselues. 4. The remedies against the ouerweening of our selues.

For the first: it may be demanded how it can be truly said, that men are of themselues meere nothing? Is he nothing that is created after the image of God, in holinesse and righteousnes? Are princes and Potentates nothing that are called Gods in Scripture? Are they nothing that prophesie, and worke miracles? *Answer. Paul* speaketh not of the gifts of God, bestowed vpon men, but of the men themselues: and of them, not as they were in the state of innocency before the fall, but as they are now in the state of corruption and apostasie, or in the state of grace, as they are considered of, in, and by themselues. Thus euen spirituall men are nothing of themselues: (for of them especially the Apostle speaketh, as it may appeare out of the first verse.)

For first, all are by nature the children of wrath, and firebrands of hell. 2. The gifts of God bestowed vpon vs, whether of nature or of grace, are not ours, but Gods, the giuer of them. Therefore no man may arrogate more vnto himselfe, then another in regard of them, seeing all of vs are but stewards, and the things we haue, are but talents, left vs to imploy to our masters aduantage. *If thou hast receiued them* (saith *Paul*) *why boastest thou thy selfe, as though thou hadst not receiued them?* 3. Be it that a man be in Christ, and sanctified, yet hee hath no greater right to the merits of Christ, nor greater part in them, then he which is lesse sanctified: for though sanctification hath degrees, and a certaine latitude, yet iustification hath none. So that a man is in truth nothing of himselfe. 1. Because he hath his being and beginning of nothing, and tendeth of his own nature to corruption & nothing. 2. In that he is not that which he imagineth himselfe to be. 3. Though he haue some gifts and graces of God, yet is hee nothing, because he is farre short of that which he ought to be, 1.*Cor.*8.2. Vpon these considerations *Abraham* acknowledgeth himselfe to be but *dust and ashes, Gen.* 18.27. *David* comparing himselfe with the magnificence of *Saul*, saith, *What am I, or what is my fathers house?* 1.*Samuel* 18.18. Nay whether

πᾶν κτιστὸν, τρεπτὸν. Damascenus.

whether we conſider man abſolutely in himſelfe, or relatiuely in reſpect of other creatures, as thoſe glorious bodies, the Sun, Moone, Starres, we may ſay with the Prophet Dauid, *Lord what is man, that thou art mindefull of him, or the ſonne of man, that thou regardeſt him? Pſal.8 4.*

Paul confeſſeth himſelfe to be nothing, in, of, or by himſelfe: but *by the grace of God* (ſaith he) *I am that I am, 1. Cor.15.10.* And againe, *I was nothing inferiour to the very chiefe Apoſtles, although I am nothing. 2.Cor.12 11.* The Apoſtle affirmeth of euery man, *which thinketh he knoweth ſomething, that he knoweth nothing as he ought to know. 1.Cor.8.2.* and of many, that they are puffed vp and know nothing. *1.Tim.6.4.* For a ſwelling conceit, and emptines, vſually goe together.

The ſecond general thing to be obſerued in the words, is this, That it is naturall for men to thinke too well of themſelues, to magnifie themſelues aboue others in their conceits, and in a manner to deifie themſelues: and to nullifie others in compariſon of themſelues: and this ouerweening of a mans ſelfe, is a branch of pride. For a man looking vpon himſelfe through the ſpectacles of ſelfe-loue, doth thinke euery ſmall gift of God, which he ſeeth to be in himſelfe, to be farre greater then in truth it is: imagining meere ſhadowes, to be ſubſtances; or molehills, to be as bigge as mountaines. For as a man that is in loue, doth thinke the blemiſhes and deformities in his loue, to be ornaments, which make her more beautifull: So theſe with *Narciſſus* are in loue with themſelues, and dote vpon their owne gifts; iudge the vices which they ſee to be in themſelues, to be vertues. *Simon Magus* though a wicked wretch, a limme of the Deuill, a ſorcerer, &c. yet had this conceit of himſelfe, and gaue it out alſo, that *he was ſome great man. Act.8.9,* to wit, *the great power of God, verſe 10.* The Church of *Laodicea*, thought *ſhe was rich and increaſed with goods; and had neede of nothing: whereas ſhe was wretched, and miſerable, and poore, and blind, and naked. Apoc.3.17.* And ſo the ſkarlet ſtrumpet thought her ſelfe a Queene, and that ſhe was out of all daunger of downefall, when ſhee was already fallen. *Apoc.18.2,7.* Yea this corruption is ſo naturall, that euen the regenerate themſelues, who are in part ſanctified, are tainted therewith: and generally, they that haue receiued greater gifts of knowledge, of ſanctification, &c. are moſt ready to ouerweene their owne gifts, except God giue them grace to reſiſt this temptation: for *knowledge puffeth vp. 1.Cor.8.1.* The Apoſtles themſelues contended *which of them ſhould ſeeme to bee the greateſt, Luke 22.24.* Yea in all ages there haue beene ſome in the

the Church ouerweening themſelues,as in Chriſts time the Iuſtitiary Phariſes : after them, the *Cathariſts*, or *Puritanes*, who both proudly and odiouſly called themſelues by that name, thinking themſelues without ſinne : the *Donatiſts*, that they weare a Church without ſpot or wrinkle : the *Iouinianiſts*, that a man cannot ſinne after the lauer of regeneration. The *Pelagians*, that the life of a iuſt man in this world, hath no ſinne in it at all : and of later times the *Semi-Pelagian* heretike, who will be ſomething of himſelfe, aud will haue ſome ſtroke in his firſt conuerſion, and will concurre with Chriſt in the worke of Iuſtification. It will be ſaid, Papiſts aſcribe all the praiſe to God. *Anſ.* So did the Phariſie, *Luke* 18.11. and yet a wicked Iuſtitiary for all that. Now all this ariſeth from ſundry cauſes : the firſt is,the bitter roote of pride,that was in our firſt parents,when as they affected a higher place,in deſiring(through diſcontentment of their owne eſtate) to deifie themſelues, and become equall to the higheſt Maieſty, in knowing good and euill.

The ſecond is, the ouermuch conſidering the good things we haue; as when the Phariſie conſidered that he gaue tithe of all that he poſſeſſed,that he faſted twiſe a weeke,that he was not thus and thus,as other men.*Luke* 18.

The third is, the comparing of our ſelues with the infirmities that we ſee to be in others : the Phariſie was puffed vp, by comparing himſelfe with extortioners, vniuſt men, adulterers, and with the Publican.

The fourth is, the falſe flattering, and applauſe of men, which ſooth vs vp in our humours, in perſwading vs to be that which in truth we are not,as the people flattered *Herod*, when they gaue a ſhout,and ſaid,*The voice of God, and not of man. Act.* 12.22.

The third point is, that they which thus ouerweene their gifts, in thinking themſelues ſomewhat when they are nothing, doe notably deceiue themſelues : as thoſe that thinke they haue the ſubſtance, when they haue but the ſhadow ; as thoſe that dreame they are Kings or Princes, being in truth but baſe perſons: or to vſe the Prophets ſimilitude, *Eſay* 29.8. *Like as an hungry man dreameth and behold hee eateth, and when he awaketh his ſoule is empty : or like as a thirſty man dreameth, and loe hee is drinking, and when he awaketh behold he is faint, and his ſoule longeth.* Men are deceiued two wayes, either by others, or by themſelues : by others, as by flatterers, they are deceiued occaſionally ; by themſelues cauſally, or properly. For he that doth iudge himſelfe to be that which indeede he is not, he may haply pleaſe himſelfe, but he doeth but

φρεναπατᾷ. ἀπατῶν καρδίαν αὐτοῦ. παραλογιζόμενοι ἑαυτούς.

please himselfe in an errour: for in truth hee deceiueth himselfe in his imagination: the Apostle *James* saith, *If any man seeme* (specially to himselfe) *to be religious, and yet refraineth not his tongue, hee deceiueth his owne heart, his religion is vaine, Iam.* 1.26. So likewise, they that are onely hearers of the word (and therefore thinke that all is well enough with them, though they be not doers thereof) *deceiue their owne selues, Iam.* 1.22. And verily this corruption is so great, that as men can be content to be deluded by flatterers, and clawbackes, which please them in their itching humours: so they willingly suffer themselues to be deceiued, euen by themselues, to the end that they may appeare to others to bee that which in truth they are not: that so they may aduance and magnifie themselues in the accoumpt of the world. For as *Alexander* the great, being in India, caused his souldiers to make and leaue behind them bittes and horse-shoes, of an extraordinary greatnesse; huge speares, massie shields, bigge helmets, long swords, and other furniture for horse and man, fitting rather Hippocentaurs, or Giants, then men of ordinary stature; and all to the end it might be said in future time, that *Alexander was a mighty Monarch indeed:* So many there be; who (setting the faire side outward) make goodly glorious shewes in the eies of men; and so would haue other to thinke of them accordingly, (farre aboue their desert) that posterity might iudge them to be that which indeed they are not: and so with *Alexander* in deceiuing others, they wittingly deceiue themselues. Which spiritual guile of deceiuing our selues in matters touching our saluation, is most dangerous, when men delude themselues, in perswading themselues falsly, that they know sufficiently that God is to be loued aboue all, our neighbour as our selues, (which is as much as al the preachers in the earth can say:) that they beleeue; when in stead of faith, there is nothing but damnable pride and presumption: that they repent, when it is nothing but deceitful counterfeiting, and hypocrisie. Besides the danger, consider the indignity of it: men can abide nothing lesse, then to be deceiued and circumvented by others; and yet, behold, they are deluders & deceiuers of themselues: and that which doth more aggrauate the indignity of it, in such things as ought to be best known and most familiar vnto them, wherein it is a shame they should be deceiued, *viz.* in the knowledge of themselues, and that which is yet more, in a matter of greatest moment, in the saluation of their soules. What maruaile therefore is it, that men should be deceiued by the seducer of all seducers, the diuell, who are so easily deceiued of themselues, or rather willing to deceiue themselues?

Plutarch. in Alexandro.

Further

Further obserue, that proud conceited persons, such as haue an ouerweening of themselues and their gifts, and of all men thinke fowle scorne to be deceiued, euen they are easiliest deceiued, yea and that of themselues: for so the Apostle saith, *He that thinketh that he is somewhat, &c. deceiueth himselfe in his imagination.*

Againe, marke hence, that no men, be their gifts neuer so rare, their callings neuer so hie, their places neuer so great, are too good to beare other mens burdens; for they that thinke themselues to be somewhat, some great men, that is, too good to put vnder their shoulders to beare the frailties, and infirmities of their brethren, doe nothing herein but deceiue themselues. Princes and Potentates of the earth are prophecied by *Esay*, chap.49. vers. 23. to be nurcing fathers, and nurcing mothers vnto the Church, not onely by nourishing and defending it, (as the nource her child) but also by bearing with the frailties and wants which are therein.

Lastly, consider that this selfe-conceitednesse, and ouerweening of a mans selfe, is the very bane and poyson of loue; for it maketh proud men thinke themselues too good to become packehorses, or drudges to beare other mens burdẽs, to become seruiceable vnto them in any duty of loue, or to tollerate their frailties or to yeeld of their right, or to suffer iniuries at their hands, or to put vp any little indignity, without stomacke and discontent: because they imagine themselues euery way better then their brethren, and therefore ought to be tollerated, but not so bound to tollerate and beare with others; So that where selfe-loue is, there is no true brotherly loue. It was well said of the Poet, *Non bene conueniunt, &c. maiestas & amor.* It may be said, may not he that is priuy to his own vertues, in conscience of his owne worth, iudge himselfe to be somewhat, that is, to be that which indeed he is, or to haue a greater measure of knowledge, grace, & other gifts, then they that haue lesse?

Answer. He may. For humility is not sottish: the master in humility cannot thinke his scholler more learned then himselfe, except he shall thinke against his conscience. For that saying, *Let* Phil.2.4. *euery man thinke better of another, then of himselfe*, must be restrained onely to equalls, and not extended to superiours in regard of their inferiours. Secondly, I answer, that the Apostle in that place, speaketh not of the giftes and graces bestowed vpon men, but of the persons themselues, and of them, not so much as they are in the account of men, as in the account of God. For he saith not, *Let euery man thinke another more learned, wiſe, diſcreete, ſober then himſelfe* (for ſo he may thinke againſt his conſcience) but *Let euery man thinke another* (that is, any other that is his brother in the Lord) *better then himſelfe*, to witte, before God. And this euery man may doe with good conſcience; for albeit another ſhall outwardly ſeeme more ignorant, negligent, backward, in matters of religion then himſelfe, yet for any thing he knoweth, he may be higher in the fauour of God, then he. And therefore though a man erre in thinking of another, better then of himſelfe, yet he ſhal not doe any thing againſt his conſcience. Thus the *Publican* accounted the proud *Phariſie* better then himſelfe. For he held him as iuſt, himſelfe not worthie to looke vp to heauen: yet herein he ſinned not, nay he is commended for it, though he erred in his iudgement of the *Phariſie*. And ſo if the *Phariſie* had reputed the *Publican* better then himſelfe, that is, higher in Gods fauour then himſelfe, he had not ſinned, nor done againſt his conſcience. For though he might iudge himſelfe more iuſt then the *Publican*, in regard of his life paſt, yet for his preſent eſtate before God he could not. Though *Dauid* knew in the particular quarrell betwixt *Saul* & him, that *Saul* was vniuſt, and he innocent, yet if he ſhould haue thought better of *Saul* in generall, then of himſelfe, he ſhould but haue done his duty.

The fourth and laſt point, containeth the remedies of this euill, which are the rather to be conſidered, becauſe it is a great ſinne, one of thoſe ſeuen which the Lord doth moſt of all deteſt, *Prou.* 7. 17. a dangerous ſinne, hauing a heauy woe attending vpon it, *Woe to them that are prudent in their owne eyes. Iſa.* 5.21. a ſinne almoſt incurable, *Seeſt thou a man that is wiſe in his owne eyes? there is more hope of a foole then of him. Prou.* 26,12. therefore the remedies are more carefully to be knowne, and applied. The remedies are ſpecially fiue.

The firſt is, to looke our ſelues in the glaſſe of the Law, which will ſhew what we are without flattery, or partiality: and by it we ſhall ſee nothing in our ſelues but the vgly ſhape of Satan, cleane defacing the image of God, and that in vs there dwelleth no good thing (as *Paul* ſaith of himſelfe, *Rom.* 7,18.) that there is nothing but vanity in our mindes, rebellion in our wills, a confuſed ataxie in all our affections, tranſgreſſion in our liues. The viewing of our harts and liues in the Law, and the conſidering of our wretched eſtate, in that we are vnder the fearefull curſe, which is a thunderbolt annexed to euery breach thereof, will driue vs out of all conceit of our ſelues, from our ſelfe-loue, and ſelf-liking:

nay,

nay, it will make vs goe out of our selues, not onely *to deny our selues*, as Christ commands, but euen to *abhorre our selues, repenting in dust and ashes*, as *Iob* did, chap. 42.6. causing vs to become flat nothing in our selues, that we may be something in Christ, as *Paul* saith, 1 *Cor*. 3.18. *Let no man deceiue himselfe: If any among you seeme to be wise in this world, let him be a foole, that he may be wise.*

Secondly, when we feele our selues to be tickled with the itching humour of selfe-loue, and selfe-liking, arising from our hidden corruption, either in regard of outward gifts, or inward graces: we must make our owne euills, sinnes, blemishes, imperfections (for there is no man but hath one or other) a soueraigne remedy against it, and so (as it were) driue away one poison with another. As to call to minde some great deformity that is in our bodies, some great infirmity that is in our minde, some crosse or misery in our outward estate, some vile and abhominable sinne which we haue committed, and the horrible punishment, to the which we are lyable by reason thereof: and no doubt but the serious consideration of these, or any of these, will be auaileable, to nippe pride in the bud, and kill the serpent in the shel: and in so doing we shall with the Peacocke, now and then cast our eyes downeward, to our feete, the fowlest and vgliest things we haue: and not alway stand in admiration of our gay feathers, and glorious traine.

Thirdly, we must consider that the things for which we looke so high, and swell so in our owne conceits, are not our owne: but lent vs for a time. *For what is there, that thou hast not receiued?* whether in gifts of body, or graces of minde? nay whether thou speake of soule, or body it selfe? *and if thou hast receiued it, why boastest thou thy selfe as though thou hadst not receiued it?* What vanity is it, for a man to be proud of another mans garment? or for a woman to bost of her borrowed haire? The wicked persecutors of the Church are reprooued for *sacrificing to their nettes, and burning incense to their yarne. Hab.* 1.16. Further, we must consider we haue not onely receiued them; but that we haue so receiued them, as that they are not our owne, with which we may doe what we list, but talents lent vs for a time, and left with vs to employ, ouer which we are but stewards and bayliffes, not Lords or Masters, and that we must be countable for the smallest gift, euen the least farthing: how we haue got it, kept it, bestowed it: the time will come when it shall be saide vnto thee, *Giue an account of thy stewardship. Luk.* 16. 2. Therefore we ought not so much to be puffed vp with the greatnes of our talents, as to be humbled with the consideration of the strict reckoning that God will require at our hands, seeing that *of him, to whom much is committed, much shall bee required.*

Fourthly, to the end we may auoyd this ouer-weening of our selues, let vs compare our selues with the maiestly of God, in whose sight we are but as silly wormes, crawling vpon the ground; nay, in comparison of whom wee are lesse then nothing, and vanitie it
Phil. 2. 10. selfe. Consider, that *to him euery knee doeth bow, of things in heauen, in earth, and vnder the earth*; and thou wilt not be so conceited of thy
Verse 11. selfe, that a silly man doth crouch vnto thee; that *to him euery tongue doth confesse*, and sing his praises, the blessed Angels crying continually, Holy, Holy, Holy, Lord God of Saboth, heauen and earth are full of thy glory: & then a short blast of wind, or popular applause, shall not so easily puffe thee vp, like an emptie bladder, or carrie thee away, as it did *Herod, Actes* 12. But to omit this odious comparison, betwixt a fraile mortall man, and the glorious euerliuing God (there being no comparison betwixt finite, and infinite) let vs neuer compare our selues with our inferiours, but with our superiours and betters, who are eminenly aboue vs in euery gift and blessing of God, in regard of whose honours and preferments wee are but base and contemptible: in regard of whose knowledge, wee are but children, and know nothing: in regard of whose riches we are but beggars, and haue nothing. For as *Dauid*, when he beheld the wonderfull frame of the heauens, those glorious creatures, the Sunne, the Moone, and the Starres, by and by made this vse of it to himselfe, to consider his owne vilenesse in regard of them, *What is*
Psal. 8. 4. *man, that thou art mindfull of him? or the sonne of man, that thou visitest him?* So when we compare our selues with others, that are as farre aboue vs, as the heauens are aboue the earth, whose gifts and graces doe as farre excell ours, as the bright sun-shine the dim candle light: we cannot chuse, but bee ashamed, and confounded in our selues; acknowledging, that there is no such cause why wee should so magnifie our selues aboue others, and nullifie others in comparison of our selues.

4 *But let euery man proue his owne worke, and then shall he haue reioycing in himselfe onely, and not in another.*

Here the Apostle laieth down another remedy against self-loue, and ouerweening of our selues and it is the fift and the last of which I purpose to intreat, and it stands in prouing and examining of a mans owne worke by it selfe, without comparing it with an other

mans

mans worke, and withall in the approouing of it vnto God. *Let euery man approoue his owne worke.* And hee giues two reasons why euery man ought to approue his owne works vnto God, and to consider them absolutely in themselues, and not relatiuely in respect of others, the first reason is in this verse, *then shall hee haue reioycing in himselfe onely, and not in another*: the second, in the next verse, *for euery man shall beare his owne burden.*

Touching the remedy. *Let euery man prooue his owe worke.* The word translated* *prooue*, signifieth also to *approoue*, as *Rom.* 14.22. *Blessed is he that condemneth not in himselfe in the thing that he approoueth,* 1.*Cor.* 16.3. *Whosoeuer ye shall approue or allow of by letters.* And so the word is vsed in English, when wee say, such a one is *to prooue a will*, that is, to approoue it.

* δοκιμάζειν. ἐν ᾧ δοκιμάζει. ἐὰν δοκιμάσητε.

The word in this place (I take it) may bee vnderstood in both senses, *to prooue our works*, and *to approoue them.* How we are to proue our workes, by taking triall and examination of them, I haue already shewed in the former verse. But we are further *to approoue them to God*, according to *Pauls* commandement, *study to shew thy selfe approued vnto God*, 2. *Timoth.* 2. 15. and his practise, in coueting alway *to bee acceptable vnto him*, 2. *Cor.* 5. 9. This approouing of our works, is a soueraigne remedie against ouerweening of our selues, for hee that alwayes stands vpon his triall, and Gods approbation, cannot bee puffed vp with selfe-loue of himselfe, or selfe-liking of his owne workes: but rather humbled with the consideration of Gods absolute iustice, and his owne imperfections, and so stirred vp with great diligence, to worke out his saluation with feare and trembling.

Now we shall approoue our workes vnto God, if we obserue these three things. First, that all our actions specially (in the worship and seruice of God) be grounded vpon the will and word of God; and not vpon wil-worship, or humane inuentions: otherwise it will be said, *Who required these things at your hands?*

Secondly, that we performe all our actions sincerely and vprightly, as in the presence of God, with an honest heart, and a good conscience: as *Abimelech* protesteth of himselfe, *Gen.* 20.5. and *Hezekiah*, *Isay.* 38.3. and *Paul*, *Act.* 23.1.

Thirdly, that they alway tend to a good end, as the glory of God, *Whether ye eate or drinke, or whatsoeuer yee doe, doe all to the glory of God*, 1. *Cor.* 10.30. and the good of our brethren, *Let all things bee done to edification*, 1. *Cor.* 14.26.

It may here be demanded, whether wee may not approoue our selues and our actions to men? To which I answer, that wee may

and

and ought. For although we may not be men-pleaſers, that is, ſuch as frame and temper our actions, and our ſpeeches ſo, as they may alway bee pleaſing to the corrupt humours, and wicked affections of men (for then we were not the ſeruants of God) *Gal.* 1.10. Yet wee are to pleaſe them in that which is good to edification, *Rom.* Matth.5.16. 15.2. 1.*Cor.* 10.33. And Chriſt commandeth, that *our light ſhould ſo* Rom.12.17. *ſhine before men, that they may ſee our good workes.* And *Paul* biddeth vs to *procure honeſt things in the ſight of all men.* And *whatſoeuer things are true, and honeſt, and iuſt, and pure; whatſoeuer appertaine to loue, and are of good report, wee muſt thinke on them, and practiſe them*, *Phil.* 4.8. Yet wee muſt ſeeke for the approbation of men, with theſe cautions.

Firſt, we muſt ſo ſeeke for the approbation of men, as that we do not ſeeke it, nor reſt in it *alone*, but withall ſeeke to be approoued of God. *For hee that praiſeth himſelfe* (and ſo conſequently, hee that is praiſed of others) *is not approoued, but hee whom the Lord praiſeth*, 2. *Cor.* 10.18. *How can yee beleeue* (ſaith our Sauiour Chriſt) *which receiue honour one of another, and ſeeke not the honour that commeth of God alone? Iohn* 5.44.

Secondly, we muſt ſeeke for the approbation of God in the firſt place; and in the ſecond place, to be approoued of men, as Chriſt did: for hee *grew in fauour*, firſt *with God*, and after *with men*, *Luke* 2.52. and the Elders, *who by faith obtained a good report*, *Hebr.* 11.2. Reade *Rom.* 14.18.

Thirdly, we muſt neuer looke for the approbation of the multitude, or acclamation of the moſt: for that cannot be done without ambition, and vaine glory, in ſeeking popular applauſe: *Woe bee to you when all men ſpeake well of you*, *Luke* 6.26. Thus Chriſt ſaith, *Hee* John 5.41. *ſought not praiſe of men.* For thoſe that are addicted to popular applauſe, and are ouer curious of their credit, immoderatly ſeeking to get and keepe a good name with all ſorts of men, while they ſeeke for fame, they loſe a good name, in ſeeking fame from the wicked, which is but a ſhadow, and loſing a good name in the opinion of the godly, which is the ſubſtance.

Fourthly, we muſt ſo farre ſeeke for the approbation of the wicked, that wee miniſter, no not the leaſt occaſion of offence vnto them, 1.*Corinthians* 10.32. *Giue no offence, neither to the Iewe, nor to the Gentile:* but to conuict their conſciences, and to ſtoppe their mouthes by our godly and vnblameable conuerſation, which may bee a preparatiue for them againſt the day of their viſitation, 1. *Peter* 2.12. *Haue your conuerſation honeſt among the Gentiles, that they which ſpeake euill of you, as of euill doers, may by your good workes*

which

which they shall see, glorifie God in the day of their visitation.

Fiftly, in doing our duties, we must not respect the iudgement of the world, neither fearing the faces, nor the censures of men. This was *Pauls* practise, 1.*Cor.*4.3. *I passe very little to bee iudged of you, or of mans iudgement:* wee must goe *through good report, and euill report*, 2.*Cor.*6.8.

Lastly, we must seeke to be approued of men, not so much in regard of our selues, as that by this meanes Gods glory may be more and more aduanced: for *our light must so shine before men, that they may see our good workes, and glorifie our Father which is in heauen, Matt.* 5.16. If wee obserue these sixe cautions, wee may with good conscience seeke to get a good name, which will be vnto vs as a precious oyntment, refreshing vs with the comfort of a godly life, *Prou.* 22.1 *Eccles.*7.3.

Thus much of the Remedy. The reason followeth, *And then shal hee haue whereof to reioyce in himselfe, and not in another.* The wordes translated to *reioyce*, signifie, to *glory:* which is more then to reioyce. καύχημα ἕξει.

There is a double ground of glorying; one, out of a mans selfe: another in himselfe. Out of himselfe, in God alone, *Let not the wise man glory in his wisedome, nor the strong man in his strength, nor the rich man in his riches. But let him that glorieth, glory in this, that he vnderstandeth and knoweth me, Ierem.* 9.23,24. 1.*Cor.* 1.31. In himselfe, in the comfortable testimony of a good conscience. *Our glorying is this, the testimony of our conscience, that in simplicitie and godly purenes, we haue had our conuersation in the world,* 2.*Cor.*1.12. The one is glorying before God; the other before men. The one, of iustification, the other of holy conuersation for time past, and constant resolution for time to come. The one in the testimony of our conscience, 2 *Cor.* 1.12. the other, in the testimony of Gods Spirit, witnessing to our spirits, that wee are the sonnes of God, *Rom.*8.16. The first is not meant in this place, but onely the second, *For no flesh can glory in his presence*, 1.*Cor.*1.29.

It will be said, This glorying in a mans selfe, is vaine glory, and a branch of pride. *Answer.* It differs from vaine glorie: first, in the foundation: for vaine glory hath for his ground our owne vertues and gifts, considered as comming from our selues, and not from God: whereas this true glorying is grounded vpon them, as they are fruites of regeneration, proceeding from our iustification by Christ, and reconciliation with God. Secondly, in the end: Vaine glory tendeth to the aduancing of our selues, in an opinion of our proper iustice, and desert. This true glorying aimeth at the glory of God alone.

Obiect.

Obiect. *Paul* reprooues thoſe that conſider their owne gifts onely, neuer comparing themſelues with others, 2.*Cor.* 10.12. *They vnderſtand not that they meaſure themſelues with themſelues, and compare themſelues with themſelues.* Therefore it ſeemes that a man by comparing himſelfe with others, may haue whereof to reioyce. *Anſwer.* He reproues the falſe apoſtles in that place for glorying in the gifts which they had, and the number of Proſelytes which they had wonne, neuer comparing themſelues with himſelfe, or any other Apoſtle, which was the cauſe they were ſo puffed vp with pride. For to compare our ſelues with thoſe that are eminently aboue vs, is a notable meanes to abate pride: as I haue already ſhewed. Whereas the meaſuring of our ſelues by our ſelues, with our inferiours, is the onely way to increaſe it. And this is it which the Apoſtle reprooues in this place.

Further, wee may reioyce, or glorie in the teſtimony of a good conſcience, if we obſerue theſe rules.

I. In our beſt deſires, endeauours, actions, wee muſt labour to feele our owne defects: that we doe not the good wee ſhould, nor in that manner we ought.

II. We muſt labour to haue euen our beſt workes, (our almes, prayers, &c.) couered with the righteouſnes of Chriſt: for it is the ſweet odour of his ſacrifice, that doth perfume all our actions, that they may be acceptable to God, being *offered with the praiers of the Saints vpon the golden altar, Reuel.* 8.3.

III. Wee muſt acknowledge all the good things we haue, the will, and the worke, the purpoſe and the power, to proceed from God alone, *Phil.* 2.13. *Iames* 1.17.

IIII. Wee muſt reioyce in them, not as cauſes, but as fruites of iuſtification: ſo that if the queſtion be, whether we be iuſtified by them, or not? we muſt renounce them, tread them vnder our feet, and account them as dung as *Paul* did, *Phil.* 3.8.

Hence we learne ſundry things.

I. That if we would haue a light heart, and paſſe our time merrily with comfort and content, wee muſt looke to approoue our hearts to God in all our actions.

II. It confutes the opinion of the multitude, who iudge thoſe that make conſcience of ſinne, and leade a more ſtrict life then the
Act.24.16. common ſort, endeauouring with *Paul*, to haue alwayes a cleare conſcience toward God, and toward men, of all others to leade a moſt melancholike, ſad, and vncomfortable life. For the trueth is, this is the onely true ioy, all other ioy is but counterfeit in compariſon: it is radicall, proceeding from the heart: the other but ſuperficiall,

ficiall', from the the teeth outward: it comforts a man in the midſt of afflictions: whereas a man may haue the other, and yet in the midſt of mirth his heart will be ſorrowfull: this is pernament and during, the other tranſitorie and fading. It is like the ioy in harueſt, *Pſal* 4. 7. and which they haue that diuide a ſpoyle. *Eſa*. 9. 3. therfore *Salomon* ſaith, it is *a continuall feaſt: Prou*. 15. 15. and *Peter* calls it *ioy vnſpeakeable, and glorious*, 1. *Pet*. 1. 8.

III. This ſhewes that there is much falſe ioy in the world, conſiſting wholly in honours, profits, pleaſures: none of which haue their ground in a mans ſelfe: and therefore being out of a mans ſelfe, they are not true and durable, but falſe and vaniſhing ioyes. Now thoſe which haue no comfort but out of themſelues, are of foure ſorts. Firſt, ſuch as reioyce, and glory in the opinion that the world hath of them, and not in the teſtimony of their owne conſcience. Secondly, ſuch as reioyce, not in their reconciliation with God, but in their blameleſſe conuerſation, in that they haue not bin open offenders, or men of ſcandalous life. *Luk*. 18. 11. Thirdly, ſuch as reioyce in the vertues of their anceſtors, as the Iewes bragged they were the ſeed of *Abraham*. *Ioh*. 8. 33. which vaine glorying of other mens vertues, *Iohn Baptiſt* reproueth, when he ſaith, *Thinke not to ſay with your ſelues, we haue Abraham for our father, &c. Mat*. 3. 9. Fourthly, ſuch as reioyce and thinke themſelues in a good caſe, becauſe they ſee others worſe then themſelues: this is right the Phariſies ioy, *O God, I thanke thee, I am not thus, and thus, or like this Publican, Luke* 18. 11. This is it which the Apoſtle directly aimeth at in this place: when men thinke themſelues iuſt, becauſe others are more wretched then themſelues: and pure, becauſe others are more defiled. Whereas other mens hainous ſinnes ſhall not iuſtifie vs and our leſſer ſinnes, ſaue onely as Ieruſalem iuſtified her ſiſters, Sodom, and Samaria, *Ezech*. 16. 51. But ſo a man may bee iuſtified, and yet condemned.

5. *For euery one ſhall beare his owne burden.*

Here *Paul* layes downe a ſecond reaſon of his aſſertion, in the former verſe, why euery man ought to prooue his owne worke, rather then to be curious in ſearching into the liues, and skanniug the actions of other men, becauſe *euery man ſhall beare his owne burden*, which is all one with that, *Gal*. 5. 10. *to beare a mans owne iudgement:* and that *Rom*. 14. 12. *to giue an account to God for himſelfe*. It is a prouerbiall ſpeech, the meaning whereof is expreſſed by the like, *Ier*. 31. 30. *Euery man that eateth the ſowre grape, his teeth ſhall bee ſet*

on

on edge. And by that which is common amongſt vs, *Euery veſſell ſhall ſtand vpon his owne bottome:* that is, euery man ſhal beare the puniſhment of his owne ſin. For as the Indian is not therefore white, becauſe the Morian is more blacke, or as the ſand-blind is not therfore ſharpe ſighted, becauſe ſome other is ſtone blind. So no man is therefore acquit of his ſinnes, becauſe others are greater ſinners: or exempt from puniſhment, becauſe others ſhall vndergoe a deeper condemnation. Therefore conſidering that euery man muſt beare the guilt and puniſhment of his owne ſinne, he ought more narrowly to looke to himſelfe then to others; and to be a more ſeuere cenſurer of himſelfe, then of another.

For the better vnderſtanding of the words, ſundry queſtions are to be diſcuſſed.

Onus rationis reddēdæ: onus infirmitatis participādæ. Auguſt. contra ſcript. Petil. lib. 3. Beda & Lumbard. in hunc locum. Hugo de S. Vict. in Gal. quæſt. 58

Firſt, it may bee demaunded, how euery man ſhould beare his owne burden, ſeeing wee are commanded to beare one anothers burdens? *Anſwer.* There are two ſorts of burdens. The firſt is, of giuing an account to God: thus euery man ſhal beare his owne burden, *For euery man muſt giue an account of himſelfe vnto God, Rom.* 14. 12. The ſecond is, of bearing one anothers infirmities, of which *Paul* ſpeakes, verſe 2. In this ſenſe a man is not to beare his owne burden: but euery man his brothers. For the Apoſtle (to croſſe the opinion of thoſe which thought a man was polluted with other mens ſinnes,) ſaith, *Euery man ſhall beare his owne burden.* And to meet with the careleſneſſe of others, who reſpect themſelues alone, neuer minding the good of their brethren: he ſaith, *Beare ye one anothers burdens.*

II. Obiect. By bearing of our owne burdens, is vnderſtood giuing an account for our ſelues vnto God. Now euery man is not to giue account for himſelfe alone, but for thoſe alſo that are committed to his charge, as the father for his childe, the maſter for his ſeruant, the magiſtrate for the ſubiect, the ſhepheard for the ſheepe, *Ezec.* 34. *His blood will I require at thy hand. Hebr.* 13. 17. *They watch ouer your ſoules, as they that muſt giue account. Anſwer.* Gouernors and ſuperiours are not to giue account for the ſinnes of thoſe that are committed vnto them: but for the ſinnes which themſelues commit, in not looking vnto them, not admoniſhing them, not reſtraining them, not taking condigne puniſhment of them for their offences. This is plainly taught, *Ezech.* 33. 8, 9. *If thou doeſt not admoniſh the wicked of his way, hee ſhall die for his iniquitie, but his blood will I require at thy hand. Neuertheleſſe, if thou warne the wicked of his way, to turne from it, if hee doe not turne from his way, hee ſhall die for his iniquitie, but thou haſt deliuered thy ſoule.*

III. Obiect.

III. Obiect. Infants which haue not ſinned after the manner of the tranſgreſſion of *Adam*, doe beare the burden of *Adams* ſinne: therefore all doe not beare their owne burden. *Anſw.* Firſt, the wordes are properly to be vnderſtood of perſonall, or actuall ſinnes, which are proper to euery man in particular, and not of originall ſinne, or the ſinne of our nature, which is common to all mankind, being propagated together with nature. Secondly, I anſwer, that *Adams* ſinne was our ſinne: and therefore ſeeing infants partake with him in the ſinne, it is iuſt with God, they ſhould partake with him in the puniſhment, and ſo beare their owne burden. For albeit the tranſgreſſion of *Adam* was his actuall and perſonall ſinne: yet it is our originall ſinne, or the ſinne of our nature: ſeeing it is ours by imputation, and propagation of nature, together with corruption. For as *Leui* was in the loynes of *Abraham*, when *Melchizedech* met him, and payed tithes in *Abraham*, *Hebr*.7.9,10. So, all mankind was in the loynes of *Adam* when he ſinned, as the branches are in the root, or in the ſeed. And therfore when he ſinned, we alſo ſinned, as the Apoſtle ſaith, *In whom all ſinned, Romanes* 5.12. For ſo are the words in the originall and not as it is commonly tranſlated, *for as much as all men haue ſinned.*

In ſeminali principio. ἐφ' ᾧ πάντες ἥμαρτον.

IV. Obiection. In the ſecond commandement, the Lord threatneth to viſite the ſinnes of the fathers vpon the children, to the third and fourth generation. Therefore they beare not their owne burden, but part of their parents burden: and parents do not beare their owne whole and entire burden, but their children for them. *Anſwer.* The clauſe in the ſecond Commaundement, of viſiting the ſinnes of the fathers vpon the children, doeth not contradict that of *Ezech*.18.19. *The ſonne ſhall not beare the iniquitie of the father, neither ſhall the father beare the iniquitie of the ſonne; the ſame ſoule that ſinneth, that ſhall die.* For they are reconciled, verſe 14.17. *If hee* (that is, a wicked man) *beget a ſonne that ſeeth all his fathers ſinnes, which he hath done, and feareth, neither doeth the like—— he ſhall not die in the iniquitie of his father, but ſhall ſurely liue.* Therefore the threatning in the ſecond commandement, is not to be vnderſtood abſolutely, as though God would alway plague the children for the fathers ſinne, but conditionally, if they perſiſt and continue in their ſinnes, walking in their waies, and treading in their ſteps. And the ſame anſwer is giuen in the ſecond commandement, that God will not viſite the ſinne of the fathers vpon the children, ſaue *vpon thoſe that hate him.* It may be ſaid, The ſinnes of the parents are not vindicated vpon the children, becauſe the puniſhment inflicted

vpon

vpon their poſteritie, is not felt of the parents. *Anſw.* Firſt, children are (as it were) a part of their parents, and therfore they being puniſhed, their parents are puniſhed with them. Secondly, it is a corraſiue and a torment to parents, to know that their children ſhall bee ſeuerely puniſhed and afflicted. Thirdly, the puniſhment of poſterity hath a relation to the parent, ſeeing God hath threatned hee will puniſh the children which walke in the wicked wayes of their forefathers, that ſo hee may teſtifie how extreamely hee abhorreth both their ſinne, and the ſinne of their progenitors. Fourthly, the parents ſinne, is oft a cauſe of the childrens ſinne, ſeeing that God in his iuſt iudgement, curſeth a wicked mans poſteritie, by leauing them to themſelues, to blindneſſe of mind, and hardneſſe of heart, that ſo they may fulfill the meaſure of their fathers, as our Sauiour Chriſt ſpeaketh, *Matthew* 23.32. And by their owne ſinnes may iuſtly pull vpon them condigne puniſhment. Laſtly, God doeth more manifeſt his wrath againſt the ſinne of the parent, by puniſhing the child.

V. Obiect. Numb. 25.4. The chiefeſt of the Iſraelies were hanged vp before the Lord, for the fornication and idolatry of the people: therefore they did not beare the burden of their owne ſinne. *Anſwer.* They were puniſhed for their owne ſinne, for they conſented to worſhip the Idoll, and commit folly with the daughters of Moab: or rather were principall ringleaders, and firſt actors in this Commicke Tragedie, as may appeare by the practiſe of *Zimri*, Prince of the family of the *Simeonites*, verſe 6. in bringing *Cosbie* a *Midianitiſh* woman into his tent, in the ſight of *Moſes* & the whole congregation. Therefore becauſe they did not hinder them from committing this fact, as they might, being in place of gouernment, but did partake with them in the ſinne, they are firſt puniſhed, and that more ſeuerely: for a thouſand of them were hanged vp the ſame day, verſe 4. the reſt of the people, to the number of three and twenty thouſand, were ſlaine by the ſword at the commandement of God, verſe 5. to which *Paul* had an eye, when hee ſaid, that *there fell in one day* 23. *thouſand*, 1. *Cor.* 10. 8. meaning of the common ſort, excluding thoſe that were hanged vp: for in all there were 24000. *Num.* 25. 9. Thus the contrarietie which ſeemes to bee betwixt theſe two places, may be better accorded, then to ſay (as ſome doe) that the pen-men, or ſcribes, failed in copying out the bookes. Or (as others) that it was ἁμάρτημα μνημονικὸν in *Paul*: or as others, that *Paul* is not contrarie to *Moſes*, ſeeing that if there were 24000. (as *Moſes* ſaith,) there were 23000. for there is no reaſon why the Apoſtle ſhould vſe the leſſe number rather then the greater, (except that

that which I haue ſaid) conſidering the greater is as round a number as the leſſe.

Obiect. VI. Dauid ſinned in numbring the people, and they were puniſhed for his ſinne: *Achan* ſinned, and the people fell ſlaine before the men of Ai: therefore euery man doth not beare his own entire burden. The like may be ſaid of the children of the Sodomits, and of the firſt borne of the Egyptians, who bare the burden of their parents ſinne. *Anſwer.* The people were puniſhed for their owne ſinnes: and ſo was *Dauid*, albeit not in his owne, but in their perſons: for God puniſhed him in his kind, in deſtroying the people with that fearefull plague, in whoſe great multitude hee had gloried ſo much. Indeede their puniſhment was occaſioned by his ſinne: but cauſed by their owne: for no man, though neuer ſo holy, is without ſinne, and therefore none but deſerue puniſhment: nay, *It is Gods mercie, that wee are not conſumed Lam.* 3. verſe 22.

And albeit all the infants periſhed in the Deluge, and in the ouerthrow of Sodome and Gomorrha, which could neither imitate, nor approoue the actions of their fathers: yet their death was deſerued. For though infants bee truly called *innocents*, in regard of actuall ſinne: yet they are not *innocents* in regard of originall: for from the wombe they carrie a woluiſh nature, which prepares them to the ſpoile, though they neuer did hurt: the Scorpion hath his ſting within him, though he doe not alway ſtrike: and though a Serpent may be handled whilſt the cold hath benũmed him; yet when he is warmed, he will hiſſe out his venomous poiſon. Mans practiſe doth cleare God of vniuſtice in this behalfe, in killing the young cubbes, as well as the old foxe: the wolues whelps, as well as the damme. Albeit if we ſpeake of their finall eſtate, and come to particulars, we are to leaue ſecret iudgements to God. The example of *Achan* is more difficult, ſeeing that for his ſinne, 35. of the people were ſlaine, *Ioſh.* 7.5. and his whole familie rooted out, verſe 25. who were not conſenting to his fact: nor guilty of his ſinne. Yet ſomething may probably be ſaid in this caſe. Firſt, that they were guiltie of this his ſinne in part, in not puniſhing theft ſo ſeuerely as they ought to haue done, which was a meanes to embolden *Achan* to ſteale the execrable thing. Secondly, that priuate good muſt yeeld to the publike; as the life of euery particular perſon to the general good of the whole Commonwealth: thus ſouldiours in the warres, redeeeme the publike peace by the loſſe of their own liues: now the manifeſtation of the glory of the wiſedome, power, and iuſtice of God, is the publike good of the whole

Church: therefore mens priuate good, euen their liues, muſt giue place to it: eſpecially conſidering hee neuer inflicts temporall puniſhment for the publike good, but hee reſpects therein the priuate good of his Elect, whom hee corrects in iudgement, not in furie. Thirdly, howſoeuer *Achan* did beare the burden of his owne ſin; this iudgement might be inflicted vpon them for their good: for temporall puniſhment, yea death it ſelfe is ſometimes inflicted for the good of thoſe that are puniſhed, as we ſee in the children of the Sodomites, many whereof (no doubt) were taken away in mercy, leſt malice ſhould haue changed and corrupted their minds: and ſometime for the terrour of others, to be a warning peece to make them take heed; and ſometime for both: as it may be it was in this particular. Fourthly, ſinne committed by a particular man, that is a member of a politike body, doeth after a ſort belong to the whole body: thus the Lord ſaith, that *Blood defileth the land, which cannot bee cleanſed of the blood that was ſhed therein, but by the blood of him that ſhed it, Numbers* 35.33. And thus *Achans* ſinne, though not knowne to the people, made the whole armie guiltie before God, till he was put to death, *Ioſhua* 7.11, 12. Laſtly, if the tithing of an army for the offence of ſome few, haue bin thought lawful and iuſt: why ſhould the death of thirtie ſixe men ſeeme vniuſt for the ſinne of *Achan*, eſpecially conſidering it was to make the people more prouident, to preuent and take heed of the like euill? If theſe reaſons ſatisfie not, yet let vs reſt in this, that Gods iudgements are often ſecret, but alway iuſt. See *Auguſt. lib. quaeſt. in Ioſh. q.* 8. and *Caluin in 7. cap. Ioſh.*

Decimatio exercitus.

Obiect. VII. If euery man muſt beare his owne burden, *Dauid* ſhall as well beare the burden of his murthering of *Vrias*, by the ſword of the children of *Ammon*, as *Saul* the murthering of himſelfe with his owne ſword; *Peter* his denying Chriſt, as *Iudas* his betraying him, &c. *Anſwer.* By the ſentence of the Law, euery one is to beare his owne burden, and to ſatisfie for his owne ſinne, in his owne perſon: but the Goſpell, (the ſecond part of Gods word,) makes an exception: which is, that they which haue their ſinnes ſet vpon Chriſts reckoning, ſhall not giue account for them againe: and thoſe that haue the burden of them laide vpon his ſhoulders (who hath borne our ſins in his body vpon the croſſe, 1. *Pet.* 2. 23.) ſhal not beare the burden of them themſelues at the laſt iudgment. Therfore true beleeuers, which haue Chriſt their ſuretie, ſatisfying the rigour of Gods iuſtice for them, ſhall not anſwer or ſatisfie for them themſelues: for they are freed by him from a threefold burden. Firſt, from the burden of ceremonies (and ſo conſequently

of

of humane lawes and ordinances) which were *a yoke* (as *Peter* saith) *which neither we, nor our fathers were able to beare, Act.*15. Secondly, from the burden of miseries, or crosses, which befall men in this life. He doeth ease vs of this burden, by his word and spirit, either in remoouing them away, *Psalm.* 81.7. or in giuing strength and patience to beare them, 2.*Cor.*12.9. or in mitigating and proportionating them to our strength, 1.*Cor.*10.13. Thirdly, from the burden of sinne, as well originall as actuall, in being made *sinne*, that is, 2.Cor.5. accounted a sinner, and made a sacrifice for sinne, for vs: as also by easing them that are heauy laden, in pacifying the perplexed conscience, *Matth.*11.28. It will be said, If Christ beare the burden of our sinnes, euery man shal not beare his owne burden. *Answ.* Both be true, and may well stand together: for *Legally*, euery man is to beare his owne burden, the Law requiring personall obedience, or satisfaction, or both. *Euangelically*, Christ, our suretie doeth beare the burden of them, and satisfie the iustice of God for them, 1.*Pet.*2.23.

Vse. Hence we learne, first, that no man can pay a ransome for his brother, or redeeme his soule from death, or satisfie the iustice of God for his sinne, seeing that euery man by the tenour of the law, is to beare his owne burden: and by the Gospel, none can bee our suretie, but Christ.

Secondly, here we see the nature of sinne, that it is a burden to the soule: for it is heauier then the grauell of the earth, and the sand of the sea. It is a burden to the wicked angels, for it weighed them from the highest heauen, and made them fall like thunderbolts into the lowest hel. To man: for as *Dauid* saith, it is *like a grieuous burden, too heauy for him to beare, Psal.*38.4. To God: for the hypocriticall and ceremoniall seruice of the Iewes, was such *a burden vnto him, that he was weary to beare it, Isa.*1.14. *Behold, I am pressed vnder you, as a cart is pressed that is full of sheaues, Amos* 2.13. To the creatures, who groane vnder this burden, being by mans sinne subiect to vanitie and corruption, *Rom.*8.20,21. Hence it followeth then, that those which feele not the weight and burden of their sinnes, are dead being aliue, as *Paul* speakes in another case, 1. *Timoth.*5.6.

Thirdly, we are not to wonder, that sinne being so heauie a burden, should be made so light a matter by carnall men: for it is a spirituall burden, and therefore no maruell, though it be not felt of them that are all flesh, and no spirit.

Fourthly, this shewes that the more a man doeth feare the burden of his sinnes, the greater measure of grace, and spiritual life he hath: and the leſſe he feeleth it, the more he is to ſuſpect himſelfe, that the graces of God doe want, and decay in him. For corruption is not felt by corruption, but by grace: and therefore the more a man doth feele the burthen of his owne corruptions, the more grace he hath.

Fiftly, by this we ſee, that the greateſt part of the world are dead in their ſinnes, in that they haue no ſenſe nor feeling of this heauie burden. There is indeede great crying out of the ſtone in the reynes, becauſe it is felt to bee a great torment to the bodie: but there is little or no complaining, of the ſtone in the heart, becauſe men want ſpirituall life, and ſenſe to diſcerne it. All men can take pittie vpon a beaſt, if he lie vnder his burden, and will be readie to helpe him vp againe. But all haue not the like ſight and ſenſe of the ſpirituall burden of ſinne, nor ſimpathy of the miſerie of their brethren, groaning vnder it.

Sixtly, whereas *Paul* ſaith, *Euery man muſt beare his own burthen*, he meeteth with the prophaneneſſe and Atheiſme of our time, when men make a mocke at the day of iudgement, and the ſtrict account that euery man is to giue for himſelfe. The Iewes were woont to ieaſt at the threatnings of God, denounced by the Prophets, and to call the viſions of the Prophets, *onus Iehouæ, the burthen of the Lord*, in a merriment, vſing it as a by-word. *Ieremie* 23. verſe 34, 36, 38. Thereby ſignifying that the threats of God, were but vaine bugs, or ſcarre-crowes, which might perhaps terrifie children, but could not hurt them. The like prophaneneſſe, infidelity, atheiſme, hath crept into the mindes of many, who otherwiſe profeſſe the Goſpel, which they teſtifie by their ſpeeches, in ſaying, they are ſure, ſinne is nothing ſo ougly, hell is not halfe ſo hotte, nor the deuill halfe ſo blacke, as preachers ſay they are: or if they bee, they are ſure they ſhall not goe loaden alone, with the burden of their ſinnes, but ſhall haue company, and ſhall perhaps abide the brunt as well as their fellows. But alas, they know not that the burden of ſin is intollerable, that it wil eternally preſſe thē down to the gulfe of hell, & that they ſhal neuer be able to be rid or eaſed of it.

Seuenthly, we are here admoniſhed to take heede of euery ſinne, for there is no ſinne ſo ſmall but hath his waight, and ſuch a waight, as will preſſe downe to the bottomleſſe pit, *Ro.* 6. 23. And though ſome be greater then others, and ſinke a man deeper into condemnation, yet many ſmall ſinnes will as eaſily condemne, as a few great. Like as ſands, though but ſmall in quantity, yet beeing many in number, will as ſoone ſinke the ſhip, as if it were laden with the greateſt burden.

Eightly,

Eightly, seeing the guilt and punishment of sinne, is so heauie a burden, we are to ease and disburden our selues thereof. And that we may doe this, we must labour to feele the intollerable weight of it, pressing, and oppressing the conscience. Therefore as those who in their sleepe are troubled with the *Ephialtes* or *mare*, feeling (as it were) a great mountaine lying vpon them, & pressing them down, would giue all the world, the weight might be remooued: So wee feeling the weight and burden of our sinnes, are to labour to bee disburdened and eased therof: and this we shall doe by our repentance toward God, and faith in Christ, *Matt.*11.28. *Come vnto mee, all ye that are weary, and laden, and I will ease you.*

6 Let him that is taught in the word, make him that hath taught him, partaker of all his goods.

In these words the Apostle laieth downe an other rule, touching the maintenance of the ministerie, and competencie of allowance for the Ministers of the word: for it seemeth that the Ministerie among the Galatians, was at that time much neglected, at least, not so respected as it ought.

In handling of the rule, I will first shew the meaning of the words; secondly, the reasons of the rule: thirdly, the obiections against it: lastly, the doctrine, and vses, that are to bee gathered from it.

The meaning.

Let him that is taught] The word translated *taught*, signifieth him that is catechized, or taught familiarly by word of mouth, or liuely voyce, as when children are taught the first principles of religion. But heere it hath a larger signification (as *Oecumenius* hath well obserued) for him that is any way taught and instructed, whether it bee in the first principles, and rudiments, or in points of greater difficultie; whether plainely and familiarly, (as Catechizers vse to doe:) or more profoundly, for the instruction of the learned.

κατηχούμενος.

κατηχούμενος, id est, διδασκόμενος.

Taught in the word] What needes this addition (may some say) is there any catechizing without the word? *Answ.* The Apostle addeth *in the word*, to shew that hee meaneth not so much the doctrine of Christian religion, contained in the Scriptures, as the doctrine of the Gospel; which by an *exoche*, or peculiar excellency, is called *the word*, *Act.*16.6. *They were forbidden of the holy Ghost to preach the word in Asia:* which is expounded, v.10. to be the preaching of the Gospel. Thus it is vsed, *Act.*14.25. *when they had preached the word*

word in Perga. Marke 4.14. *The sower soweth the word.* And so in sundry other places. And it is further called *the word of the kingdome, Mattew* 13.19. because it teacheth what is the kingdome of grace, and glory: and because it being beleeued, or (as the Apostle speakes) *being mingled with faith in our hearts,* doth make vs free denizens of the kingdome of grace in this life; and doth aduance vs to the kingdome of grace in this life; and doth aduance vs to the kingdome of glory in the life to come. Secondly, it is called *the word of God,* because he is the authour of it, and no creature, man, or Angel, 2.*Thess.*3.13. Thirdly, *the word of saluation, Actes* 13.26. because it shewes the way and meanes of attaining saluation. Lastly, the *word of life, Actes* 5.20. because it doeth not onely shew the narrow way, that leadeth to *eternall life;* but is in it selfe *a liuely word, and mightie in operation, Hebr.*4.12. For as the powerfull word of God in the beginning, did giue beeing to things that were not; so the Gospell (being the power of God to saluation to euery one that beleeueth,) doeth make new creatures, by the immortall seed of the word.

Hebr. 4.2.

Make him that taught him] *q.d* catechised him. Yet as before, it must be taken generally for any kinde of teaching, or instruction; for so the word is vsed else where in Scripture, as *Luke* 1.4. *Act.* 18.25. *Romanes* 2.18. 1.*Corinth.*14.19. so that this text giueth vs no iust occasion to speake of the originall, maner, vse, and profit of catechizing.

* τροφάς, εὔνοιαν, τιμήν.
Oecumen.

Partaker of his goods] By *goods* he* vnderstandeth food raiment, lodging, bookes, and other necessaries, without the which a Minister of the word cannot follow his calling; for *Paul* calleth these *goods*, according to the common opinion, which so iudgeth of them. *Luke* 12.19. *Soule, thou hast much goods laid vp for many yeeres. Luke* 16.25. *Sonne, remember that thou in thy life time receiuedst thy good things.*

Make them partaker] That is, communicate, affoard, giue vnto them these temporall things, seeing they giue you spirituall.

Of all his goods] Not in giuing all away, but imparting to their teachers what they stand in need of, accounting nothing too deare for them. The Papists vpon this ground, take tithes of all, as the Priestes did in the Leuiticall law: whereas *Paul* speakes nothing of tithes.

There are foure principall duties, which the people are to performe to their Pastour, three of them are recorded elsewhere in Scripture. The first is, to heare them as Embassadours sent of God, with reuerence. The second is, to obey them, & submit themselues

1.Thess.3.13.
Hebr.13.17.
1.Thess.5.13

vnto

vnto them in the Lord. The third, to loue and honor them for the works ſake. The fourth, the Apoſtle ſpeakes of in this place, to giue them not onely countenance, but alſo maintenance.

The reaſons of this rule are many and weightie.

Wee are bound (euen by the bond of nature) to maintaine our parents if they be in want; becauſe they maintained vs, and gaue vnto vs our being: *Paul* ſaith, *It is an honeſt thing and acceptable before God, for children to recompenſe their parents and progeniours,* 1 *Tim.* 5.4. Now if this bee ſo, men are bound by the ſame right to maintaine their ſpirituall fathers in Chriſt, that haue begotten them anew by the preaching of the word: as *Paul* ſaith, *Hee trauelled in paine of the Galatians, till Chriſt was formed in them, Gal.* 4. and that *hee begate Oneſimus in his bonds, Philem.* v. 10. And, 1. *Cor.* 4. 15. *In Chriſt Ieſus I haue begotten you through the Goſpell.* Hence *Paul* commendeth the Galatians, *Gal* 4 15. for that if it had been poſſible, they would haue plucked out their eyes, and haue giuen them him. And ſurely, wee owe vnto our ſpirituall parents, and fathers in Chriſt, not onely this temporall traſh, but euen our ſelues, as *Paul* ſaith to *Philem.* verſe 19. *Albeit I doe not ſay vnto thee that thou oweſt vnto mee, euen thine owne ſelfe.*

II. It is a law of nations, and a concluſion grounded vpon common equitie, that thoſe that watch, labour, and ſpend themſelues, as a candle, to giue light to others, and that for the common good of all, ſhould bee maintained of the common ſtocke by all. And the Lord chargeth all the twelue Tribes, euen all Iſrael, *Deut.* 12.1. *Beware that thou forſakeſt not the Leuite, ſo long as thou liueſt on the earth.*

III. Euery trade, calling, and condition of life, is able to maintaine them that liue therein (as experience ſhewes:) therefore wee may not thinke that the miniſtery, being the higheſt calling, ſhould be ſo baſe or barren, as that it cannot competently maintaine them that attend thereupon.

IV. The Miniſters are the Lords ſouldiers, his captaines, and 1.Cor.9.7.
ſtandard-bearers, and therefore are not to goe a warfare at their owne coſte: the Lords labourers in his vineyard, and therefore are worthy of their wages, and ought to eate of the fruite of the vineyard: the Lords ſhepheards, ſet ouer the flocke of Chriſt to feed his ſheepe, and therefore ought to eate of the milke of the flocke. And ſeeing it was forbidden, that no man ſhould muzzle the mouth of the oxe, that treadeth out the corne: ſhall we thinke that Deut.25.4.
God would haue thoſe that threſh in his floore, and ſeparate the 2.Cor.9.9,10
wheate from the chaffe, the precious from the vile, to be muzzeled, or

or not to liue vpon their labours? *For they are worthy double honour*, that is,all honour,reuerence,helpe,and furtherance, *which labour in the word and doctrine*, 1.*Tim*.5.17.

V. The Miniſters are to giue themſelues wholly *to reading, exhortation,doctrine,and to continue therein*, 1.*Tim*.4.13,15,16 they are wholly to deuote themſelues to the building of the Church, and to the fighting of the Lords battels: and therfore *not to be entangled with the cares of this life*, 2.*Tim*.2.4. Therfore they are to haue their pay,and their allowance, that ſo they may attend vpon their callings,without diſtraction.

VI. It is the ordinance of God (as *Paul* ſaith, 1.*Corinth*.9.14.) that they which preach the Goſpell, ſhould liue of the Goſpell: therefore thoſe that doe not their endeauour,and inlarge not their liberality to vphold and maintaine the Miniſtery in good eſtate, they withſtand (as much as in them lieth) the ordinance of God: beſides, they waſte and make hauocke of the Church of God: and are guiltie of the blood of all that periſh for want of inſtruction.

I adde further, it is the will of God,that the Miniſters which labour in the word and doctrine, ſhould be plentifully and liberally prouided for: (yet with moderation, that they draw not all mens wealth into their purſes, as the Pope and Church of Rome haue done into their coffers,of whom it is truly verified, *Religio peperit diuitias, ſed filia deuorauit matrem.*) which I prooue from the Leuitical law: for the whole land of promiſe, being no bigger in compaſſe then Wales,or the fourth part of England: yet yeelded vnto the Leuites, at the appointment of God, beſides the ſhare which they had out of the ſacrifices,beſides tenths,firſt fruits,&c. fortie eight cities with their ſuburbs.

It may here be demaunded,whether the Miniſters of the word are now to be maintained by common contribution,and liberality of the people,or not?

Anſwer. We muſt conſider,that if the Miniſters be ſufficiently prouided for,by ſet ſtipends, as by ſome foundation,or by the reuenewes of the Church, men are not bound to contribute vnto them,and make them partakers of all their goods; although in regard of thankfulneſſe, *they owe vnto them euen themſelues*, as *Paul* telleth *Philemon*; but onely ſuch as haue not elſe wherewith to maintaine themſelues. And we muſt conſider the reaſon why *Paul* commandeth all that are inſtructed in the word,to make them that inſtructed them,partakers of their goods, to wit, becauſe in *Pauls* time, and long after,the Church was not endowed with lands or

goods,

goods, whereby the Ministerie might be vpholden; neither had it publike Christian Magistrates, but was vnder cruell tyrants in persecution: and therefore those that were taught in the word, were to maintaine their teachers by liberal contribution, otherwise they might starue: but now the Church beeing greatly inriched, they may without contribution be sufficiently maintained of the Church goods.

And that it is much more conuenient for the Ministers to bee maintained by set stipends, arising from goods proper to the Church, then by voluntarie contribution, it may appeare by this, in that it cuts off sundry inconueniences, which in voluntary contributions, either cannot be, or are hardly auoyded. First, flatterie, and suspition of flatterie, in beeing thought to haue some persons in admiration, because of aduantage. Secondly, the poorer sort are no way disgraced by this meanes, as they should bee in contributions, except they did giue ratably as the rest. Thirdly, dissembling and deceite, in making as though they receiued little, when as they haue much, is cut off in a set stipend. Fourthly, the euill disposed would not so easily cast off their Minister, and seeke a new that would teach for lesse; or would giue nothing at all, if they were touched to the quicke, and galled for their sinnes. Fiftly, ostentation in some, in giuing much, and disdaining those that giue lesse. Sixtly, suspition of couetousnesse and filthy lucre in the Ministers, in seeming to take of those to whom they ought to giue. Seuenthly, disgrace of the Ministery, in gathering themselues, or sending others to gather the peoples liberalitie from doore to doore. Lastly, a set stipend comes nearer the order appointed by God, in maintaining the Priesthood vnder the Leuiticall law.

In the next place, I will answer the common obiections that are made to the contrarie, by such as thinke it as easie a matter, to say Seruice in the Church, as to doe seruice in the house: to stand at the Altar of God, as to followe their masters plough; to preach in the Pulpit, as to talke in the tauerne.

1. Obiect. 2. Thess. 3. 10. They which will not worke, must not eate. But Ministers neuer plow, nor sowe, nor hedge, nor ditch, nor vse any painefull labour: for of all men they haue the easiest liues: their greatest paines is to reade ouer a few bookes, or to speake a few words, once or twise a week. Therfore they are not to be maintained. *Answer.* There is a twofold labour, one of the bodie, another of the minde: now albeit the Ministers doe not weary themselues

ſelues in bodily labour, yet they are not therefore idle: for the labours of the minde, doe farre exceed the labours of the body: they are more painefull, they ſpend the ſpirits more, they conſume naturall moiſture, and bring old age ſooner. The holy Ghoſt calleth the miniſtery, *the worke of the miniſterie. Eph.*4.12. nay, *a worthy worke.* 1.*Tim.*3.1. therefore *Paul* ſaith, that *thoſe Elders are worthy double honour that labour in the word and doctrine.* 1.*Tim.*5.17. and he exhorts the Theſſalonians that they would know them that *labour* among them; and that they haue them in ſingular loue for their *works* ſake, 1.*Theſſ.*5.12,13. Hence it is that the Scripture doth vſually compare the worke of the miniſtery, to the moſt toyleſome labour that may be, as to the worke of the husbandman, to ſetting, to plowing, to ſowing, to reaping, to the labour in the vineyard: and the miniſter to a builder: to a ſheepheard, that watcheth his flocke; to a ſouldier that fighteth in the warres, &c. Againe, we may not iudge of the painefulneſſe of the calling, by the outward appearance: for ſo a man would thinke a King had the eaſieſt life of all; when as the truth is, the toyle which he takes, and the cares wherewith he is poſſeſſed, doe exceede all other cares: if a man knew the trauaile that is required to the weilding of a ſcepter, and the paine that is taken in wearing of a heauy crowne, he would hardly ſtoope downe, to take the one into his hands, or to ſet the other vpon his head. The Maſter builder doth not hew the ſtones, nor worke the morter, nor carry the rubbiſh, nor any ſuch drudgerie; but onely ſtandeth by, and directeth the workemen; and yet his labour is double to any of theirs. The Maſter of a ſhip (a man would thinke) were idle; and did nothing: he ſtands not to the tackling, he ſtirreth not the pumpe; he driueth not the oares, he ſoundeth not the deepe, he rideth not the ropes; but onely ſitteth ſtill at the ſterne, and looketh to the pole-ſtarre, and guideth the compaſſe; yet his labour paſſeth all the reſt: were it not for him, the ſhippe would runne her ſelfe vnder the water, or ſtrike vpon the rockes, or be ſplit vpon the ſands, or fall foule with another (as marriners ſpeake.) Euen ſo for all the world fareth it with the Miniſters of the word: they ſeeme to ſit ſtill, to be at eaſe, to doe nothing; and yet their labour is double and treble to other mens bodily labour, except they bee vnfaithfull, and doe the worke of the Lord negligently.

II. Obiect. Paul laboured with his hands in making of Tents, *Act.*18.3. that hee might not be chargeable to any, *Act.*20.34. Therefore Preachers are to maintaine themſelues, by their handy labour, and not be chargeable to the Church. *Anſ. Pauls* example

2.Theſſ.3.8.

prooueth

ueth not,that the miniſter ought to liue by the labour of his hands: for firſt, himſelfe receiued a contribution of the Philippians,when he was abſent from them,*Philip*.4.16.*When I was in Theſſalonica ye ſent once,and afterward againe for my neceſſitie.* Therefore if *Paul* receiued exhibition from other Churches, where he did not labour, it is lawfull for the Miniſters to receiue of thoſe whom they doe inſtruct. Secondly,conſider the reaſons why *Paul* would not take wages of the Church of Corinth,and ſome others.I.leſt he ſhould be a burden vnto them.2.*Theſſ*.3.8. *We wrought with labour and trauell,day and night,becauſe we would not be chargeable to any of you.* 2.*Cor.* 11.9. *In all things I kept and will keepe my ſelfe,that I ſhould not be grieuous vnto you.*II. That hee might giue a preſident or example to others to tread in his ſteppes.2.*Theſſ*.3.9 *Not but that we had authoritie, but that wee might make our ſelues an example to them to follow vs.* III. That he might manifeſt what his end was in teaching the Goſpel,not to ſeeke himſelfe,but the ſaluation of his hearers.2 *Cor.* 11.14.*I ſeeke not yours,but you.*And verſe 19.*We doe all things for your edification, Philip.* 4.17.*Not that I deſire a gift, but the fruit which may further your reckoning.* IV. That he might confound the falſe Apoſtles which taught not freely,but receiued wages for their labour, whereas he receiued none : or leſt they ſhould ſlander him and his miniſtery,if he ſhould receiue wages : that he did it for filthy lucre. 2.*Cor*.11.12.*But what I doe that will I doe,that I may cut away occaſion from them which deſire occaſion, that they might be found like vnto vs in that wherein they reioyce.* Therefore *Pauls* example is altogether impertinent,and prooues nothing For firſt,he himſelfe tooke wages: ſecondly, when as he refuſed it, it was vpon ſpeciall conſideration : thirdly,he did not onely permit,but alſo command that the Miniſters ſhould be maintained.

III. Obiect. Mathew 10 8 *Freely ye haue receiued,freely giue:*therefore as it was vnlawfull for the Apoſtles to take any reward for their labour,ſo is it for preachers at this day, *Anſw.* Firſt,this text is ſpecially to bee vnderſtood of the extraordinary gift of working miracles which Chriſt hauing freely beſtowed vpon them, hee would haue them to vſe freely,not ſeeking thereby to enrich themſelues by exacting or taking any thing,or to winne reputation and glory among men.Secondly, if wee vnderſtand it of the whole miniſtery,as well of preaching,as of working miracles,it is to be taken as a precept forbidding onely filthy lucre, that they ſhould not make merchandize of the word of God, ſetting it to ſale, in preaching the word with purpoſe to benefit themſelues,to feede their bellies,or to get a name and reputation in the world,which is, forbidden

bidden in other places, as 1.*Tim*.3.3. *Tit*.1.7. but for the glory of God, the diſcharge of their duties, and the ſaluation of their hearers. Great reaſon there is of this precept. Firſt, becauſe the graces of God exhibited vnto vs in the preaching of the word, are ſo pretious, that they cannot be valued at any price, all earthly things a man can deſire, are not to be compared to them, as the wiſe man ſaith; therefore *Peter* ſaid to *Simon Magus*, *Thy money periſh with thee, becauſe thou thinkeſt that the gift of God may be obtained by money*, *Act*.8. 28. 2. Becauſe it is not in mans power to ſel them, ſeeing he is not Lord ouer them, but ſteward and diſpenſer of them, 1.*Cor*.4. 1. 3. Becauſe that which God hath giuen freely, ought not to be ſold baſely: ſeeing by that meanes, that is made ſaleable, which God would haue free, which kind of merchandize is vſed in the Church of Rome at this day, in their Indulgences, wherein they ſell pardons for remiſſion of ſinnes, and ſet euen heauen it ſelfe to ſale, for a ſmall ſūme of money. Thirdly, this text muſt ſo be expounded, as that it croſſe not other precepts in this commiſſion, and that Chriſt be not contrary to himſelfe, which he ſhould be, if it were vnlawfull for preachers to take any thing for their paines: for in the 10. verſe he ſaith, *The workeman is worthy of his meate*: therefore hee may receiue it: and verſe 11. he enioynes them to enquire in euery towne where they came, who is worthy, *and there abide*. Therefore they were not vtterly barred from taking all neceſſaries, for they might take their lodging, their food, their raiment; with this they were to bee content, and more then this they might not take, though it were offered them, or forced vpon them. Thus *Elizeus* refuſed the gift offered him by *Naaman*, for curing his leaproſie, leſt Gods gifts ſhould be made a gaine, or leſt that which was giuen to ſet forth Gods glory immediatly, ſhould be an occaſion of ſatisfying mens greedy deſires.

IV. Obiect. *Math*.10.9. The Apoſtles are forbidden by Chriſt, to poſſeſſe gold, or ſiluer, &c. *Anſw*. We may not preciſely vrge the letter of the text, for ſo we ſhall make the Apoſtles practiſe contrary to Chriſts precept: and ſo he ſhould condemne himſelfe, for he had his bagge, which *Iudas* bare. He had beſides his vpper garment, *Iohn* 13.4. and coate without ſeame. *Iohn* 19.23. *Luke* 22.36. *Peter* had ſandalls, *Act*.12. *Paul* had a cloake, 2.*Tim*.4. Yea Chriſt afterwards ſaith vnto them, *But now hee that hath a bagge let him take it, and likewiſe a ſcrippe, &c.* Secondly, it was a temporary precept, giuen them in commiſſion onely for that preſent; and their going without gold, ſiluer, a ſcrip, two coates, ſhooes, a ſtaffe, ſignifies, that they ſhould goe in haſte, committing themſelues wholly to the

prouidence of God, not caring for prouision or victuals, which is signified by a scrip, by siluer and gold: nor of change of raiment, signified by two coates: nor of defending themselues against violence, by the staffe.

Vse. Here we see that there are two sorts of men in the Church, some teachers, others to be taught, called in scripture *teachers* and *hearers*. The ground of this distinction, is taken from the good pleasure of God, who hath ordained that man should be taught by man, partly because of mans weakenesse, who could not endure the glory and maiesty of God, speaking vnto him: partly, that nothing might be ascribed to the excellency of the instrument, in the conuersion of men, but that God might haue all the glory of it, as the Apostle speakes, 2. *Corinthians*, 4.7. *We haue this treasure in earthen vessels, that the excellency of that power, might be of God, and not of man.* There is set downe, *Deut.5.verse* 23. &c. a notable ground for the institution of the holy ministery by man, in stead of Gods liuely voice from heauen. And it was one of the ends which God had in giuing his law in so great maiesty, to teach vs, that it is for our good, that he doth no instruct vs with his owne liuely voice from heauen, and speake vnto vs in his owne person: and that therefore we should be content, nay desirous rather to be taught by man. For when the people desired that they might not heare the voice of the Lord any more, but that *Moses* might speake vnto them, The Lord answered, *They haue done well to say so, I will raise them vp a Prophet from among their brethren like vnto thee, and I will put my words in his mouth, and he shall speake vnto them all that I command him. Deut.*18.*verses* 17.18. This crosseth the curiosity of those, who not contenting themselues with the word of God deliuered by the ministery of man, desire that God would speake vnto them with his owne mouth from heauen. For the Israelites found it by experience, that it was a fearefull thing, full of horrour and astonishment to heare the voice of God, therefore they desire *they may heare it no more, lest they die. Deut.* 18.*verse* 16. But the Anabaptists obiect that vnder the N.T. *all shall be taught of God. Ioh.*6.*verse* 45. and *they shall not teach euery man his neighbour, and euery man his brother, saying, Know the Lord.* Therefore the publike ministery is now needlesse. *Ans.* The words must not be vnderstood simply, but *comparatiuely*, and *synecdochically*. *Comparatiuely*, that there shall be farre greater knowledge vnder the new Testament, then was vnder the old. *Isa.*11.9. The Apostle saith not, that there shal be no teaching at al (for Christ hath giuē some to be Prophets, others Pastors & techers, for the work of the

Ier.31.34. Heb.8.11.

the miniſtery, and the edification of the body of Chriſt. *Eph.* 4. 11. 12.) But that there ſhall be no neede of this kind of teaching, to catechize them in the firſt rudiments, as to teach them what God is. *Synecdochically*, not of perfect and abſolute knowledge, for we al *know but in part*, 1. *Cor.* 13. 12. But of initiate, or inchoate knowledge, which ſhall be conſummate in the life to come.

Further, vpon this diſtinction followeth, that hearers are not to intermeddle with the publike duties of the miniſtery; for euery man is to abide in the calling wherein God hath placed him, and therein to liue contented, 1. *Cor.* 7. For no man may take vnto himſelfe this honour, but he that is called, as was *Aaron*, *Heb.* 5. 4.

In comment. in 4. ad Epheſ.

For albeit it be true which *Ambroſe* writeth, that in the beginning of the preaching of the Goſpel, and founding of the Church of the New Teſtament, all Chriſtians did teach and baptize indifferently: yet afterward, when the Churches were founded, it was not lawfull, neither is it now. And though there be neither *male nor female in Chriſt, but we are all one in him. Gal.* 3. 28. namely, in receiuing of the Goſpell: yet in diſpenſing of it, there is great difference: it being vnlawfull for a woman to preach, or publikely to teach. *I permit not a woman to teach*, 1. *Tim.* 2. 12. *Let women keepe ſilence in the Churches, for it is not permitted vnto them to ſpeake*, 1 *Cor.* 14. 34. *Apocalyps* 2. 20. This condemneth the fantaſticall opinion of the Anabaptiſts, that all men may ſpeake publikely without any difference, according to the inſtinct of the Spirit, and meaſure of his gifts.

Againe, when *Paul* ſaith, *He that is taught in the word, &c. him that taught him in the word, &c.* he ſhewes what the duty of the Miniſter is, that lookes to liue by his miniſtery, namely, not to feede his auditory with Philoſophy, or fables, or lying Legends: nor to preach Poeticall fictions, Thalmudiacall dreames, Schoolemens quiddities, Popiſh decrees, or humane conſtitutions, or to tickle the itching eares of his auditory with the fine ringing ſentences of the Fathers (for what is the chaffe to the wheate?) But he muſt preach *the word of God*: for there is no word nor writing in the world beſides, that hath a promiſe to be the power of God to ſaluation, *Rom.* 1. able to make men wiſe to ſaluation. 2. *Tim.* 3. 15, to giue an inheritance amongſt them that are ſanctified, *Act.* 20. To be liuely and mighty in operation, ſharper then any two edged ſword, entring through, euen to the diuiding aſunder of the ſoule and the Spirit, the ioynts and the marrow, and to be a diſcerner of the thoughts and intents of the hearts, *Hebrewes* 4. 12. and that can make the man of God abſolute to euery good work. 2. *Timoth.* 3. 17. but onely this word

word giuen by diuine inspiration. It beeing not onely the seede by which we are begotten and borne anew, but the foode by which we are nourished: both milke for the babe, that is, a nouice in religion, and strong meate for him that is of yeares: and therefore being perfect nourishment, the bread of life for him that is hungry, and the water of life for him that is thirsty, what needes there any more? Besides no word nor writing hath the property of fire saue onely the word of God, to dispell the darkenesse of ignorance by enlightening the minde with the sauing knowledge of the truth, and to heate, yea to enflame the affection with a zeale of Gods glory, by burning vp the corruption of nature. Againe Diuinity is the Mistris, all liberall arts, tongues, histories, &c. are but handmaids to attend vpon her: now when the mistris is speaking, it is good manners for the maide to hold her peace. To this word alone the Prophets were tyed by their commission: *What I shall command thee, that shalt thou say.* And the Apostles, *You shall teach what I haue commanded you.* Christ himselfe taught nothing but that which hee had heard and receiued of his Father. *Ioh* 8.28. *Paul* deliuers nothing but that which he receiued of Christ, 1.*Corinthi.* 11.23. and taught nothing but that which *Moses* and the Prophets had written, *Act.* 26.22. *Paul* commands *Timothie* to charge the Pastours of Ephesus, *that they teach no diuers doctrine,* either for matter or manner, for substance or circumstance. Yet here we must take heede of extremities, for in some cases it is lawfull in preaching to vse Philosophy, the testimony of prophane writers, and quotations of the Fathers.

1.Tim.1.3. μὴ ἑτεροδιδασκαλεῖν Nec aliud, vt Beza, nec aliter, vt vulg. editio.

I. When we haue to deale with heathen men (who will not bee so easily mooued with the authority of the Scriptures) wee may conuict them by the testimony of their owne writers, as *Paul* did the Athenians, Epicures, and Stoikes, by the testimonie of *Aratus*, *Actes* 17. 28. and the Grecians by the testimony of *Epimenides*. *Tit.* 1.12.

II. In preaching to a mixt congregation, where some are infected with Poperie, or some other heresie, and will not receiue the doctrine deliuered, nor yeeld vnto the truth, except it haue the consent of the Fathers of the Church.

III. In handling of some controuersall point of diuinitie, shewing, that the doctrine we teach is no new doctrine, but that which was taught in the Primitiue Church, especially in speaking to the weake, who haue not as yet left their old superstition wherein they were nuzzeled.

IV. To cut off the calumniations of the malicious aduersaries, who

who muſt needs haue their mouthes ſtopped by ſome other means then by the Scriptures.

V. In the neceſſary vnfolding of the meaning of certaine places of Scripture, which without Philoſophy cannot be conceiued. In ſuch a caſe we may vſe humanity in deſcending to the reach and capacitie of the auditory, and ſo teach heauenly things, by earthly things, as our Sauiour Chriſt taught regeneration by the ſimilitude of the wind, *Iob*.3. Yet all theſe muſt be vſed, firſt, ſparingly, ſecondly, when there is iuſt cauſe, thirdly, without oſtentation, fourthly, deliuering nothing to the people, the ground whereof it is not in the word.

This ſhewes, that the maine ſcope of the miniſtery, is, to preach the word purely, and to apply it powerfully to the conſciences of men: and it condemnes all deceitfull handling of the word, and all huckſter-like dealing, in mingling wine and water together, wheat and chaffe, gold and droſſe, in peruerting it with aguiſh and ſottiſh conceits; in wreſting it with allegories, tropologies, and anagogies, & in wringing the text til they make it bleede, and ſo (as an auncient writer ſaith) preſſe the two dugges of the Scriptures, the old and new Teſtament, that in ſtead of milk they drinke nothing but blood. This teacheth the hearers likewiſe to reſt contented with the bare word, without hungring after new doctrines, as the Athenians after newes, or beeing drawne away from the ſimplicity that is in Chriſt, by the ſubtilty of ſeducers; or by deuices and quiddities of mans braine. Let thoſe therefore which loth *Manna*, and long for Quailes, remember that if God giue them their deſire, hee will alſo giue them their deſert. Let them take heede leſt he puniſh them with a famine, not of bread, nor a thirſt of water, but of hearing the word. *Amos*.8.11. And let thoſe that haue *itching eares*, in heaping vp to thẽſelues a multitude of teachers, take heede alſo that they haue not *tingling eares*, when they ſhall heare of the iudgements of God for the contempt of his word.

Voluſian epiſt ad Nichol c. Scripturarum mammillas dum durius preſſerunt, ſanguinem pro lacte biberunt.

2.Tim.4.3.

2.Sam.3.11.

Further, whereas *Paul* ſaith; *He that teacheth is to be maintained*: it is a good *Item* for all idle drones that will not labour, and all dumme dogges that cannot barke, they may not expect the maintenance which is due vnto the Miniſters: for it is generally true of all men, and much more true of the Miniſter, that *he which will not labour, muſt not eate*. And great reaſon it is that he which looketh for his hire, ſhould doe his worke: he that would liue of the ſacrifice, ſhould miniſter at the altar: he that lookes to be fed with corporal bread, ſhould breake vnto his hearers the bread of life: hee that would reape carnall things, ſhould ſow ſpirituall things, he that would

2.Theſ.3.10.

1.Cor.5.

would not haue his mouth muzled,ſhould threſh out the corne:he that would drinke of the wine, ſhould plant the grape: hee that lookes for milke, ſhould feede the flocke: that is, hee that will liue of the Goſpel,ſhould teach the Goſpel. It is a maxime not only of the *Canon law*, but grounded vnto the law *of nature*, that *beneficium poſtulat officium*, *a benefite requireth a duty*;or more plainely, *a benefice requireth an office*, and diligence in the office. They therefore that care not ſo much for the feeding of the ſheepe, as for the feeding of themſelues,and feare not ſo much the loſſe of the flocke,as the loſſe of the fleece,doe not onely violate the law of God, but euen the law of nations, and the law of nature.

Againe hence I gather,that thoſe that labour in the word and doctrine, may lawfully take wages, albeit they haue ſufficient of their owne to maintaine themſelues: it is the very equitie of this text. For if they that are inſtructed in the word, are to make thoſe that inſtructed them, partakers of their goods: then it is lawful for them which inſtruct and teach, to receiue ſomething in recompence of their labour,ſeeing that *the labourer is worthy of his wages.* Yet this one caueat muſt be remembred,that if receiuing of wages be a hinderance to the Goſpell(as it would haue beene in *Paul*)it is not lawfull: for we may not ſo vſe our libertie, as that wee thereby hinder the free courſe of the Goſpell.

We may here further perceiue the greate want of deuotion, which is in moſt men of theſe daies. For as the cry of the poore in the ſtreetes, and at our doores, is an argument that there is no mercie,no bowles of pittie and compaſſion:So,in that there are ſo many needy poore wandring Leuites, which would gladly ſerue for a morſell of bread,or a ſute of raiment, it is a pregnant proofe there is very ſmall deuotion in men for the maintenance of religion;eſpecially in thoſe which are ſo ſtraight laced,and ſhort ſleeued in beſtowing any thing for the good of the Miniſtery, and yet in keeping of hounds and hawkes,and worſe matters,in maintaining players,ieſters,fooles,and ſuch like,are very lauiſh and profuſe, to their great coſt. This hath beene the practiſe of the world, and the contemptible eſtate of the Miniſterie in former times. Foure hundred falſe Prophets were richly prouided for at *Iezabels* table, 1. *King.* 18.19. whereas the true Prophets of God in the meane time were faine to hide their heads,hauing ſcarce bread and water, and that not without danger. Well, her practiſe ſhall condemne a number of profeſſours;nay,our forefathers zeale and forwardnes, (notwithſtanding they liued in blindneſſe) ſhall condemne our coldneſſe, in this behalfe:what ſpeake I of our forefathers? euen the ſtones in the ruinated Abbeyes, and other religious houſes, ſhall riſe vp in iudgement againſt vs: for thoſe places could maintaine thirtie or fourtie idle bellies, which did nothing but nuzzle men in ſuperſtitious idolatrie: whereas now the ſame place will not competently mainetaine one or two to inſtruct them in the way to eternall life. And no maruel: for we take from the Church, as faſt as they gaue it. In old time they were wont to ſay, *What ſhal we giue the man of God?* 1. *Sam.*9. but now with the ſacrilegious churchrobbers, they ſay, *Come and let vs take the houſes of God in poſſeſſion. Pſal.* 83. 32. The Iewes were exceeding forward and liberall in their contribution to the Tabernacle; ſome brought gold, others ſiluer, ſilke, pretious ſtones; the meaner ſort, rams skins, goats haire, &c. ſo that more then enough was offered by them, in ſuch ſort that *Moſes* was forced to cauſe a proclamation to be made to ſtay the people from offering, *Exodus* 36.5.6. This their example in beeing ſo forward to contribute to the materiall temple, ſhall condemne our backwardneſſe in conferring ſo little to the Miniſters, who are the liuing temples of God, and to the miniſterie which is in the place of the altar: for looke by how much God hath diminiſhed the coſt of the altar, and the charges of the ceremoniall worſhip vnder the old Teſtament, by ſo much more doth he require the Miniſtery to be maintained, and ſpirituall worſhip furthered in the New.

Laſtly, if they that doe not put too their helping hand to vphold the Miniſterie, are to be condemned; what condemnation trow we then belongs to ſacrilegious perſons that rob the Church of her reuenewes, and deuoure holy things?

7. *Be not deceiued, God is not mocked: for whatſoeuer a man ſoweth, that ſhall he reape.*

Here the Apoſtle preuenteth ſundry ſecret obiections againſt the former precept, verſe 6. For the Galatians might pleade for goods: thēſelues in this maner. Wheras thou enioyneſt vs to make for, thoſe which inſtructed vs in the word, partakers of al our alas, we cannot doe it. It is vnreaſonable that thou exacteſt of vs: as for ſome of vs, we haue a great family and charge to looke vnto, wife and children to prouide for: and for them we muſt prouide, otherwiſe *wee denie the faith, and are worſe then infidels*, 1. *Tim.*5. 8. others are poore and needy, fitter a great deale to receiue then to giue: and thoſe that can giue are not ſo to giue, *that others may bee eaſ'd, and they themſelues pinched*, 2. *Corinth.* 8. 13. And as for the Miniſters themſelues, many of them are couetous and inſatiable, and therefore it is euill ſpent that is beſtowed vpon them: ſome of

them

them neede, not, and therefore we neede not to giue: and why doe not those that are needy, follow *Pauls* example, who laboured with his hands and got his liuing by making of tents, because hee would not be chargeable vnto any? or why doe they not leade a single life (as in former times they did) that so they may bee lesse burdensome to the Church, and more beneficial to their brethren? Besides all this, God hath promised, he will be the portion and inheritance of the Leuites; and therefore we neede not be so hastie to share with them in all our goods.

To these and all other vaine and friuolous excuses of the same kinde, made by worldlings of corrupted minds, the Apostle answereth in these words, *Be not deceiued, God is not mocked*; as if he should say, I know right well, you are very cunning in seeking out shifts and pretending reasons to excuse your faults, and to exempt your selues from the performance of the former duty, and so to couer the cursed couetousnesse of your hearts with colourable excuses: But, be not deceiued brethren, they are but figge leaues, you doe but dance in a nette, you cannot bleare the allseeing eyes of God: howsoeuer these reasons may perswade you, and goe for currant with men, yet they are but counterfeit in Gods estimate (with whom you haue to deale,) who is not mocked, nor can be deceiued, neither will be deluded with such vaine excuses: therefore take heede lest in going about to deceiue them, you deceiue your selues: for looke how you deale with them, God will deale with you: and with what measure you mete vnto them, the same he will measure to you again; *for as you sowe, so shall you reape*. So that in these wordes the Apostle doth summarily comprise these three things. First, a disswasion from this their vaine reasoning, and wicked practise, laide downe by way of preuention, *Be not deceiued*. Secondly a reason of the dehortation, shewing that these their excuses are but friuolous and vaine, *God is not mocked*. Thirdly, a confirmation or proofe of his former reason, *for whatsoeuer a man soweth, that shall hee reape*. The disswasion is laide downe in these words, *Be not deceiued*. The like phrase of speech we haue in sundry other places, as in that aduertisement which *Hezekiah* giueth the Leuites, *2.Chro.29 11. Now my sonnes bee not deceiued*: And *Paul* the Corinthians, *1.Cor.6. 9. Be not deceiued; neither fornicators*, &c. *1.Cor.15.33. Be not deceiued, euill speeches corrupt good manners*. Now men erre and are deceiued sundry waies, both in diuine and humane things (which appertaine not to this place.) Touching the deceit here mentioned, we are to know that a man may be deceiued, and that by himselfe, Mal.2.17.
two wayes. First, through ignorance, in iudging that to be sinne

which is a ſinne, as when a man is perſwaded that God is to bee worſhipped in an image: that when hee perſecutes the Saints of God, he doth God good ſeruice. Secondly, when men are ſo wickedly wilfull, that they wittingly deceiue themſelues, in thinking they can deceiue God himſelfe, and ſo cunningly handle the matter, that he ſhall not know their words, nor ſee their workes, nor vnderſtand their thoughts: that whether they doe good or euill, giue to the Miniſterie, or not; liue according to the fleſh, or according to the ſpirit, it is all one, ſeeing he conſidereth it not, and ſo promiſe to themſelues impunitie, though they ſinne willingly, as *Eue* did in putting a peraduenture, where Gods threat was peremptorie. Both theſe ſorts of deceit are here vnderſtood, ſpecially the latter.

Vſe. Hence we may obſerue the deceitfulneſſe of ſinne, which maketh men thinke all is well with them, and that there is no danger, &c. when the caſe is farre otherwiſe. This ſhewes that the *heart of man is deceitfull aboue meaſure* (as the Prophet ſaith) *who can finde it out?* or who can ſound the depth of the deceit of his owne heart? or who knowes the infinite windings and turnings which are in this intricate Labyrinth? Now this commeth to paſſe, partly by reaſon of originall corruption, which the Apoſtle ſaith is deceitfull, *Heb.*3.13. *Take heede leſt any of you be hardened through the deceitfulnes of ſinne:* partly, by reaſon of long coſtome in ſinne, whereby the heart is inured to deceit, *Pſal.*32.2. *Bleſſed is the man—in whoſe ſpirit there is no guile.* For from this double ground it cometh to paſſe, that men are ſo wittie in defrauding the Miniſters of their due, in cutting them ſhort of their allowance, in embezeling and purloining from them what they can: and ſo ingenious in inuenting probable reaſons, and plauſible arguments, to deceiue themſelues withall, in accounting all to bee gained that is thus gotten. This teacheth vs, firſt of all, to pray inſtantly that God would open our eies that wee may ſee our hidden corruptions, and that he would annoint them with the eyeſalue of his Spirit, that we may clearely ſee, and rightly diſcerne of things that differ, conſidering that ſinne doth often apparell it ſelfe with the cloake of vertue. Secondly, wee are to ſuſpect our ſelues of our ſecret ſinnes, and to aggrauate our knowne ſinnes by all circumſtances, ſeeing wee may ſo eaſily deceiue our ſelues, in flattering our ſelues to be cleare of this or that ſinne: or at leaſt not to be ſo grieuous ſinners as in truth we are. Thirdly, that it is the dutie of the Miniſter to warne the people to take heede that they be not deceiued, as *Paul* doth *Eph.*5.6. *Let no mã deceiue you with vain words: for, for ſuch*

things

things commeth the wrath of God vpon the children of diſobedience.

Againe hence I gather, that in the prime of the Church, in the Apoſtles daies, when the Church of the New Teſtament was but in founding, the Miniſtery was in contempt: and (as it may appeare out of other places) the Miniſters were not onely neglected, or contemned, but reuiled, perſecuted, accounted as the filth of the world, and the offskouring of all things, 1. *Cor.* 4. 13. or where they were better intreated, they were but abuſed, ſcorned, reputed brain-ſicke fellowes: as the Prophet was, 2, *King.* 9. 11. and *Paul, Act.* 26. 24. This hath beene, and is the account which the world maketh of the Miniſters of God, which muſt bee ſo farre from diſcouraging vs, that it ſhould miniſter rather matter of ioy vnto vs, in that we are conformable by this meanes to Chriſt our head, who was not onely neglected of all, not hauing where to reſt his head, *Luk.* 9. 58. but laughed to ſkorne, accounted a pot-companion, a drunkard, and a glutton, a ſorcerer, one that had a diuell, and was madde, *Ioh.* 10. 20. For, *if we ſuffer with him, we ſhall be glorified with him. Rom.* 8, 17.

Thus much of the dehortation: the reaſon followes to bee conſidered in the ſecond place, in theſe words, *God is not mocked,* where the Apoſtle ſhewes that their excuſes as but in vaine, becauſe God is not mocked, nor will be deluded with ſuch pretences.

Firſt here the Apoſtles dealing is worthy to be obſerued, in that, reproouing them which neglected their duty to the Miniſters of the word, he bringeth in God himſelfe taking the matter into his owne hand, making the Miniſters quarrell, his own quarrell: & this he doth, to the end we might ſee whom we haue to deale withall, & whom we doe abuſe, when we abuſe the Miniſters of the word; to wit, that we abuſe not man, but God. For albeit it bee true of all and euery ſinne, which *Dauid* confeſſeth of his owne particular murther and adultery, that it is *againſt God, yea againſt him alone, Pſal.* 51. 4. yet in theſe and ſuch like caſes which tend to the vndermining of his Church, and the decay of his religion & worſhip, hee taketh himſelfe more directly aimed at, & more nearely touched. When the Iſraelites refuſed to haue *Samuel* and his ſons to rule ouer them, the Lord ſaith, *They haue not caſt thee away, but they haue caſt me away, that I ſhould not reigne ouer them,* 1. *Sam.* 8. 7. When the Leuites were defrauded of their due, the Lord by his Prophet telleth the people, *Ye haue ſpoiled me in tithes and offerings. Mal.* 3. 8. So, in this place, when the Galatians did wrongfully with hold and keepe backe that competent allowance, that was due to their teachers, he telleth thẽ that it was a ſin tending againſt God, who is not, nor will not, nor cannot be mocked: for what wrong soeuer is done to the messenger that is sent, the same is done to his Lord that sent him: and whatsoeuer disgrace or indignitie is offered an Embassadour, the same redounds to the Prince, whose Embassadour he is. This ought to be a *Caueat* vnto vs, to take heede how wee contemne or neglect the Ministers of God, seeing whatsoeuer wrong is done them, Christ takes it as done to himselfe, *Mat.* 25.45. *Act* 9.4. This lets vs see the hainous sinnes of many that professe the Gospel, specially in this kind, who, now at this day (if euer) are ingenious in defrauding, and eloquent in declaiming against the Ministers of the word: in laughing them to skorne, as they did our Sauiour Christ, *Mark.* 5.40. and abusing them in tearmes and taunts, calling them bald priests, as young children called *Elizeus balde pate*, (no doubt following the example of their parents, of whome they learned it) *Ascend thou balde pate, ascend thou bald pate*, 2. *King.* 2.23. That they are *too full of the spirit*, as they derided the Apostles, in saying, *they were full of new wine*, *Act.* 2. verse 13. In making them their table talke, making songs of them, as the drunkards did of *Dauid*, and *Ieremie*. In scourging them with the whippe of the tongue, as the Stoicks called *Paul* a babbler, *Act.* 17. verse 18. and *Festus* a madde man, *Act.* 26. Now in that they thus scornefully abuse his Ministers, and so indignely, and disdainfully intreate his messengers, and Embassadours; what doe they els but abuse Christ Iesus himselfe, and through their sides, wound and crucifie him againe? When *Sanachereb* King of Ashur reuiled Ierusalem and *Hezekiah* the King: what sayes the Lord? *O virgin daughter of Sion, he hath dispised thee, and laughed thee to skorne: O daughter of Ierusalem, hee hath shaken his head at thee. Whom hast thou railed on, and blasphemed? and against whom hast thou exalted thy voice, and lifted vp thine eyes on high? euen against the holy one of Israel. Esay*, 37.v.22,23.

The vse. Hence we learne, that God hath an exact knowledge of all our actions, and cannot be deluded, *Prou.* 15.11. Hell and destruction are before him, how much more, &c, *Psal.* 11.4. His eyes consider, his eie liddes trie the children of men. *Psal.* 139.v.2. Hee knowes our thoughtes *long before they be*. *Hebr.* 4.12. All things are naked and bare in his sight. Reason it selfe shewes, that he which made the eie, cannot but see, hee that made the heart and minde, cannot but vnderstand the frame and motion thereof, *Psal.* 94. vers. 9.10 &c.

II. This shewes the madnesse of those which say, God heareth not, seeth not, vnderstandeth not, or which say in ther hearts,

How

How ſhould he heare? is there knowledge in the moſt high? or can he ſee through the thicke cloud?

III. Hence we are taught in our praiers, to powre forth our hearts before the Lord, without concealing ſo much as the leaſt ſinne, ſeeing we may eaſily delude men, and deceiue our ſelues, but God we cannot deceiue.

IV. It ought to be a bridle to vs to curbe and keepe in our corruptions, conſidering his eies pierce the darkeneſſe, the moſt ſecret and hidden places, yea euen the ſecret cloſets and cabinets of our hearts.

Thus much of the reaſon: I prooceed to the confirmation or proofe of his reaſon, in theſe words, *For whatſoeuer a man ſoweth, that ſhall hee alſo reape.* Where the Apoſtle prooues, that God will not be mocked with vaine excuſes; ſeeing hee will render to euery man, according to his workes, which is ſignified by this allegoricall ſpeech of *ſowing* and *reaping* ſo often vſed in Scripture, as 1.*Cor.*9.11.2. *Corinth.* 9.6. in which places, labour and coſt in doing good, and beeing beneficiall, ſpecially to the Miniſters of the word, is compared to *ſeede*; the workers to *ſeedſmen*; the Miniſters to whome this benefit is conferred, to *the tilled ground*: the gaine that accrewes vnto them thereby, to the harueſt, wherewith God will reward them, and that according to their workes, in the generall day of retribution. This metaphor of ſowing, doth elſwhere ſignifie all the morall actions of a mans life, whether they be good or euill. Of good actions *Salomon* ſaith, *he that ſoweth righteouſneſſe, hath a ſure recompence, Prouerbs* 11.18. Of euill actions hee ſaith, *hee that ſoweth iniquitie ſhall reape affliction.Prouerbes*.22.8. But here *Paul* reſtraines it, to thoſe good workes of liberalitie, which are performed in the maintenance of the miniſterie. And he calleth that which is beſtowed vpon the Miniſters of the word, *ſeede*, which beeing ſowne, doth recompence the coſt, 30. ſixty, an hundred fould: that ſo they might not think their labour loſt, nor their coſt beſtowed in vaine, ſeeing they were to receiue that which they laid forth, with aduantage.

But here it may be ſaid, This prouerbiall ſentence is not alwaies true: for ſometime *men ſowe much, and gather but little. Deut.*28.30. *Agg.*1.6. nay ſometime *they ſowe, and reape not. Mich.*6.15. Againe experience ſhewes, that, that which is ſowne, may degenerate into another kind. *Anſ.* It is not neceſſary that prouerbiall ſentences ſhould be true at all times, and in euery particular: if they bee true for the moſt part, or in that for which they are brought, it is ſufficient, as that, *Matth.*13.57. *A Prophet is not accepted in his owne* *countrie*, is for the most part true, though not alwaies. So, what soeuer a man soweth, the same commonly, and vsually, he doth reape.

But it will be said, how can a man reape that which he soweth? seeing that Christ affirmeth it to be a true saying, that one soweth, and an other reapeth? *Iohn* 4.37. *Ans.* In that one soweth, and another reapeth, it is not to be imputed to nature, but to the speciall prouidence of God: the words are to bee vnderstood of the prophets, who were the seedes men, in sowing the seedes of the Gospell; and of the Apostles, who were the reapers, whose plaine and powerfull preaching of the Gospell, did as farre exceed that of the prophets as the haruest doth the seede time. Thus the time vnder the law, is resembled to childhood, and infancie, that vnder the Gospell, to mans estate, *Gal.* 4. 1. &c, Againe, it may be said the husbandman *soweth not the bodie that shall be*, 1. *Cor.* 15. 27. therefore he reapeth not that which he sowed. *Ans.* He reapeth not the same indiuidually, but yet the same speciall bodie. It may further bee doubted of the truth of that which is signified by this prouerbiall sentence, namely, whether euery man shall receiue according to his workes, for so euery man should be condemned. To which I answer, that it is not vniuersally true, for *if the righteous commit iniquity all his righteousnes shall be no more remembred*: and, *if a wicked man turne from his sinne, none of his sinnes that he hath committed shall be mentioned vnto him. Ezecke.* 33. 13. 16. It must therefore be restrained thus, He that doth wickedly, and perseuereth therein to the end: He that doth well, and continueth in his well doing, shal receiue according to his workes; the seedes of his former sinnes, shall not grow vp to the haruest of condemnation. For it is the priuiledge, yea the happinesse of a righteous man, so to haue his sinnes couered with the robes of Christ his righteousnes, as that they shall neuer be vncouered to his shame. *Psal.* 32. *Esay*, 43. 25 Againe, it may bee hence prooued; in that sanctification in death, is perfected, originall corruption beeing vtterly abolished: and therefore though the booke of a regenerate mans conscience bee opened at the day of iudgement, yet nothing shall be found in it, but his good workes, which follow him till the resurrection. *Apoc*, 14. 13. Besides this, in the last sentence pronounced by our Sauiour Christ, *Matth.* 25. only their good workes are mentioned: *Come ye blessed of my Father, inherit the kingdome prepared for you, for I was hungrie, and ye fedde me, &c.* their sinnes and imperfections, not so much as once named, but concealed and passed ouer.

II. *Obiect.* It may be said, that neither the good nor the badde doe reape that which they haue sowne: the godly for the seedes

of

of good workes reape nothing but affliction: the wicked for the curſed ſeedes of damnable life, comfort and contentation. To which I anſwer, that it is not true, if we reſtraine it to the tearme of this life; for ſo all men reape not, as they haue ſowne: but it is vndoubtedly true of the life to come: for the iuſtice of God requires that all ſhould be rewarded according to their workes. *Romaines* 2. Hence therefore wee may gather, that ſeeing men muſt reape as they ſowe, and yet doe not reape, nor receiue their reward in this life: that there is another life after this, in which God will giue to euery one as his worke ſhall be, and therefore there ſhall be a iudgment. And becauſe the bodie was partaker with the ſoule either in doing good or euill, it is iuſt likewiſe it ſhould be partaker either of miſery, or felicity: and therefore there ſhall be a reſurrection.

III. *Obiect.* The whore of *Babylon* muſt be rewarded double. *Apoc.* 18.6. *In the cuppe that ſhee hath filled to you, fill her the double.* And the Saints pray thus to God, *Render to our neighbours ſeuen fold into their boſome. Pſalme* 79.12. Therefore it ſeemeth that ſome men ſhall not bee iudged according to their workes, becauſe they are puniſhed aboue their deſerts. *Anſwer.* Shee is rewarded double, yet not aboue, but according to her deſerts; *giue her double according to her workes*, v. 6. The meaning is not, that ſhe ſhould be puniſhed twice as much as ſhee had deſerued, (for it is the law of God that the malefactour ſhould be beaten with a certen number of ſtripes, not *aboue*, but *according to his treſpaſſe. Deut.* 25.2.) but that ſhe ſhould be tormented, twiſe as much as ſhe had tormented others. Againe, theſe phraſes and formes of ſpeech of *rewarding double*, or *ſeuenfold*, ſignifie, that God will pay wicked men home to the full (a definite number beeing put for an indefinite) as *Gen.* 4.15. *Doubtleſſe, whoſoeuer ſlaieth Cain ſhall be puniſhed ſeuen fold.* The meaning is not, that the murtherer of *Cain* ſhould bee puniſhed ſeuen fould more then he was puniſhed, for killing his brother *Abel*, (for it ſhold not haue beene ſo great a ſinne for a man to haue killed him, as it was for him to kill his brother) but that hee ſhould bee moſt ſeuerely and grieuouſly puniſhed.

IIII. Obiect. Infants haue no workes wherby they may be iudged, ſeeing they doe neither good nor euil, as the Scripture ſpeaketh of *Iacob* and *Eſau*, *Rom.* 9.11. Therefore all ſhall not be iudged according to workes. *Anſw.* Theſe phraſes of Scripture, *As a man ſowes ſo ſhall he reape: euery one ſhall receiue according to his workes*, &c. are not to be extended to al, but muſt be reſtrained to ſuch as haue workes, and knowledge to diſcerne betwixt good and euill, which infants haue not. For beſides that they are diſtitute of workes,

they

they alſo want the vſe of reaſon: and therefore they ſhall not be iudged by the booke of conſcience, but by the booke of life. For to ſay, as *Hugo de S. vict.* doth, vpon the *Rom. quæſt.* 59. that they ſhall be condemned for the ſinnes which their parents committed in their conception and natiuity, as though they themſelues had actually committed them, is contrary to that *Ezek.* 18. 20. *the Son ſhal not beare the iniquitie of the father.*

V. Obiect. But how ſhall they be pronounced iuſt, who beeing come to yeares of diſcretion, yet haue no good workes, as *Lazarus* and the theefe vpon the croſſe, who liuing leudly all his life long, was conuerted at the laſt gaſpe? *Anſ.* That *Lazarus* had no good workes, whereby he might be declared iuſt, it cannot be proued: the contrary rather may be gathered out of Scripture: and that the good theefe had no good works, it is flat againſt the text, *Luk.* 23, 40. 41. where he maketh a notable confeſſion of Chriſt, and rebuketh his fellow, labouring to bring him to the faith, which was a memorable fact of Chriſtian charity. Secondly, though it were graunted that they had no good works in action; yet they were full of good workes in affection, and by theſe they were to be iudged, God accepting in his children the wil for the deed. *Lazarus* by reaſon of his extreame pouerty, and the theefe by reaſon of the ſhortnes of time which he had to liue in the world, could not be plentifull in good workes, thereby to giue ſufficient teſtimonie of their vnfained faith: yet God accepteth a man according to that which he hath, and not according to that which he hath not, accepting the will for the deede, as he accepted the willingnes of *Abraham* to ſacrifice his ſonne, as though he had ſacrificed him indeede. *Gen.* 22.

VI. Obiect. God doth not proportionate the reward to the work, becauſe he doth reward workes which are finite and temporall, with infinite and eternall puniſhment. *Anſ.* Sinne beeing conſidered in reſpect of the *act*, as it is *a tranſient action*, is finite. But in a threefold conſideration, it is infinite. Firſt, in reſpect of the obiect againſt whom it is committed: for beeing the offence of an infinite Maieſty, it doth deſerue infinite puniſhment: for if he that clippes the Kings coyne, or defaceth the Kings armes, or counterfaiteth the broad ſeale of England, or the Princes priuy ſeale, ought to die as a traytour, becauſe this diſgrace tendeth to the perſon of the Prince: much more ought he that violates the law of God, die the firſt and ſecond death, ſeeing the breach therof doth not only tend to the defacing of his owne image in vs, but to the perſon of God himſelfe, who in euery ſinne is contemned, and diſhonoured. Secondly,

condly, ſin is infinite in reſpect of the ſubiect. For ſeeing that the ſoule is immortall, and that the guilt of ſin and the blot together, doe ſtaine the ſoule, as the crimſon or skarlst die the ſilke or the wooll, and can no more be ſeuered from the ſoule, then ſpots from the Leopard: it remaineth that ſinne is infinite in durance, and ſo deſerueth eternall puniſhment. Thirdly, it is infinite in reſpect of the mind, deſire, & intent of the ſinner, whoſe deſire is ſtill to walk on in his ſins, and except God ſhould cut off the line of his life, neuer to giue ouer ſinning, but to runne on *in infinitum*, committing of ſinne euen with greedines.

Thus hauing the meaning of the words, let vs come to the doctrine and vſe, There be two principall reaſons which hinder men from beeing beneficiall and liberall to the Miniſtery. The firſt is, becauſe they thinke all his loſt that is beſtowed that way. The ſecond is, becauſe they are afraid leſt themſelues ſhould want. To both which the Apoſtle makes anſwer in this place, comparing our beneficence in the vpholding, maintaining, countenancing of the Miniſtery to *ſeed*, to teach vs that as the husbandman doth ſow his corne in the ground, neuer fearing the loſſe thereof, but hoping for a greater increaſe: not doubting his owne want, but aſſuring himſelfe of greater plenty. So we in ſowing the ſeeds of good workes, muſt neuer dreame of loſſe or coſt, conſidering the more we ſow, the more we ſhall reape: we muſt neuer feare want, ſeeing we ſhall receiue an hundred fold. *Mark.* 10.30. If men could be perſwaded of this, that the time of this life is the ſeed time; that the laſt iudgment is the harueſt; & that as certenly as the husbandman which ſowes his ſeed lookes for increaſe, ſo we for our good workes, a recompence to the full; O how fruitfull ſhould we be, how plentifull, how full of good works? But the curſed roote of infidelity, which is in euery man by nature, doth dry vp the ſap of all Gods graces in vs, and make vs either bad or barren trees, either to bring forth ſowre fruits of ſinne, or no fruit at all, but to become vnprofitable both to our ſelues and others. For the reaſon why men are ſo cold in their liberality, ſo fruitleſſe, ſo vnprofitable, is, becauſe they doe not beleeue the promiſes of God, that he is true of his word, that whatſoeuer they giue to the poore, or the Miniſters of his word, *they lend vnto the Lord, and whatſoeuer they lay out, the Lord will reſtore to them againe. Prov.* 19.17. For if they were as wel perſwaded of a recompence at the laſt day, as the husbandman is of a harueſt, they would be more frequent in duties of charity, and more plentifull in good workes, then commonly they be.

Further let it be obſerued, that though theſe words be but *generally*

rally expounded in the verſe following, where the *A*poſtle ſaith, *He that ſoweth to the fleſh, ſhall of the fleſh reape corruption : he that ſoweth to the ſpirit, ſhall of the ſpirit reape life euerlaſting* : yet are they more *particularly* and diſtinctly ſet downe elſewhere in Scripture: as 2.*Cor.*9 6. *He that ſoweth ſparingly ſhall reape ſparingly, and he that ſoweth liberally, ſhall reape liberally* : that is, the harveſt ſhall not onely be anſwerable to the ſeed, and the reward to the worke; but greater or leſſe according to the quantity, and quality of the worke. *For euery man ſhall receiue his reward according to his proper labour.* 1.*Cor.*3.8. For the more the husbandman ſowes, the more he doth vſually reape (except God blow vpon it, in curſing the land, as he did the Iſraelites who ſowed much and gathered little) and the leſſe he ſowes the leſſe ſhall his croppe be. Euen ſo, the more plentifull we are in ſowing the ſeeds of good works, the more we ſhal reape: and the more ſparing we are, the leſſe ſhall our harueſt be. Hence I gather: Firſt, that there are ſeuerall degrees of puniſhments in Hell, according to the greatnes and ſmalnes of ſinnes : for ſome ſinnes are but as motes, others as beames, *Matth.* 7.4 ſome as gnats, others as camels, *Matth.*23.24. and therefore ſome ſhall be beaten with many ſtripes, ſome with few, and it ſhall be eaſier for them of Sodom and Gomorrha at the day of iudgement, then for them of Capernaum. Secondly, that there are ſundry degrees of glory & felicity in heauen, proportionall to mens works : for all men doe not ſow alike, neither are their workes equall; but haue ſundry degrees of goodnes in them, and therfore there are anſwerable degrees of glory wherwith they are to be crowned. This truth is taught elſ-where more plainly, as *Dan.* 12.3. *They that be wiſe ſhall ſhine as the brightneſſe of the firmament: and they that turne many to righteouſneſſe, ſhall ſhine as the ſtarres for euermore.* Therfore as there is a greater brightnes in the ſtar, then in the firmament; ſo there ſhall be greater glory in one then in an other. 1.*Cor.*3.8. *Euery man ſhal receiue his reward, according to his owne labour,* therfore ſeeing all mens labours are not alike, their reward ſhall not be alike. This is further confirmed by the parable of the talents, *Luk.*19. where the maſter of the ſeruants doth proportionate his wages to their worke, making him that had gained with his talent, fiue talents, ruler ouer fiue cities; him that had gained ten, ruler ouer ten. And wheras it may be ſaid, that all the labourers in the vineyard, receiued an equall reward, namely a penny; as well as thoſe that wrought but an houre, as thoſe that bare the burden and heate of the day. I anſwer, it is true of *eſſentiall* glory, all the elect ſhall haue equall glory: but it is not true of *accidentall* glory, therein all ſhall not be equall. Take ſundry veſſels of diuerſe bigneſſe, and caſt them into the ſea, all will be filled with water, though ſome receiue a greater quantity, others a leſſe: So, all ſhall haue fulneſſe of glory; that is, the ſame *eſſentiall* glory: though in reſpect of *accidentall* glory, ſome ſhall haue more, and ſome leſſe. Secondly, the ſcope of the parable is not to ſhewe the equality of glory, in the word to come; but that they which are firſt called, ought not to inſult ouer their brethrẽ, which are not as yet called, ſeeing they may be perferred before them, or (at the leaſt) made equall with them. It remaineth therefore for a concluſion, that there ſhall be degrees of glory in heauen, as there are degrees of torment in hell, and that as mens labours differ in goodnes, ſo their rewards ſhall be different in greatnes. Now mens labours differ in goodneſſe, three waies; in the *kind*, in the *quantity*, and in the *quality*. In the *kind*; in that ſome are more noble in their kind, ſome more baſe; as to cure the maladies of the ſoule is a more excellent worke in it kinde, then to cure the diſeaſes of the body: & therefore it hath a greater degree of glory promiſed. *Dan.* 12. 3. *They that turne many to righteouſnes, ſhall ſhine as the ſtars for euermore*. In the *quality* or manner, in that ſome are done with greater loue, ſome with leſſe: ſome with greater zeale, ſome with leſſe: ſome with greater care & conſcience to diſcharge our duties, ſome with leſſe. Now, thoſe that are performed with greater loue, zeale, care, and conſcience, ſhall receiue a greater reward: thoſe that are done with leſſe, a leſſer: for ſo is the promiſe, *Euery man ſhall receiue his wages, according to his own labour.* 1. *Cor.* 3. 8. In the *quantity*, in that ſome labour but an houre, others beare the burden and heate of the day, and ſo according to the greatnes or ſmalnes of their paines, they ſhal haue a greater or leſſer reward. He that had ſo carefully emploied his talent, that he gained with it ten others, was made ruler ouer tenne cities: and he that had taken leſſe paines, and gained but fiue, was made ruler but ouer fiue, that is, had his reward; yet a leſſe reward ſutable to his worke.

Further, as God doth reward the good workes of his ſeruants, according to the *kind*, the *quantity*, and *quality*: ſo he rewardeth ſinnes not onely according to their degree (as we haue heard) but alſo in the ſame manner, according to the nature & quality of the ſinne. 2. *Theſſ.* 1. 16. *It is a iuſt thing with God to recompence tribulation to them that trouble you.* Thus he threatneth that *to the froward he will ſhew himſelfe froward.* *Pſal.* 18. 26. And, *he that ſheddeth mans blood, by man ſhall his blood be ſhedd. Gen.* 9. 6. And, *all that take the ſword, ſhall periſh by the ſword, Matth.* 26. 92. And, *he that ſtoppeth his eares at the cry of the poore, ſhall cry vnto the Lord,*

and

and he will not heare him.Pro 21.13. And, *iudgment mercilesse shall be to him that shewes no mercy. Iam.*2.13. And, *Woe be to thee that spoilest, and wast not spoiled, and doest wickedly, and they did not wickedly against thee: for when thou shall cease to spoile, thou shalt be spoiled: and when thou shalt make an end of doing wickedly, they shall doe wickedly against thee. Esa.*32.1. *For with what iudgement men iudge, they shall be iudged, and with what measure they mete, it shall be measured to them againe. Matth.*7.2. Neither doth God barely threaten this, but he doth it in deede; in handling sinners in their kind. *Gen.*2.17. *Because thou hast eaten of the tree, cursed is the earth for thy sake, in sorrow shalt thou eate of it all the daies of thy life.* Thus God punished the filthy Sodomites in their kinde, in that, for their burning lust he *rained vpon them fire and brimstone from heauen. Gen.*19 24. *Nadab* and *Abihu* censing with *strange fire*, were consumed with fire from heauen. *Leuit.* 10. 1, 2. The like may be said of *Adonibezek*, for as he caused seuenty Kings hauing the thumbs of their hands, & of their feet cut off, to gather crummes vnder his table, so the Lord rewarded him. *Iud.*1.7. As *Agags* sword made women childelesse, so his mother was made childlesse among other women, beeing hewen in peeces before the Lord in *Galgal.* 1.*Sam.*15.33. Thus God punished the adultery and murther of *Dauid*: for as he defiled an other mans wife, so his owne sonne *Absolom defiled his wiues in the sight of all Israel*, 2.*Sam.*16 *verse* 22. and his murther in slaying *Vriah* by the sword of the children of *Ammon*, in that *the sword did neuer depart from his house.*2.*Sam.*12.10. Because the *Grecians* accounted preaching foolishnes: it pleased God (as a fit & iust punishment of this their sin) *by the foolishnes of preaching to saue them that beleeue.* 1.*Cor.*1.21. Thus as *Chrysost.* hath obserued, the rich glutton was mette with in his kind: for whereas he would not giue *Lazarus a crumme of bread* to slake his hunger, God would not giue him *a drop of water* to coole his thirst, *Luke* 16. and therefore he saith, *Hiems non semina vit misericordiam, venit æstas & nihil messuit.* Thus he punisheth spiritual fornication, with bodily pollution, because the Israelites went a whoring from God, therefore *their daughters became harlots, and their spouses whores: Hos.*4.12.13. And this is verified in the Church of Rome at this day: for as he gaue vp the heathen to reprobate minds, by reason of their idolatry; so hath he giuen them vp, as we may see in their vncleane cloysters, their Sodomiticall Stewes, their beastly brothelhouses, and the like. So they that delight in looking at *the rednesse of the wine*, shall haue *red eies*, as a punishment of their sinne. *Pro.*23.30. Thus God punished the pride of the women of Ierusalem: for *in stead of a sweet sauour, there was a stinke, in stead*

Epist.3.ad Cyriac. Micas cadentes de mensa non dedit quid mirũ si aque guttã non accepit?

stead of a girdle, a rent, in stead of dressing of the haire, baldnes, in stead of a stomacher, a girding of sackecloth, and burning, in stead of beauty. Esa. 3. 24. And thus the Lord shut vp euery wombe of the house of *Abimelech*, because of *Sara Abrahams* wife. *Gen.* 20.18. Thus the wise man saith, *Because the Israelites worshipped serpents which had not the vse of reason, and vile beasts, the Lord sent a multitude of vnreasonable beasts among them for a vengeance, that they might know, that wherewith a man sinneth, by the same also shal he be punished. Wisd.* 11.13. And this maner of punishing sinners in their kinde, *Iob* acknowledgeth to be most iust, When he saith. *If mine heart haue beene deceiued by a woman, or If I haue laid waite at the dore of my neighbour: let my wife grind vnto another man, and let other men bow downe vpon her. Iob.* 31. 10.11.

Vse. First, here we see the iustice of God in awarding the last sentence, nay his bounty and seuerity: his bounty, in recompencing men aboue their deserts; his seuerity, in punishing sinners according to their deserts. (Rom. 11.22.) For as he will deny any thing in iustice that denied to *Diues a drop of water* to coole his tongue, *Luk.* 16. 24.25. so he will recompence *a cup o cold water. Matth.* 10.42. This integrity in iudgement without partiality, is signified by *the white throne, Reu.* 20.11. and it serues as a patterne and example for all Iudges and Magistrates to follow, in laying iudgement to the rule, and righteousnes to the ballance, *Esa.* 28.17. that is, in hearing causes indifferently, and determining equally, examining them (as it were) by line and square, as the mason or carpenter doth his worke. The Grecians placed Iustice betwixt *Leo* and *Libra*, thereby signifying that there must not onely be courage in executing, but also indifferency in determining. The Egyptians expresse the same by the *hieroglyphical* figure of a man without hands, winking with his eies; wherby is meant our vncorrupt Iudge, who hath no hands to receiue bribes, nor eyes to behold the person of the poore, or respect the person of the rich. And before our tribunalls we commōly haue the picture of a man, holding a ballance in one hand, and a sword in the other, signifying by the ballance iust iudgement, by the sword, execution of iudgement. For as the balance putteth no difference betweene gold and lead, but giueth an equall or vnequall poise to them both, not giuing a greater waight to the gold for the excellency of the mettall, because it is gold, nor a lesse to the lead for the basenes of it, because it is lead. So they were with an euen hand to way the poore mans cause as well as the rich. But it is most notably set out by *the throne of the house of Dauid*, mentioned *Psal.* 122.5. which was placed in the gate of the city towards the

by

ſun riſing:*in the gate*,to ſignifie that all which came in and out by the gate of the city,might indifferently be heard,the poore as well as the rich,and might haue acceſſe and regreſſe, too and from the iudgement ſeate. *Towards the riſing of the ſunne*, in token that their iudgment ſhould be as cleare from corruption,as the ſun is, cleare in his chiefeſt brightnes.

Secondly,this confutes the common opinion of the Schoolmen, who as they truly affirme that God rewardeth his Elect, *ſupra meritum*, aboue their deſert,ſo they erroniouſly teach that he puniſheth the reprobate,*citra condignum*,leſſe then they haue deſerued.For God powreth vpon the wicked,after this life, the full violls of his wrath,puniſhing them in the rigour of his iuſtice,without all mercy,not onely according to their works,in regard of nature and quality,but in reſpect of the meaſure and quantity.

Laſtly,this doctrine ſeriouſly conſidered and thought vpon,that we ſhall drinke ſuch as we brew,reape ſuch as we ſow, & that men ſhall haue degrees of felicity,or miſery,anſwerable to their works, anſwerable to the kind of their worke,to the quantity and quality thereof;will make vs more carefull to auoid ſinne, and to be more plentifull in good workes,then if with the Papiſts,we ſhould teach iuſtification by works.

Againe,in that euery one ſhall reape as he ſoweth,that is, ſhall be rewarded not according to the fruit and ſucceſſe of his labour, but according to his labour, be it more,or leſſe, better or worſe: it ſerues(firſt of all) to comfort the Miniſters of the word, which are ſet ouer a blinde ignorant people,who are alway learning, and neuer come to the knowledge of the truth:they muſt not be diſcouraged,though after long teaching, there be little knowledge or amendment;after much paines taking,little profiting;but rather a coldneſſe, a backwardneſſe,a declinining in all ſorts & degrees. They muſt remember, that if their Goſpell beeing deliuered with ſuch ſimplicity,with ſuch aſſiduity,with ſuch euidence & demonſtration of the ſpirit,be hid,*it is hid to them that periſh, in whome the god of this world hath blinded the mindes of the infidels, that the glorious Goſpel of Chriſt ſhould not ſhine vnto them.2.Cor*.4.3,4. Beſides, let the cōſider that though they ſeeme to labour in vaine,& to ſpend their ſtrength in vaine,and that their words take no more effect then if they were ſpoken in the winde:*yet that their iudgement is with the Lord,and their worke with their God.Iſa.*49.4.remembring that God will giue to euery man according to his worke, according to the kind,the quantity,the quality thereof: and not according to the fruit,or ſucceſſe of his worke.

It may serue also as a cordiall to euery man that is painefull and faithful in his calling, though neuer so base and seruile, as to a shepheard which watcheth his flocke, or a poore drudge that attends vpon his masters busines: he is to comfort himselfe with this, that though he see no great good that comes by his labour and trauell, yet if he be obedient to him that is his master according to the flesh in all things, not with eye-seruice as men pleasers, but in singlenes of heart, seruing God; and whatsoeuer he doth, doing it heartily as to the Lord, and not to men: let him know, and assure himselfe, that *of the Lord he shall receiue the reward of inheritance. Coloss.* 3.22,23,24. And the promise is more generall, *Eph.6.5. Know ye, that whatsoeuer good thing any man doth, the same shall he receiue of the Lord, whether he be bond or free.*

It serueth further, as a comfort against inequality, whereas the wicked flourish in all manner of prosperity, and the godly lie in cōtempt and misery; for the time shall come, when euery one shall reape euen as he hath sowne. When God will punish the sins of the reprobate with eternall torment, acccording to their deserts; and crowne the good workes of his seruants, with an eternall weight of glory, aboue their desert: for piety shall not alway goe vnrewarded, neither shal impietie alway goe vnpunished, for as the *Psalmist* saith, *The patient abiding of the righteous shall not perish for euer.* And againe, *doubtlesse there is a reward for the righteous, doubtlesse there is a God that* Psal.10.18. *iudgeth the earth.* Psl.58.11.

Againe, this condemneth the damnable opinion of Atheists, who thinke al things come to passe by nature, or fortune; & that domes day is but a dreame: and that sticke not to say, *It is in vaine to serue God, and what profit is it, that we haue kept his commandements, and that we haue walked humbly before the Lord of hoasts?* as thogh good works Malach.3.14. should neuer be rewarded, nor sinne punished: albeit the Lord hath said, *Behold I come quickly, and my reward is with me, to giue euery one as his worke shall be. Apoc.22.12.*

Besides, it meeteth with the practise of those men, which sowe nothing but cockle, and yet expect a crop of wheate: or nothing but darnell, and yet looke to reape a barly haruest: that is, such as sow nothing but the cursed seeds of a damnable life, and yet looke to reape the haruest of eternall life: for as a man soweth, so shall he reape: such as he brueth, such shall he drinke; *Euery one shal eate the fruite of his owne waies, and be filled with his owne deuices, Prou.* 1.31.

It doth further detect the folly of those which fraught the shippe of their soule, with nothing but faith, resting (in carnall presumption) vpon a vaine opinion of faith, and neuer caring for good works: againſt whom S. *Iames* writeth, chap. 2. 14. *What auaileth it, though a man ſay he hath faith, when he hath no workes? can the faith ſaue him?* 20. *Wilt thou vnderſtand, O thou vaine man, that faith which is without workes, is dead?* We muſt therfore ſow the ſeeds of good works in this life, if after this life we looke to reape the haruest of eternal life: and giue all diligence by good workes, to make our calling and election ſure, that as it is ſure in it ſelfe in Gods vnchangeable decree, 2. *Tim.* 2. 19. ſo wee may make it ſure to vs, 2. *Pet.* 1. 10. and ſo lay vp in ſtore a good foundation againſt the time to come, that we may obtaine eternall life, 1. *Tim.* 6. 19.

Laſtly, it croſſeth the wicked conceit and imagination of thoſe men, that ſing a *requiem* to their ſoules, in promiſing to themſelues an impunitie from ſinne, and an immunity from all the iudgments of God, notwithſtanding they go on in their bad practiſes; and all becauſe God doeth preſently take vengeance on them for their ſinnes. For they doe not conſider, that their ſinnes are as ſeedes, which muſt haue a time to grow in, before they come to maturitie; but being once ripe and full eared, let them aſſure themſelues God wil cut them downe with the ſickle of his iudgments, as we reade *Gen.* 15. 16. They remember not what the Lord ſaith by *Ieremie*, that he will not weary himſelfe with following after theſe wild aſſes, vſed to the wildernes, which ſnuffe vp the wind by occaſion at their pleaſure, and none can turne them back, *but wil ſeeke for them, and finde them in their moneths*, that is, when their iniquity ſhall be at the full, the Lord will meet with them.

Iere. 2. 24.

8 *For, he that ſoweth to the fleſh, ſhall of the fleſh reape corruption: but hee that ſoweth to the ſpirit, ſhall of the ſpirit reape life euerlaſting.*

Heere S. *Paul* ſpecifieth that in particular, which before he had deliuered in generall, *viz.* what he meant by *ſowing*, & *reaping*. And this hee doeth by a diſtribution, or enumeration of the kinds of ſowing & reaping: ſhewing, that there are two ſorts of ſeeds which men ſow in this life, good and euill. Two kinds of ſowers, ſpirituall men, and carnall men. Two ſorts of ground, in which this ſeed is ſowen; the fleſh and the ſpirit. Two ſorts of harueſts, which men are to reape according to the ſeed; corruption, and life: as *Paul* ſaith, *If yee liue after the fleſh, yee ſhall die: but if ye mortifie the deedes of the body by the ſpirit, ye ſhall liue*, *Rom.* 8. 13. Theſe two ſorts of harueſts, being anſwerable to the feed: corruption and death, being the harueſt of the ſeed ſowen to the fleſh: life and immortalitie, of that to the ſpirit.

Tacianus the heretike, and authour of the ſect of the *Encratites*, doth gather from this and the like places, that mariage is in it ſelfe ſimply euill, becauſe it is a ſowing to the fleſh. To him we may adioyne the Popes holineſſe, *Syricius*, who reaſoneth after the ſame maner, to prooue that Prieſts ought not to marrie, becauſe (ſaith he) *they that are in the fleſh, cannot pleaſe God, Romanes* 8.8. where he condemneth all marriages as vncleane, both in the Cleargie, and the Laitie. *Diſtinct.* 82. (Vnderſtanding, as though *Paul* ſhould ſpeake properly of *ſeed*, and of the *fleſh*,) But worthily was *Tacianus* his opinion confuted, and he condemned for an heretike: for the Apoſtle ſpeaketh not of the works of nature, but of corrupt nature, which ouerturneth the diuine order which God ſet in nature, in the creation. Beſides, the Apoſtolike writer ſaith, that *marriage is honourable among all men*; (not the firſt onely, but alſo the ſecond, third, &c. and among Cleargy men as well as others:) and therefore the marriage bed being *vndefiled*, that is, being vſed in holy manner, is no ſowing to the fleſh, but to the ſpirit, as Popiſh *doctours are enforced to confeſſe. Laſtly, *Paul* ſaith not, *Hee that ſoweth to the fleſh, ſhall of the fleſh reape corruption*: but, *he that ſoweth to his fleſh, &c.* Now no man (except hee be worſe then a bruit beaſt) doth abuſe himſelfe by ſowing to his owne fleſh, (as *Ierome* ſaith vpon this place.) Others, by ſowing to the fleſh and ſpirit, vnderſtand the following after the fruites of the fleſh and of the ſpirit, mentioned in the former chapter, ver. 19.22. But this expoſition cannot ſtand in this place; becauſe the illatiue particle *(for)* in the beginning of the verſ, ſheweth euidently, that theſe words depend vpon the former, as an exegeſis, or expoſition thereof, where *Paul* ſpake not generally of all, but particularly of thoſe workes which ſerue directly to vphold the miniſtery.

Hebr.13.3.

* Catharinus in Comment. in hunc locū.

By ſowing to the fleſh therefore the Apoſtle meaneth nothing els, but to liue in the fleſh, to walk in it, to take pleaſure in it, to follow the deſires of it, and to fulfill the luſts therof. More plainly; it is wholly to giue & addict a mans ſelfe to the pleaſures, profits, honors, and preferments of this life, & to ſpend himſelfe, his ſtrength, and wit in compaſſing of them, hauing little or no reſpect of the life to come, how he may compaſſe the rich purchaſe of the kingdome of heauen: which who ſo doth, ſhall reap nothing at the harueſt, but corruption: that is, ſhal haue for his reward, eternall death, vnderſtanding by corruption, the corruption of good qualities, not of the ſubſtance. On the contrary, to ſow to the ſpirit, is to liue in the ſpirit, and to walke according to the ſpirit, and to mortifie the deeds of the fleſh by the ſpirit, and to doe thoſe things, which otherwiſe we would neuer doe, if we were not mooued and ledde by the ſpirit] as to beſtow a mans goods, his labour and trauell, his ſtrength, his wit, and all, in thoſe things that may further true religion and pietie, with relation to eternall life: which whoſoeuer doth, ſhall reape life euerlaſting, as a iuſt recompence of his worke, according to the mercifull promiſe of God.

Chatharinus in ver. 10. Rhemenſ. in v. 9. Bellar. de iuſtif. cap. 3.

Here ſundrie obiections are to be anſwered, for the clearing of this text. Firſt, the Papiſts reaſon thus. Workes are ſeedes: but ſeedes are the proper cauſe of the fruite: therefore good workes are the proper cauſe of eternall life, and not faith onely. So that as there is a hidden vertue in the ſeede, to bring forth fruite: ſo is there a dignitie in good workes, to merit eternall life. *Anſw.* Firſt, as in a parable, ſo in a ſimilitude, whatſoeuer is beſide the ſcope and drift thereof, (as this their diſpute is) prooueth nothing. The ſcope of the ſimilitude is this, that as he which ſoweth wheate, ſhall reape wheate: ſo he that ſoweth to the ſpirit, ſhal of the ſpirit reape life euerlaſting; and as he that ſoweth tares, ſhall reape nothing but tares: ſo he that ſoweth to the fleſh, the curſed ſeedes of a wicked life, ſhall of the fleſh reape nothing but corruption: and as he that ſoweth plentifully either of theſe, ſhall reape a plentifull harueſt of either of them: ſo he that ſowes the ſeede of a godly, or wicked life, in plentifull manner, ſhall reape a plentifull increaſe, either of miſerie, or felicie. VVhen the Papiſts therefore reaſon thus: Seedes are the cauſe of the fruite, and haue in them a hidden vertue, whereby they grow, and bring forth fruite: therefore good workes are the proper cauſe of life, and haue a dignitie and excellency in them, whereby they are worthie of eternall life: they miſſe of the drift, and intent of the Apoſtle, and ſo conclude nothing. Beſides, this their collection, and diſcourſe, is contrarie to their owne doctrine. For they teach that good workes are meritorious by merit *of condignitie*: which may be vnderſtood 3 waies, either in regard of the dignitie of the worke alone; or in regard of the promiſe of God alone and his diuine acceptation: or partly in regard of the dignitie, and excellencie of the worke; partly in regard of the promiſe of God. Now albeit ſome of them hold, that good workes doe merit in reſpect onely of Gods promiſe, and mercifull acceptation, as *Scotus*, *Ariminenſis*, *Durandus*, *Vega*, *Bunderius*, *Coſter*, and the like: others, in reſpect partly of their owne worthineſſe, partly of Gods promiſe, and acceptance, as *Bonaventure*, *Biel*, *Driedo*, *Clingius*, *Ianſenius*, *Bellarmine*, &c. it beeing the common receiued opinion among the Schoolemen (as *Bensfeldius* witneſſeth:) yet none of them (excepting onely *Caietan*) affirme that they are meritorious only *in regard*

of

of the dignitie of the worke: which notwithſtanding the Rhemiſts, and others, labour to prooue out of this ſimilitude, vrging the analogie betweene *ſeed* and *good workes*, contrary to the current and ſtreame of their own Doctors. Thirdly I anſwer, that good works are ſeeds, yet faith is the root of theſe ſeedes: and in that good workes are made the ſeedes of eternall life, it is to bee aſcribed to Gods mercifull promiſe, not to the merit of the worke: for in that we, or our workes, are worthy of the leaſt bleſſing, it is more of Gods mercy, then our merit. Fourthly, the Apoſtle ſheweth onely who they are that ſhall inherite eternall life; and the order how life is attained: but not the cauſe wherefore it is giuen. It will be ſaid, not only the order, but the cauſe is ſet downe, as it may appeare by the *antitheſis*: for as ſowing to the fleſh, is the cauſe of deſtruction, ſo ſowing to the ſpirit, is the cauſe of eternall life. *Anſw.* It is true in the one, but not in the other. For firſt, ſinnes or works of the fleſh, are perfectly euill, as being abſolute breaches of the law, and deſerue infinite puniſhment, becauſe they offend an infinite maieſtie: whereas workes of the ſpirit, are imperfectly good, hauing in them wants, and imperfections, (there being in euery good worke a ſinne of omiſſion,) comming ſhort of that perfection that is required in the law: they being good and perfect, as they proceed from the ſpirit of God; imperfect and vicious, as they come from vs. Euen as water is pure, as it proceeds from the fountain: but troubled, as it runneth thorow a filthy channel; or as the writing is imperfect and faultie, as it comes from the yong learner, but perfect, and abſolute, as it proceedeth from the Scriuener which guideth his hand. So that if God (ſetting aſide mercie) ſhould trie them by the touchſtone of the word, they would bee found to be but counterfeit. And if he ſhould weigh them in the ballance of his iuſtice, they would be found too light. Secondly, there is a maine difference betwixt the workes of the fleſh, and the works of the ſpirit, in this very point; in that the works of the fleſh are our owne works, and not the workes of God in vs: and ſo wee deſerue eternall death, by reaſon of them, they being our owne wicked works: whereas good works proceed not from vs properly, ſeeing *we are not ſufficient of our ſelues to thinke any* [*good*] *thing as of our ſelues*, 2. *Cor*.3.5. but from the ſpirit of God, who worketh in vs both the will and the deed; and are his workes in vs: therefore being not ours, wee can merit nothing by them at the hands of God. Thirdly, obſerue, that it is not ſaid, he that ſoweth to the ſpirit, *ſhall of that which he hath ſowen, reape life euerlaſting*, but, *ſhall of the ſpirit reape life euerlaſting.* Where wee ſee the Apoſtle attributes nothing to our works,but to the grace of Gods spirit. Lastly,*Rom.* 6.23. the holy Ghost putteth manifest difference betweene the works of the flesh, and of the spirit, in respect of merit,when hee saith,*The wages of sinne is death: but eternal life is the gift of God.* Hee saith not,that eternal life is the reward of good works,but *the gift of God.* Now in the reward of sinne,there is merit presupposed: in the gift of eternall life,nothing but grace and fauour.

Obiect. II. God giueth eternall life according to the measure and proportion of the worke, v.7. *As a man soweth, so shall he reape,* 2.*Corint.*9.6. *He that soweth sparingly,shall reape sparingly,and hee that soweth liberally, shall reape liberally,* 1.*Cor.*3.8. *Euery one shall receiue his proper wages according to his owne labour.* Therefore in giuing eternall life,he hath no respect of the promise or compact, but of the dignitie and efficacie of the worke. *Answer.* Fulnesse of glory, called by Schoolemen, *essentiall glory,* is giuen onely for the merits of Christ, in the riches of Gods mercie, without all respect of works. *Accidentall glory,*(when one hath a greater measure of glory,another a lesse, as when vessels of vnequall quantitie cast into the sea,are all filled,yet some haue a greater measure of water,some a lesse) is giuen,not without respect of workes: yet so,as that it is not giuen for works,but according to works,they being infallible testimonies of their vnfained faith in the merits of Christ. If it be said,that eternal life is giuen as a reward,meritoriously deserued by good workes,because it is said,*Come ye blessed: for I was hungry, and yee gaue mee meat, Math.*25. I answer,it is one thing to be iust,another thing to be declared and knowne to be iust. We are iust by faith,but we are knowne to be iust by our workes: therefore men shall bee iudged at the last day, not by their faith, but by their works. For the last iudgement serueth not to make men iust that are vniust,which is done by faith,but to manifest thẽ to the world what they are in deed, which is done by workes. Men are often

Gal.1.3. Ierem.17.8. Math.3.10.

compared to trees in Scripture. Now a tree is not knowne what it is by his sap,but by his fruite: neither are men knowne to bee iust by their faith,but by their works. Indeed a tree is therefore good, because his sap is good: but it is knowne to be good by his fruit. So,a man is iust,because of his faith, but he is knowne to bee iust by his good works: therefore seeing that the last iudgement must

Apoc.20.12.

proceed according to euidence that is vpon record,(*for the bookes must be opened,and men must be iudged of those things,that are written in the bookes*) all must be iudged by their workes, which are euident and apparent to the view of all men,and not by their faith, which is not exposed to the sight of any. And hence it is that the Scripture

ture ſaith, we ſhal be iudged *according to our works*, but it is no where ſaid, *for our good workes*. Gregorie ſaith, *God wil giue to euery one according to his workes: but it is one thing to giue according to workes, an other thing, for workes.* For workes are no way the cauſe of reward; but onely the common meaſure, according to which God giueth a greater or leſſer reward. Take this reſemblance. A King promiſeth vnequall rewards to runners (the leaſt of which would equall the riches of a kingdome) vpon condition, that hee which firſt commeth to the goale, ſhall haue the greateſt reward; the ſecond, the next, and ſo in order. They hauing finiſhed their race, the King giueth them the reward according to their running. Who would hence but childiſhly inferre, that therefore they merited this reward by their running? And whereas they vrge that text, *Math.* 25. *Come yee bleſſed, for I was hungrie, and yee fedde mee:* I anſwer, firſt, that the word [*for*] doeth not alway ſignifie a cauſe, but any argument or reaſon taken from any Topick place: as *Rom.* 3.22,23 *The righteouſnes of God is made manifeſt vnto all, and vpon al that beleeue. For there is no difference: for all haue ſinned, and are depriued of the glory of God.* Where *ſinne* is no cauſe of the righteouſneſſe of faith, but only an antecedent, or adiunct, common to all men. So when we ſay, *This is the mother of the child, for ſhe will not haue it diuided.* There [*for*] doeth not implie the cauſe, as though her refuſing to haue it diuided, did make her the true mother of it: but onely the ſigne, that ſhe was the true mother indeed. Secondly, be it granted that it implieth the cauſe, yet not the meritorious cauſe: for good works are ſaid to be cauſes of eternall life, not as meriting, procuring, or deſeruing any thing at the hands of God, but as they are the kings high way to eternall life, God hauing prepared good workes, that we ſhould walke in them. If a King promiſe his ſubiect a treaſure hid in the top of a ſteep and high mountaine, vpon condition that hee clime and dig it out: his climing and digging is the efficient cauſe of enioying the treaſure, but no meritorious cauſe of obtaining it, ſeeing it was freely giuen. If it be further ſaid, that the word [*for*] doth here ſignifie the cauſe, as wel as in the words following, *Goe yee curſed, —— for I was hungry, and ye gaue me no meat:* ſeeing our Sauiour Chriſt ſpeaketh after the ſame maner, of the reward of the godly, and puniſhment of the wicked. I anſwer. The paritie of the reaſon ſtands in this, that as by good workes we come to eternall life, ſo by wicked works, we run headlong to perdition. The diſſimilitude is this, that euill works are not only the way, but alſo the cauſe of death: good works are the way, but not the cauſe, as *Bernard* ſaith, they are *via regni, non cauſa regnandi.*

In Pſal. 142. Reddendum cuiq; ſecundũ opera, ſed aliud eſt ſecundũ aliud propter opera reddere

Obiect. III. Here God pr[illegible]ternall life to good works: therefore good works merit etern[illegible] *Answ.* There is a double couenant, *Legal*, and *Euangelical*. In [illegible]egall couenant, the promise of eternall life is made vnto works. *Doe this and liue. If thou wilt enter into life, keepe the commandements.* But thus no man can merit, because none can fulfill the law. In the *Euangelicall couenant*, the promise is not made to the worke, but to the worker; and to the worker, not for the merit of his worke, but for the merit of Christ, as *Apoc.2.20. Be faithfull vnto the end, and I wil giue thee a crowne of life:* the promise is not made to fidelitie, but to the faithfull person, whose fidelitie is a signe that he is in Christ, *in whom all the promises of God are yea, and Amen,* that is, most certaine and infallible. Secondly, if any thing be due to workes, it is not of the merit of the worke, but of Gods mercifull promise. *Augustine* saith, *God made himselfe a debter, not by owing any thing, but by promising.* Thirdly, no reward is due to workes of regeneration, vpon compact and promise: first, because we are not vnder the couenant of works, in which God doth couenant with vs vpon condition of our obedience: but vnder the couenant of grace, the tenor of which couenant runneth vpon condition of the merits of Christ apprehended by faith. Secondly, though wee were vnder the legall couenant, yet we merit not, because our works are not answerable to the law. Lastly, whereas the pillars of the Romish Church teach, that the promise made vpon condition of performing the worke, maketh the performer to merit, is very false. This is not sufficient to make a meritorious work: it is further required, that the work be answerable and correspondent in worth & value, to the reward: as if one shal promise a thousand crowns to him that wil fetch a little water out of the next wel; it is debt indeed in the promiser, but no merit in the performer; because there is no proportion betweene the worke, and the reward.

2.Cor.1.20.

In Psal.31. [illegible] debẽdo, [illegible] mit-tẽ[illegible] Deus se fecit debitorẽ.

Bellar.de Iust. lib.5.c.3.

Obiect. IV. Sowing to the spirit, is a good worke, and reaping eternal life, the reward: but reward presupposeth merit: therefore sowing to the spirit doth merit eternall life. *Answer.* There is a double reward, one of *fauour*, another of *debt*, *Rom.4.4. To him that worketh, the wages is not counted by fauour, but by debt.* So saith *Ambrose, There is one reward of liberalitie and fauour: another reward, which is the stipend of vertue, and recompense of our labour.* Therefore *reward* signifieth generally any recompence, or any gift that is bestowed vpon another, whether it be more or lesse, whether answerable to the worke or not, whether vpon compact, or otherwise: for the Scripture maketh mention of reward, where there are no precedent workes, as *Genesis 15.1. Feare not Abram, I am thine exceeding great*

μισθὸς κατὰ χάριν. μισθὸς κατ' ὀφείλημα.

Epist.1.lib.1. Alia est merces liberalitatis & gratiæ: aliud virtutis stipendium, laboris remuneratio.

great reward, thas is, thy full content and happinesse. *Psal.* 127. 3. *The fruit of the wombe is a reward*, that is, a blessing, and a free gift of God. In this sense (I grant) eternall life is a reward. Yet it is no proper reward, but so called by a *catachresis*, which yet is not an *intollerable catachresis* (as *Bellarmine* either ignorantly or malitiously affirmeth) but easie and familiar; for in the phrase of the Scripture, eternall life is called a reward, in a generall signification, when it is vsed absolutely, and not relatiuely, to signifie the heele, or end of any thing: and so the Hebrew word which signifieth a *heele*, signifieth also a *reward*, because it is giuen when the worke is ended: And eternall life hath this resemblance with a reward, in that it is giuen at the end of a mans life, after that his trauell and warfare is ended. Thus the Greeke words, which signifie *a reward* and *an end*, are vsed indifferently one for the other. 1. *Peter* 1.9. *Receiuing the end of your faith, the saluation of your soules*, that is, (as *Beza* hath fitly translated it,) *the reward of your faith*: for to translate it, *the end of your faith* cannot agree to the word *receiuing*, for we receiue not an *end* but *a reward*. Thus reward signifieth a free gift, or free remuneration, as when the master giueth his seruant something for his faithfull seruice (though done vpon dutie) when as hee oweth him not thanks, much lesse reward. *Luke* 17.9. *Doth hee thanke that seruant, because hee did that which was commanded vnto him? I trow not.* Thus God giueth vs eternall life, not because hee is bound in iustice so to doe, (for hee oweth vs neither rewards, nor thankes for our labour, because *when wee haue done what wee can, we haue but done our dutie, vers.* 10.) but because his goodnesse, and mercifull promise made thereupon, doth excite him thereunto. And yet eternall life is called a reward, because it doth as certainly follow good works, as though it were due. And good works are mentioned in the promise, because they are tokens that the worker is in Christ, for whose merit, the promise shalbe accomplished. And it is further called the reward or fruit of our faith, (as here the haruest) because it is the way and meanes of obtaining it.

De iustif. l.5. c.3.

Hekeb. Psal. 19 12. Acharith. Prou. 23.18.

μισθὸς. τελός.

τὸ τελὸς τῆς πίστεως.

II. Eternall life is called a reward of good workes, not *causally*, as procured by them, but *consequently*, as following them. For albeit it be giuen *properly*, for the merit of Christ apprehended by faith: yet it is giuen *consequently* as a recompence of our labours: as an inheritance is giuen to the heire, not for any duty or seruice, but because hee is the heire: yet by consequent it is giuen in recompense of his obedience. *Hee that forsakes father and mother, —shall receiue a hundred fold more in this life, and in the world to come eternall life, Marke* 10.29,30.

Non αἰτιατικῶς vel causaliter: sed ἑπομένως siue consequutivè.

III.

III. Reward doth not alway preſuppoſe debt, but is often free, for whereas it is ſaid, *Math.* 5.46. *If you loue them that loue you, what reward ſhall ye haue?* It is thus in *Luke* 6.34. *What thanke ſhall ye haue?* by which we ſee that *reward* doth not alway ſignifie due debt, but thankefull remembrance, and gracious acceptance.

ἀνταπόδοσις τῆς κληρονομίας.

IV. *Coloſſians* 3.24. Eternall life is called *the reward of inheritance*, whereby is ſignified, that it is not giuen, for our workes, but becauſe we are the ſonnes of God by adoption. *Bellarmine* anſwers, that it may be both *a reward*, and *an inheritance*: *a reward*, becauſe it is giuen to labourers vpon compact: *an inheritance*, becauſe it is giuen to none, but thoſe that are children. But the word ἀνταπόδοσις tranſlated *reward*, ſignifieth a gift freely giuen without reſpect of deſert, it beeing all one with δόσις, as *Baſil* teacheth vpon the 7. pſalme.

V. The Scripture teacheth that God giueth rewards foure waies. Firſt, he giueth reward of due debt, in reſpect of merit: thus he giueth eternall life, as a reward due not to our merits, but to the merit of Chriſt: for none can merit at the hands of God, but hee which is God. Secondly, he giues a reward, in reſpect of his free and mercifull promiſe, and thus he rewards onely beleeuers. Thirdly, he giueth rewards to hypocrites, infidels, heathen, &c. beeing neither bound by his owne promiſe, nor by their merit; when they performe the outward workes of the law, and leade a ciuill life conformable thereto, as when *Ahab* humbled himſelfe before the Lord, 1. *King.* 21. And this God doth to the end he may preſerue humane ſociety, and common honeſtie, and that he may teſtifie what hee approoueth, and what he diſliketh. Laſtly, hee giueth good ſucceſſe in interpriſes, and attempts, according to his owne decree, and the order of diuine prouidence: which metaphorically is called a reward, *Ezek.* 29. v. 19. 20. becauſe it hath a ſimilitude thereunto, as when wicked men through ignorance, doe that wickedly, which he hath iuſtly decreed ſhall come to paſſe, ſuffering them to fill their houſes with the ſpoyle of the poore, which they haue for their worke, as a man hath wages for his honeſt labour. Thus the ſpoyle of Iudea, is called the hire or reward giuen to *Tiglath Pelaſſar* for his Syrian warre. *Iſa.* 7. 20. and thus the ſpoyle of Egypt, is ſaid to be wages giuen *Nebuchodonoſar*, for his ſeruice againſt Tyrus.

Further, let vs here obſerue the different maner of ſpeech which the Apoſtle vſeth, in ſpeaking of the fleſh and of the ſpirit. Of the former he ſaith, *He that ſoweth to his fleſh, &c.* Of the latter, *He that ſoweth to the ſpirit, not to his ſpirit*, by which is ſignified, that what good

good ſoeuer a man doeth in being beneficiall to the Miniſterie, in following the Goſpel,&c. he doeth it not by any goodneſſe that is in himſelfe, but by the ſpirit of God,who in euery good motion workes in vs the will,and in euery good action the deed,*Phil.*2.13. therefore no man ought to flatter himſelfe in this reſpect, or to thinke highly of himſelfe,as though he had attained an extraordinary meaſure of ſanctification,either for affecting, or effecting any thing that is good: ſeeing whatſoeuer good thing is in vs,is the gift of God,as *Ierom* ſaith. On the contrary,what euil ſoeuer a man doth,he doth it of himſelfe,God being neither the author, the furtherer,nor the abetter thereof.

Et Primaſius in hunc locũ. Dei dona ſunt quæcunque bona ſunt.

Againe,we hence learne,that all vnregenerate perſons,are ſowers to the fleſh,becauſe that before their conuerſion they doe nothing but thoſe things which are pleaſing to the fleſh: ſo that dying in that eſtate,they can reape nothing but corruption: therfore it hence followeth,that Philoſophers,heathen,and all meere ciuill, and naturall men,being ſuch as neuer ſowed to the ſpirit,ſhal reape nothing but corruption,death,and condemnation,contrary to the opinion of ſome ancient,and moderne writers.

Further, obſerue heere, that though there bee ſome that are *Neuters* in religion, luke-warme Goſpellers, halting betweene two opinions, ſuch as are neither fiſh nor fleſh: yet in morall duties there are no *Neuters,* nor *mediators*: for all men are ranged into one of theſe two rankes, either they are ſowers to the fleſh, or to the ſpirit.

Here alſo wee ſee who are true worldlings indeed; to wit, *ſuch as mind earthly things,* in ſpending themſelues, their ſtrength, and wits, vpon the world, hauing all their care for it, and all their comfort in it: in the meane time,hauing little or no taſte of the ioyes of the world to come, becauſe they make their Paradiſe here vpon earth, and neuer looke for any heauen after this life. As alſo who are ſpirituall men, namely, ſuch as walke in the ſpirit, who though they liue in the world, in theſe houſes of clay, yet are not of the world, becauſe they ſet not their affections vpon it, but haue their conuerſation in heauen,where Chriſt ſitteth at Gods right hand. Phil.3.19.

This ſerues firſt of all, to diſcouer vnto vs our owne eſtate,whether we be indeede carnall, or ſpirituall: for if we ſowe to the fleſh, that is, be alway poring,and digging in the earth with the mole, ſetting our affections vpon it, not referring the bleſſings of God, to his glory, and the furtherance of the Goſpell, but to ſerue our owne corrupt deſires: we are fleſhly minded,(though we pretend

this,

this, and that, and proteſt neuer ſo much)and continuing in this eſtate, wee can expect nothing but the harueſt of death and condemnation. Whereas on the contrary ſide,if we ſauour the things of the Spirit, by ſetting our affections vpon them, and ſeeking thoſe things that are aboue, eftſoones lifting vp our hearts by ſecret groanes and eiaculations,for the enioying of them,we are ſpirituall men, and ſhall vndoubtedly in due time reape the harueſt of eternall life.

Secondly,this bewraies the paucity of ſpirituall men,euen where the Goſpel is profeſſed: and how the world ſwarmes with multitudes of carnall,and fleſhly minded men.For as in former times before the flood,*they eate,they dranke,they bought, they ſold,they planted, they built*,that is,wholly addicted and deuoted themſelues to theſe things: So in theſe latter daies(which our Sauiour Chriſt propheceied ſhould be a counterpaine of the former) the multitude generally in euery place doe wholly imploy and ſpend themſelues, in thinking,in affecting,in taking,in ſeeking, in following of worldly things,ſeldome(God knowes)or neuer minding the kingdome of God,or the righteouſnes thereof,nor practiſing the Apoſtles rule,*ſo to vſe the world as though they vſed it not.* 1.*Cor*.7.31.

Luk.17.17.

Againe,here we ſee how the wiſedome of God is counted folly, among worldly wiſe men: and how the wiſedome of the world is fooliſhneſſe before God. For if a man ſow to the Spirit, in not following blind reaſon,nor corrupted affection, nor faſhioning himſelfe to the guiſe of the world,nor ſeeking his owne good ſo much as the good of others,but denying himſelfe, forſaking all(in his affection)for the Goſpel of Chriſt, and contemning this temporall traſh, in regard of the heauenly treaſure; he is accounted in the world but *a foole*: whereas God accounts him truely wiſe: for hee is the wiſe merchant man, *who hauing found a pearle of a great price, went and ſold all that he had, and bought it.Math.* 13.46.For the leſſe he laieth vp for himſelfe vpon earth,the more he treaſureth vp for himſelfe in heauen: and though hee ſeeme to ſowe vpon the waters,yet after many daies he ſhall finde it againe.Whereas they that minde nothing but the world, in ſowing to the fleſh, are reputed *wiſe* and *prouident men*: when as God accounts them ſtarke *fooles: Thou foole, this night ſhall they fetch away thy ſoule, and then whoſe ſhall thoſe things be which thou haſt prouided*? and then it followeth,*So is he that gathereth riches to himſelfe, and is not rich in God.* For the more they treaſure vp riches, the more they treaſure vp to themſelues wrath againſt the day of wrath.*Rom*.2.5.and fat themſelues againſt the day of ſlaughter.*Iam*.5.5.

Luk.12.20.21

Laſtly,

Laſtly, we are here warned to take heede of the Diuells ſophiſtry. It is a notable policie, one of the cunnineſt ſtratagemes the Diuell hath, in good things commanded, to ſeuer the meanes from the ende: and in euill things forbidden, to ſeuer the end from the meanes. He laboureth to ſeuer the meanes from the end, by perſwading a man that he may come to the end though he neuer vſe the meanes, that he may reape eternal life, though he neuer ſow the ſeedes of the ſpirit in this life. But we muſt know, that as he which runneth not at all, can neuer gaine the garland: he which laboureth not in the vineyard, the labourers wages: he that neuer ſowes, can neuer reape. So he that runneth not in the race of Chriſtianity, ſhall neuer attaine the crowne of happines, and felicity: he that laboureth not in the Lords vineyard, the recompence of reward: he that in this life ſoweth not of the ſpirit, ſhall neuer after this life reape life euerlaſting. For we may not dream of a good harueſt, without a good ſeede time, of ſowing nothing to reape ſomething, or ſowing tares to reape wheate. Againe, he ſeuereth the end from the meanes, by perſwading men that they may vſe the meanes and neuer come to the end, that though they ſow to the fleſh, yet they ſhall not reape corruption. Thus he perſwaded *Eue*, that though ſhe did eate of the forbidden fruite, yet ſhe ſhould not die the death, nay ſhee ſhould not die at all, but her eyes ſhould be opened, and ſhe ſhould be as a God himſelfe, knowing good and euill. But we are to be vndoubtedly reſolued of this, that God hath linked with an yron chaine, the pleaſure of ſin, and the puniſhment thereof: that as he that followes a riuer, muſt needs at length come to the Sea: ſo he that followes the courſe and ſtreame of his ſinnes, muſt needes come at the length to the gulfe of eternall deſtruction.

9. *Let vs not therefore be weary of well doing: for in due ſeaſon we ſhall reape, if we faint not.*

In theſe words, the Apoſtle expounds the fift generall rule appertaining to all ſorts of men: and in it he aſcendeth from the *hypotheſis* to the *theſis*, that is, from the *particular*, to the *generall*, ſhewing that we ought not to faint in any good courſe, either in doing good to them that labour amongſt vs, and are ouer vs in the Lord, and admoniſh vs; nor yet in beeing beneficiall vnto others. And this verſe dependeth vpon the former, (as the word *therefore* doth imply) by way of neceſſary illation, and conſequence: for ſeeing that they which continue in well doing, in ſowing to the ſpirit, ſhall of

the

of the ſpirit reape life euerlaſting. v. 8. therfore no man ought to be wearie of well doing. It conſiſteth of two parts: of a rule, or precept, in the former part of the verſe, *Let vs not therefore be weary of wel doing*: and a reaſon of the rule, or a motiue to incite vs to the performance thereof, in the latter part: *for in due ſeaſon we ſhall reape, if we faint not.* In the rule, the Apoſtle ſpeakes that plainely, which in the former verſes he had deliuered more obſcurely: for here he expoūds himſelfe, what he meant by *ſowing to the ſpirit,* namely, *doing of good,* or (as it is in the next verſe) *doing of good vnto all,* which may alſo appeare by that which followeth, *we ſhall reape, if we faint not,* that is, we ſhall reape the fruit of that which we haue ſowne to the ſpirit, if we faint not: therefore to ſow to the ſpirit, is nothing els, but to doe good. Now by *well doing,* the Apoſtle meaneth not onely the outward worke, whereby our neighbour is furthered, helped, relieued; but the doing of it alſo in a good manner, and to a good end; ſo, as it may be a good worke indeede, not onely profitable to our neighbours, and comfortable to our ſelues, but acceptable to God. This is a moſt neceſſary precept: for moſt men are ſoone weary of a good courſe, like to theſe Galatians, *who began in the Spirit,* but being weary of that walke, turned aſide, and *made an end in the fleſh. Gal.* 3.3. Like *Ephraim* and *Iudah, whoſe goodnes was as a morning cloud, and as the morning dewe which vaniſheth away. Hoſ.* 6.4. This weariſomneſſe in well doing hath ſeaſed vpon the moſt: euen vpon all drowſie profeſſours, (which are the greateſt part,) as may appeare by this, in that ſome, if they be held but a quarter of an houre too long, or aboue their ordinarie time, are extreamely weary of hearing the word. And as for duties of mercie, and liberality, putting vp iniuries, and tolerating wrongs, they are ready to make an end as ſoone as they begin. And as for Praier and thanſgiuing, and other parts of the worſhip of God, moſt men ſay in their hearts with the old Iewes, *what profit is it that we keepe his commandements, and that we walke humbly before the Lord of hoſts? Malach.* 3.14. nay they count it a *wearineſſe* vnto them, and *ſnuffe thereat. Malach.* 1.13. Hence it is, that the Holy Ghoſt is ſo frequent in ſtirring vs vp to the performance of all good duties, with alacrity and chearefulnes, and ſo often in rouſing vs from that drowſines and deadnes, wherewith we are ouerwhelmed. *Luke* 18.1. Our Sauiour Chriſt propounds a parable to this end, to teach vs, *that we ought alwaies to pray, and not to waxe faint. Eph.* 3.13. *I deſire* (ſaith *Paul*) *that ye faint not at my tribulations.* 2. *Theſſ.* 3.13. *And ye, brethren, be not weary in well doing.* And ſo in this place, *Let vs not therefore be weary of well doing.*

Now the reaſons which make men ſo weary of well doing, are

in

in *generall* these three. First, the strength of the flesh, which euen in the regenerate is like the great gyant *Goliah*, in comparison of poore *Dauid*. Secondly, the weakenesse of the Spirit, and spirituall graces. Thirdly, the outward occurrences, and impediments of this life. In *speciall* they be these. First, men by nature are wolues one to another. *Esay* 11.v.6. and so they continue, till this woluish nature be mortified, and renued by grace, being so farre from helping, furthering, releeuing, tollerating one another, or performing any other duty of loue, that contrarily, they are ready to bite, and deuoure one another. *Gal.* 5.15. Secondly, oftentimes it commeth to passe, that other mens coldnesse doth coole our zeale, their backewardnesse slacketh our forwardnesse. Thirdly, many thinke it a disgrace and disparagement vnto them, to stoope so low, as to become seruiceable vnto their inferiours. Fourthly, there are many things which discourage vs from well doing, either the party is vnknowne vnto vs, as *Dauid* was to *Nabal* (for which cause he would not relieue him in his necessity:) or else seemeth vnworthy of our helpe, being such as through riot, harlots, lewde company, hath brought himselfe to miserie and beggerie. Or such as reward vs euill for good, hatred for our good will: or such as are querulous, alwayes complaining, though neuer so well dealt withall: all which make men cold in the duties of loue. Fiftly, some there be which faine dangers and cast perils, which hinder them from doing the good they should: *The slothfull person saith, a lyon is in the way, &c.* Lastly, the manifold occasions and affaires of this life, doe so distract the minde, as that a man is soone wearied, yea in the best things. Besides, many see no reason why they should spend themselues, in doing good vnto others.

Now to all these obstacles, and pul-backs, we are to oppose the Apostles precept, *Let vs not be weary of well doing.* For verily, if the consideration of these small occasions, and rubbes that lie in our way, daunt and dismay vs, and so stoppe our course, wee shall neuer be plentifull in good workes: wee may haply put our hand to the plowe, but a thousand to one we shall looke backe againe: with *Lots* wife cast a long looke toward Sodome; and with the Israelites Gen.19.26 in our hearts turne againe into Egypt. Luke 9.62 For as *he that obserueth the winde shall not sowe, and as hee that regardeth the cloudes, shall not reape. Eccles.* 11.4. So he that regardeth the ingratitude of some, the euill example of others, the manifold distractions, and occurrences of this life; and shall cast perils in carnall wisedome, of this, and that trouble, or inconueniencie, that may ensue, shall neuer doe his duty as he ought.

And

And assuredly, he that fainteth in a good course, and giueth it ouer before he come to the ende, is like vnto the slothful husbandman, who hauing plowed and tilled, and in part sowed his ground, giueth ouer before he haue finished it; and so, either the parching heate doth wither it, or the nipping cold kill it, or the fowles of the aire deuoure it.

Now most men are sicke of this disease, which shewes the greatnesse of our corruptions, and that the best Christians haue a huge masse or lumpe of sinne in them, and but a sparke of grace; in that they are seldome or neuer wearie in scraping together of riches, in following their pleasures, in pursuing honours, aud hunting after preferments: and yet are quickely wearie in duties of pietie, iustice, and mercie, albeit they haue an vnspeakable reward annexed vnto them.

Well, whatsoeuer the corrupt practises of men be, let vs learne our dutie, to goe forward without wearinesse, nay to do good with chearefulnesse, as *Paul* saith of himselfe, *Philippians* 3. *forgetting that which is behind, and indeauouring himselfe to that which is before.* Let vs consider that it is the propertie of a liberal minde, *to deuise of liberall things, and to continue his liberallity, Esay.* 32. 8. Neither is this all, not to be wearie, or to persist and continue, but we must proceede on from strength to strength, and *bring forth more fruite in our age, Psal.* 92. 14. as the Church of *Thiatyra*, whose workes were more at the last, then at the first, for which shee is worthily praised by our Sauiour Christ, *Reuel.* 2. 19. It was the *motto* of *Charles* the fift, *Plus vltra*, and it ought to be euery Christians *motto*, to striue to perfections, and as the Apostle exhorts vs, *To be steadfast, immoueable*, and not to make stay there, but to be *aboundant alwaies in the worke of the Lord*, 1. *Cor.* 15. 58. And that we may doe this indeede, we must set this downe as a certaine conclusion, that we wil not recoile, nor giue backe, come what will come: and withall we must labour to quicken our dull and drowsie spirits, to girde vp the loynes of our mindes, to strengthen our weake hands, and our feeble knees, by publike and priuate exercises of reading, praier, meditation, conference, &c.

Thus much of the rule: now followeth the reason of the rule, or the motiue to incourage vs to the performance of this dutie; *for in due season we shall reape, if we faint not*: as he should say more fully, thus, Let vs be assured of this, that continuing and increasing in well doing, our labour is not lost, nor spent in vaine. 1. *Cor.* 15. 58. for though wee imagine that we labour in vaine, and spend our strength in vaine, (as the Prophet speaketh) yet *our worke is with the*

Lord

*Lord, and our labor with our God, Esa.*49.4. And albeit we may seeme to our selues & others to cast away our goods, in being beneficial vnto some, and (as the wise man speaketh) to sow vpon the waters; *yet after many daies we shall find them again, Eccles.*11.1. In the motiue there be three things contained. First, the reason it selfe, which is a promise of reward, *We shall reape.* Secondly, the circumstance of time, when this haruest shall be reaped, wee shall reape *in due season.* Thirdly, the condition that is required on our parts, that wee may reape, *if wee faint not.* Of these in order, and first of the reason or promise it selfe.

Wheras the Apostle to the end we may not be weary of a good course, doth encourage vs to proceed on, by setting before our eies the promised reward, I gather that we may encourage, animate, and excite our selues to the performance of all good duties, by the consideration of the heauenly haruest, which we are to reape, and the crown of glory we are to receiue after this life; as the husbandman doth sow, in hope that hee shall reape: and though seed time be painfull and chargeable vnto him, yet he giueth not ouer for all that, but comforteth himselfe with the expectation of the haruest, which will fully quite his cost, and recompence his labour. That this is a truth, it may appeare by sundry arguments: by *precept*, by *promise*, by *practise*, by *reason*. For *precept*: It is the commandement of Christ wee should *make vs friends of vnrighteous Mammon*, or of the riches of iniquitie, *that when we shall want, they may receiue vs into euerlasting Tabernacles, Luke* 16.9.

For *promise*, besides this place (which is very pregnant to this purpose) *Paul* exhorts seruants, *that whatsoeuer they do, they would doe it heartily, as to the Lord, & not to men, knowing that of the Lord they shall receiue the reward of inheritance, Col.*3.23,24. And generally *what good thing soeuer a man doeth, the same shall he receiue of the Lord, whether hee be bond or free, Eph.*6.8. *He that forsakes father & mother, &c. for Christs sake, shall receiue a hundred fold more in this life, and in the world to come life euerlasting, Math.*19.29. These and the like promises were to no purpose if it were not lawfull for vs to looke for the reward, and if we might not by considering of it, incite and stirre vp our selues, to greater alacritie in the course of Christianitie, in making vs more feruent and frequent in the duties of pietie.

Thirdly, it may be prooued by the *practise* of the Saints of God: *Abraham* was contented to forsake his natiue countrey at the command of God, and to dwell in a strange land, yea, and that in tents, *because he looked for a citie hauing a foundation, whose builder and maker is God, Hebr.*11.v.9,10. *Moses* esteemed the rebuke of Christ greater riches then the treasures of Egypt, *because he had respect vnto the recompense of reward*, verse 26. Christ (whose example is without all exception, being *exemplum indeficiens*, as the Schoolemen speake) did sweeten the bitternesse of the crosse with the consideration of the glorie which a little after hee was to enioy; for so the Apostle saith, that *for the ioy that was set before him, hee endured the crosse, and despised the shame, Ebr.* 12.2. The Colossians are commended by the Apostle, for that they continued and increased in faith to God, and loue to man, *for the hopes sake that was laid vp for them in heauen, Col.* 1.5. And *Paul* shewes this to haue bin the practise, and to be the dutie of al the Saints of God, *so to run that they may obtaine*, 1.*Cor*.9.24.

Lastly, it may be prooued by *reason*. For first, that which is the end of our actions, ought to bee considered of vs, as a meanes to stirre vs vp to the attaining of this end: therfore seeing the end of our faith and hope, is eternall life, *Rom*.6.22. *Ye haue your fruit in holinesse, and the end euerlasting life*, 1.*Peter* 1.9. *Receiuing the reward of your faith, the saluation of your soules*: Therefore wee may, nay wee ought to cast our eyes vpon it, and to direct all our actions for the attaining of it. Secondly, if the labourer worke, not in regard of the common good onely, but also with respect of his wages: hee that runneth a race, to attaine the garland: if the husbandmen set and sow, plant and plow, in hope to reape a haruest, and to receiue some fruite of his labours: It is lawfull for Christians also to doe good in regard of eternall reward; for that is the Apostles reason, 1. *Cor*.9.25. *They that trie masteries abstaine from all things, that they may obtaine a corruptible crowne; but we for an incorruptible.* It is S. *Iames* his reason, *Iames* 5.7, 8. as the husbandman waiteth for the precious fruite of the earth, and hath long patience for it, vntill hee receiue the former and the latter raine; *So must we be patient, and settle our hearts, for the comming of the Lord draweth neere*, and hee will recompence euery man according to his workes. Thirdly, if it bee lawfull for a man to abstaine from sin, for feare of eternall punishment, and torment in hell, (as we know it is,) *Math*.10.28. then it is lawfull to doe good, in hope of eternall reward. It will be said, that it is the propertie of a mercenary hireling to looke for a reward. I answer, it is the property of a hireling to looke *onely*, or *principally* for his hire, either not minding the glory and honor of God, or lesse respecting it, then his owne priuate aduantage; so that when the hope of his gaine is gone, he leaueth his charge, and flieth away: like the Popish Monkes, who were right hirelings indeed: for they minded nothing but their owne commodity, according

ding to the old saying, *No peme, no Pater noster.* But to looke to the recompense of reward in the second place, after the glory of God, the performance of our dutie, and discharge of a good conscience, is no propertie of a hireling; seeing God hath promised to giue *to them which by continuance in well doing, seeke honour, and immortalitie, eternall life, Rom.*2.7.

By this that hath bene said, we may see the impudencie of the *Rhemists*, who in their marginall notes vpon *Luke* 14.1. *Ebr.*11.26. and *Apoc.*3.5. doe notably slander vs and our doctrine, in auerring that we teach, that no man ought to do good in respect of reward: the like may be said of Cardinall *Bellarmine*, *Binsfeldius* and others. For this is our constant doctrine, that we may, and ought, to stirre vp our dulnesse to all chearefulnesse, in the discharge of our dutie, by setting before our eyes the reward which is promised. Yet so, as that wee ought not *onely*, nor *principally*, to respect the reward: for the zeale of Gods glory, the care and conscience wee haue to discharge our dutie, ought rather to moue vs to be plentifull in good works (in lieu of thankfulnesse vnto God for the riches of his mercy) then the greatnesse of the reward; seeing we ought to doe our dutie, though there were no heauen, no hell, no reward, no punishment, no deuill to torment, no conscience to accuse; the very *loue of God ought to constraine vs, 2.Cor.*5.14. And heere wee must with thankfulnes acknowledge the endlesse loue and mercy of God towards vs, seeing that when hee might exact strict obedience without any promise of recompence for our labor: nay, when he might shiuer vs in pieces with his yron scepter, yet as *Ahashuerosh* did to Queene *Esther*, hee holdeth out his golden scepter vnto vs in the preaching of the word, that wee might lay hold of it, and by it apprehend eternall life. Yea it pleaseth him to winne vs by gifts, to incite vs by rewards, to allure vs by promises, in giuing his word, that if we giue, we may look to receiue (though not for our merits, yet through his mercy:) if wee bestow transitory goods, wee shall receiue a durable substance; if a cup of cold water, Gods kingdom, *Math.*10.12.

De Iustificat l.5.c.8. de Iustif. & mer. Sect.4. memb.5. concl.15.

The second generall point, is the circumstance of time, when we shall reape, to wit, *in due time*. This due time may be vnderstood in part, of this life: for godlinesse hath the promise of this life, as well as of the life to come, and the workes of mercy haue bin euen in this life recompensed to the full. The widow of *Zarepta* for entertaining the Prophet *Eliah*, was miraculously sustained in the dearth: *the meale in her barrell did not waste, and the oyle in her cruise did not diminish*, 1.*Kings* 17.16. And so the *Shunamite*, for the like kindnesse shewed to the Prophet *Elizeus*, being barren, obtained a sonne: and when he was dead, shee obtained him to life againe, 2. *Kings* 4. as the widow of *Sarepta* did hers at the prayer of *Eliah*, 1. *Kings* 17.23. For as God doth alwaies giue to his children in this life the first fruits of his spirit: so he doth often giue them the first fruits of their labours, as a taste of their future felicitie, and an earnest of that happinesse which after they shall fully enioy. Our Sauiour Christ saith, he wil reward them an hundred fold in this life. *Math.* 19. But *this due time* is properly meant of the life to come, which hath two degrees, the first is at the day of death, when the soule entreth into happinesse: the second, at the day of iudgment, when both soule and body (being reunited) shall be put in full possession of eternall glory and felicitie: for then they shall bee rewarded according to their workes, not so much as a cup of cold water which they haue giuen to relieue the Saints of God, but shall bee recompenced to the full, *Math.* 10.42.

Vse. Seeing God hath set downe a set and certain time when we are to reape, it is our dutie with patience to expect it, as the husbandman doth, who hauing sowed his field, doeth not looke for a crop the next day, or weeke, or moneth: but patiently expecteth the haruest, that he may receiue the precious seed of the earth. For he is too vnreasonable, who hauing sowed in *September*, looketh for a crop in *October*: hee must wait for the moneth of *August*, till the haruest, and in the meane time endure storme and tempest, wind and weather, snow and raine, haile and frost. So we must sow our seede, and sow plentifully, still expecting the fruite of our labour with patience, till the great haruest come, the great day of retribution, in which God will separate the wheate from the chaffe; gathering the one into his garners, and burning vp the other with vnquenchable fire, *Mat.* 3.12. Let vs consider the example of God, who doeth patiently expect, and (as I may say) waits our leasure when we wil turne vnto him, *that hee might haue mercy vpon vs*, *Esay* 30.8. hee waiteth at the doore of our hearts, & standeth knocking to bee let in, *Apoc.* 3.20. nay, hee calleth vnto vs standing without, *Open vnto me my sister, my loue, my doue, my vndefiled: for my head is full of dew, and my locks with the drops of the night, Cant.* 5.2. *Woe vnto thee Ierusalem, wilt thou neuer be made cleane? when will it once be? Iere.* 13.27. More particularly, Gods waiting and expecting is set downe in Scripture by sundry degrees. First, hee waiteth *all the day long, Esay* 65.2. *I haue stretched out my hand all the day long, to a disobedient and gainsaying people.* Secondly, 40. daie together, *Yet* 40. *daies and Nineue shall be destroied, Ion.* 3.4. Thirdly, *all the yere long*, as the husbandman

doth

doth; *I looked for grapes, and loe wilde grapes. Esa.* 5 4 Fourthly he expecteth our amendment, *many yeares together. Luk.* 13.7. *Behold, these three yeares haue I come and sought fruit on this figge tree, and finde none.* Fiftly, the Lord suffered the manners of the Israelites fourtie yeares in the wildernesse. *Psal.* 95.10. *Act.* 13.18. Sixtly, the long sufferance of God (as *Peter* saith, 1. Epist. 3.20.) did patiently expect the conuersion of the old world, all the while the Arke was in preparing for the space of *an hundred and twentie yeares.* Seuenthly, he expected the Canaanits, and Amorits, for the space of *foure hundred, yeares*, yea he suffered all Gentiles to wander in their owne waies, & in the vanity of their minde almost for *three thousand yeares together. Act.* 14.16. Now if God bee so patient in expecting our amendment from day to day, from yeare to yeare; we ought to be patient in expecting the accomplishment of his promises day after day, and yeare after yeare, as we are commanded. *Habac.* 2.3. *Though the vision tarrie, yet waite for it, for it shall surely come, and shall not stay*: and though it be long before we reape any fruite of our labours, yet let vs with patience expect it, for in due season we shall reape, if we faint not. For, if God wait vpon vs, not for his owne good, but for ours; what a shame is it, that we will not waite vpon him, in tarrying his good leisure, for our owne good? The dumme and sensles creatures may set vs to schoole in this point: for they expect *with a feruent desire to be deliuered from the bondage of corruption, into the glorious liberty of the sonnes of God. Rom.* 8.19, 20. and as the word signifieth, they expect with a longing desire, euen with *thrusting forth their heads*, as the poore prisoner that is condemned doth, who eftsoones putteth forth his head out of the window, in a continuall earnest expectation of the gracious pardon of the Prince. It is our parts therefore to waite as *Dauid* did, who saith of himselfe, *Psal.* 69.3 *I am wearie of my crying, my eyes faile me whilst I waite for my God.* For if we giue ouer our patient expecting, and faint in our minds, seeking to anticipate this DVE TIME, this period which God hath prefixed in his vnchangeable will, (more immutable then the lawes of the Medes and Persians) a thousand to one but we runne for helpe, either to the witch of *Endor*, as *Saul* did, 1. *Sam.* 28. or to the wizzard of *Pethor*, as *Balack* did, *Numb.* 22. or to the sorcerer or figure flinger of *Babel*, as *Nebuchadnezzar* did, *Ezek.* 21.21. or if all these faile, (as commonly they doe) we either breake out into open blasphemie, as the King of *Israel* did, 2. *King.* 6.33. *Behold this euill commeth of the Lord, should I attend on the Lord any longer?* or in the depth of discontent, we play the desperate part of *Razez*, and lay violent hands vpon our selues. 2. *Macchab.* 14.41.

ἐτροποφόρησε, not ἐτροφοφόρησε, as some would haue it.

ἀποκαραδοκοῦντες.

μὴ ἐκλυόμενοι.
*Oecumen. in hunc locum, & alij.

The third thing to bee considered, is the condition required on our part, that we may reape in due time, set downe in these words, *if we faint not.* The words in the originall are thus: we shall reape in due time, *not fainting*: which may be (and are of * some) taken in a double sence: either as *a promise*, or as *a condition.* As *a promise*, thus, If we be not weary of well doing, we shal reape in due season without all fainting and wearinesse, either to the body, or minde, that is, we shall reape with all ioy and comfort, as it is *Psal. 126. 5, 6. They that sow in teares, shall reape in ioy: and they that went weeping and caried precious seed, shall come againe with ioy, and bring their sheaues with them.* As *a condition*, that if we continue constant in wel doing to the end without fainting, we shall reape in the time that God hath appointed: and in this sense it is to be taken in this text, to wit, *conditionally*, as it is well translated, *if we faint not.*

Wee are further to consider, that there is a double fainting, one of the bodie, another of the minde. The bodily fainting which commeth by labour, and toyling, is not here meant, seeing it doth nothing impeach the goodnesse of the worke, (it is an argument rather of the soundnesse and sinceritie thereof:) but the spirituall fainting is that which is to be feared, because it maketh our labour all in vaine. And this spirituall fainting is twofold: the first is, the slacking and remitting somewhat of our course, and this hath, and doth befall the Saints of God, as we may see in the example of the Church of Ephesus, *which left her first loue, Apoc. 2. 4.* Yea all the Saints of God haue their *turbida interualla*, troubled and distempered fits, sometime in the full, sometime in the wane, sometime zealous and forward in the seruice of God, sometime againe heauy and backward, &c.

The second is such a fainting and languishing, that we cleane giue ouer our course, of which *Paul* speaks, 2. *Cor.* 4. 16. *Therefore we faint not, but though our outward man perish, yet the inward man is renewed daily.* And the author to the Hebrews, *we must consider Christ, who endured such speaking against of sinners, lest we should be wearied, and faint in our soules, Hebr.* 12. 3. And againe, v. 5. *Despise not the chastening of the Lord, neither faint when thou art rebuked of him.* This fainting is meant in this place.

Finis coronat opus.
Of all vertues it is only constancie is crowned.

Whereas S. *Paul* saith we shall reape, *if we faint not:* he signifieth, that wee must perseuere and continue to the end, otherwise wee cannot looke to reape the haruest of eternall happinesse. It is nothing but constancie and continuing in well doing, that doeth crowne all our good workes. *Bee constant* (saith our Sauiour Christ to the Church of Smyrna, *Apoc.* 2. 10.) *and I will giue thee the crowne*

of

life. Ierome saith, It is the propertie of true vertue, *not to beginne well, but to ende well. Paul* blameth these Galatians, for beginning in the spirit, and ending in the flesh: and Christ shewes what a shame it is to him that beginneth to build and cannot finish it: it is as good neuer a whit, as neuer the better: nay his condition is better that neuer began, *then that of Iudas*, whose ende was worse then his beginning. *Leuit*.3.9. the taile of the sacrifice was commanded to be offered vpon the altar, by which was signified, that in euery good worke, we must not onely begin, but continue in it to the end, and sacrifice the end of it to God, as well as the beginning: otherwise we lose our labour, and misse our reward, therefore Saint *Iohn* biddeth vs *looke to our selues, that we lose not the things which we haue done, but that wee may receiue a full reward*, 2.*Iohn* v. 8. The labourers in the vineyard came at sundry times, some in the morning, others at the third, others at the sixt, and ninth, others at the twelfth houre of the day, yet none receiued the labourers wages, but those that continued in the work to the end, *Mat*.20. God is *Alpha* & *Omega*, and therefore requireth a good end, as well as a good beginning, and it is our dutie not only to obey the commandement of Christ, *Venite ad me, come vnto me*, *Mat*.11.28. but that also, *manete in me, abide in mee*, *Iohn* 15.4. for he onely that continueth to the end, shall bee saued, *Math*.24 13.

Non cœpisse, sed perfecisse virtutis est.

Further, whereas the Apostle saith, *Wee shall reape, if wee faint not:* It may be demaunded, whether the Saints doe so faint at any time, that they finally fall away? To which demaund I answer in a word, that they doe not, nay, they cannot *totally* and *finally* fall from grace. For first, if any thing should make them fall away, it is sinne; but they cannot sinne, because the seed of regeneration and grace remaineth in them, 1.*Iohn* 3. 9. And though the Church sleepe, yet her heart waketh, *Canticles* 5.2. And if any thing make them faint, it is affliction and persecution; but these and all other crosses *worke together for the best vnto them that loue God, Romanes*, 8.28. And therefore these are no hinderances, but furtherances rather to their saluation. Secondly, they are built and founded vpon the promise of God, *I will put my spirit into their hearts, so that they shall not depart from me*, *Ierem*.32.40. Therefore Christ doeth so preserue them by his power, preuent them by his grace, guard and guide them by his spirit, that they shall neuer fall away, and that none shall plucke them out of his hand, *Iohn* 10. I adde further, that they are built vpon the trueth and fidelitie of his promise, *God is faithfull, and will not suffer you to be tempted aboue that you bee able, but will giue the issue with the temptation, that ye may bee able to beare it*, 1. *Cor.* 10. 13. Thirdly, vpon the prayer of Christ, who prayed, that they might bee *kept from euill, Iohn* 17.15. that they might *bee one in the Trinitie, as hee in the Father, and the Father in him*, verse 21. that they *may bee with him, and see his glorie*, ver. 24. Now Christ was alway heard in that which hee prayed for, *Iohn* 11.42.

Lastly, vpon the life of Christ, which is communicated to all his liuing members, *Gala.* 2. verse 20. *When Christ which is their life shall appeare, then shall they also appeare with him in glory, Col.* 3.4. *Quest.* If they cannot altogether faint and fall away, why doeth the holy Ghost make a doubt of it, as though they might? *Answer.* It is the will of God to mooue vs to perseuerance, and to stirre vp our dulnesse by such speeches, that we should not be wanting to our selues in the vse of the meanes.

10 *While we haue therfore time, let vs do good vnto all men, but specially to them which are of the houshold of faith.*

In these words the Apostle doeth iterate the conclusion propounded in the sixt verse, as also in the ninth verse immediatly going before; that wee should doe the good wee can, while we haue time; and withall hee doth illustrate it both by *the obiect* to whom we must doe good, & by *the circumstance of time*, how long we must continue therin. And herein he answereth a secret demand, which might be made vpō the former rule; for wheras it might be thoght that the Gentiles which professe not the same religion with vs, were to be neglected, or at least, not so respected (as we reade, *Actes* 6.1. the Grecians were neglected of the Ebrews in their daily ministery) the Apostle answereth, that we must not restraine our bountie and goodnesse only to those that are of the same religion with vs, but enlarge it vnto all, *We must doe good vnto all men, but specially to them of the houshold of faith.*

In the words we may consider three things. First, the dutie it selfe, *Let vs do good.* Secondly, the obiect or persons to whom wee must do good, which is laid downe comparatiuely, *we must do good to all, specially to those that are of the houshold of faith.* Thirdly, the circumstance of time, when and how long we are to doe good, *whilest we haue time*; of these in order, and first of the dutie.

This generall dutie of doing good, is recommended vnto vs by sundry arguments. The first may bee taken from the maine end and scope of a mans life in this world, which as *Paul* signifieth in this place, is nothing else but *to doe good*: and this doing of

good

good standeth in three things: the first concerneth God, in praising, magnifying, and adoring his holy name. *Dauid* had an eye to this end, whē he desired to liue for no other end, but that he might praise God, *O let my soule liue, and it shall praise thee.* The second concerneth our selues, in seeking the kingdome of God, and the righteousnesse thereof, by making our calling and election sure by good, 2. *Peter* 1.10. This end of a mans life *Salomon* intimateth, when hee saith, *Let vs heare the ende of all; feare God, and keepe his Commaundements, for this is the whole dutie of man, Eccles.* 12. verse 13. The third concerneth our brethren, in doing good vnto them so farre foorth as possibly we can in the compasse of our calling: for it is the end of euery mans calling, in seruing of men to serue God; and this is that which *Paul* vrgeth in this place, *to bee beneficiall vnto all.*

The second may bee taken from the example of God himselfe, *Wee must doe good to them that hate vs, that wee may bee the children of our heauenly Father, Matthew* 5. ver. 44.45. For we are more conformable vnto God in doing good vnto others (it being an essentiall propertie in God to doe good to euery man, seeing that euery creature doeth drinke, or at the least taste of the sweet cuppe of Gods goodnesse, *Psalme* 145.v.9.) then in receiuing good from them: for he receiueth nothing from vs, as *Dauid* saith, *My goodnes reacheth not to thee, Psal.* 16.2. To the example of God we may adde the example of godly kings. The chiefest praise and commendation of *Hezekiah* and *Iosiah*, is noted by their goodnes. Concerning the rest of the acts of *Hezekiah*, and his GOODNESSE, they are written —— 2. *Chro.* 32.32. Concerning the rest of the acts of *Iosiah* and his GOODNESSE, doing as it is written in the Law of the Lord, behold, they are written —— 2. *Chron.* 35.26,27. And this excellent name of *goodnesse*, or *bountifulnesse*, was (as it may seeme) by the law of nations, ascribed to Princes and Potentates, in that it best beseemed them, as in name, so in the vertue it selfe, to expresse the diuine nature of God by, and therefore they were called, *ἐυεργηται*, that is, bountifull benefactors, or gracious Lords, *Luke* 23 25.

The third is drawne from testimonie, diuine and humane. Our Sauiour Christ saith, *It is a blessed thing to giue, rather then to receiue, Actes* 20.3. that is, to doe good, rather then to receiue good. * *Nazianzen* saith, that a man doeth resemble God in no propertie so much, as in doing good. And the heathen Oratour *Demosthenes* could say, that (a) doing of good, and speaking the truth, makes vs most like to God himselfe.

* Orat. 27. de pauperum amore, ὐδὲν ὕτως ὡς τὸ εὐποιεῖν ἄνθρωπος ἔχει θεȣ̃.

a τὸ εὐεργετεῖν καὶ ἀληθεύειν.

But

Bonum prophylacticum vel conſeruatiuũ: congregatiuum: cõmunicatiuum.

But to conſider this more particularly, *Goodneſſe* is threefold, *Preſeruing, Vniting, Communicating*: in all which particulars we are to practiſe this dutie. And firſt, for the *preſeruing goodneſſe*: we muſt do good not onely to our ſelues, but to others alſo, in labouring to keepe and preſerue them from the contagion of ſinne, from falling from grace, or back ſliding from their holy profeſſion, by all good meanes, as by good example, and by gracious ſpeeches ſeaſoned with ſalt, *&c.* as *Barnabas* did, *who comming to Antioch, and ſeeing the grace of God that was giuen them, was glad, and confirmed them therein, exhorting them that with purpoſe of heart they would cleaue vnto the Lord.* *Act.* 11.12. and for this cauſe (as I take it) it is added, v.23. *that hee was a good man, and full of the holy Ghoſt, and faith.*

The *Vniting goodneſſe*, is likewiſe to be practiſed, in ſetting men at Vnity, in reconciling thoſe that are at variance, in making peace and amity, where there is nothing but enmity and diſſention: for, for this cauſe Chriſt calleth *peace-makers the children of God.* *Mat.* 5. 10. becauſe herein they liuely reſemble the goodneſſe of God their heauenly Father, as any ſonne doth reſemble any quality or propertie in his naturall father: for he maketh men to be of one mind in an houſe, *Pſal.* 67.

The *communicating goodneſſe* (being eſpecially vnderſtood in this place) hath foure degrees. Firſt, for *temporall things* we muſt communicate to the neceſſities of the Saints, *Rom.* 12.13. And for *ſpirituall bleſſings*, we muſt remember the ſaying of *Peter*, *Let euery man as he hath receiued a gift, ſo miniſter the ſame vnto others, as good diſpoſers of the manifold fold grace of God*, 1.*Pet.* 4.10.

Secondly, we muſt be plentifull in the works of mercy, not contenting our ſelues with this, that wee are beneficiall to ſome in releeuing them in their wants and neceſſities: but wee muſt be rich in good workes, 1.*Tim.* 6.18. *Charge them that are rich in this world, that they be not high minded, that they doe good, and be rich in good workes, ready to diſtribute and communicate.* Wee muſt bee like *Tabitha* (or *Dorcas*) who cloathed the poore with the garments which ſhee made at her owne proper coſt and charges, *Actes* 9.39. and for this cauſe the holy Ghoſt giueth this teſtimonie of her, that *ſhee was rich or full of good workes and almes which ſhee did*, verſe 36. like to the vertuous woman, *Prouerbes* 31.20. who openeth the palme of her hands to the poore, and ſtretched out her hands to the needy: like *Iob*, of whom it is ſaid, that the loines of the poore bleſſed him, *Iob* 31.20.

Thirdly, wee muſt bee *much in goodneſſe* (as the Scripture ſpeaketh of God) that is, abundant in goodneſſe, in communicating

vnto

vnto others abũdantly those blessings which the Lord hath stored vs withall: not onely in louing our brethren, for which the Thessalonians are commended, that their loue one towards another did abound; but in a liberall supplying of their wants, as *Paul* exhorts the *Corinthians*, that *as they did abound in faith and loue, so they would abound in rich liberality*. 2. *Cor*. 8.7. as good *Obadiah* did, in spending his liuing, and venturing his life, in hiding an hundred of the Lords Prophets, from the furious rage of wicked *Iesabel*. 1. *King*. 18.13.

Lastly, we must be *exceeding* or *superabundant* in goodnes; in exceeding measure (if it may be) in doing good: like the poore widdow who had rather want her selfe, then be altogether wanting in contribution to the treasurie of the Lords Temple: and therefore though it was but two mites which shee cast into the *Corban*, yet Christ preferred it before all the rich mens offerings being put together, in that they gaue of their *superfluitie*, but shee of her *penurie*, cast in all that shee had euen all her liuing. *Luk*. 21.4. It is well said by *S. Ambrose*: *We must relieue the wants of others according as wee are able, and sometime euen aboue our abilitie*; as *Paul* witnesseth of the *Corinthians* to their great commendation, *that to their power, and beyond their power they were willing*. 2. *Cor*. 8.2.

Offic.l.2.c.28 Necessitates aliorum quantum possimus iuuare debemus, & plus interdum quam possimus.

Further, in doing good, we must obserue these rules. I. We must doe good of that onely which is our owne: for we may not cut a large and liberall shiue of another mans loafe (as the common saying is) we may not steale from one, to giue to another: or deale vniustly with some, that we may be mercifull to others: or robbe *Peter*, to cloath *Paul*. The Lord abhorreth euen burnt-offering, if it be of that which is gotten by rapine and (o) spoile. *Esa*. 61.8. and hence it is that *David* would not offer burnt offering without cost, of that which was not his owne. 1. *Chron*. 21.24.

o holocaustũ de rapina.

II. We must doe good with chearefulnes and alacritie, *for God loueth a chearefull giuer*. 2. *Cor*. 9. *Ambrose* saith fitly and finely to this purpose, *Well-doing ought to proceede from well-willing*: *for such as thine affection is, such is thy action*. Therefore if we giue, we must doe it freely, otherwise it is no gift: for what more free then gift? therefore wee may not play the hucksters in doing good, for that doth most blemish the excellencie of the gift: for as *Lactantius* saith, *Danda beneficia non fœneranda*.

Offic l.1.c 30 Beneficentia ex beneuolentia manare debet, affectus tuus nomen imponit operi tuo.

Institut.diuin. lib.2.cap.12.

III. Wee must so doe good, as that we doe not disable our selues for euer doing good; but may continue in well doing, and as the *Psalmist* speaketh, *bring forth more fruite in our age*. *Salomon* commands that the streames of our wells should flow to others, yet so, as

Psal 92.14.

as that the fountaine be ſtill our owne.Pſal. 112.5.*A good man is mercifull, and lendeth,and will guide his affaires with iudgement*; that is,he will ſo diſcreetly diſpoſe and order all his actions, as that hee will keepe himſelfe within his compaſſe; ſo beginning to doe good,as that he may continue : therefore the wiſe man ſaith, *In the houſe of the wiſe there is a precious treaſure, and oyntment, but a fooliſh man deuoureth it. Prou:*21.20.All the diſciples that were at Antioch, ſent ſuccour to the brethren which were in Iudea,in the great famine that was in the time of *Claudius Cæſar*,yet *euerie man according to his abilitie. Act.* 11.29.for according to *Pauls* rule, we muſt *not ſo giue,that others bee eaſed,and we our ſelues pinched.*2.*Cor.*8.13.

IV. We muſt doe all the good we can poſſibly within the compaſſe of our callings, and hinder all the euill. It will bee ſaid, God (whoſe examdle wee are to follow) doth not all the good he can, neither doth he hinder all the euill. Therefore we are not bound to doe all the good, or preuent all the euill we can. I anſwer, in this particular we are not to imitate the example of God, and that for three cauſes. Firſt,becauſe we are ſubiect to the law, *Thou ſhalt not doe euill that good may come of it.Rom.*3.8. whereas God is not bound nor ſubiect to any Law,no not to his owne law,but is aboue it,and hath power to diſpence with it.Secondly,becauſe he is able to draw good out of euill, light out of darkeneſſe ; which we cannot doe. Thirdly,becauſe God is the *Generall* good,*we particular*. Now there is great difference betwixt theſe two,for it belongs to the nature of the *particular good*,to procure all the good that may be ſimply to euery one,and to hinder all euill : whereas to the nature of *the generall* or *vniuerſall good*,three things appertaine. Firſt, that all things ſhould be good in ſome meaſure of goodneſſe.Secondly,that ſome things ſhould be better then others.Thirdly,that thoſe things that are defectiue in goodneſſe,that is,*euills*, ſhould be ordained to the common good : as in a well ordered houſe,all the parts thereof are good in their kind. Secondly, ſome better then others, as *Paul* ſaith,*In a great houſe there are veſſells of gold and ſiluer,of wood and ſtone, ſome for honour,and ſome for diſhonour.*2.*Tim.*2.20. Thirdly,thoſe that are deſtitute of goodneſſe,as *ſinkes,draughts*, and other like places (ſeruing for baſe,though neceſſary vſes)are ordained to the common good of the whole houſe,which it cannot want. And therefore if the maſter builder (to preuent theſe particular euills) ſhould leaue them out of his building, hee ſhould preiudice the common good of the whole houſe,which cannot be without them.

Thus much of the firſt part, namely the duty : Now I proceede to proſecute the ſecond,which ſhewes firſt to whom we muſt doe

good,

good, and ſecondly the order to be obſerued therein. *Wee muſt doe good vnto all,but ſpecially to thoſe which are of the houſhold of faith.* Touching the firſt; It may ſeeme,that ſome among the Galatians were of the Phariſes minde,who thought they were bound to loue their friends, but not their enemies; or of this perſwaſion that they were not bound in conſcience to doe good vnto the heathen amongſt whom they liued,as being profeſſed enemies of Chriſt,and open perſecuters of his Church. But *Paul* teacheth them and vs another leſſon,when he commands vs *to doe good vnto all*;ſutable to that of our ſauiour Chriſt,*loue your enemies,bleſſe them that curſe you, doe good to them that hate you, pray for them that hurt you and perſecute you.Math.*6.44. Let vs conſider the good *Samaritans* practiſe: Albeit there was mortall hatred betwixt the Iewes and the Samaritans.*Ioh*.4.6. yet he ſeeing his deadly enemie wounded and halfe dead, had compaſſion vpon him; powred wine and oyle into his ſoares,bound vp his wounds, ſet him on his owne beaſt, brought him to an Inne,and made prouiſion for him; the like ought we to doe,euen to our enemies,as occaſion ſhall ſerue,*Luk*.10.30. For if we muſt do good to our enemies beaſt,his oxe or aſſe going aſtray, in bringing him home againe; *Exod* 23.4.Much more ought wee to doe good to our enemy himſelfe. For the more beneficiall and communicatiue we ſhew our ſelues to bee,the greater goodneſſe we ſhew to bee in vs, as the fountaine which powreth forth his ſtreames vnto all,& the candle which ſtandeth vpon a candleſtick ſhineth vnto all,and not to it ſelfe being couered with a buſhell.

The reaſons why wee ought to doe good vnto all, (euen to our enemies) are principally *foure.* The firſt may bee taken from the grounds of loue and beneficence,which are in all men, euen in the wicked themſelues; now the grounds of loue are ſpecially *three:* the firſt is the image of God, which beeing in all men, yea euen in prophane perſons in part, ought to be the loadeſtone of loue to draw our affection vnto it. The ſecond is communion and fellowſhip in the ſame nature, and therefore wee ought to bee beneficiall vnto men, becauſe they are men; and though wee will not doe good *homini*,yet we muſt doe good *humanitati*,as the Philoſopher ſaid.The third is participation in the death of Chriſt,in that all men haue part in Chriſt as well as we(for any thing wee know.) Secondly God (whoſe example wee are to follow, as hath beene Math.5.45. ſaid) is good,and bountifull vnto all, cauſing his ſunne to ſhine as well vpon the badde as the good,and his raine to fall as well vpon the ground of the vniuſt, as of the iuſt, beeing kinde vnto the vnkinde and to the wicked. Thirdly,we muſt doe to others as wee would

Math.7.12. would they ſhould doe to vs. Therefore if wee being in diſtreſſe, would be glad to receiue good at the hand of a wicked man, wee ought in the like caſe to doe good vnto him. Fourthly, our profeſſion and the reward which we looke for, require this at our hands; for if we doe good vnto them onely that doe good vnto vs, or if we be friendly to thoſe onely that doe good vnto vs, what ſingular thing doe we? for euen the Publicanes doe the like; and ſo hauing our reward here in this life, wee can expect none other after this life, *Math.* 5.47.

The ſecond point, (which containeth the order to be obſerued in doing good,) is laid downe in theſe words, *Let vs doe good to all, but ſpecially to thoſe which are of the houſhold of faith.* By *them of the houſhold of faith*, wee are to vnderſtand thoſe which by faith are of the ſame family with vs, namely, of the ſame Catholike Church vpon earth; *the houſe of God* being often put to ſignifie the Church of God, as 1 *Tim.* 3.15. The houſe of God is called *the Church of God, the ground and pillar of trueth, Hebr.* 3.2. *Moſes was faithfull in all Gods houſe*, that is, his Church: and thus this phraſe is expounded, *Epheſ.* 2.19. *Yee are no more ſtrangers and forreiners, but citizens with the Saints, and of the houſhold of God.* So that by them of the *houſhold of faith*, we muſt vnderſtand onely the *faithfull*. Indeed among men, not onely children, but alſo manſeruants, and maidſeruants are counted to be of the family; but God accounts them to be of his houſe, that are Saints by calling, and ſonnes by faith. The reſt are baſtards, and not ſonnes, they are (it may be) in the houſe, but not of the houſe: for true ſauing faith, doeth characterize thoſe that are of the *familie of faith*; euen as fanaticall dreames, fantaſticall opinions, allegorizing of the literall ſenſe of the Scripture, denying the reſurrection of the fleſh, do characterize thoſe that are of the *Family of loue.*

Hauing the meaning, conſider the dutie, which is, to doe good principally to the faithfull, the Saints and ſeruants of God, that is, wee muſt doe good vnto them before others, and more then to others, which are not of the ſame family; as *Dauid* ſaith, *My wel doing reacheth not to thee, but to the Saints that are in the earth, and them that excell in vertue, Pſal.* 16.2,3. For it is all one as if the Apoſtle ſhould haue ſaid, As it is fit and conuenient, that they that are of the ſame family ſhould be helpfull and beneficiall one vnto another, rather then to thoſe that are of another family: So it is requiſite, that thoſe which are members of the ſame body, nay ſons and daughters, brethren and ſiſters, hauing the ſame God for their father, the ſame Church for their mother, Chriſt for their elder brother, begotten of the ſame immortall ſeede, nouriſhed with the ſame milke of the word, and looking for the ſame bleſſed inheritance: ſhould rather be beneficiall one to another, then to thoſe that are forrainers and ſtrangers, no way linked vnto them by the bond of faith.

Now the reaſons why we ought ſpecially to doe good to them of the houſhold of faith, may be theſe. Firſt, becauſe God loueth all his creatures, ſpecially mankind, moſt eſpecially the faithfull, vpon whom he doth beſtow the riches of his loue, yea himſelfe alſo: for though God be *good vnto all,* Pſal. 145.9. yet in a ſpeciall ſort he *is good to Iſrael, to them that are of a pure heart.* Pſal. 73.1. *He is a Sauiour of all men, ſpecially of thoſe that beleeue.* 1. *Tim.* 4.10. Secondly, becauſe whatſoeuer is done to one of Gods Saints, is done vnto him, *Matth.* 25.44. Thirdly, in reſpect of the excellencie of their perſons, in that they are *ſonnes of God, heires of his kingdome, members of Chriſt, Temples of the holy Ghoſt, &c.*

Further, in that all the faithful are called a houſhold & a family, this teacheth vs that as we haue one bed and one board, one bread to feede vpon, and one cup whereof all drinke: ſo we ſhould haue one minde and one heart, we ſhould cleaue together, and hold together: for if they of the *Family of loue* ioyne together, why ſhould not we which are of the *family of faith* hold together? If thoſe of the kingdome of darkeneſſe combine themſelues together, as it is *Pſ.* 2.2. *The kings of the earth band themſelues, and the Princes are aſſembled together, againſt the Lord, and againſt his Chriſt,* Act. 4.27. *Doubtleſſe againſt thine holy Sonne Ieſus, whom thou haſt annointed, both Herod and Pontius Pilate, with the Gentiles and people of Iſrael gathered themſelues together.* Pſal. 83.5.6.7,8. *They haue conſulted together in heart, and haue made a league againſt thee; The tabernacles of Edom, and the Iſhmaelites, Moab, and the Agarims, Geball, and Ammon, and Amalech, the Philiſtims with the inhabitants of Tyrus: Aſhur alſo is ioyned with them: they haue beene an arme to the children of Lot.* How much more therfore ought the children of light to accompanie and conſort together? But the children of this world are wiſer in their generation then the children of light. Nay the bruite beaſts may condemne vs in this point: for cattell heard together, ſheepe flocke together, fiſhes ſhole together, and (as the prouerbe is) birdes of a feather will flie together. What a ſhame is it therefore for vs, that are of the ſame family of faith, to fall out, making a rent in the coate, and a diuiſion in the body of Chriſt, by ſeparating our ſelues one from another, in affection of heart, and practiſe of life?

Againe, this may miniſter comfort to all the faithfull beeing vnder the croſſe, to conſider that they are of Gods family; and therefore

fore neede not doubt of the prouidence of God, but that he will prouide things necessarie for them, *for he that prouideth not for his owne, and specially for them of his family, hath denied the faith, and is worse then an infidell.*

Lastly, in that the faithfull are called *a family*, it sheweth that they are but few, euen a handfull in comparison of the world; for what is a familie to a countrie or a kingdome? Indeede I grant, if those of the family of faith, be considered by themselues, they are many. *Matth.* 8.11. *I say vnto you, that MANY shall come from the East and from the West, and shall sit downe with Abraham, Isaac, and Iacob in the kingdome of heauen.* Nay they are innumerable. *Apoc.* 7.9. *After these things I beheld, and loe, a great multitude, which no man could number of all nations and kindreds and people and tongues, stood before the throne, and before the Lambe, cloathed with long white robes, and palmes in their hands.* But beeing compared with infidels, which shall bee condemned, they are but few, *Math.* 7.13.14. *Enter in at the straite gate: for it is the wide gate and broad way that leadeth to destruction, and MANIE there bee which goe in thereat: Because the gate is straite, and the way narrow, that leadeth vnto life, and FEW there be that finde it. MANY are called, but FEW chosen.* Here they are called *a family, and a little flocke. Luke* 12.32. *and a remnant, Rom.* 9.27. Let the Papists therefore brag of their Vniuersalitie and multitude, as much as they list, in the meane time, let vs not feare to ioyne our selues to the little flocke of Christ, and with them to goe on in the straite way to eternall life.

The order which we are to obserue in doing good to others, is elsewhere more distinctly set downe in Scripture: and it stands in these degrees. First, and principally, a man must do good to those *of his familie*, as to wife, children, seruants, 1.*Tim.* 5.8. *If there be any that prouideth not for his owne, and* especially *for them of his houshold, hee hath denied the faith, and is worse then an infidell.* Secondly, after those of our familie, we must doe good to our *parents* and *progenitors.* 1. *Tim.* 5.4. *If any widow haue children or nephewes, let them* (that is, those children or nephewes) *learne first to shew godlinesse toward their owne house, and to recompence their parents.* Marke, they must first doe good to their owne house, and then in the second place to their parents, that is, their fathers and mothers, if they be children; their grandfathers and grandmothers, if they be nephewes. Thirdly, after the two former, we must doe good to *our kinred.* 1.*Tim.* 5.8. *If any prouide not for his owne—he hath denied the faith,* &c. where by *owne*, we are chiefely to vnderstand, those poore widowes that are neare of blood, or kinred vnto vs; or generally all those that are

μάλιστα, not well translated, Namely.

προγόνοις, not well translated Kinred.

are of our kinred in the flesh, who are therefore called *ours*, because they doe more neerely concerne vs, as being linked vnto vs by the bond of nature. They that are of our kinred, are to be respected, and relieued of vs in the third place, if they bee of the houshold of faith; otherwise the Saints of God, which are neither kith nor kinne vnto vs, are to be preferred before them. Fourthly, of strangers and forreiners, we are to doe good to the *faithfull* before others. Fiftly, and lastly, wee must be beneficiall *to all*, whether friends or foes, of our kinred, or strangers, of the house of God, or otherwise, as God in his prouidence shall offer them vnto vs: for so *Paul* saith, *Wee must doe good vnto all men.* It will be said, we are to loue all men alike (seeing we must loue our neighbours as our selues) and therefore wee must doe good to all men alike, not respecting the faithfull more then others. I answer, our loue of our brethren, is lesse or greater, either in respect of the *obiect*, in wishing a greater or a lesse good vnto them: and thus we must loue all men alike, in wishing to them eternall life, : or in respect of *the intention of our loue*, in hauing a greater desire of the good of some, then of othersome: and thus we are not bound to loue, or to doe good to all alike. For as *S. Bernard* saith, *Meliori maior affectus, indigentiori maior effectus tribuendus.*

This doctrine inuested with the former examples, may shame the base, seruile, and beggerly liberalitie of the common sort of men, which professe the Gospel, whose hands are tied to their purses, and their hearts locked to their chests, who are so extreamely miserable, that they neither doe good to others, nor yet to themselues. Secondly, it condemneth them which are so vnnaturall, that they forget all dutie to their kinred and acquaintance in the flesh. Thirdly, those that will doe good to none, but to those that haue done good to them: this is right the Pharisies righteousnes, to loue our friends, and hate our enemies; the goodnes of the Publican, to lend to those, of whom they looke for the like. Lastly, those who are so full of the poison of malice and reuenge, that being once incensed, they can neuer be appeased, till they crie quittance with those that offend them.

The third thing to be considered in the words, is the circumstance of time; *we must doe good to all, while we haue time.*

Here sundry points are to be obserued.

I. If wee must doe good while wee haue time, we must make a holy and profitable vse of our time, (the rarest iewell and greatest of all earthly treasures) because time will not alway last: and therefore wee must take time while it is time, seeing time and tide will tarry for no man. Let vs consider what a shame it is, that the children of this world should be wiser in their generation then wee, who professe our selues to be the children of light. The Marriner or sea-faring man who obserues winde and weather, taketh the opportunity of the time: the trauiler or way-faring man takes day before him, and trauaileth while it is light. The Smith striketh the yron while it is hot, for when it is cold, it is too late to strike. The Lawyer taketh his time, to wit, the Tearme time, for entertaining of his Clients, and following of his suits: for when the Tearme is ended, his time is gone. Now it is alway Tearme time with Christians, euery present day, euen this present time, is their Tearme time: therefore if wee will not shew our selues more carelesse and negligent, nay more absurdly foolish, or desperatly madde then all men, we must take the opportunity that is offered to doe good, and vse the precious time which God in mercy affordeth vs, to his glory, our comfort, and the good of others. Time and opportunity of doing good, is hieroglyphically resembled by the head of a man that hath locks of haire before, which a man may take hold of, but hath none behind; whereby is signified, that when opportunity is past, there is no possibility left to doe good. We must not therefore let slippe any good occasion, but take hold of it at first, when it is offered. Hence it is that the Apostle, *Hebr.* 3. 13. biddeth vs *exhort one another, while it is called to day*. And the wise man, *Prou.* 3. 28. *Say not to thy neighbour, goe and come againe, and to morrow will I giue thee, if thou now haue it*. For he may dye, and so cannot come againe, or by thy delaying of him, may be discouraged from comming, or thou maist be hardened against him, or maist with the rich man in the Gospel, bee suddainly taken away from thy riches, or thy riches taken from thee. Our Sauiour biddeth vs *walke in the light, while wee haue light. Ioh.* 12. 35.

Fronte capillata est, post est occasio caluo.

II. If we must doe good while we haue time, we must obserue the Apostles golden rule, *Ephes.* 5. 16: *Redeeme the time*: which is nothing else, but so to employ it, and vse the benefit of it, as that we suffer it not to slippe away from vs without fruite or profit, either for sloth and idlenes, or by reason of vaine and transitory pleasures, or other occasions of this life: but to gaine that time we formerly lost by negligence, with double diligence, yea to redeeme it with the losse of our ease, our pleasures, our profits. And we shall the better practise this dutie, if we consider that time is *short, precious, irreuocable*: it is *short*, and therefore to bee guided by diligence: it is *precious*, and therefore to be redeemed by an high estimate and account of it, in not beeing too lauish of it: in bestowing it vpon our

our friends, not vpon our enemies : in placing it as a iewell in our golden age, and wearing it in our new garments, as the robes of Chriſt his righteouſneſſe,and not (as a pearle in a ſwines ſnowt)in the rotten ragges of ſinne and wickedneſſe. Laſtly it is *irreuocable*,and therefore it is to be redeemed by taking the opportunity thereof.

III. *Paul* commanding vs to doe good while we haue time, would haue vs know times and ſeaſons ; to obſerue the ſhortnes of time,to number our daies that we may apply our hearts to wiſedome. The not knowing and obſeruing of time, is a ſinne much inueighed againſt by our Sauiour Chriſt, *Math*. 16.3. *O hypocrites, you can diſcerne the face of the skie, and can yee not* * *diſcerne the ſignes of the times? Luk*.12.56. *why* * *diſcerne ye not this time* ? the Lord doth preferre the very bruite beaſts before his people,becauſe they know their appointed times and ſeaſons, whereas his people knew not the time of mercy and grace, which was offered vnto them. *Euen the Storke in the ayre knoweth her appointed times, the turtle, and the crane,and the ſwallow, obſerue the time of their comming,but my people knoweth not the iudgement of the Lord.Ier*.8.7. And Chriſt threatneth Ieruſalem,that one ſtone ſhould not be left vpon another, *becauſe they knew not the time of their viſitation.Luk*.19.44. And verily of all follies and ignorances,this is the greateſt, not to know the day of our viſitation,the acceptable time,the day of ſaluation,when God offereth mercy, by riſing early and calling vs by the miniſtery of his word,and ſtretching out his hands all the day long.*Rom*.10.21. For if he ſtand at the doore of our hearts,and knocke by the ſound of his word outwardly, by the motion of his Spirit inwardly, by his threatnings,by his promiſes,by his iudgements,by his mercies, by his tolerance and long ſuffering,and yet for all that we will not open nor liſten vnto him, we ſhall ſtand with the fiue fooliſh virgins, and knocke at his mercie gate, and ſay, *Lord, Lord, open vnto vs*,when it will be too late, when heauen ſhall be ſhut againſt vs.*Math*.25.11,12.For,for this cauſe among others,they are called *fooliſh virgins*, becauſe they conſidered not the time of the bridegroomes comming.

* διακρίνειν.
* δοκιμάζετε.

Here it will be ſaid,obſeruing of time is forbidden.*Gal*.4.10.*Yee obſerue dayes, and times, and moneths, and yeares, I am afraid of you, leaſt I haue ſpent on you labour in vaine. Anſw*. There is a twofold obſeruing of time *good*,and *euill* ; *lawfull*, and *vnlawfull*. Vnlawfull and ſuperſtitious,is either *Iewiſh*,or *Heatheniſh* : the *Iewiſh*, and ſuperſtitious obſeruation of times, is, when religion is placed in the keeping of them, in an opinion that they bind the conſcience to the

the strict obseruing of them, as their Iubilies, feasts of the Passeouer, of weekes, of Tabernacles, Calends, new moones, &c. *Heathenish*, when times are obserued in respect of good, or badde successe: as when men make two (*i*) vnluckie dayes in euery moneth, in regard of health: when they count leape-yeare ominous, as *Valentinian* did, who beeing newly created Emperour, would not come forth and shew himselfe the bissext of Februarie. Not (*k*) to marry in the moneth of May. To obserue Planetarie houres, and Climactericall yeares, the Horoscope or time of a mans birth, and the position of the heauens at that time. Both these kindes are forbidden. *Paul* was afraid of the *Galatians*, first, because they obserued *dayes and moneths and yeares*, that is, Iewish ceremonies, and beggerly rudiments. Secondly, because they obserued *times* or *seasons*, that is, heathenish superstitions mentioned before. And assuredly, besides the vnlawfulnes of this practise, it is also vaine euen in the iudgement of the heathens themselues. *Alexander* the Great, commanded the Macedonian souldiers (which had not beene accustomed to fight in Iune, because it had beene ominous vnto them) that they should call it *Iuly*, and so got the victorie ouer *Darius*. *Lucullus* beeing to fight with *Tigranes* vpon an vnlucky day, in which *Cepio* was ouercome of the *Cimbrians*: I will (said he) make it fortunate to the Romanes, and got the victorie. And who knoweth not that the selfe same day hath beene fortunate or luckie to some (as they vse to speake,) vnfortunate and vnluckie to others? The same day was *Crassus* slaine by the Parthians, and *Pachor* king of Parthia taken by *Ventidius*. The same day was vnto *Pompey*, the day of his birth, and the day of his death. The same day was to *Fredericke* the second, his coronation day, and his funerall day.

i Egyptian dayes.

k Mense malum Maio nubere vulgus ait.

Δαισιός.

μία τῶν ἀποφράδων.

The lawfull obseruing of time is two fold; *Humane*, *Diuine*. *Humane* is three fold, *Naturall*, *Ciuill*, *Ecclesiasticall*. *Naturall* is, the obseruing of the motion of the sunne, the moone, & the starrs, whose reuolutions make times and seasons, dayes, moneths, yeares: the obseruing of the foure quarters or seasons of the yeare, spring, summer, autumne, winter: The Eclipses of the sunne and moone: the full moone, the wane, the change: The time of cutting timber, of planting, sowing, &c. in obseruing wherof, a great part of Astronomie, Philosophie, and husbandry is imployed.

Ciuill is, when times are obserued in regard of pollicie, or of the good of the Common wealth, as Faire-times, market times, tearme times, &c. the Spring, as fit time for Kings to goe foorth to warre, 2.*Sam*. 4.11. The keeping of Lent, Fasting dayes, Ember weekes, all are in a ciuill respect for the breed of cattell, the main-

maintenance of nauigation, and the plentie of all things.

Ecclesiasticall, when set times are obserued in the Church for order sake, without superstition, or opinion of worship: as among the Iewes the feast of Purim, *Eph*.9.26. the feast of the Dedication, *Ioh*. 10.22. Amongst Christians, festiuall daies: as the feast of the Natiuitie, of circumcision, of the resurrection, and ascension of Christ: these and such like solemnities, appointed for our thanksgiuing and humiliation, are not vnlawfull, if they bee enioyned by lawfull authoritie, and kept in good manner.

Diuine is, when vpon the consideration of the shortnesse and vncertaintie of our liues, wee prepare our selues against God shall call vs, and *so number our daies that we apply our hearts to wisedome*. *Psal*.90. Or, obseruing the day of Gods mercifull visitation, we take the opportunitie and vse the meanes that is offered, for our conuersion and saluation. Or, obseruing the time of Gods visitation in iudgement and indignation, we hide our selues vnder the couert of his wings. *Prou*.22.3.

IV. Hence we learne, that there is no possibility of doing good, or beeing beneficiall vnto others after this life, for *Paul* biddeth vs doe good *while we haue time*, thereby insinuating, that after death, all possibilitie of doing good is cleane cut off. The time allotted to doe good, beeing included within the limits of this life, *The dead that dye in the Lord rest from their labours*. *Reuel*. 14.13. Therefore no good workes are performed after this life. *Paul* beeing aged and readie to dye, the tearme of his life beeing almost expired, saith, *I haue finished my course*, 2. *Tim*.4.7. which could not be truely said, if hee were to performe any good workes after his death, 2. *Corinth*. 5.10. *Wee must giue account for all things wee haue done in the body*, that is, *in this life*. Where it is to bee obserued, that the Apostle speaking of all the workes whereof wee are to giue account, doth confine them within the compasse of this life; therefore no workes can bee done after this life be ended. Let vs heare the testimonie of the auncient. *Cyprian* to *Demetrius*. *Quando istinc excessum est, nullus locus pœnitentiæ est, nullus satisfactionis effectus*. Ierome. *Dum in præsenti sæculo sumus, siue orationibus, siue consiliis invicem posse nos coadiuvari; cùm autem ante Christi tribunal venerimus, non Iob, non Daniel, nec Noe rogare posse pro quoquam, sed vnumquemq; portare onus suum*. And againe, *In hac vita, licet nobis quod volumus seminare: quum transierit, operandi tempus auferetur, &c*. Hence I gather two things. First, that the doctrine of Purgatory is a meere fable, because there is no time after this life be ended, left to doe good, either to our selues or others, and therefore not to worke righteousnesse, to

ἐν τῇ ζωῇ ταύτῃ ὁ καιρὸς ἐστὶ τῆς ἐργασίας: ἐκεῖ δὲ οὐκ ἔστι. Oecumen.

to repent, or to satisfie the iustice of God, which the popish sort say is done in Purgatory. But what should I stand to batter the paper walles of Purgatory with the canon of the Scripture, which were long agoe burnt to ashes, by the fire of the word?

Secondly, seeing all opportunitie, nay all possibilitie of doing good is confined in the compasse of this life, euery man must follow the counsel of the wise man *Salomon, All that thy hand shal find to doe, doe it with all thy power; for there is neither worke nor inuention, nor knowledge, nor wisdome, in the graue whither thou goest, Eccles.9.10. Dauid* saith, *in the graue no man wil or can praise God.* And this is the cause wherefore *Paul* doeth so instantly vrge all men to take the present opportunitie, *Behold, now is the acceptable time: behold, now is the day of saluation, 2.Cor.6.2.*

V. Hence we are taught to account euery day, euen this present day, as the day of death, or the day of iudgement: for we must doe all the good we can *while we haue time*, now our time is the instant, or present time, for we are vncertaine whether we shall liue till to morrow or no, *Iam.4.14.* Therefore looke what we would doe at the houre of death, if wee were now at the last gaspe, panting for breath, or if we did see Christ comming in the clouds to iudgment; the very same thing we ought to do euery day, with like zeale and feruencie of spirit, to praise and magnifie the mercy and goodnesse of God; with like feare and trembling, to worke out our saluation, and to seeke reconciliation; with like loue and sinceritie of affection, to be beneficiall vnto our brethren, &c.

VI. This doctrine meeteth with all miserable minded men, who hauing great meanes and opportunitie of doing good, yet let slip, or rather cut off all occasions that might induce them thereto, who in a bruitish mind like to the swine, neuer doe good, nor profit any, till their dying day. I speake not against the laudable custome of bequeathing goods to *godly vses*, by a mans last will and testament; but against those that do little or no good all their life long, till the houre of death: Let these men consider, that as the late repentance of malefactors, a little before their death, is commonly but a ceremoniall repentance: so *the funerall beneficence* of those who giue little or nothing all their life, is vsually no free, but a formall, and extorted gift: formall, in doing as others do: extorted, in that it is giuen to stop the mouth of an accusing conscience; The *vitall beneficence* is that which God accounteth of, and by so much to bee preferred before the other, but how much it doth euidently declare a more liuely faith in the prouidence of God, and a more vnfained loue of our brethren. Againe, they giue testimony, that

Who be men of good wills, but bad deeds

they

they truſt not in vncertaine riches, but in the liuing God. Laſtly, they haue the benefit of poore mens praiers, (to whom they are beneficial,) which otherwiſe they ſhould want.

VII. The circumſtance of time hath heere the force of an argument, for it inforceth the exhortation much, that we ſhould doe all the good wee can, and take the benefit of the opportunitie, becauſe time will not alway laſt: the holy Ghoſt in ſundry places of Scripture, from the conſideration of the ſhortneſſe of our time, enforceth the duties of faith, repentance, new obedience, as 1.*Cor.*7. v.29,30,31. *And this I ſay brethren, becauſe the time is ſhort, hereafter that both they that haue wiues, bee as though they had none: and they that weepe, as though they wept not: and they that reioyce, as though they reioyced not. Hebr.*3.v.7,8. *To day if yee will heare his voice, harden not your hearts:* and v.13. *Exhort one another daily, while it is called to day.* The godly in all ages haue practiſed this dutie. *Peter* knowing that the time was at hand, that hee was to lay downe his tabernacle, ſtirres vp himſelfe to greater diligence in his calling, and ſaith, *I will not be negligent to put you in remembrance of theſe things, ſo long as I am in this tabernacle, ſeeing I know the time is at hand that I muſt lay it downe, as our Lord Ieſus Chriſt hath ſhewed mee,* 2.*Pet.* 1.12,13,14. The Church prayeth thus to God, *Teach vs to number our dayes,* that is, ſo to conſider the ſhortneſſe, vncertaintie, and vanitie of our life, *that wee may apply our hearts to wiſdome, Pſal.*90.12. But wicked mens practiſe is cleane contrary, for they take occaſion vpon the ſhortneſſe of their time, to liue as they liſt, to take their pleaſures, and to follow the luſts of their hearts: therefore they ſay, *Let vs eat and drinke, for to morrow we ſhall die. Eſay* 22.13. *Our life is ſhort and tedious, and our time is as a ſhaddow that paſſeth away —— Come therfore and let vs enioy the pleaſures that are preſent. Wiſd.* 2. verſ. 1,5,6. And hence it is, that ſome ſpend their time in eating and drinking, and going gorgeouſly, and faring deliciouſly euery day; other in gaming, carding, dicing, rioting, reuelling, and (as the tearme is) in ſwaggering, wherein they follow their father the diuell, who is therefore more full of wrath, *knowing that hee hath but a ſhort time, Apocal.* 12.12. To theſe wee may adde all ſuch idle perſons, as follow no vocation, or trade of life, but day after day, and yeare after yeare, are ſtill deuiſing new paſtimes (as they call them) to trifle the time away. Theſe men haſten the iudgements of God, and pull it vpon them before God inflict it. It is a great iudgement of God for a man to bee in that caſe, that *in the morning hee ſhall ſay, would God it were euening, and in the euening, would God it were morning, Deut,* 28.67. In this caſe is euery idle loiterer, who through idlenesse is weary of himselfe, and grieued the time passeth away so slowly: and to these *qui nihil agunt*, wee may ioyne them *qui malè agunt*, and those also *qui aliud agunt*, all which are condemned in this text; and against them *Titus* the heathen Emperour shall rise in iudgement, and shall condemne them, because hee remembring on a time as he sate at Supper, that he had trifled away the day in doing nothing, said, *Amici, hodie diem perdidi: Friends, I haue lost this day.*

11 *Yee see how large a letter I haue written vnto you with mine owne hand.*

Here beginneth the conclusion, being the third generall part of this Epistle, consisting of two parts: an *Insinuation*, in the 11. verse, and a *Recapitulation* in the verses folowing. He insinuateth himselfe into the minds of the Galatians by a twofold argument. First from the largenesse of his Epistle, *Ye see how large a letter I haue written*: secondly, from the instrumentall cause, in that he writ it *with his owne hand*: where hee giues authoritie to it, and a kinde of eminencie aboue his other letters. And in both he commendeth his diligence, loue, and care which he had of them.

ἴδετε. The word translated, *ye see*, is ambiguous, and may be taken either as a commandement, *See how large a letter I haue written*: or as an assertion, *Ye see*—. The like ambiguitie is in the word φαίνεσθε, *Phil.* 2. 5. and may be read either thus, *amongst whom you doe shine*: or *see that you shine as starres*. It is not materiall in whether exception it be taken, seeing the sense is all one.

The fist argument to moue the Galatians to attention, and acceptation of *Pauls* paines, and good affection, is taken from the
πηλίκοις. largenes of his Epistle. The word in the originall translated *large*,
* In Psal. 118 is strangely wrested by sundry interpreters, without cause. * *Hilary* referring it to the loftinesse of sentences: *Hyperius* to the profundity and depth of matter: *Ierome* to the greatnes of the character: *Chrysostome* and *Theophylact*, to the badnes of his hand, as not being able to write well; *Haimo* to the Hebrew character, in which hee
πηλίκος οὗτος ἡλίκος. wrote: whereas the word doth not onely signifie *quality*, but as properly *quantity*, as *Heb.* 7. 4. *Consider how great this man was.* And the word that answereth vnto it, signifieth as wel quantitie, as quality.
ἡλίκον ἀγῶνα. ἡλίκον ὕλην. *Coloss.* 2. 1. *I would ye knew what great fight I haue*—*Iam.* 3. 5. *Behold, how great a thing a little fire kindleth?* The plaine & simple meaning therfore of *Paul* is this, that he neuer wrote so long an Epistle with his owne hand vnto any Church, as vnto them. Hee writ indeed the Epistle to *Philemon* with his owne hand, but that was short in compa-

compariſon of this. And he wrote larger Epiſtles to other Churches, as to the Romanes, Corinthians, &c. but by his Scribes, not with his own hand. Therfore ſeeing this is the longeſt, and largeſt letter that euer *Paul* writ with his owne hand, it ought to be more regarded, and better accepted: So that as his paines were greater in writing, our diligence ſhould bee greater in reading and obſeruing the ſame.

This ſhewes *Pauls* great care of the Churches, not onely when he was preſent, but when he was abſent. How painefull he was being among them to winne them to the Goſpel, how fearefull when hee was abſent from them, leſt their minds ſhould bee leauened by falſe teachers: how faithfull both preſent and abſent.

And it may ſerue as a preſident to all Paſtours, hauing cure of ſoules, to vſe the like diligence and conſcience in their Miniſterie; that being abſent in body from their charge vpon neceſſary occaſions (as *Paul* was) yet they would be preſent in ſpirit with them: & preſent by their letters; that ſo they may teſtifie to al the world, that they haue a greater care of the flocke, then of the fleece.

It further teacheth vs, that if the Miniſter being caried with diſcreet zeale for the good of the Church, goe further either in word, or writing, then he intended, or is thought fit by ſome: (as it ſeemes *Paul* did in this place, for what needs this large letter (may ſome ſay,) a ſhorter would haue done as well) that we are not to cenſure him, or limit & preſcribe him. It had bin a great fault in the Galatians, if they had found fault with *Paul* for his large letter; and in the diſciples and Iewes if they ſhould haue blamed his long Sermon, which continued at one time from morning to night, *Acts* 28.23. at another time, from the cloſing of the euening til midnight, *Acts* 20.7. And ſo it is in many hearers, who are too curious and ſtrict in preſcribing and limiting their teachers to the time, longer then which they cannot patiently endure. And in ſtinting them, in vrging this or that point, in ſaying hee miſſed his *Rhetoricke*, his *Epimone* was too long, he was ouerſeene in dwelling ſo long vpon the point: it had bin better, a word and away, &c.

His ſecond argument is taken from the inſtrumentall cauſe, that he *wrote it with his owne hand.* * *Haimo* ſaith, it is the opinion of the Doctors, that *Paul* wrote not this whole Epiſtle with his owne hand, but onely from hence to the end: which opinion is confuted by the very text, *You ſee how large a letter I HAVE WRITTEN with mine owne hand:* ſpeaking of the whole Epiſtle, in the time paſt: or if of any one part more then of another, of the former part, rather then of the latter. Secondly, his aſſertion is

*In hac Epiſtola ſicut tradunt Doctores, ac hoc loco vſq; ad finem, propria manu ſcripſit.

not

not true,for (if we except *Ierome*) none of the Ancients (as I take it) are of that opinion. Not [b] *Ambroſe*,who ſaith, *Where the whole writing is his owne hand,there can be no falſhood.* Not [c] *Chryſoſtome*,who ſaith, *To the reſt of his Epiſtles he did ſubſcribe, but this whole Epiſtle he writ himſelfe.* Not *Primaſius*,vſing the word *perſcripſit*,that he writ it through with his owne hand. Not [d] *Theodoret* , affirming that *it ſeemes Paul writ the whole Epiſtle.* Not [e] *Theophylact*,who bringeth in *Paul* ſpeaking to them in this manner; *I am enforced to write this Epiſtle vnto you with mine owne hand.* Not *Oecumenius*,who calls it, ἰδιόχειρον ἐπιστολὴν, an Epiſtle written with his owne hand. Not [f] *Anſelme*, who paraphraſing the text,ſaith,it is all one as if he had ſaid; *This Epiſtle I writ with mine owne hand.* And a little before, *Not with the Scribes hand,but with mine owne hand* : (albeit *Anſelme* cannot ſo preiudice his aſſertion,who liued long after him.) Not the author of the Commentary vpon the Epiſtles aſcribed to *Ierom,Tom.*9.for he vpon the 2.*Theſſ.*3.17.ſaith plainely, [g] *With theſe words hee ſubſcribes all his Epiſtles,excepting that to the Galatians, which hee writ from the beginning to the end with his own hand.* And vpon theſe very words which we now entreat of, [h] *See how I am not afraid; which of late time haue written with mine owne hand.* (Where by the way, wee may obſerue,that *Ierome* is not the author of thoſe Commentaries, being ſo contrary to himſelfe.) This I confeſſe is a light matter,and not to be ſtood vpon, were it not that ſome are too haſtie to ſwallow whatſoeuer comes in their way, vnder the title of the *Doctours*. It muſt therfore be as a *caueat* vnto vs,not to be too credulous in beleeuing euery one that ſhall auouch this or that to be the opinion of the Fathers,no though it be affirmed by a Father, eſpecially by ſuch a one as draweth neere the dregs,as *Haimo* doth.

It is certen then,that *Paul* writ this whole Epiſtle with his own hand : the reaſons are theſe. Firſt, that it might appeare vnder his hand, that he was no changeling, but the ſame man that he was before, in that he did not preach circumciſion, or the obſeruation of Iewiſh ceremonies,as the falſe Apoſtles ſlandered him.*Gal.*5.11. Secondly,that this his letter was not counterfaited by another,and ſent in his name,as the falſe Apoſtles might haue obiected,and the Galatians ſuſpected. Thirdly,that he might teſtifie his ſincere loue towards them,and how he did (as it were) trauaile in paine of thẽ, till Chriſt were formed in them, ſhunning no labour that might further their ſaluation.

We may hence further obſerue a threefold difference of the bookes of Scripture in the new Teſtament. Some were neither written by an Apoſtle,nor ſubſcribed:as the Goſpel of *Marke*,and

Luke

[b] Vbi holographa manus,falſum dici non poteſt.
[c] In cæteris ſubſcribebat quidem, hic verò totam ipſe ſcripſit.
[d] Totam (vt videtur) hanc ſcripſit Epiſtolam.
[e] Etſi ſum minime apprimè ſcribendi peritus: compulſus ſum tamen vel mea manu hanc ad vos Epiſt. ſcribere.
[f] Epiſtolam iſtam ſcripſi ego propriã manu. Non Notarii manu,ſed mea.
[g] His verbis omnes Epiſtolas ſubſcribebat : excepta Galatarum,quam ex integro manu propria perſcripſit,———
[h] Intelligite quàm non timeam,qui literas manu mea nuper ſcripſi.

Luke. Some ſubſcribed,but not written : as the Epiſtle to the Romanes,and others. Some both written,and ſubſcribed : as this Epiſtle, and that to *Philemon,* verſe 19. *I haue written it with mine owne hand : I will recompenſe it* ——. Now that *Paul* ſubſcribed euery Epiſtle with his owne hand, hee himſelfe witneſſeth, 2.*Theſſalon.* 3.17. *The ſalutation of mee Paul with mine owne hand, which is a ſigne in euery Epiſtle*(that it is mine, and not forged in my name by another)*ſo I write ; The grace of our Lord Ieſus Chriſt bee with you all.* In which place he warneth the Theſſalonians againe of falſe teachers, and forged letters : for, 2.*Theſſalon.*2.2.hee had beſought them *they would not be troubled by ſpirit,nor by word,nor by letter, as though it came from him*——.And here he ſhewes how they may know whether the Epiſtle be his or not : if it haue this ſigne,it is mine,els it is counterfaite: for this note or marke is to bee found in all and euery one of my Epiſtles.Now theſe words[*which is a ſigne in euery Epiſtle*]cannot bee meant(as ſome are of opinion)of the former words onely, viz. *The ſalutation of me Paul with mine owne hand.* Firſt,becauſe hee ſaith, it is a ſigne in euery Epiſtle,whereas it is onely to be found.1. *Cor.* 16.21.*Galat.*6.11.*Col.*4.18. 2.*Theſſ.*3.17.*Philem.* v.19.and not in any other of his Epiſtles. Secondly,the words,*ſo I write*,ſhould bee falſe, if they be referred onely to the former words, becauſe that manner of ſalutation ,is not to be found in euery Epiſtle,(as I haue already ſhewed.) And except they bee referred to the words following,*The grace of our Lord Ieſus Chriſt,&c.*they haue either none, or a very hard conſtruction.Thirdly,if *Pauls* ſalutation(which he affirmeth to bee a certaine note of his Epiſtle) bee vnderſtood of theſe words, *The grace of our Lord Ieſus Chriſt, &c.*it agreeth vnto all(as *Anſelme* confeſſeth)whereas being meant of the former words onely, it doth not agree to all, but to a few : and yet *Paul* makes it, a generall,infallible note,and ſigne of euery Epiſtle.Beſides, *Ambroſe* and *Primaſius*, in their Commentaries vpon the place, as alſo the Author of the Commentaries which goeth vnder *Ieroms* name, affirme, the ſigne whereby we may know *Pauls* Epiſtles from counterfeite,and forged Epiſtles,to conſiſt in theſe words : *the grace of our Lord, &c. Chryſoſt.*and *Theodoret* likewiſe ſay, that *Paul calleth the ſalutation,a benediction,or bleſſing,which is in the end of the Epiſtle* : and a little after,*Hence we learne that he was accuſtomed to write theſe words, The grace,&c.in ſtead of adiew or farewell vnto them.*And *Haimo*(long after)expounds theſe words,*ſo I write,how?* (ſaith he)*euen thus as it followeth,The grace of our Lord, &c.*I graunt it is probable that *Paul* writ his owne name in the end of euery Epiſtle (whether in the Greeke tongue,and in the Hebrew characters(as *Haimo* affirmeth)

Salutationem appellauit benedictionem quæ in fine ſita eſt. Hinc ergo diſcimus,quod hoc, Gratia Domini,&c. pro eo quæ eſt vale ſcribere conſueuerat.

I leaue

I leaue it as vncertaine) and that by the ſalutation or ſigne of his Epiſtle, his name written with his owne hand, is in part to bee vnderſtood: yet it is not onely nor principally meant. The certaine ſigne therefore of his Epiſtles, is beſide the ſubſcription of his owne name, the farewell that he giues them in theſe words, *The grace of our Lord Ieſus Chriſt be with you all*, or the like to the ſame effect; I ſay to the ſame effect, becauſe theſe very formall words, are not to bee found in euery of *Pauls* Epiſtles. Therefore *Caietan* is farre wide, who taketh the entire and formall ſalutation, as it is litterally ſet downe. 2.*Theſſ*.3.17. to bee a note that the Epiſtle is his, ſo that if it want any one word, either the Epiſtle is not *Pauls*, or there is ſome defect in the text: for hereupon hee concludes that the Epiſtle to the Coloſſians onely, hath ſomething wanting in the farewell or ſalutation, becauſe it is ſaid, *Grace be with you*: and not *the grace of our Lord Ieſus Chriſt be with you*, as it is in all his other Epiſtles. But firſt, it is an vntruth, for they are not onely wanting in the Epiſtle to the Coloſſians, but alſo in the firſt to *Timothy*, and in that to *Titus*, where it is onely ſaid, *Grace be with thee, Grace be with you all.* Secondly, it is a flat miſtaking of the text, for *Pauls* meaning was not in euery Epiſtle to tye himſelfe preciſely to ſo many words and ſyllables: but to commend them to the grace of Chriſt: ſometime making expreſſe mention of Chriſt, ſometime concealing his name: yet ſo as that it is alway vnderſtood, though not expreſſed.

Coloſſ 4.18.

1.Tim.6.21.
Tit.3.25.

12 *As many as make a faire ſhew in the fleſh, compell you to be circumciſed, onely becauſe they would not ſuffer perſecution for the croſſe of Chriſt.*

From hence to the end, is laid downe the ſecond part of the concluſion, which I call a *Recapitulation*, wherein the Apoſtle doth very artificially (as orators are acuſtomed) repeat thoſe things which he would haue ſpecially to be remembred, the maine points handled in the Epiſtle. Firſt, that neither circumciſion is neceſſary to iuſtification, nor the ceremoniall law to ſaluation. Secondly, that the falſe Apoſtles vrging the obſeruation of the law as a thing neceſſary to ſaluation, ſought not herein Gods glorie, or the edification of their hearers, but their owne eaſe, and freedome from the croſſe, and perſecution. Thirdly, that Chriſt crucified is the onely thing that iuſtifies a ſinner without the workes of the Law. Fourthly, that the true religion ſtandeth not in outward things, but in the renouation of the inward man.

In this verse and the next following, *Paul* describes the false apostles by fiue properties: three whereof are laid downe in this verse. The first is, that *they make a faire shew.* The second, that *they compell them to the obseruing of their deuised religion.* The third, the end and scope they aime at, that they may alway bee in the Sunshine, liuing at ease, and hauing the world at will; *onely because they would not suffer persecutions for the crosse of Christ.*

First, the Apostle saith, that *they make a faire shew in the flesh*: which is taken diuersly, for it signifieth sundry things. First, to make an outward glorious shew according to the flesh, as that they were true Israelites, of the seed of *Abraham, &c.* Of which boasting *Paul* speakes, 2. *Cor.* 11. 18. *Seeing that many glory after the flesh, I will glorie also. They are Israelites, so am I: they are the seed of Abraham, so am I.* Secondly, to please the Israelites, which are after the flesh, and to approue themselues vnto them, which held the keeping of the ceremoniall law. Thirdly, to vaunt themselues to the Iewes, and them of the circumcision, of the Galatians, whom they had circumcised in the flesh, as beeing made proselites, and wonne to their profession by their meanes. Lastly, to pretend great zeale and religion in outward obseruing of the law, standing in carnall rites and bodily exercises, as circumcision, meats, purification, and the like: which carnall rites the Apostle opposeth to spiritual worship, *Rom.* 12. 1. and to the new creature, v. 16. of this chapter: and bodily exercise (which profiteth little) to true piety, and the sincere practise thereof, which is profitable for all things, 1 *Tim.* 4 8. The words may be taken in all these acceptions, though principally in the last.

Here wee haue a notable propertie of false teachers, which is, to set a faire face vpon the matter, to carrie all before them with a smooth countenance, and in outward appearance to excell. For as Satan, though a blacke deuill, an angel of darkenesse, doeth change himselfe into a white deuill, as though he were an Angell of light, so that a man can hardly distinguish his wicked suggestions, from the good motions of the spirit of God, and therfore may say, as *Iosua* said to the Angel, *Art thou on our side, or on our aduersaries? Iosh.* 5. 13. So his instruments *transforme themselues, as though they were the Apostles of Christ, and Ministers of righteousnesse,* 2. *Cor.* 11. 13, 15.

In the olde Testament, false prophets were accustomed outwardly to conforme themselues to the habite and attire of the holy men of God, in wearing a rough garment, as *Elias,* and the rest of the Prophets did, *Zachar.* 13. 4. Vnder the new Testament,

ſtament,in the time of Chriſt, the Phariſies in hypocriſie, vnder a ſhew of long prayer, deuoured widdowes houſes, *Matthew* 23. 14. In the Apoſtles time, falſe teachers with their will-worſhip, as *Touch not, taſte not, handle not*, (which had a ſhew of wiſedome in voluntary religion, and humbleneſſe of minde, and not ſparing the body) did vndermine the Religion of God, *Coloſſians* 2.21,22,23.

And after that, in the primitiue Church, the heretikes called *Cathariſts*, vnder a ſhew of holineſſe, faſting, prayer, &c. did ſowe moſt damnable hereſies in the Church.

And as in former times, the Iewes vnder the glorious titles of *the children of Abraham, the ſchollers of Moſes, the Temple of the Lord, the Temple of the Lord*, made many Proſelytes by deceiuing the ſoules of the ſimple: So, at this day, vnder the glorious titles of the Church, of Councells, Fathers, Antiquitie, Conſent, Vniuerſalitie; the pretended Romane Catholikes haue enſnared many a ſimple ſoule: and no maruaile, conſidering that theſe are the times of which Chriſt foretold, that falſe prophets ſhould deceiue (if it were poſſible) the very Elect, *Mat*.24.24. and of which Saint *Paul* prophecied, that Antichriſt ſhould come, *through the efficacie of Satan, with all power, and ſignes, and lying wonders, and in all deceiueableneſſe of vnrighteouſneſſe, among them that periſh*, 2. *Theſſ*.2.9,10. And all this is done by outward ſignes and ſemblances, which our Sauiour Chriſt tearmeth *ſheepes cloathing*, and it ſtands in theſe foure particulars. Firſt, in great ſwelling titles, as the onely true Catholike Church, the Vicar of Chriſt, the Oecumennicall Biſhop: moſt Profound, Illuminate, Angelicall, Seraphicall Doctours: Ieſuites, the only true followers of the doctrine, and example of Ieſus, &c. Secondly, in pretended zeale, and deuotion, whereby they would perſwade, that their religion is the onely true religion: all others, which ſwarue from it, are nothing but falſe and fabulous: and this they doe three wayes. Firſt, δοξολογία; by hauing God alwaies in their mouthes, crying in hypocriſie with the falſe prophets, *Lord, Lord, Math*.7.22. or as the Ieſuiticall faction doe, *Ieſu, Maria*. Secondly, πιθανολογία, with enticing words, conſiſting in probable reaſons, and perſwaſiue arguments, *Coloſſ*.2.4. Thirdly, χρηστολογία, with faire and flattering words, to deceue the hearts of the ſimple, *Romans* 16.18. By which three meanes the Ieſuits haue preuailed much in Princes courts, in theſe latter dayes, *Apoc*. 16.14. Thirdly, in the glorious outſide of holineſſe of life and conuerſation, in not ſparing the body, by whipping of themſelues, as *Baals* Prieſtes launced themſelues till the

Math.7.15.

the blood gushed out, 1. *Kings* 18.28. in strict fastes, canonicall houres, hard fare, badde lodging, course apparell, and such like. Lastly, in rare and excellent gifts of prophecy, tongues, eloquence, miracles, &c. And thus they make *Pauls shew of godlinesse*, 2.*Tim.* 3.5. to bee *Peters cloake of wickednesse*, 1. *Peter* 2. 6. so that as the diuell with faire words put *Eue* into a fooles paradise, till at length he had driuen her out of the terrestriall Paradise, and made her also hazard the celestiall. So his ministers false teachers, by faire and flattering speeches, deceiue the minds of the simple, and cause them to fall from their owne stabilitie.

μόρφωσιν εὐσεβείας. ἐπικάλυμμα κακίας.

By this wee may see how hypocrites and false teachers, stand especially vpon outward things, as externall rites and ceremonies, *which are but deuices and doctrines of men, Matthew* 15.9. The Pharisies made much adoe about washing of the outside of the cup, and of the platter, when as the inside was full of rapine and all vncleannesse, *Matthew* 23.25. very curious about washing of their hands before meat, *Mark* 7.3. and yet carelesse to wash their hearts from wickednesse, *Ierem.* 4.14. precise in small matters, as in tything of mint, annise, and cummine; but profane in the practise of the waightier things of the law, as iudgment, mercie and fidelity, *Matth.* 23.23. whited tombes, faire without, and filthy within, verse 27. Thus the Popish worship consisteth especially in outward things, which may please the senses of carnall men, as in vocall, and instrumentall Musicke, to please the eare: censings and perfumes to delight the smell: guilding and painting, with other sights and spectacles, to affect the eye. And at this day, in the Masse (which they account the very marrow of their Mattins) there is nothing but dumme shewes, histrionicall gestures, and trickes fitter to mocke apes withall, then to edifie the people. For whereas in former time they were wont to say, *Let vs goe heare a Masse*: now the common saying in Italie is this, *Let vs goe see a Masse*. Let vs therefore trie the spirits before we trust them, and especially in matters of religion, follow Christs precept, *not to iudge by the outward appearance, Iohn* 7.24. But to iudge of Prophets by the fruite of their doctrine, *Matth.* 7.16. and of their doctrine by the touchstone of the word, *Isa.* 8.20. so that though the diuell transforme himselfe into an Angell of light; nay, though an Angell from heauen preach any other thing, beside that we haue receiued from Christ, we must hold him accursed: and in so doing we shall follow Christ his practise, *who was prudent in the feare of the Lord, and did not iudge by the sight of his eyes, nor reproue by the hearing of his eares, Isai.* 11.3.

The

The ſecond note and marke of theſe falſe teachers, is, that *they compell men to be circumciſed.* The word *compell*, hath great emphaſis, for it ſignifieth, that they did not conuince the iudgement, or perſwade the will, and affection of the Galatians, but enforced them againſt their wills; for though circumciſion bee nothing of it ſelfe (as *Paul* ſaith) yet to be compelled to receiue circumciſion, and to place iuſtification in the vſe of it, and ſinne in the neglect of it, is the ready way to ouerturne Chriſt, the foundation of our ſaluation. *Gal.*5.4.

Here ſundry queſtions are to be anſwered. Firſt, it may bee demanded, whether it be lawfull to compel men to embrace religion, as the falſe Apoſtles compelled the Galatians to circumciſion? *Anſ.* The Magiſtrate may and ought to compell obſtinate Recuſants to profeſſe true religion: for he is *cuſtos vtriuſq; tabulæ*, and therefore is to haue care that true religion be profeſſed, and the contemners thereof puniſhed. An example hereof we haue in good King *Ioſiah* who *cauſed all that were found in Ieruſalem and Beniamin*, (that is, all his ſubiects) *to ſtand to the couenant which he made with the Lord*, nay which is more, *he compelled all that were found in Ieruſalem to ſerue the Lord their God.* 2.*Chron.*34.32,33. among which multitude many there were (no doubt) which did like better of Idolatrie, then of Gods worſhip, as the word *compelled*, doth import. The King that made the great ſupper, commanded his ſeruants to *compell the gueſts to come in vnto him.* *Luke* 14.23. whence *Auguſtine* gathereth, that it is the Magiſtrates dutie to compell Recuſants, ſchiſmatikes, heretikes, and ſuch like, to the hearing and profeſſing of the word. But here three things are commonly obiected againſt this doctrine.

Obiect. 1. To compell men to embrace true religion, is to make them goe againſt their conſcience, which the Magiſtrate ought not to doe: as ſome Papiſts haue affirmed, that they would not for ten thouſand worlds compell a Iew to ſweare that there were a bleſſed Trinitie, becauſe hee ſhould be damned for ſwearing againſt his conſcience, although the thing were neuer ſo true. *Anſ.* I. If it were ſo hainous a ſinne to compell any to embrace true religion, becauſe it is againſt their conſcience; why doe Popiſh Prelats, and Magiſtrates, compell Proteſtants (and that by exquiſite torments) to reconcile themſelues to the Church of Rome, to ſweare obedience to the Pope, to acknowledge Tranſubſtantiation, and to heare Maſſe, which they know are directly againſt their conſcience? II. If they will not compell men to doe any thing, (though neuer ſo good or godly,) becauſe it is againſt their conſcience: why ſhould they not

be

be as ſcrupulous in reſtraining them from doing that which is vnlawfull, becauſe they are perſwaded in conſcience they ought to doe it? For if they compell men to omit that which they beleeue to be good, becauſe they know it to be euill, (as their owne practiſe prooueth, in that they will not ſuffer Proteſtants to pray publikely in a knowne tongue, nor receiue the Sacrament in both kinds, &c.) why doe they not compell them alſo, to doe that which they know to be good, though they thinke it to be euill? III. The Magiſtrate is to compell men to embrace true religion, or to puniſh thē for their obſtinacy in not harkening to the word, becauſe he is to vſe the meanes to reclaime them, & to win them to a loue and liking of the truth. Now ſo long as they are vrged to heare the word, there is hope they may be wonne againe: and experience ſhewes (as *Auguſtine* teſtifieth of the *Donatiſts*) that they which did profeſſe religion at the firſt meerly by compulſion, may afterwards (by the mercy of God) profeſſe it onely for deuotion. And what though ſome come not to learne, but to carpe and cauill? yet God may caſt the net of his mercy ſo farre ouer them, that contrary to their purpoſe they may bee caught. IIII. If the Magiſtrate who may compel them, and ſo reclaime them, do ſuffer them to continue in their errours or hereſies, without controlment, he is guilty of their ſinne: but by compelling them, he hath diſcharged his duty: for albeit they beeing compelled, doe diſſemble and play the hypocrites, doe lie, and forſweare themſelues; that is not the Magiſtrates ſin, who intendeth nothing but their conuerſion and ſaluation, it is their owne proper and perſonall ſinne.

Obiection. II. Men ought to be perſwaded to embrace religion, and induced to beleeue, but not compelled, for the wil can not be compelled. *Anſ.* True it is, the will cannot be compelled; and as true is it likewiſe, that the Magiſtrate cannot compell any to beleeue: for when a man doth beleeue, and from his heart embrace true religion, he doth it willingly: notwithſtanding meanes are to be vſed, to make them willing that are vnwilling, and the meanes is, to compell them to come to our aſſemblies, to heare the word, and to learne the grounds of true religion: for it is Gods commandement men ſhould *proove the ſpirits*, 1. *Ioh*. 4. 1. that ſo they may know the truth, and cleaue vnto it. *Auguſtine* ſaith fitly, and finely to this purpoſe, *Quod autem vobis videtur, invitos ad veritatem non eſſe cogendos, erratis neſcientes Scripturas, neque virtutem Dei, qui eos volentes facit, dum coguntur inviti.* Secondly, when Papiſts receiue the Sacrament, ſweare allegeance to their Prince, preſent thēſelues in our congregations, who knowes that they doe theſe things a-

Perſuaderi vult fides, non cogi.

Contra Gaudent Epiſt. 2. lib. 2. c. 17.

 gainſt

gainſt their conſcience? nay rather we ought in charitie to thinke that they are perſwaded in conſcience they may do them, when by oath and proteſtation they confeſſe ſo much. But be it, they did all in hypocriſie, ſhall the execution of godly lawes therefore ceaſe, becauſe hypocrites will not obey, but in diſſimulation?

Obiect. III. The Magiſtrate by compelling Recuſants to the outward profeſſion of religion, maketh them to play the hypocrites, to counterfeit, and diſſemble. *Anſwer.* The Magiſtrate in executing the lawes, hath no ſuch intent: but only that they might heare the word, beleeue it, and be ſaued. Againe, Proteſtant Recuſants in other countreys, are not allowed by Papiſts, to alleadge their conſcience for their refuſall: but are compelled either to conforme themſelues, or to vndergoe cruell torments: no more may ſuch pretence of conſcience excuſe the Papiſts, or other heretikes, but that they ſhould receiue the ſame meaſure which they mete to others.

II. *Queſt.* How can it be truly ſaid, that the falſe apoſtles compelled men to receiue circumciſion, ſeeing *Titus was not compelled to be circumciſed? Gal.*2.3. *Anſw.* That place maketh nothing againſt the text in hand: the meaning is, that *Paul* for his part was ready to haue circumciſed *Titus* (as he did *Timothie, Act.*16.3.) rather then offend the weake brethren. But when it came to this point, that they would vrge circumciſion, as a thing neceſſary to ſaluation, *Paul* refuſed to doe it, *for all the falſe brethren that crept in,* v.4 that is, notwithſtanding they laboured by all meanes to bring it in vſe againe. Neither did the Apoſtles vrge it, or require it, as a thing neceſſary to ſaluation.

III. It may be demanded, whether that circumciſion being ſo vehemently vrged by the falſe apoſtles, might not haue bene vſed? *Anſwer.* It might not. For albeit it be in it ſelfe a thing indifferent, and ſo it skilleth not, whether a man bee circumciſed, or not, (as *Paul* ſaith) *Circumciſion is nothing, and vncircumciſion is nothing:* yet beeing vrged as a matter of abſolute neceſſitie, as without which men could not be ſaued, *Actes* 15.1. it ought not to be vſed. The like may bee ſaid of all indifferent things, if they be made eſſentiall parts of Gods worſhip, or neceſſarie to ſaluation; as the vſe of meates and drinkes, obſeruing of times and ſeaſons, wearing this or that habit, or attire: forbidding of marriage to ſome orders of men. For when things indifferent are made neceſſarie, the nature of them is changed. Vpon this ground *Ezekiah* brake in pieces the brazen Serpent, when the Iſraelites began to worſhip it, 2.*Kings* 18.4.

Firſt, let vs obſerue out of theſe words, *they compell you to be circumciſed*, that *Paul* doeth not onely vſe Chriſtian pollicie, but dealeth very rhetorically, excuſing the Galatians, as though they were conſtrained againſt their wils to doe as they did: and laying all the blame vpon the falſe apoſtles: and ſo doeth cloſely alienate their affection from theſe ſeducers, who would haue them circumciſed, either by voluntary ſubmiſſion, or by violent compulſion: the like godly pollicy we ought to vſe in dealing againſt heretikes, & falſe teachers, that the peoples minds may be eſtranged from them, and take no loue of their doctrine, nor liking of their perſons.

Here we haue a ſecond note of falſe teachers, which is, not onely to retaine ceremonies themſelues, but to vrge them vpon others, and conſtraine men to the obſeruing of them. for they were more earneſt and forward in vrging circumciſion (their owne deuiſe) then the keeping of the morall law: and ſo are all ſeducers. The Phariſies did vrge their owne ceremonies, as waſhing before meat, waſhing of potts, cups, and beds, &c. more then the commandemẽt of God. And the Papiſts vrge the Lent faſt more ſtrictly, then faſting from ſinne, which is the only true faſt, *Iſa.* 58.6. And their owne ſtories doe ſhew, that men haue bin more ſeuerely puniſhed, for eating fleſh vpon good Friday, then for committing of ſimple fornication, or following of ſtrange fleſh. They ſtand more in vrging the outward worſhipping of an image, or a piece of bread, then the inward ſpirituall worſhip. And as they haue made the Saints daies equall with the Sabbath daies, ſo haue they made the prophanation of them an equall ſinne, and haue puniſhed it with equall puniſhment.

It is further to bee obſerued, how they abuſe circumciſion; for whereas by Gods ordinance it was but a *ſeale of the righteouſneſſe of faith, Rom* 4.11. they peruerting the end of it, make it a meritorious cauſe of ſaluation; and therefore *compell men to bee circumciſed*: it is Gods worke, they make it their owne worke, yea ſuch a work as by which they hope to bee ſaued. And this their dealing may fitly bee paralleled by the Popiſh practiſe at this day, in making baptiſme, which is but a ſigne and ſeale of grace, to bee the proper, immediate, and phyſicall cauſe of conferring grace by the worke wrought. Almes, prayer, and faſting (which are but ſignes and teſtimonies of iuſtification) to be cauſes thereof. Nay their owne deuiſes, of confeſſion, ſatisfaction, ſupererogation, to be meritorious cauſes of iuſtification and ſaluation.

Laſtly, ſee heere how the peruerſeneſſe of the corrupt heart of man, doeth thwart the ordinance of God. As long as circum-

Apella Iudæus.

cision was commaunded by God, most abhorred it; for the heathen testifie so much, that the Iewes were odious for it. But now beeing abolished, they take it vp againe; receiue it, and vrge it as a thing necessary to be obserued vpon paine of damnation. Whereas if God should enioyne it again, they would (no doubt) account it as an heauy yoke, which neither they nor their fathers were able to beare. This improuing of that which God commands, and approuing that which he forbids, argues the great corruptiō of the heart, and that the wisedome of the flesh is not onely an enemie, but euen flat *enmity against God, Rom.* 8.7. It must therefore therfore teach vs to captiuate our reason, and to subiect our wills to the wil of God in all things.

The third property of the false Apostles is, the teaching of circumcision, that is, of false doctrine; *because they would not suffer persecution for the crosse of Christ*, that is, for preaching the true doctrine of the Gospel, concerning Christ crucified. It may be demanded whether it was necessarie that those which taught not circumcision, but spake against it, should be persecuted? To which I answer, that it was necessary, according as *Paul* affirmeth *Gal.* 5.11. *If I teach circumcision, why doe I yet suffer persecution?* The reason was this. The Romane Emperour had giuen liberty to the Iewes to liue according to their owne lawes, and that without molestation or disturbance, in all places of the Romane Empire, so that if a Iewe became a Christian, he had the priuiledge of a Iewe, so long as he kept the ceremoniall law, and taught no departing from *Moses*: wheras they which taught, that ceremonies were abrogated, and that men were iustified onely by faith in Christ, wanted this priuiledge, and so were persecuted of no men more then of the Iewes, either by themselues, or by incensing others against them. 1. *Thess.* 2.15.16. The false Apostles therefore to auoide persecution, coyned a new Gospel; in matter of saluation, ioyning Christ and *Moses*, iustification by faith, and by workes. So that here we haue another character and marke of false teachers, which is, to labour by all meanes to enioy the world, and to eschewe the crosse, and rather then they will suffer persecution, to make a hotch-potch of religion, as we may see, not onely by this particular, but by the course of the history of the Church, and in latter times, by the *Interim* vnder *Charles* the fift, and the sixe articles vnder *Henrie* the eight: by our mediators and reconciliators, who either (as it is said of old *Conciliator*) labour to accord fire & water: or else like hucksters mixe wine and water for their owne aduantage: & by all neuters and mungrils in religion, who houer in the wind,

Hieron in Comment. in hunc locum.

because

because they would stand sure for all assaies, or winne the fauour of great men, that they might not stand in the way of their preferment. This is the sinne of the multitude among vs, who desire to haue Christ, but they will none of his crosse: they would bee with him vpon mount *Tabor*, but not vpon mount *Caluarie*, crowned with glory, but not crowned with thornes.

Further, we may hence gather an essentiall difference of the true and false teachers: the one seekes the good of the Church, the other seeks themselues: the one the glory of God, the other their owne glory. It is obserued by Popish priests and others, that though the Iesuits pretend they doe all things *in ordine ad Deum*, yet they intend themselues, dooing all things *in ordine ad seipsos*: it beeing the marke they shoote at in all their Machiauelian plottes and pollicies, that they may haue *cum dignitate ocium*, a Lordly command, and a laisie life.

Againe, here we see that the loue of the truth, and of the world, the feare of the face of man, and the feare of God can neuer stand together. As also how dangerous a thing it is to be addicted to the loue of the world: for it hath beene alwaies the cause of reuolt, in that men neuer imbraced religion so, as that they could be contented to suffer persecution for the profession of it, nor lay downe their liues in the maintenance thereof. *Math.* 13.21. *As soone as tribulation or persecution commeth, by and by they are offended.* Whereas we ought to haue the same minde that *Paul* had, who knowing that bonds and imprisonment aboad him, yet passed not for them, neither was his life deare vnto him, *Act.* 20.23. and was not onely ready to be bound, but to dye also, for the name of the Lord Iesus. *Act.* 21.13. The reasons which should make vs willing to take vp our crosse and follow Christ, are these. First, it is a great mercy and fauour of God, that we are accounted worthy to suffer any thing for his sake. *Act.* 5.41. *The Apostles departed from the councell reioycing that they were accounted worthy to suffer rebuke for his name.* Secondly, it is a meanes (by the mercifull promise of God,) to procure and obtaine the blessings of this life. *Mark.* 10.30. Thirdly it hath blessednesse annexed to it, with a promise of assistance and helpe of Gods Spirit, 1. *Pet.* 4.11. *If ye be rayled on for the name of Christ, blessed are yee, for the Spirit of glory and of God resteth vpon you, which on their part is euill spoken of, but on your part is glorified.* Lastly, the end of the crosse, is glory vnspeakeable, *If we suffer with him, we shall also be glorified with him. Rom.* 8.17.

Further, whereas Saint *Paul* linketh together persecution, and the preaching of the crosse, we may see that the profession of the

Goſpel,and perſecution,doe either goe hand in hand,or do follow one another inſeparably ;for *as many as will liue godly in Chriſt Ieſus, muſt ſuffer perſecution.* 2.*Tim*.3.12. *Moſes* is ſaid to haue *choſen rather to ſuffer affliction with the people of God, then to enioy the pleaſures of ſinne for a ſeaſon. Heb.* 11.25. Where wee ſee that affliction is the lot and portion of the godly. The reaſon hereof is two-fold. The malice of the Diuell who is alway nibbling at the heele, *Gen*.3.15. And the hatred of the malignant Church (the diuels ſeede) euer maligning the Church and people of God. The diuell maketh warre with the remnant of the womans ſeede, which keepe the commandements of God, and haue the teſtimonie of Ieſus, *Apoc*. 12.17.The malignant Church perſecuteth the Church of God, as we may ſee in their types, namely, in *Cain* hating and perſecuting *Abel*; *Iſmael, Iſaac*; *Eſau, Iacob*. Which they did onely *becauſe they ſaw their owne workes to be euill,and theirs to be good.* 1. *Iohn*.3.12. And if it be demanded, why thoſe that preach the word plainely and powerfully to the conſciences of men,in euidence of the ſpirit, are ſo extreamely hated and maligned ? *Anſ*. It is for no other thing, but *euen for the workes ſake*,for which they ought to be reuerenced, 1.*Theſſ*.5.13. and becauſe *they prophecie not good vnto them,but euill,* 1.*King*.22.8.that is,preach not pleaſing things,by ſowing pillowes vnder their elbowes,and lulling them aſleepe in the bed of ſecuritie,but denounce the iudgements of God againſt them, and ſo diſquiet and trouble their guiltie conſciences. And what (I beſeech you)is the reaſon why thoſe that make conſcience of ſinne, are ſo maligned of the wicked world,and branded with the blacke names of *Puritans*, and *Preciſians*, but this, which our Sauiour Chriſt giueth, *Ioh.* 15.19. *Becauſe they are not of the world,therefore the world hateth them* ? Now all this commeth to paſſe, by reaſon of that enmitie which God hath put betwixt the woman,and the ſerpent;his ſeede,and her ſeede.*Gen*.3.15.

This teacheth vs,firſt, that we ſhould ſuſpect our ſelues,that our hearts are not ſound,nor our practiſe ſincere, when all men ſpeake well of vs : for true profeſſion is alwaies accompanied with perſecution. *Woe bee to you, when all men ſpeake well of you. Luke* 6. *verſe* 26.

Secondly, that we muſt not bee diſcouraged in our profeſſion, though there be neuer ſo many that make oppoſition,or ſo mighty that raiſe perſecution againſt vs. Though they tell vs as they did *Paul*, *Act*.28.22. *Concerning this ſect, we know that euery where it is ſpoken againſt* : or take vs vp with *Nicodemus*, *Iohn* 7. 52. *Art thou alſo of Galile ? ſearch and looke, for out of Galile ariſeth no Prophet.* In

theſe

theſe blaſts and ſtormes of temptations, wee ought to make that ſaying of Chriſt our anker hold, *Bleſſed is hee that is not offended in mee, Math.*11.6.

Laſtly, that we thinke it not ſtrange when we find affliction, or meet with perſecution, 1.*Pet.*4.12,13.

13 *For they which are circumciſed, keepe not the Law, but deſire to haue you circumciſed, that they might glorie in your fleſh.*

Heere the Apoſtle preuenteth an obiection, which might bee made againſt the former concluſion, verſe 12. For it might be ſaid, *Paul* did them wrong in ſlaundering them, to vrge circumciſion onely becauſe they would auoid perſecution, when as they did it, as zealous obſeruers of the law. To this he anſwereth negatiuely, that whatſoeuer they did pretend, they intended no ſuch thing. And he proueth his former aſſertion, by two arguments, and withall deſcribeth the falſe apoſtles by two other properties. His firſt reaſon may be framed thus: If they did vrge circumciſion as being zealous of the law, and hauing conſcience of the obſeruing therof, they would keepe it themſelues, as well as compell others to the keeping of it. But they keepe it not themſelues. Therefore they vrge it not in conſcience to haue it obeyed, but for ſome ſiniſter end. The ſecond reaſon is this. They that propound no other end to themſelues, in vrging of circumciſion, but vanting and boaſting in the fleſh: they ſeeke not the obſeruation of the law: But theſe ſeducers, vrge circumciſion, and other ceremonies, that they might glory in the fleſh: Therfore they ſeeke not the obſeruation of the law. So that heere we haue two other properties of falſe teachers. The firſt is, *to compell men to the obſeruing of that, which they will not obſerue themſelues.* For thus theſe ſeducers vrged the ceremoniall law. Reſembling herein the Scribes and Phariſies, *who bound heauie burdens, and grieuous to be borne, and laid them on mens ſhoulders, wheras they thẽſelues wold not mooue them with one of their fingers, Mat.* 23.4. The Popes and Prelates of the Romiſh Church, are notorious in this kind, in vrging men to make conſcience of that, which they themſelues will not keepe, to practiſe that which they will not performe, and to beleeue that, which they count falſe, and fabulous. For firſt, they ſtrictly require regular obedience to bee performed of their nouices, and others, to their Generals or gouernours, ſpecially to the Vicar of Chriſt, and See of Rome; whereas they will not bee ſubiect to the higher powers as they ought,*Rom*.13.1.nor obedient to gouernors,as it is required, 1.*Pet.* 2.13,14. Nay,their practise is notorious in these foure particulars. First,in freeing children from obedience to their parents. Secondly,in exempting their shauelings from subiection to the ciuill Magistrate. Thirdly,in freeing subiects from their oath of alleageance to their Soueraignes. And lastly,by aduancing that man of sinne aboue all that is called God, or worshipped,and giuing him power to depose Princes,to dispose of crownes and kingdomes, and to impose lawes which shall properly binde the conscience; yea to tread Kings and Emperors vnder his feet, and cause them like vassals to hold his stirrop. Againe,they compel others to fast,especially in Lent,when as they in the meane time feast;their fast being to eat fast,and drinke fast, in mortifying the flesh with their Indian capons,and peacocks,and that vpon Good Friday;whereas to eat white-meates vpon that day,should bee in others a mortall sinne. Further,they beare the poore people in hand,that Indulgences are meanes to remit sinnes; and that those that are excommunicated by the Pope,are in a damnable estate: whereas many of them, account Popes Bulles to be but *bulla*, meere trifles, and such as buy them,starke fooles;witnesse the speech of the Duke of Valence,bastard to Pope *Alexander* the sixth, who hauing lost certaine thousand crownes at a throw at the dice;Tush(said he)these are but the sinnes of the Germans. And that of *Charles* the fift (though a fauourer and maintainer of the Romane religion) who being menaced by Pope *Paulus* the third, with excommunication, if hee would not yeeld vp Playsance into his hands, let him vnderstand by his Embassador,that he would thunder at S.*Angelo* with his canons and artillery,if he would needs be thundring out his excommunications. Lastly,they vse confession of Purgatory,almost as an article of faith,wheras some of them are so farre from beleeuing it, as that they thinke there is neither heauen, nor hell; witnesse the speech of Pope *Leo* the tenth to Cardinall *Bembus*: *O Bembus,what riches haue wee gotten by this fine fable of Iesus Christ?* By this wee are contrarily admonished to practise that we professe: the Ministers of the word especially,ought *verba vertere in opera*, (as *Ierome* speaketh) that is,to turne words into workes, that their liues may bee reall Sermons to the people: for otherwise they pull downe with one hand,as fast as they build with another. Let vs consider how *Peters* bad example, is said to haue compelled the Gentiles to liue as the Iewes,*Gal*.2.14. For actions abide, and are of force,when words passe as the wind.

O Bembe, quantum nobis profuit fabula ista de Christo?

Moreouer,vpon this dependeth another propertie of seducers,

which

which is, to ſet a faire gloſſe vpon the matter, and to make the world beleeue, they doe theſe and theſe things, for ſuch and ſuch ends (as theſe falſe teachers did, pretending religion & conſcience, but intending freedome from the croſſe, and their owne vaine glory) whereas they meane nothing leſſe: like *Herod*, who made ſhew of worſhipping Chriſt, when his purpoſe was to haue deſtroied him, *Math.2.* This propertie and practiſe is, and hath bene vſuall, ſpecially in the Church of Rome. For generally, they would haue the world beleeue, that the Popes triple crowne and Hierarchie of that See, is for the maintenance and defence of the Goſpel: whereas all the world knowes, it is onely to keepe their kitchins hote, to vphold their Perſian pompe, and ambitious tyrannie. Particularly, there be two politike practiſes of theirs, which proue the point in hand. Firſt, it is well knowne, that Popes haue neuer ceaſed from time to time, to ſolicite the Princes of *Europe*, to maintaine the holy warre, (as they call it) pretending the recouerie of the holy land out of the hands of the Turkes and Saracins: (when as (at leaſt in the beginning) they intended nothing leſſe, but that by this meanes they might ſet the Eaſt and Weſt together by the eares, whileſt they played their parts at home in Italy. The ſecond is, their Shrift, or auricular Confeſſion, which they practiſe for this ende (as they ſay) that they may pacifie diſtreſſed conſciences, by abſoluing them of their ſinnes: when as the truth is, they firſt brought it into the Church, and doe ſtill continue it in a politicke reſpect, as being the onely way in the world, to know all the ſecret purpoſes, plots, pollicies, and practiſes, that are either in Church, or Commonwealth.

We are therefore here admoniſhed to take heed of diſſembling, in making Chriſtianitie a cloake of impietie, or to pretend one thing, and intend another, like the heart pointing vpward, and poiſing downeward; for that will be a farre fowler ſolœciſme then that which the heathen committed with his hand, in pointing to heauen, when hee ſpake of the earth. But let vs alway labour for ſinceritie, to be at leaſt that which we pretend to be, or rather like *Salomons* Temple, whoſe windowes were larger within then without, and not like the glow-worme, making a faire glittering ſhew of that which we haue not.

14 *But God forbid that I ſhould glory, ſaue in the croſſe of our Lord Ieſus Chriſt, whereby the world is crucified to me, and I vnto the world.*

In theſe words *Paul* comes to the *Reddition* of the diſſimilitude betwixt him and the falſe Apoſtles,his glorying and their. In them we may conſider two generall points. Firſt, wherein hee would not glory *in nothing, ſaue in, &c.* Secondly, the thing wherein he would glory, *In the croſſe of Chriſt*, whereof he renders a reaſon in the words following, taken from the effects which the croſſe wrought in him,For,*by it,the world was crucified to him,and hee vnto the world.*

For the firſt : To *glorie*, implies three things. Firſt, to reioyce, exult,and triumph in a mans ſelfe,in regard of ſome good thing,or ſome ſuppoſed good.Secondly,to bewray this great exultation, by ſpeech,or action,or both. Thirdly, by boaſting of it, to looke for praiſe and applauſe of men ; which glorying(according to the nature of the obiect,and the end) is either good or euill. For if it haue a right obiect,namely,*the croſſe of Chriſt* : and a right end,*the glorie of God*,it is good ; otherwiſe it is euill : ſuch as was this glorying of the falſe Apoſtles,and all other carnall glorying,which is not in the Lord : for it is nothing elſe but *vaine glory.Vaine* I ſay,firſt, in regard of the things wherein men glorie,which are either ſuch as are not, as when a man boaſteth of that which hee hath not, but would ſeeme to haue : or ſuch as hee hath not of himſelfe .1.*Cor*.4.7. or ſuch as haue no continuance,but are tranſitorie and fading, as all earthly things are,ſeeing man himſelfe is but *as graſſe,and all the glorie of man,but as the floure of the field.Iſay*,40.6. Secondly,it is *vaine* in regard of man,from whom we looke for glorie,and admiration, ſeeing his iudgement is erroneous.Thirdly,in regard of the end,in not referring it to the maine and proper end,the glory of God,and the good of his Church. The Prophet reduceth all thoſe things,
Ier.9.23. wherein we ought not to glorie, to three heads : *wiſedome, ſtrength, and riches* : all which we haue receiued, and therefore ought not to boaſt of them,as though we had not receiued them. In particular, wiſedome is not to be gloried in, ſeeing it is very defectiue, whether we ſpeake of ſpeculatiue wiſedome, ſtanding in contemplation, or practicall, conſiſting in action : For in arts and ſciences, as alſo in the ſecrets of nature, our ignorance is greater then our knowledge.He that knowes not that he knowes nothing in theſe things,let him reade the booke of *Iob*,chap.28.and 37,and 38.And as for wiſedome in diuine things, *Wee know nothing as wee ought to know.* 1.*Cor*.8.2. *for wee know but in part, and ſee but as in a glaſſe, darkely.*1.*Cor*.13,12. And as for practicall wiſedome, ſtanding in pollicie,it is not demonſtratiue,but meerely coniecturall,and therfore we cannot build vpon it,conſidering in it there is the concur-

rence

rence of ſo many cauſes that are caſuall, and of ſo many mindes which are mutable. *Salomon* the great polititian had experience hereof; for he thought that by ioyning affinitie with his neighbor Princes round about him, and taking their daughters to bee his wiues, hee ſhould eſtabliſh his owne houſe, ſtrengthen his kingdom, and draw the heatheniſh Idolaters to the worſhip of the true God. But all things fell out contrary to this his plot and proiect: for it was ſo farre from winning others to imbrace true religion, as that it drew him to idolatrie: and ſo farre from ſtabliſhing his houſe, or ſtrengthening his kingdome, as that it was the cauſe of the rending of the one, and the ruinating of the other. *Conſtantine* the Great was perſwaded, that by building the citie of Conſtantinople in the confines of Europe and Aſia, and there placing one of his ſonnes, as his Lieutenant to keepe his court, hee ſhould fortifie his Empire as with a wall of braſſe: But he was deceiued, for the building of new Rome, was the decay of the old, and the diuiding of the Empire, was the deſtruction thereof: So that it is truly ſaid, Policie is often the ouerthrow of politie.

Now if wiſdom may not be gloried in, much leſſe may ſtrength, ſeeing that *wiſedome is better then ſtrength, Ecclеſ.* 9.16. ſeeing that the greateſt ſtrength of man, is not comparable to that of Behemoth, *Iob* 40. and other bruite beaſtes: ſeeing it is but the ſtrength of fleſh: ſeeing no power nor might, can deliuer from wrath in the day of wrath. Of all the puiſſant princes, and plotting polititians, the *Pſalmiſt* ſaith, They are ſo vaine, that if they bee laid vpon the ballance, euen vanitie it ſelfe will weigh them downe, *Pſal.*62.9.

And as for riches, beſides that they make vs neuer a whit the better, (nay oftentimes much worſe) they are alſo vncertaine. *Salomon* ſaith, *They make themſelues wings like an Eagle, and flie away, Pro.*23.5. They may not vnfitly be compared to *Ionas* his gourd, which flouriſhed in the morning, yeelding him content and delight, but ſhortly after (to his great griefe,) it was ſtricken by a worme, and withered away. The like may be ſaid of honours, and pleaſures. For what more vaine then to glorie in honour, which is not in a mans power, ſeeing as the Philoſopher teacheth, *Ho-* Ethic. l.1.c.5. *nour is not in him that is honoured, but in him that honoureth:* and therefore Courtiers are compared to counters, which ſtand ſometime for pounds, ſometime for pence, beeing now aduanced, now debaſed, according to the pleaſure of the Prince. *Haman* to day high- Eſther 7. ly honoured in the court at Shuſhan, the next day hanged vpon a tree. To omit the examples of *Iob*, and *Nabuchodonoſor*, (in whom

we

we may see the mutability of worldly dignitie.) Consider it in the glasse of these examples. First of *Geliner* a puissant Prince of the Vandals, who was brought so low, that he was enforced to request his friend to send him a loafe of bread, a sponge, and a harpe: a loafe, to slake his hunger: a sponge, to drye vp his teares: a harpe, to solace him in his misery. Of *Bellisarius*, (for prowes and honour, the onely man then liuing,) who came to that miserable estate, that hauing his eyes put out, hee was led in a string to beg by the high way side, crying *Date obulum Bellisario.* And of the victorious Emperour *Henerie* the fourth, who had fought 52. pitched fields; and yet was driuen to that exigẽt, as that he became a suter for a poore Prebend in the Church of Spira, to mainetaine himselfe in his old age. And as for worldly pleasures, least cause is there that any man should glory in them, seeing they are more vanishing then the former: seeing they are common to vs with bruite beasts: seeing they are mingled with much griefe and vexation, for *in the midst of laughter the heart is sorrowfull. Prou.* 14.13. And lastly, seeing they leaue a sting behinde them, for the end of pleasure is nothing but paine, as *Salomon* saith, *The end of reioycing is mourning.* For feasting and banquetting are often turned into surfeiting and vomiting: drinkings into palsies: lusts into goutes, &c. And if pleasures were but onely painefull, the matter were the lesse; but they are also sinnefull, *Hebrew.* 11.25. and therefore in no wise to bee gloried in.

Procopius.

Prou. 14. 13.

By this we see that *Paul* had iust cause in this earnest manner, to say, *God forbidde that I should glorie but in the crosse of Christ*, considering that this boasting in outward things, is not onely a fault of vanitie, but also of impietie, as may appeare by these reasons. I. God hath expressely forbidden it. *Ier.* 9.23. *Gal.* 5.26. II. Hee hath alway seuerely punished it, as in *David*, for numbring the people in a vaine-glorious minde. 2.*Sam.*24. In *Ezekias*, for shewing his treasures in a brauery to the Embassadours of the King of Babel, *Isay* 39. In *Herod*, for ascribing to himselfe the glory proper to God alone, *Act.* 12. III. The Saints of God haue alwaies abhorred it, as *Paul* doth in this place, and 2.*Cor.* 11.30. *If I must needs glorie, I will glory in mine infirmities*, as if he should say, I will be farre from carnall boasting. IV. The heathen by the light of nature haue condemned it: the Grecian Orator calls it *an odious, and burdensome thing.* And the Romane Orator prooues it to be most true by his owne practise, making his words which flowed from his mouth, as sweete as hony, to taste as bitter as wormewood, by interlacing his owne praises.

φορτικὸν τί καὶ ἐπαχθές. Demost. de Coron.

Obiect. I.

Obiect. I. *Paul* gloried in ſomething beſides the croſſe of Chriſt, when he ſaid , *It were better for him to die, then that any ſhould make his glorying vaine.* 1.Cor.9.15. *Anſ. Paul* in glorying doeth diſtinguiſh his calling, from his perſon ; *Of ſuch a one I will boaſt, of my ſelfe I will not boaſt,* and, *I was nothing inferiour to the very chiefe Apoſtles, although I am nothing.* 2. Cor.12.5.11. Of his perſon or perſonall gifts hee boaſteth not : but onely of his Apoſtolicall calling, and his faithfull diſcharge thereof: to the end he may ſtop the mouthes of the falſe Apoſtles. Thus to confeſſe the good things wee haue, to the glorie of God, being vrged thereunto, is lawfull boaſting; nay it is ſometime neceſſarie, making much for the maintenance of the Goſpell, as *Pauls* boaſting made much for the good of the Church of Corinth. Againe, there is a twofold lawfull boaſting, one before God, another before men. *Romanes* 4.2. Of the former the Apoſtle ſpeakes in this verſe: of the latter in the 2. *Cor.* 12. He gloried not in the teſtimony of a good conſcience, before God, but onely before men. Before God he gloried in nothing , but in the ſauing knowledge of Chriſt, and him crucified. And whereas it may be ſaid, that this his boaſting in regard of the falſe Apoſtles, as alſo his glorying in the teſtimonie of his conſcience. 2. *Cor.* 1.12. and in his infirmities. 2. *Corinthians* 11.30. were not in the croſſe of Chriſt: I anſwer, they were: for his glorying ouer the falſe Apoſtles, in teaching freely , was in the good and proſperous ſucceſſe of the Goſpel, which is the doctrine of the croſſe, and his glorying in the teſtimonie of his conſcience ; in that it was waſhed by the blood of the croſſe , as *Paul* ſpeakes , *Col.* 1.20. In his afflictions, in that they were the afflictions of Chriſt, and he by them made conformable to him.

But it will be ſaid, that he gloried in his reuelation, in his paines and trauell, in preaching the Goſpel, and in the multitude of Churches which he had planted. *Anſw.* Firſt, he did it being vrged thereunto ; ſecondly, he did it to defend his calling, and the credit of the Goſpel: and therefore this boaſting was not vnlawfull ; nay it was neceſſarie, and in the Lord. For when wee are compelled, we may confeſſe the good things wee haue, if we doe it ſparingly , and for the edification of others, that they may be bettered by our example: and that they ſeeing our good workes, may glorifie God our heauenly father. *Matth.* 5.16.

Here we ſee what glorying is vnlawfull ; namely, when men aſcribe vnto themſelues either that which they haue not , or more then they haue, or as proceeding from themſelues, their wiſedome, ſtrength , induſtrie, in ſacrificing to their owne nets, and burning

incenſe

incense to their owne yearne, *Habac.*1.16,or in boasting of them without necessary cause, either for their owne vaine-glory,as *Nebuchodonosor* did,*Dan*.4.or not for Gods glory,as *Herod* did, *Act.*12. And if this glorying be so great a sinne, surely boasting in wickednesse(as *Doeg*.did,*Psal.*52.1.)must needes be most damnable : as when the greatest swearers and swaggerers, count themselues the best companions:The greatest Idolaters,and superstitious persons, most religious : the greatest oppressours,surfeiters,drunkards,fighters,most valiant and couragious,&c. Now this may be done three waies,either ignorantly,as when *Paul* gloried in his cruell persecuting of the Saints before his conuersion, *Act* 26.11. or presumptuously,when men glory in wickednesse, notwithstanding they bee perswaded in conscience,that it is euill : and then it is the sinne of Sodome,*Isa.*3.9.or maliciously, to despite God, and then it is the sinne against the holy Ghost.

The second point to be considered in the words, is, the thing wherein he will glorie, called here *the Crosse of Christ* : *Saue in the Crosse of our Lord Iesus Christ.* The words in the originall translated *saue*,are exceptiue : as if he should say,I will glory in nothing except in the crosse of Christ : and exclusiue,onely in the crosse of Christ, and in nothing els. Albeit they are sometime aduersatiue, as *Gal.*2. 16.and *Apoc.*21.27.*There shall enter into it no vncleane thing* εἰ μὴ, *but they that are written,&c.* where the words are not exclusiue : for then it would follow that some which worke abhomination,should enter into heauen :)but aduersatiue as *Math* 12.4.and *Luke* 4.20 which may serue(by the way)to cleare the text, *Ioh.*17.12. *Those thou gauest me haue I kept, and none of them is lost,but the child of perdition*: that is,*but the child of perdition is lost*.For the words, εἰ μὴ (as I take it)are not so well translated by the exceptiue coniunction *nisi*, as by the aduersatiue *sed*: seeing heere is no exception made of *Iudas*,as though he had beene giuen to Christ, and afterward had fallen away: which exposition must needs be made, if the words be read,*nisi filius perditionis*.

Further, by the Crosse of Christ, the Apostle vnderstandeth synecdochically, the all-sufficient, expiatorie, and satisfactorie sacrifice of Christ vpon the crosse, with the whole worke of our redemption : in the sauing knowledge whereof he professeth he will glorie, and boast. For *Christ is made vnto vs wisedome, righteousnesse —that as it is written, He that glorieth, should glorie in the Lord*: euen to make boast of him all the day long, as the Psalmist speaketh. And the reason why *Paul* professeth that he will glorie onely in the Crosse of Christ, is, because Christ crucified is the treasurie, and store-

Marginal notes: εἰ μὴ. — εἰ μὴ ὁ υἱὸς τῆς ἀπωλείας. — 1.Cor.1.31.

ſtorehouſe of the Church: ſeeing that in him are hid, not only the treaſures of wiſdome and knowledge, *Coloſſ.*2.3. but of bountie and grace, *Iohn* 1.16. and of all ſpirituall bleſſings, *Epheſ.*1.3. For firſt, by Chriſt crucified, we haue reconciliation with God, remiſſion of ſinnes, and acceptation to eternall life. Secondly, we haue the peace of God which paſſeth all vnderſtanding, peace with God, with Angels, with men, with our ſelues, with the creatures. Thirdly, we recouer the right and title which we had in the creation to all the creatures and bleſſings of God, 1.*Cor.*3.22. Fourthly, all afflictions and judgements, ceaſe to bee curſes and puniſhments, and become either trialls, or corrections. Laſtly, death it ſelfe is no death, but a ſleepe: for all that die in the Lord, are ſaid to ſleepe, and to reſt vpon their beds, *Iſai.*57.2. Indeed, if wee looke vpon death through the glaſſe of the Law, it is the very downefall to eternall deſtruction: but if we conſider it as it is changed by the death of Chriſt, it is but a paſſage from this tranſitorie life to eternall life. Chriſt by his death hath taken away ſinne, the ſting of death: ſo that though it ſeaze vpon vs, yet (hauing loſt his ſting) it cannot hurt vs. So that in a word, in *Chriſt crucified*, are all things that a man can glory of. If wee would glory in knowledge and wiſdome; he is the wiſdome of the Father, ſeeing that all treaſures of wiſdome and knowledge are hid in him: and therefore *Paul* deſired to know nothing among the Corinthians, *but Chriſt and him crucified*, 1.*Corint.*2.2. for this knowledge is eternall life, *Iohn* 17.3. If in the loue and fauour of great men: by him we are highly aduanced into the loue and fauour of God, *Epheſ.* 1.6. If in honors and riches; by him we are made Kings and Prieſts, *Apoc.*1.6. If in libertie; by him we are deliuered from the hands of our enemies, Sinne, Satan, &c. *Luke* 1.74. If in pleaſures, comfort, and content; he is our felicitie, in him we are complete, *Coloſſ.*2. By him wee haue right *to thoſe things which eye hath not ſeene, eare hath not heard, neither can the heart of man conceiue.* It may be ſaid, why doth *Paul* glory in the ignominious death of Chriſt, rather then in his glorious reſurrection, triumphant aſcenſion, and imperiall iuriſdiction now ſitting at the right hand of the Father? *Anſwer.* Theſe are not excluded, but included in the Croſſe: yet he nameth the croſſe rather then them. Firſt of all, to ſhew that vpon the croſſe, Chriſt did fully finiſh the worke of our redemption: for beeing now ready to giue vp the ghoſt, he ſaid, *It is finiſhed, Iohn* 19.30. this made *Paul* to deſire to know nothing but Chriſt, and him crucified, 1.*Cor.*2. For in his humiliation ſtands our exaltation; in his weakeneſſe ſtands our ſtrength; in his ignominie, our glory; in his death,

August.de verb.Apost. Serm.20.

death,our life. Secondly, to shew that he was not ashamed of the crosse of Christ, though neuer so ignominious in the eyes of the world.It had beene no great thing for *Paul* to haue gloried in the resurrection,ascension, wisedome,power, and maiestie of Christ, wherein the world can and doth glory. But to glorie in the shame-full, contemptible, accursed death of the crosse, was a matter of great difficultie, and the worke of faith, iudging that which the world counts ignominious, to bee most glorious: that which the learned Philosophers counted foolishnes, to be the wisedome of God. 1.*Cor*.1.24.

The Popish sort abuse this text two waies.First,in applying it to the *transient crosse*.Secondly,to the *permanent* or *materiall crosse*. To the *transient crosse*, in that they glorie in it: First,as hauing a vertue in it,(when it is made in the ayre,)to driue away Diuells.Secondly, beeing made in the forehead to be as an amulet against charmes, blastings, and other such like casualties. To the *materiall crosse*, when they adorne it with golde and iewels, and so cause it to bee carried in great pompe before them.Whē the *Crucigeri* weare it in their hats in a white,redde,or greene colour. When they put their confidence in it,and pray vnto it,*Holy Crosse,saue vs*.This is Popish and carnall glorying in the crosse; and not spirituall, in the death of Christ vpon the crosse, of which onely the Apostle speakes in this place.

The reason why he would glory in nothing but in the crosse of Christ, followeth to be considered, in these words, *By which the world is crucified to me,and I vnto the world*.It is taken from a double effect,which Christ,or the crosse of Christ, wrought in him: (for the words,δι' οὗ,*by which*, may be referred to either indifferently.) The first,*to be crucified to the world*: the second,*the world to be crucified to him*. By *the world*,we are not to vnderstand the frame of heauen and earth, nor the creatures, nor mankind: but honour, riches, pleasures,fauour, wisedome,glorie, and whatsoeuer is opposed to the kingedome of Christ,and the new creature.*To be crucified to the world*,is to be dead vnto it,to despise and contemne it,to count all the glorie of it to be no better then dung,in respect of Christ and his righteousnesse,as *Paul* did,*Phil*.3.8.The world is said *to be crucified to vs*,when it hates and persecutes vs,and accounts vs the filth and the off-scouring of all things. 1.*Cor*.4.13.Yet here obserue that we are crucified to the world, and the world to vs, by the vertue of the death of Christ,after a different manner.We are crucified to the world,properly by the spirit of Christ,weaning our affections from the loue of this world. The world is crucified to vs, by the death of of Christ, improperly, and by accident, in that we are made such as the world cannot but hate and persecute: for seeing we are made new creatures, and chosen out of the world, therefore the world hateth vs, *Iohn* 15.15.

Heere we see who those are that can truly glorie in the crosse of Christ, namely those that are dead to the world, and the world to them: such as feele the power of the spirit of Christ crucifying the flesh in them, with the affections and lusts. Others can no more glory of the crosse of Christ, then he that glories of the victorie which his Prince hath gotten ouer his enemies, himselfe in the meane time beeing a vassall, and slaue vnto them.

Secondly, that it is not sufficient for a Christian, that the world is crucified to him, except he also be crucified to the world, neither louing the world nor the things in the world.

Thirdly, that to be crucified to the world, is not to professe monasticall life, and to be shut vp in a Monastery: but to renounce the world, and the corruptions that are therein, both in affection of hart, and practise of life.

Fourthly, we are taught to carry our selues to the world, as crucified aud dead men, not to loue nor like it, to seeke or affect it, but to renounce & forsake it, with al the vanities, delights, & pleasures thereof: and to be as dead men to our owne wicked willes, and to our carnall reason, letting them lie dead in vs, & suffering our selues to be ruled, ordered, and guided by the Spirit of God: making his will our will, his word our wisedome.

Fiftly, by this we may examine our hearts, for if we haue our affections glued to the world, and set vpon the honors, pleasures, profits, and preferments thereof, we are worldlings indeed: for they that are Christs are crucified with Christ. *Gal* 2.20. and haue crucified the flesh, with the affections and lusts. *Gal.* 5.24. and therfore must needs be crucified to the world. A man that is hanged vpon a gybbet, ceaseth from his thefts and murders: So all that are indeed crucified with Christ to the world, cease from their old offences. For as the Apostle reasoneth, if we be risen with Christ, wee ought to seeke the things that are aboue, and not the things that are vpon the earth. *Col.* 3.1, 2. So if we be dead with Christ from the vanities of the world, we ought as dead men to abstaine from all worldly lusts, which fight against the soule. 1. *Pet.* 2.11.

v. 15. *For in Christ Iesus neither circumcision auaileth any thing, nor vncircumcision, but a new creature.*

Here the Apoſtle prooues his former aſſertion, v.14. that he neither did, nor ought to glory in any thing, ſaue in the croſſe of Chriſt, becauſe nothing is of any account in the kingdome of God, but a new creature. And this he prooues by the remoouall of all thoſe things, that are either oppoſite to, or diuers from a new creature, ſignified by *circumciſion* and *vncircumciſion*. And withall he laies downe two concluſions. The firſt is, that *in Chriſt Ieſus*, that is, in the kingdome of grace, *neither circumciſion, nor vncircumciſion are any thing*, that is, are neither acceptable to God, nor auaileable to ſaluatiō: Vnder theſe two ſynecdochically cōprehē-ding all outward priuiledges, and prerogatiues, dignities, and regalities, or whatſoeuer can be named: vnder *circumciſion* compriſing the prehemineñce of the Iewe, and the profit of circumciſion, which was much euery way, *Rom.* 3.1. ſeeing that *to them appertained the adoption, and the glory, and the couenants, and the giuing of the Lawe, and the ſeruice of God, and the promiſes. Rom.* 9.4. Vnder *vncircumciſion* containing the Gentiles, with all their wealth, wiſdome, ſtrength, Lawes, pollicy, and whatſoeuer is of high account, and glorious in the eies of the world. All which he excludes and accounts as *nothing* in reſpect of regeneration. *For that which is highly accounted of among men, is abomination in the ſight of God. Luk.* 16. 15. Therefore wiſedome, wealth, nobility, ſtrength, are nothing. 1. *Cor.* 1.26. Outward callings, as to be King or *Kaſar*, Prophet or Apoſtle. Outward actions of faſting, almes, prayer. Nay, kindred and alliance, as to be mother or brother of Chriſt, is nothing: for if the bleſſed virgine had not borne Chriſt in her heart, as ſhee did in her wombe, ſhe ſhould neuer haue beene ſaued. *Luk.* 11.27, 28. and if his kinſmen had not beene his brethren by ſpirituall adoption, as well as by naturall propagation, they ſhould haue had no inheritance in the kingdome of God, *Mark.* 3.33.34. Nay, the outward element of baptiſme, without the inward grace, is of no force; for it is *not the waſhing away of the filth of the fleſh* (that is acceptable to God) *but the ſtipulation of a good conſcience, which maketh requeſts vnto God.* 1.*Pet.*3.21. And if the communicant at the Lords table, doe not eate *panem Dominum* as well as *panem Domini* (as *Auguſtine* ſpeaketh) that is, if he doe not receiue Chriſt ſpiritually by the hand of his faith, as he doth corporally receiue the element by his bodily hand, he *receiueth vnworthily, and ſo eateth and drinketh his owne iudgement.* 1.*Cor.*11.29. Now the reaſon why theſe outward things are nothing auaileable, is, becauſe the things that are accounted of with God, are ſpirituall and eternall, not temporall and carnall, as theſe are: which as they ſhall vtterly ceaſe in the kingdome

kingdome of glory, *Matth.22.30.* (*for then Chriſt will put downe all rule, authority, and power. 1.Cor.15.24.*) ſo are they not of any moment or account in the kingdome of grace, as *Paul* teacheth. 2. *Cor.5.16.Gal.3,28.Coloſſ.3.11.* It may be ſaid, theſe priuiledges and outward things, as Prince, and people; Maſter, and ſeruant: bond, and free, &c. haue place in the kingdome of grace, ſeeing Chriſtianity doth not aboliſh nature, nor ciuill pollicy. To which I anſwer, that man muſt be conſidered two waies, in reſpect of the outward, or inward man. Conſider him as he is a member, in ciuill ſociety, as of the family, Church, or Common-wealth: there are ſundry differences of perſons, as bond, free; magiſtrate, ſubiect; poore, rich &c. in which ſenſe the Apoſt. exhortation taketh place, *Wiues, ſubmitte your ſelues to your huſbands. Coloſſians 3.18. Children, obey your parents, verſe.20. ſeruants, be obedient to your maſters, verſe 22.* But if a man be conſidered in reſpect of his ſpirituall eſtate, as he is a member of the inuiſible, or Chatholique Church, vnder ſpiritual gouernment, conſiſting *in righteouſneſſe, peace of conſcience and ioy in the holy Ghoſt. Rom.*14.17. there is no diſtinction of calling, condition, or ſexe; *for we are all one in Chriſt. Gal.3.verſe 28.* or *Chriſt is all and in all things. Coloſſ.3.11.* in that though we be many, yet are we but one body in Chriſt. *Rom.12.verſe 5.* ſeeing we are quickned with one ſpirit. *Eph.4.verſe 4.* The Popiſh opinion therefore which teacheth that there be ſome outward callings and actions which commend vs to God, as to leade a ſingle life, to faſt, to vow voluntary pouerty, to performe regular obedience, to profeſſe monkery, to be buried in a friers cowle, or to abſtaine from theſe and theſe meates, is here condemned, when *Paul* ſaith, that outward priuiledges will not ſerue the turne, and that *meate commendeth vs not to God.1.Cor.8.8.*

Againe, neither this nor the like places *Gal. 3.ver.28.Col. 3.11.* do any thing fauour the Anabaptiſticall fancy, of bringing in an anarchie, that is, an ataxy into Chriſtian ſociety; by taking away chriſtian magiſtrates, and diſtinction betwixt maſter and ſeruant: for by the ſame reaſon we may confound the ſexe of man and woman; for *Paul* ſaith, *there is neither male nor female, but we are all one in Chriſt:* the meaning thereof is this, that although in reſpect of our inward or ſpirituall eſtate before God, there be no ſuch difference: yet that hindreth not but there may be in reſpect of our outward eſtate.

Further, we learne from hence, that no man is to thinke highly of himſelfe in regard of outward priuiledges, as birth, honour, wealth, fauour, nor to glory in them. *Ier.9.23.* rich men muſt not be high minded. 1.*Tim*.6.17. Nay, the King may not lift vp his mind aboue his brethren.*Deut*. 17.20. *Pauls* example is notable, who accounted all the priuiledges which he had before his conuersion, whilest he was a Iew, (as that he was a citizen of *Rome*, a Pharisie, a great Rabbin, instructed by *Gamaliel*, of the tribe of *Beniamin*, circumcised the 8. day &c.) and after his conuersion beeing a christian (as that he was an Apostle, takẽ vp into the 3. heauen &c.) to be as nothing, or worse then nothing, euen as *losse or dunge* in respect of beeing a new creature in Christ, that is, in respect of iustification, and sanctification. And therefore we may not set our minds too much vpon outward things, as riches, honors, pleasures: seeing they are not auayleable to saluation.

Besides, this teacheth al those that are but in mean & base estate, to be content: for outward priuiledges auaile nothing: outward wants and miseries, hinder nothing. If a man be rich, he is nothing the nearer, & if he be poore, he is not a whit the further off: it is the pouerty of the spirit, which makes a man rich in grace: for though the poore man be the rich mans slaue, yet he is the sonne of God, and fellow heyre with Christ: and though the rich man bee the poore mans master, yet he is the seruant of Christ, as *Paul* saith, *he that is called beeing a seruant, is Gods free man: and he that is called being free, is Christs seruant*. 1.*Cor*.7.22.

Lastly, this crosseth the opinion of the multitude, who thinke that if a man be increased in riches, graced with fauour, aduanced with honour, that he is a godly, wise, religious man; and that religion which he professeth, is the truth. This is nothing else but *to haue the faith of our Lord Iesus Christ in respect of persons*. *Iames* 2. *verse* 1.

The second conclusion is, that the new creature is the onely thing that is acceptable to God. *Circumcision, &c. auaileth nothing, but a new creature*. By the *new creature*, the Apostle vnderstandeth the image of God, or renouation of the whole man, both in the spirits of our minds, and in the affections of our hearts, which is also called *the new man*. We shall the better conceiue it by the contrary, namely, by *the old man*; which is, want of knowledge in the minde, and delight in ignorance: want of subiection and conformitie in the will, and rebellion withall: want of holines in the affections, and pronenes to euill. *The new man* then, is the restoring of al these defects. For the vnderstanding hereof, cōsider, that there are three things in the soule. The substance of the soule: the faculties, or powers of the soule: and the qualities of these faculties. Now neither the substance nor faculties are lost by the fall, but onely the

the qualities of the faculties: as when an inſtrument is out of tune, the fault is not in the ſubſtance of the inſtrument, nor in the ſound, but in the diſproportion, or iarre in the ſound: therefore the qualities onely are renewed by grace. Theſe qualities or habits, are either in the Vnderſtanding: or will and affections. The qualitie in the vnderſtanding, is *knowledge, Coloſſ.*3.10. *Yee haue put on the new man, which is renewed in knowledge, after the image of him that created him.* In the will and affections, they are principally two, *righteouſneſſe*, and *holineſſe*, both which are in truth and ſynceritie, without all hypocriſie. *Eph.*4.22. *Put on the new man, which after God is created in righteouſnes, and true holines*: where *holines* and *righteouſnes*, are oppoſed to concupiſcences, and luſts of the old man: *Truth* (which hath relation to both) to ſpirituall guile, and diſſimulation: ſo that each of theſe qualities, haue two parts, a want of the contrarie euill, and a poſitiue qualitie or habit of goodneſſe. *Holineſſe* reſpecteth God, and containeth all duties of pietie, conteined in the firſt table: *Righteouſnes*, reſpects man, and the creatures, and compriſeth all the duties enioyned in the ſecond table. *Truth* reſpecteth the manner how both the former are to be practiſed, viz. with an vpright and ſincere heart, free from all hypocriſie and deceit. Theſe three making a perfect harmonie in all the faculties of the ſoule: *Holineſſe* performing all the duties of pietie: *righteouſnes* the duties of humanitie: *truth* ſeaſoning both the former with ſinceritie.

But (ſome may ſay) how is the new creature oppoſed to all externall things, or ſaid to be of any force in the kingdome of Chriſt, ſeeing it is not auaileable to iuſtifie a man before God, being ſtained with manifold imperfections? For anſwer whereof, we are to know, that outward things are ſometime oppoſed to Chriſt, and his righteouſneſſe, as *Col.*3.11. *There is neither Iew, nor Grecian, circumciſion nor vncircumciſion, &c. but Chriſt is all, and in all things.* ſometime to faith, as *Gal.*5.6. *Neither circumciſion auaileth any thing, nor vncircumciſion, but faith which worketh by loue.* ſometime to the new creature or ſanctification, as in this place, and 1.*Cor.*7.29 *Circumciſion is nothing, &c. but the keeping of the commandements of God.* But the ſenſe is all one, for they are oppoſed to Chriſt, as to the matter of our iuſtification: to faith as to the inſtrument apprehending it: to the new creature, as to the ſigne of them both.

Further, whereas both here, and 2.*Cor.*5.17. the image of God is called *a new creature*, (or as it is in the originall [καινὴ κτίσις] *a new creation*) the meaning is not, that either the ſubſtance, or faculties of the ſoule are created anew; but that the worke of regeneration is wholly to be aſcribed to God alone, (not as though we were ſtocks or ſtones without life or motion) but becauſe God doth create theſe new qualities in vs, quickning vs when wee were dead in ſinne, and working in vs both the will, and the deede. *Philip.2.13.*

If regeneration then bee *a new creation,* it muſt needes follow, that before our conuerſion we were not onely dead, but euen flat nothing, in godlineſſe, and grace. By which we ſee what to iudge of the *Semi-pelagian* hereſie, which teacheth, that a man by an *internum principium,* may diſpoſe himſelfe to will that which is truely good: and that man is not *ſtarke dead* in ſinne, but onely *ſicke* or *wounded,* and *halfe dead,* as the man which fell among theeues, *Luk.* 10. or as a priſoner that is ſhackled and manackled, who can walke of himſelfe, if his fetters be taken from him: ſo we (if Chriſt looſe the chaines of our ſinnes) haue power of our ſelues to mooue our ſelues. Which doctrine we know is moſt iniurious to the mercy of God and moſt derogatorie to the merits of Chriſt, ſeeing it makes him in the worke of our ſaluation, to bee but *cauſa remouens prohibens,* which (as Logicians teach) is but *cauſa ſine quâ non,* which in truth is no cauſe at all. So that they make themſelues their owne Sauiours, and Chriſt to be but an inſtrument whereby they ſaue themſelues: for if hee doe but remooue the impediment, they without any more adoe, are able to mooue and act themſelues. When as the conuerſion of a ſinner is as great a worke as the creation of heauen and earth: for *Paul* calleth it here *a new creation.* Nay, here is a greater power required (if I may ſo ſpeake) then that whereby the world was created. For though an infinite power be required as well to the creating of the great world, as the re-creating or regenerating of the leſſe world, as our Sauiour Chriſt ſignifies, *Mark* 2.9. *Whether is it eaſier to ſay to the ſicke of the palſie, Thy ſinnes are forgiuen thee, or to ſay, Ariſe, take vp thy bed and walke?* yet the holy Ghoſt ſeemeth, of the two, to make it more difficult, to create a new heart, then a new world, in that ſpeaking of the creation of the world, he ſaith it was made by the word of God, *By the word of the Lord were the heauens made. Pſal.*33.6. or by his fingers, *when I conſider the heauens, the workes of thy fingers. Pſal.*8,3. or by his hands, *Pſalm.*102.25. *The heauens are the workes of thy hands.* But the redemption of man, and the conuerſion of a ſinner, is ſaid to be wrought by the *arme of God.* Marie in her *Magnificat,* ſaith, *He hath ſhewed ſtrength with his arme. Luk.*1.51. nay, hee was faine to ſet his ſide to it, and it made him ſhed many a teare, and ſweat as it were *drops of bloud trickling downe to the ground. Luk.* 22. 44. Before our conuerſion, we are like the drye bones, *Ezek.*37. for

as

as when the winde of God came vpon them,bone came to bone, and were ioyned with ſinewes, and couered with fleſh, and had their ſenſes reſtored: ſo when the Spirit of God,like the fauonian winde,bloweth vpon vs,it reuiueth vs againe; giuing vs a new life, new ſenſes,a new heart,new wills, and affections: for *all old things paſſe away,and all things become new.*2.*Cor.*5.17. For it openeth the eyes of our vnderſtanding,making vs diſcerne of things that differ. *Eph.*1.18. *Philip.*1.10. it boareth a new eare of obedience in vs, *Pſal.*40.6.and giueth vs a new taſt,not to ſauour the things of the fleſh,but of the Spirit.*Rom.*8.5.

Further, this ſerues to detect the natuall Poperie of the multitude,and of our owne hearts,when we perſwade our ſelues(though falſely)that though we goe on in our ſinnes,yet that we can repent when we liſt. When as the Prophet ſaith, *O Lord I know that the way of man is not in himſelfe*: and *Paul* ſaith,that it is as great a worke to create a new heart,as to create a new world: for regeneration is *a new creation.* 2.*Corinth.*5.17.*Auguſtine* ſaith well,*He that will grant pardon to him that repents, will not alway giue repentance to him that ſinnes.*

Ierem.10.23. Qui dabit pœnitenti veniam, non dabit peccanti pœnitentiam.

Againe,in the ſenſe that *Paul* calleth the image of God,a *newe creature*,or the new man,and *corruption* the old man: we grant,that our religion is new,and Popiſh religion is old. For as the new man is the reſtored image of God, in which *Adam* was firſt created, though afterwards defaced by *his owne inuentions, Eccles.*7.31. So our religion is the reſtored or reformed doctrine firſt taught by the Apoſtles,which afterward was corrupted by mens deuices.Albeit, in *Tertullians* ſenſe,ours is the old religion,and theirs the new: as the image of God is the old man,and corruption the new.

Quod antiquiſſimum, id veriſſimum.

Vſe. If we be not changed in our liues,but remaine old *Adams* ſtill,euen the ſame men we were before, in minding,willing,affecting earthly things, and faſhioning our ſelues to the guiſe of the world; we are no new creatures, though wee promiſe and proteſt neuer ſo much: we are but hypocrites, deceiuing others, and our ſelues alſo.For where this new creature is, there is a change in all the faculties and powers of ſoule and body: the minde is not ſet vpon the world,but mindeth heauenly things: the will,affections, and conuerſation of the whole man,is in heauen. *Philip.*3.20. For the Spirit of regeneration is like the leauen which a woman tooke and hid in three pecks of meale till all was leauened: for after the ſame manner,by a ſecret operation it altereth the mind, will,affections. *If any be in Chriſt*,(ſaith the Apoſtle) *he is a new creature, old things are paſſed away,behold,all things are become new.* If therefore we be be new creatures,why leade we not a new life? if we be changed in affection,why are we not changed in conuersation?

But by this wee may perceiue that all which are Christians in profession, are not Christians in conuersation: all that are washed with the outward element of water,are not washed with the inward baptisme,the lauer of regeneration: as first, those that are as good fellowes (that is,as badde) as euer they were before, and make no conscience of sinne. Secondly,such as are no more but ciuill honest men, like those honest women which raysed persecution against *Paul* and *Barnabas*, and expelled them out of their coasts. *Act.* 13. 50. Thirdly,worldly wise men which sauour of nothing but the world. Lastly,such as haue some loue and liking of the word, and are in some sort outwardly conformable thereunto, hauing some legall sorrow for sinne arising from legall terrours: but haue no thorow change nor renouation.

Lastly,we may not maruell if the world hate and maligne those that are new creatures: seeing they neither mind nor affect the same things. For there can be no true loue,where there is contrarietie of iudgements,wills, affections,which hath bene,is,and will bee betwixt those that are borne of the flesh, and those that are borne of God,*Gene.*3.15.

16 *And as many as walke according to this rule, peace shall be vpon them,and mercy, and vpon the Israel of God.*

Heere *Paul* commends this glorying in the crosse of Christ,and studie of pietie, in becomming a new creature, as the onely rule of faith and manners,which all teachers and hearers were to obserue, and follow: Enforcing the keeping and obseruing of this double dutie,by the fruit and benefit that comes thereby,specified heere by *peace* and *mercy*. In the words two things are generally to be considered: First, the dutie of walking,in these words,*As many as walke according to this rule:* Secondly, the reason or motiue to the practise thereof, in these, *Peace shall bee vpon them, and mercy:* which is amplified by the generalitie thereof, that is, shall light vpon *as many* as walke according thereto,and *vpon the Israel of God.* The dutie is,that wee walke according to this canon, or rule: the * word translated *walke*, signifieth not simply to walke, but to walke warily and circumspectly (as it is expounded, *Ephes.* 5.15.) or to walke by rule in order, and measure, without treading aside but making straight steppes to our feete, *Hebrewes* 12.13. *Pauls* rule which we must walke by, is faith in Christ, called here glory-

* στοιχήσ.

ing

ing in the croſſe of Chriſt: and repentance towards God: called regeneration, or the new creature: which is rightly called a rule of faith and manners, of things to bee beleeued, and practized, becauſe by it all doctrines and actions are to bee examined: nay, the Scripture is therefore called *Canonicall*, becauſe it ſets downe an expoſition of this rule: there being nothing from the firſt chapter in *Geneſis*, to the laſt words in the *Apocal.* which aimeth not at one of theſe two, either repentance towards God, or faith in Chriſt.

Heere all Miniſters are taught what rule to follow in preaching the word, or building the Church of God, namely faith and repentance, the doctrine of the croſſe, and conuerſion, or the new creature. And all hearers according to what rule to order their liues and actions. For this metaphor of walking, and that by a rule or line, ſhewes that wee are trauellers or pilgrims, that this world is a ſtrange countrey, that we are to go to another, that the world is an endleſſe labyrinth, in which we ſhall for euer loſe our ſelues, except we be guided by this rule.

And heere wee ſee that there is a certaine rule for regulating of all things appertaining to faith and manners, though wee cannot apply it nor vſe it as wee ſhould: The fault is in vs, not in the rule.

Whereas *Paul* ſaith, as many as walke according to *this rule*, hee ſhewes, that Chriſtians haue but one onely rule which they are to follow, and according to which they muſt frame their liues; for the Apoſtle exhorts vs that *wee all proceed by one rule*, *Phil.* 3.16. Therefore the Papiſts doe notoriouſly offend not onely in wreſting, peruerting, and breaking this rule, but in making other new Lesbian rules, which they preſcribe as neceſſarie to bee followed: as the rule of S. *Francis*, of S. *Dominicke*, S. *Auſten*, S. *Ierome*, &c. holding one mans baptiſme better then another, one mans profeſſion holier then another, one mans rule perfecter then another: following any rule rather then Chriſts, and ſo diuide his ſeameleſſe coat. And that theſe ſundry rules of Monks are vaine and wicked, it may appeare. Firſt, becauſe they agree not with this rule of *Paul*, they being many, it but one: it directing & leading to Chriſt, they leading to by-paths, obſcuring the merit of Chriſt, and preſcribing many things partly friuolous, partly impious, contrary to faith & good life. Secondly, in that they agree not among themſelues; euery ſect hauing his owne proper orders, and contending their owne to be better, holier, perfecter thē the reſt. Thirdly, in that they diuide into diuers ſects, thoſe that ought to be all one in Chriſt, for which cauſe

cause *Paul* calles the Corinthians carnall, in holding some of *Paul*, others of *Apollos*, 1.*Corinth*.3.4. For how can they bee spirituall, who in speech, action, habite, and attire, profession and conuersation, professe nothing but Schisme and dissention? *Ierome* against the Luciferians, saith, *Sicubi audieris eos qui dicuntur Christi, non à Domino Iesu Christo, sed à quoquam alio nuncupari, puta Marcionitas, Valentinianos, Montenses, Campates, scito non Ecclesiam Christi, sed Antichristi esse Synagogam.* that is, *Wheresoeuer thou shalt heare those that are called Christians, not to haue their name from our Lord Iesus Christ, but from some other, as Marcionites, Valentinians, Montenses, Campates, know this much, that they are not the Church of Christ, but the Synagogue of Antichrist.* Nay further, solitary life, in leauing the societie of men, and sequestring themselues from all companie, which is the ground, and generall practise of Monkish Eremites, (for Cœnobites to speake properly, are no Monkes, as the word teacheth) is against the very light of nature it selfe. First, because it is naturall for men to liue together; nay it is the ground of the family, the Church and Common wealth. There was neuer nation so barbarous or sauage, but endeauoured to liue together by associating themselues, in cities, townes, villages, caues, woods, tents, or some other way, according to the custome of the countrey: which generall practise of all, argues the impression of nature in all. Secondly, speach is giuen men for this end, that they might conuerse together: for it were little or nothing auaileable if men should liue alone, and conuerse with none. Thirdly, sundry vertues bestowed vpon men, as iustice, fortitude, loue, and friendship, should be giuen in vaine, if men should liue solitarie, sequestred from all company. Fourthly, mans imbecilitie argues thus much; for whereas all other creatures are armed by nature, as the Bull with hornes, the Boare with tuskes: other with teeth, feathers, swiftnesse, &c. man is borne feeble, and naked, not able to prouide or defend himselfe, but onely by helpe of others, which is an argument that hee is borne to liue in ciuill societie, and to be holpen by others. Lastly, man is borne to doe good to himselfe and others, in some estate and calling, 1.*Corinthians* 7. But hee that liueth alone, can doe no good to others, nor receiue good from them: For whereas they plead for themselues, that they leaue their particular callings, and betake themselues to Hermitages, that so they may renounce the world. I answer, that to renounce the world, is not to leaue their places and callings, whereunto God hath called them, but *to renounce the corruption that is in the world through lust*, 2.*Pet*.1.4. These and the like reasons made the

the Philoſopher to ſay, That hee which left the ſocietie of men, and betooke himſelfe to a ſolitarie life, was either a God, or a beaſt. Ariſtot.Polit. lib.1.cap.2.

By this wee may ſee what Lesbian rules they follow: and how that which they account the higheſt degree of perfection, is in truth the depth of abomination: that it hath beene the cauſe of much wickedneſſe, as of idleneſſe, hypocriſie, whoredome, ſodomitry, beſides the cruell murthering of many poore innocents. Therefore let neither their hypocriſie, nor the Churches pretended authoritie, nor the long receiued cuſtome, any thing mooue vs, but that leauing them, we follow the rule of *Paul* in this place: for they that walk according to it, *peace ſhall be vpon them and mercy*. By *peace*, wee are to vnderſtand outward peace, as proſperitie, and good ſucceſſe in all things wee goe about. For *whatſoeuer they doe, ſhall proſper*, *Pſal.* 1.3. And peace with the creatures; as firſt with the good Angels, *Coloſſ.* 1.20. who *are miniſtring ſpirits, ſent foorth to miniſter, for their ſakes that ſhall be heires of ſaluation*, *Hebr.* 1.14. *pitching their tents about them*, *Pſal.* 34 7. *and bearing them in their hands as the nurſe her child*, *Pſal.* 91.12. Secondly, with the godly. The Prophet ſaith, that in the kingdome of Chriſt, *the wolfe ſhall dwell with the lambe, the leopard ſhall lie with the kidde, &c.* that is, men of fierce, ſauage, and woluiſh natures, ſhall bee ſo changed by grace, as that they ſhall liue peaceably and louingly together. Eſay 11.6. Thirdly, with the wicked their enemies, partly becauſe they ſeeke to liue in peace, as *Dauid* ſaith of himſelfe, *I labour for peace*, *Pſalm.* 120.7. partly, becauſe God ſo inclines their hearts, as that they are peaceable. Laſtly, with the beaſt of the field, and all the creatures. The Lord promiſeth to make a couenant with the wild beaſts, and foules of the heauen, in behalfe of his people, that they may ſleepe ſafely, *Hoſea* 2.18. But the peace which is principally meant in this place, is *peace of conſcience*, which paſſeth all vnderſtanding, *Phil.* 4 7. which is peace with God, being reconciled and at one with him, *Rom.* 5.1. *Being iuſtified by faith, wee haue peace with God.* And peace with our ſelues, which is threefold, as it is oppoſed to a threefold diſſention in man. The firſt is, when the will and affections renewed by grace, are obedient to the minde enlightened by the ſpirit, and at peace therewith: oppoſed to the diſſention that is betwixt rebellious affections, and naturall reaſon. The ſecond is, when grace (though ſtrongly aſſailed) giueth corruption the foile, whereupon followeth the calming and quieting of the minde, oppoſed to the combate betweene the fleſh and the ſpirit. The third is, when the conſcience perſwaded of remiſſion of ſinnes, and reconciliation

with

with God, ceaseth to accuse and terrifie, and begins to excuse, and comfort vs: opposed to the conflicts that a distressed conscience hath with legall terrours, and the anger of God. By *mercie* (which is the cause of this peace) are vnderstood, all spirituall blessings, which flow vnto vs from the loue and fauour of God in Christ, as remission of sinnes, iustification, sanctification, and eternall life it selfe. The words *ἐπ' αὐτοὺς, vpon them,* haue great emphasis, signifying, that these blessings come downe from heauen, and light vpon them that follow this rule, and that they cannot bee hindered by the malice of men.

Let the Pope then anathematize, curse, and excommunicate vs, both Prince and people, because wee tread not in the steps of his faith, but in the faith of our father *Abraham*, and walke not according to his rule, but according to this rule of the Apostle: for wee need not feare his thunderbolts nor curses, seeing *the causelesse curse shall neuer come, Prou.* 26.2. for what though hee curse, if God doe blesse? It was the thing that comforted *Dauid* being cursed of his enemies, in that *though they did curse, yet God would blesse, Psal.* 109.28 and let vs comfort our selues in this, that *he will curse them that curse his people, Gen.* 12.3.

Againe, if peace and mercie shall bee vpon them that walke according to this rule, then wrath and indignation shal light vpon those that follow any other rule, or deuise any other way, or set downe any other meanes of saluation besides, or contrary to this. False therefore is the opinion of *Pucksius*, that if a man leade an outward ciuill life, he may bee saued in any religion, the Iew in his Iudaisme, the Turke in his Mahometisme, the Heathen in his Paganisme. For they that walke not in this way, according to this rule, doe but weary themselues in endlesse Labyrinths: and so walking without line or rule in *their crooked waies, shall bee led with workers of iniquitie, when as peace shall be vpon Israel, Psal.* 125.5. Other vses are made of mercy and peace, Pag. 10. and 11. to which places I referre the Reader.

The Aposte addeth, that peace and mercie shall bee vpon all them that walke according to this rule, *and vpon the Israel of God.* There is a double Israel mentioned by *Paul, Israel according to the flesh,* 1.*Cor.* 10. 18. and *the Israel of God:* as there is a twofold Iew, one outward, in the flesh: another inward, in the spirit, *Rom.* 2.28, 29. By *the Israel of God,* the Apostle meaneth all such as are like to *Nathaniel,* who was *a true Israelite, in whome there was no guile, Iohn* 1.47. whether they bee the faithfull Gentiles, or beleeuing Iewes. And hee makes mention of the Israel of God, partly by reason of the

the aduersaries, who bragged so much of their father *Abraham*, and that they were the onely true Israelites, and yet were no Israelites, because they troad not in the steps of the faith of *Abraham*: partly, for the weake conuerts, who thought it a hard thing to bee seuered from the society of those to whō the promises were made: partly for vs Gentiles, that wee might know that *all are not Israel, which are of Israel, Rom.* 9.6. but that all they which are of faith are blessed with faithfull *Abraham, Gal.* 3.9. seeing that God is no accepter of persons, *Act.* 10.34.

17 *From hencefoorth let no man put mee to businesse: for I beare in my body the markes of the Lord Iesus.*

Heere the Apostle laies downe his last admonition, preuenting an obiection that might be made by the false apostles, or the Galatians. For whereas it might be said, that *Paul* sought himselfe, and the world, shunned persecution, and therfore ioyned circumcision to Christ, to please the Iewes, and followed not his owne rule, ver. 16. he takes away this obiection with great authoritie, when hee saith, *From hencefoorth let no man put mee to businesse.* And withall he addes a reason of it, *for I beare in my bodie the markes of the Lord Iesus:* as if hee should say, The bonds, the imprisonments, the stripes, wounds, and scarres in my bodie, doe sufficiently testifie my fidelitie in my ministery, for if I had preached circumcision, I should not haue suffered persecution. The words may be, and are taken in a double sense. First thus, The false apostles, and you Galatians (by their instigation) haue bin troublesome vnto me, by false accusations, and slanderous imputations, as that I taught circumcision and the obseruation of the ceremoniall law, as a thing necessary to saluation, and so you haue made a reuolt from my doctrine, and by that meanes haue doubled and tripled my labour & paines among you: But from hencefoorth cease to be troublesome vnto me, you may take experiment and proofe from me; the marks that I beare in my body, doe sufficiently witnes and seale the truth of my doctrine, and my fidelitie in mine Apostleship, as also whose disciple I am, *Moses*, or Christs, and what rule I follow, Iudaisme, or Christianisme. Secondly, they carie this sense, I haue said, that they which walke according to this rule, in glorying onely in the crosse of Christ, *peace shal be vpon them, and mercy, and vpon the Israel of God.* And I say againe and againe, that we ought to striue and contend for it, to obserue & keep it as a thing most necessary to saluation: τοῦ λοιποῦ, as for other things not necessarie to saluation, as circumcision, &c.

Let

Let no man trouble mee in the execution of mine Apostolicall function, or hinder the course of the Gospell, by vrging any other doctrine or ceremony contrary or diuerse from this, as necessarie to saluation: This one thing is necessary, other things are needlesse and fruitlesse in comparison, therefore neither I, nor the Church of God ought to be troubled with them. This latter sense I take to bee more agreeable to the text. Some make the sense to be this, I haue had many troubles and conflicts; and haue many markes and scarres in my body inflicted by persecutours: therefore be no more troublesome vnto mee: for it were too much to adde wormewood to my gall, affliction to affliction. Heere wee see the condition of the Apostle, and the estate of all faithfull Ministers; that it is full of trouble and molestations. For as they are accounted men of turbulent spirits, disquieters of the state, as *Elias* was, 1.*Kings* 21. and *Ieremie*, chapter 15.18. and *Paul*, *Actes* 16. 20. and 21.28. So they are most troubled with factious opposers, and false teachers, who labour to bring into the Church, things partly needlesse and superfluous, partly hurtfull and pernicious. Thus the false apostles troubled the Pastours and Church of Galatia, *Galat.* 5.10. and the Churches of Antiochia, Syria, Cilicia, *Actes* 15.24.

Secondly, consider how that the most and greatest troubles of the Church, haue beene for matters, not of substance, but of circumstance, partly not necessary, partly contrary to the rule: which notwithstanding haue beene vrged with fire and fagot, as things most necessary.

Lastly, hee that stands foorth for the defence of Gods truth (as *Paul* did, and all Ministers ought to doe) must let goe all circumstances, and looke to the substance. Not with *Martha*, to trouble himselfe about many needlesse things, when as one thing onely is necessarie.

Luke 10.41.

The reason followeth in these words: *For I beare in my body the markes of the Lord Iesus.*

στίγματα. Vide Lipsium de militia Romana, lib. 1. dialogo 9.

The word in the originall translated *markes*, doeth properly signifie prints with a hote yron. But it is here vsed generally to signifie any blemish, scarre, or marke whatsoeuer, whether such as was wont to bee set vpon seruants bought with money (which among the Iewes was a hole in the eare pearced with a naule, *Exod.* 21.6. *Deut.* 15.17.) or vpon slaues taken in the warres, as the Samians set vpon an Athenian captiue the signe of an owle: and the Athenians vpon a Samian, the signe of a ship: or vpon malefactors, as a hole in the eare, an F. in the forehead, a brand in the hand. Or

such

ſuch a marke, as ſome thinke was ſet vpon *Cain*, *Gen.*4.15. or the marke of God, *Ezek.*9.4. or of the beaſt, *Apoc.*16.2.

The markes of Chriſt are of two ſorts, either *inward* and *inuiſible*: or *outward* and *viſible*. The *inuiſible markes* are two. The firſt is, Gods eternall Election, which is called Gods *ſeale* or *marke*, 2.*Tim.* 2.19. *The foundation of God remaineth ſure, and hath this ſeale, The Lord knoweth who are his.* All the Elect are marked with this marke, *Apoc.*7. and by it Chriſt knoweth and acknowledgeth them for *his ſheepe*, *Iohn* 10. The ſecond is, regeneration, or the imprinting of the defaced image of God in the ſoule. By this marke, (which is *the true indeleble character*, neuer to be blotted out) are all beleeuers ſealed, 2.*Cor.*1.22. *Epheſ.*1.13. Theſe inuiſible markes of Election and Regeneration are in the ſoule, and therefore not here meant: for hee ſpeakes of bodily markes, *I beare in my bodie the markes* ——. The outward viſible markes are two fold: *Typicall*, or *Reall*. *Typicall*, as circumciſion, which was a marke ſet in the foreskinne of the fleſh, *Rom.*4.11. The blood of the Paſchall lambe, wherewith the houſes of the Iſraelites were marked, when the firſt borne of the Egyptians were ſlaine by the deſtroying Angel. And Baptiſme is of the ſame kind: for by Baptiſme Chriſtians are diſtinguiſhed from Iewes, Turkes, Infidels whatſoeuer. *Reall markes* of Chriſt, are either in his *naturall*, or in his *myſticall bodie*. In *his naturall bodie*, the wounds which were giuen him in his hands, feet, and ſides, which he ſhewed to his Diſciples after his reſurrection, *Iohn* 20.27. which whether they be now to be ſeene in his glorified body (as ſome affirme) or aboliſhed (as others,) I leaue to the Reader, as a thing vncertaine, and meerly coniecturall, ſeeing there is nothing in Scripture either for it, or againſt it, that doeth neceſſarily conclude it. But of theſe markes, the Apoſtle ſpeaketh not in this place. The marks in his *myſticall bodie*, are thoſe, which are in his members, as wounds, ſcarres, whippings, maimedneſſe, &c. of which we reade, 2.*Cor.*4.10. *Euery where wee beare in our bodie the dying of our Lord Ieſus*: and, 2.*Cor.*11.24, 25. *Fiue times receiued I fourtie ſtripes, ſaue one: I was thrice beaten with rods, once ſtoned, &c.* And theſe the Apoſtle heere calleth *the markes of Chriſt*, becauſe they are inflicted for the profeſſion of Chriſt, and the Goſpel: as the wounds and ſcarres of a ſouldier, may bee called his Princes wounds and ſcarres, becauſe they are had in his cauſe and quarrell. Now thoſe in his naturall body differ from theſe in his myſticall: Firſt, in that they are meritorious, for *by his ſtripes wee are healed*, 1.*Pet.*2.24. Theſe in his myſticall bodie, are glorious in the ſight of God (as the death of his Saints is;) yet not meritorious. Secondly,

thoſe

thoſe in his naturall body, were propheſied of before in particular, *Pſalm.* 22.16. *They pierced my hands and my feete.* Theſe in his myſticall bodie onely in generall, that wee ſhould be conformable vnto him.

In this place *Paul* ſpeaketh of the latter onely, which were in his owne perſon; and this he doeth, not to put any merit in them, (as S. *Francis* did) but to teſtifie himſelfe to bee a faithfull ſeruant of Chriſt. And he further meeteth with the falſe apoſtles, who would needes haue had the Galatians circumciſed, that ſo they might glorie in the fleſh, as hauing ſet the marke of circumciſion in the foreskin of their fleſh. As if he ſhould ſay, I ſet not markes in other mens fleſh, to glorie of them, as the falſe apoſtles doe, but I beare about in my bodie the markes of the Lord Ieſus, theſe are the ſignes of mine Apoſtleſhip, and arguments of fidelitie in my Miniſterie, which I ſet not in other mens fleſh, but haue in mine owne.

Here we ſee what we are to thinke, and what vſe we are to make of the wounds, ſcarres, and blemiſhes that are in any of the Saints for the profeſſion of the Goſpell, and maintenance of the trueth. Firſt, that they are the ſufferings, wounds, and markes of Chriſt himſelfe (as *Paul* tearmeth them here, and *Coloſſ.* 1.24.) ſeeing they are the wounds of the members of that bodie, whereof he is the head. Secondly, they haue this vſe, to conuince the conſciences of perſecutors, and wicked men, that they are the ſeruants of Chriſt, which ſuffer thus for righteouſneſſe ſake, for which cauſe they are here mentioned by *Paul.* Thus he prooues himſelfe to be a member of Chriſt, by the afflictions which hee ſuffered for his ſake, 2. *Cor.* 12. Thirdly, if men be conſtant in their profeſſion, namely in faith and obedience, they are banners of victory. Therefore no man ought to be aſhamed of them, no more then ſouldiers of their wounds and ſcarres: but rather in a holy manner to glory of them as *Paul* did. For as it is a glorie to a ſouldier to haue receiued many wounds, and to haue many ſcarres, in a good cauſe, in his Princes quarrell, and for the defence of his countrey: So it is a glorie for a Chriſtian ſouldier, to haue the markes of the Lord Ieſus in his bodie, as of wounds, ſcourges, bonds, impriſonment, for the profeſſion of the truth. Therefore *Conſtantine* the great, (as the Eccleſiaſticall hiſtorie records) kiſſed the holes of the eyes of certaine Biſhops, (which had them put out by the Arrians, for the conſtant profeſſion of the faith of Chriſt) reuerencing the vertue of the holy Ghoſt which ſhined in them.

This makes nothing for the *fratres flagellantes*, who glory in the markes

markes which they make in their fleſh,by whipping of themſelues. For firſt,it is not the puniſhmēt(as *Cyprian* ſaith)but the cauſe that makes a Martyr. Secondly,the markes which men ſet vpon themſelues contrary to the Law, *Leuit,* 19.28. are not the *markes of the Lord Ieſus* : but thoſe onely which are ſet vpon them by others, for the profeſſion of the truth. Thirdly,this whipping and afflicting of themſelues,being but will-worſhip,in not ſparing of the body,*Col.* 2.23.is no better accepted of God,then the ſuperſtitious practiſe of *Baals* prieſts,launcing themſelues with kniues,till the blood guſhed out. 1.*Kings* 18 28.

Againe,if this be the glorie of a ſeruant of Chriſt, and a note of conſtant profeſſion,what ſhall we ſay of them who haue not onely their conſciences ſeared with a hot yron,but by drinking,whoring, rioting,&c.get the markes of *Bacchus* and *Venus* in their bodies ? For if theſe be the markes of Chriſt, thoſe muſt needes bee the markes of *Satan.*

Laſtly, hence we are taught a ſpeciall dutie,and that is,to ſuffer bodily affliction in the profeſſion of the truth : and though bonds and impriſonment abide vs in all places,not to paſſe for them, ſo that we may fulfill our courſe with ioy, according to *Pauls* example,both here,and *Act.*20.24 as alſo in his commandement to *Timothie,Suffer affliction as a good ſouldier of Ieſus Chriſt.*2.*Tim.*2.3.The reaſons are theſe. Firſt,by ſuffering bodily affliction, wee are made conformable vtno Chriſt, and fulfill the reſt of the afflictions of Chriſt in our fleſh.*Col.*1.24.Secondly,they teach vs to haue a ſympathie & fellow feeling of the miſeries of our brethren, to remember thoſe that are in bonds,as thogh we were bound with them,& thoſe that are in affliction,as though we alſo were afflicted in the body.*Heb.*13.3. Thirdly,our patient enduring of affliction,doth not onely ſerue as a preſident & example to others to ſuffer patiētly,but alſo is a notable means to confirme them in the truth.2.*Cor.* 1.6.*Philip.*1.14. Laſtly,they ſerue to ſcoure vs that are earthly veſſels,from the ruſt & filth of ſin,that cleaues ſo faſt vnto our nature.

18. *Brethren,the grace of our Lord Ieſus Chriſt,be with your ſpirit, Amen.*

Here, the Apoſtle concludes his Epiſtle with his vſuall farewell, commending the Galatians to the grace of God,and wiſhing vnto thē all things *appertaining to ſpirituall life & godlines.*1.*Pet.*1.3.which he ſignifieth here by *grace.* There is a two-fold grace mentioned in Scripture, Grace which makes a man gracious or acceptable to God,*gratia gratum faciens* : and grace which is freely giuen, *gratia* *gratis data.* *Gratia gratum faciens*, is the fauour and loue of God, whereby he is well pleased with his elect in Christ, and this grace is in God himselfe, and no qualitie infused or inherent in vs: and it is truly called *the first grace*, as beeing the cause of all other subsequent graces. *Gratia gratis data*, is the free gift of God bestowed vpon men, whether naturall, or supernaturall: naturall either in the state of innocencie, before the fall, as originall iustice, &c. or in the state of apostasie, since the fall, as the gift of illumination. *Ioh.* 1,9. and such like: Supernaturall, either common gifts, as the gift of miracles, prophecying, tongues &c. or sauing graces, as the grace of election, effectuall vocation, iustification, adoption, glorification &c. all which are called *the second grace*, because they flow from the first, as the streame from the fountaine. Thus *Paul* distinguisheth them, *Rom.* 5.15. calling the former *the grace of God*, the latter *the gift by grace*. Now grace in this place is not to be restrained onely to the benefit of our redemption, as it is, 2. *Cor.* 13.13. where the grace of Christ is distinguished from the loue of Cod, and communion of the H. Ghost: but to be vnderstood of the fauour and loue of God, which is the *first grace*: and of the sauing grace of regeneration, which is *the second grace, or the gift by grace.* And it is called *the grace of our Lord Iesus Christ*, first, because he is the fountaine of it. *Iohn* 11.16. *Of his fulnes all we haue receiued and grace for grace.* Secondly, because he is the conduit or pipe, by which it is conuaied vnto vs. *Ioh.* 1.17. *Grace and truth came by Iesus Christ:* for he is our propitiator by whom alone we receiue *grace*, that is, the fauour of God, and reconciliation: *for grace*, that is, for the fauour and loue which God the father bare vnto his sonne; we beeing accepted of God, and *beloued in his beloued. Eph.* 1.6. Christ is further called [*our Lord*] in fiue respects. First, by right of creation. *Iohn* 1.3. *All things were made by him.* Secondly, by right of inheritance. *Hebr.* 1.2. *He is made heyre of all things. Psal.* 2.8. *I wil giue thee the Heathen for thine inheritance, and the endes of the earth for thy possession.* Thirdly, by right of redemption. 1. *Cor.* 6.20. *Ye are bought with a price*, which is neither siluer, nor gold, but the pretious blood of Christ. 1. *Pet.* 1.18,19. and this hee performed by a double right, namly, *by right of proprietie*, as a King redeemes his subiects, the master his seruants: or by *right of affinitie*, as the father may redeeme the sonne, one brother another, and one kinsman another. Fourthly, by right of conquest, *Luk.* 11.21. *When a strong man armed keepeth his palace, &c. but when a stronger then he commeth vpon him, and ouercommeth him, he taketh from him all his armour wherin he trusted & diuideth the spoile.* Lastly, by right of contract and marriage. *Hos.* 2.16. *Thou*

shalt

shalt call me Ishi,and shalt not call me Baali. and v.29. *I will marrie thee vnto me for euer in righteousnes,iudgement,mercy, and compassion, I will marrie the vnto me in faithfulnes,and thou shalt know the Lord.*

The Apostle proceeds and saith, the grace of our Lord Iesus Christ *be with your spirits.* For the better vnderstanding of which phrase,we are to know,that Man consisteth of two essential parts, of *soule*,and *bodie.Eccles.*12.7.*Dust*(that is,the body)*returnes to the earth, whence it was taken: and the spirit returns to God that gaue it.* Albeit the Apostle elswhere deuideth man into three parts, *spirit, soule*, and *bodie*, when he prayeth for the Thessalonians, *that their whole spirit, and soule, and body, may be kept blamelesse, vnto the coming of Christ.* Where he subdiuideth the soule into two parts, reason, or vnderstanding, which he calleth *the spirit*: will, or affection,which hee tearmeth(by the common name agreeing to both) *the soule*: God hauing giuen reason to see, and will to seeke,after that which is good: that reason hauing eyes might guide the will that is blinde, and goe before, that it might follow. So that the spirit and soule are not two seueral substances,but one and the same(euen as the body & the flesh are one bodie) and yet are they distinguished for doctrine sake.*Heb.*4.12.the word of God is said to *enter through, euen to the diuiding asunder of the soule and the spirit.* and *Eph.*4.17. 18. the Apostle distinguisheth the soule into three Faculties, *the mind, cogitation, heart*: when he saith the Gentiles walked in the vanitie of their minds, and had their cogitations darkened, because of the hardnesse of their hearts: by *minde*,meaning the *hegemonicall* part or vnderstanding: by *cogitation*,the inward senses, as memorie, phantasie.&c.and by *heart*,the affection.

1.Thess.5.23

νοῦς, διάνοια, καρδία.

Now by *spirit* in this place,is not ment the vnderstanding alone, or the soule alone, but by a *synecdoche* the whole man is vnderstood, albeit the soule principally be ment, because it is the proper subiect of grace: for grace beeing a spirituall thing is placed immediately and properly in the spirit, or mind of man; and in the bodie accidentally, where it doth bewray it selfe by outward actions. Secondly, for that, as the seate of grace is in the mind; so the sense and apprehension of it is there likewise, and not in the body. Thirdly, as *Theophilact* saith, *Non ait vobiscum, quid ita? abigens eos à rebus hisce, arguensq; non à lege hos spiritum, sed à gratia accepisse.* So that, it is all one, as if he should haue said, *The grace of our Iesus Christ bee with you all*: as it is *Philip.*4.23.and 2.*Thess.*3.18. as it may appeare by the like: for that farewell which *Paul* giues *Timothie* in his latter Epistle, *The Lord Iesus Christ bee with thy spirit*, 2.*Tim.*4.22. is all one with that in his former, *Grace be with thee.* 1.*Tim.* 6. 21. And that

Mens cuiusq; is est quisq;

ſalutation *Philem.*15. *The grace of our Lord Ieſus Chriſt bee with your ſpirit*, is all one with that *Coloſſ.*4.18. *Grace be with you.*

Hence that phraſe and forme of ſpeech in our Engliſh Liturgy, or Common praier booke,(though miſliked by ſome, and cauilled at by others)hath his warrant and ground,when the Miniſter ſaith, *The Lord be with you*; and the people anſwer, *And with thy ſpirit*, wiſhing the ſame to him, that he to them, that God would bee with his ſpirit,that is, with him.

Againe, marke how the Apoſtle as he did beginne with grace, chap.1.3.ſo he doth end with grace,to teach vs firſt of all,that our ſaluation is placed in it alone, for the beginning,the progreſſe,and the accompliſhment thereof: for election is of grace, *Rom.* 11.5. and vocation is of grace,2.*Tim.*1.9. and iuſtification, *Rom.*3.24. and glorification. *Rom.*6.23. Secondly, that Chriſt is to haue all the glorie of this grace, whereby wee are ſo highly aduanced into the fauour of God, both for the beginning, continuance, and ending, without aſcribing any part thereof to our ſelues, or any other creature. Thirdly, that all our ſalutations and greetings, our adieues, and fare-wells, ought to bee grounded in the grace of Chriſt, otherwiſe they are but carnall: and therefore the Apoſtle biddeth the Chriſtians to ſalute one another *in a holy kiſſe*, or (as Rom.16.16. *Peter* ſpeakes) with *the kiſſe of loue.*1.*Pet.*5.14.

This confutes the Popiſh Doctors, who doe not onely aſcribe the beginning of their ſaluation to themſelues, in co-working with God in their firſt conuerſion: but alſo the ende and accompliſhment of it,by workes of condignitie, which(as they ſay) are meritorious of eternall life.

Further, obſerue, with what *Emphaſis* the Apoſtle concludes Heb.3.5.6. his Epiſtle: Firſt oppoſing Chriſt the Lord of the houſe to *Moſes* who was but a ſeruant in the houſe.Secondly,the grace of Chriſt to inherent iuſtice, and merits of workes. Thirdly,the ſpirit,in which he would haue grace to be ſeated,to the fleſh,in which the Apoſtles gloried ſo much.Laſtly,brotherly vnitie one with another,implied in the word *bretbren*,to the proud and lordly carriage of the falſe apoſtles ouer them.

The Concluſion.

In the ende of all, it is added,in the *Greeke*,and *Siriacke* copies, that this Epiſtle was *written to the Galatians from Rome.* Which poſtſcript ſeemes to be erroneous and falſe: for firſt, there is not a title in the whole Epiſtle, that giueth the leaſt inkling that it ſhould haue beene written from *Rome:* whereas in all the reſt, which are written from thence, *Paul* makes mẽtion of his bonds & impriſonment

ment. Secondly, the varietie of copies argues the vncertentie of it, ſeeing in ſome copies it is ſaid to haue bin *ſent from Epheſus,* as *Caietan* and *Hyperius* affirme, in their Commentaries vpon this place. Thirdly, *Baronius* (if his authoritie be of any waight in this caſe) af- Annal. Tom. 1.p.657 l.26. Antuerp. firmeth that it is not likely or credible that it was written from thence. But, be it granted that this poſt-ſcript were true indeede; yet it is no part of Canonicall Scripture, as not being written by the Apoſtle, but added afterwards by the Scribes which copied out the Epiſtles. Neither is this onely true of poſt-ſcripts, but alſo of Inſcriptions or Titles prefixed before Epiſtles, they are no part of holy writ. This may eaſily be prooued in particular: for 1. touching Poſtſcripts, the Greeke copies agree in this, that the firſt Epiſtle to the Corinthians, was *written from Philippi, and ſent by Stephanas, Fortunatus, Achaicus, and Timotheus:* when as it is certen, it was written from *Epheſus.* For firſt, chap. 16. 5. he ſaith, *He will come to them when he ſhall goe through Macedonia.* Therefore *Paul* was not then at *Philippi,* a chiefe citie in *Macedonia.* Secondly, in the 19. of the ſame chapter he ſaith, *All the Churches of Aſia ſalute you,* which ſhewes plainely, that when *Paul* writ this Epiſtle, he was at *Epheſus* in *Aſia,* not at *Philippi* in *Europe.* Thirdly, v. 8. he ſaith, *hee will abide at Epheſus till Pentecoſt,* therefore he was not then at *Philippi.* Fourthly, that it was written before the tumult in *Epheſus* raiſed by *Demetrius* and his complices, and ſo conſequently before his comming to *Philippi:* as alſo that it was ſent by *Timotheus* and *Eraſtus,* it is manifeſt, v. 10. of that chapter, being compared with *Act.* 19. v. 21, 22. Laſtly, the *Syriacke* tranſlatour agreeth with me, in affirming that it was written from *Epheſus;* and ſo doth *Baronius Annal. tom.* 1. *pag.* 494. *l.* 39. Againe, the poſt-ſcript of the 2. to the Corinthians hath, it was *written from Philippi of Macedonia, and ſent by Titus and Luke:* whereas the *Rhemiſts* (if wee may giue any credit to their teſtimony, who elſewhere make titles part of the Canonical Scripture) ſay, it was *written at Troas,* as it is thought. And *Baron. annal. tom.* 1. *pag.* 590. *l.* 51. *Antuerp.* thinkes it was written at *Nicopoli,* vpon this occaſion, that in his former Epiſtle from Epheſus, promiſing to come vnto them as he paſſed through Macedonia, & comming not, 1. *Cor.* 16. he doth in this excuſe himſelfe, 2. *Cor.* 1. 15. 16, 17. compared with 2. *Cor.* 7. 5. Neither is it a good reaſon to prooue that *Titus* carried this Epiſtle (as it is in the poſt ſcript) becauſe *Paul* ſaith, *hee ſent Titus to them, and another with him.* 2. *Cor.* 8. 18, 22. and 12. 18. for *Paul* ſpeakes of *Titus* his comming vnto them before that time: neither may it be thought that *Titus* was ſent the ſecond time vnto them, cōſidering that departing frō *Macedonia,* & taking *Titus* with him, he left him in *Creete*. See *Cæſar Baron.annal.tom.*1.*Antuerp*.p.591.l.40.Beſides, the *Rhemiſts* controll the ſubſcription of the firſt Epiſtle to the Theſſalonians,which hath it thus, *The firſt Epiſtle to the Theſſalonians,written from Athens*.For in their preface,they are bold to affirme,that *it ſeemeth rather to haue bin written at Corinth, then at Athens*: and they giue this reaſon of it, becauſe after the ſending of *Timothy* to *Theſſalonica*,*Paul* and he meete not at *Athens* againe,but at *Corinth*. And *Baronius* affirmeth, that it ſeemes to haue beene written preſently after that *Sylus* and *Timotheus* came to him to *Corinth*,out of *Macedonia*, by comparing *Act*.18.5.with 1.*Theſſ*.3.6. *Annal.tom*.1.*pag*.457 *l*.1. And *Emãnuel Sa* doth cenſure the Syriacke poſtſcript,which ſaith it was ſent from Athens by *Timothy*,ſeeing that *Timothy* was then abſent. The like they affirme in the argument of the ſecond Epiſtle. for albeit the Greeke poſtſcript hath it, that it was written from *Athens*, yet they rather thinke it was *written from Corinth*, where *Paul* aboad a yeare and ſixe moneths, *Act*.18.11.becauſe the title is like vnto the firſt Epiſtle,*Paul and Syluanus,and Timotheus,&c*.And *Baronius* ſaith,that it ſhould be written from Athens, *impoſſibile eſt affirmare*; becauſe it was written ſoone after the former,as may appeare by the inſcription, *Paul and Syluanus and Timotheus*,(they continuing together:) but the former was written from *Corinth*, (as hath bin prooued,) and therefore the latter: ſpecially conſidering that *Paul* went from *Athens*,and aboad at *Corinth* a yeare and a halfe, and returned not backe againe to *Athens*,but went to Epheſus. *Annal.tom*.1.*pag*.457.*l*.28.

Adde hereunto,that whereas the poſtſcript of the firſt to *Timothy* ſaith,it was *written from Laodicea the chiefe citie of Phrygia Pacaciana*, the *Rhemiſts* notwithſtanding in the argument, affirme that it is vncertaine where it was written: and though it be commonly ſaid to haue beene written at *Laodicea*,yet it ſeemeth to bee otherwiſe, becauſe it is like hee was neuer there, as may be gathered by the Epiſtle to the Coloſſians which was written at Rome in his laſt trouble,a little before his death: for *Coloſſ*.2.1.*Paul* ſeemes to inſinuate that he was neuer at that *Laodicea of Phrygia*,neare to *Coloſſos* and *Hierapolis*,and that they neuer ſaw his perſon. Beſides,neither *Plinie* (who writeth after *Paul*) nor any other ancient claſſique author,doth make mention of *Phrygia Pacaciana*,ſo that it ſeemeth to haue bin ſo called long after *Pauls* deceaſe: the firſt mention that is made of it(as ſome haue obſerued)being in the acts of the fifth Synode of Conſtantinop. *Baronius* is of opinion that it was written from *Macedonia.tom*.1.*pag*.564.grounding his coniecture vpon 1.*Tim*.1.3.*as I beſought thee to abide at Epheſus,when I went into Macedonia*;

cedonia; ſo doe.—The ſame doth *Athanaſius* affirme, in his Synopſis, and *Theodoret* in his preface vpon that Epiſtle.

Againe, the ſubſcription of the 2. to *Timothy*, that it was *written from Rome vnto Timothy the firſt Biſhop elected of the church of Epheſus:* cannot well ſtand, as ſome thinke, with that of *S Paul*, 2. *Timothy* 4. 5. *Doe the worke of an Euangeliſt*, ſeeing that Euangeliſts were not tyed to perſonall reſidencie, to abide in one place (as Biſhops and paſtors are) but were to goe from place to place, to confirme the Churches planted by the Apoſtles. But the diſcuſſing of this argument, whether *Timothy* were an Euangeliſt properly ſo called, and whether the ſame man could not be an Euangeliſt, and a Biſhop, requireth a longer diſcourſe, then can bee affoarded to this ſhort treatiſe. Laſtly, the poſtſcript of the Epiſtle to *Titus*, ſaith it was *written from Nicopolis of Macedonia*: the deuiſers of which aſſertion ground their opinion vpon *Titus* 3. 12. where *Paul* ſaith, *be diligent to come to me to Nicopolis, for I haue determined there to winter*: miſtaking the text, for he ſaith not, be diligent to come to me to Nicopolis, for I haue determined *here* to winter, (as beeing there already) but I haue determined *there* to winter. By which it is plaine that when *Paul* wrote to *Titus*, he was not at *Nicopolis*, (as the poſtſcript affirmeth,) and ſo we ſee the text which they alleadge for them, maketh moſt againſt them. And this is the iudgement and reaſon of *Baronius, Annal. tom.* 1. *pag.* 575. *l.* 33. *Antuerp.* howſoeuer *Claudius Eſpencæus* ſhifts his fingers of it, and paſſes it ouer in ſilence.

Thus much concerning *Subſcriptions*: a word or two touching *Inſcriptions* or *titles* prefixed before Epiſtles. That theſe bee no part of Scripture written by the Apoſtles, but added to the Epiſtles by ſome others, it may appeare by theſe reaſons. Firſt generally, if titles were *canonicall* as well as the epiſtles themſelues, the Fathers would neuer haue doubted (as they did) whether *Paul* were the author of the Epiſtle to the Ebrewes or not, ſeeing in all copies ſaue one (as *Beza* hath obſerued) it beareth his name: but ſome of them aſcribe it to *Barnabas*, as *Tertullian*: others to *Luke*, as *Ierome* witneſſeth, others to *Clement*: *Oecumenius* intitleth it only thus, *The Epiſtle to the Ebrewes*, without adding the name of *Paul* or any other as the penner of it: and ſo *Hentenius* a papiſt doth tranſlate it out of *Oecumenius*. Secondly, ſome Epiſtles (as thoſe ſeauen written by *Iames, Peter, Iohn, Iude*) haue vnfit titles prefixed before them, in that they are called ſometime *Canonicall*, (ſpecially of the Latine Church) and ſometime *Catholicke* (chiefly of the Greeke Church:) neither of which were euer giuen them, by any Apoſtle, or Apoſtolique writer. For firſt, touching the title *Canonicall*, it may ſeeme ſtrange that this inſcription ſhould euer haue bin appropriated vnto thẽ, which is common with them to the whole word of God: as though in them were contained a more perfect and abſolute rule of doctrine and manners, of things to be beleeued and practiſed, then in the other bookes of holy writ; conſidering that ſundry Diuines (albeit erroniouſly I confeſſe) haue bin ſo far from giuing vnto them this preheminence aboue the reſt of the bookes of Scripture, that they haue altogether reiected them, as no part of Canonicall Scripture: by name, the Epiſtle of *Iames*, the 2. of *Peter*, the 2. and 3. of *Iohn*, and that of *Iude*, of all which it was doubted in ancient time, as we ſee in *Euſebius*; and the Syrian Church receiueth them not to this day, as being not in the Syriacke tranſlation; and *Caietan* a Popiſh writer, & the *Lutherans* at this preſent, reiect them, as may appeare by their writings. Secõdly, that this inſcription was added to theſe Epiſtles without ſufficient ground, and warrant of reaſon, may appeare, in that no reaſon can be giuen why theſe ſeuen ſhould bee called *Canonicall*, rather then the Epiſtles of S. *Paul*, or that to the *Ebrewes* (whoſoeuer was the penner thereof.) For whereas the ordinary Gloſſe ſaith, they are called *Canonicall*, becauſe they were receiued into the Canon with the other Epiſtles; by that reaſon they ſhould be no more *Canonicall* then the reſt, nay, not of that authentical, at leaſt of that vndoubted authority the reſt are of, ſeeing they hardly obtained to bee regiſtred in the Canon with the reſt as *Canonicall*. Laſtly, this title was neuer giuen to theſe Epiſtles by the Greeke Church (which was more ancient) but onely by the Latin Church, as might be prooued by manifold teſtimonies, if it were a thing neceſſary to bee ſtood vpon. Neuertheleſſe, howſoeuer this inſcription cannot be defended, yet it may be excuſed, & tolerated, as a title of diſtinction, to diſtinguiſh them from the other epiſtles. As we ſee the Iewes diuiding the old Teſtament into foure parts: the firſt they called the law, or 5. books of *Moſes*: the 2. the former Prophets, *viz*. *Ioſhua*, *Iudges*, 2. bookes of *Samuel*, two books of the *Kings*: the 3. the later Prophets, as *Eſay*, *Ieremie*, *Ezechiel*, and the ſmall Prophets: the 4. they called *Kethubim*, which in Engliſh is as much as the *Scriptures*, not as though thoſe 11. bookes were more properly Scripture, then the *Pentateuch* of *Moſes*, or the bookes of the former and later Prophets: but onely for diſtinction ſake they were ſo called. And they are tearmed of the Seuentie, and of the Greeke Church ἁγιόγραφα, that is, *holy writs*, not becauſe they had a peculiar holines proper to them aboue other parts of Gods word (ſeeing all Scripture is equally giuen by diuine inſpiration) nor as though the amanuenſes of theſe bookes were more holy then the other pen-men of the holy Ghoſt (nay, contrarily it is doubted by ſome, of *Salomon*, who penned three of theſe bookes, whether he were elected or reiected; whereas it is not doubted of the reſt:) but only (as I haue already ſaid) to put a note of diſtinction betwixt them and other books, in naming of them, as **Hugo de S. Vict.* hath well obſerued.

* Tom.1. per tot. Elucid. c. 12. quia nullam habent ſpecialem proprietatem quâ diſtinguantur à cæteris, commune nomen quaſi proprium obtinent.

In this ſenſe this title Canonicall, may be giuen to theſe Epiſtles without danger: but if wee ſhall vnderſtand it in any other ſenſe, we ſhall be ſo farre from being able to defend it, that we ſhal not be able to excuſe it.

The ſecond title which is giuen them, is, that they be called *Catholike*, which inſcription is as vnfit as the former: for they are ſo called (as ſome would haue it,) becauſe they were written, and directed to the whole Catholike Church, conſiſting both of Iewes, and Gentiles. But that is not true, ſeeing *Iames*, chap. 1. 1. directeth his Epiſtle only to the 12. tribes that were diſperſed, and not to the Gentiles. And *Peter*, who was an Apoſtle of circumciſion, 1. Epiſt. 1. 1. writeth onely to the ſtrangers the Iewes, that dwelt here and there throughout Pontus, Galatia, Cappadocia, Aſia, & Bythinia. Others thinke they are tearmed *Catholike*, for that they were not ſent to one man, or family, or citie, or countrey: but generally to the whole bodie, company, or ſocietie of the Iewes, whereſoeuer diſperſed ouer the whole earth. But neither in this ſenſe can they fitly, or truely be tearmed *Catholike*: foraſmuch as two of theſe ſeuen, *viz.* the ſecond and third of *Iohn*, were written to particular perſons, the one to the elect *Lady*, the other to *Gaius*. And by this reaſon the Epiſtle to *Timothie*, that to *Titus*, and *Philemon*, may bee called *Catholike*, as well as theſe.

Again, be it granted, that they were all directed to all the Iewes, yet I ſee not why the Epiſtle to the *Ebrewes* may not as well challenge this title to be called *Catholike*, as any of theſe ſeuen, conſidering it was written to all the Iewes, and only to the Iewes.

Thirdly, others affirme them to be called *Catholike*, becauſe they containe Catholike doctrine, ſuch as appertaineth to all men generally, of what eſtate, place, condition, or calling ſoeuer they bee. But in this ſenſe all *Pauls* Epiſtles, may be called *Catholike Epiſtles*. *For whatſoeuer is written, is written for our learning, that we through patience and conſolation of the Scriptures, might haue hope, Rom. 15. 4.*

Secondly, the word *Catholike* is not ſo ancient: for *Pacianus* an ancient Father ſaith, it was not vſed in the Apoſtles daies. His words are theſe. *Sed ſub apoſtolis (inquies) nemo Catholicus vocabatur: eſto, ſic fuerit, vel illud indulge, cū poſt apoſtolos hæreſes extitiſſet, diuerſiſq; nominibus Columbam*

Biblioth. ſacræ tom. 3. ad Sympronian Nouatian. de Cathol. nomine Epiſt. 1.

Columbam Dei atque reginam lacerare per partes, & ſcindere niterentur; nonne cognomen ſuum plebs Apoſtolica poſtulabat, quo incorrupti populi diſtingueret vnitatem, ne intemeratam Dei virginem, error aliquorum per membra laceraret? that is, *But thou wilt ſay, vnder the Apoſtles no man was called Catholike: well, bee it ſo, yet admit this withall, when after the Apoſtles there were hereſies, and men began to rend in pieces, and diuide Gods Doue, and Queene, by ſundry different names, did not the Apoſtolike people require their ſurnames, whereby they might diſtinguiſh the vnitie of the vncorrupt people, leſt the error of ſome, ſhould rend in ſunder Gods vndefiled virgin?* where we ſee *Pacianus* doeth freely grant, that this ſurname *Catholike*, was not in vſe in the time of the Apoſtles. Which teſtimony *Baronius* doeth notably diſſemble, in ſhewing the original of this name out of *Pacianus*; affirming, but not proouing it to be as ancient as the Apoſtles. Now this error hath not only befallen the Latine, & Greeke copies, but the Syriacke likewiſe, as may appeare in the title prefixed before the moſt ancient Syrian tranſlation, where we ſhall find theſe words, *The three Epiſtles of the three Apoſtles, before whoſe eyes our Lord was transfigured, Iames, Peter, Iohn.* In which inſcription be couched 2. foule errours. Firſt, in that this tranſlator maketh but 3. Epiſtles of *Iames, Peter, and Iohn*: whereas there are ſixe, he omitting the 2. of *Peter*, the 2. & 3. of *Iohn*, (as alſo that of *Iude*) as no part of holy Scripture; and therfore the Syriack Church (as I haue already ſaid) doth not receiue theſe Epiſtles into their canon vnto this day. The ſecond is, in that he affirmeth *Iames* before whom our Sauiour Chriſt was transfigured in moũt *Tabor*, to be the author of this Epiſtle. For that *Iames*, before whom Chriſt was transfigured in the mount, was *Iames* the ſon of *Zebedeus*, and brother of *Iohn*, *Mat.* 17.1. *After ſix daies, Ieſus tooke Peter, & Iames, and Iohn his brother, and brought them vp into an high mountaine, and was transfigured before thẽ.* Which *Iames* could not poſſibly be the penner of this Epiſtle, for he was ſlaine by King *Herod* long before the deſtruction of Ieruſalẽ, & the diſperſion of the 12. tribes, *Act.* 12.2. *About that time Herod the King ſtretched forth his hand to vexe certaine of the Church: & he ſlew Iames the brother of Iohn with the ſword.* Therfore *Iames* the authour of this Epiſtle, was *Iames* the ſon of *Alpheus*. For to faine an other *Iames* the brother of our Lord, as ſome haue done, is childiſh, ſeeing it is plaine by ſundry places of the new Teſtament, that there were but two of that name mentioned in ſcripture, *Iames* the ſon of *Zebedeus* called *Iames* the greater; and *Iames* the ſonne of *Alpheus*, brother to *Iude*, called the leſſer, and brother of our Lord.

Annalium tom.1.p.349. Antuerp.

GRATIAS TIBI DOMINE IESV.

COMMON PLACES HANDLED IN THIS *Commentarie*.

The first figure shewes the page, the second the line.

27 Of

A Table

A Table of all those places of Scrip- *ture which are briefly expounded* in this Commentarie.

I. Cor.

An

An exact Table of all particulars contained *in this Commentarie.*

The first figure shewes the page, the second the line.

A

B

We

What

D

Good

Rea-

H

The

M

N

O

P

T

A TABLE.

FINIS.